Вп. о. Дорогому Григорієви Лаврієви

Срдечно і глибоко шаную

з вірою, за волю України

о всіх людей, де живе

народній дух

Андрій

(Квітень, 1989)

Ukraine
and the Subjugated Nations:
Their Struggle for National Liberation

Yaroslav Stetsko after the proclamation of Ukrainian Independence on June 30, 1941.

Ukraine
and the Subjugated Nations:
Their Struggle for National Liberation

Selected Writings and Speeches
by
Yaroslav Stetsko
Former Prime Minister of Ukraine

edited by John Kolasky, M.A., B.Ped.

Philosophical Library
New York

Library of Congress Cataloging-in-Publication Data:

Stetsko, Yaroslav S.
  Ukraine and the subjugated nations.

  Translated from Ukrainian.
  1. Ukraine—Politics and government—
1945-   2. Soviet Union—Territorial
expansion.   3. National liberation movements—
Soviet Union.   I. Kolasky, John.   II. Title.
DK508.84.S74   1988   947'.71   87-6948
ISBN 0-8020-2537-3

Foreword
by John Wilkinson M.P.
Chairman, European Freedom Council

It is a daunting task to write an introduction to this collection of articles by my old friend, the late Yaroslav Stetsko. Daunting, because few words can truly express the commitment shown by Yaroslav in his fight to free, not only his beloved Ukraine, but also all countries which are denied their freedom by the Soviet Union.

Throughout his life Yaroslav endured great injustices and suffered profoundly for his beliefs. His experiences in Ukraine during the Stalinist purges, the German occupation, and his subsequent deportation to the Sachsenhausen concentration camp for refusing to work with the Nazi regime are all reflected in his writing. He always rejected totalitarianism, was a passionate advocate of national self-determination, and was declared Prime Minister of a free Ukraine in 1941 when the Red Army retreated from the Germans.

After the Second World War Yaroslav continued his fight against world Communism from Munich, sustained and encouraged by his heroic wife Slava. To many Ukrainians both within and outside Ukraine, he remained their legitimate leader. He worked tirelessly until his death, promoting the causes of Ukraine and the other Captive Nations, championing the right for individuals as for nations that they should both be free. Inspired by a deep, personal Christian faith as well as a profound sense of history, Yaroslav was a symbol for those who wished to see the downfall of Bolshevism and the oppression and sorrow which it inflicts.

It was my very humble privilege to have known Yaroslav. He was a true patriot, outstanding politician, and great friend and colleague in both the Anti-

5

Bolshevik Bloc of Nations and the European Freedom Council. He will be sadly missed by his many friends and admirers throughout the Free World.

His memory, however, will be kept alive not only by his friends and countrymen but also by this collection of articles which span many years and topics. In them the reader will find one of the finest critiques of Communism and oppression coupled with Yaroslav's undying call for the freedom of his beloved Ukraine. There can be no better memento of what Yaroslav Stetsko stood for than his own words.

Preface

by Bertil Haggman
Helsingoborg, Sweden

When asked to write this introduction to the thoughts of Yaroslav Stetsko I was both pleased and somewhat hesitant. To write such an introduction is an important task. "His life," in the words of President Ronald Reagan, "burnt brightly with the love of liberty in an age darkened by totalitarian tyranny." How, in these few pages, to give full justice to the diplomat, the statesman, and the man Yaroslav Stetsko and his ideas?

The diplomat worked tirelessly not only for the freedom and independence of his beloved Ukraine and its people but for all nations subjugated by Russia. It was in the tradition of Hetmans Ivan Mazepa and Pylyp Orlyk in the eighteenth century, both connected with my own country, with Sweden, in opposing Russian imperialism.

As a statesman he was in the great line of famous Ukrainians of the twentieth century: Symon Petlura, Yevhen Konovalets, Gen. Taras Chuprynka, Roman Shukhevych and Stepan Bandera, all brutally murdered by Soviet Russia.

Yaroslav Stetsko paid a heavy price for his struggle for Free Ukraine: three and a half years in the Nazi concentration camp of Sachsenhausen during World War II. His "crime" in the face of Hitler and Stalin was to work for the re-establishment of Ukrainian independence and to serve as its first Premier after the June 30, 1941 proclamation of a free nation.

Mr. Stetsko survived the ordeal to become a member of the Presidium of the Leadership of the Revolutionary OUN and leader of the Anti-Bolshevik Bloc of Nations, founded in Ukraine on liberated territory in 1943 and later re-established in the West. From 1968 he was the leader of OUN.

7

What made Yaroslav Stetsko unique among statesmen of the twentieth century was his constant emphasis on the importance of the Western cultural heritage as opposed to totalitarianism and messianic Soviet-Russian imperialism. Hellenic, Roman and Christian ideas are the basis of our culture, our civilization. If these ideals are forgotten the road will lead to the destruction of the West. I often heard him complain, both privately and in speeches, that we seemed to forget that heritage and that Westerners were afraid of ideas, of ideology.

Yaroslav Stetsko constantly reminded the leaders of the West that there was only one way to peace in the world. That way was the dissolution of the Russian empire, and that empire could only be dissolved with the aid of the subjugated nations under Russian oppression. The policy of national liberation of the subjugated nations was the only way to avoid nuclear wars. Thus it was only natural that Mr. Stetsko supported President Reagan's Strategic Defense Initiative (SDI).

In reality the Reagan Doctrine, as reiterated in the Presidential speech of February 4, 1986, was an expression of the ideas Mr. Stetsko had for so long advocated. It was an irony that he so shortly before his death was to hear the leader of the Free World talk of what he had been fighting for all along: "To those imprisoned in regimes held captive, to those beaten for daring to fight for freedom and democracy, for their right to worship, to speak, to live, and to prosper in the family of free nations, we say to you tonight: you are not alone, freedom-fighters. America will support with moral and material assistance your right not just to fight and die for freedom but to fight and win freedom.... This is a great moral challenge for the entire Free World."

Zbigniew Brzezinski, in an interview in 1984, said that the multinational reality of the Soviet Union is its Achilles heel. The liberation struggle of the subjugated nations in the Russian empire is the best protection against nuclear holocaust. Moral, political, and if necessary military support for the national liberation process in Ukraine, Estonia, Latvia, Lithuania, Georgia, and all other oppressed nations behind the Iron Curtain, can eliminate the threat of nuclear war. In reality, it is the true peace movement of today.

Let us pause to ponder the fact that the Russian "prison of peoples" grew from around 15,000 square miles in 1462 to 8.6 million square miles in 1914. It continued to expand after the Communists took power. In books, speeches, and essays Yaroslav Stetsko reminded us tirelessly of the expansionist driving force of the heirs of the tsars. The Kremlin leaders have reached much further than the emperors of Russia could ever dream of with footholds in Asia, Africa, and Latin America, and have an impressive number of fleets roaming the seas of the world. This should make us ponder the words of the famous British geographer Sir Halford Mackinder, who in the beginning of this century issued the following warning:

"Who rules East Europe commands the Heartland:

"Who rules the Heartland commands the World-Island (i.e., Eurasia):

"Who rules the World-Island commands the World."

The West has accepted the policy of containment as a guiding light in the East-West conflict. But it is the policy of surrender. In the words of Professor

James Burnham, who wrote in the spirit of Mr. Stetsko: "If the Communists succeed in consolidating what they have *already* conquered, then their complete world victory is certain.... What this means is that liberation is the only defense against a Soviet world victory." Men like Yaroslav Stetsko have had a profound influence on the thinking of many leaders of the West, an influence that, had it been converted into practical policy, would have changed world history. Thus far his thinking has not, because it cannot become the policy of the West but because those leaders so far have not been able to convert the ideas into political action. The 1980s have in many ways proved the ideas of liberation to be right. For the first time since World War II the tide has really turned against Marxism-Leninism. All over the world, including in the Third World, peoples realize that Marxism is not the wave of the future, does not hold the promise of progress. And there can be no peace without freedom for the subjugated nations. Thus the publication of Mr. Stetsko's works is timely indeed as we approach the end of the twentieth century. The growing insight of the importance of liberation as an alternative to nuclear holocaust will place this book among those books that forged the Free World. Mr. Stetsko will be remembered not only as a fighter for his beloved Ukraine but as a representative of ideas bound to save the West. That is the great legacy of Yaroslav Stetsko, one of the great men of this century.

As a young student I first met Mr. Stetsko when he visited Sweden in 1964 with his wife and co-fighter, Mrs. Slava Stetsko. They had come to pay tribute to Sweden's contribution to the struggle against expansionist Russia and for freedom of the peoples under the tsars. At that time Mr. Stetsko struck me as a man of great dignity, the dignity one associated with great thinkers and statesmen. His visit to Sweden that summer over twenty years ago drove Nikita Khrushchev, who was there too on the invitation of the Swedish Government, to new heights of rage. No doubt Mr. Stetsko, by his mere presence in the same country as the Russian ruler, contributed to the downfall of Khrushchev that same year.

May this book have the very large readership it deserves. The ideas of Yaroslav Stetsko will continue to be a guiding light not only to Ukrainians but to all in the West who love liberty. Every since World War II they have served as an inspiration to those Western leaders who feel that free peoples worldwide have an obligation to aid their subjugated brothers and sisters.

CONTENTS

List of Illustrations

Editor's Note

The activities of Yaroslav Stetsko in the Ukrainian revolutionary nationalist movement span nearly half a century. With the assassination of Stepan Bandera in 1959 by the KGB agent Stashynsky, Stetsko emerged as the leading spokesman in the Western world of the cause of Russian-occupied Ukraine and other submerged nations.

The material in this collection covers a period of more than thirty years. It includes a wide variety of subjects from culture to politics and it indicates both a wide erudition and a fundamental understanding of religious, social, economic, political, and international problems.

The articles and speeches reveal the author's deep conviction and dedication, as well as his personal modesty and abiding Christian faith.

Selection was complicated by a number of factors. Since the articles and speeches were directed to various readers and audiences at different intervals of time, there was considerable repetition of the author's basic theses. The classification according to subject matter was made somewhat difficult by the fact that each article or speech usually dealt with more than one topic. Consequently, deletions and abridgments were made in many articles without altering the trend of the author's discourse.

One article, which dealt at length with two distinct topics, was divided and placed under two separate subject headings.

The names of organizations, institutions, and movements are given in full the first time they are used, followed by their abbreviated forms in brackets. Thereafter, only the abbreviation is used. A list of abbreviations with their full titles is provided at the beginning of the collection.

Yaroslav Stetsko arriving in Taipei (center). With him is Prof. Lin Tsiu-sen, a translator (left) and Dr. Ku Cheng-kang, President of the Asian Peoples Anti-Communist League (APACL). (October 9, 1955).

Abbreviations

ABN: Anti-Bolshevik Bloc of Nations
APACL: Asian Peoples' Anti-Communist League
CIAS: Comité International d'Information et d'Action Sociale
CPSU: Communist Party of the Soviet Union
CSSR: Czechoslovak Socialist Republic
DUN: Legion of Ukrainian Nationalists
EFC: European Freedom Council
FRG: Federal Republic of Germany
GDR: German Democratic Republic
GPU: State Political Administration (Soviet Secret Police 1922-1923)
KGB: Committee of State Security (Soviet Secret Police 1954-)
MVD: Ministry of Internal Affairs (Soviet Secret Police 1946-1953)
NATO: North Atlantic Treaty Organization
NEP: New Economic Policy
NKVD: Peoples Commissariat of Internal Affairs (Soviet Secret Police
            1934-1938)
NTS: Russian Solidarists' Organization
OUN: Organization of Ukrainian Nationalists
SUM: Ukrainian Youth Association
SVU: Union for the Liberation of Ukraine
UAPTs: Ukrainian Autocephalous Orthodox Church
UHVR: Ukrainian Supreme Liberation Council
UNO: United Nations Organization
UPA: Ukrainian Insurgent Army
USSR: Union of Soviet Socialist Republics
UVO: Ukrainian Military Organization
WACL: World Anti-Communist League

I
The Church, Religion, and Moral Values

On the Threshold of the Atomic Age

Countless critical essays and works have been written on the subject of the "Dark Ages," but the positive factors of that era are not stressed sufficiently. The Inquisition, the intolerance which prevailed at that time, serfdom, and feudalism have quite rightly been condemned, but the fact has frequently been overlooked that, apart from these evils, the Middle Ages also gave the world certain creative forces and ethical values: the belief in all that is good and noble which created the magnificent monuments of culture which are still admired by us today, the typical figures of the knight and the monk, the ideal of a sublime love which can only be won by chivalry. But, unfortunately, the heroic and altruistic qualities, the spirit of self-sacrifice and the noble virtues of medieval man were overshadowed by the atrocities of the Middle Ages.

If one enters the Escorial and beholds the pantheon of kings or the royal palace with its austerity of style, if one enters the monastery buildings and sits in one of the halls and listens to the interesting arguments propounded by the president of the Spanish syndicates, José Solis Rutz, as he criticizes the modern social and economic order of liberal capitalism, by endeavoring to protect the worker and demanding cooperation between all social classes of the nation and the elimination of exploitation—one cannot help but feel how absolutely essential it is that the present ruling class in economic life should allow itself to be ruled by the spirit of a new Middle Ages—by austerity of morals, faith in God, and renunciation of an extravagant way of living—in order to be able to wage a victorious fight against Bolshevism.

The atmosphere of the Escorial constantly reminds one of the fact that, without a new spirit, without new ideas, without the rebirth of Christian ethics, and without the furtherance of national consciousness, there can be no solution of internal, national, and social problems in the true sense of justice. Liberal capitalism has denied the nation from the ideological point of view by taking the unlimited egoism of the individual as the basis for social and economic life. The economy of a nation, however, does not allow the egoism of individual persons a free hand, but represents the basis of the material existence of the nation. Bolshevism preaches materialism, but, unfortunately, there are many people in the West who convert materialism into reality. Man is becoming more and more obsessed by the idea of "prosperity"; a fierce competition has begun for the material things of this earth, for the amassing of huge riches, for unlimited material wealth, and for hedonism, as if man had only been created in God's likeness in order to lead a life of luxury and brutally oust his own fellow-countrymen in the competition for the luxuries of life. It is not Christian doctrine with its eternal and unchanging truth that has become obsolete; the Christians themselves have ceased to be Christians. Modern Christians disregard Christian doctrine, despite the fact that they constantly use fine phrases about God, "social justice," "brotherliness," "peace," "humanity," etc.

Christian moral standards have indeed come to a sorry pass when the advocates of our modern age believe that the greatest evil of the Middle Ages was the knights' wars, in which each individual personally risked his own life and the conquered were as a rule spared, and are of the opinions that the modern type of war, conducted against women and children, is "noble." The development of morality is by no means keeping pace with the present technical progress of civilization. Man invented the atomic bomb, but has no qualms about using it against old persons, women, and children, or, in fact, against the unarmed population as a whole. For practically forty years, the evildoers of the Kremlin have, with the aid of modern technical science, been enforcing an unheard of terrorist regime on the subjugated peoples and nations and are now threatening the entire Free World with this same regime.

The atomic age, one might assume, should bring with it the further liberation of man from his dependence on the powers of Nature, the improvement of living conditions, and should create pre-conditions which allay man's fear of over-population, inasmuch as it opens up new sources of the energies needed by mankind. The French Senator, Michel Yver, who is a member of the Commission for Foreign Affairs of the Council of the French Republic, gave an excellent technical survey of the possible means of bringing about a coordination of European interests as regards the use of atomic energy for peaceful economic purposes. Unfortunately, however, he did not mention the political aspect of this problem and entirely overlooked the existence of a despotic major power. But this major power possesses destructive atomic weapons which it can use against the Western world whenever it sees fit, if the latter concentrates its attention above all on the peaceful use of atomic energy and neglects its own armament and the policy of liberation towards the peoples enslaved by Moscow. It seems, incidentally, as if it were perhaps too soon to attempt to deal with the problem of

Europe's economic and social status in general in the atomic age, since we are still on the threshold of this age and cannot as yet clearly visualize what consequences the manifold use of atomic energy for peaceful purposes would have. We cannot as yet foresee whether such a use of atomic energy would make more or less human labor available and what the results would be as regards unemployment, for instance, and reduction of working time etc. As far as the destructive power of atomic energy is concerned, the only two examples we have which give us some idea of what would happen if the old type of atomic bomb were dropped are Hiroshima and Nagasaki. But what about the new type? Nor do we, for instance, know what would happen if an unintentional explosion were to occur in an atomic plant "for peaceful purposes."...

We are still only on the threshold of the atomic age, yet already a tragic problem confronts us: scores of nations and hundreds of millions of human beings in slavery! Such is the result when man, grown too self-confident and presumptuous through his own intellect, loses his faith in the world hereafter and in human feelings and, seeing that he has discovered a new source of energy, becomes convinced that he alone is able to rule the world and determine its existence. A philosopher in ancient times once said that the state should be ruled by philosophers. But at present the physicists and chemists seem to think that they alone are the ones who should rule the universe. Should the future elite of the state really consist of thousands of specialized technical experts who would be able to control the use of atomic energy? Should philosophy be replaced by technical science or technocracy? This kind of presumption was apparent in the well-known collective letter by Einstein and his colleagues in which they warned the world of the danger of an atomic war and insisted on so-called coexistence, since "we possess the means of destroying the world." Mortal human understanding has neither created the world nor will it destroy it. Man is bound to fulfill his duties to God and to his native country regardless of whether the world is threatened by an atomic war or not, for it is not the physical but the spiritual and eternal life which determines man's true being. And man's duty to his native country must not be set against his duty to God.

The fact that Spain five years ago first decided to arrange annual congresses of the intellectual and political elite of Europe, who, on the strength of their recognition of national characteristics and national independence are endeavoring to unite Europe in the spirit of Christian ethics, as the first step towards a world union, represents a valuable contribution to the furtherance of a closer Christian and national union of Europe. Such a group of prominent European personalities, who have meanwhile, thanks to the congresses, become well acquainted with one another, now exists and represents an important factor in the anti-Bolshevik fight for the positive aims of a heroic, national, and social Europe which is so multifarious as regards its national aspect, yet so homogeneous from the intellectual and spiritual point of view. Europe is where the fight is being fought for the European character and spirit—for the freedom of the creative individual, for the recognition of human dignity, for national characteristics, for the heroic moral principles of the individual, and for Christian culture, the heart of which is man's creative ego.

The members of the congress in the Escorial, in their endeavors to bring about the union of Europe, are, however, well aware of the fact that Europe is neither bounded by the Oder nor the Vistula. And they are furthermore aware of the fact that little success can be hoped for from Strasbourg—in view of its adjustment to constantly changing international constellations, to the status quo of an "amputated" Europe (which includes the elimination of so ancient a European cultural nation as Spain), and to socialist, liberal, conservative, and other contradictory party formulas. As long as the present spirit prevails, as long as an exclusively egoistic attitude predominates instead of a joint effort, and as long as economic interests only are the decisive factor instead of the nobler aims of a human mission, all the projects for the European community, though they may be drawn up with the best of intentions, will be bound to fade into comparative insignificance. In view of the dreadful Muscovite menace to the existence and character of Europe, what significance can the fixing of tomato prices possibly have—which, according to the statement made by the Italian Ambassador, Ugo Sola, was the reason why certain Italian and French negotiations were broken off! There is not a single European problem which can be solved integrally as long as one tries to solve it on one half of Europe, whilst the other half continues to be the object of Eurasian Muscovite extermination. In any case, there is no large-scale problem to be solved as long as a Russian empire continues to exist, which includes about 800 million people in its sphere of influence.

The European Center of Documentation and Information deserves the greatest credit and praise for always including the burning questions of international politics on its agenda and, as for instance at the 1955 Congress, for its frank and comprehensive discussion of the problem of so-called coexistence (in which connection its resolutions were in complete agreement with the fundamental principles of our anti-Bolshevik fight for freedom). Such resolutions have, of course, at present only a theoretical value; but they are nevertheless of considerable significance, inasmuch as the members of the congress who approve them in this way pledge themselves morally to act accordingly and to do their utmost to influence the governments of their respective countries in this direction.

Yaroslav Stetsko
ABN Correspondence,
October-December 1956, p. 13

The Church of Martyrs

Christianity has been existing in Ukraine for more than 1,000 years. It has fostered a profound faith in God among the people, and has begotten abiding moral principles, and nourished a new culture and erudition.

In December 1917, Communist Russia invaded Ukraine, and in 1919-1920 occupied the eastern provinces of this country. The Soviets were bent on extirpating Christianity from these regions. They published aggressive anti-religious propaganda and terrorized the people with threats of exile, torture, and death.

First, the Communists attacked the Church in Eastern Ukraine. Within 10 years, from 1921 to 1931, they unjustly arrested and ruthlessly murdered 34 Ukrainian Orthodox bishops, with the Metropolitans Vasyl Lypkivsky and Nicholas Boretsky at the head, and more than 3,000 priests. Hundreds of thousands of the faithful were inhumanly tortured in prisons or deported to concentration camps in Siberia; a greater part of these innocent people died martyrs to their faith; the remainder still endures the appalling trials and hardships of imprisonment.

The Russians destroyed 80 percent of the churches (many contained precious historical relics, as for example the Golden Domed Michalivsky Monastery in Kyiv from the 12th century); other churches were despicably converted into warehouses, theaters, and convention halls; monasteries were desecrated and cemeteries profaned.

By 1930 the Communists had completely liquidated the Ukrainian Orthodox Church.

Though Article 123 of the Soviet Constitution, which is binding in Ukraine as well as the USSR, explicitly recognizes freedom of religion, during the first Red occupation of Western Ukraine (1939-1941), the Communist regime overtly persecuted the Church, arresting many Ukrainian priests and ruthlessly murdering 27 of them.

This anti-Christian terror adopted more hideous means of exterminating Christianity in Ukraine during the second occupation of this country beginning in 1945. On April 11, 1945, the Soviets arrested the Metropolitan of Halych and Archbishop of Lviv, Joseph Slipy; 80-year-old Bishop Gregory Khomyshyn; Bishop John Latyshevsky; Bishop Nicholas Charnetsky, C.S.S.R.; and Bishop Nykyta Budka. On June 25, 1946, Bishop Josaphat Kotsylovsky, OSBM, and Bishop Gregory Lakota were imprisoned. All these bishops were condemned to forced labor for 8 to 10 years and even life. Some of these bishops (for instance, Bishop Gregory Khomyshyn and Bishop Josaphat Kotsylovsky) later died from maltreatment in prison. When Archbishop Joseph Slipy's or other bishops' terms expired, they were not released from prison.

In the autumn of 1947, the Communists murdered Bishop Theodore Romza (Uzhorod, Carpathian Ukraine), and in 1950, the Bishops Paul Gojdich, OSBM, and Basil Hopko (Pryashiv, Czechoslovakia), were imprisoned. On January 15, 1951, Bishop Paul Gojdich was tried and unjustly condemned to forced labor for life. Bishop Basil Hopko is now in a concentration camp.

Altogether, ten Ukrainian Catholic Bishops have been liquidated by the Reds.

In 1946, the Soviets forbade the legal continuance of the Ukrainian Catholic Church in Ukraine. Thus, in the 20th century, it has been reduced to the sorrowful plight of the "Church of the Catacombs," as was the early Church during the Neronian persecution.

Two thousand secular priests and monks were arrested and deported to slave labor camps for rightfully refusing to acknowledge the Russian Orthodox Church as their head. The Russians abolished all five dioceses of the Ukrainian

Catholic Church and persecuted mercilessly the Ukrainian laity for remaining steadfast to its Christian heritage, Church and Faith.

I request that the non-Communist governments propose to their delegations in the United Nations that the condition of the persecuted Church in Ukraine be placed on the agenda of the United Nations Assembly.

> A memorandum to all national non-Communist Delegations in the United Nations concerning Religious Persecution in Ukraine.
> ABN Correspondence,
> August-September 1956, p. 11

The Kremlin Attacks the Vatican

Devout and orthodox Catholics believe in the infallibility of the Pope in all matters pertaining to the dogmas of religious faith and moral principles if he proclaims them *ex cathedra*. In other matters even the Pope may be mistaken, and for this reason devout Catholics may be permitted to criticize certain views expressed by the Pope, provided that they do so with all due respect and also recognize the incontestable authority of His Holiness in all matters pertaining to the dogmas of religious faith and moral principles. The author of this article is a devout and orthodox Catholic and he regards the authority of the Pope as inviolable. In spite of this fact, however, he considers himself justified in questioning the prudence of the course adopted by the Vatican in its relations with the Kremlin. In our opinion there was a marked difference between the decisions reached by Pope Pius XII and those of Pope John XXIII. Pope Pius held the view that water and fire were incompatible. He excommunicated the Communists since he regarded them as incorrigible atheists. He rightly regarded Communism and religion as incompatable ideologies. He considered Communism, its role and its character, from the universal point of view. Pope John XXIII, on the other hand, viewed Communism from the Italian standpoint. In his opinion, the party led by Togliatti was by no means a fifth column of a foreign power, but an Italian political party. He did not regard it as a non-Italian party, as the party of Moscow.

True, many Italians vote for the Communist Party and nevertheless go to confession and Holy Communion. This attitude is determined by moods and emotion, vacillating sentiments, outbursts of enthusiasm, and inconsistent views. In spite of this fact, however, one cannot draw any concrete conclusions from it as regards world Communism as a system—a system which fundamentally was, is, and always will be anti-religious. In their views and practical measures the Communists' leaders assess religion as the opium of the people. And this unchangeable fact should always be borne in mind.

The Vatican should not draw any practical conclusions with regard to Communism as a system determined by the Russian mentality from a change in attitude, not of Communism as a movement, but of individual adherents of Communism as a social, economic system, or in view of the deceptive watchwords pertaining to the attitude towards religion which are at present being uttered in Italy. One cannot make a pact with the Russian atheists, the actual initiators of the persecution of the Church, of nations, and of individuals. The blessing pronounced upon the leader of militant atheism, Khrushchev, through Adzhubey and his wife ("for your closest relatives") both amazed and depressed us. True, one can pray for sinners and criminals, but one should not conduct conversations with them as if they were one's partners. For Khrushchev has not been converted and become a Paul with whom the representatives of Christ could conduct talks. In our opinion, agreements with the Communist system, which is nothing but a form of Russian godless colonial rule in the countries enslaved by Moscow, are illusory and futile. The Vatican aims to obtain religious freedom for the Catholic faith, but at the same time is prepared to acknowledge the existence of the Communist regime. But our argument is: one of the inherent characteristics of Communism is the negation of religion as an uncompromising enemy in spiritual, ideological, and moral respects.

The Russian Bolsheviks persecute and will continue to persecute religion, not because Marx and his theory furthered religious persecution by barbarous methods, but because the Russian mentality as reflected in Bolshevism was always the same, even before the phenomenon of Marxist doctrine. Although Marx adopted a negative attitude towards religion, in his works he did not by any means demand the destruction of religion by violence, a method which the Russian Bolsheviks are so fond of practicing. For this is solely a privilege of the Russians and their disciples in the whole world, for whom the Kremlin is a kind of Mecca. Various Muscovite sects, as for instance the "Dukhobory," "Molokany," "Byeguny," "Stranniki," and "Nemolyaki," paved the way for Communism as a ruthless, barbarous system of society. All these sects were fervent advocates of this system long before the forcible introduction of Bolshevism.

Even the Russian philosopher N. Berdyaev admits that Bolshevism is an organic creation of the Russian mentality, a typically Russian national phenomenon. The talented Ukrainian paintress Maria Bashkirtseva, who died of tuberculosis at the age of twenty-four, prophesied Communism in Russia eighty years ago when she characterized the Russians as a people with an organic tendency to Communism. Kostomarov, the famous Ukrainian historian of the 19th century, stressed the superficiality of the religiosity of the Russians, their religious atheism, the nihilism and corruption prevalent in the theological colleges.... And the French aristocrat A. de Custine ascertained in the 19th century that the sons of the Russian priests were for the most part anti-religious organizers. Atheists such as Dobrolyubov and Chernyshevsky came from Russian clergymen's families. In 1620 a Swede, Botvin, raised the question as to whether the Russians were Christians at all. Peter I ordered all Russian civil servants to attend church and threatened them with punishment if they did not do so.... Byelinsky wrote to Gogol that his opinion that the Russians were pious was erroneous. On the contrary, the Russians, as he pointed out, were godless. Two famous Russians, Stepniak and Bulgakov, affirmed that the atheism of the Russians was a kind of religion. And Stepniak added that the Russians believed that the Devil was God's helpmate.

Precisely because of its character there can be no fundamental change in the Russian Communist system. This system cannot exist without the persecution of religion. Nor can it negate its true character, since otherwise it would be ruined. In the 1920's the New Economic Policy (NEP) of the Russian Bolsheviks was introduced and the Ukrainian Autocephalous Orthodox Church (UAPTs) was at first tolerated. For this Church Ukrainian ecclesiastical heroes, the Metropolitans Lypkivsky and Boretsky and other ecclesiastical dignitaries, were to die as martyrs. Within a few years the Russian Bolsheviks liquidated these ecclesiastical dignitaries and their Church, which had previously been sanctioned by the Bolsheviks themselves. After the Ukrainian clergy had openly shown themselves to be militant Christians of the UAPTs, they were obliged to lay down their lives in prisons and slave-labor camps, where they were either tortured to death or shot. The same fate will undoubtedly befall the two Catholic Churches and, above all, the Ukrainian Greek Catholic Church, if their priests, who are at present active underground, should openly carry out their ecclesiastical tasks and duties. Internal—national, religious, cultural, social, and economic—forces, which threaten to destroy the Russian empire and its regime from within are at present bringing pressure to bear on the Kremlin. For this reason the Kremlin must now act cautiously and must offer a substitute NEP in the religious and cultural sector in order to be able to expose these forces more easily later on and thus destroy them. The Kremlin aims to expose and liquidate the new Chuprynkas, the new Greek Catholic Lypkivskys and Boretskys, who are secretly active in the underground in the name of Christ. It is thus the perfidious intention of the Kremlin to expose these fighters by pretending to make various concessions. By releasing the Ukrainian Metropolitan Slipy from imprisonment the Kremlin wanted to give the West, which has been lulled by the coexistence idea, new "proof" of a change in its regime. It is conceivable that Cardinal Mindszenty, Archbishop Beran, and the Ukrainian martyr Bishop Hopko will also be released in the near future, but at the same time the Kremlin will continue to close down and destroy numerous churches in the Soviet Russian sphere of influence, to kill men such as Bandera, and to prepare new murders secretly. The hypocrisy of the Kremlin is only too evident. Other "concessions" will probably follow in the very near future if the "proof" provided in the case of Metropolitan Slipy or Cardinal Mindszehty should not suffice to deceive the naive West and to divert its attention from the eventuality of a surprise attack by the Kremlin on the West.

Caveat consules! We warn the West against Moscow's deceptive game, against the outbreak of a sudden war, against an unexpected advance on the part of the Red Russian troops against Western Europe, and against another world war, which, if the West is not vigilant enough, might well destroy it in these dangerous times.

We should always bear in mind that "alleviations" of every kind which are conceded to the Ukrainian or to any other Catholic Church, whilst, at the same time, the Ukrainian Autocephalous Orthodox Church is persecuted, might result in a division amongst the Ukrainians, which would in turn lead to entirely unnecessary disputes in the denominational sector. The Vatican should realize that Moscow by its "concessions" to the Ukrainian Catholic Church is endeavoring to cause a certain disorientation in order to be able to persecute the other heroic Church of Ukraine, the Ukrainian Autocephalous Orthodox Church, more ruthlessly, since it has no intention whatever of making any "concessions" to this Church. It is an established fact that the priests and faithful of the Ukrainian Autocephalous Orthodox Church are languishing in the prisons and concentration camps of the USSR. But the Kremlin does not mention them at all. That great Metropolitan Lypkivsky died as a martyr. Has the Vatican thought of these martyrs and heroes who laid down their lives for Christ? It grieves us profoundly to think that it has not done so. On the other hand, a blessing was bestowed through the Adzhubey family on that criminal Khrushchev, who, during the period that he was governor-general of Ukraine by the grace of Stalin, liquidated both Ukrainian Churches. Neither Mrs. Bandera, the wife of the Ukrainian leader murdered by Moscow, nor her children received the Pope's blessing. This is the sad truth!

I do not wish to disparage the authority of the Pope, the supreme head of the Catholic Church in which I believe. But precisely because I believe in this Church I consider it my duty to tell my brothers of the same faith the truth. Some persons might point out that the question at issue is a political one. This is not true. The Church should not concern itself with transitory political matters but with truth and moral principles, with noble ideals. I do not regard the attitude adopted by certain Vatican circles as correct—namely, that ecclesiastical policy should enable the faithful to enjoy freedom of religious practices under every state's political, ideological, and social system and should not let them become martyrs. This is a purely abstract theory and is equivalent to reducing religion completely to the level of formalism, whilst the true nature of religion is not taken into account at all.

The true nature of religion does not consist merely in visiting church, for one can also pray in prison or in a slave-labor camp. The true nature of religion is the fight for truth even though one may not be in a position to take the Holy Sacrament. The time has now come to wage the fight for the realization of Christian truth here on earth and in all spheres of life. The Ukrainian national liberation idea and Ukrainian freedom-loving nationalism are inseparably bound up with militant Christianity. And this nationalism strives to realize the Truth of God on earth, inasmuch as it defends the right of Ukraine and of other peoples enslaved by Moscow to national independence, to freedom of the individual, and to social justice. The entire purport of the Ukrainian ideas can be summed up in the following words: God, fatherland, truth, honor, freedom, and justice.... The essential difference between our conception of Christian practices and that of certain Vatican circles lies in the fact that we are of the opinion that Christianity should in principle and in all spheres of life oppose Communism and should not, by means of the recognition and tolerance of the main principles and fundamental phenomena of the Russian Bolshevik system in many spheres of life, strive to obtain a "minimum of freedom" for formal religious practices. True, we do not believe that there is any people on whom the curse of God rests to such an extent that it could never partake of the truth of Christ wholly. But we cannot by any means reconcile ourselves to the thought that there are certain circles in the

Vatican which are of the opinion that militant atheists and persecutors of Christ, namely the bulk of the Russian people, could become overnight a nation of crusaders. If that were the case, all the subjugated nations which are tortured and persecuted because they defend the truth of Christ would in future be led by the Russian sham Pauls regardless of the fact that the saints, heroes, and martyrs of our day—men like Metropolitans Lypkivsky and Slipy, Petlura, Chuprynka, Bandera—were killed or imprisoned by the Russians.

The opportunism which has seized part of the Western Church and some of its hierarchs casts a shadow on this terrible epoch.

Attempts are being made now to reach a modus vivendi with the Antichrist, who, according to the Gospel of St. Matthew, tempted the Son of God and promised Him the kingdoms of the world. But Christ withstood this temptation.

At first the West began to evade the fight for the truth of Christ in everyday life, and now it capitulates, by way of experiment, directly to the Antichrist. But capitulation on the part of the West to a life of ease and comfort, to the "golden calf," may also lead to capitulation to another "calf" as personified by the aggressive evil of the Kremlin. Martyrdom is to be avoided for the sake of the peaceful exercise of formal religious practices.

The question at issue is not that the Catholic churches behind the Iron Curtain, in the USSR, should be opened but that the truth of Christ should triumph. For the churches may be opened, but truth nevertheless continues to be persecuted. Truth must be realized in all spheres of our life. Is the Vatican really convinced that the Kremlin would agree to a realization of Christian truth in all spheres of our life? One must bear in mind Moscow's old watchword: "Moscow is the third and last Rome; there can never be a fourth Rome."

The seven million Italians who, as a result of the weakness of the Church in ideological, moral, and altruistic respects and in consequence of the lack of a profound Christian faith and firm will to fight for justice and against evil not only in formal sermons but also in deeds, have become pro-Communists, cannot cast a shadow on our militant Church, on our holy Kyiv, a center of the rebirth of Christianity in the world. We who may perhaps already tomorrow be the victims of Khrushchev's crimes herewith solemnly and openly declare that we will spare no sacrifice for truth and that we will enter into no coexistence with the tyrants, not even for any ephemeral concessions, which are nothing but a diabolical temptation on the part of the Antichrist.

We know only too well that Moscow will never renounce the Ukrainian territories of its own free will. We shall have to drive Moscow out of Ukraine by force and punish the tyrants.

The Ukrainian Church can only be really free in an independent Ukrainian state, but not in a Russian prison of peoples. For it has never been and never will be possible for the Ukrainian Church to be free as long as the national freedom of Ukraine is crushed under the heel of the Russian overlords. Even though the whole world may fall round Khrushchev's neck, we, the Ukrainian nationalists, will defy Moscow, for we prefer to fight and to die rather than to see our people and our Church degraded. We shall never shake hands with the hangman of Ukraine, not even if all the churches in Ukraine should be opened (which we, incidentally, consider most unlikely), for the occupant of Ukraine can only be driven out of Ukraine with the aid of Ukrainian weapons.

We bow down in reverence before the great self-sacrifice and noble personality of the sorely tried Metropolitan Joseph Slipy, of whom the entire Christian world and not only the Catholic Church can rightly be proud, for he has become the symbol of resistance against militant atheism for the whole of Christianity, just as the first Christians and the apostles of Christ in the days when people were not concerned with things of secondary importance but with the main issue, faith in God and in Christ and the willingness to die for this faith. Metropolitan Joseph Slipy is a martyr of militant Christianity, both of Catholicism and of Orthodoxy, for during the many long years of his imprisonment he was undoubtedly a spiritual father and a comforter to Catholics, to members of the Orthodox Church, and to Protestants alike—in short, to all those who believe in Jesus Christ. They all regarded him as an indomitable, undaunted, great, and incomparable spiritual leader and a good shepherd of the Christian flock. The Orthodox Ukrainians likewise venerate Metropolitan Slipy. And the faithful of the entire Christian world see in him the new spirit of a martyr and an example worthy of being imitated. He not only strengthened the Christians in their faith by his conduct as a martyr, by his sufferings and his unbroken spirit, but the Mohammedans, the Buddhists, and all those who believe in God regarded him as a spiritual comforter, as a modest but great man who was prepared to endure suffering for us all. In view of Metropolitan Slipy's great merits, it is all the more surprising that certain circles in the Vatican have so far failed to recognize them, for he has not yet been honored even with the title and rank of a cardinal.

We Ukrainian Christians shall be grateful to the Almighty if the divine providence entrusts our Metropolitan, who already belongs to the whole of Christianity, with a great mission in the entire Ecumenical Church. We are firmly convinced that the intrigues and temptations of the Devil, of which St. Matthew speaks, will be defeated if a great martyr for God and for man, for the honor and dignity of the individual, for his native country, and for all his fellow-sufferers, a great Christian and Ukrainian, Metropolitan Slipy, is chosen as the leader of the great crusade of faith and of militant Christianity against the Russian Antichrist. We are firmly convinced that the temptations of Satan will then be overcome and that he will not achieve his aim.

In its fight for the rebirth of the world, for its de-barbarization and for its Christianization, Christianity must be led by martyrs and ascetics, by heroes and fighters. In view of this fact, the demand that the minimum of freedom should be granted for the exercise of formal religious practices seems very petty and insignificant. Far more important matters are at issue: the supremacy of Christ or of the Antichrist, but not a coexistence between the two.

The heroism and the martyrdom of millions of persons for Christ and for their fatherland, for man, created in God's image, today predestine Kyiv to give the West a new stimulus. For at this stage Kyiv might well assume the lead of the Christian crusade against the destructive forces of the Antichrist to the honor and glory of the entire Ecumenical Church. This city, the city of St. Sophia, which was blessed by Christ's Apostle St. Andrew, should fulfill this duty towards the city of the Apostle St. Peter. It is by no means a Ukrainian but a Russian theory that "there will never be a fourth Rome," for there will always be only one Rome—Moscow. But in the interests of the Ecumenical Church in our day Kyiv should occupy the position which it deserves, as a vanguard of heroes and martyrs, headed by the Ukrainian Metropolitan and martyr Joseph Slipy, in a crusade of militant Christianity.

In view of the great danger which threatens the Church and the tasks which must necessarily arise out of this situation, faintheartedness and hesitancy must be cast aside. The light of the rebirth of mankind shines forth from the Ukrainian Christian East in the catacombs. *Ex Oriente lux*—even though it is an Orient which at present is forced to be active underground!

The Ukrainian Review,
No III, 1963, pp. 89-96

The Longing for Eternal Values

For forty years the diabolical system of Bolshevism has been endeavoring to eradicate from the human soul faith in God, the longing for eternal values, for absolute truth, and for a deeper meaning of life than the one preached by dialectical materialism. But it is inborn in human nature to put its creative powers in intellectual, social, and cultural respects to the test in every way.

Man is only really free if he has free choice. And the essence of this freedom includes the possibility of being able to engage in free activity and to make a free decision. This possibility of a choice between alternatives is thus characteristic of the free will of every individual.

In its diabolical presumptuousness, Russian Messianism—Bolshevism—does not hesitate to defy human nature and the divine teachings of Christ. It does its utmost to eradicate completely from the human soul all religious and national elements, the personal characteristics of the individual, his ties with old, established traditions, his longing to be independent in his decisions and to be able to dispose at his own free discretion of his own person, his material and intellectual achievements.

The dynamic character of Ukrainian Christianity constitutes the main obstacle to the intellectual enslavement of Ukraine by materialistic Russia, whose passive and superficial Christianity in the past helped to achieve the victory of anti-Christian Bolshevism, which is organically allied to the Russian mentality and cannot therefore be regarded as an imported product of Western Communism—a fact which, incidentally, was admitted and explained at length by the Russian Christian philosopher N. Berdyaev in his works *The Middle Ages* and *The Meaning of Communism*.

The enemy knows only too well who it is who is digging the pit he will fall into. For this reason he has launched a fierce attack on liberation nationalism—that is to say, on the predominating idea of our age—and on heroic Christianity, this ever-dynamic and elementary force of the intellectual and moral rebirth of man and, indeed, of all peoples.

These two forces behind the Iron Curtain, which are so closely allied to each other, represent a deadly danger to the Bolshevik rulers, to the empire and to its ideological, materialistic, and atheistic foundations. The Russian Bolsheviks even admit this in their publications. The fact that the Red Russians are forced to try to combat the ideas which inspire the individual people is clear proof that the activity of the national, religious, cultural, and social underground movements in their various forms has assumed a dangerous character. This circumstance could no longer be concealed and the Russians have thus been obliged to try to combat it systematically. But one can neither hide a vulnerability nor get rid of it. And it is this vulnerability which will eventually cause the downfall of the empire of the Antichrist.

The Failure of Militant Atheism

Even the revival of the state-controlled Russian "Orthodox" Church is nothing but proof of the failure of godless Bolshevism in its anti-Christian fight. Nor can this be altered by the fact that Bolshevism is doing its utmost to use this new type of state-controlled orthodoxy, in keeping with the example set by the tsars, for the purposes of Russian imperialism and Messianism according to the motto "Moscow is a third Rome and there can never be a fourth!" In spite of all this, however, the "opium of the people" (religion), which has allegedly been eradicated completely, cannot be destroyed in the human soul. On the contrary, what disappears from the human soul is the dialectical materialism that was to take the place of religious metaphysics and philosophy. Moscow does not want to admit the rapid growth of religiosity among the subjugated peoples, such as Ukraine, Lithuania, etc., in the form of their true Churches, which are steadily increasing in strength, namely the Autocephalous Orthodox and Catholic Churches, which are not dependent on the so-called "all-Russian" Patriarch. The Bolshevik press is resorting to attacks directed against "Jehovah's Witnesses" as the most dangerous "confession," since it is the one which can most easily be accused of dependence on American funds and connections with American tourists, etc. The fact that the Soviet press constantly sounds the alarm and, after an alleged triumph of Marxism and "enlightened" atheism for the past forty years is still obliged to stress the prevalence of "religious prejudices" is undoubtedly proof of the intensification of religious feeling, which is above all in evidence to a large extent amongst the younger generation.

Izvestiya of September 16, 1960 published a reply to "Uncle Matviy," who wrote a letter to the Soviet press in which he condemned a mother who abandoned her child in order to lead a more comfortable life. He wrote as follows: "It is undoubtedly a base trick. But what is the cause for such behavior? Materialism alone is to blame. A religious person—that is to say, a really religious person and not the type of person about whom the papers write in order to make people turn away from religion [the writer is most certainly referring to the state-controlled orthodoxy of the Russian "Patriarch"]—would never have allowed himself to be carried away to such an extent. But what can the materialists do in such a case? If someone has already been born with negative qualities, what ideas must he adopt in order to change his ways? Religion is the only idea that can influence the human soul. And many examples of this can be seen in our everyday life. If one is a convinced materialist, one regards oneself as a product of various chemical processes—that is to say, that one should enjoy life to the full. Think logically, comrades! In the Bible man's godless attitude—'Let us eat and drink, for tomorrow we shall die'—is already reproved."

"Uncle Matviy" circulated his letters by the dozens until he was finally arrested.

The Russian rulers are greatly disquieted that the nationalists circulate anti-atheistic and anti-Bolshevik leaflets, which very often have been written on a typewriter and are left lying about intentionally in railway compartments and pushed through letter-boxes. In this connection the journal *Voprosy Filosofiyi* ("Problems of Philosophy"), No, 8/60, writes: "From the ideological point of view those persons must be exposed who are seeking to mislead the Soviet people by writing anonymous letters and secretly smuggling anti-Soviet literature into letter-boxes."

In another Soviet paper of May of last year, mention was made of a letter by Yuriy Kuleshiv, who "affirms in all seriousness that no one except God could have created man"; Kuleshiv is of the opinion that everyone "should go back to the Christian faith...."

The Soviet press also refers to the printing in secret of prayer-books and other religious writings. From our own sources we have learnt of secret religious messengers who "with their staff in their hand" wander from village to village and from town to town proclaiming the Word of God....

We frequently hear reports to the effect that agents of the Russian secret police inform the "refractory" Ukrainian Catholic priests, who have remained loyal to their Church and its hierarchy and who after their return from exile continue to fulfill their priestly duties in secret, that they can continue their religious activity, but on one condition: namely that they must subordinate themselves to the Russian "Patriarchate." Otherwise they will be banished to Siberia again. Such threats have, however, failed to impress priests. One could quote many other cases of religious activity by the two Ukrainian Churches and many other examples of the intrepidity and steadfastness of their priests, who refuse to allow their spirit to be broken by the threats of godless Moscow.

The paper, *Young Communist* (No. 11, 1960) published a statement by a mother who said that she sent her children to church so that "religion would help her to bring up her children to be honest, decent-living beings." Seeing that their father had been killed during the war, she would not have been able on her own to raise her children to be modest and hard-working had not her faith in God helped her....

The fight for the soul of the individual and, above all, for the soul of youth is being continued with the greatest possible intensity. Moscow is doing its utmost to delude the youth of the subjugated peoples with a vision of Communism (which actually is already in decline). Moscow is endeavoring to prove to them the "objective truth" of dialectical materialism, but obviously without success, for no doctrine is more unscientific. And youth, incidentally, longs for eternal, divine, and transcendent values, which do not belong to this world....

The Victory of the "Remnants" of the Past

The Secretary of the Central Committee of the Komsomol, S. Pavlov, recently sounded the alarm: "It has been ascertained recently that religion and its servants are the active instigators of bourgeois ideology in the villages..." Izvestiya (October 6, 1960) and other Soviet papers try to divert the attention of the population from the Catholic and Orthodox underground Churches. They attack above all Protestant sects of every kind, since they find it easiest to affirm that these sects entertain relations with the United States of America. Thus they are able to attack religion from the secular point of view, for the "ideologists of Jehovah's Witnesses are the American imperialists." The Soviet press likewise attacks the Mennonites, the Seventh-Day Adventists, and many others, which they accuse either of collaboration with the Nazis or of espionage activity on behalf of the Americans. The press launches these attacks because Moscow is unable to combat successfully the ideological and religious re-awakening and rebirth of Christianity.

All this proves the complete failure of militant atheism on the one hand, and an increasingly intensive search for eternal values on the part of man, who constantly longs for God, on the other. Forty years of godless Russian tyranny have not succeeded in eradicating from the human soul what has been inborn in it for thousands of years, namely the longing for eternal truth and what is good.

Young Communist (No. 10, 1960), for instance, writes: "The young people who have been infected by the remnants of the past must be re-educated." But it is not worth the effort! No human or diabolical force can succeed in obliterating what is divine in the human soul. God created man in his own image. In view of this, how futile and base the efforts of the Russian satraps in this connection seem! Foreign tourists reported that a group of active members of the Komsomol forced their way into St. Volodymyr's Cathedral in Kyiv during the Easter Mass in 1960 and tried to interrupt the service by making a noise and bawling. On the other hand, it is an established fact that in 1955 five hundred Ukrainian women in the concentration camp in Kingir (Kazakhstan), assuming that their courageous action would deter the Russian hangmen from slaughtering their insurgent fellow-prisoners, threw themselves in front of the tanks of the Russian atheists and were crushed to death singing religious and patriotic songs. These brave women remind one of the early converted Christians, who, whilst they were being torn to pieces by wild animals in the forum of the Roman Colosseum, sang hymns in praise of Christ.

In its edition of June 3, 1960, Izvestiya mentioned a religious underground center in Irkutsk which was extending its activity to the whole of Siberia. It also reported that this center possessed underground printing offices and disseminated propaganda affirming that people should leave the collectives without delay and should not take part in the elections held by the godless Soviets. According to reports by foreigners who have been released from Soviet concentration camps, Ukrainians constitute about 40 percent of the total number of prisoners and persons exiled to Siberia, whereas Russians only constitute 8 to 10 percent (and the majority of these are criminal prisoners). There can likewise be no doubt about the fact that it is precisely the Catholic and Orthodox Ukrainians who are the driving force of the religious rebirth in Siberia.

The religious underground movement in the Baltic countries is also constantly growing. The journal *Ogonyok* (September 25, 1960) reported that there were two secret Catholic convents in Kaunas in Lithuania. "In these convents," so the periodical wrote, "there were icons of the 'Crucifixion' in every cell.... Amongst the two dozen 'Brides of Christ' there were two laboratory assistants of the medical school, a nurse from the local hospital, two students from the college of technology..... Their wages and scholarship money were handed over to the Mother Superior. The nuns are not allowed to have any possessions of their own. Theaters, cinemas, clubs, and places of amusement—the internees are deprived of all these things since they are regarded as 'sinful.' The strict rules of these convents demand that the members should take the vow of eternal virginity. Very often these fanatics try to convert their colleagues at the medical school and college of technology to their faith."

What is the Real Purpose of Life?

As can be seen from these facts, neither Communist propaganda nor re-education in the spirit of Marxism has succeeded in eradicating religion. In its victorious advance Christianity is bursting asunder the fetters with which the Russian atheists are trying to chain the souls of the subjugated peoples. The most important point in this respect is that the younger generation is adhering to the Christian faith and is courageously defending its ideals. The young people of the subjugated countries, who are being tormented by state-controlled education and training in the spirit of materialism, long for higher ideals and seek the purpose of life, not in everyday and material things, but in eternal values and ideals.

Writing to the Soviet press, a Valentyna Zarytska affirms: "Frequently in the evenings I ponder on the question of what the real purpose of life is. Everyone must have some aim in mind. We see no aim before us. In short, we long for a life full of strong and ardent enthusiasm. But we do not feel such enthusiasm. Can there be such a thing in our day as strong and ardent enthusiasm?... You will retort—uncultivated virgin regions, the cultivation of Siberia. But there, too, the new settlers become old settlers and their life becomes stereotyped and monotonous...."

Another periodical published the following letter: "I am interested in the question as to why man lives at all. He eats, sleeps, and works. Why does he do all this? Should one swim against the current? But it is boring always to swim with the current!... How can one find out what is the real purpose of life?..."

The answer to these profound questions which occupy the minds of the people behind the Iron Curtain has been simplified most crudely by Khrushchev in his ruthlessly empirical attitude promising a "piece of meat" as an addition to the Communist ideology, or constantly repeating: "We must catch up with and overtake America in the production of material goods."

There is something more than tragicomic about the huge propaganda sloganeering "Catch up with and overtake America" which one sees on the walls of wretched hovels where large families live in one tiny room.

In any case, this demand can never be realized in the USSR, nor can it be an incentive in the lives of persons who are seeking the way to God and to eternal values and not solely the way to acquire American refrigerators, television sets, luxury cars, and other transient comforts of our life in this world. All the propaganda about "sputniks" and "luniks" has prompted youth to turn its thoughts towards divine and eternal values and to ask with ever-growing insistence: "What is the origin of the cosmos? How did man originate? Who created this fly which, even though it is so tiny, has a life of its own and flies about in space?"

As a result of technical achievements and nuclear physics, man again and again recognizes the eternal values and the eternal power of God, the Creator of this world. The "sputniks" and the "luniks" and even the "landing" of human beings on Mars or on the moon are by no means a guarantee of the superiority and predominance of one social economic order or another, or of a certain philosophy, but on the contrary are further proof, and so far perhaps the most effective proof, of the existence of the secret of the universe and of God.

And, incidentally, the grandiose development of nuclear science and the growing interest of youth in this field are no proof that youth has abandoned its idealist and philosophical attitude or has lost interest in metaphysics. In ancient times attempts were made to discover the divine secret of the universe through the philosophies of Socrates, Plato, Aristotle, and Kant, or the philosophical ideas of Thomas Aquinas, which were based on the divine revelation. Nowadays, nuclear fission, the research into thermonuclear energy and outer space constitute youth's approach to a further recognition of the divine through the discovery of new laws and of new wonders of God's world order. Just as in former times it was, above all, the humanistic scholars who showed those who thirsted for knowledge the approach to a recognition of the secrets of the universe, it is now nuclear physics and medical science which guide youth in its search for truth to the divine mystery of the universe and of creation.

Methods change with the times. Tomorrow, the king of sciences, philosophy, will take the place of nuclear physics and medical science in this respect. But be that as it may, until the end of the world man will continue to seek to discover the original phenomenon of human existence and the fundamental secret of the divine order of the world.

The younger generation behind the Iron Curtain does not accept the technical achievements of the Soviet Union as proof of the "superiority of Communism over capitalism," but regards them as the solution of one more of the countless secrets of the universe which corroborate the antithesis of atheism, namely the divine Omnipotence that has created all things out of nothing and by its own will. Thus, though the "sputniks" and "luniks" draw the attention of the people subjugated in the USSR to the heavens in a physical sense, this nevertheless also occurs from the philosophical and transcendental aspects and means the acceleration of the end of godless Bolshevism. The "metaphysics of Communism" have long been moribund in the collective soul of the younger generation of the enslaved peoples and the mysticism of the Russian mission is regarded as something alien by these youths. The "big Russian brother who makes the rest of the world happy" and the "piece of meat as an addition to the theory of Communism"—all this is unequalled cynicism. The "piece of meat" and "more butter"—slogans which Khrushchev on one occasion, in one of his speeches, hurled at the leftist extremists—cannot take the place of the search for eternal truth, for the cause of our existence. In the subjugated countries Communism has proved a complete failure in the ideological respect; all that has remained is the inquisitional methods of the Soviet secret police.

For this reason the Russian periodical *Literature and Life* expresses considerable alarm and affirms that a "hard fight is being conducted." "This fight seems to be much harder than we imagined...." Which is undoubtedly true, for no one has ever won the fight against the Christian faith. And this also applies to satanic Moscow!

Some time ago, the prominent Ukrainian ideologist Prof. Dr. Dmytro Dontsov wrote about the journey of an unknown apostle of God's teachings through Ukraine, about the significance of certain "rumors," about mysterious incidents in Ukraine, and about mysticism in the life of the Ukrainian people—a life that is one constant struggle.

American authors wrote about a "miracle in the concentration camp in Vorkuta." MVD agents tried to force some Ukrainian Catholic nuns, who had been abducted to this camp in the Arctic Circle, to work for the atheistic occupation regime. The nuns refused to do so. By way of punishment they were then forced to endure the icy Siberian cold without clothes for three whole days. At the same time, cold water was poured over them. The nuns prayed and sang hymns and survived these inhuman tortures. The MVD hangmen were so disturbed by this miracle that they eventually took the nuns back to their barracks and did not molest them again.

This miracle in Vorkuta is merely a premonitory sign of an approaching, new, divine order, which will be built on the ruins of the godless Russian colonial empire.

"Rumors" about the end of the world, mysterious heralds—"those with a pilgrim's staff," as they are called in Ukraine, mystic happenings—all this directs the attention of the population to something that is exactly the opposite of transitoriness. Jehovah's Witnesses, which of all Protesant sects talks most about the end of the world, owes its popularity mainly to the mystic nature of its prophecies. Various versions of apocryphal Bible stories are told and rumors of various miracles are circulating.

We have received a number of authentic reports about the circulation of pastoral letters written by the internal Ukrainian Catholic hierarchs and about the heroic attitude of that martyr Metropolitan Dr. Joseph Slipy! An ascetic in the truest sense, he refused all help (parcels from abroad) and alleviation of his lot as a prisoner, since he did not want to live under better conditions than his faithful flock. His attitude and his unbroken spirit can indeed be compared to the spiritual courage of the priests of the early Christians. Surely all this is proof of the complete failure of militant Bolshevik atheism?

Religion and militant Christianity are, above all, alive amongst the peoples who have been subjugated, humiliated, and deprived of all their national and human rights. The paper *Komsomolskaya Pravda* wrote ironically about "living apostles." At the same time, it exhorted the population to combat the "incredible rumors" which are circulating in the enslaved countries and in particular in Ukraine (in Mykolayiv and Odessa, for instance). One of these rumors alleges that girls who wear red coats should be killed.

These and similar rumors are being circulated orally house to house and from place to place. They give rise to a feeling of alarm, tension, and the expectation of something unknown. The hysteria frequently occasioned by "sputniks" and "luniks" is by no means proof of enthusiasm about the "Communist achievements," but rather the expression of the feeling that prevails amongst the population, namely that something mysterious will happen in the near future.

In its edition of October 6, 1960, *Izvestiya* reported that religiosity had increased to immense proportions in the region of Krasnodar. It accused the Orthodox faithful of acting as henchmen to the "fascist occupants, of anti-Soviet subversive activity, of violation of the Soviet legislation, of criminal offenses," etc. Since Soviet Russian propaganda, however, designates every patriotic deed that is performed by a member of an enslaved people and not by the ruling Russian people as activity on behalf of the "fascists and Americans" or as a crime, it is quite obvious that religious feeling and patriotism go hand in hand. A woman teacher recently wrote in *Teacher's Newspaper* that she had read a notice in the press to the effect that some people had broken with religion. "Why," she asked, "does the press never report that someone has gone back to Christianity and why does it never say for what reasons the person in question has begun to believe in God again?..."

St. Sophia versus the Kremlin

The Bolshevik atheists who ridicule religious mysticism as "superstition and prejudice" are themselves obliged to capitulate before it. Unintentionally they espouse this cause themselves, for they are incapable of exterminating the longing in man's soul for all that lies beyond this world, for what is shrouded in mystery—the longing to understand the secret of our existence on earth. For this reason the notorious "dedication of youth" has been introduced in the Soviet Zone of Germany.

The paper *Soviet Estonia* in its edition No. 132 propagates a "Komsomol marriage ceremony" instead of a solemnization in a church, and a kind of "summer days" for youth instead of baptism; it advocates a kind of code of "Soviet customs," to be worked out and published in a compilation. It is not so long ago since Bormann and other blasphemers adopted a similar procedure under the banner of the swastika. They presented newly-married couples with a copy of Hitler's *Mein Kampf* instead of a Bible and propagated senseless "old Germanic customs": these also included the blasphemous obituary speech made by Hitler at the grave of religious-minded Hindenburg, which ended with the old Germanic words "enter Valhalla...." Why should thousands of "pilgrims to the Kremlin" pray to the mummies of Lenin and Stalin in the Moscow mausoleum if people have no longing for mysticism?

Literaturnaya Gazeta ("Literary Gazette") of October 15, 1960 complains that the Orthodox faithful with ever-increasing conspiracy are holding secret meetings in the forests. Such epithets as "Christ-sellers," which are applied to those who are dissatisfied with and opposed to the regime, are certainly in strange taste. They are used to designate those persons who establish contact with foreign tourists and give them pictures and similar things as presents. Other contemptuous designations are also used, as for instance "Nibocho," which is applied to those persons who "are neither in favor of God nor the Devil" because they have apparently been disappointed by dialectical materialism and therefore seek truth outside the Communist Party. The press of the Soviet Union, which is centrally and strictly controlled by the Russians, likewise talks about "political vagabonds" who seek a "higher life," as well as about "preachers of free life" who carry on "senseless conversations about a fusion with Nature" and "boast of their theory of a higher form of life."

These comments refer to the philosophically-minded young people of Krasnoyarsk. The organ of the Central Committee of the Komsomol of Ukraine reports from the town of Kryvy Rih that five young engineers held secret meetings on the banks of the River Saksahan in order to discuss rumors from abroad and news items broadcast by foreign stations. With considerable indignation the press quotes a remark made by one of these young people who was searching for truth, that he "had not been by any means profoundly moved by the flight of the cosmic rocket." There can be no denying the fact that the fiercest attacks on the part of the atheists of the Kremlin are directed against Christian Ukraine, against a country whose eternal city Kyiv from time immemorial was the symbol and the center of Christian culture in Eastern Europe. As a symbol of faith in God, Kyiv to an ever-increasing degree has become a fortress against Moscow, the symbol of militant atheism and the capital of the Antichrist.

It is precisely Ukraine that is putting up the fiercest resistance against Russian aggression in the national, religious, and social sphere. But here, too, Ukraine is being robbed in a shameful manner inasmuch as its efforts in the fight against the Antichrist are ascribed to the advocates of atheism, the Russians. Every effort is made to conceal the heroic Christianity of Ukraine from the Free World.

None of the Ukrainian bishops broke down during their imprisonment. They all sacrificed their lives courageously and worthily for Christ, and those who are still alive languish, unbroken in spirit, in Soviet concentration camps. But no mention whatever is made of these facts. Under the tortures inflicted by the police the Ukrainian Metropolitans Joseph Slipy and Vasyl Lypkivsky were not in the least broken spiritually. The Free World, however, seeks refuge in a strange silence as regards the martyrdom of these intrepid Ukrainian ecclesiastical dignitaries.

The Ideological Downfall of Marxism

The Soviet Russian journal *Ogonyok* recently sounded the alarm because religiosity is steadily growing amongst the young people of Lithuania. In the town of Birzhay, for instance, a priest "organized" a Catholic "club" for children in his house. This "club" was attended by twenty children from the local school. After having been "re-educated" they began to attend church as "zealous believers."

Similar conditions prevail in the Caucasus, where the Bolsheviks are carrying on an equally intensive atheistic propaganda campaign. They use atheistic exhibitions, special films, broadcasts, articles in the press, lectures, and holidays in order to prevent the people from devoting any time to religion. But all these efforts on the part of the Red Russians will prove futile.

In the Soviet Russian journal *Rodina* ("The Fatherland"), No. 4, VII-VIII, 1960, a woman writer called Markova published a review of the film *Ivanna*, which is full of blasphemous hatred directed against the Ukrainian Catholic Church and its late Metropolitan Count Andreas Sheptytsky. As in the Caucasus, so, too, in Ukraine, a foul campaign of militant atheism has recently been launched with the intention of bringing discredit upon the Church by defamation and lies. If the "out-of-date" is already past and done with, then one does not need to conduct vile and defamatory propaganda against it. Nor is it necessary to represent the Metropolitan, a servant of God, who is to be canonized by the Vatican in the near future, as a "German collaborator and informer" and to slant the film against a Christian faith that is already "dead." In her review F. Markova stresses above all the revenge which the Metropolitan allegedly took on a woman partisan. This partisan had refused to continue to serve the Ukrainian "bourgeois nationalists" and the priests, who were nothing but "German collaborators." When she realized the "true" character of the Ukrainian Catholic Church, she joined the Reds and helped them to liberate three hundred prisoners of war from a German prison camp. Allegedly the Metropolitan, with the help of her father, who was also a priest, succeeded in handing her over to the German occupation forces. When she was standing on the gallows with the noose around her neck, she begged that her hands be freed from the fetters. Then "in a rage she tears her chain from her neck and with obvious contempt throws the cross on it onto the ground."

"This final and highly dramatic scene in the film leaves a deep impression on the beholder. It is permeated with great optimism and reveals all the greatness and spiritual strength of a person who sacrifices his or her life for their own people." With these words the godless Markova ends her review of *Ivanna*, which was produced specially for Ukraine.

The author of the scenario is the Russian V. Belyaev, who, together with Mykhaylo Rudnytsky, on a previous occasion published a libelous attack on the Ukrainian Catholic Church and, above all, on its Metropolitan Count Andreas Sheptytsky.

As was announced by the Soviet press, Inna Burduchenko, the actress who played the part of the heroine in *Ivanna*, was burnt to death in an accident while shooting her next film. This piece of news was soon common knowledge in Ukraine. And the Ukrainian people regard the tragic death of the actress as God's punishment for her blasphemy and contempt for the cross.

"For practically two years Klevtsiv was forced by circumstances to be active in the remote and sinister underground," wrote *Izvestiya* and other Soviet press organs. "Imagine a small and damp mud-hut, which he burrowed out of the ground with the perseverance of a beaver...." Klevtsiv printed leaflets, he traveled as a courier with "holy instructions," broke with his family, and became the "pioneer of a secret religious sect," which successfully developed its activity in Siberia. It can be assumed that this "sect" was an Orthodox or Catholic community consisting of prisoners exiled to Siberia, which would be far more difficult to combat than any other sect.

With such reports as these, the Bolsheviks themselves answer the question as to whether such films as *Ivanna* are likely to be a success in Ukraine (which "supplies" 40 percent of the deportees, totalling 17 million, in the prison camps).

And in Turkestan Comrade Mukhitdinov, a humble and loyal servant of Moscow, will not be able to replace the profound mysticism of Islam and the Turkestanians' faith in God by "cotton festivals" (*Pakhta Bairami*).

Moscow is obliged to admit the ideological downfall of Marxism and dialectical materialism, as well as the enormous growth of religiosity amongst the population. The underground process of fermentation must indeed be powerful if even the Soviet press sees itself obliged to polemicize with the Orthodox faithful by publicly attacking them. This would hardly be necessary if there were only a few isolated cases of religiosity amongst the people.

The future world will belong not to the godless Russians, but to the militant, freedom-loving nationalism of the subjugated peoples, which is based on heroic Christianity.

The Ukrainian Review,
No. II, 1961, pp. 11-23

The Ecumenical Council and the Expectations of the Faithful of the Persecuted Church

Not only the Ukrainian public but also others in the West have approved of the protest by the Ukrainian bishops in the Vatican against the presence of the delegates of the Russian Orthodox "Church" as observers at the Ecumenical Council. A wide response by the world press to this protest clearly indicates that the Ukrainian ecclesiastical dignitaries can count on the moral support of the freedom-loving, anti-Communist West, since human rights, human dignity, and the right to freedom of religious faith are recognized there.

The Ukrainian nationalist liberation movement, which in its fight for the freedom of the Ukrainian people upholds the Christian and national ideas as a vital force in the life of the Ukrainian people, is greatly perturbed at certain measures adopted by some Vatican circles, which are endeavoring to establish a kind of modus vivendi with the atheistic governments, since they obviously hope that these governments will make certain temporary concessions of a local nature for the churches in the regions in question. But one should bear in mind that these governments will on principle continue to maintain a hostile attitude towards the Church as well as towards the rights of individuals and peoples. For it is obvious that neither their doctrine nor they themselves as representatives or servants of the Russian atheistic, imperialistic center are likely to accept or adopt any fundamental changes.

The Ukrainians have indeed set their hopes on the noble plans of Pope John XXIII and Pope Paul VI, aimed at the restoration of Christian unity, for there could not be a finer and more magnanimous idea than this amongst the Christians at the present time. Nevertheless, we are of the opinion that the course which certain circles of the Vatican intend taking in order to carry out the papal plan in practice does not always seem to be right. For these circles for inexplicable reasons are—as far as Orthodoxy is concerned—attaching most importance to the question of the Russian Orthodox Church. With the help of this Church the circles who are at present influential in the Vatican are hoping "to convert the East." And these circles are dazzled by this illusion to such an extent that they are obviously—and on the strength of so-called realistic considerations—also pursuing a policy of opportunism with regard to the present "Orthodox" Russian "Church," which is headed by the "Patriarch" Alexey. A few years ago we were perturbed when Vatican diplomats refused to continue to recognize the diplomatic representation of (non-Communist) Lithuania and Poland and based their refusal on international legal considerations which were of secondary importance. Later we learned from the press that the Pope received an official representative of Communist Poland in audience. The spokesman of the Union Secretariat, which is headed by Cardinal Bea, is reported to have stated that, in the event of certain preconditions being fulfilled, there would be a possibility of the Vatican entering into diplomatic relations with the USSR. Can it be that the Vatican circles still believe in something in which not even the children in Ukraine believe—namely, that structural changes are possible in the atheistic regime which is now led by Khrushchev and which until recently was led by Stalin? As regards this subject one only needs read what that disillusioned Yugoslav Communist Djilas says in his book *Conversations with Stalin*:

Stalin's successors are continuing his work; the inner structure of their regime is composed of the same elements, of the same ideas, conceptions, and methods which

prompted Stalin.... Even today, after the so-called de-Stalinization, one can unfortunately only reach the same conclusion as in former times: those who want to live
and survive in a world which is different from the world created by Stalin are
obliged to fight. For Stalin's world has not ceased to exist; its character and its power
have been preserved unbroken.

Can it be that this truth, which is so obvious to Djilas, has not been comprehended by these Vatican circles?

Are not the ruthless suppressions of the Polish, Hungarian, and German
revolts as well as of numerous riots by Ukrainian prisoners in the Soviet Russian
concentration camps, the persecution of the Ukrainian churches, the arrest and
imprisonment of Ukrainian priests and their Metropolitan, the incarceration of
individuals and the genocide committed against entire peoples, the tyranny and
enslavement, the murder of Stepan Bandera and Lev Rebet—which was organized by Shelepin, the deputy Prime Minister of the USSR—the militant atheism,
and other similar conditions sufficient proof that the attitude and the policy of
the Soviet Russian regime remain unchanged? Does all this indicate any "structural changes in the regime" and prompt us to assume that some form of
coexistence with this atheistic regime is possible? For the Church of Christ there
can never be any coexistence with the forces of evil—not even if the entire world
were to agree to such a coexistence. For the Church must always combat the
forces of evil. Nor can it change its attitude for the earthly well-being of its
believers, even though they might be persecuted for their religious faith. No, the
Church must constantly defend the truth and God and must combat the undue
importance attached to material values, love of ease and comfort, and worldly
pleasures. And in this respect priests and ecclesiastical dignitaries should set the
faithful believers an example.

Even the mention of the possibility of the Vatican entering into diplomatic
relations with the USSR, though this is to depend on the fulfillment of certain
preconditions, creates the illusion that structural changes are possible in the Red
Russian empire. This merely confuses and misleads the faithful and is, in any
case, reprehensible. And it shakes the trust of the faithful in the Catholic
Church, which has always been a citadel that was inaccessible to destructive,
Russian, Communist, masonic, and "progressive" ideas. Do certain opportunist-
minded ecclesiastical dignitaries allow the commandments of this citadel, the
possibility of making a compromise with the Devil? Can it be that this citadel
houses the wooden horse of Troy?

Strictly religious dogmatic problems are not within our province. The decisions reached by the Ecumenical Council in this respect are accepted by faithful
Catholics. But, as regards the question of an anti-Communist attitude, the
faithful are on the side of the Ukrainian ecclesiastical dignitaries, on the side of
the uncompromising fighters against Communism, on the side of the champion
of a spiritual crusade against atheist Moscow—Cardinal Ottaviani, who rejects
all possibility of a "coexistence" with the Russian tyrants and their "Church" and
thus defends the Ukrainian priests and faithful who have been incarcerated.

We always assume that unity of action on the part of the Christian churches in their fight against atheism, as represented by Moscow, is possible. A unity in dogmatic questions depends upon the Grace of God and also upon the tedious and systematic work of many years, but unity in the fight against militant atheism, against tyranny and slavery, and for the rights of the individual as a being created in the divine image, and for the freedom of religious faith, is now more than ever possible and real and, indeed, imperative. It is extremely regrettable that the invitation of representatives of the Russian "Orthodox Church" to the Ecumenical Council has made all this impossible. For the presence of the delegates of the Kremlin, attired in priestly robes, in the Vatican created an entirely different atmosphere for the discussions held by the Council elders. For the Council cannot become a council of the militant Church against the godless on a global scale if the Moscow representatives of the godless regime continue to be present, since all condemnation of this regime, which is hostile to man, would arouse opposition on the part of the "observers." Moscow has unfortunately succeeded in paralyzing the militant Church in the West. For this reason the Council is at the moment not in a position to defend uncompromisingly every religion which is being persecuted in China, Korea, Vietnam, the USSR, Albania, and in other countries, and to condemn the persecutors, for the representatives of the "Church" from the USSR who are taking part in the discussions of the Council would defend the "freedom" of religion in the USSR and thus ridicule everyone else. It is hardly likely that any great, historical decisions will be reached at present as regards a crusade of the spirit and of the idea against atheism and against the persecution of religion behind the Iron Curtain. This has incidentally been corroborated in a cynical and symbolical manner by the Moscow "Patriarch" Alexey (who has his representatives at the Council), who at a diplomatic reception held recently in Moscow kissed Nikita Khrushchev like a brother, a man who liquidated the restored Ukrainian Autocephalous Orthodox Church (UAPTs) and the Ukrainian Catholic Church, and who has murdered hundreds, in fact thousands, of priests and true believers in Ukraine. And this man, the hangman of Ukraine and, above all, of the two Ukrainian Churches, is kissed by the "Patriarch," who, incidentally, has been decorated with the highest Soviet order. Meanwhile, the representatives of the "Patriarch," without the least respect and in complete disregard of the ritual of kissing the Pope's ring which is customary in the Christian world, merely shake hands with His Holiness.

The assertion that the delegates of the Russian "Church" at the Ecumenical Council are representatives who are not connected with the Soviet government, since the Church is separated from the State on the strength of the Constitution of the USSR, and that the ecclesiastical delegates cannot therefore be held responsible for the crimes of the Bolshevik regime, is nothing but a sophism of dialectical materialism, which likewise blinds the initiators of the invitation. In this connection the fact must be borne in mind that the Ukrainian Autocephalous Orthodox Church and the Ukrainian Catholic Church were not liquidated solely by the Russian secret police. The Lviv "Council," which "decided" to conclude a "union" with the Church of Moscow, was arranged not only by the NKVD but also by "Patriarch" Alexey. This same "Patriarch" appointed his supporters as bishops, enforced his supreme authority on the Church which had been liquidated by applying violence, and transformed the Catholic priests who had been in danger of being shot into "Orthodox" priests. Alexey worked hand in hand with the NKVD. He designated Stalin, the most ruthless persecutor of Christianity of all time, as "God's anointed." If Alexey believes in God, why did he not defend the Ukrainian priests who died for Christ? He should not have placed terrorized Ukrainian Catholic priests and even priests of the Ukrainian Autocephalous Orthodox Church under his "jurisdiction," for he must have been aware of the fact that this was not a case of a "voluntary conversion"; these unfortunate priests were "converted" by means of NKVD guns. The representative of the Patriarch of Constantinople, Professor of Theology Dm. Trakous, designated the observers of the Russian Church as "political agents who are endeavoring to bargain over the 'peaceful coexistence' between the Soviet state and its Catholic subjects."

As has already been pointed out, the fact that representatives of the Russian "Church," of the Church which is morally and in practice responsible for the terrorization and persecution of the Ukrainian Churches, are taking part in the Council in the Vatican, is undermining the morale of the faithful of the two Ukrainian Churches. The man who approved of the arrest of the Ukrainian Catholic Metropolitan and of the Ukrainian Orthodox priests who were not prepared to recognize the Patriarch of Moscow (and who was extremely pleased that the Ukrainian Churches were liquidated by the NKVD), the man who gave Stalin his blessing and recently kissed Khrushchev, the man who tried to persuade the Ukrainian Metropolitan to betray the Ukrainian Church by offering him the highest post in the Moscow Patriarchate—this same man, as if to ridicule all Christians, sends his delegates to the Ecumenical Council in the Vatican, while numerous Ukrainian Catholic and Orthodox priests and many of the faithful still linger in Communist Russian dungeons and forced labor camps.

Those Vatican circles which decided to invite the Russian "Orthodox Church" to the Ecumenical Council have in the meantime no doubt realized that they made a sad mistake in assuming that "the experience of the past two thousand years" would be able to outwit the cunning of a "Communism merely a hundred years old." For they themselves were outwitted by the Russians, who by cunning methods managed to get the Patriarch of Constantinople, Athenagoras, excluded from the Council so that they might remain the sole spokesmen of "Orthodoxy." If only the genuine and true Orthodox Churches, and in particular the persecuted Churches, were taken into consideration in this respect, then the participation of representatives of the Ukrainian Autocephalous Orthodox Church as observers in the Ecumenical Council would naturally be extremely desirable. In that case the delegates of the "Patriarch" Alexey would have no business to be present amongst the Council participators.

Incidentally, a straight and uncompromising course, as well as dogmatism, should remain firmly anchored within the Church, but opportunism, tactical considerations, and relativism are out of place. Principles and not tactics must rank foremost. The path to unity does not lead via opportunism and collaboration with the "Church" which supports the government of tyrants and atheists and what is more serves the aims of the regime of the atheists, but via a crusade against these tyrants and persecutors of religion, these modern Neros and Diocletians.

The hopes of certain Vatican circles for the "conversion of the East" via Moscow (Russia) would be realizable given a certain precondition: namely that the Catholic Church changes its spiritual structure fundamentally and becomes a refuge for servilism and Caesaropapism and an instrument of Russian world Messianism, with a Russian Pope and the Kremlin instead of Rome as the center of the Catholic Church.

The opinion naturally obtrudes itself that the Ecumenical Council will not succeed in fulfilling the noble intentions of Pope John XXIII if the militant Church in the catacombs behind the Iron Curtain is not allowed to express its views at this Council. It would be fatal if the confidence of the faithful in the Catholic Church, in its capacity hitherto as a bulwark in the fight against godlessness, tyranny, slavery, and moral degeneration, was shattered. And there is danger of this being the case if the guiding principles pursued hitherto in this fight and the uncompromising rejection of all collaboration and any kind of "dialogue" with the advocates of the atheist regime and of slavery are undermined. For the strength of the Catholic Church always lay in its uncompromising fight against the forces of evil and in the dogmatic and indisputable emphasis of its truths, which are based on divine revelation. And the Church has never made a pact with the Diocletians and Neros, nor with the heathen pontiffs, but has always fought with the weapon of the spirit, of faith, of the Christian idea, and of martyrdom for the victory of its truths. It never aimed to establish any coexistence with tyranny, tyrants, and blasphemers. The Church of Christ prefers to be persecuted rather than to enjoy protection. The Church always forgave those who were converted and even made them its champions; the Sauls became Pauls, but the Church never sought to make any pacts with the Sauls. It never allows itself to be humiliated, nor did it ever negotiate with those who persecuted its faithful, or with those who negated the Church itself.

In our opinion the Church should also defend social rights, as many of the great Popes have done, and it should further the realization of social justice by preaching idealism, self-sacrifice, and altruism, and, at the same time, opposing egoism and hedonism both in practice and in every other respect. It should not ignore the national rights of the subjugated peoples, but should support them, for this, too, is part of the realization of divine justice.

We had hoped that the present Ecumenical Council would advocate the protection of all the persecuted churches in the world and the freedom of religious faith. We were firmly convinced that the Catholic Church would initiate the union of all Christians in the fight for God on earth and for the defence of His laws.... We likewise felt justified in hoping that the Council would issue a renewed appeal for a crusade of the spirit and the Christian idea for the rebirth of Christianity in the spirit of the early centuries of its existence—for a different and more austere mode of living, for purity of morals, for ascetism, for social and national justice, and against hedonism and materialism, against the moral degeneration which is becoming increasingly widespread in the West; for the rebirth of religious faith and moral principles, for the liberation of the individual from the fetters of godlessness and indifference, for a new way of life for individuals and for peoples, for a new and courageous approach on the part of the entire Christian Church, of the universal Church towards the persecuted Church, since this Church must be regarded as the standard-bearer of our day.

We expected a fighting spirit to manifest itself against the Antichrist, who dared to undertake a campaign against Christ and against all the religions of the world.

Above all, we expected a spirit of regeneration to manifest itself, and, in the second place, resolutions and decisions, which were to serve as a basis for unity. That is to say, in the first place a unity in spirit, in a definite attitude to life, in the primacy of self-sacrifice, asceticism, and of heroism "for our nearest neighbors" in the fight against the atheism which dares to attack the whole world and which has as its allies religious indifference and the priority of materialism over idealism. For the Christian Church will never speak the same language as the Diocletians and Neros, or as the chief pontiffs such as the atheist Alexey, just as the early Christians had nothing in common with the heathens.

The Metropolitan Count Sheptytsky, the Metropolitan Lypkivsky, and the Metropolitan Slipy revealed the same courageous attitude which was manifested by the leaders of the early Christians. To us they are an example worthy of imitation.

We are gratified that our Ukranian ecclesiastical dignitaries candidly and openly voiced the truth in Rome. In this respect they have the full support of the entire Ukrainian people, regardless of any difference in religious faith. For our Ukrainian prelates defended truth and also indicated the course which Western Christianity should follow.

Our arguments would not be complete and it would be a serious omission on our part if we did not quote in conclusion the noteworthy statement which our prelate, Archbishop Dr. Ivan Buchko, made on the occasion of a press conference held in Rome on October 30, 1962, when he told German journalists:

> The Ukrainian prelates were always unswerving in their faith. None of them ever betrayed Christ or the Church. They all sacrificed their lives for their religious faith. Only one of them, namely the successor of the Metropolitan Sheptytsky— Archbishop Joseph Slipy—is still alive today in exile. He is the great but also the unknown absentee in this assembly of the Council. It seems to be more acceptable to some persons if his name and also the name of the persecuted Church are passed over in silence. If we were living in the days of the Apostles, St. Peter would languish a long time in Herod's prison. But in those days the Church prayed for him.... We Ukrainian bishops are now forced to reveal the truth about the situation behind the Iron Curtain. But many persons accept this situation as though it only concerned us. From the worldly point of view we have nothing more to lose. But in spite of this, our Church continues to live on in secret and to train new persons who can indeed be called true and devout Christians. Nevertheless we consider it our duty to warn all those who fail to assess godless Communism rightly. The decalogue intended for young Communists contains the following passage: "Do not forget that the clergy must be regarded as the fiercest enemies of the Communist state. Fight religion on every occasion. He who is not a convicted adherent of the godless movement is not a

good Communist. For atheism and Communism are inseparable. These two ideals constitute the basis of the Soviet government."

But has this "basis" been established after forty-five years of Soviet Russian rule?! No! For in the hearts of the faithful faith and hope are still alive. And it is this faith which enables them to endure sorrow and suffering. And it can be assumed that it is thanks to this suffering that we here in the West are still free. It is by the Grace of the Holy Ghost that we are able to send delegates to this Council from all over the world and that we are able to assemble here in order to bear the Cross of Christ and also help our brothers to bear it.

The Ukrainian press has devoted appropriate attention to these courageous words by the Archbishop of the Ukrainians in exile. We trust that his words will meet with the response that they deserve in the circles to which they are addressed. The attitude of the entire Ukrainian people in this respect is the same as that expressed by Archbishop Buchko in so impressive and convincing a manner.

In conclusion we wish to stress that our criticism is directed not against the Catholic Church as an institution but against certain ecclesiastical dignitaries. For we know only too well that the Church can never reconcile itself to Communism—for the two are as different as fire and water. But some ecclesiastical dignitaries are such opportunists and so calculating that they are either not capable of seeing, or refuse to see, the danger which threatens and interpret the self-satisfied and deceptive smiles of Alexey or Nikita as an indication of a change for the better. The Church as an institution, however, will never follow the course adopted by these opportunist dignitaries.

For this reason we hope that the third session of the Vatican Ecumenical Council in the autumn of 1964 will not disappoint the hopes of the incarcerated, persecuted, and subjugated Christians, but will show the whole world that the Church is the eternal protector of the righteous who suffer, fight, and die for it and for truth.

The Ukrainian Review,
No. II, 1964, pp. 27-35

The Ecumenical Council and the Liberation Movement Behind the Iron Curtain

Without doubt, the greatest event in the history of the world was the birth of Jesus Christ. Notwithstanding the differences that exist among the Christian churches, the attention of the faithful, as well as the faithless, is focused on the happenings that transpire in the Church of Christ. All this occurs in spite of the fruitless attempts on the part of the unbelieving world, which, out of fear of the militant Christ, acts as a luring devil to suppress the victorious emergence of

Christ from the underground of the subjugated world. Truth cannot be vanquished by the forces of evil and of destruction.

Many hopes are attached to the Catholic Church's Ecumenical Council, which has become a major event in the life of the entire Christian world. Representatives of other churches are also present at this Council in the capacity of observers.

So far, however, the hopes of the Martyr Church have not been entirely fulfilled. The fight against bellicose and aggressive godlessness, however, should be a matter of supreme importance, not only for the Catholic Church, but for this era as a whole. This extremely important matter has not yet been put on the agenda in all its momentous significance. The fight against militant godlessness should form the most permanent common basis for a unity of action on the part of all Christian and other churches. What is essential about this unity is not only a formal approach and ritualistic assimilation among the churches—these are unessential matters. What is of fundamental importance is the common fight for the belief in God-Christ. For this reason, merely formal reforms would have no permanent success, unless all Christian churches were united in, and sparked by a spirit to fight for the victory of belief over unbelief, of Christ over the Antichrist.

The people are not only interested in knowing whether Ukrainian Catholic bishops have the same insignia of their Supremacy as the Orthodox bishops have, or whether they should kneel during Holy Communion, or whether they should use bells. They are interested in much more momentous matters, in the essence and rebirth of a deep belief in Christ and in the realization of Christ's truths in all aspects of life.

Victory will be carried by that Church which produces more ascetics, martyrs, apostles of faith, and militant crusaders. Like the early Christians, the priests of this Church should live exemplary lives, both for the ideas of Christ and in the ardent service of their country. The attractive and captivating power of the Church and the unity of all Christian churches depends on the rebirth of deep faith, on high ethical values, on self-sacrifice, on the willingness to make sacrifices in daily life, and on the realization of all that which Christ demanded of us. The heroism and martyrdom of our two underground churches—the Ukrainian Catholic Church and the Ukrainian Orthodox Autocephalous Church—have a strong appeal to all truly faithful and genuine Christians. The battle cry of these fighters, who die but do not submit, acts as an inspiration for a moral and spiritual rebirth.

In my opinion the central aim of the Council should be the rebirth of Christian faith in the spirit of the first centuries of Christianity, austerity of the priests, apostolic activity by daily deeds, and finally the revival of the inspiring forces of faith and of a strict moral life.

Our Metropolitan confessor, the Great Archbishop Joseph Slipy, has rightly raised the matter of the Ukrainian Catholic Patriarchate, which our church has long deserved. Our Bishop Sapelak has also rightly demanded that the Council speak up on behalf of those who are persecuted and martyred for Christ and that it condemn Moscow, which is suppressing our Churches. It is to be hoped that the Council will speak out emphatically against godlessness, against the persecution of the Church, and against genocide. It would be very sad if this were not done. It is possible that the Council will reserve such a statement to the very end, to forestall a premature ushering out of Alexey's Russian observers, or perhaps there are fruitless and hopeless negotiations being carried on with the tyrants behind the scenes, in the naïve hope of obtaining concessions. Everything is possible, even the most bizarre.

It is, however, by no means exclusively a question of the Council condemning Moscow once. We do not doubt that this will be done, for how could it be omitted when even some Marxist Socialists condemn Moscow for its persecution of the Church? What is most essential, however, is that all the decrees of the Council, that every step which it takes, reveals a new spirit, which will give new life and new vitality to the fight against godlessness, which will activate the assistance to the churches fighting in the underground, to the martyrs, to the persecuted, and to those who are punished in the service of God and their country. A spirit of active offensive must radiate from the Council. This spiritual offensive must be directed against those who commit homicide and genocide (exactly as Christ will speak out against them on the Day of Judgment), those who are responsible for the death of seven million people through starvation in Ukraine, who have exterminated millions of people in concentration camps, who have crucified bishops, monks, priests, and the faithful, who have robbed, desecrated, and destroyed the churches, and murdered the wives and children of those who fought for the independence of their countries and the freedom of humanity.

A fighting spirit should emanate from the Council. This militant spirit should be directed against philistinism, hedonism, materialism, egoism, religious indifference, and atheism, for these vices are spreading on both sides of the Iron Curtain. The deficiencies and frailties of the free community, but especially of misplaced priests and prelates should also be strongly stigmatized by this spirit.

If legal stations are not permitted to transmit radio programs to the East, then dozens of underground radio stations should be set up in the Free World to transmit programs directed against the tyrants behind the Iron Curtain in the name of Christ, the Christ of the Day of Judgment, to instill the peoples with hope and to call them to battle with their cross in their hands. Hundreds and thousands of priests and monks—new Peters of Amiens—should voluntarily step forth in the fight against the godless; they should make use of illegal means to gain access into the empire of the Antichrist; there they should fight fearlessly for their faith and for God's word, just as the Holy Apostles Peter and Paul did; they should announce the Day of Judgment to the tyrants. To this end, monasteries with hundreds of heroic monks following Christ's teachings should be set up in the free world, on the initiative of the Council. For there cannot be a rebirth of faith as long as the various camps of faith are not inspired by a mission and a mystic sense, and as long as these do not become a reality. The power of Christianity lies in its offensive promulgation and propagation of the eternal and infallible truth. This campaign of the spirit, of the idea, of faith, launched by thousands of preachers of Christ, is to be an appeal to man's conscience, an appeal that shall proclaim the great mission of the fight against egoism and hedonism.

Its emanating force should reach into the realm of Antichrist.

This is what the world awaits from the Council.

A Council with daily press reports which do not leave meaningful imprints on man's consciousness would be only too reminiscent of the United Nations.

The Council should be a secret clerical assembly at the final session of which great truths, which will awaken man to a new sense of life, must be proclaimed; new ways to fight philistinism, injustice, evil, godlessness, and crime, new ways to protect the subjugated, the righteous, and the persecuted must be shown; and the eternal truths of Christ must be given fresh vitality to enable them to revive nations and individuals. The world is yearning for such a proclamation by the Council.

The peoples need a lofty, holy secret, a lofty, mystic sense of life; they are tired of being intimately exposed, day by day. The "Councils" of the godless, whether they take place in the Kremlin or in Peking, are always secret, "mystical." They do not want to become a part of daily affairs.

The great offensive of the spirit, of the idea, of belief in Christ must begin with the cross and be followed by the sword.

The great offensive of Christ, courageous, fanatical, launched in the name of eternal truths at the risk of individual lives of the missionaries on both sides of the Iron Curtain, will unhinge the foundations of the Communists and the Antichrist himself will be thrown into the eternal fires of hell.

We are waiting for an idealistic, spiritual, and moral offensive from the Council, and not solely prayers for peace. The highest purpose is not peace, but the victory of Christ's truths, of justice for nations on earth. This is also God's truth, for it cannot be the will of God that the Ukrainian nation should languish under the yoke of the atheist and the tyrants who are crucifying Christ anew.

The Ukrainian Review,
No. IV, 1964, pp. 10-13

Where Eternity Lives

Nationalism—Key to a Solution

The threat of Communism is very strongly felt throughout the Asian countries through which our ABN delegation passed on its recent journey to the Far East. One of the apparent reasons for this is the lack of social and agrarian reforms. To attract and deceive the local population, clever Soviet strategists use anti-feudal slogans. Communist strategy aims to convince Asian peasants that the main purpose of Communist activity is to seize large landed estates and to divide the land among them equally. The agrarian reforms introduced in Taiwan, therefore, could well serve as an example to other Southeast Asian countries. Moreover, national and social revolutions should be promoted—that is to say, social justice from the nationalist point of view should be sought. In essence, this means that people of one nation must not be social enemies; but must strive for social reforms within the scope of their own national unity. It can no longer be denied that social reform movements based on the various Asian religions—Hinduism and Mohammedanism—have failed. Hence nationalism must be revived and become the inspiring force of opposition against Communist advance, and not the Buddhist philosophy of non-resistance to evil. The State Department of the United States of America, which neither forms any alliance with Nationalists nor creates suitable conditions for them to gain power, places many obstacles in the way of such a revival. The Diem regime in Vietnam is the best example.... During our travels we met an American professor from Chicago who told us that Americans are partially responsible for the corruption in Asia. But the fact is that Nationalist movements are the least corrupted—e.g., Chiang Kai-shek's Nationalist China.

We had occasion to meet several Europeans who had a troubled conscience about colonial policies, but, quite frankly, in comparison to some native representatives who were U.S. State Department protégés, the British or other West European "colonial masters" cannot be regarded as corrupt. To place the entire blame for the present situation in Asia on one country—on the British nation or some other West European "colonial power" of yesterday—is, quite objectively speaking, unjust. This is all the more so because the constant repetition of phrases about European "guilt" causes the whites in Asia to react unreasonably. They are ashamed of all their achievements, even of the fact that the whites were decidedly instrumental in helping to develop Asia....

Furthermore, it is the "whites" who are often exploited in Asia today. Practically all Americans and Westerners are regarded as wealthy by some Asians, and hence free booty!... In the meantime it is the "white" man who is working the hardest in a climate that is an utter horror to him while some natives while away their time in play, cabarets, and idleness....

A "white" man in Asia wants to expiate all his past sins, but he often goes about it with his eyes shut. For instance, he sometimes supports governments that are in fact much worse for the broad masses than former colonial lords. If the Westerners repenting former colonial power were not afraid of Nationalism in Asian countries and ceased regarding the "democratic phrasemakers" as their only partners, but instead gave their support to Nationalists, a victory over Communism would be assured. Nationalists in Asia regard every member of their nation as their brother, while "liberal democrats" in Asia regard only themselves to be brothers....

To be sure, a great task was accomplished by Protestant—mainly Scandanavian—missions; Catholic missions have left a deep-rooted mark.... But they are so very few.

Observing what England and Holland brought to Asia, I must admit that it was not merely colonial exploitation.... They were not Muscovites.... I am not trying to defend imperialism, but neither can I bring myself to believe that all who came here from the West were criminals in search of personal gain....

There are no colonial lords in Italy, but the south of the country lives in poverty. Here again it was a Democratic-Christian movement that failed; Christian democrats were not able to bring about social reforms in Sicily by liquidating large landed estates. As I sit here, in a plane which lifts us over the clouds, nearer to God, I recall the wax-glued wings of Icarus that melted under the burning sun.... Yet I do not share the opinion that asks: Why go to the Moon as long as there is poverty on Earth?... It is the great spirit of Man that ever yearns to know more, to discover new secrets of the Universe.... Yet if Bolshevism, and Russian imperialism in particular, could be destroyed, then thermonuclear armament would take less of the nations' budgets and new projects could be launched and continued. For instance, the irrigation problems of the Sahara and Gobi deserts, the problems of Pakistan and India.... The Earth is not depleted and exhausted; it is merely that the efforts of mankind are directed elsewhere.... The irrigation of the Sahara desert is not really in contradiction to man's efforts to reach the Moon. If the human brain did not strive to achieve what appears to be impossible it would surely deteriorate. Hence it was with pleasure that I read the statement by the astronaut Colonel Glenn: "Only my great belief in God gave me the strength to overcome my fear and all mental and emotional strains while starting my flight into orbit. I am firmly convinced that every astronaut must have a strong belief in God or in an ideal. But the belief in God is superior.... There is order in the Cosmos, and this is one of those great things in the universe which prove to me that God exists. There must be a higher Power which gives the stars their paths and sees to it that the stars keep to this plan...."

The Longing for Eternity

Because of the Pakistan-Indian conflict, our air route was changed, and for this reason we had to spend several extra hours in Bangkok, Istanbul, and Athens before going, as scheduled, to Rome. While admiring magnificent temples and pagodas in Bangkok—the center of Buddhism—and seeing the terrible mediocrity all around, the inability to comprehend the eternal values created by the human spirit in the past periods of great faith, I was suddenly struck by the question "What noble tribute will *our* generation pay to eternity?" Just like the fathers and forefathers of these mortals around us who now leisurely sip Coca-Cola and throw admiring glances at the human, all too human, "art"—perhaps in the shape of Sophia Loren—I was thinking how could they have created such monumental beauty, before which we, Europeans, stand in awe....

Facing other situations while in the Far East, we were constantly conscious of the fact that we *were* Europeans, that this world was not our world, that our understanding of *human dignity*, rooted in Christianity, ancient Greek and Roman culture, is not the understanding of the majestic culture of Buddhist Rome—Bangkok....

Especially in India this feeling strongly prevails. How erroneous the existing appraisal of India could be! For a European, who is used to view India through the image of Gandhi and Rabindranat Tagore, it is hard to realize the extent to which sex dominates the spiritual in India. How amazingly far are we Christians and

Europeans from India, and yet the Japanese are just as far from India! The nation of kamikaze and samurai! Asia is not monolithic, but heterogeneous.

It seems that the philosopher was absolutely right when he spoke about the transient character of culture. Cultures are born, reach a point of culmination, and then die out.... And yet it is painful and sad to have to admit that the philosopher—a tragic pessimist—was right.

It was painful suddenly to see St. Sophia Cathedral, which is now a museum in Istanbul! A monumental structure containing uncared for, priceless treasures of art—Byzantine art. I felt so much at home while looking at and admiring these treasures of art, living through the centuries of the existence of this Cathedral, and yet painfully conscious of the fact that nobody cares to restore this church.... Christianity is in a lethargic sleep when such a treasure is allowed to deteriorate. My thoughts carry me across the Black Sea to my native Cathedral of St. Sophia, in Kyiv, which I have seen only in pictures... and I am overcome by emotions: we are of the Byzantine rite. Greece is closer to our hearts than Rome. Icons familiar and dear to us—and not tri-armed crosses, as we are for some reason made to believe—are there at St. Sophia Cathedral....

Turkish sultans thought that their mosques would cast a tall shadow over St. Sophia Cathedral, but the shadow fell short. The blue Mosque of Sultan Ahmed, the Mosque of Suleyman the Great outshine St. Sophia with their glitter, but not with their originality. Everything here is an imitation of St. Sophia. And the sultans were not ashamed to admit it. They wanted to outdo the Cathedral in style, but the first Cathedral remained unique. And even the best imitation is unable to dim its glory.

And my thoughts turn to St. Peter's Basilica in Rome, the largest in the world, but even here we have an imitation of St. Sophia Cathedral, which, it seems, will remain forever as the original, most imitated Cathedral throughout the ages.... Here, too, stands St. Irene's old church, older than St. Sophia, and also turned into a museum. Disappointing and sad! Sad, for the Christian world is making no effort to restore St. Sophia Cathedral, it is not being cared for, it lies forgotten....

The same sad feeling stayed with us during our short stopover in Athens, as we practically ran to see the Acropolis.... We looked.... Large monumental ruins... but out of these ruins an ancient culture spoke to us in silence.... Athens leaves a stronger impression than ancient Rome. Immediately one senses that Rome was an imitation. Majestically completed—no, still to be completed—spiritual culture! Standing before the Acropolis how deeply do I feel that we are Europeans! More deeply, as I begin to realize that here Europe was born. We are now standing before Pallas Athena and thoughts grip me with such intensity that I am momentarily overcome. What beauty! What a perfect symbol of spiritual knowledge, and how strange it is to stroll by and walk on paths used by immortal Athenians.... We are on the Agora.... And as we look at a reconstructed model of the Acropolis, Agora, and many other buildings and temples—we are sad and sad again. For if the Western world is able to invest astronomical sums in senseless films, degenerate television programs, sports stadiums, golden beds ornamented with precious stones—for the wife of Ghana's Minister of Finance—why is it that the Acropolis and the Agora are not reconstructed?... Yes, I had similar thoughts while standing before St. Sophia's Cathedral, for they stem from the same roots.... Socrates and Plato, the greatest of philosophers—both shared a belief in one God, both prepared the world for the arrival of God's Son. Is it not possible to start a Foundation for the Rebuilding of the Acropolis just as the Ford, Rockefeller, and other foundations exist? For anybody who once visits the Acropolis and wants to believe in greatness, in the genius of mankind, is reminded at once of the creative human spirit. Suddenly, how ridiculous all theories of historical and dialectical materialism appear, when compared to the greatness created by human genius! We stroll again, the paths used by Plato, Socrates, Stoics, and Pericles, Phidias, Praxiteles, and again we fail to understand how it is that the poverty-stricken Greeks, rushing by with their oxen, are the descendants of real titans of spirit!

The Ukrainian Review,
No. IV, 1966, pp. 79-83

Where Eternity Lives (Conclusion)

Herder once said that Ukraine is the future Hellas. How meager seem the views of the learned "occidentalists" for whom Europe ends at the Curzon line! It is when I think of Hitler's death factories and the tyrannical "occidental" rule of the Nazis in Ukraine or Poland that the truly European and Christian greatness of Ukraine comes into relief. Europe would not exist without ancient Hellas, nor without Christianity and ancient Rome.

It is not by chance that Ukraine adopted Christianity from Greece because it is the most essential integral part of "Europeanism." Ancient Greece and Christianity are inseparably joined together. Before coming to Rome, the Apostles, and especially St. Paul, preached in Greece. Again it is not by chance that the modern teachings of Thomas of Aquinas or Fr. Pierre Teilhard de Chardin are based on the Greek Fathers of the Church. We must give special acknowledgement to those of our bishops, especially His Eminence Joseph Cardinal Slipy, and to those of our priests, such as the Rev. Dr. Lypsky, who are working towards maintaining a pure Eastern rite in our religious practices which are so closely tied in with Greece. Both the Parthenon and the Hagia Sophia are, first and foremost, an emphasis on the spiritual and the mystical, a unique proof of the continuity of the creative expression of human genius inspired with the belief in the transcendental.

When one looks at the priceless ruins on the Acropolis of the marble temple to Athens Parthenos, the virgin patron of Athens, built during the reign of Pericles (448-432 B.C.) by the famous architects Iktinos and Callicrates, under the artistic direction of the incomparable Phidias, or at Phidias' own Athena sculptured in gold and ivory, with that expression of classic Hellenic calm and depth of artistic expression, inspired by the idea of eternal faith in divinity, then one experiences a profound spiritual closeness, a kinship of the people of Herder's future Hellas with those of ancient Hellas. The truth of the unbroken unity of transcendental values—symbolized by the Acropolis and the Parthenon (whose priceless sculptures were plundered in 1801 by the British Ambassador to Constantinople, Lord Elgin, for the British Museum in London) and by the Hagia Sophia, a temple to the true God who had been discovered in principle by both Socrates and Plato, inspired with God's grace—was acquired by Ukraine directly from the primary source, and not through the Roman prism, as was done by the Germanic peoples, the Anglo-Saxon, and other "occidental" nations.

To the degree that Ukraine is Europe, so to a greater degree the fountainhead of spiritual Europe is Ancient Hellas, with her Plato, Aristotle, Homer, Aeschylus, Sophocles, Euripides, Herodotus, Thucydides, Myron, Phidias, Praxiteles, Lysippus—without Roman instrumentality, without the Roman Empire. Just as for Plato this world was merely a reflection of the transcendental world of ideas, so the spiritual life of Rome was in real life the reflection of the real cultural life of Hellas, an imitation of it.

Of course, one must not underestimate Roman civilization, especially the legal norms and institutions of Rome, valid even to this day, which were based on Hellenic spiritual culture and their social and political order. The Roman legal code became an integral part of Europeanism; it also forms the basis of the Magdeburg Law, which was also abided by in Ukrainian cities. But without its Hellenic philosophical basis, Roman law would not have become the primary source of Europe's law-consciousness.

Ukraine lies closer to the sources of Europe, closer to the sources of fundamental Christianity, than so-called occidental Europe, including Germany. St. Sophia in Kyiv is closer to the Hagia Sophia in the city of Constantinople. In Ukraine the cross over the trident of St. Volodymyr the Great symbolizes the unity of the spiritual greatness of ancient Hellas and Christianity, whose basis was laid by Plato (427-347 B.C.), the creator of metaphysical and ethical idealism, in his teachings about goodness, truth, and beauty as the highest ideals; by the Stoics, the followers of Zeno (d. 265 B.C.), whose ethics were so close to those of Christianity; by monumental artists and dramatists; by the unsurpassed Homeric epics; by historiographs; and by all the other creators of unattainable spiritual heights.

When we stand in the portals of the Hagia Sophia we know, or rather feel in our hearts and souls, that we are of "Greek origin." The icons to the Mother of God, the crosses, not at all tri-armed (though for some reason some people try to convince us that these are typically Byzantine), are near to our spiritual mentality, there is greatness in the greatest modesty. This is a true temple of Christ....

Maybe most like it among those Western churches known to me where a man can pray undisturbed by unnecessary clutter and glitter is the cathedral in Toledo, where there are priceless art treasures, including those of El Greco. Precisely—El Greco; not a Spaniard, not a Roman, but a Greek in essence with a Spanish name. It was the great El Greco, who, in my opinion, was the only one capable of creating a painting of the Crucifixion which reaches the soul....

It would be a mistake to think that I am speaking of present-day Greeks.... Not at all.... I am speaking of *eternal Hellas*, from which the present-day Greeks differ as much as the Italian carabinieri differ from the Roman legions.... Intermingled with Arabs, Phoenicians, Vandals, all sorts of Africans, and Near Easterners, they are the merry dwellers of Italy and not of the *Imperium Romanum*. They do not think at all about imperial greatness; they think only about their cafés, great operas, carefree "canzoni and canzonnetti"; not about Mucius Scaevola; not about Romulus and Remus, who had fed on a she-wolf's milk; not about Caesar, who in those ancient times crossed the Alps with his armies; not about Scipio— but about Capri, Caruso, Gigli, Mario Lanza, Sophia Loren, and hedonistic, passing things; they do not think about the proud and stern Cato.... Old Rome is dead to them, both the Rome of the victors and the Forum Romanum and the Rome of the catacombs....

But this is not our concern today; we are concerned with the assertion that Hellas's values came directly to Ukraine and into Georgia (and the Caucasus as a whole), around which values great legends of ancient Greece, including the Iliad, the legend about the Golden Fleece of Jason, and various others, were woven— proofs of a connection with the geographical complex of Hellas.... Georgia, based on Hellenic and (partly) even on Roman eternal values, is more "Europe" than Germany, which first found ancient Greece and perceived its eternal values through ancient Rome. Therefore it is ridiculous to look for our "Europeanism" among the Germans or the Romans, when we were closer to the source, to the beginning, than the so-called Occident of Latin culture.

We are proud of the fact that we are not of Latin but of Hellenic culture, which is more spiritual and nearer to the divine than the pragmatic culture of Rome. There is nothing in this assertion which depreciates ancient Rome, whose concept of legal institutions based on the spiritual values of the Greeks is also native to us; we are only emphasizing how much more naïve are all those publishers of *"Der Europäische Osten"* and the "specialists" in Eastern European history from the University of Munich and other such places with whom it has often been our luck to argue at international conferences—as, for example, in Bolzano—and who proved that they do not understand the Europeanism of Eastern Europe—that is, Ukraine, Georgia, and other countries, which have more affinity in their national cultures and philosophy of life to ancient Hellas, to fundamental Christianity, than the so-called Germanic or Romance peoples.

It is time to give the death blow to the legend about the identity of "Occidentalism" with "Romanism." The same should be done with the legend about "true" Christianity, which is supposed to be identical with Roman, Protestant-Anglican, or Evangelical-Lutheran Christianity. One must destroy the legend propagated by Germanic or Romance thinkers (with whom I have often argued at conferences of intellectuals of Western Europe) that Europeanism is identical with Catholicism, and Roman at that, and with Protestantism.... If the essential element of Europeanism, Occidentalism, is ancient Hellenism, without which there is no Europe, then it is just out of this Hellenism that Ukrainian Orthodoxy and Oriental Catholicism grew; they are nearer to the philosophical, artistic, and cultural sources of Hellas than Roman Catholicism and Protestantism. St. Paul's most profound philosophical and religious thoughts on Christianity are addressed to people of Hellenic culture. The appearance of St. Andrew, Christ's Apostle, brother of St. Peter, on the hills of Kyiv, is of the same order of reality, profoundly metaphysical and messianistic, as any analogical occurrence of religious meaning anywhere else. It is ridiculous to try to prove the Europeanism of Ukraine to some conceited Germanic pseudo-intellectual "übermensch" when Ukraine is nearer to the fountainhead of Europe—ancient Hellas and Hagia Sophia—than Germany.

Especially profoundly symbolic are the facts that Hagia Sophia is now a museum and not a free temple of the Lord, that the holy places of the man-God are found in those countries in which worldly power is in the hands of non-Christians.... When will the Holy Land have a Christian Government? Maybe it was Christ's plan that in ever renewing suffering our faith in Him would be justified?! *Ceterum censeo*: it is better for the Church to be persecuted than protected. If the proof of true faith is endurance and preservation of faithfulness to Christ in suffering, then maybe this great trial which was placed on St. Sophia in Kyiv and on her people is to be a proof of the fact that the first shall be the last and the last, first?! How odd that the Second Ecumenical Vatican Council forgot to remind the world that St. Sophia in Kyiv is the symbol of today's catacombs and that our age, as His Eminence Joseph Cardinal Slipy said, is the age of a persecution of Christians without precedent in the history of the world.

I do not know Mount Athos, but we all know of the famous Ukrainian monks Ivan Vyshensky and Theodosius Pechersky, and it seems to me that to essentials of our Christianity belong not the glitter and the purple but the caves of Kyiv's Lavra, asceticism, and the sword of Zaporozhian Cossacks—the only order of the Christian Orthodox East, the only national, Christian, military republic of its kind.

Later, in another set of circumstances, but with an identical goal, arose the Ukrainian Insurgent Army—an army of warriors for Ukraine and Christ. General T. Chuprynka placed this army under the protection of the Mother of God, following in the traditions of Zaporozhska Sich. Let us remember a legion of martyrs-ascetics: Lypkivsky, Boretsky, the Servant of God, Metropolitan Andrew Sheptytsky, Bishop M. Charnetsky, and numberless others. Let us remember 500 women in Kingiri, who, with religious and nationalistic songs on their lips, died under the treads of Russian tanks.... No, the Christianity of the future Hellas (according to Herder) is more profound than the occidental form.... Christianity is in man's experience; not only in teachings—because God's teachings are the same to everyone.

The world of ideas of the Old Testament with its hedonistic aspects is in such contrast with the New Testament that it seems to me that Plato's world of ideas, a product of a great mind and an unsurpassed metaphysical and ethical idealist, is a hundred times nearer to the New Testament. Therefore, one could consider him as the idea-forerunner, philosopher-prophet of Christianity rather than the authors of certain sections of the Old Testament. There is proof of this—especially in the Gospel of St. John! In it the teachings of Christ are presented unsurpassably in all their divine greatness. There are a number of things in it that are close to Plato and the Stoics in the human sphere, in the sphere of people of the Apollonian type—not of the Dionysian, to whom the Old Testament is closer! In the teachings of the great minds of Hellas there is no revenge, no sensual passion, no sexual paeans, no extolling of that which Christ's faith and morality try to overcome. In my understanding, Plato is nearer to us Christians than Jewish religious teachings.

*

We are approaching Rome, nearing the center of what is called occidental Christianity. The monumental greatness of Rome, the metropolis of a bygone empire, overpowers Athens. The arch-cathedral, the Basilica of St. Peter, the largest and the most splendid in the world, puts Constantinople's St. Sophia in the shadow. But Constantinople's St. Sophia, in its originality, Christian mysticism, profound spiritualism, is nearer and dearer to us. It is less earthly, less glittering outwardly, and for some reason it seems closer to God.... And how real is the parallel between ancient Hellas and ancient Rome! Completely analogical— as between Occidental Roman and Oriental Greek Christianity. But then the many-sidedness of integral Christianity come together into a harmonious whole. In its purest forms, the monastic spirit came to the West from the East and the Eastern Fathers greatly enriched theological thought while striving for a complete contemplation of Christian truths.

Our thoughts found live evidence when, while still enraptured by ancient Hellas and the Hagia Sophia, we unexpectedly found the "Studion"—the monastery of the Studite monks on the shores of Lake Albano. Here seven monks, under the direction of the Prime Archbishop, His Eminence Joseph Cardinal Slipy, began their monastic existence of penance, mortification, and sanctification, according to the precepts set forth by St. Theodore Studite. Here is laid the basis of our iconographical school. The monastery is also becoming the center of spiritual practices.

The first "Studion" was built on the Bosphorus 1500 years ago. Its most famous abbot, St. Theodore Studite (759-826), revived monastic life in the East with his precepts (the "Typicon"). He encouraged all those who were being persecuted at the time, especially for honoring holy icons, to come to Ukraine. This was noted by His Eminence Joseph Cardinal Slipy in his speech to the Pope.

Two hundred years later, in the famous Pecherska Lavra (Monastery of the Caves) in Kyiv, which had been founded by Metropolitan Ilarion and St. Anthony Pechersky, the abbot, St. Theodosius, introduced the Typicon of St. Theodore the Studite. As a result, this monastery became the spiritual, intellectual, and ecclesiastical center and had an important influence on the public life of the realm of Kyiv. According to the traditions of the Holy Cross Society monasteries, the Studite order is subject to the head of the archdiocese, and not directly to the Vatican.

The "Studion" is to become in Rome what it once was in Constantinople because the organization of the Studite order has not changed; only at this time the most convenient place of settlement for the Studites fathers is Rome, as was stated by the Prime Archbishop in his epistle to the Studite on the feast of St. Anthony Pechersky (July 10, 1964) in the monastery of St. Theodore the Studite on the shores of Lake Albano. In his attempt to draw nearer to Greek and ancient Kyivan sources, church institutions, and traditions; in his plan for a patriarchy and the re-creation of the "Studion" from above the Bosphorus; and in his restoration of the "Typicon" of the monks of Kyiv's Pecherska Lavra and of St. Anthony and Theodosius Pechersky, the Prime Archbishop, quietly and without fanfare, proved himself a great Catholic in the spiritually religious sense.

A few more discussions with some of our bishops about the Patriarchy and the problems of the Vatican Council; some conversations about present political matters with some Italian politicians; a distribution of our declarations as to the problems of the Council to the international press accredited by the Council; a few more meetings with some foreign fathers of the Council and members of the representations of the ABN—and we are in Bonn, a large village of one of the economic powers of the world.

Spiritual claustrophobia, the lack of endless space which is so strongly felt on the Acropolis or on the mountainside of the "Studion" in Rome, an exclusively empirical point of view in political dealings, the absence of the elusive in politics, which is more art than science—all this brought us down to earth, reminding us that people live more for the present than for the eternal. And it was sad to think that the proof of man's immortality and the striving of his soul towards the unknown were left somewhere beyond the horizon like a magic dream. Before us again the ordinary and the commonplace, so endlessly removed from the genius that built that pagodas of Bangkok, the Hagia Sophia, the Blue Mosque of Sultan Ahmad, the Parthenon, Athena Nike, the Pantheon, the Colosseum, the Basilica of St. Peter, our St. Sophia and Pecherska Lavra in Kyiv, and—reminiscences from the point of view of the eternal—the "Studion" on Lake Albano.

But still, we are happy that there is someone who in this terrible era of hedonism and luxury on the one hand, and suffering and martyrdom on the other, did not forget people not of this world: Sts. Anthony and Theodosius Pechersky, the great Metropolitan Ilarion, St. Theodore Studite, his followers of the last decades in Ukraine—the first Archimandrite of the revived Studite order, the Servant of God, Andrew, the Archimandrite Clement, brother of Metropolitan Andrew, both martyrs for Christ....

The Prime Archbishop stated in his epistle: "Maybe during these times it would be a good idea to begin our humble task with iconography which is forgotten and forbidden in the East.... Showing Rome and the whole world the greatness of our icon, its piety, its heavenly anticipation, the Studites will find a sure way to their hearts and will regain for themselves their old respect and love...." And only someone who had been lucky enough to see hundreds of ancient icons in the Byzantine Museum in Athens understands the profundity of this modest thought. But certainly each of us has seen the icon of the Mother of God of Vyshhorod, plundered from Ukraine and renamed by the plunderers "Vladimirska," and therefore each of us knows the delight taken in it by the Christian world. And we understand the importance of the task which, among many others, was given by the Prime Archbishop to the new Ukrainian "Studion" on the shores of Lake Albano—in Rome only for the time being.

It is a good thing that there is someone among the Ukrainians who reminds men of things not of this world, not only in words, but in deeds. This could be done only by someone who suffered for eighteen years in the empire of the Antichrist, in prison and concentration camps—the Prime Archbishop, a Ukrainian, who, unbroken by tortures, is a great proof of the invincibility of the Ukrainian spirit, of strength of character, and of firmness of faith in God and Country.

Before us is a unique duty: to permeate the present with the eternal, to see the present in the mirror of eternity and in this sense to shape it.

The Ukrainian Review,
No. II, 1967, pp. 70-77

The Present-Day Vatican and Ukraine

Although we find it unpleasant to write on the subject, *salus rei publicae suprema lex*—the good of Ukraine is our first and foremost concern. We are writing about the Pope not as the Head of the Catholic Church who has the authority to pronounce upon faith and morals, upon the teachings of Christ which are mandatory for every true Catholic, but as we would about a statesman and politician, because to a great extent the present Pope is playing this role.

In numerous speeches the Pope has drawn attention to and appealed for the redress of injustices suffered by those who are oppressed, underprivileged, or persecuted, but his references apply only to people who live in countries of the Free World, where in some places injustice, racial discrimination, and other evils are unfortunately to be found.

Many times we have heard the present Pope condemn nationalism without, however, differentiating between the *liberating* nationalism of the *enslaved* nations and the chauvinist "nationalism" of the *ruling* nations. We have heard a list of all the evils caused by nationalism, as if such evils were also attributable to the liberating nationalism of enslaved and oppressed nations. The present Sovereign of the Vatican City-State appears not to see the differences between, for example, racialist Nazism, Russian chauvinism (i.e., imperialistic "nationalism"), and the nationalism of little Estonia, Georgia, indestructible Ukraine, or other nations which have fallen victims to the insatiable imperialism of chauvinist nations. Even Moscow, in all its baseness, differentiates between *liberating* nationalism and *imperialistic* nationalism. Red China too makes the same distinction; Charles de Gaulle was also able to see it. But, unfortunately, Pope Paul VI does not want to see the difference between what is noble and good and what is evil and base. *Liberating* nationalism, the fight for the deliverance of one's own nation from the foreign yoke, is in accordance with God's commandment. The duty to fight for one's friends is placed on our conscience by Christ himself. However, the Pope does not see this. For him the nationalism of liberation, the honorable struggle for justice, equal rights, and the independence of all nations of the world, does not seem to exist. Pope Paul VI visited the United Nations

Headquarters, but there he did not even mention Ukraine, Georgia, Turkestan, Armenia, Bulgaria, Lithuania, Latvia, and other enslaved nations. The Pope also forgot about us, the enslaved, at Christmas and Easter. He sent out his Easter greeting in Russian (although, as we all know, there are only a handful of Russian Catholics), but had no greeting for the Ukrainian Catholics, of whom there are several million, in their own language. The Pope made use of many languages for this purpose, so as to stress ecumenism but neglected Ukrainian. Is he the Pope of all nations and peoples, or only of the *ruling* nations, including the Russian?

His trips to Geneva, to India, to Bogotá, to the countries of Africa, his speech in defense of the technicians in Biafra, the special audience granted them—all these are noble acts, but they concern people on this side of the Iron Curtain only.

On the occasion of the fiftieth anniversary of the Russian Patriarchate, Pope Paul VI sent a letter of congratulation to "the most holy patriarch of Moscow and the whole of Russia" Aleksei, known to be the Kremlin's servant, who blessed Stalin as a "messenger from God." This helped the patriarchs to liquidate our Ukrainian Autocephalous Orthodox Church and our Ukrainian Catholic Church, by putting them under his "protection." How tragic, then, that for the Pope he is "most holy"!

The Pope sends telegrams to Biafra, Jordan, and other countries in the Western hemisphere to give moral support to the unfortunate, while we and other nations under the Russian yoke are ignored. Why is the Pope silent when the Russians cruelly persecute the underground Ukrainian Church, which is within his jurisdiction, when Father Superior Velychkovsky (it is said he has the title of Archbishop) was arrested, together with numbers of priests and of the faithful, and was taken to prison in Moscow? Why does he say nothing?

Why does the Eastern Congregation, to which our Catholic Church belongs, remain silent? Why is the State Department of the Vatican silent? Why is the Congregation for the Union of Churches silent? Is it because in the Russicum there are actually people from the Moscow patriarchate, which supports the atheist regime and in the name of which Aleksei approved of the invasion of Czechoslovakia? Is it because Cardinal Willebrandt is engaged in talks about establishing contacts and an exchange of representatives between the Vatican and the Russian patriarchate, since it would be awkward for the Vatican to accredit its representatives to the Kremlin? Is it because the Kremlin's representative would in fact be the "patriarch"? Do our Catholic Church and its martyrs, with Velychkovsky at the head, have to be sacrificed on the "altar" of diplomatic relations between Moscow and the Vatican? Maybe that is why at the airport in Rome during Nikodym's flight to Moscow he was greeted by *no less than two cardinals* from the Eastern Congregation and the Congregation for Union? Is it possible that we are living in a time when the Pope reigns in the Vatican for the sake of the ruling nations alone?

It is as if our martyred Catholic Church "does not deserve" to nominate His Eminence Cardinal Joseph Slipy as patriarch, because that church has had to be sacrificed to the Russian patriarch, whom Pope Pius XII referred to as a servant of evil. The present-day Vatican is silent while martyrs for the Church of Christ are suffering in Ukraine and all the other countries where the Russian boot treads and where the "patriarch" Aleksei reigns. But the Vatican did not always discriminate between these countries. Pope Benedict XV, who understood the importance of Ukraine, specified her particular role as a vanguard of Christianity in Eastern Europe. The Vatican politicians of today deliberately forget this, but the fact remains that there have been Popes who understood the specific importance of Ukraine and other countries enslaved by Moscow.

In the Russicum, which seems to have become the gathering place for all Aleksei's emissaries, plans are being made for the return of the Russians, and through them the return of the "East".... Blessed believers! This will happen when the capital of Catholicism is no longer Rome but Moscow, when Aleksei or his successor Nikodym becomes the "Pope" of the Catholics too!

When will the Pope finally speak out in defense of the martyr for the faith Velychkovsky, and of all those who are persecuted for Christ's faith, *for their loyalty to the Apostolic See*, which is headed by Pope Paul VI?

When will the Pope defend our writers, poets, scientists, intellectuals, artists, priests, and the Red Cross workers of the Vladimir prison, who are being persecuted in concentration camps; when will he defend Dr. Volodymyr Horbovy, a dying old man who has spent twenty-three years in Mordovia without a trial, or the martyr Katrya Zarytska, whose only "fault" lies in the fact that she was a worker of the Ukrainian Red Cross and for this "crime" has spent twenty years in prison?

We are waiting for a word of protest from the Pope, we Ukrainian Catholics who consider His Holiness Pope Paul VI the Head of our Church too, we Ukrainian Christians who believe that the Pope should defend our persecuted Ukrainian Autocephalous Orthodox Church.... Our criticism is not aimed at the institution of the Head of the Church, the authority of which is acknowledged by Ukrainian Catholics, and *we do not link the functions of the successor of the Disciple Peter* with the policy of the present Head of the Church, Pope Paul VI. But because the present Pope has entered *the political sphere of action*, and because he underestimates our nation and our Church, we must complain to the Pope, who is also the Head of our Catholic Church, about his neglect of our martyred Church and nation.

Christ was on the side of those who are persecuted and oppressed, and not on the side of the persecutors and oppressors. We ask not only for a Pope of the ruling nations and peoples, but for a *Pope of those who have been martyred and deprived of their freedom*, who are fighting for the truth, *for justice and independence, for Christ and against the atheists from the Kremlin*.

When will we find a Pope for the enslaved, a Pope to deputize for Christ who came to earth *to teach us to fight evil, and not to sign pacts with the persecutors of the faithful of His Church?*

ABN Correspondence,
November-December 1969, pp. 27-29

For the Ukrainian Catholic Patriarchate

Petition submitted to His Holiness Pope Paul VI by Yaroslav Stetsko, former Prime Minister of the Ukrainian State Government in 1941

His Holiness
Pope Paul VI

Your Holiness:

We, the Ukrainian Catholics, beg to submit this petition to Your Holiness in the hope, that Your Holiness and the Ecumenical Council's consent to our appeal will strengthen our martyrized Churches of both confessions: the Ukrainian Catholic Church and the Ukrainian Orthodox Autocephalous Church, which have continued to exist in the modern catacombs in Ukraine, and among the Ukrainians deported by the atheist Muscovite regime to the wastelands and concentration camps of Siberia and Kazakhstan.

In filial devotion to Your Holiness, we beg to ask, most humbly, that the Ecumenical Council attach supreme importance to the following matters:

A) That the mobilization of the entire religious world, and, particularly, of the Christian world be achieved by a unity of *action*, which will embrace all religious bodies, but particularly those of the Christian Churches, against militant atheism. According to our modest opinion, the regeneration of Christian militancy is what is most needed in the struggle against militant atheism at the present time;

B) That the central role in the contemporary Christian world of the militant Christian Churches in the catacombs, and, especially, of the Ukrainian Catholic Church, should be defended and honored in the Council's decisions. The Ukrainian Catholic Church lost nearly all its hierarchs by martyrdom because they remained faithful to Christ and the Apostolic See until their death. In addition, it lost many priests and thousands upon thousands of the faithful. The prelates, many priests, and thousands upon thousands of the faithful of the Ukrainian Autocephalous Orthodox Church were martyred in the struggle for the victory of Christ's truth. It is only fitting, therefore, that the Ecumenical Council pay tribute to the sufferings for Christ of the faithful—the priests and prelates of the Christian Churches—in the catacombs, for the *true spirit of the Christian Churches of modern times* is exemplified by the catacombs of Christian Ukraine and other Christian nations that are enslaved by the Antichrist;

C) That the Ecumenical Council exclude the representation of Moscow's Patriarchate (i.e., the representatives of the Council for the Affairs of the Russian Orthodox Church of the Council of Ministers of the USSR) from participating in the Council as observers. Moscow's Patriarchate helped to destroy the Ukrainian Catholic Church and the Ukrainian Autocephalous Orthodox Church and, at present, continues to be subservient to the regime of the Antichrist. The presence of these observers at the Council paralyzes the possibility of the emergence of a firm attitude, backed by uncompromising schemata, concerning the struggle of Christianity against the Antichrist of Moscow;

D) That the Ecumenical Council initiate a great movement for an ideological, spiritual, and moral regeneration, especially in the free Christian world, by opening a new front of action against the domination of material values in life, not only of the faithful, but also of some priests, and against the displacement of idealism by hedonism. This must be done by restoring the old and militant principles of Christianity, which are indispensable in the present struggle against the false doctrines of the Antichrist of Communist Moscow;

E) That the Ecumenical Council direct the attention of the Churches and the peoples of the Free World to the martyrized and militant Churches, the Ukrainian Catholic Church and the Ukrainian Autocephalous Orthodox Church, which continue their existence in the catacombs of Ukraine and in other countries of the Kingdom of the Antichrist. They should be distinguished as examples of a genuine devotion to Christ, and their sacrifices should be honored as a great contribution to the final victory of Christ's Truth on the ruins of the Kingdom of the Antichrist;

F) Concerning the Ukrainian Catholic Church, we beg to ask Your Holiness, most humbly, that a Patriarchate of the Ukrainian Catholic Church be created. The Archbishop Major Metropolitan-Confessor Cardinal Joseph Slipy, who faithfully defended Christ's Truth in a dignified manner through eighteen years of imprisonment, should be the Patriarch of the Ukrainian Catholic Church, which has been uncompromisingly militant against the Kingdom of Antichrist and its Kremlin Orthodox "Church."

In contemporary Ukraine a Patriarchal See of the militant Ukrainian Catholic Church could be established only in the catacombs, or the Vorkuta concentration camp, where the Metropolitan-Confessor was recently interned, but since the Metropolitan-Confessor has become an emigrant, his return to Ukraine, during the reign of the Kingdom of the Antichrist, is utterly impracticable and purposeless. Metropolitan Cardinal Slipy, therefore, as a Patriarch, should have his See established in the Free World—in Rome.

In addition, we humbly ask Your Holiness that, for the purpose of the struggle against the Kingdom of the Antichrist in which many of our brothers and sisters, mothers and fathers, the whole of our faithful Ukrainian people have been suffering, the Archbishop Major, H.E. Cardinal Joseph Slipy, be allowed to interrupt his silence to tell the world about the sufferings and martyrdom of the people faithful to Christ, to our Church and to our fatherland, about the sufferings of all the enslaved Churches, nations, and peoples, and to warn the world against the dangers of coexistence with the devil, by pointing out the Hell which he has created on the earth and, at the same time, pay tribute to the sacrifices, heroism, and martyrdom suffered in the struggle for Christ, for the freedom and independence of Ukraine and of other enslaved nations.

We also beg to ask that the Metropolitan-Confessor, who has been, not only for us, but for all Christians, a glorious example of martyrdom for Christ and our spiritual leader, be not caused to have any contact with the authorities of the Antichrist. Such contacts are contrary to his aureole as martyr and spiritual leader of the Ukrainian people in the struggle against the Antichrist and his power. This is disgusting for all those who believe in the final victory of the Truth of Christ.

We humbly ask Your Holiness to listen to our petition, and we pray that the Almighty God show His Grace and Benevolence to Your Holiness. We most humbly ask Your Blessing.

We remain in filial devotion to Your Holiness.

Yaroslav Stetsko
Former Prime Minister of Ukraine

Submitted on Sept. 21, 1964

On the Protection of Traditions
of the Ukrainian Catholic Church

Memorandum Sent to Cardinal Testa
by Mr. Yaroslav Stetsko

Munich, 25th June, 1965.

His Eminence
Gustavo Cardinal Testa,
The Sacred Congregation for the Eastern Church,
The Vatican

Re: Perpetual obligations arising from the Berest Union of 23rd
December, 1595, and the decisions of the Universal Second Vatican
NFRe: Council of the Catholic Church

Your Eminence,
As Head of the last independent Ukrainian Government on Ukrainian territory in 1941, which initiated the war on two fronts against atheistic Bolshevism and Nazism and had the blessing of the Servant of God, the Metropolitan Andrey Sheptytsky, and moral support of our present spiritual leader, the Metropolitan Confessor Joseph Cardinal Slipy, I take the liberty to submit to Your Eminence some objections against the introduction of certain innovations in the Ukrainian Catholic Church in the USA and other countries, which contradict the Berest Union with the Apostolic See and the Council Decree on the Eastern Catholic Churches.

His Holiness Pope Clement VIII, on the reestablishment of the unity of the Ukrainians with the Holy See, guaranteed in the name of the Holy See in his bull of 23rd February , 1596, "Decet Romanum Pontificem," as well as in the documents, approved by him, of the Berest Synod attended by the Ukrainian bishops of that time, headed by the Metropolitan of Kyiv and Halych, Michael Rohoza, to respect the traditions and the rites of the Ukrainian Greek-Catholic Church. The Union was concluded on the basis of the principles laid down by the Ecumenical Council of Florence.

The Holy See granted to the Ukrainians all the rights, liberties, and privileges that had been enjoyed by them up to then, and confirmed them in all their ecclesiastical usages in the administration of the Holy Sacraments, and in the performance of the ritual acts, which had since ancient times been accepted in Ukraine, insofar as they were not contrary to the dogmas of the Catholic Church.

Of late, however, some Ukrainian bishops and priests, in particular in the USA, have been acting in contradiction to these principles. For instance, the new (Gregorian) calendar and other innovations are being introduced into the Ukrainian Catholic Church; there are attempts to introduce a non-Ukrainian language, English, into our liturgy, thus violating § 23 of the Decree on Eastern Catholic Churches of 21st November, 1964, and in no lesser measure openly contradicting the accords of the Berest Union.

Permit me, Your Eminence, to touch in a few words on the following points:

1) The historico-juridical status of the Ukrainian Catholic Church on the basis of the accords binding on both parties:

On 12th June, 1595, the Ukrainian bishops held a synod in Berest under the leadership of the Metropolitan Michael Rohoza and on this day drafted a letter to the Pope concerning the conditions of reunification, in which it was particularly emphasized:

"...siquidem Sanctitas Vestra administrationem sacramentorum, ritusque et caerimonias Orientalis Ecclesiae integre, inviolabiliter, atque eo modo quo tempore unionis illis utebamur, nobis conservare, confirmareque pro se et successoribus suis, nihil in hac parte innovaturis umquam dignetur...." ("Your Holiness will allow us to retain any administration of sacraments, rites, and ceremonies of the Eastern Church, in the form in use at the time of union, wholly and inviolably, and to confirm in your name and that of your successors, and never to introduce innovations in this part....")

In the bull of 10th January, 1595, "Unio Nationis Ruthenae cum Ecclesia Romana" ("Union of the Ruthenian [Ukrainian] Nation with the Roman Church"), § 10 states: "...atque ad majorem charitatis nostrae erga ipso significationem omnes sacros ritus, et caeremonias quibus Rutheni Episcopi, et Clerus juxta Sanctorum Patrum Graecorum instituta in Divinis Officiis, et Sacrosanctae Missae Sacrificio, ceterorumque Sacramentorum administratione, aliisve sacris functionibus utuntur, dummodo veritati, et doctrinae Fidei Catholicae non adversentur, et communionem cum Romana Ecclesia non excludant, eisdem Ruthenis Episcopis, et Clero ex Apostolica benignitate permittimus, concedimus, et indulgemus." ("...and, therefore, for the greater significance of our love, we permit, yield, and allow to the Ruthenian bishops and clergy, from the Apostolic Grace, all those sacred rites and ceremonies used by the Ruthenian bishops and clergy as well as the institutions of the divine services of the Holy Greek Fathers, and the holding of the sacred Mass, and the administering of the other sacraments, or other sacred functions, provided that the truths and doctrines of the Catholic faith are not contradicted, and they do not exclude communion with the Roman Church...."

In the papal "Breve" of 7th February, 1596, Pope Clement VIII informed the Metropolitan Michael Rohoza that he had granted all the requests and demands of the Ukrainians. By the bull of 23rd February, 1596, the Pope confirmed the Metropolitan in the possession of his rights of jurisdiction. He confirmed that the Metropolitan of Kyiv and Halych could confirm and institute all suffragan Bishops in the name of the Holy See, as soon as they were appointed to this office. Pope Clement VIII was even gracious enough never to ask the Ukrainian Catholic Church to include the word "filioque" in its Creed, considering as sufficient the solemn promise of the Ukrainian bishops that they would defend in principle the Catholic doctrine of the origin of the Holy Ghost in the Father and the Son.

King Sigismund III issued a manifesto on 29th May, 1596, in which he proclaimed the completed Union and added: "The bishops have brought nothing new from Rome, nothing which will hinder your salvation, no changes in your religious rites. To the contrary, all your dogmas and rites have remained untouched, conforming to the authority of the Apostles and of the Councils, and to the teaching of the Holy Greek Fathers, revered by you, whose feast days you celebrate." (*Annales Eccl. Ruth.*, p. 227.)

One of the conditions put forward by the opponents of the Union, which was stressed by Prince Ostrozhsky, was the demand for the retention of the old calendar. For this reason alone the Ukrainian bishops had to plead for the retention of the old (Julian) calendar. On 10th October, 1596, the Synod of Berest issued a synodal message signed by the Ukrainian bishops and the Metropolitan, Michael Rohoza himself, by which the union of the Ukrainian Church with Rome was promulgated in the entire metropolitanate.

In this we read the following: "*...so that, at the same time, we may preserve the rites and ceremonies of the Greek-Ruthenian Church, that no alterations be carried out in our churches, but that all be left in accordance with the traditions of the Holy Greek Fathers for time eternal, which the Holy Father has indeed granted us and for which he has sent us the relevant privileges and documents....*"

2) On the present juridical status

From the documents of the Berest Union it is clear that neither individual bishops, nor priests, nor, even less so, parish congregations have the right to carry out any alterations regarding the rights and privileges guaranteed in the Berestia Union. Moreover, the practices introduced in the USA contradict the decree adopted by the Second Vatican Ecumenical Council on the Eastern Catholic Churches (§§ 19, 23, 24, 9, 6, 2).

Any changes concerning the decisions of the Berestia Synod of 8-10 October 1596 can only be carried out by an analogous institution of the Ukrainian Catholic Church, that is to say by the Synod of Ukrainian bishops—and not only those living outside Ukraine—headed by His Beatitude Joseph Cardinal Slipy, according to § 10 and in agreement with §§ 7 and 9 of the Decree.

Hence I question the validity of the changes and innovations carried out in the USA as contrary to the accords of the Berest Union and the decisions of the Second Ecumenical Vatican Council. I consider it as an action "without legality" when a decision by a congregation or an instruction on the part of a bishop can alter the rights and privileges guaranteed by the Apostolic See with regard to the entire Church and nation. According to the meaning of § 7, section 3, and in accordance with § 10 of the Decree on Eastern Churches, the Ukrainian Greek-Catholic bishops in the USA also are subject to the jurisdiction of Archbishop Major Joseph Cardinal Slipy.

On the basis of the new juridical position in the Ukrainian Greek-Catholic Church and in connection with the recognition of the institution of Archbishop Major whose rights equal those of a Patriarch (§ 10), the legal status of the Ukrainian Catholic Church within the framework of the entire Catholic Church is similar to its status at the time of the Berest Union of 10th October, 1596, and of 23rd December, 1595.

The changes carried out in the USA contradict the spirit and the wording of §§ 19 and 9 of the Decree on Eastern Catholic Churches, and of §1 as well.

Ukrainian Catholics consider a synod of Ukrainian Catholic bishops (and not only those living outside Ukraine), headed by Archbishop Major Joseph Cardinal Slipy, as an equivalent of the Berest Synod. The Ukrainian Church is active not only outside Ukraine, but also in the catacombs. The will of that Church, too, has to be respected. No individual bishop or two or three bishops have the right to introduce changes in our Church without a decision by the Synod of Ukrainian Catholic bishops headed by the Major Archbishop. Changes introduced in any other way amount to an infringement of the rights and privileges guaranteed by the Berest Union and by the Decree on Eastern Churches, and are illegal.

Moreover, our teaching Church, the Synod of Bishops, has had to take into account and must take into account the will of the Ukrainian people, which is at present engaged in a prolonged struggle for Christ's Church and is opposed to any Latinization or Americanization of our Church. The emigré community is only a small part of the many-million-strong Ukrainian people, and the hierarchy has to listen to the will of the entire Ukrainian people.

3) On the actual situation

The confusion in various Ukrainian Catholic parish congregations in the USA in connection with the changeover of the calendar and the forcible introduction of the English language causes deep concern, especially in Chicago and Cleveland....

Similar mistakes in the past have already had unfortunate consequences....

The underground Ukrainian Catholic Church in Ukraine, as well as the Ukrainian Autocephalous Orthodox Church, celebrate their feast days in accordance with the old calendar. In families of mixed confessions disagreement and discord will reign, just as in purely Catholic families, after the introduction of these innovations, because some are celebrating according to the old calendar and some according to the new one. Instead of combating atheism, the believers of the same Church and of the same confession are fighting each other, and are at odds with the hierarchy, as is the case, for example, in Chicago.

In the USA, as a matter of fact, it is only a question of a single feast day in the year [Christmas, 7th January], which falls on an ordinary working day, because apart from Christmas there are no other religious holidays in the USA which do not fall on a Sunday. It is not much of a sacrifice for Ukrainians to devote one weekday in the year to a religious service, to forgo wages for that day, in order to be united in prayer with our Catholic Church in the catacombs of Ukraine and with our Orthodox brethren, with our Orthodox Church, which also lives and is active in the catacombs of Ukraine.

The changes mentioned above also contribute to the weakening of the ecumenical movement, *since the overwhelming majority of Ukrainians are of Orthodox belief and our Orthodox Church follows the old calendar.* The Apostolic See is always urging ecumenical reconciliation, but in homogeneous Ukrainian communities of the faithful in the USA the supporters of the new and the old calendar are in dispute. Under such conditions, it will be more than difficult to strive for a rapprochement and reconciliation with our Orthodox Church. First of all, it is necessary to restore unity among the Catholic faithful who are in dispute concerning the calendar, which is essentially a dispute about much deeper things, for the introduction of the new calendar is *merely a pretext for Latinization and Americanization of our faithful and our Church.*

The reasons for these attempts to introduce alterations are not so much religious arguments, but rather Americanizing tendencies in the form of calendar reforms.

I consider it my duty to emphasize that even in the past the Apostolic See, striving for multiplicity in unity, had no intention of Latinizing or supporting Latinization of other rites, or to act against traditions. Pope Urban VIII, in his bull of 7th February, 1624, had already forbidden changing one's rite and adopting the Latin rite without a special, separate permission of the Holy See. Pope Paul V issued a similar prohibition on 10th December, 1615. The Decree on the Eastern Catholic Churches of the Second Ecumenical Vatican Council goes even further in this direction.

At the same time I should like to question the attempts to introduce English into services instead of Ukrainian, amongst various congregations in the USA, since, exactly as in the case with the calendar reform, this contradicts the decision of the Decree (§§ 1, 2, 19, and 24). § 2 clearly notes that the Catholic Church attaches great importance to the traditions of each particular Church and their ritual being left untouched, and remain unchanged and whole. In § 23 and § 24 faithfulness to the Eastern traditions is emphasized and stressed, and it is pointed out that the introduction of the mother tongue into the divine services is reserved for the Patriarchs with the Synod, or the Synod of the bishops of each Church respectively.

In § 19 it is clearly stated that the transfer of feast days for each Church lies within the competence of the Synod concerned, and not in the hands of individual bishops which naturally also refers to the reform of the calendar. Hence the so-called reforms carried out in the USA and elsewhere in these matters are illegal both in the light of the Decree of the Ecumenical Council of the Catholic Church and the Union of Berest....

In view of the fact that the jurisdiction of the Archbishop Major of the Ukrainian Catholic Church, Joseph Cardinal Slipy has not entered into force, there is not uniformity within our Catholic Church.

4) Legally justified demands

In submitting to the Sacred Congregation for the Eastern Churches, or respectively to other appropriate juridical institutions of the Apostolic See, my objections regarding the changes carried out in the Ukrainian Catholic Church in the USA and elsewhere, contrary to the accords formulated in the Union of Berest, which are binding (and act as her rights and privileges) on both the Ukrainian Catholic Church and the Apostolic See, which by its decisions and accords took upon itself in the person of Pope Clement VIII unambiguous obligations with regard to the Ukrainian Catholic Church and the Ukrainian people, and referring in particular to the Decree of the Second Ecumenical Vatican Council on the Eastern Churches, I wish to put forward the request that:

a) all instructions issued by any ecclesiastical or any other authority in the USA or elsewhere in contradiction of the accords of the Union of Berest, and

b) all the innovations introduced in the USA or elsewhere contradicting the decisions and the spirit of the Decree on the Eastern Churches of the Second Ecumenical Vatican Council

be rescinded and annulled by the Apostolic See as illegal.

With this in mind I refer to § 4 of the Decree, in which the Council grants the right for recourse to be made to the Holy See, which as the highest arbiter extends its care over the ecumenical movements, as well as to § 6 of the Decree in which the Council, led by the Holy Father, decided that those who have deviated from the ancient traditions are duty bound to revert to them.

As Prime Minister of the last independent Ukrainian Government on Ukrainian soil, and in the name of lay Ukrainian Catholic faithful, may I at the same time make the following request:

a) that in accordance with §§ 10 and 7 (especially Section 3) Archbishop Major Joseph Cardinal Slipy be enabled to exercise effectively his jurisdiction with the Synod of Ukrainian Catholic Bishops, to direct all ecclesiastical matters of the Ukrainian Catholic Church abroad, and in accordance with § 23 of the Decree to regulate the problem of the language used in services, since here and there some bishops are beginning, on their own authority, to introduce the use of English in some churches although it is not the mother tongue of Ukrainians;

b) that the Apostolic See create the institution of the Ukrainian Catholic Patriarchate thus giving a monolithic form to the Ukrainian Catholic Church and making of her a radiant center in the struggle against atheism.

I beg Your Eminence to accept expressions of my profound respect.

Yours very truly,

Yaroslav Stetsko
Former Prime Minister of the Ukrainian
State Government in 1941
Ukrainian Information Service
London, 1971

II
Eulogies and Funeral Orations

The Heroic Death of Taras Chuprynka

We have just received the tragic news that Lt. General Taras Chuprynka, commander-in-chief of the Ukrainian Insurgent Army (UPA) and leader of the Ukrainian Liberation movement, has fallen as a hero on the soil of his oppressed native country. He was killed in an action with MVD troops who had located and attacked his headquarters.

This short announcement adds the name of one more martyr to the glorious record of those who have died for the freedom of Ukraine—Petlura, Konovalets, Lypkivsky, and Sheptytsky. It is a blow not only to the Ukrainian people, but to all those behind the Iron Curtain who are bound together with Ukraine in a common fate and a common fight for freedom. Above all, the resistance troops of the nations in the Anti-Bolshevik Bloc of Nations, who are proud to have had the honor of fighting side by side with his fellow-countrymen in the front founded by Chuprynka, mourn his loss. That is why all our national flags are lowered at the grave of this hero of the Ukrainian fight for freedom, as a token of our great admiration and gratitude. General Chuprynka fell not only for his native Ukraine. His heroic death concerns all of us. In order that his death may not be in vain, we feel bound to swear that now, more than ever, we shall not yield until the crusade for national freedom and independence has reached a victorious conclusion.

It may be that Western opinion may think it sufficient merely to note the date of this flaming danger signal on our dark horizon and then to proceed with the order of the day. Compromising with the world's enemy in the Kremlin and preserving "peace" at the cost of our people's life and freedom are still items on this order of the day. A "peace" which permits insurgent armies to wage a desperate fight for freedom and to let heroes like Taras Chuprynka be shot down

73

by the agents of tyranny because they stand up for the right of their compatriots to life and freedom is a disgrace to our civilized world.

The West may find an excuse for its indifference. It probably lacks the proper perspective to be able to see this event in its right proportions and to grasp its significance. Only those who have lived behind the Iron Curtain and have had personal experience of the Bolshevik regime can realize what it means to organize resistance in a country enslaved by Soviet Russia, to form an army of insurgents, to defy and fight tyrants for years. They alone can imagine what it is like for a responsible leader to command a national revolution under the nose of Bolshevik bloodhounds and to look death hourly in the face every day for years. If public opinion in the West is otherwise indifferent to the heroic death of this fearless champion of the Ukrainian Liberation Revolution, it should at least be warned by it. The same bells that toll in the hearts of all oppressed nations for the death of General Chuprynka are ringing the alarm for a fresh attack and the West would do well to take note of the signal.

General Taras Chuprynka's life is a record of patriotism, duty, and conflict. He was born in 1907, his civilian name being Roman Shukevych. Immediately after graduating from the Technical College, he became a leading member of the Ukrainian Military Organization (UVO), to which he had already belonged as a student. In 1929 he took over the military department of the Organization of Ukrainian Nationalists (OUN). In the years 1938-39 he played an active part in organizing the military association, "Ukrainian Carpathian-Sich." In 1943 he was elected chief of the staff of the OUN and then commander-in-chief of the UPA. In November of the same year, the Anti-Bolshevik Bloc of Nations (ABN), uniting the revolutionary movements of the peoples oppressed by Moscow, was founded at his suggestion. In July 1944 he was elected President of the secretariat of the Ukrainian Supreme Liberation Council (UHVR), and general secretary for military affairs in this the supreme revolutionary organizaton in Ukraine. He held the Golden Cross and the Golden Military Cross (First Class).

May the memory of General Taras Chuprynka live forever! His heroic death is a significant milestone on the path of national revolution in Ukraine and other oppressed countries.

ABN Correspondence,
October 1950, p. 1

Address Delivered at the Funeral of Stepan Bandera
on October 20, 1959

In 1926 Symon Petlura was murdered in Paris; twelve years later, in 1938, Evhen Konovalets was assassinated in Rotterdam; and in 1950 the same fate befell Taras Chuprynka in Bilohorshcha (Ukraine). Today, nine years later, we stand at this open grave here in Munich, at the coffin of Stepan Bandera....

Four tragic dates in the recent history of Ukraine, four great men, each of them a noble and outstanding personality, four pillars of fire in heroic self-sacrifice for the Ukrainian cause of freedom and state independence.

Each of them died at his post by the hand of the Russian occupant, by the treacherous cunning that is typical of all Moscow murderers of every era and every state system. Moscow has not the courage to take up an open fight with the champions and representatives of the noble idea of freedom cherished by Ukraine, the idea of right and justice, the idea of universal freedom; Moscow resorts to the course of cunning and secret murder. But Moscow's triumphs in the long run are not permanent. Moscow, which personifies the forces of evil, destruction, and ruin, robs us of our best men, but their spirit and their ideas live on.

Moscow is endeavoring to break our spirit and, by forcibly taking Stepan Bandera from our midst, believes that the Ukrainian nation will thus be spiritually crushed and overwhelmed by despair, will renounce the ideas of the man who has been murdered and will abandon its national fight for freedom.

Such hopes are futile! The deceased was the very personification of the ideas of the entire Ukrainian nation, of the ideas which inspire it, of the ideas for which it suffers and for which millions of Ukrainians have already sacrificed their lives. The name of Bandera has become the symbol of the present anti-Russian fight of Ukraine for its state independence and for human freedom. In the course of his revolutionary activity, Stepan Bandera for many years held the leading posts in the Ukrainian organized liberation movement and distinguished himself by his great spirit of self-sacrifice, his courage and determination—to begin with in the UVO, then in the OUN. As his country's leader and territorial UVO commander, and, later, as the leader of the entire OUN and as President of the Executive Committee of the Units Abroad of the OUN, in which posts he molded the political character of the OUN and gave it its form of organization. Neither the fact that he was sentenced to death, nor the years he spent in German concentration camps, nor the martyrdom inflicted on his two brothers in Auschwitz and on his brother-in-law could make him swerve from his revolutionary course; he continued to pursue his path unwaveringly, regardless of obstacles or failures.

He derived his great moral strength from his profound religiosity. Christianity was an inalienable part of his spiritual strength, and his entire activity was characterized by his faith in God and his Christian moral principles. His patriotic nationalism was inseparably united with his Christianity. He was fully aware of the fact that Moscow, the center of aggression, was an atheist nation, hence so much more dangerous for Ukraine, because it aimed at a physical and spiritual ruination of his beloved motherland.

Today we bid farewell to the mortal remains of Stepan Bandera, but in our hearts and the soul of the Ukrainian people he will live on forever!

In the name of the entire Organization of Ukrainian Nationalist revolutionaries on this side of and beyond the Iron Curtain, in the name of the whole of fighting Ukraine, in the name of the survivors of the old guard of the Ukrainian national revolution, who for over thirty years fought side by side with you at the front—and as a personal friend—I bid you, our loyal comrade and leader, farewell as you pass over into the realm of everlasting life.

As a last greeting I bring you water from the Black Sea, from the Ukrainian sea, which is as stormy as your whole life was!

And next to it I place a handful of soil—from Ukraine! It will always remind you of our native country!

May foreign soil rest lightly on you!

The Year of Chuprynka vs. the Year of Lenin
Part One

On March 5, 1950, on the field of glory in battle against the MVD troops in Bilohorshcha near Lviv, died the Commander-in-Chief of the UPA General Roman Shukhevych-Taras Chuprynka, Head of the Supreme Executive Board of the OUN and Chairman of the General Secretariat of the UHVR.

With his death the most heroic period in the history of the UPA came to an end; a nationwide uprising terminated. But the revolutionary liberation struggle did not cease. It assumed new forms, adopted new methods, and became more intensive, designed for an extended period of time and with the aim of preparing not only the national liberational revolutionary insurrection in Ukraine, but simultaneous coordinated uprisings of other nations subjugated by Russia in the USSR and the satellite countries. The most striking traits of the second period of the revolutionary liberation struggle in the last quarter century are mass uprisings, strikes, and actions of prisoners in concentration camps, which characterize the liberation drive until 1959. At about that time we entered the third stage— the intensification of the revolutionary struggle in Ukraine with the help of demonstrations by workers and students, armed clashes with the Russian occupation forces, and the unusual heightening of the ideological and cultural struggle of the young intellectuals, poets, and artists of Ukraine against the Russian and Communist domination. Two worlds stand in opposition to each other distinctly and clearly, Kyiv, vs. Moscow, as two opposing poles.

The basis for the contemporary epoch was created by the heroic epic of the OUN-UPA, which were led from 1942 to 1950 in Ukraine by Taras Chuprynka (Tur, Lozowsky). Of course, our revolutionary liberation struggle stems from and is based on the traditions of the Liberation Struggle of 1918, as well as on the whole history of our heroic struggle for our national identity, for the sovereignty of our nation, and for the development of all its creative forces and potentials.

What made the figure of the Commander-in-Chief of the Ukrainian Armed Forces so strong? He had great passion for the army, for the expansion of military forces. From this angle we must view the entire growth through the decades of this unusual figure in the modern history of Ukraine. This, however, does not preclude his other outstanding attributes: a politician-revolutionary of high quality, a statesman, a strategist of the total national liberation political revolution, and first of all a remarkable leader-strategist of the modern type of warfare: insurgent-guerrilla warfare.

The modern age is at the same time the age of ideology and the age of thermonuclear weapons. It would seem that these are two opposing tendencies in the development of the world. On the contrary, however, in the ideological struggle which is being waged in all corners of the world it is impossible to use the all-destructive thermonuclear arms to achieve victory of these or other ideas. From this stems the only solution: the guerilla-partisan strategy. In its basis lies the ideological and political strategy to captivate by definite ideas the broad popular masses, the peoples, which serve as the basis for this type of strategy. General Roman Shukhevych-Chuprynka grasped the meaning of the age by his great intuition as a military strategist and politician, statesman, and revolutionary. He expanded the nationwide revolt to unheard of proportions. In a public statement in Rome Josyf Cardinal Slipy, who at that time lived in Ukraine as a free man, gave the size of this army, as half a million strong. General Chuprynka, whose *nom de guerre* had become legendary, being aware of the general trend of the epoch, merged the national idea with the social into one indivisible whole. Under his able leadership, the OUN, the initiator of the UPA began to place strong emphasis on the social aspects of revolution. UPA defended the varied interests of the nation and the individual. It fought for the socio-economic interests of the people, defended them against forced deportation by both Germans and Russians for slave labor, took away grain supplies which were collected by means of teror, hindered attempts to draft our people into the Soviet army or the German slave auxiliary units. Stressing the socio-political elements, the Commander-in-Chief of the UPA and the Head of the Supreme Executive of the OUN from 1943 placed national political liberation in the forefront, for he was conscious of the fact that with the assumption of power by the Ukrainian people on Ukrainian territory, social liberation would take place simultaneously and social justice would prevail. The UPA-OUN were practicing what they preached. They were building a state on territories conquered by Ukrainian arms where the power of the occupants did not penetrate. There all branches of a full-fledged state life were developed.

From a historic aspect one can speak about two revolutions which were unusually similar: the period of Khmylnytsky and its successor, the revolution initiated by the OUN—UPA, manifested in particular in the period of the nationwide rising of the UPA when it had been commanded by General Chupyrnka. Two great epochs, two revolutions. The latter has been just set in motion by the OUN-UPA and is waiting for its triumphant end. The ideas of the great statesman Mazepa and the social reformer Paliy have been put into life by the leader of the Ukrainian national and social liberation revolution of our times, Taras Chuprynka.

The foreign-policy aspect of this revolution was a two-front war of OUN-UPA. The anti-German war which began on June 30, 1941 and the continuation of the anti-Russian one became a great signal for other subjugated peoples to unite in a common front against both aggressors: Germany and Russia. As a member of the Ukrainian State Government of 1941, in the capacity of Assistant to Defense Minister General Vsevolod Petrov, who had won fame in the Liberation Struggle of 1918, Roman Shukhevych was the co-creator of the historic Act of 1941. The general was conscious of the fact that without the armed forces there could be no talk of renewal of statehood. He built them up by first becoming the commanding officer of the Legion of Ukrainian Nationalists (DUN), which was temporarily created within the framework of the Germany army in order to train cadres for his own independent army of the future. When the Germans failed to live up to the conditions for creating military units within the framework of their army and demanded the oath of allegiance to Germany or the Führer, instead of an oath of allegiance to the Ukrainian state, Roman Shukhevych cleverly transferred the well-trained cadres of DUN into the underground, thus immediately creating a backbone of our two-front army, the Armed Forces of Ukraine—the UPA.

Roman Shukhevych was a determined advocate of the armed forces. He was their moving force in the OUN Executive as well as their untiring organizer together with his future Chief of Staff of the UPA, General Dmytro Hrytsai, and his successor after the latter's heroic death, Yu. Hasyn. This dedication to the armed forces permeated the whole being of the General. As a leading member of the UVO he stressed the importance of military struggle at every opportunity. Personally, he was unusually courageous, but at the same time cool and calculating, systematically planning each military deed or action. As a young member of UVO he participated in the most heroic deeds of UVO of a military nature against the representatives of powers occupying Ukraine. Unafraid to take risks, a brilliant performer and at the same time a great conspirator, he was always successful. As a military secretary for the Regional OUN Executive in Western Ukraine he planned, organized, and performed the most dangerous military operations, which were always great successes for the OUN-UVO, which at that time became the military arm of the OUN. Roman Shukhevych, in his youth one of the greatest fighters at the services of the OUN-UVO in the style of Zhelyabov-Perovsky-Kybalchych, was never uncovered by the occupying power, although the acts which he performed himself or which he organized within the framework of the UVO or later OUN-UVO received worldwide publicity as deeds of the UVO-OUN. He was silent as a great anonymous fighter. He remained anonymous as the leader of the Ukrainian Revolution—as the Head of the Supreme Executive of the OUN (Tur), Commander-in-Chief of the UPA (Taras Chuprynka), Chairman of the General Secretariat of UHVR (Lozovsky), and initiator, together with the late Rostyslav Voloshyn, of the First Conference of the Subjugated Peoples in November 1943, which served as the organizational basis for ABN. Only after his heroic death on March 5, 1950 on the field of battle with the Russians did his name become known to the whole world. His modesty was unprecedented. He, the Commander-in-Chief of the greatest insurgent army of World War II, did not care about military rank of any kind. Only after Stepan Bandera had placed this matter on the agenda of the UHVR were Taras Chuprynka, the Commander-in-Chief, and D. Perebyinis, the Chief of Staff, raised to the rank of general.

Roman Shukhevych as the Regional Commander of OUN in Ukraine, in the so-called General-Governorship and at the same time a military secretary of the Supreme Executive of the OUN, was in the center of the organization of the Marching Groups of OUN—this political army of the brave, which together with the cadres throughout Ukraine had inspired the broad popular masses and has included them in the struggle against the occupying powers. He had an uncommon sense for the practical. He was one of the creators of the great strategically political and militarily insurgent plan of action for various situations which could prevail in Ukraine during World War II.

He liked the military profession above all and had a deep political understanding of it. He wanted to unite deeds and ideas. When spring set in in Carpatho-Ukraine in 1938, he appeared there after illegally crossing the border and began to expand the Carpatho-Ukrainian "Sich" (army) together with Col. Kolodzinsky-Huzar, who was the Chief of Staff of the Carpatho-Ukrainian Sich, which was heroically defending the independence of the Carpatho-Ukraine. Roman Shukhevych was as fearless as the late Zenon Kossak, who, in answer to demands of the German Consul at Khust that our army in Carpatho-Ukraine capitulate, answered in the style of the Roman Cato: "There is no such word in the Ukrainian dictionary."

Imprisoned several times by the Polish occupation regime, and in 1936 sentenced to four years' imprisonment for membership in the OUN at the trial of the Regional Executive of OUN in West Ukraine—that is, at the trial of Stepan Bandera and his associates—he maintained complete secrecy and great attentiveness and did not provide any material evidence which could be used to convict him for military acts. In prison he was a good friend and companion who always rose in defense of his fellow-prisoners and kept everybody's spirits high by his cheerful disposition, sense of humor, and daring in his relations with the prison guards.

Rarely are generals and commanding officers good politicians and statesmen. Roman Shukhevych was one of those exceptional figures, who posessed the talents of a military strategist, a politician, and a statesman. What is more, among the leading individuals associated with our revolution at that time, he was the most conciliatory in relation to other political parties and groupings, although he never crossed the boundary line of revolutionary-political adherence to principles.... On the other hand, he was very strict and inexorably just, determined and energetic, qualities which a leader and a commander of the revolution had to possess. He found practical application for the revolutionary-liberation concept of the ABN as the only possible and realistic road to liberation without foreign intervention and foreign legions.... The Great UPA raids into the countries neighboring on Ukraine, including the Caucasus in 1949, were proof of his orientation toward simultaneous, coordinated, national liberation revolutions and uprisings.

Widespread political activity among the soldiers of the Soviet army and the armies of the satellite states, his own radio station in the Carpathians, negotiations and treaties with other underground armies (as for example the Polish Home Army) or with the General Staff and the commanding generals of the Hungarian Army and the Rumanian government (which wanted to save itself before the Russian hordes) all testified to the political farsightedness of Roman Shukhevych, and in particular were proof of our expanding power, of the revolutionary potential of the Ukrainian people.

The Ukrainian statehood proclaimed on June 30, 1941 continued to exist under the protection of UPA arms on the Ukrainian territories controlled by it. The functions of the arrested State Government were taken over by the UHVR, created in June 1944 for that very purpose, and it conducted negotiations on the basis of inter-state relations between Ukraine and her neighbors. At that time Ukraine existed as a real fact.

What a great force it was is attested to by the death in battle with the UPA of the German S.A. Chief of Staff General Lutse, the Russian Marshall Vatutin, and the Vice-Minister for Military Affairs of the "people's" Poland, General Walter Swierczewski. What is more, in May 1947, three states, the USSR, CSSR, and Poland, signed a military pact calling for mutual destruction of insurgent Ukraine, the UPA-OUN. A pact of three Communist states against the forces of Ukraine, including Russia, which was one of the victors in the war with Germany! The OUN-UPA-UHVR and the front of the subjugated nations (ABN) mobilized against the Russian occupying power—included UPA raids into East Prussia, Latvia, Byelorussia, Poland, Slovakia, and other countries—was such an explosive force that it threatened to topple the empire and its Communist regime from inside. Russia was more certain of victory over Germany, which was not driven by any ideas which could inspire the peoples but only by conquest, while Ukraine was bringing revolutionary ideas which inspired our whole nation as well as all the other subjugated nations. The First Conference of the Subjugated Nations in 1943 called on all the subjugated peoples of Europe and Asia to unite in a common front against both tyrannies. It condemned the common front with one tyranny against the other tyranny, but called for a common struggle against all tyranny. It was a historic signal for the Allies, who lost the Second World War in a political sense.

As a result Russia became afraid of the revolutionary potential of Ukraine, of the great improvisation of our nation, the nationwide insurrection, the UPA, and its mobilizing ideas, which knew no boundaries, transgressed Ukraine's frontiers and encompassed the whole subjugated world of nations and individuals under Russian rule.

ABN Correspondence,
May-June 1970, pp. 7-10

The Year of Chuprynka vs. the Year of Lenin
Part Two

At that time, side by side with the military pact of the three states, a bacteriological and chemical war was launched by Russia, through MVD troops, directed personally by Khrushchev, against fighting Ukraine, against the UPA, against our people, who supported the UPA-OUN. Children, women, and old people—all of them were in the front lines in the struggle against Russia.... Mass deportations, raids, provocations, Russian partisans at the UPA's rear supplied from the air, an avalanche of MVD troops, and Russian divisions of the Soviet Army—all this was aimed at the destruction of fighting Ukraine. This was the struggle of the heroic Ukrainian people, which has no equal in the history of the world, against the victor in a world war, thanks to the Allies, over such a military power as Nazi Germany.

Blood ran in streams.... This army of the nation of heroes, as it was called by the great Commander-in-Chief in one of his orders, which has no equal in the history of mankind was commanded by an unequalled strategist of insurgent-guerrilla warfare, the most modern type of warfare in the thermonuclear age— General Taras Chuprynka. A great unifier of ideas and deeds.... This was manifested even in his assumed name: the head of the Insurgent Center of the Central Ukrainian Territories in the 1920s was Hrytsko Chuprynka.

When the unconquerable population of the so-called Zakerzonnya (Lemky region) put up such staunch resistance to forced resettlement, Stalin became alarmed and stopped mass deportations from West Ukraine, for he feared that the flames of revolution were going to envelop the entire prison of nations. *And it was not the German bombers but the Ukrainian liberation ideas which threatened to blow up the Russian empire from within.*

At the head of this fierce and heroic struggle in Ukraine and in the empire stood the Commander-in-Chief of the Armed Forces of Ukraine. He was opposing Stalin. He personified the gigantic struggle of the Ukrainian nation against the aggressive Russian nation. Chuprynka vs. Stalin, Kyiv vs. Moscow, St. Sophia and St. George vs. the Kremlin, Ukraine vs. Russia! The Red Russian partisans led by Kovpak were thrown at the UPA's rear and the UPA had to fight them while fighting the German occupants. The UPA defeated Kovpak's bands so that when the opportunity presented itself they were glad to march through some regions of Ukraine under cover of darkness, fleeing in the wake of the brave army of Ukraine. The "raids" of the Red Russian partisans in Ukraine were no more than random attacks of robber-gangsters against the daring population of Ukraine, which supported the UPA-OUN. Kovpak and his bands looked like thieves and robbers who, after stealing somebody else's property or killing a defenseless man in his sleep, bragged about their thieving, gangster "courage." In the long run the common attacks by both the Germans and the Russians against the organized OUN-UPA were to no avail. Only after Germany had capitulated while Russian friendship with the Allies continued uninterrupted, and when the activities of the OUN-UPA continued to expand and grow in strength, did Russia together with her allies, the CSSR and Poland, throw her forces against the UPA-OUN. The ABN against the Russian prison of nations! For its final dissolution into independent national states within the ethnographic boundaries of the subjugated peoples! Taras Chuprynka projected a new world on the ruins of the empire. He proposed and strove for a new political map of Europe, Asia, and the world after the destruction of the Russian prison of nations and the Communist system.

And it is not an accident that we are now putting forth a slogan: The Year of Chuprynka against the Year of Lenin! This year marks the twentieth anniversary of the heroic death on the field of glory of the leader of our liberation army and the defender of the most noble ideas of the nation and the individual, and the 100th anniversary of the birth of Lenin—the founder of the most barbaric prison of nations.

Chuprynka vs. Lenin in the historio-ideological cross-section of our epoch in world dimensions—two symbols, two systems of ideas, two conceptions, two pictures of life. The world of truth, freedom, goodness, justice, human and national rights, the acknowledgment of man as a creature like unto God, a nation as the cornerstone in the construction of the world, the national state as the principle of organization of the new world, religion as the source of morality and the projection of the supernatural, eternal life—this is the world of General Chuprynka—against the world of deception, terror, arbitrariness, genocide, injustice, and exploitation, the trampling of human and national rights, the downgrading of an individual making him into a member of the herd, the world prison of nations and individuals, militant atheism and philosophical material-ism, which does not acknowledge the immortality of the human soul—this is the world of Lenin. As the deceived and Bolshevik-infiltrated circles, even in the Free World, are getting ready to celebrate Lenin's centennial, let us offset this, in this year of Chuprynka, by his image with its ideas, the ideas of fighting Ukrainians of Kyiv, versus the figure of Lenin with his criminal aims, the aims of Russia, the aims of Moscow to ruin and destroy the world of goodness and truth, freedom and justice.

Let us show Ukraine to the world, let us show our national underground Christian militant Kyiv, our St. Sophia and St. George, against Russia, against Moscow, against the Kremlin. Kyiv and Moscow—let them show themselves to the world in this year of Chuprynka in the cross section of the many-sided world ideological struggle of two opposing concepts of life, of two opposing worlds.

At mass demonstrations or at any other opportunity let us carry banners with the name of Shukhevych-Chuprynka in contrast to the name of Lenin. Let the demonstration with signs bearing the names of Chuprynka, Bandera, and Petlura, clash in the streets of cities of the Free World with those bearing the names of Lenin, Stalin, Marx, which are the symbols of the world of crime and the downfall of man.

Just as the Zaporizhian Sich under Baida-Vyshnevetsky was placed under the protection of the Blessed Virgin Mary, so our army under General Chuprynka was placed under the protection of Mary the Patroness. In the early morning and evening all of Chuprynka's warriors gathered in prayer to their Creator begging Him for protection and the victory of their just cause. Fighting against the armies of the atheist Russians, our army had its own chaplains who fell in battle with the cross in their hands just as their companions, their soldiers, fell with arms in their hands.

Taras Chuprynka stood for equal rights for all citizens of Ukraine, regardless of race, religion, and national origin, provided they are loyal to the Ukrainian Government.

The UPA defended the Jews, who were being annihilated by the Nazis. Hundreds and hundreds of OUN-UPA members were executed by the Germans for sheltering the persecuted Jewish population. The UPA accepted into its ranks all volunteers, such as Jewish doctors, and anyone who wanted to fight for a Ukrainian state against Nazi or Russian barbarity. Creating national units within the framework of the UPA, its Commander-in-Chief aimed at mobilizing the armed forces of other subjugated peoples into separate national armies against the Russian and German invaders. This was part of a plan for a common armed front of the subjugated nations. His proposal is applicable even today. The armed struggle will determine the fate of the subjugated nations, the fate of Ukraine. This is a firm guiding principle which was left to us by the Commander-in-Chief of the Armed Forces of Ukraine—General Roman Shukhevych-Chuprynka.

So few instances are recorded in history in which the Supreme Commander remained with his army on the field of battle without leaving his native land and died a hero in the struggle with the troops of the aggressor. "We—the Command of the Organization of Ukrainian Nationalists—are remaining in our native land with our people," wrote the Head of the OUN Command, Tur (in "The Declaration of the OUN Command after the End of World War II"), "to continue unchangeably our liberation struggle, without leaving our people...."

As the Commander-in-Chief of the UPA, the Head of the Ukrainian Underground Government, in contrast to the puppet "Government" of the Ukrainian SSR, the Head of the OUN Command in Ukraine died near Bilohorshcha, on native soil, defending it against the brutal Russian barbarians. The ancient example of Leonidas at Thermopylae comes to mind. We also recall Nelson in the Battle of Trafalgar. We think about a modern Svyatoslav, who perished while defending his native Ukrainian land from the wild Pechenigs-Russians.

It is not known where the last remains of our Supreme Commander are to be found, for the Russian barbarians are afraid of him, even after death. They are afraid that his grave will become a site of pilgrimage for thousands upon thousands in Ukraine. But to no avail. The time will come when the last remains of our modern-day Svyatoslav, who fell at the head of his warriors in the defense of his native land, will be found, and they will find their final resting place in the Ukrainian Pantheon, in our holy and eternal city of Kyiv. But before this happens, it is our sacred duty to fight against Russia at every opportunity, and with all methods, forms, and means in order to avenge the death of our Great Heroes.

Long live the Sovereign, United Ukrainian State!

Death to the Russian empire in all its forms!

Long live the Ukrainian Insurgent Army!

Eternal glory to the Supreme Commander of the Armed Forces of Ukraine, General Roman Shukhevych-Chuprynka!

ABN Correspondence,
July-August 1970, pp. 10-12

III
Special Addresses, Appeals, Articles, and Interviews

Interview in Ottawa

Q. — Mr. Stetsko, what is the ABN?

A. — The full name of our organization is "The Anti-Bolshevik Bloc of Nations." We are active in the satellite countries and within Russia proper. Our aim is the liberation of subjugated states and peoples from Communist rule.

Q. — What is the basis of your appeal inside Russia?

A. — The same as it is in, say, Poland — Liberation. It is something forgotten —Soviet Russia is an empire containing many peoples who speak different languages and have different cultural traditions.

It contains, in short, many conquered nations, which are entitled to a separate national existence. Ukrainians, for example, are just as much interested in national independence as Poles or Czechs. Our underground is active wherever people feel this need.

Operations

Q. — How do you operate?

A. — In many ways, depending upon circumstances. In mountainous areas and in others where the terrain is favorable, we wage guerrilla warfare. Where this is not possible, we publish and distribute propaganda, undertake sabotage where and when feasible, do what we can to embarrass the secret police. We also maintain our own Intelligence organization.

Q. — Do you undertake large-scale military operations?

A. — Not now. This was possible during the war and for a year or so afterwards when conditions were still turbulent. In 1946, we were still able to fight pitched battles with Russian units. We later were forced to revert to the kind of tactics which we used before the war.

Q. — It is sometimes suggested that most members of the ABN were wartime collaborators of the Nazis.

Fought Both

A. — This is not true. We loathed both and we fought both. I and many others in the ABN spent years in German concentration camps, where our treatment was not, to say the least, sympathetic.

Q. — Many people in the Western world distrust reports of resistance and opposition to Communism behind the Iron Curtain. What is your comment on that?

A. — I can understand the mistrust. But it is regrettable. The opposition is genuine. It exists. Our Underground movement is genuinely active—as the MVD is well aware. Our Intelligence reports, smuggled into Western Europe, seem to be treated as reliable.

Q. — How do you keep in touch with your organization when you are far from Russian or satellite territory?

A. — We maintain an efficient courier system. Couriers carrying important documents and messages slip out of Communist territory — often into Germany. It is not easy. We have lost many good messengers. The distances and risks are great. A disadvantage of the system is that it virtually ceases to operate in wintertime, due to cold and snow.

Q. — Do you maintain radio communication?

Dangerous

A. — No. At the moment, a two-way communications system would be dangerous.

Q. — In what areas is opposition to Russian Communism the strongest?

A. — Outside the USSR, I would say that Poland and Czechoslovakia contain the strongest resistance. The ABN is also very active in Hungary. Inside the Russian empire, the key areas are Ukraine and Byelorussia. Our movement is strongest of all in Ukraine. And this is important—don't forget that one Soviet soldier of every four is a Ukrainian.

Q. — Would you say that a majority of Ukrainians are anti-Communist?

A. — Beyond any doubt. Our movement could not have survived, let alone reach formidable proportions, if this were not the case. And I would say this —that in my opinion there are more devout Communists in Canada and the United States than there are in Ukraine with its population of 40,000,000.

Q. — In the event of war, could Stalin count upon the loyalty of the Ukrainian troops?

Distrust

A. — Certainly not. The Soviet rulers have always had good reason to distrust Ukrainian troops. Russian policy is to keep them in the Far East —Siberia —where they could cause as little trouble as possible.

Q. — *Do you believe that if war did come, that Soviet Russia would be defeated?*

A. — Yes — but only if the Free World accepts the assistance of the Ukrainians and other enslaved peoples who wish their freedom.

Q. — *How could this be done?*

A. — By assuring them that, following a victory, the path to independence would be free of obstacles. The Western Powers should make it clear to any nation which, by majority vote, seeks this status.

Q. — *Is anything along these lines being done now?*

Too Cautious

A. — No. Your foreign offices and external affairs departments are too cautious. They are afraid of annoying those whom they call "the Russian people." They won't or can't recognize the fact that many whom they could describe as Russians are nothing of the sort. They ignore the fact that of the entire population of the Soviet Union two people out of every five are non-Russians. These non-Russians are natives of fourteen once-independent states. Does the West believe that this "new nationalism" which is admitted to be sweeping the whole of Asia has passed the Soviet Empire by? It hasn't. Nationalist feelings are strong among these large minorities.

Q. — *Is Titoism an important factor behind the Iron Curtain?*

A. — In the satellite states, yes. But not in the Soviet Union. Anti-Communists oppose all forms of Communism. And that includes Tito.

Q. — *What, in your view, would be the most effective means of avoiding a Third World War?*

A. — I think that this can best be done by exploiting the weaknesses of Stalin's polyglot empire. The Free World should pay at least as much attention to struggling Nationalist movements in one Ukraine and the Baltic States, for example, as the Politburo lavishes upon French Indochina and Iran.

More and better propaganda should be directed behind the Iron Curtain. The ground is ready for the seeding. Despite packed concentration camps, there is discontent even among the Russian Communists themselves. As long as the Politburo cannot confidently expose the Soviet Empire to the strains and stresses of war there will be peace.

Truth on the March, Toronto:
Canadian League for Ukrainian Liberation, 1953, pp. 28

The Pilgrimages
to Peking and Belgrade

It is no mere coincidence that the same delegation from Moscow which last year went on a pilgrimage to Peking has this year visited Belgrade. On both occasions the delegation was headed by the First Secretary of the Communist Party, Khrushchev, a fact which indicates beyond all doubt that the questions at issue were not merely confined to inter-state relations with Red China and Yugoslavia, but also concerned the solution of certain fundamental problems in the reciprocal relationship of the three main centers of Communism. It is true that Yugoslavia, compared to the Soviet Union or to Red China, is a relatively slight factor as far as its sphere of influence is concerned, but morally and politically it must be regarded as important.

We know that the USSR has tried to lay down the law everywhere, but its attempts to do so in Yugoslavia and previously in Red China have not been successful. This fact, however, is not of any decisive importance as far as the international political function of Communism and the further development of Russian imperialism are concerned. Even in the event of an open conflict between West and East, the existence of Tito's Yugoslavia would contribute towards the confusion of the West as regards the course and nature of the psychological war, rather than to the success of a genuine liberation policy.

The fact that Khrushchev and Bulganin, upon arriving at the airport in Belgrade, promptly took the blame for the breach with Tito themselves, and in doing so made Beria the scapegoat, may quite possibly indicate that they had already reached a secret agreement with Tito before they set off for Belgrade.

In the event of a war, Tito will by no means be anxious to see the West victorious, since the existence of his regime depends for the most part on the continued existence of the USSR. The position of the United States, however, as far as the Yugoslav riddle is concerned has now become extremely complicated; if Tito has already definitely gone over to Khrushchev's side, then the USA by continuing to provide Tito with aid, would actually be helping Moscow; if the USA on the other hand discontinues its aid to Tito, such a step might prove disastrous for America's policy and would most probably drive Tito to join forces with the USSR. Paradoxical though it may sound, to help or not to help in this case seems to be equally dangerous.

Even if Tito has not reached a secret agreement with Moscow and should refrain from doing so in the future, he will, with Moscow's blessing, now busy himself as the champion and advocate of "active coexistence," which definitely aids the present trend of Russian foreign policy.

It is very doubtful whether a development of this kind would be in keeping with the interests of the West! The present Russian endeavor to set up a "neutral zone" which, beginning with Finland and Sweden, would extend via Germany, Austria, and Yugoslavia as far as Egypt and India, and would quite possibly also include Italy and even France, is a deadly menace to the West. The Kremlin is obviously seeking to set up a new "Cordon Sanitaire" for itself, after the model of the Versailles Treaty, save that in this case the "cordon" would now be located 500 miles further west.

Any concessions which Moscow might make to the satellite countries by withdrawing the Soviet troops, but retaining the Communist governments, would never really ease the tension in the international political situation. Even if the Moscow Bolsheviks were to sanction or put up with a "National Communist" variant in all the countries which now have a Communist government, these countries would after all, like Peking and Belgrade, still continue to be dependent on Moscow, and at the critical moment would be more closely allied to the Soviet Union than to the West.

And what is more, the emancipation of these states from their position as satellites might, to a certain degree, even prove advantageous to Moscow; for statements such as those made by Red China's Minister of War, for example, at the Warsaw Conference—namely that in the event of conflict the population of China, numbering 600 million, would support the USSR—might well, since they are statements which are made voluntarily and by a sovereign power, be far more important in aiding the consolidation of the Communists' position and assisting Red propaganda than the parrot-like speeches made by Cyrankiewicz, Zapotocky, or by other Moscow puppets.

The West, however, is seriously mistaken if it hopes to achieve a political success in the Communist satellite countries, in the course of "active coexistence" by active trade relations and increased economic influence. The Communist regimes of these countries and their trade and industrial corporations, either camouflaged as cooperative or not, will be astute enough to carry on trade on a large scale with the West and, at the same time, use the economic and financial means obtained in this way to consolidate the Red regime and suppress any resistance—and will then, at the critical moment, join forces with the Soviet Union. Western trade relations with Red China would, it is true, diminish the latter's economic dependence on the Soviet Union, but would not result in Red China's political severance from the Kremlin.

The existence of two or even three main centers of Communism does not by any means denote a weakening of the movement, but, on the contrary, under the present circumstances might consolidate Communism even more. By using clever new catchwords—as, for instance, "People's Republic of China" or "Balkan Federation"—Soviet Russian imperialism might even occupy and mislead the Free World more successfully than by direct action on the part of Moscow, whose practices so far are, in any case, of bad repute.

As long as the Soviet Russian empire continues to exist as the stronghold of world Communism, subsidiary sources of Communism will be able to exist in other countries. It is only when the main center and source in the USSR has been destroyed and that country has been disintegrated into independent national and democratic states, that the elimination of the Communist regimes of Mao Tsetung and of Tito will no longer present any problems.

Neither coexistence nor atomic war should be adopted as the watchword of our times, but a definite and steadfast policy of liberation, which will help the nations at present enduring the Red yoke of Moscow, Peking, and Belgrade to attain their freedom. Otherwise the Western world will be in danger of becoming utterly confused and of being completely taken in and led astray by hypocritical and crafty catchwords, which are inspired either directly or indirectly by Moscow and are disseminated throughout the world.

The Ukrainian Review,
No. III, 1955, pp. 3-5

For a United Front

"Coexistence"

"Coexistence" is a deceptive term which is used for the purpose of lulling the Free World into security, undermining its morale, and then subsequently attacking it by surprise. The aim of "coexistence" is to show the peoples subjugated by Russia, who are fighting for the disintegration of the Russian empire, whatever its color, into sovereign states within their own ethnographical boundaries, that the Free World has approved of the subjugation of these peoples. In this way the suspicion of the subjugated peoples is to be aroused as regards the Free World, which bargains away the freedom of nations and individuals. The "co-existence" policy aims to destroy the united and universal front of all of freedom-loving mankind on this side of and beyond the Iron Curtain. Its purpose is to help Moscow to attack the Free World when the opportunity seems ripe to the Kremlin and to exploit the attitude of mistrust and suspicion towards the West on the part of the nations subjugated by Russian imperialism and Communism.

Methods Russia Understands

I am of the opinion that the policy of friendship with Russia and the Red Peking Government which is being pursued by the Indian Government is harmful for the Indian nation, since the latter's vigilance as regards the menace of Russian imperialism is thus impaired. Peace can never be maintained if the Free World pursues a policy of concessions towards Russian imperialism and Mao Tse-tung. Russia will only yield to pressure.

And various examples in history illustrate this fact. The history of the nineteenth and twentieth centuries proves beyond all doubt that whenever Russia, in the course of a conference or congress, renounced some territory or other that she had annexed, she merely did so either because she had suffered a military defeat or else was threatened by military force if she refused to cede the territory in question. It was only Germany's ultimatum at the peace conference of Brest-Litovsk in 1918 which forced Lenin and Trotsky to renounce their claims to the Baltic States, Poland, and Ukraine. It was only the fact that Poland, Finland, and Ukraine proclaimed their national rights in 1917 and made it plain that they would, if need be, resort to military force if their national aspirations were disregarded that compelled the Kerensky Government to yield. It was only the British convoys in the Sea of Marmara and the stern warning of the British Cabinet during the Turko-Russian War of 1878 that prompted Russia during the Congress of Berlin to renounce her Balkan booty and abandon her Dardanelles plans much against her will. It was only the fact that Japan had been victorious in the war which led to the eviction of Russia from Korea and Manchuria at the peace conference at Portsmouth. And it was only thanks to England's firm attitude that Russia was evicted from North Persia and Greece after World War II.

There have never been nor are there any other methods of forcing the Russian imperialists to cede territories which they have annexed.

Peace can only be achieved if the Russian empire is disintegrated into independent national states within their own ethnographical boundaries and the Russian state is established solely within the ethnographical boundaries of the Russian nation. Siberia is not part of Russia and must be detached from the latter. The independent states of Ukraine, Turkestan, Byelorussia, of the peoples of Caucasia, Idel-Ural, of the Baltic peoples, and of all the satellite countries in Europe and Asia must be restored once more.

Mao and Titoism

It does not seem to me that Mao Tse-tung could ever become the Tito of Asia. All the more so since it cannot be assumed that Tito has really severed his connections with Russia and is genuinely on the side of the West. In my opinion, Tito will take sides with Russia should it come to a decisive conflict with Russia. Tito is well aware of the fact that the free democratic West, should it prove victorious in such a conflict, would never permit the despotism which prevails in the Balkan States to continue. Tito is a typical adherent of "coexistence" for the simple reason that he is hoping to land a big haul by fishing in troubled waters— those of the free West and those of despotic Russia. The Free World must openly support the cause of the national state independence of the Croats, Serbs, and Slovenes as well as the reunion of Macedonia with Bulgaria in order to win over these peoples for the fight against Communist despotism and imperialist artifices.

The age of empires is past. No one nation may subjugate another. This is the fundamental attitude of the ABN, which rejects all cooperation with Russian imperialists, whatever their political tendency, and neither cooperates nor will ever cooperate with any Russian group, even though the latter may be anti-Communist, since there is no emigrant Russian political group which is not imperialist in tendency.

The source of evil in the world today is not merely Communism, but Russian imperialism.

Basic Ideas for Victory

The Free World must support the idea of independent national states for the peoples of Europe, Asia, and Africa; it must reject imperialism; and, above all, it must advocate the idea that the Russian empire should be disintegrated into national states of all its nations within their ethnographical boundaries. The Free World must under no circumstances allow an unjust social order to prevail in the countries of Asia and Africa. It must call a halt to every form of colonial policy and every form of feudal social order, and must support the endeavors of the nations to achieve independence; in addition, it must, above all, support the champions of the cause of the national liberation of the peoples in the empires, and also the champions of an anti-feudal and anti-Communist social order, who are striving to restore the just social and national traditions of all the dependent and colonial peoples of Asia and the entire world. As long as the Free World supports imperialistic ideology in any form whatsoever, it will never conquer Russian imperialism. It is futile to try to fight an unjust ideology by means of some other unjust ideology—especially in our time, in the era of the anti-Communist world revolution.

Japan and the West

It would be a mistake to attempt to introduce a social order in Japan which is not in keeping with the national characteristics and spirit of that country—an order which is a complete contradiction of the national and religious traditions of this industrious nation. Moscow and the Red Peking Government will, of course, try to make Japan adopt India's policy; they will try to buoy Japan up with vain hopes of economic prosperity, and, above all, will try to persuade Japan to play a double game.

Perhaps the wisest thing the West can do is to give Japan back her full sovereignty in every respect and admit her into the family of nations of the Free World which enjoy equal rights. And, incidentally, the past must be forgotten. The West should help Japan to solve her difficult economic problems; it should bear in mind the national dignity of this great nation and should not constantly remind the Japanese nation of its recent defeats, but should adhere to the principle that the age of empires is past and that no nation in the world may subjugate another.

Unity of Freedom-Loving Nations

It is undoubtedly essential that the freedom-loving anti-Communist forces of all the peoples of the free and subjugated world should be united. But I believe that this can only be achieved if the full sovereignty of the nations of the world is recognized—that is to say, on the basis of a clear and firm conception of national state independence, and not on the basis of a purely negative and vague anti-

Communist ideology. In this anti-Communist world bloc there must be no room for any Russian imperialists, who are only intent upon replacing the Communist regime with a new form of subjugation. Not a single subjugated nation within the USSR will join a world bloc directed against Communism if this bloc is not at the same time also directed against the Russian empire, for it is high time that the latter be liquidated. It is impossible to justify the Russian empire in an era in which the British, French, and Dutch empires are ceasing to exist. It is impossible to persuade the nations that they should fight against Communism only that they may be forced to put up with Russian imperialists of other political trends or with other conquerors in the future, instead of the Russian Red imperialists of today. The nations are not fighting in order to exchange iron fetters for golden ones, but in order to rid themselves of all fetters for good!

It is wiser to have a small circle of advocates of just national states who are capable of winning over the peoples completely, than a medley of all kinds of anti-Communists who have no clearly defined and positive ideology and no sound ideas on the setting up of a just social order in the future. Vague watchwords have never yet led to victorious revolutions; on the contrary, revolutionary organizations have always succeeded in stirring and winning over the masses by the lucidity of their ideas. The motto of our age must be the fight to bring about the downfall of imperialism. And the national idea is the symbol of our age. Millions will die in the future fight, and in order to justify this sacrifice before God and history these millions must die for the cause of absolute truth, national state independence, social justice, freedom of the individual, and faith in God!

Hitler advanced eastwards in pursuit of his conquest plans, and the revolutionary national liberation organizations of the peoples subjugated by Russia opposed him, regardless of the fact that he was an anti-Communist, solely because no one had any desire to fight for the German empire and a new form of subjugation. The UPA conducted a two-front war—against Hitler and against Stalin, against Hitler's "New Europe," which was merely a camouflage for the German empire, and against the USSR, the Russian empire.

We warn the Free World not to cooperate with the so-called anti-Communist White Russian imperialists, for, at the crucial moment, they will join sides with the Kremlin. At the outbreak of World War II Kerensky affirmed that he was exhorting the West and the Russians to fight on Stalin's side, since it was "better to have a cruel dictator than to help partition the Russian empire."

It is impossible to unite the imperialists and the nationalist democrats in one bloc, just as it is inconceivable that one should fight for the preservation of the Russian empire and for its disintegration at one and the same time.

New Role for the United Nations

The Western major powers, together with Free China, must see to it that the USSR and the Communist governments of Moscow's satellites are excluded from the United Nations, and, in doing so, must base their arguments on the principles of the UN Charter, which stipulates that those guilty of aggression and genocide may not be members of the UN. Instead of these Communist governments, the authorized representatives of the national liberation organizations and exiled governments of the peoples living in Moscow's sphere of influence must be admitted to the United Nations as members. The representatives of Ukraine, Byelorussia, Turkestan, Czechia, Poland, Bulgaria, Slovakia, Rumania, Georgia, the Baltic countries, Serbia, Croatia, Korea, Vietnam, Hungary, and of all the other nations subjugated by Moscow and by Communism must become members of the United Nations, as well as all the other nations and countries, such as Japan, which are not yet members of this organization.

The United Nations must become an organization for the struggle against the Russian empire and Communism, not an organization for the "coexistence" of the free states and the subjugated states. It must be reorganized on the basis of equality of rights for all nations, great and small alike, so that the feeling of equality will give all nations the strength to fight in unity for the great causes, for the freedom and national state independence of all nations, for social justice for mankind, and for a universal freedom for the individual. The United Nations must become a world union whose activity is conducted in the same spirit as that of the Asian Peoples' Anti-Communist League (APACL) and the Anti-Bolshevik Bloc of Nations (ABN).

Trends in Russia—the Free World's Opportunity

The development of the international situation in the Kremlin points to the trend to maintain an absolute dictatorship, as has always been the case in the history of Russia, which has never been democratic and whose people have never known freedom—as compared, for example, with the Ukrainian nation, which for more than a thousand years has advocated the idea of personal freedom and has never set up a despotic regime in its own country.

It is really immaterial whether the Kremlin dictatorship is that of one man or of a group of persons. The Communist Party, the personification of Russian imperialism, is in power and continues to remain the actual dictator. The marshals and generals are leading members of the Party and owe their power to the Party. It is completely immaterial whether the absolute ruler is a Party member in civilian attire or in the uniform of a marshal. In any case, he is a member of the Party which dictates.

The vulnerable spot of the Russian empire is the national problem—that is to say, the revolutionary national liberation aims of the subjugated peoples who are fighting to achieve the disintegration of the empire into national states. The unnatural Communist social and economic system is steadily being weakened and undermined by radical resistance on the part of the subjugated nations and peoples.

A change in the Kremlin Government will in no way influence Russia's relations with the Free World, since the constant aim of all Russians is to conquer the whole world. At the 20th Congress of the Communist Party the rulers of the Kremlin criticized Stalin in order to deceive the Free World and to make it appear as though they had changed for the better, to throw dust in the eyes of the subjugated nations and to try to make them believe that Stalin alone was responsible for genocide and despotism. But the fact must not be overlooked that Khrushchev, Kaganovich, and Molotov were governors of Ukraine for many years and that the three of them were responsible for the death of millions of persons there.

It is characteristic of the rulers of the Kremlin that they criticized Stalin for having falsified the history of the Communist Party and for having wrongly assessed capitalism, etc., but not for having annexed half of Asia and Europe, nor for having subjugated millions of persons of various nations, nor for the fact that the foreign countries which were occupied and annexed as a result of Stalin's policy were not liberated later on. The theory according to which the proletariat can attain power solely by violence was condemned and Bulgaria, Poland, and Czechoslovakia were quoted as examples of this theory, but the fact was "overlooked" that the Russian army brought Communist power into these countries by means of their bayonets.

Mikoyan's theory, according to which Communism has come to power in the West as a result of elections, is an admission of the complete bankruptcy of Communism, since a comparison with the "elections" in Poland, Czechoslovakia, and Bulgaria is bound to lead to the conclusion that Russia's army will have to be present when the Communists take over power in the West.

A complete loss of faith in the victory of the Communist revolution was apparent at the 20th Communist Party Congress, and from what was implied in the speeches that were made it is obvious that the rulers of the Kremlin have staked all on the Russian army, on sheer Russian imperialism, and on the hardiness of the Russian soldiers. The latter are to effect the "liberation" of the proletariat in the Western countries, just as was the case under Voroshilov's command in Hungary and under Zhukov's command in Eastern Germany, where "free elections" and the "evolutionary" assumption of power by the Communist Party have taken place. This same program is to be carried out in Italy or France after the Russian divisions have effected an invasion under the command of Koniev.

The Western world must proclaim a charter of national freedom and the independence of the nations; it must support the revolutionary national liberation movements behind the Iron Curtain; it must support the underground resistance movements politically, morally, technically, and militarily, and must be ready to intervene actively in every breach which occurs beyond the Iron Curtain in order to widen such breaches and create situations similar to those created by the Russians in Indochina when they supported Ho Chi Minh, or in Greece when they supported Markos. The greatest danger lies in waiting passively and not acting, in the hope that an internal conflict will put an end to the despotism of the Kremlin.

Instead of idly looking on when Beria was liquidated and while confusion reigned after Stalin's death, instead of keeping silent when the German workers in East Germany revolted and the Ukrainian internees in the concentration camps in Vorkuta rebelled, instead of assuming the role of a silent spectator while the Ukrainian, Lithuanian, Georgian, Turkestanian, or Byelorussian insurgents fought, the West should have taken an active part in all these processes in order to destroy the Russian empire from within and, with the aid of the national revolutions of the subjugated nations, should have opened up the surest way to lead to the destruction of Communism. Instead of helping those units of the Ukrainian Insurgent Army which, in their legions, their weapons in their hands, fought their way out of Ukraine and through to Western Germany in order to show the world that Ukraine is in a state of political ferment, the occupation forces of the Western powers put the Ukrainian insurgents in isolation camps in Western Germany.

On this side of the Iron Curtain Moscow only has Fifth Columns on its side; on the other side of the Iron Curtain, however, the West has whole nations on its side. And all that is needed is a little careful thought on the part of the West and these mighty dynamic forces within the Russian imperium will explode.

We revolutionary nationalists of the peoples of Eastern Europe and Soviet Asia were very pleased to hear Marshal Chiang Kai-shek's conception of liberation—the conception of a national revolution as the only true way to destroy Communism and the Russian empire without thermonuclear weapons or a world war....

The Ukrainian Review,
No. II, 1956, pp. 76-84

Let Us Be on Guard

American friends of captive nations! Friends of those now in bondage of Russian Imperialism and Communism!

The national liberation movements of the subjugated peoples regard the US Congress Resolution on Captive Nations Week as a far-reaching historical event in the present psychological and political anti-Bolshevik struggle and as a fitting basis for the future solution of international problems once the Russian empire has been liquidated.

On behalf of the Central Committee of the Anti-Bolshevik Bloc of Nations, which organization is the coordination center of the liberation movements of Ukraine, Hungary, Turkestan, Byelorussia, Bulgaria, Georgia, Armenia, Slovakia, Czechia, Latvia, Lithuania, Estonia, Rumania, Croatia, Serbia, Cossackia, and other enslaved nations, I welcome and applaud the initiative of the US Congress and declare ourselves in full agreement with its Resolution.

It is our earnest hope that this Resolution will become the basis of a practical liberation policy by the US Government.

In the present global political conflict between the world of tyranny and the world of freedom, between the Russian Communist concept of a Soviet World Empire and the concept of a world order with free and independent national states, the US Congress has courageously placed America on the side of justice and national independence.

To approve and advocate the preservation of the reactionary Russian empire in an era when empires are declining and ideas of national independence are spontaneously gaining ground in the world would not only be a historical anachronism but also a direct threat to the freedom and security of the United States.

By stressing the national problem of the Captive Nations, the US Congress has revealed the vulnerable spot of the Russian prison of nations. At the same time, the United States, thanks to the action of its Congress, may acquire a true ally in the enslaved nations, which, with the support of the West, would help to annihilate Bolshevism from within without provoking an atomic war.

The recognition of the common fate and the need for freedom and liberation of all the nations enslaved by Moscow, regardless of when they were enslaved, is a far-reaching political diagnosis on the part of the US Congress, which should become the fundamental guiding principle of a concrete liberation policy, inasmuch as it rightly treats Russia as a ruling force and not as an enslaved nation.

World politics today revolve around the subjugated nations, which constitute the key force in the present conflict between opposite worlds and also the first fighting front in the ceaseless anti-Bolshevik struggle. This liberation front must be given active support as well as military help by the Free World. There must be no passivity on the part of the West, as there was during the October revolution in 1956 in Hungary.

In 1953-56, and again in October 1959, in Temir-Tau in Kazakhstan Ukrainian, Byelorussian, Lithuanian, Estonian, and other prisoners in the concentration camps revolted against Soviet Russian tyranny. But elsewhere, on other fronts, the spirit of coexistence dominated, thus making moral support for the freedom-fighters, not to mention any other form of support or help, entirely impossible.

The failure of the Paris Summit Conference, the humiliation of the USA, the shooting down of unarmed American planes, the personal insults hurled at the President of the United States by Khrushchev, all would in the past have at least led to the severance of diplomatic relations with the Moscow gangsters, if not to an outright ultimatum of war. But now? *Quo vadis, Occident?*

Not only the enslaved nations, but also America needs friends in the fight against Communist aggression in defense of its way of life and the eternal values of mankind—freedom, justice, and independence.

The angry and hysterical reaction of Khrushchev to the proclamation of Captive Nations Week was an indication that the United States had found the key by which to destroy Bolshevism. Hence, now is the time to strike—now is the time for an active policy of liberation.

From the moral and legal point of view the proclamation of the Resolution may have a tremendous significance, provided that the next step be taken toward a conclusive result. All the nations of the Free World should follow the example of the United States and issue similar proclamations.

At the same time, the peoples of the Free World should put spiritual values before materialistic goals; they should seek the purpose of life in noble and heroic deeds and should put aside the comforts of life and look for their destiny in the struggle against evil and slavery, for good and justice, for freedom and for the triumph of the divine truth. Their aim should be, not peace at any price, but the victory of truth and justice on earth.

The subjugated nations have nothing to lose, but everything to win! They are not asking anything for themselves from the Free World. They are fighting for their God-given rights on their soil, for free government that will guarantee them freedom and will help them to realize a just social and economic order. By helping them the Free World is also helping itself.

Moscow talks about the independence of the African and Asian peoples, to whom the West is conceding independence to an ever-increasing degree. Why does the free West, fail to talk about the right to independence of the nations subjugated by the USSR?

Why do the governments of the West refrain from advocating the disintegration of the most ruthless colonial empire in the world—the Russian empire—whilst, at the same time, they approve or advocate the dissolution of the Western empires which are much more humane in character than the Russian empire? Has not Russia subjugated highly civilized peoples, as for instance those of East Germany or Ukraine, Lithuania or Hungary, Georgia or Bulgaria!

We appeal for the development of an offensive in psychological war for a liberation policy to be actively supported.

"Captive Nations Week" should not be confined to the USA, but should be introduced in all the other countries of the Free World. The cause of freedom and independence of all the nations subjugated in the USSR and in the satellite countries should be actively supported.

A coordination center of psychological warfare should be set up in the Free World in joint effort with the representatives of the national liberation movements behind the Iron and Bamboo Curtains.

A freedom manifesto should be drafted by this coordination center and proclaimed as a Magna Carta of the independence of nations and the freedom of individuals.

Steps should be taken to bring about the disintegration of the last empire in the world, the Russian empire, into independent national states of all the subjugated nations, as the main aim and objective of the political war of the free and the subjugated worlds.

The national liberation revolutions of all the peoples subjugated by Russian imperialism and Communism should be supported actively and wholeheartedly.

I repeat—the Free World should actively and with every means available support a coordinated national liberation of the subjugated nations behind the Iron and Bamboo Curtains and should regard this as the only possible alternative to an atomic war.

The policy of coexistence should be rejected by the peace-loving Western world as a trap designed by Moscow, since it is bound to lead to a surprise atomic war.

The United Nations Organization, which is adjusting itself more and more to a policy of coexistence, should be reorganized as an anti-Bolshevik world organization, with the immediate exclusion of Russian representatives and their satellites; as an organization in which the authorized representatives of the nations subjugated by Moscow are included.

Diplomatic, cultural, economic, and other relations with Moscow and the Communist bloc should be severed. No "summit" conferences should be held, for Russia's objective in such conferences will always be to obtain recognition of the status quo of enslavement. Such recognition can only demobilize and undermine the Western world's relations with the enslaved nations. The status quo is regarded by the Russians as merely a stepping-stone to further conquests.

The United States is already threatened not merely from Siberia but from the very American continent—namely, from Cuba. Khrushchev aims to attack America by every possible means, and one of these means is "peaceful coexistence."

In the morass of coexistentialism he commits crimes against humanity which appear to leave the conscience of the Free World unmoved. A shocking crime was committed by the Bolsheviks not long ago when they murdered the leader of the Ukrainian Liberation Movement, Stepan Bandera, who symbolized the struggle for freedom of Ukraine.

Let all freedom-loving people in the world unite in the fight against Russian imperialism and Communism for the freedom of individuals, for the cause of justice and independence of all nations!

Let us be on guard, for the enemy is already at the gates!

Address delivered in Philadelphia to
mark Captive Nations Week
ABN Correspondence,
September-October 1960, pp. 4-6

Curious Facts about the Cold War

In this barbarous world of ours man longs for the ideals of Christ. In the underground movement in Ukraine the Christian faith, for which people yearn so much in this age of evil, violence, murder, torture, falsehood, terrorism and tyranny such as never before existed in the history of mankind, is experiencing a rebirth. Regrettably, however, the Western world completely ignores this mighty underground movement in Ukraine and other subjugated countries. On the contrary, it plays up to the supporters and imitators of Tito and Gomulka, to the Communist "opposition" and to "potential National Communists." The West endeavors to convince the genuine godless Marxists that Bolshevism is not genuine Marxism; at the same time, however, it never occurs to the West to support the uncompromising fighters against militant Bolshevism and for the Christian faith in Ukraine and elsewhere. There is not a single broadcasting station in the territory of the major Western powers which would ever think of addressing a message in a national and Christian spirit to the peoples enslaved by Moscow.

Those who wish to "correct" Bolshevism are not concerned with the welfare of freedom-loving mankind, but, on the contrary, are furthering an even more successful dissemination of Bolshevism in the world. In spite of this, the West shows considerable interest in these persons and tries to curry favor with them, instead of according this favor to those who, on grounds of principle, oppose both Bolshevism and Russian imperialism in every form. The advocates of the Russian empire in this era of the decay of all other empires, as well as the Bolshevik collaborators who, thanks to their participation in the "people's fronts," have enabled the Red Russians to deceive the world (as if the Russian Red Army had occupied the countries in question in accordance with the wish of the "democratic group"!) and have, by reason of the will of official circles in the West, become the "spokesmen" of the peoples enslaved by Bolshevism. Surely a curious fact, which is unprecedented in the history of mankind.

Moreover, the Russians with their usual mendacity affirm that, in every country in which Communism has assumed power, it did so at the explicit wish of the people in question. But these Red Russians trip up on their lies. For the Communist parties in all the subjugated countries are over-enthusiastic in their praise of the services of the Red Army, to which they owe the introduction of the Communist regimes in their countries. Thus, they admit that Communism is nothing but an imported product. Tito, too, admits that the Russian Red Army helped him to assume power in Yugoslavia. Where, therefore, is this "will of the masses," who allegedly introduced "socialism" into their countries themselves?! The pride of the "big brother" dictates that the Russians should ignore all reproaches regarding the forcible introduction of Communism in Ukraine, Hungary, Bulgaria, Slovakia, or other countries and should call a spade a spade!

It is a futile undertaking to repeat all these truths to those who are in charge of government affairs in the West. Neither the fact that one was imprisoned for years in Nazi concentration camps and one's health and vitality were impaired nor the fact that one is a national freedom fighter and a Christian are of any avail: one is stamped as a "Nazi" for the rest of his life. One can produce all kinds of proof that the fight in Ukraine is waged under the banner of freedom-loving, enlightened nationalism and Christianity and that hence one is justified in demanding that the West should support Ukraine and those who have never betrayed these ideals but have suffered and fought for them and even today still continue this fight—all these arguments will fall on deaf ears.

But in spite of this depressing state of affairs, it is precisely the national liberation idea, the yearning for eternal and divine values, the fight for freedom of the individual and peoples, for social justice, for creative freedom, for the ownership of private property by the working man as the basis for his genuine independence, the fearless fight of youth against the doctrine forced on it by those in power, and the searching of youth for truth which will destroy the realm of tyranny.

Who Was Responsible for the Revolt in the Concentration Camp of Vorkuta?

The emigre White Russian imperialists are now also beginning to adopt some of these ideas, although they were advocates of "corrected" Marxism until recently. Their organ *Posev* (No. 40/60), for instance, writes as follows:

> The plans of the government are opposed by our entire Christian culture, histori-
> cal traditions of the past, the yearnings and hopes of the nation, and, last but not
> least, by man's nature. The living and active forces of our society not only oppose
> the intentions of the Government, but also attack them, since they regard the fight
> for the liberation of the individual as their aim and mission. The fight for man's soul
> constitutes the main tenor, the meaning and essence of all ideological and political
> campaigns which are carried on nowadays.

Until recently the Russian-exile solidarists never so much as mentioned Christianity, but propagated a "corrected Marxism" of the type advocated by Khokhlov. Now Khokhlov himself, at a conference of the solidarists, talks about the
fight under the banner of God! Was it not the Khokhlovs of the GPU, NKVD, and
MVD who murdered countless innocent persons? Was this done in the name of
Christ?

From "corrected Marxism" via "general humane humanism" to Christianity! A
long path, but one travelled at great speed by the advocates of the Russian
empire! But this is not the end! The "white" Russian imperialists are now
advocating private ownership of production, national traditions, as well as affinity with the monuments of "our history," "old churches and edifices, fortresses
and museums," etc. All this, however, on one condition—namely that the "green
mountains of the national resorts of the Caucasus, the Carpathians, the Urals,
and of the Altai Mountains, which, since there are no owners, are turning into
dismal, bare, gray crags," should remain the property of a "better" lord and
master (i.e., the Russian solidarists) for all time. For, allegedly, there are no
enslaved peoples in the Russian empire; in fact, there is no Russian imperium at
all, but only one indivisible "Mother Russia."

The Russian imperialists on principle used certain watchwords and in this way
sought to conceal their true character. Just as Lenin in former times talked about
the "self-determination of peoples," including their "secession from Russia," so,
too, the Russian organization of solidarists, the NTS, today preaches a "general
humane humanism" and even a "Christian culture" on the basis of coexistence
and harmony, as advocated by the emigrant Russian philosopher just as the
Bolsheviks once talked about the partition of the large estates and then forced
the Ukrainian farmers, whom they had deceived, to join the collectives. The NTS
people also talk about the "soul of the individual," but this soul may not evince
any national feelings except Russian ones. They also talk about national traditions, but they only mean Russian ones. Whenever the Russian solidarists
mention any tradition belonging to the subjugated peoples, they put down the

achievements of the latter's fight against Bolshevism to the account of the Russian people.

Hence, the NTS people term themselves "Christians, nationalist solidarists, humanists, and advocates of private property, champions of human rights." Precisely these Russian solidarists and "worshippers of Christ," who refuse to admit the existence of the individual peoples within the USSR, are preparing this new paradise! But, at the same time, they threaten to join forces with Khrushchev in a common front of the Russian people if the West should refuse to guarantee the inviolability of the imperial frontiers of the Russian prison of peoples. And these "solidarists" write as follows in *Posev* (No. 41/60):

> The Russian people demand a guarantee for the inviolability of the Russian frontiers once the revolution has been effected. Before the last world war the Russian people expected this guarantee.... The statutes of a Russian student underground organization in Moscow demanded, as their first point, an immediate guarantee for the inviolability of the Russian frontiers after the revolution had been carried out. During the last world war, the soldiers of the Soviet army did their utmost to establish this claim. Up to the outbreak of the October Revolution, complete equality of rights was enjoyed by all the peoples who inhabited Russia. The NTS organization can have nothing in common with those who long for the disintegration of Russia.

Then why so much empty talk about "general humane humanism," "Christian culture," "freedom of the individual," and "man's soul"?

Russia continues to remain unchanged in its mendacity, immeasurable rapacity, and terrorism!

Heine once said that the chief ally of the Devil was the liberal intellectual who does not believe in the Devil. One might well say the same thing of the NTS organization, which bases its program for the preservation of the Russian prison of peoples on the "liberal" traditions of tsarist Russia, which carried out countless massacres amongst the enslaved peoples. The NTS in no way differs from the Communist Party of the Soviet Union. The NTS solidarists are, in fact, even more reactionary, for they do not even admit the existence of the individual peoples in the Red Russian empire, a fact which the Communist Party of the USSR does not venture to deny, at least not on paper. The difference between the NTS and the Communist Party of the USSR is the same as that between Peter I and Lenin, or between Malyuta Skuratov and Yezhov. History repeats itself!

The NTS is thus trying in vain to put down the facts of resistance in Ukraine, Georgia, Turkestan, Lithuania, and Estonia to its own account. And the Russian solidarists are trying in vain to ascribe the organization of the revolts in the concentration camps of Vorkuta or Temir Tau to themselves or to Russians (as is affirmed in *Posev*, No. 47/60).

This naive attempt to adorn oneself in the eyes of the world with borrowed plumes is futile. Sooner or later the world will see through this Russian ruse....

No one in the world has ever heard anything about armed insurgent resistance against Communism in the Russian ethnographical territory. But the UPA, on the other hand, has become known all over the world!

The Ukrainian Review,
No. II, 1961, pp. 29-31

Accusation against Khrushchev before the UN

Subject: Protection of Human Rights of the Ukrainian People against Assassinations on the Territory of the German Federal Republic, Instigated and Organized by the Russian Government in Moscow. Crimes Committed against the Ukrainian People by the Russian Government with the Assassinations of Stepan Bandera, Leader of the Organization of Ukrainian Nationalists (OUN), and Dr. Lev R. Rebet, noted Ukrainian writer and journalist.

Honorable Sirs:

On October 12, 1957, Dr. Lev Rebet, a prominent Ukrainian writer and journalist, was murdered in Munich, West Germany, and on October 1, 1959, Stepan Bandera, leader of the Organization of Ukrainian Nationalists, was murdered.

These two criminal acts were committed by KGB agent Bohdan N. Stashynsky on the direct orders of the Russian Government in Moscow, through General Alexander N. Shelepin, then Chief of the KGB, and now one of Khrushchev's closest aides in the Central Committee of the Communist Party of the USSR.

Soon afterwards, the order was given to Stashynsky to make his next victim the President of the Anti-Bolshevik Bloc of Nations, Mr. Yaroslav Stetsko, the former Prime Minister of the Independent Ukrainian Republic proclaimed in June 1941.

The weapon which KGB agent Stashynsky used in these two murders was a double-barrelled squirt gun loaded with potassium cyanide, which was provided by the KGB headquarters in Moscow.

The specially trained KGB agent Stashynsky, after killing these two Ukrainian leaders and freedom fighters, received the "Order of the Red Banner" by a decree of the Presidium of the Supreme Soviet of the USSR of November 6, 1959, which was bestowed upon him by Alexander Shelepin, the KGB Chief himself.

Stashynsky gave himself up to German Federal Republic authorities on August 13, 1962. He was tried and sentenced, according to the German Federal Republic Penal Code §§ 47, 49, and 211, to eight years' penal servitude for the murders of Stepan Bandera and Dr. Lev Rebet.

Both in the *Oral Opinion* and *Written Motivation* (StE 4/62, verdict of October 19,

1962) of the Stashynsky trial of the Federal High Court in Karlsruhe, it was unequivocably stated that the real murderers responsible for these two crimes were those who had planned and ordered them. The members of the Russian Government in Moscow trained the murderer, selected the victims, the time and method of murder, instructed the KGB agent to carry them out within a limited space of time, and gave him the instrument designed in the Academy of Science of the USSR in Moscow and the means with which to carry out the murders. The award of the medal to Stashynsky after the murder of Bandera proved that the real criminals who killed the two Ukrainian leaders were the Russian Government leaders in Moscow.

Political assassination and murder have always been the chosen weapon of the Russian Communists in combating their political opponents and adversaries. It should be recalled that, in May 1926, a Russian agent in Paris killed Simon Petlura, head of the Ukrainian national government in exile. In 1938, also in May, another Russian agent slipped a time-bomb into the coat-pocket of Col. Eugene Konovalets, head of the Organization of Ukrainian Nationalists, in Rotterdam, Holland, which exploded and killed the Ukrainian leader instantly.

The fact that Moscow constantly sends trained agents to annihilate Ukrainian nationalist leaders in foreign countries outside the USSR obviously demonstrates that Moscow actively fears Ukrainian nationalism.

The foregoing account of the murder of Ukrainian national leaders shows that the Russian Government, even though a member of the United Nations, maintaining diplomatic relations with the German Federal Republic, issued orders to commit the murders on German territory in direct violation of international law. Furthermore these actions by the Russian Government show a direct violation of the principles of basic human rights and fundamental freedoms as laid down in the *Universal Declaration of Human Rights* and the *Charter of the United Nations*.

Therefore, the Ukrainian Delegation of the Anti-Bolshevik Bloc of Nations appeals to the Commission on Human Rights for the protection of human rights, ignored and consistently violated by the Russian Government in its power-drive for world domination.

Therefore, the Ukrainian Delegation of the Anti-Bolshevik Bloc of Nations asks the Commission on Human Rights to act as judge in this matter and to deliver its opinion in accordance with the principles laid down in the *Universal Declaration of Human Rights* and the *Charter of the United Nations*, showing the undeniable guilt of the Russian Government in these murders.

Supplementary Information:

Ukraine is situated in the southwestern portion of the East European lowland, on the shores of the Sea of Azov and the Black Sea, and extends westward beyond the Carpathian Mountains to the Tyssa River. It covers an area of 945,000 sq. km. The population in January 1961 numbered 43,091,000.

The Ukrainians enjoyed their independence during the periods of the great Ukrainian Kyivan State of Volodymyr the Great (981-1015) and Yaroslav the Wise (1018-1054). This ideal motivated the career of the Ukrainian Hetman

Bohdan Khmelnitsky (1648-1709) and the great Hetman and patriot Ivan Mazepa (1648-1709). In 1918 a Sovereign State of the Ukrainian People's Republic
was proclaimed, with the Central Rada as its head.

Immediately after the declaration of independence the Russian Bolshevik
government in Moscow planned a campaign for the total annihilation of the
Ukrainian Independent State. Accordingly, the Bolsheviks organized a puppet
Soviet government in Kharkiv composed chiefly of non-Ukrainians and on
December 29, 1917 they officially acknowledged their own creation, the Ukrainian SSR, and promised "the brotherly Republic all possible support in its struggle" against the Ukrainian Central Rada. The Russian Government severed its
relations with the Ukrainian Central Rada, and ordered its armed forces and food
and requisitioning brigades, which by now were ready for action, to advance
against Ukraine in full force—to move in their first aggression in the expansion
of the territorial base of the revolution. The first practical application of the
Bolshevik self-determination theory was thus put to the test.

Although the forces under the Ukrainian Central Rada's command had, on
several occasions, shown heroism in their efforts to stop the invaders they were,
as a result of being outnumbered, inadequately equipped, and disorganized by
revolutionary ideas, no match for the Bolshevik forces, which on their southwes-
terly move had occupied one Ukrainian city after another.

The national spirit of the Ukrainians did not die. Military defeat of the Ukrainian armies in the War of Independence did not weaken the struggle for the
liberation of the Ukrainian nation. The Ukrainian War of Independence was of
immense importance in the formation of the Ukrainian National State. The
independence of Ukraine proclaimed during that war became the basic dogma of
political faith of the Ukrainian people.

Again, on June 30, 1941, the Independent Ukrainian Republic was proclaimed
with Yaroslav Stetsko as its head. But the German Nazi Government planned to
turn Ukraine into a German colony. Hitler ordered the arrest of the Prime
Minister of the proclaimed Independent Ukrainian Republic and the members of
his Government; they were sent to German concentration camps, where most of
them were murdered.

As an agricultural country, Ukraine is well known as the "breadbasket of
Europe" or as the "granary of the Russian Empire," and she provides food for
domestic needs and contributes a great share for export. In addition to rich coal,
iron, manganese ore, salt, and other mineral deposits, which comprise the basis
of Russian industry, Ukraine includes a considerable part of Russia's industrial
enterprises and a large proportion of the Russian railroad network. In view of
these and many other factors, it is evident that the Russian Bolsheviks will not
tolerate Ukrainian national aspirations towards separatism.

The process of retarding Ukrainian scientific and cultural development and the
Russification of university-level schools in Ukraine are being carried out with all
the pressure which the Russian apparatus is able to muster. This action is
accompanied by incessant propaganda about the "beneficial influence of the
socialist culture of the Great Russian people on the development of Ukrainian
culture."

The Russification of the Ukrainian population goes hand in hand with a mass exportation of Ukrainian specialists, scientists, and considerable numbers of peasants and workers beyond the borders of the Ukrainian SSR, and the importation of Russian specialists, scientists, and administrative personnel into Ukraine.

Today as never before, the Ukrainian population is scattered. The Russian Government has worked relentlessly to liquidate or break every leader who has refused to bow to its all-embracing rule.

The liquidation of Stepan Bandera, the leader of the Ukrainian Nationalists, who was a symbol and the watchword of the Ukrainian liberation struggle, was a major move in Moscow's attempts to obliterate the Ukrainian Nationalists. Stashynsky's assignment was cold-blooded political assassination, but elaborate precautions were taken by the Russian Government in Moscow and by the KGB to avoid the possibility of connecting the murder plots with the Kremlin.

The Ukrainian Delegation of the Anti-Bolshevik Bloc of Nations appeals to the Commission on Human Rights to extend its active support in behalf of the non-Russian enslaved peoples in their fight for freedom to enable them to overthrow the tyrannical Russian Communist rule and thereby to regain their national freedom and independence.

Yours respectfully,
Yaroslav Stetsko
Former Prime Minister of Ukraine
ABN Correspondence,
January-February 1964, pp. 12-15

What Now?

We have before us the arguments on which the verdict pronounced by the German Federal High Court in Karlsruhe in the trial of the assassin Bohdan Stashynsky, who murdered Stepan Bandera and Dr. Lev Rebet, is based and in which emphasis is particularly placed on the fact that the main perpetrator is the Government of the USSR, headed by Khrushchev and his right-hand man, Shelepin, who was recently appointed Deputy Prime Minister and who is the only person—apart from Khrushchev—to be a member of both the Secretariat and the Presidium of the Communist Party of the USSR.

The following arguments are cited in the opinion of the Federal High Court: "Stalinism is dead. But individual murderous terrorism still lives on. The real change which has taken place thus has not the least connection with lawfulness; the Soviet secret service no longer commits murder arbitrarily and of its own accord. Murder is now only carried out *at the explicit orders of the Government*. Political murder *has* now, as it were, *become an institution*.... The political leadership of the Soviet Union, the leadership of a world power which is wont to be proud of its history and civilization...the political leadership of a country that is a member of the United Nations and entertains correct diplomatic relations with the German Federal Republic, considers it expedient to have murder by poison, decided at least on a Government level, committed on the sovereign territory of the German Federal Republic as a State order. On the certain assumption that this crime would not come to light, this same leadership acts in defiance of all international rules of decency, of the German penal laws, and of its own laws in order to liquidate a political opponent. But every political murder, like a political lie, is in the end directed against its instigator.... This court is now obliged to ascertain with regret that the political leadership of the Soviet Union also officially orders and has murders carried out on German territory."

We have only quoted a short passage from the verdict pronounced by the Supreme Court of Justice of the German Federal Republic, but it is a verdict that is unique and unparalleled in the jurisdiction of the free world.

This same court, against whose verdict there can be no appeal, has ascertained beyond all doubt that *the Government of the USSR*, headed by Khrushchev and Shelepin, *bears the main responsibility for the murders of Stepan Bandera and Lev Rebet*, and for this reason the court condemns this Government morally and legally. The fact that Shelepin has been appointed to the extremely important post of chairman of the Control Commission of the Government and of the Communist Party of the USSR indicates fairly clearly the extent to which he has been of service to Moscow as the chief of the KGB secret police. It is indeed a mockery of the administration of justice throughout the whole world to appoint a person who is directly responsible for these murders to such a post. The Government of the USSR derides the fact that the Supreme Court of Justice of the German Federal Republic has condemned both morally and legally a member of the Government of the USSR as a criminal. The police of any country which such a criminal enters should immediately arrest him on the strength of warrants of the Interpol and extradite him to Germany.

The Supreme Court of Justice of the German Federal Republic has ascertained that:

a) the Government of the USSR has violated the sovereignty of the German Federal Republic in spite of the fact that it entertains diplomatic relations with Bonn;

b) the rights of the individual in the territory of the German Federal Republic have been ruthlessly violated by the Government of the USSR. In addition to these two murders, Shelepin also gave an order that a third murder be organized and carried out, the murder of Yaroslav Stetsko, who lives in the territory of the German Federal Republic.

The public of the Free World hopes that the Government of the Federal Republic of Germany will:

a) send a protest to the Government of the USSR through the German Ambassador to Moscow. Under normal circumstances, one should on the strength of the court's verdict, break off diplomatic relations with such a government of criminals;

b) submit the entire material of the Karlsruhe trial to the International Court of Justice at The Hague in order to protect the sovereignty of one's own territory and the rights of the individual in this territory;

c) submit the entire case to the Committee for Human Rights in the United Nations, since both the German Federal Republic and the USSR have signed the Declaration on Human Rights in the United Nations Organization;

d) instruct the German section of the International Jurists' Commission, which recently examined the administration of justice in Spain and published extensive documentary material on this subject, to undertake to collect and publish documentary evidence regarding the violation of Germany's sovereign rights and of human rights on German territory by a state which entertains normal diplomatic relations with the German Federal Republic;

e) instruct the Chief Public Prosecutor of the German Federal Republic to consequently demand the extradition of Shelepin as a criminal through the Federal Government in Bonn in order to take legal proceedings against him in Germany—that is to say, in the country in which he has committed his crimes, two cases of actual murder and one of attempted murder.

To cite an example in this connection: if in some state other than the USSR a center of international conspirators and assassins were discovered, who were organizing and having crimes such as murder, abduction, etc., carried out, and their chief was exposed as the instigator and organizer of these murders, then the Government of the German Federal Republic would most certainly demand the extradition of such a criminal. The fact that the chief perpetrator in this case is a Vice-Premier is of no account, for a gangster's crime remains a gangster's crime and murder remains a murder, and the abduction of individuals remains abduction, regardless of whether this gangster's crime is perpetrated by Al Capone or Shelepin. If Al Capone were to enter French territory and from there organize robberies and murders in Germany, the Bonn Government would undoubtedly demand his extradition once they discovered that the members of his gang had murdered someone in Germany.... For this reason it is appropriate that I myself, as the person who was also to be murdered at Shelepin's orders, should request that the Government in Bonn demand the extradition of the Vice-Premier of the USSR, Shelepin, the person who planned, organized, and issued the orders for the murder of the two freedom fighters, Stepan Bandera and Lev Rebet.

It is in this case a question of a moral and legal attitude towards the murders and organizers of the murders, as was incidentally stressed, in a manner that was objective and also unique in the history of political trials, by the Supreme Court of Justice of the German Federal Republic under the presidency of Dr. Heinrich Jagusch—namely, that the murders in question must be imputed to the Government of the USSR. The Federal High Court designated the criminal Stashynsky as an "assistant" and pointed out that the main perpetrators were Shelepin and the Government of the USSR. The German Federal Government should draw the logical conclusions from this opinion if its does not want to leave the Federal High Court in the lurch. Either Stashynsky is the main perpetrator, in which case he should be sentenced to two terms of life-imprisonment, or if, *according to the conception of German jurisdiction,* he is only to be regarded as an "assistant," then the *main perpetrator* must be sentenced accordingly—that is to say, the Chief Public Prosecutor of the German Federal Republic, with the aid of the Government in Bonn, must take the necessary legal measures in order to ensure that the main perpetrator is extradited. In his arguments the President of the Third Court of Criminal Appeal of the Federal High Court, Dr. Heinrich Jagusch, very courageously and very rightly said that there were no reasons why one should cast the blame of the main perpetrators on Stashynsky. *For the main perpetrators would not be able to escape from their guilt, just as no one in the long run can escape just punishment.*

At the moment it is imperative that Interpol, on the strength of the precise legal indictment drawn up by the Chief Public Prosecutor of the Federal High Court and with the cooperation of the German Federal Government, should issue a warrant for the arrest of the criminal Shelepin and likewise of "President" Voroshilov (who at the instigation of Khrushchev, in his capacity as head of the Government of the USSR, signed the confirmation for the murder) and should endeavor to arrest these criminals as soon as they appear in territory that is accessible to the Federal Chief Public Prosecutor—that is to say, in any country of the Free World. In this respect the fact that they are leaders of the "mighty USSR" is not of decisive importance. What is above all important is that *these individuals should be branded by the disgrace of vile crimes* and that uncompromising anti-Communists, basing their arguments on the legal opinion of the court, for these additional reasons should thus be justified in demanding the exclusion of the Soviet criminals from international organizations. For no one will be so naive as to expect a concrete result from such a decision. The essence of the matter lies rather in a *moral and legal* exposure and condemnation, for the most effective and important factor in the fight against Bolshevism at present is *moral mobilization.* From this point of view the verdict of the Federal High Court is of great historical significance, even though the length of the sentence pronounced on Stashynsky is naturally from our point of view by no means sufficient, since the "assistant" should in any case have been sentenced to fifteen years' imprisonment. But this fact is only of secondary importance provided that action is taken against the Government of the USSR and provided it is not hushed up or dropped completely, so as not to complicate American and Russian negotiations regarding Berlin. Ukrainian and pro-Ukrainian circles in the West are acting rightly in demanding that the Government in Bonn should take these measures. Demands by telegram and in writing to this effect are most certainly justified, for this is a matter which has roused public opinion all over the world and cannot be postponed indefinitely. *The verdict pronounced in Karlsruhe should be the beginning* but by no means the end of the action taken on account of the murder of Stepan Bandera and Lev Rebet. Nor should the Government in Bonn alone take the initiative. The United Nations and also the Governments of the USA and of Canada, in which countries there are countless Ukrainians, should also take action accordingly.

In addition, as a person who was likewise to be murdered at Shelepin's orders (and this fact was ascertained by the Federal High Court), and *in the name of all those who are threatened by the fate of Stepan Bandera and Lev Rebet, I request the*

German Federal Government to afford all persons legal and concrete protection against the measures planned against them, such as murder and abduction, by the Vice-Premier of the USSR and chief criminal, Shelepin, the chairman of the supreme Control Commission of the Soviet Union and of the Communist Party of the USSR. I base this request on the facts ascertained by the Federal High Court, which stated that I was also to be murdered by order of the Government of the USSR. It is less important that the measures of the German Government should lead to actual success. What is more important is that the law should be respected and that human rights, which the German Federal Republic had promised to respect, should really be protected. My request is not based on any political fact, if the German authorities do not wish to take such facts into account, but is made on the strength of human rights and in the name of these human rights.

Let us assume, for example, that the German police learn that a group of gangsters is planning to rob and murder a German. The police will most certainly surround the house in which the German lives and protect him against these gangsters. If, on the other hand, there is no doubt about the fact that the Government of the USSR carries out such crimes, why should not the Government of the German Federal Republic, in whose territory the freedom fighters now find themselves as a result of the aftermath of World War II, for which both Russia and Germany are responsible, protect these freedom fighters? And one of these persons was a prisoner in the Nazi concentration camps until he was liberated by the Allied forces.... Nor did he come to Germany of his free will, since he was arrested in Lviv and imprisoned by the Gestapo in Berlin and in the concentration camp in Sachsenhausen.

We—prisoners of the Nazi concentration camps—think we are justified in pointing out that various countries, not without evident reason, extradite Nazi criminals at the request of the countries concerned so that these criminals may be sentenced. Hence we ask: why can one not demand the extradition of Russian Bolshevik criminals such as Shelepin, seeing that the Supreme Court of Justice of democratic Germany has objectively ascertained Shelepin's guilt?

If the Government in Bonn fails to draw the logical conclusions from the Karlsruhe verdict, then the Bundestag, the Federal Parliament, should take this matter up. In view of the fact that the Bundestag discussed the matter of "Spiegel" with considerable interest and attention on three occasions, it should likewise protect the sovereignty of the German Federal Republic, in whose territory the assassins who receive their orders from the Government of the USSR behave as if they were at home. And the Bundestag should also protect the human rights which Khrushchev violates not only in his own sphere of influence but also elsewhere, inasmuch as he orders the murder of freedom fighters on German soil. For after all, the freedom fighters are also human beings, even in the world of today, which has become shallow and materialistic as a result of its inordinate desire for pleasure.

Upon receiving the *written* opinion and verdict of the Federal High Court, the German Federal Government and the Bundestag should take action immediately.

It is to be hoped that competent Congressional committees in the USA which investigated Khrushchev's crimes and also published valuable documentary material on this subject will also investigate the murders in Munich. The documentary material of the Federal High Court which is placed at the disposal of the US Congress will suffice to condemn the gangsters of Moscow at least morally....

Stepan Bandera laid down his life not only for the freedom and independence of Ukraine, but also for the security and independence of the Free World, including the Federal Republic of Germany. Will this Free World make an effort to condemn his murderers?

We—the freedom fighters of the enslaved world—do not intend to wait. We must act without delay, regardless of how the Free World and its responsible leaders react to our opinion.

The Ukrainian Review,
No. I, 1963, pp. 6-11

Under Their Banners We Shall Be Victorious!

The resolution adopted by the US Congress to erect a monument in honor of Taras Shevchenko in Washington, as well as the proclamation of "Captive Nations Week" on the basis of a disintegration of Soviet Russian empire into national independent states, is evidence of the American nation's solidarity with the national liberation ideals of the Ukrainian nation and its unsurpassable standard-bearer, Taras Shevchenko.

As former Prime Minister of the Independent Government of Ukraine, I wish to express my warmest thanks to former Presidents Eisenhower and Truman for honoring the great son of Ukraine who, by virtue of his heroic martyrdom, his ideas, his powerful word, became a symbol of freedom. Today, the greatest nation of the world is erecting a monument to the son of a serf, whose spirit, however, was always free, though he experienced external freedom for only ten years of his life. He was the son of the invincible Ukrainian soil.

I also wish to express my appreciation to the Ukrainians in the USA for their willingness to make sacrifices and for the great pains they have taken with respect to the erection of this monument and the organization of this celebration. This day has become a historical event in the relations between the American and the Ukrainian peoples—what is more, in the relations between the American and the subjugated peoples. For, first and foremost, the author of the powerful poem "Caucasus" was a champion of the freedom and independence of the peoples dominated by Moscow and of all suppressed and tormented human beings. In the name of the Central Committee of the Anti-Bolshevik Bloc of Nations, as its President, I greet all subjugated peoples, in the name of the realization of Shevchenko's ideals, for then there will be no more slaves—only free individuals. The Russian prison of peoples will collapse and independent states of free nations will come into existence. The entire subjugated but unconquered Ukraine will rejoice not only that this monument was erected—owing to the efforts and material sacrifices made by the Ukrainians living in the US—but most of all that we here in the Free World, together with sympathetic circles, are honoring Shevchenko's memory, the memory of the unfalsified Shevchenko, of Shevchenko as the standard-bearer of the anti-Muscovite fight for the rights of the Ukrainian nation and of other subjugated nations. We must think especially of today's fighting Ukraine and do our best to support her in this struggle.

An exceptionally gifted man who opens new horizons for the growth of humanity and whose creative spirit and artistic works give birth to ethnically good ideas in aesthetic forms which lift man to heights marking the border between the Creator and nature—to heights that almost reach the Creator—such a man is a genius. An exceptionally gifted man of strong character and firm moral values who by the strength of his will fills the vacuum between that which is possible and that which is desired stakes his life for "his friends." An exceptionally gifted man of mental or artistic power who opens new horizons for the growth of humanity, an exceptionally gifted man who elevates the altruistic elements in man and makes them the meaning of his existence and who overcomes the egoistic instinct for self-preservation, a man for whom self-sacrifice does not constitute a perversion of man's basically egoistic tenor, but which becomes the very meaning of his life—he is a hero.

The attributes of a hero and a genius, united in one and the same figure—are nonethless shining polestars on the dark firmament of the history of a people, of a nation, and of all humanity. Such a person is a national prophet who points the way to the future.

A genius, a hero. a prophet of a nation, a son of a serf, a giant among giants—and not solely for the Ukrainian nation....

The unveiled monument is a tribute to that which is eternal in Shevchenko, a tribute to his universal values. One of these universal values is also the present fight of the Ukrainian nation, a fight kindled by Shevchenko himself, for freedom and independence, for the victory of Christ's Truth on earth, for our God-given rights, which are trodden underfoot by the Moscow Antichrist, a fight against the embodiment of evil on earth, against atheist Moscow, the center of the people's prison.

Kyiv's fight is carried on under the sign of the Cross, for the new world of truth, of justice, of freedom, a fight whose watchword is "the liberation of our brothers and a glorious victory" over Moscow. This fight is carried on in the interest of the entire world.... Kyiv's legend, like that of our eternal city is vitally alive to this very day in all of Shevchenko's works....

It is not enough to be sympathetic toward Shevchenko's ideals—we must fight for them....

The victory of the eternal, of truth, is not brought about spontaneously, but by the effort of those who believe in it.... This monument, therefore, is also to be regarded as an impetus to the present fight against Russia, the peoples' prison. For Shevchenko is not solely the past and not solely the future; he is the present uniting with the past by the fight for the future....

For this reason, this celebration today is also a powerful anti-Russian demonstration: the fighter cannot be honored in any other way. In terms of its purpose and its goal, this celebration must lead to a strengthening of the present front of an uncompromising anti-Muscovite fight, excluding any kind of coexistence with the world of tyranny and annulling present coexistence, for Shevchenko was an uncompromising fighter who from the depth of his heart hated Russia as much as he loved Ukraine, was proud of her, and willing to suffer on her behalf.

Here today, we want to indict Moscow most sharply for the falsification of Shevchenko's ideas. We want to deny Moscow and the hangman of Ukraine, Khrushchev, the right to act on behalf of the peoples subjugated in the USSR. They honor Shevchenko maliciously and hypocritically and slanderously desecrate the memory of the great fighter for Ukraine and of other subjugated peoples by attempting to appropriate him for themselves. Moscow must be desperate if it finds it necessary to try to appropriate Shevchenko, the greatest admirer of Hetman Ivan Mazepa.

The Shevchenko monument stands beside that of Washington, whom Shevchenko admired—and far away from here, on the Baltic Sea, in distant Stockholm, stands the monument of another great man, whom Shevchenko honored as Mazepa's ally, Charles XII. The symbolic act of honoring Charles XII by placing a wreath on his tomb in the name of the Ukrainian people, an act which called back to mind Mazepa's great deeds, forced an infuriated Khrushchev to publicly attack those who honored Mazepa's ally in the name of Ukraine. It is the common front of the Western world with the subjugated peoples, led by Ukraine, that Moscow fears most of all.

Moscow is afraid of the mysticism of this fight; Moscow is well aware that the revolution of the spirit in the sense of a rebirth of life's heroicism, the yearning for greatness, an anti-materialistic revolution of the spirit, is the prerequisite for a successful political and military fight.

It is in this sense that I wish to greet this manifestation today: it is to be a step forward toward the Free World's understanding of Ukraine's importance and of Shevchenko's message, of the greatest anti-Muscovite fighter and revolutionary, a step forward toward the preparation of a new Konotop. Shevchenko's most ardent desire will become a reality only when in Kyiv opposite the monument of the great Bohdan, a monument is erected to the greatest hater of imperialist Moscow, Hetman Ivan Mazepa, whom Shevchenko so deeply honored and admired. Under Shevchenko's and Mazepa's banners we shall be victorious!

Speech at the Reception in Washington
on the Occasion of the Unveiling of the
Shevchenko Monument
The Ukrainian Review,
No. III, 1964, pp. 13-15

Are Russians Striving for Revolutionary Changes in the USSR?

Among the various negative phenomena prevalent in the Western political world, particularly disturbing is the view that it is impossible to achieve victory over the present Communist regime in the USSR without the Russians being in a common front with the subjugated nations, without their participation in the revolutionary struggle. Yet, we know from history that in the revolutionary movements of the Russian tsarist empire the major role was played mostly by Ukrainians. The present Russian opponents of the regime are not even thinking about revolution, only about reforms and evolution. Hence, counting on such fiction is an unjustifiable self-deception, all the more since the aim of the Russian dissidents is the preservation of the "one and indivisible" empire and the revival of the era of the Black Hundreds under the leadership of a new Denikin, Wrangel, or Kerensky.

There is absolutely no doubt that if Ukrainians and members of other subjugated nations do not start an armed struggle on Russian ethnographic territory, there will never be any revolution there. In 1917 in Petersburg the revolution against tsarism was carried out by regiments composed of Ukrainians (the Volhynia, the Preobrazhensk, and the Izmailiv), and later the March national revolution was crushed by Lenin's October counterrevolution.

In the present processes of opposition on Russian territory the major part is also played by dissidents of non-Russian descent—Gen. Hryhorenko, Daniel, Litvinov, Ginsburg, Sinyavsky, Pasternak, Tarsis and others. This movement, as we shall see further, has absolutely no support from the Russian people. This is confirmed by the Russians themselves. Any hopes that the Russians will rebel, that they are in a revolutionary frame of mind and can start an armed struggle, are illusory, even if one does not consider the fact that their aim is strictly "one and indivisible" in character and therefore there is no basis for a joint front with them.

An average Russian is a Ryazan muzhik—as Admiral Gorshkov styles himself—who, having climbed out from behind the stove niche, is proudly sailing the seas inspired by Russian messianism. And which of the Russians can oppose such a messianic attitude of the Russian people?

Berdyayev wished to give the Russian people a "Christian" imperialistic mission. He can find new adherents of his chauvinistic theory among the Russians even now, but no partners among the subjugated nations. Today the Berdyayev groups in the USSR are without any significance and do not have any influence, for why should the Russians hope for "pears on the willow," when their Bolsheviks have their hands on the southern fruits of the Mediterranean Sea and the Indian Ocean.

A genuine strategist of the national liberation revolution cannot build his plans on wishful thinking and make the victory of national forces dependent upon the inevitability of revolution by reactionary Russians, for this is tantamount to waiting for the imaginary divisions of Gen. Wenk in the fantasy of Hitler, who expected them to check an attack....

Sakharov proposes a rejection in international politics of the "empirical conjunctural method"—that is, a maximal consolidation of their positions by the superpowers wherever possible. He suggest a renunciation of such measures, which create maximum obstacles for the opponent, because, allegedly, it is necessary to take the "general good" and the "general interests" into consideration. He proposes a change of the "structure of ownership and society" in the West—that is, a change of the system. A similar thing is demanded by the leftist Leninist-Maoist, Baader-Meinhof Gang in West Germany.

In general, the plan projected by Sakharov has the objective of saving the Russian empire, of leading it out of the blind alley and into the open, of making it more acceptable to the West. This is all the more mandatory since—as he writes in his "Appeal" to Brezhnev, Kosygin, and Podgorny, dated March 19, 1970—the bankruptcy of the Soviet economic system and its backwardness in comparison with the USA are so great that "we simply live in another epoch."

The so-called Committee on Human Rights in the USSR does not even deny the legality of the established Russian Bolshevik Government; it only wants to "correct" it. An entirely different alternative is chosen by the "numerous representatives of technical intelligentsia of the Estonian SSR" in its elaboration "To Hope or to Act?" They say: "But finally the inevitability to act will arise. And then it will be necessary to direct tank divisions not to Prague and Bratislava, but to Moscow and Leningrad!" Thus, the tiny Estonian nation through the lips of a segment of its intelligentsia raises the question of the necessity of armed retribution against the Russian Bolshevik rulers at a time when the Russians reject in principle any revolution in the USSR.

Another Russian group (in the so-called Leningrad Program in the article "Time Presses" by Zorin and Alekseyev) does not believe in the possibility of USSR's democratization from the top, but urges achieving "political democracy" only by pressuring the Government from the bottom; i.e., it rejects armed struggle and revolution. The authors of this program write that the leaders of the USSR have a choice of either agreeing to genuine reforms or of risking a global rocket contest.

"The Program of the Democratic Movement of the USSR," which was allegedly signed by "democrats of Russia, Ukraine, and the Baltic region," is also aimed at saving the "one and indivisible" Russian empire and at preserving it at all costs, this time in the guise of a "Union of Democratic Republics." It is a liberal democratic program patterned on those of the West, with paeans to American capitalism. As a typical program of liberal, bourgeois, capitalist democracy, it considers socialism in the USSR as conservatism and therefore proposes a liberal democracy of the Euro-American type as a substitute for socialist conservatism of the CPSU. The program's authors acknowledge only a "peaceful evolution of society," rejecting the revolutionary road of toppling the Bolshevik regime and its system as "irresponsible, criminal, and historically unjustifiable." Their "illegal" forms of struggle are only allegedly conspiratorial, secret groups which would organize strong, mass, but peaceful pressure of the public upon the "leadership of society...."

Sakharov's action won immediate support from the NTS (Natsionalny Trudovoy Soyuz—a Russian emigre political organization) for, according to its publication *Posyev* (No. 12, 1972), the NTS members have the same aim as Sakharov, while "the dialectical controversy with Sakharov, democratization from above and independent liberation from below, is to be found only in the method and means of achieving an end." The NTS supports democratization from below, yet it also supports and accepts democratization from above.

Neither Sakharov, nor the NTS, nor the so-called Leningrad group, nor the "democrats" from the "Democratic Movement," nor the editors of the *Viche* (V. Osypov and Co.) acknowledge the existence of the national problem in the USSR. They either pass it over in silence or simply reject it. Osypov, the editor of *Viche*, having served his sentence, defends as a matter of principle "constitutional rights" alone. He favors regaining from the regime "the right of the loyal opposition to exist" within the framework of the Constitution. Moreover, he even says that "an announcement of even a declarative war against the Soviet regime is a grave mistake." The chief means of activity of this dissident "Berdyayev group in Leningrad" is to be "the struggle with particular excesses of the Government, legal defense of the Soviet Constitution against its official opponents."

Thus, only the expectations of "democratization" of the Russian Bolshevik system and Government by way of evolution, with the assistance of pressure from the top or bottom, the struggle of the legal and loyal opposition in the USSR alone characterize the entire oppositional movement of the Russian loyalists as a movement of opposition to "His Tsarist Highness" Leonid of the Kremlin (Brezhnev).

On the territory of Russia there was only one small group—the "All-Russian Social Christian Alliance for People's Liberation," headed by Ogurtsev and Sad— which did not attempt to reform the "Soviet Government," but wished to liquidate it with the help of military power. It was immediately infiltrated by provocateurs and crushed in 1968. It considered itself a military and political organization which was to topple the regime in an armed conflict and introduce a Social-Christian order. The positions of this group were religious and national and anti-socialist. Because the USSR had found itself in a blind alley, which is confirmed by Sakharov, this group proposed "revolution as the only way out." But its activity ended with the declaration itself. It failed to find any positive response or support within the Russian popular masses.

How far removed are all those Russian "dissidents" from the Ukrainian Insurgent Army (UPA), which organized a nationwide uprising even during the horrible terror of the tyrant Stalin.

In the West it is now common to speak about the so-called third emigration from the USSR, but there are few Ukrainians among the emigrés. They are primarily Russians and Jews, emigrés by the grace of the Russian Bolshevik regime, allowed to go abroad for various reasons and on various occasions, although many of them had been members of the so-called movement of opposition, even of Sakharov's Committee (Medvedev, Chalidze). But Ukrainians are not allowed "to emigrate," but are deported to the North to prisons and concentration camps.

The fact is that both the "oppositionists" in Russia and the NTS abroad confirm that the Russian people do not wish to remove the Bolshevik Government by force. It is also a fact that the so-called movement of opposition in Russia has absolutely no support among the Russian people. The NTS itself reports that the "oppositionists" in Russia are a group totalling about three to five thousand persons. In Ukraine, on the other hand, the national liberation movement is a nationwide movement supported by the Ukrainian people as a whole.

The Russian "oppositionists" who emigrated in 1971-72 with the approval of the Russian Bolshevik regime frankly state that the "Russian people" do not want a revolution, and this means that there are absolutely no reasons to count on their participation in the revolutionary struggle of the subjugated nations—if only against the regime, without even mentioning the dissolution of the Russian empire, which is an unquantified precondition to a joint front with the Russians.

I. Agruzov, in an article "Let's Consider" (*Posev*, No. 8, 1972), speaks decisively against revolution in the USSR. He comes to the following conclusions: "There are no grounds to maintain that economic reasons can serve today (in peacetime) as a motive for large uprisings which could change into a revolution.... The universities are not the disseminators of new social and political ideas. *Samizdat* circulates in universities, but is not published there. It contains no specific student materials. As long as people able and willing to fight for political causes do not come forth from the centers of science and culture, so long are there no grounds to believe that revolution is possible.... The development of science and technology and the growth of cadres of scientific and technical intelligentsia connected with it do not lead automatically to the liberalization of the regimes.... Rejecting the present regime of the CPSU, today's generation of Russians is afraid of new experiments.... The people fear the masses and themselves.... The Communists have forgotten about world revolution. Their spirit of messianism, and the desire to make people happy have weakened.... The Communists turned into bureaucrats and usurpers inside the country.... The anti-Communists have become internal exiles, good scholars, reformists...."

With such tales Agruzov attempts to turn the West's attention away from the Russian Bolshevik threat. He pretends not to know that the Russian navy is occasionally stronger than that of the USA, that for the first time in its history Russia dominates the Mediterranean Sea, is gaining control in the Arctic and the Pacific oceans, penetrating into the Indian Ocean, Bangladesh, the Near East, Cuba, Chile, the countries of Africa, undermining defense capabilities of France, Italy, and other European and American countries, infiltrating West Germany. Agruzov tries to reassure the West with his tale that the Russian Communists "have forgotten about [world] revolution," that their "spirit of [Russian] messianism has weakened, that they are "afraid of war and revolution just as the people themselves who are afraid of any upheavals...." It seems that the Russian people are quite well off in their modern empire and that they prefer Bolshevism to any revolution and change. "Our better contemporaries", writes Agruzov, "reject violence as a means of struggle for human rights. Revolution is inseparable from violence. Therefore they reject revolution." He says that in the USSR a struggle is carried out only "for the consolidation of human rights and legality...."

There is no clear "yes" or "no" among the people. "There is no hatred toward the CPSU." The people do not want "fratricide...." "It is a mistake to think that power is concentrated in the hands of a small group of people.... It is delegated to millions of functionaries.... There are no such people who would be ready to take over authority in the country; the people do not see them...."

The author advises the NTS "openly to refuse to follow a revolutionary path of struggle," for "an internal armed conflict is contemptible for our people and country...." The NTS should declare "the formation of a lawful, multinational democratic state," placing an accent not on the struggle with the present regime, but on 'solidarity of the society.' The main thing is not the struggle with the old [the Bolshevik regime], but the solidarity with the new, to creat the new"—i.e., to change the outward appearance of the present Russian Bolshevik empire in order to save it from collapsing. In other words, to repeat what the Bolsheviks had done with the tsarist empire.

The tendency of Agruzov's deliberations is quite clear; revolution is impossible in the USSR; the Russian people are happy with their regime. The latter is true, but it is a lie that the nations subjugated in the USSR do not long for revolution, rejecting it as "violence" (over whom?). To the contrary, for them it is the only realistic way to achieve liberation.

Lulling the West by the illusion that the Bolsheviks "have lost their messianism," have given up the idea of world conquest and world revolution, that Moscow has ceased to be the center of aggression and imperialism is a deception taking the shape of a modern Russian Trojan horse. If the Western statesmen, and with them Western public opinion, accept this Trojan horse they will be digging their own graves.

It is a different story with the peoples subjugated in the Russian Bolshevik empire. They are experienced; nobody can deceive them with a Trojan horse anymore, and therefore they have chosen the only sure path toward their national and social liberation—the revolutionary path. Uprisings in concentration camps, in Temir-Tau, Kingiri, disturbances in Novocherkask, Dnipropetrovsk, Dniprodzerzhynsk, unrest in many localities of Ukraine and Turkestan— all these are only a part of the kindling fires from which a huge blaze engulfing the entire Russian empire can develop. After all, in Kingiri the Ukrainian heroines attacked Russian tanks with bare hands.

Let us also recall the insurrection in Hungary, in Poznan, in Berlin, the events in Czechoslovakia, the revolt of the workers in Poland which resulted in the downfall of Gomulka, the reaction in Ukraine during the Hungarian revolution....

Even at the peak of Stalinist tyranny uprisings broke out in concentration camps where Ukrainian political prisoners, participating in the liberation struggle, were confined. The Hungarian revolution became a proof that an insurrection is possible at the time of the greatest terror and under the harshest conditions.

Particularly eloquent is the fact that Agruzov tried to "prove" to the West that the threat to the Western world from the Russian Bolshevik aggressors has also disappeared, that revolution is impossible in the USSR because nobody wants it, for all have reconciled themselves with the reality, at a time when the West too became aware of the powerlessness of terror in the countries of the Russian-subjugated peoples.

Agruzov wants to create the impression that his "diagnosis" pertains to all peoples within the USSR—to the oppressor as well as to the nations he oppresses. In reality, it is simply a crime to transfer the estimate of the Russian nation-oppressor to the nations it subjugates. And any orientation toward the "revolution" of the Russians is both naive and false. Making the victory of the national liberation revolutions dependent upon the revolution of the Russians means driving the revolutionary forces of the subjugated nations into a corner.

Of course, the weakening of the regime in the present Russian empire, even by the internal Russian opposition, is to a certain extent useful for our liberation struggle. However, the real road to our liberation is the Ukrainian national revolution and a common front with other nations subjugated within the USSR, which are fighting for the downfall of the Russian empire and the reestablishment of their sovereign states.

Opposition movements among the Russians against the regime, conflicts and ferments weakening the regime can facilitate the liberation struggle of the subjugated nations, all the more if they are simultaneous. However, this does not mean that a revolution in the USSR is impossible without a joint front with the Russian opposition and therefore it is necessary to seek an understanding with the Russians at all costs, in spite of the fact that they totally reject national liberation and attempt to preserve the Russian empire.

ABN Correspondence,
May-June 1973, pp. 5-10

Our Answer to Peaceful Coexistence

The building up of our own forces, common coordinated revolutionary liberation action, systematic preparation of armed uprising—psychological, political, and military—the disintegration from within of the Russian empire and the Communist system; this is our answer to so-called peaceful coexistence of the Free World with the world of tyranny.

Outside this empire, in the Free World, it is necessary to mobilize the anti-Russian and anti-Communist forces which see in the policy of so-called peaceful coexistence a threat to the Free World and are turning their attention to the importance for the Free World of the struggle for liberation of the subjugated nations.

The extension of territorial conquests and political influence by Russia into the sphere of the Free World is a consequence of so-called peaceful coexistence.

We are living on a volcano. In particular because some groups in free societies have renounced their inherited national ideals and traditions, the feeling of social and national justice within their own nations, the idealistic principles of life, and have accepted the idolization of Mammon with its cult.

I shall now deal briefly with methods used by Moscow and Communism for decomposition of what is still the free part of the world.

Decomposition is the preliminary condition for guerrilla warfare strategy or a sudden attack from outside. For the time being the methods of decomposition are the following: penetration by agents, quislings, and traitors into the life of the sovereign nations, into all spheres of public life, into state administration, political parties, television, theaters, cinema, universities, schools, and even churches so that by deceit, blackmail, or bribery the Russian style of internationalism, the decline of patriotic attitudes, the establishment of the creed of materialism, the cult of money, luxury, demoralization, narrow egoism, and hedonism can be spread.

Hence our task: to concentrate our attention upon the young generation, which should be brought up in the spirit of the world heroic traditions of our nations, the ideas of patriotism, social justice, heroic humanism, and should imitate our great historic personalities instead of the symbols of the world of hostility— Lenin, Mao, Ho Chi Minh, and Che Guevara.

To start our own positive action, to encourage our youth to demonstrate on the streets of cities to show their solidarity with the subjugated nations and to defend their own traditional values.

To accept the challenges of the pro-Communist elements at the universities for the defense of idealistic values, to counteract the nihilistic contents of mass media propaganda, and to defend true and real values.

To support within all the churches and in religious life general trends which are against dialogues and coexistence with atheist Moscow and Communism.

To work for a change of policy by the free governments in the direction of adopting the policy of liberation.

To advocate the discontinuance of all relations with the USSR and the Communist regimes, the more so after the Russian invasion of Czechoslovakia and the cruel persecution of the cultural workers of the subjugated nations, especially in Ukraine, from where we have received a great deal of documentation published recently in two books in England: *The Chornovil Papers* and *Internationalism or Russification?* by Ivan Dzyuba.

To initiate parliamentary debates about Russian colonialism and the situation in the subjugated countries.

To help the subjugated nations to fight Moscow on the territories of its domination and in the countries in which Communist dictatorship rules and enslaves other nations (as for example Croatians, who aim at their independence).

To try to get facilities in this and other countries for systematic or occasional radio transmissions to the countries behind the Iron Curtain.

To organize in the free countries:

a) Study groups and seminars, not only on so-called Sovietology—i.e., the systems and doctrines of lies and deceit—but also on the subject of the national revolutionary movements of the subjugated nations, so that the young generation becomes aware of the active forces fighting Russian imperialism and Communism behind the Iron Curtain and feels encouraged by them. (And above all the young generation should firmly grasp the fact that the USSR is a Russian empire, and not a monolithic state, and that, for instance, Yugoslavia or the CSSR is a conglomerate of nations.)

b) Mass meetings of youth with speeches and lectures about the problems of the subjugated nations, methods and ideas of the struggle against Communism and Russian psychological infiltration in the Free World.

c) Means for the publication in Western and Eastern languages of works which circulate secretly or illegally in the subjugated countries and give evidence of a growing liberation movement.

To consider the ideology of national liberation as the main motivating power in the age of decolonization and the basic precondition for the social liberation and the defeat of Communism, the system of total enslavement of human beings.

To launch a campaign of information about ways and means of combating Russian aggression in the Free World, enlisting its help for the liberation struggle of the subjugated nations, pointing out the advantages to the free nations to be found in the liberation struggle.

To seek support of official representatives of the various nations, parliamentary and public opinions of the Free World.

To impress upon the conscience of all nations the importance of the fact that every nation, including all the nations subjugated in the Soviet Union, the satellite countries and Yugoslavia (nations with ancient cultural traditions in Europe and Asia) have the same right to their own state independence as have other peoples in the world.

How can one explain the reluctance to declare similar rights valid for the nations imprisoned in the Russian empire which systematically enlarges its territories by new subjugations of European and Asiatic countries?

Why should the era of Western colonialism come to an end while Russian colonialism flourishes in Europe and other continents?

ABN Correspondence,
May-June 1970, pp. 7-8

The Helsinki Agreements Should Be Annulled

The Helsinki Agreements were initiated by the Politburo of the Central Committee of the Communist Party of the Soviet Union in Moscow with the aim of receiving international recognition of the gains made during the Second World War:

—of consolidating the inviolability of the frontiers of the modern Russian empire, including the neocolonial satellite states.

—of preserving the integrity of territories dominated by Russian imperialism.

—of securing non-interference in the so-called internal affairs of the Russian colonial empire in Europe, Asia, and on other continents.

This has been the only part of the Helsinki Agreements observed by both sides, the West and the Bolsheviks. What irony!

The Russian empire, the USSR, has discarded all other pledges on human rights and the fundamental liberties of peoples and individuals in its sphere of domination.

In the hope of being personally involved with President Carter in the human rights campaign, there were formed in Ukraine, Lithuania, Georgia, Armenia, and Moscow groups for monitoring the implementation of the Helsinki Agreements.

These groups demanded the realization of the national and human rights of their peoples. The Ukrainian, Lithuanian, Georgian, and Armenian groups in particular did not stop at the Third Basket for the implementation of human rights. They reached to the sources of oppression, the existence of the USSR, the Russian colonial empire, and demanded national independence of their peoples, the disintegration of the empire in the age of the fall of empires throughout the world, according to the relevant UN Declaration on decolonization.

On the instructions of the Politburo and the USSR Government, the KGB smashed all national groups "for the implementation of the Helsinki Agreements." The pogrom against these groups continues today, even on the eve of the Madrid conference. The Politburo and the USSR Government in fact have made a laughingstock of the Helsinki Agreements, having achieved what they desire most: the recognition by thirty-three states in Europe and North America—without any peace treaty!—of the inviolability of all the present territorial acquisitions of the Russian conquerors.

The Helsinki Agreements came after the suppression of the 1949 uprising of Ukrainian prisoners in Vorkuta, the 1953 uprising of workers in East Germany, the defeat of Hungary and Poland in 1956, and the invasion of Czechoslovakia in 1968, after the smashing of the revolts of Ukrainian and other inmates of the concentration camps, after the erection of the Berlin Wall, after the suppression by brute force of the uprisings of Ukrainian working people in Novocherkassk, Novodzerzhinsk, Dnipropetrovsk, and the Donbas, and after the suppression of the workers' revolts in Poland in 1970 and 1976.

False Security

Can one speak about security and peaceful settlement of misunderstanding? If so, then how does one explain Russian aggression in Angola, Ethiopia, Zanzibar, Vietnam, Kampuchea, Laos, and numerous other countries on various continents? Is this security?

And on the eve of the review of the fulfillment of the Helsinki Agreements: aggression against Afghanistan and genocide by napalm bombs and bacteria? The Helsinki Agreements and hundreds of thousands of drowned refugees of Communism in Vietnam—is this security? Is this the indivisibility of security and peace?

The murder of the fighters for the rights of the individual and the nation, of priests, cultural workers, and political fighters, the members of the Organization of Ukrainian Nationalists and the Ukrainian Insurgent Army, thousands deported to Siberia and imprisoned.... All this took place after the Helsinki and Belgrade meetings!

Without another world war the Russian imperialists have been causing disorder inside the free nations with the help of peripheral and local wars and social subversion, including the terrorist factions of the Red Army. And the Western nations seem to be helpless and frightened like rabbits facing a python!

But at the same time the Russian empire is a colossus with clay feet. It is being destroyed by the revolutionary national liberation movements of the oppressed nations, with Ukraine at their head. The oppressed nations constitute a majority in the USSR and this means also in the Soviet army. If we add also the satellites, the the relation of forces would be three to one in favor of the subjugated nations against the Russian oppressor nation.

The policy of detente is bankrupt. The strategy based on the balance of power has been a deception, for the Russians have superiority in nuclear and conventional armaments.

The West has underestimated the most important factor: the neglected power of the oppressed nations which are tearing apart the Russian empire and the Communist system from within. The West has written off these people, its most determined allies, as the decisive force of our age.

Liberation nationalism, militant religion, the national idea coupled with the social—these are the forces that will destroy the imperial system.

We demand: instead of the policy of detente with the Russian imperialists and Communist tyrants, *a policy of liberation of the oppressed nations*, as an alternative to nuclear war!

Detente will lead to a world-wide holocaust, while the policy of liberation leads to a lasting and just peace!

The Russian empire is advancing by stages in its march for the conquest of the world. It achieves its aims piecemeal, stage by stage. Its strength lies in the ethical, ideological, and political weakness of the West, in the lack of the Western nations' political will to lead a struggle. The Russians have been occupying more and more countries by force of arms while shouting about their desire for peace. The West continues to capitulate before Russia.

Therefore, we propose to the non-Communist participants who reviewed the implementation of the Helsinki accords to start a war of nerves against the Soviet Union now.

Instead of accepting the Politburo's proposition of summit meetings, which would confirm one more Russian conquest, that in Afghanistan, *they should declare null and void the agreements made in Helsinki.*

Agreements broken by one side do not bind the other side. This is a simple truth!

If anyone wishes to call this a provocation, then the only show of provocation against the USSR is passiveness, lack of counteraction, lack of any action in general, and lack of political will to wage a struggle. Regrettably, this is typical of the West.

ABN Correspondence,
March-April 1981, pp. 1-4

Ukrainian Independence Day in the American Congress

I would like to begin by thanking the Congress of the United States for adopting the Captive Nations Resolution on July 17, 1959 and for reaffirming your commitment to the principles therein over the course of the last twenty-two years. I am particularly pleased that the resolution was adopted unanimously and I expect that this resolution, which remains in the interests of not only the subjugated nations but also the entire Free World, will be an integral component of the United States foreign policy.

Allow me to express my heartfelt appreciation to the Hon. Edward J. Derwinski, the Hon. Samuel Stratton, and to Dr. Dobriansky for organizing today's commemoration of the fortieth anniversary of the Declaration of the Reestablishment of the Independent Ukrainian State. I would also like to convey my sincere gratitude to the Hon. William Green for introducing a resolution in the House of Representatives designating June 30, 1981 as Ukrainian Independence Day. The future will justify the support that you are demonstrating today for the liberation of Ukraine by commemorating the latest period of Ukrainian statehood, which began with the Reestablishment of the Independent Ukrainian State on June 30, 1941 and lasted through 1951.

It is my conviction that the events of June 30, 1941 were of historical significance not only for my own nation, but also for all other subjugated nations. The proclamation of the Restoration of Ukrainian Statehood of June 30, 1941 marked the beginning of a period in our history known under international law as the *Ukrainian Underground State*. As a result of this proclamation the Ukrainian nation launched a two-front war of liberation against Nazi Germany and Soviet Russia—two of the greatest imperialistic, totalitarian, and military powers of the twentieth century. The act of June 30, 1941 and the subsequent struggle to consolidate the renewal of Ukrainian statehood are a manifestation of the unshakeable will of the Ukrainian nation to achieve the restoration of its freedom and independence.

The Ukrainian Government, created following the proclamation of independence, included not only representatives of the OUN under the leadership of Stepan Bandera, but also national democrats, socialists, social revolutionaries, and individuals not affiliated with any party. On the initiative of the OUN, a parliamentary body was formed under the chairmanship of Dr. Konstantyn Levytsky, a national democrat and former prime minister of the Western Ukrainian National republic of 1918. The present patriarch of the Ukrainian Catholic Church, Cardinal Joseph Slipy, was a leading member of Parliament, while Metropolitan Count Andreas Sheptytsky was elected honorary president. Both the primate of the Ukrainian Catholic Church and the metropolitan Polikarp Sikorsky of the Ukrainian Autocephalous Orthodox Church issued pastoral letters in support of the newly-formed Government. The new Ukrainian Government enjoyed the total support and loyalty of all strata of the Ukrainian nation. This was the only democratic government and parliament in continental Europe at that time.

The ideological and political foundation upon which Ukrainian statehood was restored in 1941 was contained in a manifesto issued in 1940 by the Organization of Ukrainian Nationalists, which stated: "We Ukrainians have raised the banner of struggle for the freedom of nations and man.... We struggle for the dignity and freedom of man, for the right to openly profess one's beliefs, for freedom of all religious demonstrations and full freedom of conscience.... We struggle for the right of the working man to openly profess his political convictions...for freedom of assembly and the establishment of political, social, and professional organizations...." Furthermore, the manifesto called upon the revolutionaries of other subjugated nations to join forces with the Ukrainian nationalists in the struggle to destroy the Soviet Russian empire. This was the origin of the ABN. It also stood as a challenge to Nazi Germany at the time when both totalitarian powers, having divided Europe between themselves, were at the zenith of their might.

The newly-formed Government had the support of the Ukrainian nationalist military formation and numerous insurgent units throughout Ukraine, which immediately engaged the Soviet army on the field of battle. Having secured the main radio station in Lviv, the Revolutionary Government informed the nation of the restoration of Ukrainian statehood. Upon learning of these momentous developments, the Ukrainian population openly and enthusiastically endorsed the new Government at mass assemblies in towns and villages throughout the country.

Consequently, the Nazis were forced to divulge their imperial-colonial aims. Following a period of tempestuous activity of consolidation of the newly-formed state, myself and other members of our Government, as well as several leading members of the OUN including its leader Stepan Bandera, were arrested by the Gestapo and sent into the concentration camps. Later, the Gestapo murdered three members of the Government. Subsequently, the OUN went underground to continue the struggle for Ukraine's independence.

On behalf of our Government, I sent my last letter of protest against the Nazi military occupation of Ukraine to the German Reich's chancellor in October 1941 from the police prison in Berlin. In that letter I warned that Germany's war in the East would be lost within three years, resulting in the Russian Communist occupation of vast areas of central Europe. Despite this projection, I openly stated that Ukraine and the other freedom-loving subjugated nations would never cease their just struggle for liberty and independence.

On three separate occasions I was confronted with an ultimatum from the highest levels of the German Reich to revoke the declaration of Ukrainian state independence, to resign as Prime Minister, and to dismiss the Government. Each of these demands was adamantly rejected.

A state of war existed between Germany and Ukraine. Many thousands of Ukrainian nationalists and other patriots were executed upon capture, hundreds of thousands were put in prisons and concentration camps. A two-front war against the Russian and German occupiers of Ukraine was fought by the OUN and by the UPA. Operating underground, the Ukrainian Supreme Liberation Council continued the work of the arrested Government.

By the autumn of 1941, thousands of members of the OUN had been executed, many more thousands had been imprisoned by the Nazis, who were acting on orders from Berlin such as these:

From the
Service Command of the
Security Police and of
the Security Service S/5

Headquarters
November 25, 1941

To the advanced posts of
Kyiv, Dnipropetrovsk,
Rivne, Mykolaiv, Zhytomyr,
and Vinnytsia.
Subject: Organization of Ukrainian Nationalists
(Bandera Movement)

It has been ascertained that the Bandera Movement is preparing a revolt in the Reichscommissariat which has as its ultimate aim the establishment of an independent Ukraine. All functionaries of the Bandera Movement must be arrested at once, and, after thorough interrogation, are to be secretly liquidated as marauders.

Records of such interrogation must be forwarded to the service command C/5.

Heads of commands must destroy these instructions on having made a due notice of them.

(Signature illegible)
SS-Obersturmbandführer

The Ukrainian underground state and the mass armed struggle continued from 1941 to 1951. The Ukrainian Supreme Liberation Council, as the natural extension of the Ukrainian Government, exercised national authority for a decade on various parts of Ukrainian territory. The sovereignty of revolutionary authority was preserved through the military underground of the Organization of Ukrainian Nationalists and the Ukrainian Insurgent Army.

The scope of the struggle has been acknowledged by Russians and Germans alike. For example, Nikita Khrushchev wrote in his memoirs that, and I quote:

During the second half of the war he [Stepan Bandera, leader of the Ukrainian liberation movement] fought against both us and the Germans. Later, after the war, we lost thousands of men in a bitter struggle between the Ukrainian nationalists and the forces of Soviet power.

A German general, Ernst Koestring, also reported that, and I quote again:

The military organization known as the Ukrainian Povstanska Armiya [the Ukrainian Insurgent Army] was formed with the aim of establishing an independent Ukraine, controlled neither by Moscow nor by Germany.... When western Ukraine was recaptured by the Red Army, the OUN, and the UPA called upon the Ukrainian masses to fight against the Bolsheviks—the Russian enemy. German officers who fought their way back to us in 1945 reported that the plight of the Red Army was similar to ours: it controlled only the towns and the main communication routes, while the country itself remained in the hands of the resistance movement.

The contemporary international situation is particularly grave. The expansion of Russian imperialism is well known to us all. Policies of friendship, appeasement, containment, convergence, and detente have proven to be useless in stemming the centuries-old brazen Russian imperialism which aims at complete world domination.

But the West must realize that within the Russian empire there exists a new ideological and political revolutionary superpower—the subjugated nations— which is destroying the empire from within. The processes of disintegration of the Russian empire are at different stages in the various subjugated nations.

Taking this factor into consideration, the following points should be included in western political and military strategy:

1) The Free World should engage Soviet Russia in the struggle of ideas and ideologies by recognizing the liberation movements of the subjugated nations as the legitimate representatives of these countries at all international forums including the United Nations;

2) The West should provide access for the national liberation movements to the various forms of mass media to facilitate communication with their countrymen behind the Iron Curtain on a mass scale;

3) Assistance should also be provided in the form of military training as well as other political, material, and technological means of support;

4) All of the nations of the Free World should proclaim a Great Charter of Independence of all the nations subjugated by Russian imperialism and communism.

The danger of nuclear holocaust cannot be negotiated away. Soviet Russia has skillfully exploited Western fears of nuclear war by blackmailing the West into meekly aquiescing to ever-increasing conquests. Our strategic alternative is based on the knowledge that the subjugated nations within the Russian empire represent a vast untapped force, which, in a common front with the nations of the Free World, provides the strategic raison d'etre for defeating the last remaining empire. Synchronized national liberation revolutions within the Russian colonial empire are the only alternative.

I would like to end my address to you, ladies and gentlemen, with the words of an unforgettable personal friend of mine and an outstanding British military thinker, Major General J.F.C. Fuller, who wrote:

Only the unity of the Western nations and their agreement with the national liberation movements behind the Iron Curtain can ensure final victory.... The reason should be obvious. It is that the Kremlin is living on a volcano, and it knows that the most explosive force in the world is not to be found in the hydrogen bomb, but in the heart of the subjugated peoples crushed under its iron heel....

Address to the Members of
the Congress the United States,
Washington, D.C., July 15, 1981
ABN Correspondence,
September-October 1981, pp. 1-4

IV
International Events

The Hungarian October Revolution

The revolution in Hungary is of worldwide historical significance. It has once again revealed Moscow's true character and has disclosed the falsity of "peaceful coexistence" as a tactical maneuver on the part of the Kremlin rulers, who are exactly the same imperialist and genocidal murderers as their teachers and masters, Lenin and Stalin, were. Hungary has exposed the so-called de-Stalinization even for people such as Nenni and Bevan. Moscow's soul has been revealed in all its tyrannical barbarity as never before. Moscow without its mask—this is the meaning of the Hungarian revolution, as far as all the pacifists in the West are concerned.

The determined cry of the heroic masses in Hungary—"Down with the Russians!"—has shown everyone that the question at issue is a most concrete one and that what is at stake is Muscovite imperialism, the Muscovite urge to conquer and subjugate the entire world, the Russian people as the pillar and support of this imperialism. Not "Soviet imperialism" and not the "Soviet people", which do not exist, but something perfectly obvious, the Russians as a nation.

The other cry of the Hungarian's fight for freedom, "Down with the very form of Communism," has likewise unsparingly exposed the entire treacherous game of national Communism, which at heart remains an ally of Moscow and will in the end always side with Moscow, since it will never be able to assert itself politically, socially, or economically without Moscow's aid and support; for national Communism, should it retain the collective system (and it will be *forced* to

129

do so in any case, in keeping with its very nature), will be obliged to face the opposition of the peasantry in the immediate future, and for the sake of its self-preservation will be obliged to "appeal" to Moscow for help, which is what Geroe and Kadar have done. This is an unwritten law which no true Communist can evade. What is more, Hungary has clearly shown that the working classes are by no means in favor of a social Communist program, whether it be carried out according to Stalin's or Tito's pattern. The revelation of this truth to the whole world is the heaviest blow Moscow, that alleged "Mecca of the proletariat," has so far suffered. And Moscow will, in fact, never recover from this blow, for the myth about Moscow as the "protector of the world proletariat" has been shattered for all time.

In addition, the attack carried out by the Muscovite armies against the "Workers' and Peasants' Government" of Hungary headed by the Communist Nagy has revealed that a ruthless and brutal Muscovite imperialism which is much worse than the imperialism of tsarist times is behind all the fine phrases about socialism and the liberation of the working classes. In the eyes of the dependent colonial peoples of Asia and Africa, Moscow has also exposed itself as out-and-out imperialist which is not in the least concerned about the freedom of Tunisia or Malaya, but is solely interested in seeing the so-called liberal imperialism of certain Western major powers replaced by the inhuman imperialism of Moscow, which spares neither women nor children, neither workers nor the poorest peasants.

Hungary has shown that Moscow is not interested in "coexistence," but in conquering the world by resorting to the most brutal means. Moscow's regime of terrorism in Hungary has indeed given all the pacifists and advocates of coexistence a nasty shock; in fact, even the most convinced supporters of Moscow were horrified when they realized that Moscow is prepared, if need be, to destroy the entire world by means of atomic weapons once the time is ripe for its attack—seeing that it did not hesitate to suppress the heroic Hungarian revolt by a cruel and brutal armed force which is unparalleled in the history of the world.

Though events in Hungary may have caused the peoples of the West to change their opinion about Moscow, it is not the fine phrases voiced in the forum of the United Nations which are of the most far-reaching historical significance, but the resolution passed by the International League of Free Trade Unions in which the free workers of the whole world proclaimed their boycott of the Soviet Union. This was the most fitting answer which the freedom-loving workers could have given Moscow. Whereas countless employers in the West are intent upon doing business with Soviet Russia, the workers refuse to do so, since they consider business with such a partner as beneath their dignity. They refuse to accept the idea that one can even do business with cannibals. Moscow has aroused the anger and indignation of all working classes which are spiritually and morally sound. This fact may well play an extremely important and decisive part in the event of another world war—which Moscow will most probably sooner or later try to provoke—for the antagonism of the working classes will result in the complete liquidation of the so-called Fifth Columns as the *ideological* representatives of Moscow's policy.

The Hungarian revolution has likewise revealed the enormous forces at work in the soul of a nation, forces undreamt of in the West. It has furthermore shown that a general national revolt can well be carried out in Moscow-ruled countries and may under certain circumstances be successful. It has proven that the method of preparing a national revolt of this kind should not be in the nature of a conspiracy but in the nature of an appeal to the people, who then take up arms. The revolution in Hungary was *spontaneous*, a fact which proves that Moscow has neither succeeded in exterminating the national characteristics in the soul of the Hungarian people nor in "re-educating" the youth of Hungary, which has played a leading part in the revolution, in the Communist manner. We have on numerous occasions stressed that our method—that is to say the method of the anti-Bolshevik fighters for freedom—of preparing an armed revolution of the people should not be in the nature of a conspiracy and should not aim to bring about a "court revolution," but should be a revolt of the masses which should destroy the empire and its system from within. In this respect our prognostications have been fully corroborated. Neither the youth nor the masses in Hungary have allowed their mental and spiritual outlook to be influenced by Communism, but in their innermost hearts have remained true to their own selves. Neither historical nor dialectical materialism has left any noticeable trace on the national soul of the Hungarian people, and Muscovite imperialism, which hid behind Marxist doctrines and aimed to Russify Hungary, has proved to be powerless from the ideological point of view.

Hungary has given the world a classical example of a revolution in Soviet-ruled territory—without the aid of a vast network of underground organizations (which could easily be wiped out by a terrorist system of government), but with the help of striking and appealing slogans which reflect the aims of the entire nation and reveal the root of the evil. In this way the youth of Hungary has inspired and won over the factory workers and has become the organizing force of the revolution.

What Hungary has accomplished is to be regarded as a national war, rather than as a revolution. Actually there has been no indication of a civil war, since no part of the Hungarian people has actively opposed the general revolt. It has literally been a national war against the Moscow occupants, whom not even a fraction of the people has supported. The mere handful of mercenary politicians of the Janos Kadar type or the few thousand secret police agents and spies are not worth taking into account, for there are rogues in every nation.

The Hungarian war of liberation lasted about a month and is still going on in the form of a partisan war. In this connection it is interesting to note that the Polish state was liquidated by Hitler in three weeks, though the military superiority of the German forces in Poland was much less than that of the Russians in Hungary! And, incidentally, the Hungarians have for the first time in the history of their country resorted to a *Marxist* remedy against the oppressor—namely, to the method of a general strike. The fact that a general strike, a measure recommended by Marx and Engels as the main weapon to be used against the "capitalists," is being used successfully, and, we hope, decisively, against a government which calls itself "Workers' and Peasants' Government" and claims to be bringing

mankind the "salvation" of socialism, may sound paradoxical, but it is nevertheless true; a national strike directed against Russian imperialism and Communism
has proved to be far more effective than all the "humane" lamentations of the
United Nations and of the entire West.

A general strike is thus possible within the Soviet sphere of influence, provided
that the *entire people* rise up against their national, social, and economic oppressor.
Never in the history of the capitalistic epoch has there been such a powerful
national campaign as that of the Hungarian people against the Kadar
Government—that is to say, against Moscow's outpost in the West. And this
fight is, of course, in the first place not a social and economic fight, but a *national*
fight for the national liberation of the Hungarian working classes, as the representatives and protectors of the whole nation, from a foreign yoke. The Hungarian war of liberation has clearly proven that national subjugation is the root of all
evil including the social and economic. Had Soviet Russian troops not marched
into Hungary, there would be no Communist regime there now, for the Hungarian people would have wiped out all the Communist traitors and their mercenary
hirelings completely, within a few days' time.

The course which the Hungarian revolution has taken has clearly shown that
the non-Russian troops of the Soviet Army are by no means eager to fight
against the liberation movements of other nations. The many "deserters," in
particular among the Ukrainian soldiers of the Soviet Army, the Soviet tanks
which fired not on the insurgents but on the enemy, and the rumors which have
been spread intentionally among the detachments of Soviet soldiers to the effect
that they were to be used not against Hungary but on the Suez front—all these
facts imply that a war against a national revolution is extremely unpopular in the
Soviet army.

The Hungarian war of liberation has evoked an enormous response on the part
of all the peoples subjugated by Moscow. Hungary has proven that Moscow is
weak internally and that even a spontaneous revolt by the people against its
terrorism and tyranny could be successful, provided that it is carried out simultaneously and in coordination by the subjugated peoples. In that case it would be
possible to destroy the Russian empire from within without needing much help
from the West. A new spirit is beginning to inspire all the peoples subjugated by
Moscow, who are gradually realizing that they, too, possess weapons—as the
soldiers of the Hungarian army, who used their weapons not against their own
fellow-countrymen but against the latter's oppressors.

The Hungarian national revolution against Moscow has not been in vain; on
the contrary, it represents a huge step forward on the path to the liberation of
the non-Russian peoples of the Soviet Union. Moscow will never be able to
recover from this mortal blow. Not even the Soviet-loving Indian socialists and
not even Jawaharlal Nehru, often acting as Moscow's foreign policy tool, venture
to justify the action of the Bolsheviks in Hungary.

We consider it futile to waste words of indignation against the Western
powers, which have left Hungary to her fate. In our opinion the present government circles of the Western powers are not fit to represent their peoples, but are

merely opportunists and unscrupulous "pacifists"; but we leave it to their own people to pillory them, which they will no doubt do in the near future.

Events in Hungary have likewise corroborated a statement which we have made on several occasions—namely, that an atomic war can be avoided if the Free World actively and effectively supports national wars of liberation and national revolutions within the Bolshevik sphere of influence. If this were the case, a revolutionary chain reaction would make itself felt throughout all the countries subjugated by Moscow and would destroy the Soviet Russian prison of nations from within. Whether political circles in the West learn a lesson from events in Hungary or not, at least the Hungarian October Revolution has not been in vain. The Bolshevik "October Revolution" in 1917 brought darkness, slavery, and death to the world; the Hungarian war of liberation in October 1956 represents an impetus to vast, constructive changes in the whole world and introduces a new chapter in the history of the world and in the history of Eastern Europe and Ukraine.

The Ukrainian Review,
No. IV, 1956, pp. 3-8

Limits of Atomic Warfare

Hungary's revolutionary fight for freedom has shown that the liberation of the nations subjugated by Moscow can only be achieved by means of the integral liberation and simultaneous national revolutionary insurrection of all the nations within and outside the USSR which are subjugated by the Kremlin The separate liberation of any one nation is impossible, all the more so if the Free World maintains a passive attitude.

The riots organized by the prisoners in Vorkuta, Kingiri, and Norilsk on the initiative of the Ukrainian fighters for freedom, the workers' insurrections in Berlin and Poznan, like the revolt in Hungary, have shown that a national revolution is possible even under the conditions of Russian Bolshevik terror. The most important achievement of all these insurrections is the fact that the people have overcome their fear of the totalitarian Russian and Communist system. This change of attitude on the part of the masses is a factor of the utmost importance which will prove decisive for the future fate of the Soviet regime. The fact that the younger generation and the workers have now become the vanguard of the revolution is evidence of the complete failure of materialistic training, of the Marxist-Leninist doctrine of class conflict and of the theory of the dictatorship of the proletariat. The weapon of Marx and Lenin in the fight against capitalism and the guarantee of a capitalistic defeat—a general strike— has, in the hands of the workers, become the most dangerous weapon against Marxism-Leninism as the expression of modern Russian imperialism. The younger generation, on whom Communism had set all its hopes, has now become the champion of the national anti-Communist and anti-Russian fight for freedom. The mask worn by Communism as a disguise for the Russian lust of conquest has been torn aside. Communism of every kind, including national Communism, has been rejected in principle by the masses of the farming and working classes and by the younger generation.

"Down with the Russians! Down with Communism of every kind!" were the leading slogans of the revolution for freedom. The fact that about 15,000 Ukrainian soldiers of the Soviet Army went over to the side of the Hungarian freedom fighters—a fact which, incidentally, was reported in the world press—proves that the USSR is no longer to be regarded as a monolithic unit. And it also brings home to the world the fact that 53 percent of the soldiers of the Soviet Army are non-Russians, who will join forces with the national fighters for freedom against the Russian subjugators. The precondition which would speed up this process would be the proclamation of a Great Charter of State Independence of the Nations and, above all, the disintegration of the Russian empire into national states.

The fact that Ukrainian, White Ruthenian, and other non-Russian soldiers of the Soviet Army went over to the side of the insurgents clearly shows that the vulnerable spot of Bolshevism, as a form of Russian and, in fact, any imperialism, is definitely the national problem. This leads to the logical conclusion that the anti-Bolshevik and anti-imperialist national idea of liberation, embodied in the national, democratic state sovereignty of every one of the peoples subjugated by Moscow (whether in the USSR or among the so-called satellites) and a just social order for the welfare of the workers and farmers are the guiding principles of the liberation revolution. The disintegration of the Russian empire, whatever its political color may be, and the elimination of every form of Communism and every system of social and economic exploitation are, therefore, the main aims of every future revolution in Eastern Europe which can count on success.

It must be borne in mind that the Russians in the USSR only constitute 47 percent of the population, and this is not even counting the population of the so-called satellite countries, which amounts to 88 million. These figures likewise indicate the importance of the national problem in the Bolshevik-controlled territory.

The fact that Kossuth and not Horthy has become the symbol of the present national revolution in Hungary is, moreover, an indication of the social nature of this revolution and of its anti-Moscow attitude. Kossuth was the hero of the Hungarian war of liberation which was waged against Russia in 1849, when the army of the Tsar, in keeping with the spirit of "enlightened despotism" of the absolute rulers at the time, put down the national rising.

If one sets one's hopes on national liberation revolutions, then it is logical that there must be planned and systematic action among the soldiers of the Soviet Army so that they accordingly direct their weapons against the subjugator and go over to the side of the revolution. The Hungarian revolution is, in the first place, a war of liberation against alien, in this case Russian, occupation. Moreover, every form of imperialism towards neighboring peoples is alien to the

Hungarian revolution; it is solely the idea of liberating their own people, without any claims of "historical pretensions" to foreign countries, which has mobilized the Hungarian masses. The recipe for success is the releasing of national revolutionary chain reactions in all the countries subjugated by Moscow, which process must be actively supported by the Free World. The preparation of this synchronized and coordinated liberation campaign requires such active support on the part of the West, for Moscow and Bolshevism are not only our enemies, but also the enemies of the whole world.

An essential precondition for the success of the revolution is the setting up of a political planning center, which would be acquainted with the treacherous and sly methods of Russian imperialism. It was precisely the fact that there was no such center which made itself felt during the Hungarian revolution. Both regular divisions and divisions of the insurgents stood by inactively in Hungary, while the Russians slyly carried on negotiations regarding the transfer of their troops and at the same time concentrated new forces, only to arrest the Hungarian commanders who had been invited to take part in these negotiations, in this way to undermine the revolution from the military point of view. There can be no doubt about the fact that Nagy, who, since he himself is a Communist trusted Moscow, was to blame for this state of affairs. The national revolutionary representatives of the anti-Communist and anti-Russian attitude which prevailed in Hungary would not have committed the mistakes made by Nagy, who, after all, was only a supporter of but not an active fighter for the revolution. Nagy's Communist mentality and his pro-Russian attitude were likewise obvious when he naively trusted Kadar and left the Yugoslav embassy; even the lesson he should already have learned failed to cure him of his blindness. Furthermore, it was obvious that Kadar was "the wooden horse of Troy" that had been smuggled into Nagy's Government by Moscow, but Nagy, a national Communist who had been trained to respect Moscow's "magnanimity," failed to realize this. Thus, the consequence to be drawn by the West is, that if it wishes to be victorious over Russian imperialism, it must set its hopes only on the national liberation forces and not on the national Communist ones.

The relaxing of the regime of the so-called satellites to the limits of Titoism means the collapse of every kind of liberation policy. The masses will spontaneously exceed these limits and in the end will have to face Russian tanks. For this reason, the only method which promises success is the drawing up of an extensive plan for the final revolution, confrontation with Bolshevism—that is to say, for the preparation of the national liberation revolution, organized by national forces who have never collaborated with Communism or Russian imperialism.

The preparation and planning of this form of national liberation revolution eliminates the "tragic surprises" which occurred in the case of Hungary, since it includes as its main aim large-scale, general, and completely anti-Communist and anti-Russian "surprises."

It is a precondition for the successful coordination of the revolutionary fight for freedom of the subjugated peoples that the national liberation organizations and centers in exile, as representatives of the national liberation forces in their native countries, should be regarded by the Western major powers as contracting parties, instead of these same powers allowing them to be destroyed from within by subversive activity, as was the case so far.

The West shall give its support on the strength of its recognition of the national liberation idea—that is to say, the disintegration of the Russian empire and of all other artificial and forcibly created state structures of several nations of the same type in the Muscovite sphere of influence into national states, within their own ethnographical frontiers and with a just, democratic social order. The representatives of the national fight for freedom are to be treated by the West as partners with equal rights. This means that the West should place the means of conducting a psychological war at the disposal of the representatives of the liberation movement and should allow them a free hand in planning and carrying on this war in keeping with the organized liberation insurrection; it also means that the method of trying to exert purely tactical and cyclical pressure on the Kremlin which has been practiced by "Radio Free Europe," "Radio Liberty" and "The Voice of America" should cease. A positive attitude on the part of the West towards the plan to destroy the Bolsheviks from within by means of national liberation revolutions and technical support of the cooperation of the national liberation organizations with their representatives abroad would make a systematic, coordinated and synchronized action possible, would facilitate the political and strategic planning and organizing of the liberation revolution, and would result in a double exchange of ideas from the point of view of the subjugated countries and the free countries. "Radio Free Europe," "Radio Liberty" and "The Voice of America" have given encouragement to the subjugated peoples, have held out hopes to them and made promises, but at the crucial moment have left them in the lurch; they have treated the freedom fighters of Hungary as their helpmates, only to acquiesce to the partition of the world into two parts and to continue to respect the status quo, a fact which at present characterizes the main aim of American policy.

A change of attitude on the part of the West as regards the splitting up, demobilization and discrimination of the representatives of the liberation fight in exile would lead to an intensification of the fight in the subjugated countries, in accord with the slogans which are proclaimed by the representatives of the liberation fight in exile.

The chain reaction of revolutions would destroy the prison of nations from within. In order that this aim may be achieved, however, the Free World must give its support from without and must approve of and agree to the plan of the national liberation organizations, on the basis of the ideology of the ABN.

The UPA has again resorted to measures to prevent the transportation of reinforcements for the Muscovite occupation troops in Hungary via Ukraine and to stop the deportation of Hungarian freedom fighters from Hungary to Russia via Ukraine. This is the beginning of a chain reaction, but it is one which is not coordinated.

The aim of the Western world should be to set its hopes on the national liberation revolution and to prepare them by means of a coordination center of the national, revolutionary liberation organizations, on this side of the Iron

Curtain, which represent the fundamental principles of national state independence, democratic freedoms and social justice, as well as by definitely excluding an agrarian social order in favor of big landowners or an industrial social order in favor of capitalism and by opposing every form of Communism. Experience has already proved that big landowners and capitalists, like all forms of "classical" capitalism, are definitely a thing of the past.

The recipes resorted to by the statesmen of the West, which above all prescribe practical indifference to the processes going on behind the Iron Curtain and definitely stress non-intervention and the fact that one should wait and see how events develop and turn out, are certainly favorable to Bolshevism. The example of Hungary has shown that "waiting and seeing" have led to the genocide of the Hungarian people.

Not only do the states of the West want us to act as a cat's paw for them, but they also want to achieve temporary successes at our expense by bargaining with the USSR.

The UPA, the riots in Berlin and Poznan, and the insurrections of the Ukrainian prisoners in the concentration camps of Vorkuta, Kingiri and Norilsk have shown that it is possible, with the help of national liberation revolutions, to destroy the Russian Bolshevik empire from within and thus prevent an atomic, that is, a world war. The policy of liberation is the means to prevent such a war, the policy of co-existence, on the other hand, is the surest way to start an atomic war, which would logically break out as a result of coexistence.

It stands to reason that revolutionaries and revolutions cannot be suppressed by atomic bombs.

ABN Correspondence,
March-April 1957, pp. 1-2, 11

After the Cuban Crisis

Public opinion the world over, formed by numerous mysterious forces, is still acclaiming President Kennedy's victory in the Cuba conflict as an event of far-reaching historical significance. But none of the prominent publicists who voice their opinion in this respect trouble to subject the true nature of this event to a thorough analysis.

Just before the US Congressional elections were due to take place, President Kennedy made some fairly drastic statements in order to influence public policy. And he partly succeeded in doing so. True, Khrushchev had the bases for his ground-rockets on Cuba demolished, but at what price? President Kennedy on his part promised not to intervene in Cuba. He guaranteed the further existence of Fidel Castro's Communist regime, that is to say, he recognized the right of Russia to intervene in the affairs of the American continent. Hence the legality of Castro's regime is guaranteed not only by Russia but also by the USA. And herein lies Khrushchev's victory. He may have liquidated the rocket bases on Cuba, but President Kennedy on the other hand promised that he would make no attempt to liquidate the Communist regime in Cuba. In other words, Cuba will continue to remain a center for the dissemination of Communism on the American continent which has been recognized as legal by the USA. What right has Moscow to intervene in the affairs of the American continent, and why does President Kennedy recognize the right of the Russians to be allowed to have a say in the Western hemisphere? True, Khrushchev has had rocket bases on Cuba demolished—if we accept this as the truth! But at the same time he has forcibly obtained the right to solve—together with the Americans—those problems which exclusively concern the Western world and moreover constitute the most internal affairs of the American continent. But that is not all!

For Khrushchev is now posing before the whole world as a "peacemaker," and the world press is singing his praises for having "saved peace" and for having protected the world from the horrors of an atomic war. Is this really true? Khrushchev had stowed away weapons in Cuba which were intended for an attack against the USA; he thus wanted to keep America in check by the threat of an attack on New York, Washington, and other towns if President Kennedy was not prepared to make any compromises—that is to say, concessions in Moscow's favor. And Khrushchev has actually obtained a concession by force, for he has secured the right to be allowed to have a say in American problems.

The Russians once owned Alaska, and in the days of the tsars they usurped the right to intervene in the affairs of Venezuela. They also sought to obtain the right to be allowed to have a say in decisions pertaining to the affairs of America. President Kennedy has now at last conceded this right to Moscow by promising Khrushchev that he will not attempt to liquidate Castro's Bolshevik regime in Cuba, which threatens to disintegrate the whole of America by force. Surely this can hardly be described as a victory on the part of the USA!

Incidentally, it is perfectly obvious that Khrushchev could not in any case have risked a world war, for his actual power lies in his policy of intimidation. Russia has always—both in the tsarist era and at the present time—been wont to yield under pressure of the strength of her opponents. Moscow is afraid of revolutions within its empire, since it knows only too well that the peoples enslaved by the Russians would rise up in revolt immediately should an opportunity present itself. For this reason Khrushchev could not afford to risk a world war on account of Cuba. It is by no means true that Khrushchev saved peace, as the opportunists of the Free World, who have been caught in the propaganda net of the Kremlin, so persistently proclaim to the world. For it was the Kremlin that would have caused a war by setting up rocket bases in Cuba which were directed against the USA. After this provocation Khrushchev had his rocket bases dismantled—if this is true and the rockets are not still concealed in subterranean hiding-places—and thereupon the naive world was beside itself with joy and enthusiastically acclaimed Khrushchev as a peacemaker! It is indeed most regrettable and disappointing that the Western world allows itself to be deceived in this way.

It is quite possible that Khrushchev is also hatching other plans; for it is highly probable that, having intimidated President Kennedy with the rocket bases on

Cuba, he wanted to force him to make further concessions, as for instance in Berlin, Vietnam, etc. For everyone must surely be aware of the fact that South Vietnam is slowly but systematically passing into the hands of the Communists, whilst Laos is almost completely ruled by them. And the same danger threatens Berlin. It will probably not be long before a Russian-American compromise is reached with regard to the former capital of Germany, for the following facts seem to indicate this possibility.

The Secretary-General of the United Nations, U Thant, has dropped the question of Hungary from the agenda of the UN and, at the same time, has prohibited broadcast programs to this country, whereas Kadar has invited the UN Secretary-General to Budapest. Hence Kadar is apparently approved of by the UN and thus also by the USA. This obvious triumph was undoubtedly achieved by Khrushchev during the Russian-American dispute regarding Cuba.

Khrushchev is allegedly a peacemaker. But why does no one raise the question as to what right he had to set up rocket bases on Cuba and why he set them up! One can draw the following parallel: a thief raids your house. You chase him off the premises with the threat that you are going to shoot him. The thief makes off but he reserves the right to decide who is to be the owner of your house. And you are glad that you have overpowered the thief.

The Russians raised the demand that, in exchange for the withdrawal of their bases from Cuba, the US bases in Turkey and Italy should be liquidated. And though it appears that the Americans did not accept this demand, they in fact have, for the bases are being liquidated.

President Kennedy could have completely overcome Moscow, for under the present conditions it would by no means want to risk a world war. As we have already pointed out, Moscow is terrified of revolutions breaking out in its empire. Hence it is not solely due to the USA that Khrushchev undertook to withdraw his rocket bases on Cuba. Though it may sound strange to the West— peace was saved by Ukrainians and by the other enslaved peoples, whom Moscow fears so much. No wonder Khrushchev was alarmed when he found himself confronted by the risk of a world war. Peace was saved for the Western world by the rebellious miners in the Donets Basin and the Ukrainian dockworkers in Odessa, who refused to load the ships bound for Cuba, and also by the Ukrainian nationalist revolutionaries who organized these miners and dockworkers. Peace was saved by Ukraine and by the other peoples enslaved by Russia, by their constant fight for liberation, for which reason Moscow rightly fears lest its empire, enforced by violence, might be destroyed.

The West should be grateful to the heroes of Ukraine and to the other subjugated peoples for having saved its peace. It is indeed most regrettable that the Western world still fails to comprehend the invincible spirit which spurs on the subjugated peoples to continue their uncompromising fight against the Russian subjugators. The sooner the West realizes this fact, the more will it and true peace on earth benefit.

The Ukrainian Review,
No. I, 1963, pp. 3-5

A Year of Disappointments

The Hungarian revolution evoked a considerable response all over the world. The immediate reaction of the Western communities was excellent. The trade unions demanded the severance of all connection with the empire of tyranny and a general boycott of everything connected with the Russian Communist peoples' prison. But before a year had passed, all had been forgotten. The statesmen of the West deplore the downfall of the same Zhukov who ruthlessly crushed the Hungarian revolution, inasmuch as they regard him as "better" than Khrushchev, and Khrushchev, on the other hand, who is just as much a hangman as Zhukov, for unfathomable reasons as "better" than Malenkov. As is well known, Malenkov was dismissed from office at the beginning of 1955 because he wanted to expand the light industries at the expense of the heavy industries which Khrushchev considered of primary importance. Why then should the Free World prefer Khrushchev to Malenkov? Why should it put its trust in this hangman of Ukraine, who affirms "urbi et orbi" that he is as good a Stalinist as Stalin himself? And why, on the other hand, should a Russian chauvinist and Moscow satrap such as Zhukov, whose ultimate aim was the final Russification of the Soviet empire and a large-scale attack on the Free World, be more acceptable to the latter than Khrushchev, who, incidentally, likewise aims to consolidate that Soviet empire and also to fetter Titoslavia to this imperium? And why should the possible formation of a new Cominform, whose task would be to continue its subversive activity in the countries of the Free World, according to plan, and systematically be regarded as proof of a love of peace?

Can it be that one has already forgotten the era of the NEP (the "New Economic Policy" of 1921-1927), when there were far greater "facilities" than is the case today? The NEP "thaw," however, could not be compared with the Gomulka regime, still less with the Khrushchev regime. But the question obtrudes itself as to whether this "thaw" was due to the "good will" of the Bolshevik hangmen and not to the necessity which faced them, of having to save themselves and their system from sudden ruin. But even today the West still sets its hopes on the Khrushchev regime instead of on those processes which force Khrushchev to veer in his course in order to lessen somewhat the ever-increasing pressure from below—that is, on the part of the peoples subjugated by Moscow. During the past years Stalin's birthday was passed over in silence by the Moscow official Party organ *Pravda*, but this year it paid homage to him as the "outstanding champion of the cause of Communism, as a loyal Marxist and Leninist, and as an unswerving revolutionary." In Stalin's native town a museum is to be founded which delegations from all the countries of the Soviet Union and from abroad are to visit. Radio Moscow has announced that it will wage a "relentless war" on "all those who defame Stalin." Thus, Khrushchev's "de-Stalinization" is formally coming to an end.

The Free World rejoiced at Khrushchev's victory over his rivals, for this was supposed to be the beginning of a "peaceful course." Meanwhile, Khrushchev stabilized his monocratic power by eliminating those rivals in the Party Presidium who had *any* ideas of their own and in this way might cause internal differences of opinion. Surely, the elimination of rivals and the equalization of state power is not so much proof of the weakness of the Party but rather of the centralization of the State, which, rid of all opposition, will concentrate on the annexation of new territories with even greater energy. In this respect it is immaterial whether Khrushchev happens to be the last descendant of the old worthies. In any case, the process of consolidation in the Party Presidium has increased. But is this to the advantage of the West? It is surprising that the open rejection of the suggestion of the NATO Conference still allows the West to entertain further illusions regarding negotiations "on the highest level" (which is what Khrushchev is trying to force on President Eisenhower). On what basis? Exclusively on that of the status quo. This means that the Soviet Russian empire would continue to exist not within its framework of 1939, but within that of 1957—that is to say, with the inclusion of its "zones of influence" in Asia, Africa, and elsewhere, as it sees fit. This is nothing more than a demand for the complete capitulation of the Free World. And it is indeed disgusting that in this connection the press of the Free World talks about the "successes" of the NATO policy so far and about those of the Free World. In the NATO resolutions this time, not a word is mentioned about the satellite states, nor about Poland, for whose sake the war with Hitler was started, nor even about Hungary, for whom crocodile tears were shed.

And what about Sputnik? It is true that it is an outstanding scientific achievement. But is the fact borne in mind that this achievement has cost the blood and sweat of millions of slaves? Could this invention have been achieved without the starvation of scores of millions?

The world will fall into an abyss unless at the last moment men are found who have the courage to shoulder the responsibility for bold decisions in an uncompromising fight against Bolshevism and who will not content themselves with the status quo, but will face and fight tyranny. The sooner this happens, the better. There is no possibility of a coexistence of long duration; only one side can be victorious, and to temporize is grist for the mill of Bolshevism. On the quiet, the West sets its hopes on the internal downfall of Bolshevism, without, however, making the least attempt to help to bring about this process. If it does not support the national liberation movements in the USSR it cannot count on the automatic collapse of Bolshevism. What, then, is it hoping for? It does not want to pursue an active policy of liberation: in fact, it agrees with the status quo, and it does not know how to counteract Moscow's aggression either in Asia or in Africa. Kennan once again recommends a suicidal policy on the basis of the capitulation of the West, inasmuch as he tries to make the Free World believe in the fatal idea that a decade of Communist rule has changed the national soul of the peoples in the satellite countries to such an extent that they are no longer interested in establishing states in which the individual enjoys freedom, but have become accustomed to slavery and, therefore, must be crossed off the list of freedom-loving peoples and must be regarded as permanent slaves. Thus, neither the Hungarian revolution nor the Poznan riots, neither events in the Soviet concentration camps nor the two-front war of the UPA have taught the West a lesson!

It is true that the Hungarian revolution was crushed not solely because the West failed to help Hungary (for, in view of the character of the present leading political elite, its help could not be counted on at all), but for quite different reasons. Like every revolution that has been crushed so far, the Hungarian revolution was defeated because its internal revolutionary principle was too limited. Instead of turning to the indifferent West, one should concentrate one's attention on the East, on the peoples subjugated by Moscow, whom one could fire with such enthusiasm that they join in the fight. In order to be successful, the Hungarian revolution—and we do not wish in any way to disparage its unexampled heroism—should have advocated *universal* national and social ideas, which would have fired other peoples with enthusiasm and prompted them to join in the fight and should have had a strategic plan regarding the annihilation of the entire Soviet empire and not solely a limited, local plan which was only concerned with Hungary. The Hungarian revolution was neither a revolution of the French type from the ideological point of view, nor a revolution of the Bolshevik type as regards its extent and impulse. What was lacking in this revolution of heroes was a broad standard of discernment on the part of the leading political elite, which should have realized the organic connection between the Hungarian national fight for freedom and the simultaneous fight for freedom of Ukraine or Turkestan; hence its failure.

The fact that the other peoples subjugated by Moscow were not ready to fight is another matter. An immediate and decisive victory would only have been achieved had a revolution broken out simultaneously in all the countries ruled by the Soviet Union; but the Hungarian revolutionaries had not yet acquired the political discernment needed to deal with such a question. And, incidentally, the Hungarian revolution was too spontaneous to have a broad political and strategic plan. Nor are the Hungarian national emigrants in any way to blame for this fact for the tasks which confronted the Hungarian revolution outgrew the efficiency of the Hungarian people, who had never been faced by such far-reaching tasks— just as the external world had never been as indifferent to heroism, martyrdom, and the noblest ideas as it was on this occasion. And the Ukrainians, for instance, who have had an enormous lot of experience as regards revolutions, would probably not have behaved any differently in exile if they had been faced by a similar situation. That is why the leading political class needs to have a revolutionary doctrine which it has not only worked out most carefully, but has also adopted as its own; but where could the inexperienced—but nevertheless heroic—Hungarians have obtained such a doctrine?

Throughout Hungary national and social ideas—and also ideas of a heroic humanism—should have been proclaimed, ideas which would pertain to all peoples and not only to the Hungarians. Radio stations and all means of propaganda should have turned not so much to the West as to the peoples subjugated by Moscow, so that the latter, themselves having become insurgents, would then exhort all those who value freedom and human dignity to join in the revolution. It would be better to count on the non-Russian troops of the Soviet Army, on the Ukrainian, Turkestanian, Georgian, and other insurgents rather than on American paratroops, on Chiang Kai-shek, Ngo Dinh Diem, and Syngman Rhee rather than on Eisenhower. The Hungarian revolution was defeated the moment Nagy, under pressure on the part of politically inexperienced revolutionaries, decided in favor of neutrality—namely when he announced Hungary's resignation from the Warsaw Pact. This was a gesture in the sense of Western orientation, a gesture which was to create a situation "acceptable to both sides"—something like the fantastic German neutrality according to Ollenhauer.... In order to win over the other subjugated peoples to their side, the Hungarian revolutionaries should have exhorted them to join in the life and death struggle against Moscow; instead of which, however, their declaration of neutrality acted as an immediate damper on the desire of these peoples to support the Hungarian revolution. The peoples subjugated by Moscow were forced to realize that it was a question of a local fight without a wide horizon and without inclusion of national revolutions throughout the entire Soviet Union and in Moscow's sphere of influence. It is no good resorting to half-measures in such a situation; one must stake all, just as Cromwell, Lenin, and Kemal Atatürk did, and just as Khmelnytsky did, who said, "Two walls will collide and one of them will collapse." The heroic Hungarian revolutionaries failed to realize this motto in its wider sense; and, actually, Nagy allowed the Hungarian revolution to become isolated from the fight for freedom of all the other subjugated peoples.

Indeed, it was a cardinal error that the revolution from beginning to end was headed by men such as Nagy, who, instead of having all sorts of Kadar adherents shot, calmly allowed out-and-out Rakosi supporters to demobilize the revolution. One is horrified, on reading General Kiraly's memoirs in the February (1957) issue of *Life*, to learn how very naive and trusting Nagy was as regards Moscow, how he believed right to the end that Moscow was acting sincerely, and how he forbade General Kiraly to fire on the Russian tanks when the latter—numbering 4,000—had already begun to re-enter the capital. And how naive were such men as Maletar of Istvan Kovacz—undoubtedly men of outstanding personality, but trained in the Communist spirit—who believed the treacherous Russians when they affirmed that they would withdraw.... No, national Communists will never be able to conduct a revolution directed against Moscow successfully, for they are ideologically too dependent on Moscow.

There were obviously various other reasons for the failure of the Hungarian revolution, but we do not wish to discuss them here; our intention to stress the facts which are usually overlooked completely and which are becoming more and more apparent when regarded in relation to the past year—just as is the case with respect to the entire historical significance of the Hungarian revolution. As matters stand, even if the Hungarian revolution had pursued the course which we advised above, this would by no means have been a guarantee for its immediate and decisive success, for the collapse of the Russian empire, which, after all, is the only possible way to achieve the genuine and permanent liberation of the Hungarian people and of the other subjugated peoples. No, the matter is not as simple as all that, and it is by no means out of the question that it was precisely the other peoples subjugated by Moscow who in the autumn of 1956 were not ready to start a simultaneous revolution. And yet, every national anti-Bolshevik revolution should aim to achieve this simultaneous outbreak: if it does so, its chances of success will be far greater than if it only appeals to the West for help, for political events in the world during the past year have gradually caused or, at least, ought to cause the West to have some doubts as to the wisdom of its choice of methods of "containment," "coexistence," and other compromises. Whichever part of the world one considers—Northwest Africa, Egypt, Syria, or Indonesia— wherever Bolshevik infiltration has only or mainly had to face Western defense methods, it has had an easy game in this respect in 1957, for neither the Bolshevik nor any other form of totalitarianism can be defeated successfully by half-hearted and ideologically incomplete countermeasures.

ABN Correspondence,
May-June 1958, pp. 9-10

Adenauer or Garibaldi?

Free elections or revolution? A plebiscite on paper, or a plebiscite of bloodshed? Ollenhauer's and Ulbricht's delegations at a roundtable together, or armed masses in the streets of Berlin?

As far as their political initiative on the anti-Bolshevik front is concerned, the Governments of the Western major powers have gotten into a blind alley. Almost every week Moscow puts forward new propositions, which in essence always remain the same, and Mr. Eisenhower, Mr. Macmillan, and Mr. Adenauer hasten to express their attitude to them; their political opponents in the Free World, however, never tire of stressing the "necessity" of new counter-propositions, again and again—either on the strength of the so-called Rapacki plan, or on the strength of the possibility of conducting direct negotiations with the Pankow Government.

On the other hand, however, it is an absolute certainty that Moscow does not intend to accept any compromise on the German problem. Germany's unification is only acceptable to Russia provided that the whole of Germany becomes a satellite of Russia; and for this reason the Russians are not likely to sanction free elections or any other formula which might make any regime other than the Communist one possible in the united Germany. Nor are the Russians likely to accept the idea of a neutralization of the united, free Germany, since a people numbering more than 70 million is bound to abandon its neutrality sooner or later; Germany is not Austria, let alone Switzerland. Moscow will thus do its utmost to uphold the status quo, and all the propositions of a union which it puts forward or inspires have one and the same aim—namely, to disseminate propaganda, to mislead those who are naive, and to spread defeatism and confusion. The possible withdrawal of Russian troops from East Germany, provided that the American and British troops were withdrawn from West Germany at the same time, would be no risk for Moscow, but, on the contrary, solely an advantage; for, in the event of an open revolt against Ulbricht and Grotewohl, Soviet tanks from Poland would enter Berlin within a few hours' time—"at the invitation of the legal government of a sovereign state" (as has already been the case in Budapest); on the other hand, the withdrawal of American troops would cause a psychological shock, the far-reaching effects of which cannot be estimated, not only to Germany, but also to the entire West European world. Such a step would also cause considerable disappointment and, above all, arouse a feeling of distrust towards the USA among the nations subjugated by Russia, and in this way the status quo would be strengthened still further.

Excluding the possibility of a Third World War, there is, therefore, no genuine way of bringing about the reunification of Germany, save by means of a revolution, or, to be more precise, by a revolutionary war of liberation; for the reunification of Germany means the liberation of the Soviet Zone of Germany and its incorporation in the Federal Republic of Germany. It is true that in principle Mr. Adenauer's formula of "free elections" is flawless, but, under the given circumstances, it is not feasible and, in fact, utopian. It is absolutely impossible for Moscow to make any concessions whatever in this direction— both for ideological and political reasons. What a disgrace it would be for the idea of Communism as such, if the suppressed majority of the population in the so-called "German Democratic Republic" were to opt for "capitalism" (which is what would undoubtedly happen in the event of free elections there, as the Kremlin knows only too well). On the other hand, it goes without saying that a shifting of the Iron Curtain eastward would create a favorable psychological situation for anti-Russian revolts in Poland, Hungary, Ukraine, etc. Not to mention the strategic and economic results of the liberation of the Soviet Zone of Germany.

In no case and under no circumstances will the Russians agree to free elections. The fact that they recently made the problem of Berlin a current one again is merely a diversive maneuver, and their peculiar "ultimatum" merely a piece of bluffing. It is a propaganda trick, which relies on the naiveté and ignorance of its victims, in particular, of the Afro-Asian peoples, who have not the least inkling of the Party career of an Ulbricht or a Pieck in Soviet Russia and so far have failed to realize that no Communist party (apart from the Russian one) is a party of the nation in which it exists since all serve Soviet Russian imperialism.

In the present Berlin crisis a strong American "no," together with a threat of armed intervention, would make Khrushchev smart.

And thus the whole affair would blow over. Not negotiations but firmness is the only prescription for Russia.

The only genuine way to achieve a reunification of Germany lies in the liberation of the Soviet Zone of Germany, by means of universal support (armed support, too) for a possible revolt by the Germans in the Soviet Zone—by means of support on the part of the Western major powers, including the Federal Republic of Germany. Any other plan is merely self-deception. The reunification of Germany had a good chance to materialize in June 1953, when the non-Russian soldiers of the Soviet Army, in particular the Ukrainians, and the German soldiers of Ulbricht and Grotewohl refused to fire on the insurgent German workers. On that occasion, the American divisions should have hastened to their aid. However, they waited, while the revolutionary masses bled to death. The USA failed completely, just as it failed later on as regards Poznan and

Budapest and, previously, as regards the Ukrainian Insurgent Army (UPA). If the Berlin uprising of June 1953 were to be repeated, is the Free World prepared not to fail this time? And if not—what, then, is the sense of the whole psychological war?

But are the masses of the nations subjugated by Russia also prepared to resort to an armed revolt? No, not under the present conditions behind the Iron Curtain and, above all, not in view of the present policy of the Western Powers. But the time is near for a wave of popular wrath to break out, for the striving for national freedom and independence and social freedom and justice cannot be crushed for ever. And in view of this approaching hour, the national revolutionary forces of the subjugated peoples should already have a coordinated and synchronized plan and act accordingly.

There can be no denying the fact that Chancellor Adenauer had contributed enormously to the reconstruction of Germany, and that he is expanding the armed fighting forces of the free Germany in the right way, and is right in holding them in readiness as a trump-card for all negotiations; but it is essential that there should be concord between the fighting forces of free Germany and the insurgent Germans of the Soviet Zone, and this is a task which will require new forces. Germany will need a German Garibaldi, who will have to achieve what the German Cavour failed to accomplish.... And yet, the personalities of Cavour and Garibaldi remain inseparable in the history of Italy.

But nowadays the regionally limited liberation of any one nation from the Russian yoke is a sheer impossibility. Just as the problem of Berlin cannot be solved without the liberation of the Soviet Zone of Germany, so too the German reunification in freedom cannot be achieved without the permanent liberation of other nations which have been deprived of their freedom by Moscow, and without the disintegration of the Russian empire as such. Either the liberation of all these nations is achieved by the united efforts of all, or else the entire world which is still free will be inundated by the dark and sinister Russian element. Without a free Warsaw, Budapest, Sofia, Prague, Pressburg, etc., there can be no free East Berlin; without a free Kyiv, Minsk, Tiflis, or Tashkent, the present satellite states will sink to the level of "national" republics of the U.S.S.R. (as has already happened in the case of Estonia, Latvia, and Lithuania). There is no indication that Chancellor Adenauer is aware of this fact. And herein lies the tragedy and impracticability of all the plans cherished by the Western Powers regarding the reunification of Germany and the anti-Communist fight in general.

Hardly anyone in the West believed in the possibility of mass revolts in Berlin, Poznan, Budapest, in the Soviet concentration camps in Vorkuta, Norylsk, Mordovia, etc., and in what happened in Tibet and various West Chinese territories until they actually happened. Tomorrow further revolts will take place. Only a statesman who, in his action, takes heed not only of the present, but also, and above all, of the morrow will have a lasting influence on the history of his people.

ABN Correspondence,
January-February 1959, p. 3

Prospects of a Franco-German Alliance

During his recent stay in Paris the President of the Anti-Bolshevik Bloc of Nations (ABN), Yaroslav Stetsko, had an opportunity to answer a number of questions put to him regarding current political problems. We publish some of these questions and answers below.

QUESTION: *In your opinion what part will the German-French alliance play in the anti-Bolshevik fight on a global scale?*

ANSWER: The liquidation of the French and German conflict—if this proves to be of a permanent nature—will undoubtedly strengthen the anti-Russian front. The purpose of the traditional orientation of France's foreign policy to "Great Russia"—that is to say, to the Russian empire as an ally of France—was to establish the political balance of power and the security of France in the face of Germany as a world power. For decades France's foreign policy counted on the Russian empire as an anti-German scourge in East Europe. Unfortunately, however, France overlooked the fact that individual national states such as Ukraine, Byelorussia, the Caucasus, and many other states, which were more prepared to defend their independence and freedom rather than intolerable Russian slavery, could have been her permanent allies. Germany under Hitler's regime lost the war not because there was a Russian empire, but because she ignored the idea of national freedom. Nor would an alliance on the part of France with the Russian empire have been of any avail to France if Germany had wholeheartedly and genuinely supported the explosive forces within the Russian empire. This was, unfortunately, not the case; hence not only Germany but also the Allies lost the last war. Incidentally, Bismarck's so-called pro-Russian policy was in principle anti-Russian, for it was based on Bismarck's constant fear lest Germany be encircled and strangled by Russia.

A reconciliation on the German front deprives the supporters of an indivisible Russia of their "patriotic" argument, according to which the preservation of the Russian empire is imperative in order to maintain a balance of power against the "constant" German enemy. In view of the actual international political situation, the French and German agreement concentrates its main forces against the main enemy, thus eliminating the remaining secondary fronts.

A permanent and genuine elimination of the French and German conflict will result in a completely different constellation of the European ratio of power and will objectively further the idea of the disintegration of the Russian empire, while, at the same time, rendering all activities for "patriotic" motives on the part of the Russian imperialists who are domiciled in various Western countries impossible.

QUESTION: *Practically all international meetings have the "unification of Germany" on their agenda. So far, however, the West has not achieved any positive result. Do you think that a separate liberation of Germany can be achieved?*

ANSWER: A separate liberation of any one of the countries enslaved by Russian imperialism is impossible. Still less can there be such a possibility in the case of East Germany which would bring about its reunification with the Federal Republic of Germany, since in this way a major power would be created in the heart of Europe; Russia lives in dread of this happening. For the Russian rulers in the Kremlin know only too well that the German people are industrious and, above all, versatile. Incidentally, Moscow will never cede a single strip of territory that it has once occupied. Moscow will only yield under pressure of force. The fact that Moscow will refuse to consent to a unification of Germany if it is to become anti-Communist has been made plain beyond all doubt by Stalin, Molotov, and Khrushchev. Djilas, too, corroborated this fact in his recent book. Hence it is surprising that there are still persons in the West who talk enthusiastically about a unification of Germany through the medium of negotiations. There has never been nor will there ever be such a possibility. For a unification "in freedom" would mean a liquidation of Communism in the East Zone of Germany—that is to say, in the so-called German Democratic Republic. And Moscow is hardly likely to reconcile itself to this idea and to accept the inevitable ideological, social, and political collapse of its system which would then ensue.

QUESTION: *Do you not believe that those persons who consider the possibility of a unification of Germany by peaceful means are thinking of the withdrawal of the Russian Bolshevik army of occupation from Austria after the war?*

ANSWER: A Communist system could never have been realized in the occupied territory of Austria, whereas the withdrawal of the West European Allied Forces and the neutralization of Austria has split up the NATO countries from the strategic point of view, inasmuch as the invasion of Austria on the part of Soviet Russian forces from Hungary is now possible. In any case, there can hardly be a comparison between Austria and Germany, for the former has a population of only 7 million, while the population of the latter numbers 70 million.... All the empty talk about a "unification of Germany in freedom and peace" is merely a self-deception. In this case one should talk not about a unification, but about a liberation. And a liberation can only be brought about through the medium of national liberation revolutions, which should be supported in all the enslaved countries, including the enslaved part of Germany, in every possible way by the West. If, in spite of all this, one still considers the East Zone of Germany to be a privileged country among the enslaved countries, then one is bound to come to the conclusion that there are still some Germans who erroneously regard themselves as members of a great and superior people. The East Zone of Germany will not be liberated before Ukraine, for example, is liberated.

QUESTION: *During recent years Moscow has been intent upon aggravating its relations with the West in order to carry on in a strained atmosphere negotiations, which were advantageous for Moscow. It used this tension, for instance, to bring up the Berlin question. Do you think any temporary stabilization of the situation as regards Berlin is at all possible?*

ANSWER: The situation as regards Berlin is at present such that it could only be "stabilized" if Berlin itself were engulfed. A permanent stabilization will only be possible after the collapse of the Russian empire. In the former case the complications would merely spread further westwards. In other words, the result would be not a stabilization but, on the contrary, further complications. In the latter case—that is to say, if the source of trouble were eliminated—peace would at last reign in the world. For as long as the Russian empire has not been destroyed, there can be no peace in the world. A way out of the blind alley, for which the Germans themselves are in part to blame, would have been the legal incorporation of Berlin in the German Federal Republic. This would still be a possibility today, for the Russians are not likely to risk a war on account of Berlin. The incorporation of the former capital of Germany in the German Federal Republic would then exempt Bonn from the tedious argument regarding the continued observance of the occupation statute, for this was laid down by the four occupation powers in the Potsdam Agreement.

Constant repetition of this argument regarding the valid and binding force of the Potsdam Agreement puts the German Federal Republic in the outmoded position of being under the control of an occupation statute, whereas this statute has long since been abolished in free Berlin. Actually a statute of partnership is in force there, while the German Federal Republic is still obliged to defend this statute from the point of view of the Potsdam Agreement. From the point of view of international law this argument is simply untenable. For one cannot legally argue against the presence of the *defenders of the freedom* of West Berlin—that is, the three allies of Germany—on the strength of the Potsdam dictate. For this reason the legal incorporation of a free Berlin in the Federal Republic as a new "Land" of the "Bund" is imperative. This step would most certainly not lead to war. Nor would a war ensue if the Allied Forces were to pull down the "Wall" in Berlin, or to march through the East Zone and thus ignore the controlling organs of the so-called German Democratic Republic. Moscow would not venture to start a world war as long as it was not convinced that the disintegration of the West had progressed to such an an extent that it would capitulate because it was afraid of atomic bombs. And at present the West has no intention of doing Moscow this favor.

QUESTION: *During the past few years some politicians in West Europe have attached considerable importance to the problem of the unification of Europe. In this connection they talk about a "supra-national" government but make no mention whatever of the nations under Russian-Bolshevik occupation. Do you think that the supra-national conception of a united Europe could be realized in practice?*

ANSWER: Those Western circles who seek to unite Europe and, in doing so, eliminate national characteristics and disregard national sovereignty—that is, the national interests of the countries in question—are in reality *anti-European*. For the idea of a united Europe can only be a truly European idea if it is based on the harmonization of the national interests of all the peoples of Europe, as well as on recognition of and regard for the essential intellectual, cultural, and political elements of every nation, and on many-sidedness and differentiation in unity. The existence of a *Europe of national countries*—and not a supra-national Europe—is certainly justifiable. Indeed we should endeavor to set up such a Europe. The idea of a nation and respect for human individuality as a fundamental part of the organic existence of every nation (without which all evolution is impossible) are conceptions created by Europe itself. And those who negate these conceptions are introducing anti-European elements into the world of European ideas.

Europe cannot be created out of assimilation—unlike the USA, which has been created out of the fusion of multinational elements; for Europe is the sum total of separate national individualities, which throughout the centuries have become one with its soil, and for this very reason, too, there can be no fusion of its peoples to form a so-called "Soviet" people. It is only by uniting national organisms which have formed in the course of centuries that a new Europe can be created. Otherwise one will seek to inject into Europe anti-European ideas under the guise of a unification of Europe, and the superior strength of one nation among many weaker nations will then be furthered with fine phrases about a solid and sound unification. Incidentally, Hitler also aimed to effect such a unification and he was certainly obsessed by the idea of a "new Europe."

QUESTION: *Lively discussions are held by Western politicians about the admission or inclusion of England in the United Europe. If this idea should materialize, would England's inclusion strengthen the organic structure of Europe?*

ANSWER: Yes, it would do so considerably, for it would mean a certain protection for the weaker nations among the three stronger ones. On the other hand, a certain "levelling process" might take place, in which case, after a certain time, the Walloons might become French and the Flemish people might become Germans. With her traditions and her regard for the national "ego," England would strengthen the organic element of an organized yet differentiated Europe very considerably....

QUESTION: *Certain leading political circles in France have recently broached the problem of an organically united Europe. What is your opinion in this respect?*

ANSWER: The present French conception of Europe for the most part takes into account the idea of its organic unity and not that of an anti-national Europe—that is to say, not that of a Europe which does not consist of national countries and is merely a geographical designation. The French who today support the idea of a differentiated Europe are, from the ideological point of view, more sincere Europeans than their opponents, who regard the national element as something outmoded which is allegedly holding up the unification of Europe. Recognition of individuality and respect for human dignity and for the freedom of the individual—that is to say, characteristic European ideas—thus render the Marxist socialist unification of the world and the victory of Marxism impossible, just as recognition of the idea of the nation prevents the victory of imperialism on a global scale and the enslavement of the world, which is what Moscow is aiming to achieve.

Just as there can be no European world without recognition of the individual and the nation, without the ancient Greek and Roman ideas and without Christianity, so too there can be no United Europe without the inclusion of the East European countries, including Ukraine and Georgia. If Europe only extends as far as the territory where the knout of the Russian barbarians at present enforces order, then it will rapidly head towards its own destruction, and the West European states will inevitably be transformed into colonies of anti-European Russia in the very near future.

Europe exists wherever men suffer for its ideas and sacrifice their lives for them. Togliatti in Rome and Thorez in Paris are traitors to Europe, even though they are European; but the Ukrainian prisoners in the tundras and taigas of Siberia are the champions and heroes of Europe.

QUESTION: *You not only visit the countries of Western Europe but also other continents and meet many prominent politicians of the Free World. We should be interested to hear whether, in your talks with such prominent foreigners, you have ascertained an appreciation of the ideas for which the ABN is fighting.*

ANSWER: For years we were decried as Nazis, reactionaries, chauvinists, etc., simply because we undauntedly championed the national idea and the universal idea of the independence of peoples and freedom of individuals. In due course our forecast began to prove true. Decades have elapsed since then. The collapse of the empires ensued relentlessly, and the victory of the national principle as regards a new order of the world can no longer be contested. *Freedom-loving nationalism has become a dominant idea and the motto of our epoch.*

The conceptions of territorial expansion, frequently disguised, and the forms of new empires have suffered a complete defeat. At the international conferences in various continents which I have attended, the ideas advanced by us have on practically every occasion carried the day. Other countries are showing more and more understanding and sympathy for these ideas. We are undoubtedly gaining more and more ground.

The abnegation of Russian colonialism is no longer a matter with which only the ABN occupies itself. Official spokesmen of the free nations also express ideas similar to those supported by the ABN. From countless talks which we have had with politicians of the Free World it is obvious that our causes and our ideas are assuming more and more significance in the world of today.

QUESTION: *I am afraid I have taken up a good deal of your time, but I should nevertheless like to ask you one more question. What is your view of the policy of the US State Department regarding the peoples enslaved by Moscow, a policy which surely is contrary to the resolution adopted by the US Congress?*

ANSWER: Sooner or later, the foreign policy of the US Government will in practice be obliged to defend our ideas and to become a policy of liberation. And this will be the case as soon as the genuine Americans and not the naturalized spokesmen of un-American interests, who belong to the camp of the supporters of the "indivisible Russia," are able to assert themselves.

Not the false policy which the State Department is pursuing at the instigation of Dean Rusk and which is harmful to the interests both of the USA and of all freedom-loving mankind, but the policy of the US Congress which is contained in its resolution of "Captive Nations Week" will be victorious in the end. For the US Congress, and not Dean Rusk, who merely happens to be the person who at the moment holds the post of Foreign Minister of the greatest world power, is the true representative of the will of the freedom-loving American people.

The most barbarous colonial empire in the world, the so-called USSR, will inevitably and relentlessly be destroyed. The historical process of our day will not come to a halt at the borders of the world of tyranny. The Russian prison of peoples will be destroyed from within by national, freedom-loving, anti-imperialist, anti-colonial, anti-Russian, and anti-Communist ideas and by the peoples languishing in the USSR who are inspired by these ideas.

Historical nemesis will undoubtedly overtake the Russian barbarians and they will be justly punished for the inhuman atrocities which they have committed against civilized mankind. If this does not occur during our lifetime, future generations will at least live to see this happen. And we are convinced that it will most certainly happen, for after darkness comes light!

Reported by B. Vitochynsky
ABN Correspondence,
November-December 1962, pp. 5-9

Ukraine and the Russian Invasion of the CSSR

Russia was motivated by two factors in attacking the CSSR: the fear of upheaval and possible revolt in Ukraine and the need for Moscow to move its strategic military bases close to the boundaries of the American sphere of influence—West Germany and neutral Austria. In Ukraine the situation has been at the boiling point for years. The presence of Russian troops in the CSSR, which now encircle Ukraine from Poland, Hungary, and the CSSR, gives Moscow a greater chance to put down revolts in Ukraine, and possible chain reactions of analogous revolts in other enslaved countries, than an open border with the CSSR. The CSSR has a Communist regime, but until a short while ago was not occupied by Russian troops. This could have given American troops an opportunity to advance into the CSSR, to surround the "GDR," and to wedge Western forces into the Russian imperial structure, thus strengthening the revolutionary course in Ukraine with all its consequences. The attaining of a new strategic position by Moscow through the occupation of the CSSR, and in particular the placement of its troops at the frontiers of the German Federal Republic and Austria, creates a new balance of power in Europe. Moscow has made a flank attack on the "GDR," as well as the surrounding of the Russian Army by the American forces through the CSSR, impossible, and has at the same time put the United States in danger of a thermonuclear war if the US forces were to march into the CSSR, where they would come into direct conflict with the Russian Army. Once more Churchill's old plan has fallen through. As is widely known, Churchill wanted to land troops in Yugoslavia during World War II so as to prevent the Russians at least from entering central Europe. Amidst changed conditions the Russians have once more blockaded the old British concept of wedging itself into the Russian sphere and breaking up Russian strategic military power, which is now becoming master of central Europe without the West being a threat to Russia as the British had hoped. More than that, Russian missiles can be found along the frontiers of free Germany and Austria and the whole NATO radar system is of no use. Russia is strategically dominant in the center of Europe. She has a 3:1 military advantage in conventional arms in comparison with NATO.

When we take into account the build-uo of the navy, which now stands second to that of the United States, the domination of the Mediterranean (where the

Russian navy is equal in strength to the American Sixth Fleet), the acquisition for the Russian empire of bridgeheads in Egypt or Algeria, the opening to the Indian Ocean, and the threat of the Russian fleet to the Italian ports, there is no doubt that Russian strength has grown externally, however weak it is internally.

In a broader political scheme, the occupation of the CSSR is a prerequisite to possible armed intervention in West Germany. There is no doubt that Russia has her own solution to the German problem: bringing together the "GDR" and FRG into one entity under a pro-Russian government, united under the Communist, pro-Russian flag. No suggestions from Bonn will appease Russia, because she does not and will not have any intention of conducting talks with Bonn. She does not need a national German but a satellite government. This is part of the political plan of Russia to prepare the ground for armed intervention in Germany. The first prerequisite has been carried out. Russian airborne paratrooper divisions have been posted on the frontiers of the CSSR. The politically "legal" preparation has begun. Moscow declares that "according to its obligations, which result from its treaty in Potsdam, the members of the anti-Hitler coalition are responsible for prohibiting German militarism and Hitlerism from rising again" (*Pravda*, 19. IX. 1968). The reference to its responsibilities towards the UN Charter gives a "legal" basis for armed intervention. Articles 53 and 107 of the UN Charter single out Germany as a permanent enemy, against which other countries which have signed the original Charter of the UN can intervene. By referring to these articles in 1948 the USSR by its veto prevented the UN from investigating the Berlin blockade; in 1960 the USSR also made impossible the debate about the position of German prisoners of war by citing Article 107 of the Charter. Moreover none of the countries of the great anti-Hitler coalition has declared that these articles are unlawful or are not obligatory. Even now, when the Russians have declared that they have a right to intervene in the internal affairs of Germany because "Nazism and militarism" are being revived, not one of the Western powers stated clearly and unequivocally that these articles of the UN Charter are now completely inapplicable. And so, at the request of Bonn, London stated: "In this situation articles about enemy countries cannot be applied," but in which situations they can be applied London did not say. Paris stated that Moscow's interpretation is "deceptive and inaccurate" but what the accurate interpretation is Paris did not say. Washington stressed that Articles 107 and 53 do not give Moscow the rights to "intervene" unilaterally by using arms in the Federal Republic of Germany...." But Washington was silent as to whether a multilateral intervention is possible. Instead, the Russians, in accordance with the opinion of their international jurist D.B. Levin, interpret the Potsdam treaty in a way which gives each signatory the right to intervene independently and individually, because each carries a separate responsibility for Germany as a whole. In this sense Moscow also explains the articles of the UN Charter. "International law is a form of class warfare," says D.B. Levin, and this means that it is also possible to intervene at any moment under the pretext of the interest of the proletariat or of some angry intellectuals hurt by "militarism and Nazism." In actual fact the answers of the Western allies not only gave no help to Bonn, but made the situation even more complicated, because not one of the powers stated clearly that *under no circumstances* could the Russians interpret Article 53 and 107 of the UN Charter or the Potsdam treaty as they see fit; on the contrary each left a little opening for Moscow.... Is this not a straightforward invitation to intervention?

The experience with Hungary in 1956 at the time of President Eisenhower and Dulles and the experience with the CSSR at the time of Johnson and Rusk manifest that the United States will not intervene on behalf of the victims. The USA is adhering to the conception of a world divided into two parts. In all probability it would not take armed action against Russia if she were to march into West Germany stating that in accordance with the UN Charter and the Potsdam treaty Russia was "preventing" the rebirth of "Nazism and militarism," and would be ready to negotiate in connection with the removal of her troops as soon as a really "democratic" government has been set up.... Of course, as a result of these talks the Russian divisions would remain on the Rhine "together with" the American and other forces.... With such a "conciliatory" posture the United States would not risk a nuclear war, because Moscow's retaliation would follow immediately. The conventional forces of NATO are outnumbered three to one, a substantial risk—with the present policy of neglecting to support the national liberation movement of nations subjected in the USSR and the satellite countries a risk too great to be taken. Therefore the United States would in all probability be willing to begin talks. From this point of view, the recent espionage affairs in Germany also have their significance. They are in a way also connected with Moscow's plans—for instance, the preparation of a *putsch* and with the help of the pro-Russian conspirators attempting a coup d'état, for the "protection of the world against the revival of German militarism and Nazism." Moscow's help is indispensable, so to speak. Under such a pretext Russian troops can enter West German territory.... It is possible that an admiral and a general would ask for "help" from Russia.... This far-reaching intelligence affair is consistent with political and "legal" preparation for intervention in Germany. A "blitzkrieg" in Germany carefully worked out from a strategic point of view, so as not to come into contact with the American forces, which could be blockaded by parachute formations' securing of key positions in Germany and in Bonn, would not necessarily lead to a nuclear war—if a direct clash with the American army is avoided.

Therefore, the occupation of the CSSR is a stepping stone from which it would be possible to overrun West Germany, and this means the rest of Europe. England, France, Italy, and Spain are capable of successfully opposing Russia even without help from the United States, but without the economic and military strength of Germany they are incapable of successful resistance—even more so when the nations enslaved by Moscow, the strongest explosive power inside the Russian prison of nations are completely disregarded. But at the moment nobody considers them as having military and political potential!

We are prepared to wager that Brezhnev agreed to Novotny's removal and allowed Dubcek's reformism in order to give a pretext to the army for marching in, for it is clear that this was impossible under the Stalinist rule of Novotny. Then the plans of Moscow could have been exposed all too clearly! But now everything is revolving around the so-called liberalization, "the deviation from the positions of Marxism-Leninism," but nobody mentions the fact that Russian divisions have been posted on the borders of the free part of Germany and Austria, that rockets can be found all along the borders of free Germany. Russia could have used economic sanctions against the CSSR but she did not. It is uncertain whether the West would help because one ultimatum from Moscow would be enough for Prague not to make concessions to the West. Moscow was concerned about having its military formations in the strategically important positions in Bohemia, in the center of Europe. At the same time, it wanted to surround Ukraine, by stationing its army in the CSSR, the only open window, militarily speaking!

Washington was again silent as in 1956. If the Russians were to occupy West Germany with the help of a carefully thought out plan, I am not sure that the Americans would try to expel them! Surely there are no conventional armed forces in Western Europe that could be an effective counterweight to the Russian forces. Therefore the West is afraid of a nuclear war, a fear that the Russians are counting on. But they are not prepared to do the most important thing—that is, support the national liberation revolutions of the subjugated nations so as to break up the Russian prison of nations and the Communist system from the inside, without a nuclear war.

There is, however, no doubt that Ukraine has held and still holds a key position in this. To surround it by her military forces from the CSSR as well has been an aim no less important to Russia than establishing a stepping stone for the conquest of further parts of Europe, or what remains of it. Of course this grasping action has its disadvantages for Russia. But they are less grave than those about which the Western press is shouting—namely, the decomposition of the Communist parties and the break-up of the world Communist movement. It is both good and desirable that the world Communist movement has been splintered, has no unitary leadership, and so on. But this is not decisive. Why? Let us not forget that the crushing of the Hungarian revolt in 1956 has not noticeably weakened the position of Russia in that respect. The condemnation of Moscow's aggression towards the CSSR by some Communist parties is dictated by the pressure of public opinion of those countries and not by the convictions of the leaders of the parties. They would be pleased to find some excuse for Moscow, to help save face before the public opinion of their own nations! It is not the achievement of the true "Communists," or "true Marxists," but the pressure of the popular masses whose support they want to obtain! More than that, even India did not condemn Moscow for such naked aggression!

A consequence of the conflict between Moscow and Peking is rivalry in assistance given to Hanoi. Ho Chi Minh receives more aid from two separate sources than he would if the two were completely united.

In Latin America, for example, as long as objective conditions for the existence of the Communist Party are not removed, as long as national and social justice is not attained, as long as a new vision of the great and the magnificent both in the national and social areas is not given, as long as a new or renewed faith in one's nation and a Christian faith which fights for national and social justice is not attained, these broad popular masses will not understand the essence of the conflict with Moscow, and even though they have seen Russia's aggressive acts towards the CSSR, for them the events around the CSSR will be remote, incomprehensible, and Communism will not grow weaker!

Disputes between the Communist parties and Moscow are helping to strengthen their parties' positions among their supporters, who, one can assume, are not working for Moscow.

The crushing of the Hungarian revolt did not reduce the number of members in the Italian Communist party, although here and there some criticism was expressed by its leaders toward the Communist party of the Soviet Union.

The Communist party of France did not decrease in number either, because the number of seats in parliament is not a decisive factor, but a result of voter preference, and does not reflect the true strength of a given party in the broad circles of workers or other strata of society. The gist of the matter is whether the Communist parties which today are critical of the invasion of the CSSR will take the side of their own countries in the event of a conflict with Russia or will be her acting fifth columns. Thorez showed that his loyalty to Russia was greater than to his own country when he sabotaged the defense system of France during the attack by Hitler because at that time the latter was an ally of the USSR!

A greater loss for Moscow than the decomposition of the Communist Party is the systematic realization by the patriotic circles of the West that only an armed showdown with Russia will save their countries because Moscow is always acquiring new countries and new strategic positions (the Mediterranean, the Arab world, part of Latin America, Africa, and Asia). One can only imagine what the fate of subjugated non-Communist countries and the treatment of their leaders would be when we see what fate met the CSSR, Moscow's protegé Dubcek, and the hero of the USSR General Svoboda....

When the Russian military fleet can be found in Alexandria and is blocking the Suez, when it has ports in Algeria and can blockade Gibraltar, when it has access to the "soft" heel of Europe, as Churchill called it—Italy—when nuclear warheads can be found in the Sudetes, what is the chance of France or Italy to defend itself without including the subjugated nations in a broad, jointly conceived, and mutually realized anti-Russian revolutionary liberation front of the whole of freedom-loving mankind? This is also the only chance of saving the Free World. The slow realization by the West of the importance of the enslaved nations, and of the Russian domination of the Mediterranean is a benefit of the invasion of the CSSR. A revolution of the subjugated nations can save the West and the present task of the Free World is to support it. More than ever before it appears that *whoever helps us helps himself!* Time is on our side now, because of the faults of Russia herself. The world's salvation lies in the fight of subjugated nations, in their uprisings! Their driving force is UKRAINE, therefore once again Ukraine has become the revolutionary problem of the world! That is why Moscow prompted its puppets Shelest and Podgorny to be "uncompromising" in connection with the invasion of the CSSR. There is also the other side of the coin: nuclear warheads from western regions of Ukraine have been moved further to the west, which at least partly removes the danger of destroying a certain part of Ukraine.

Contradiction follows contradiction in the imperialistic aggression of Moscow! But Moscow cannot avoid them.

However hard Moscow would scheme, however hard it would try to hide the importance of Ukraine, Ukraine's key position will always come to the fore. This happened on the occasion of the events surrounding the CSSR. The widening of the occupational zones by the Russian army is instrumental in the weakening of pressure on countries subjugated in the USSR. The troops which are in the CSSR or GDR, or in Poland, cannot be in Turkestan or in Ukraine. The forces of the KGB which have to look after the freedom-loving Czechs and Slovaks, the Germans, Poles, or Hungarians, or which can be found on the frontiers of China, cannot be in Ukraine. The ratio of Russians to non-Russians cannot be changed, regardless of the policy of the Diaspora, the forced resettlement of members of individual nations; the ratio of Russians to non-Russians of one to three still remains when the satellite countries are taken into account. If so, then the relationship between the conventional forces of NATO in Europe and the Warsaw Pact could be changed basically to three to one if the West would support the policy of liberation. The policy of liberation lessens the human military potential of Moscow because the fighters in the Soviet army who are not of Russian origin and soldiers in the satellite armies tend to sympathize more with the West.

In this way the balance of the conventional forces of NATO in Europe with the Warsaw Pact changes to the benefit of NATO in the ratio of something like three to one, if we also take into acount the fighters of the subjugated nations who, as it was at the beginning of the German campaign in the East, began to go over to the side of Germany until it became obvious that Germany was the invader and was not helping to liberate them.

It is possible that even the situation in the CSSR would have had a different outcome if the Czechs and Slovaks felt that the West was supporting them. There is no doubt that in those circumstances the Czechs and Slovaks would have put up armed resistance against the Russian invaders. Of course armed resistance by the Czechs and Slovaks would have resulted in many casualties but it would have given rise to a great legend of heroism and courage and would perhaps have directed the events onto a different course for it is not known what would have happened if the Czechs and Slovaks had fought. One cannot judge where the casus belli is nor when the chain reaction of revolts will begin. It is not possible to calculate and foresee everything rationally.

We have no intention of denying the fact that Dubcek and Svoboda wanted some liberalization, as did Gomulka in his time. But we do not cease to maintain that Gomulka saved Poland for Russia. In our opinion Dubcek, Svoboda, and Smrkovsky objectively carried out this function. The CSSR has been forced to remain a power in the Russian bloc and the role of a go-between, whether he wanted it or not, was undertaken by Dubcek. The people trusted Gomulka for a short while after he had been freed from prison, but he could not free himself from the pressure of ideas of the Russian world. In the same way neither Dubcek nor the hero of the USSR Gen. Svoboda will be able to do this. If it had not been for this trust in Dubcek the Czechs and Slovaks would have risen up in arms and it is unknown how Russian aggressive action would have ended! It is possible that the Hungarian repression would have been repeated, but even that would have left a more grandiose historic landmark and a signpost for the future.

It is possible that this would have led to.a chain of revolutions and in turn to the fall of the empire, but complications with the West cannot be ruled out because there would arise the problem of volunteers from the Free World, who would rush to the help of the victims. Nobody can foretell what consequences blood shed for the truth can bring even suddenly and instantly! Every nation has its own style. The Czech nation has its own. However, we do not think that the descendents of Huss would be silent if they had not trust their leaders. But Communists can never be leaders in a liberation fight against the center and Mecca of their ideas—Moscow. They are its slaves to a greater or lesser extent.

No nation can ever free itself from Russian yoke by a separate, isolated fight, without common aims and without synchronized insurgent revolts. Without the realization of the concept of the ABN there will be no freeing of nations because whoever does not support it has to count on foreign bayonets. The events around the CSSR and the Hungarian revolution of 1956 have shown that the American bayonets no longer stand for freedom but for the *status quo*.

ABN Correspondence,
March-April 1969, pp. 11-16

The Second Capitulation of Germany

We have before us a document: the treaty between the Federal Republic of Germany and the USSR about cooperation and the renunciation of the use of force. Its contents are: recognition by Germany of the *status quo* created by the Russian victory on the battlefield, without any *quid pro quo* on the part of the Russians. In fact this is a second capitulation of Germany to the Russians. Germany, or more precisely Bonn, or still more precisely the SPD-FDP Government, on behalf of the Federal Republic, recognizes the existence of two German States, although one of them is an outright Russian colony: the setting up of West Berlin as a de facto separate unit, for Berlin deputies have no vote in the Parliament; the renunciation of all claims to the German territories occupied by Poland and Russia, as well as Czechoslovakia. Moreover, without a recognition by the Russians even on paper, even in the form of a declaration of the right to self-determination, to the reunification of both parts of Germany, the FRG and the "GDR," in one German State. The Russians even failed to promise to pull down the Berlin wall, to democratize even to some extent the "GDR," to ease the visits between the two parts of Germany, or to repatriate the remaining Germans from the concentration camps. The Bonn Government has accepted all the Russian demands simply for the sake of "improving the atmosphere," creating conditions for cooperation, for mutual exchange of economic, scientific, and cultural "goods."... Russians want to receive from the FRG industrial products, assistance for the construction of factories on the territory of the USSR, every possible advantage from the second-strongest trading and the third-strongest industrial country in the world. The FRG will supply them with the necessary industrial goods for everyday use as well as with components for the armaments industry, and the Russians will concentrate their industrial potential primarily in order to overtake the USA in armaments and to prepare a possible war with Peking, if in the meantime no understanding between the USSR and Communist China is reached. After twenty-five years, when almost the entire world has forgotten that Germany had lost the war, during a fundamental change of attitude of the world to the FRG, which is regarded in Europe as an important anti-Russian factor, when the FRG had become a partner of the USA and the strongest military and economic partner in NATO after the USA and in the European Common Market, after the FRG became a friend of France and Great Britain, and particularly the USA, the Bonn Government has reminded the world by its second capitulation in Moscow that Germany had lost the war and has to go on paying for it.... Is this näiveté, treason, stupidity, or Machiavellianism?

The prime mover of the present German foreign policy—and not only foreign policy—is a former outstanding leader of the Communist Party of Germany and a former Russian collaborator—Wehner. Chancellor Brandt also used to belong to the left-wing socialist opponents of Kurt Schumacher, a socialist, for many years prisoner of Nazi concentration camps, but an ardent patriot who hated Russians and Communists. Brandt and Wehner are both former emigrants who did not take any particular interest in the fate of Germany in the past.... There are other members of the present government who were also left-wing social-ists; there are also former Nazis....

Surely Wehner is not so näive as not to be able to grasp the essence of the matter? Who better than he knows the Russians, when he used to sit for many years in Moscow at the Comintern HQ with Ulbricht, whose wife was formerly Wehner's first wife?... Wehner knows what he wants. Is his dream a left-wing "people's democratic Germany" united under his chancellorship in alliance with Russia?

Each treaty has two partners: I give so that you give too. The FRG has given everything, but what has it obtained from the Russians now? Lenin taught: one step backwards, two steps forwards! Even if the Berlin wall had been pulled down, this would not have meant a success, because in 1961 it was not there yet! And there is no unification of Germany either. This is Moscow's art, to make two steps forward, perhaps to go back one step, but nevertheless to make one firm step forward. Meanwhile Brandt went even further. He failed to achieve the destruction of the Berlin wall, or an improvement of conditions in the "GDR," or the security of West Berlin, or the recognition at least in the form of a declaration of the right of the German people to self-determination and reunification of Germany in freedom.... But he did recognize unconditionally the status quo. He explains that he did this in the hope that the Russians would now have confi-dence in Bonn and would meet him halfway on other fundamental problems. He has recognized the Oder and Neisse and the loss of East Prussia, Pomerania, Silesia, and the Sudetenland and the partition of Germany, and the admission of two German states into the UN, even without deciding the matter of who would represent West Berlin in the UN, although until now Western Allies recognized West Berlin as part of the FRG. And now? Will it be a free city like Danzig? A blank check has been signed.... Thus the Wehners trust the Russians for the sake of "peace and quiet" and hand themselves over to the mercies of Moscow—voluntarily, unnecessarily.

By surrendering its trumps Bonn wishes to gain the friendship of Russian imperialists. But they have intentionally forgotten that there are enslaved nations which make up over a half of the population of the USSR, and with the population of the satellite states, the relation of forces is one to two to the Russians' disadvantage. Hence Bonn seeks friendship not with the enslaved nations, but with their enslavers. The SPD-FDP follows in the footsteps of the Nazis. Is Brandt copying Hitler? This means that Germany is again losing her natural friends—the enslaved nations—while she herself continues to be partly enslaved. This is a consequence of the underestimation of the importance and the role of the subjugated nations in the struggle for a better world, in the vanguard of which stands Ukraine. Germany again binds herself with tyranny against its victims. Hitler's pact with Stalin is repeated. History does not teach anything. Does the SPD-FDP hope to achieve liberation with the help of the enslaver?

Thus the SPD-FDP has missed the opportunity to win the friendship of the subjugated nations for Germany. The FRG is placing itself today on the side of despotism, of the subjugator against the subjugated, recognizes the status quo fully in Russia's favor, thus guaranteeing the state of enslavement of all the countries in the USSR and the satellite states! By this treaty Moscow has achieved in advance the liquidation of any second front in western Europe. And Russia already has fronts in Asia—China, the Near East—the Mediterranean Sea, and the most dangerous front: the subjugated nations headed by Ukraine. FRG guarantees the inviolability of her frontiers, including the "GDR." Russia can transfer some of her divisions to the Chinese frontier and increase the pressure on the subjugated nations. The Federal Republic of Germany favors an agreement with its enemy. And what will the USA say? Surely the time will come when Moscow demands the withdrawal of the US, British, and French troops from the FRG, now that a treaty renouncing the use of force exists. What is the need then for the allied troops when Russia is becoming a friend of the FRG? And then pressure after pressure will come, blackmail after blackmail.

And Senators Fulbright and Mansfield will repeat in the US Senate tomorrow: why keep troops in West Germany, when there is an agreement between Moscow and Bonn? And Moscow will demand that atomic weapons be removed from Germany, because there is an agreement.... An agreement...Moscow has all the blackmail trumps in its hands because it did not take upon itself any obligation even on paper; it is only Bonn that has made concessions! The complex of a lost war after a quarter of a century when the entire world has almost forgotten it has again been brought back to the public mind by Wehner-Brandt in a gratuitous second capitulation of Germany to Moscow. Without any reason and sense. And all this has happened because statesmen have fallen into a hopeless lack of vision, because they see only RUSSIA, but do not see the tremendous explosive force in that empire: the subjugated nations—their natural allies in the struggle against Russia for the liberation also of the enslaved part of Germany.

Finally, does Moscow really plan a preventive war against China, and want to have a safe West European flank and rear? Or does Wehner perhaps intend in Machiavellian spirit, according to Stalin's style, to maneuver Moscow into a war against China, giving up positions in Germany in order thus to encourage Russia to attack China, in the belief that her European flank is safe, and in this way to bring about a war of attrition between Russia and China? It was how Stalin planned things when he concluded the non-aggression pact with Hitler. The Ribbentrop-Molotov nonaggression pact provoked a war of Germany against the Allies because Hitler had safety with Russia. Does Wehner speculate similarity, combining the variant—the Hitler-Stalin pact (in the present situation Brandt-Kosygin), thus encouraging Russia to begin a preventive war against China with a future variant: Bonn-Peking-Washington (in which we do not believe)? On Russia's part the war can be either atomic or conventional with the threat of an atomic war, which should compel China to capitulate. Does Wehner intend that in this way Moscow should involve itself in a prolonged war with China and—deceiving Moscow by its capitulation—Bonn will utilize the opportunity of Russia's weakening in a war with China in order to exert pressure on Moscow to gain concessions during the latter's exhaustive war with China? But Moscow also has its own political and strategic staffs and Wehner knows this better than anyone as a former member of the Politburo of the CP of Germany and of the Presidium of the Comintern. One remembers when Stalin put pressure on Ribbentrop to make Hitler agree to the occupation of the Baltic States and additionally to the occupation of another Baltic port by Russia—but Ribbentrop procrastinated. Having asked Hitler by telephone, he received immediately an answer favorable to Stalin. Rejoicing, Ribbentrop went to see Stalin, shouting out: "The Führer has agreed!" An expression of fear appeared on Stalin's face. He understood that Hitler had ulterior motives when he so easily agreed to Moscow's demand. Does Wehner, an experienced decade-long communist leader, really hope to maneuver Communist Russia into a preventive war against China and to gain from it?

More than once we have expressed our view on the Moscow-Peking conflict and consider it reasonable. If one is to abstract from the political stupidity of German leaders, a scandalous opportunism, and the atavistic pro-Communist complex of the present-day leaders brought up on Marxism-Leninism, one thing perhaps remains to explain the reason for the second capitulation of Germany to Russia despite the extremely weakened position of Russia in connection with a number of fronts which she now has: a naïve Machiavellianism of Wehner and Brandt. For "to renounce voluntarily and without compulsion one quarter of German territory which has legally belonged and still belongs to the State territory of Germany, to sanction politically the partitioning of the remaining legal territory, and to take upon oneself the obligation to respect the subjugation of 17 million Germans by an alien totalitarian domination," writes Baron Guttenberg, the most important German Christian foreign policy maker after

Strauss—moreover "by a freely elected German government"—is something nightmarish....

The Bonn Government continually stresses that it has obtained an agreement of the governments of the USA, Britain, and France to the conclusion of the pact, but it has forgotten the objections in nuances on the part of these Governments. How can a government of another country forbid a sovereign country to make these or those moves? But this is not the point. Surely neither Britons, nor Frenchmen, nor Americans can be greater, more fanatical, more consistent defenders of German interests than the Germans themselves. In addition, none of these states desires, for instance, economic competition from a strong, united Germany. Why should Nixon or Pompidou be more papist than the Pope himself? A great part of German public opinion cannot understand it, however. And why should British or American troops shed their blood for Germany when Germans have no wish to do so?

The political naïveté of the politicians brought up in the Marxist spirit has no bounds. How can they think in patriotic, national categories when not long ago not the nation but the class was everything for them? And Lenin was an idol no less than Marx.

However it may be, the USA, Britain, and France have to recognize that the real permanent allies of the freedom-loving nations and peoples of the entire world are and will remain forever the *nations enslaved by Russia* headed by *Ukraine*!

The Ukrainian Review,
No. III, 1970, pp. 2-7.

Why Brussels?

Why have we chosen Brussels for our present Conference? Not accidentally. It is a West European center in many respects. It is the home of NATO, of the significance of which freedom-loving mankind must be urgently reminded. At the same time it has to be reminded of the role of nations subjugated by Russian imperialism and Communism, which defend universal freedom—more precisely, the freedom of the Free World, in particular of the rest of free Europe. A prominent military theorist of the West and a great Englishman, Gen. J.F.C. Fuller, wrote uniquely of the importance of the ABN beside NATO, as well as of the importance of my homeland, Ukraine, in his works *Russia Is Not Invincible*, *How to Defeat Russia*, and others, and I don't have to repeat his thoughts. Excerpts of his works are to be found even here, and can serve as information for the interested. As usual, Gen. Fuller was neither a prophet in his home country nor in Western Europe. His military doctrine was applied in the first years of the war by Guderian and Zhukov and his concepts of modern warfare are applied today by Moscow and Peking.

In this country, and in this capital city in particular, the problem of Europe is very acute. But of what Europe?... Some are beginning to identify the rest of

Europe with Europe in general. Excluded are Ukraine, Byelorussia, Lithuania, Latvia, Estonia, Hungary, Czechia, Slovakia, Georgia, Armenia, Bulgaria, Rumania, Poland, and even East Germany. The border of Europe is determined by the boot of the Russian aggressor. What remains of free Europe are only scraps. But we want to remind the world that Europe is where European ideals are defended by blood and life—and those ideals are: the idea of a nation and its independence, the idea of a man, his virtue, dignity, and the heroic idea of Christianity. The ideals of Europe have been defended in uprisings of Ukrainians, Byelorussians, Caucasians, and other prisoners in concentration camps of Siberia, in the Hungarian revolution in 1956, in Vorkuta in 1956, in Berlin in 1953, in Prague and Bratislava in 1968, and recently in Kyiv, Minsk, and Tbilisi by underground fighters of the courageous young generation.

European ideas are also defended by the USA, and its foundations were laid by our ancestors. They have become the general property of all mankind. And on the fields of Vietnam Vietnamese nationalists defend them against the advance of tyranny.

Europe was great when it was great in its ideals, faithful to them, and reflecting them...when it was faithful to itself. Europe should act according to the principle of "noblesse oblige."

Europe can become an independent, vital force and a deciding factor in world politics when the Russian empire is dissolved into independent states of nations presently enslaved in the empire, and when not only France, Belgium, Great Britain, or Germany, but equally an independent national Ukrainian state, Byelorussia, the Baltic states, Georgia, Hungary, Bulgaria, Rumania, Croatia, Albania, Poland, Slovakia, Czechia, and others become partners of an integral Europe, and when parliaments of these independent states arising on the ruins of the Russian empire and the Communist system in free elections will decide on the principles of cooperation and mutual aid for European countries finally liberated from tyranny and slavery. They constitute billions of people and dozens of nations.

To get Europe into its place again it is imperative for the remaining free nations of Europe to understand that:

1) their future destiny depends entirely on the destiny of nations enslaved by Russian imperialism and Communism in the USSR and in the satellite countries;

2) Russian and Communist aggression threatens distinctly to engulf them;

3) they must at least formulate moral and political opinion in order to induce their governments to abolish the policy of so-called peaceful coexistence with tyrants ruinous to freedom-loving mankind, and start by all possible means the policy of liberation.

Thus here, in the center of the West European community and in the center of NATO—in this quiet and snug capital—in the face of the historic responsibility burdening us as well as the statesmen who meet here frequently, we thought it necessary to say this....

And this is the reason why we are in Brussels.

ABN Correspondence,
January-February 1917, pp. 9-10

Russian Agression in Afghanistan

Nothing unexpected has happened. Moscow has occupied Afghanistan, just as it had planned for years—this was well known. At present, Moscow's strategic plan for conquering the world is at the following stage: to occupy Africa's geopolitical, strategic, economic, and, in part, her human resources, especially in Central and Southern Africa, and to systematically occupy the Near and Middle East, especially the oil fields, in that manner economically blockading all of Western Europe.

Free Europe, in the progression of civilization, will automatically fall within the axis of Moscow if this strategic plan of Russian imperialism is actualized. Part one of this plan concerning Africa is being actualized on a full scale with the help of Cuban, East German, and other "satellite" mercenaries. At the same time, Afghanistan was being invaded and taken over by Moscow in stages. Since their plans regarding Amin (Moscow's former lackey president in Afghanistan) obviously fell through, they then had him liquidated and occupied Afghanistan, which could have been foreseen.

At the same time the uncalculating Ayatollah Khomeini has further complicated the matter with his senseless conflict with America, which can only have negative consequences for Iran. This conflict can only be in Moscow's favor. Iran is a multinational state of a population of 35 million; 15 million are Persians, 10 million are Azerbaidzhanians, 4-5 million are Kurds, 2 million are Arabs from Khuzestan, and a million are Baluchis in Baluchistan. Hence, Moscow holds in its hands the key to the destruction of Iran. We know of the disruptions in Tabriz, Azerbaidzhan, in Kurdistan, and soon Moscow will be coming "to the aid" of the Azerbaidzhanians or the Kurds "to create" puppet states for themselves and eventually unite these states with the Azerbaidzhan in the USSR—or they may create a separate "state," which will be a satellite of Moscow with Tabriz as its capital. Of a population of 20 million in Afghanistan, only 60 percent are ethnically Afghan, whereas the remainder consists of Pathanians, Mongols, Tadzhiks, and Turkmen. Everywhere the central question is the National Question, followed by the Religious Question. In this case Islam, which is experiencing an unusual dynamic rebirth and, if united with nationalism, can become a volcanic power. First and foremost, this power will explode within the Russian empire. Nationalism, united with religion, is a very significant force, continuously ignored by the US and Western Europe, which we have been stressing for years.

Faced with a real threat from Russian imperialist aggression, the Khomeini conflict with the US makes little if any sense from the point of view of the interests of Iran. Until the present, the US reaction to this conflict has not been well thought-out and is motivated, perhaps, by its lack of knowledge of the current situation in Iran. Khomeini must apply terror, because he must somehow control the national liberation movements of the subjugated nations. The Shah had the same problem. But, he can no longer do anything about it now. Even Khomeini's call to Islam will not suffice, because his Shiite group is not a unifying force, and secondly, only Islam united with the idea of national liberation can be victorious. One imperialist minority group (8 percent) can never achieve such victory. In the name of one minority Islamic religious group, Islamic peoples were subjugated, such as the Azerbaidzhanians or the Kurds—this is a contradiction in itself. A call to unity in the name of one minority religious group is of little value, but a call for the unity of Islam in harmony with the idea of national liberation is an indomitable force against Russian tanks and bombers.

What should the US and Free Europe have done with regard to Afghanistan or Iran—which is also threatened by the Russian empire—or in general with regard to all the oil-rich countries?

In a direct, straightforward answer on Afghanistan, the US should have militarily liberated Cuba, and thus dismantled the second part of Russia's strategic plan—e.g., Cuba as the bastion of Russian imperialism in Latin America—and, concurrently, placed the Cuban mercenaries in Africa in a position where they would have to automatically transfer their loyalty to the national forces of the African nations, thus undercutting Moscow's plan in Africa. We were very pleased to learn that this same proposal was also offered by the British M.P. David Atkinson not long ago in London.

The US should stop waiting and give military assistance to the Afghan Insurgent Army. The responses of the US concerning Afghanistan have been generally positive until now, but they do not suffice. In contrast to the lack of dignity and national pride in American politicians and capitalists, we are amazed by the great outpouring of such national pride in the American workers, who refuse to load Russian ships despite the pleadings of President Carter. These are the true spokesmen of the great American nation, who were educated by the great American patriot, the leader of their trade unions—the late Mr. George Meany.

For the last few years, we have been urging a boycott of the Moscow Olympics, and we were the first to bring this matter to the forefront. Now, we are indeed pleased, that several world leaders are also proposing such a boycott, especially the British Prime-Minister, M. Thatcher, and the President of the United States of America—J. Carter. However, we are puzzled by the naiveté of some people, such as the chief of German sports—Mr. Weyer, who continuously states that "sport has nothing to do with politics." If the athletes of the entire world want to march in front of tyrants—whose hands are bloodied with the murder of millions of people, who do not have the smallest iota, not only of national dignity, but human dignity as well—then this is a matter of their (the athletes') moral degradation and degeneration. Every lamb chooses for itself its butcher. This is not democracy, but anarchy, when a government states that athletes themselves ought to choose whether they want to compete on a sport field in Moscow covered with human blood!

In Iran there are 15 million Persians and 18 million non-Persians. Similarly, in the USSR there are at most 120 million Russians and 150 million non-Russians. Moreover, Islam is also erupting in the USSR, while Washington remains silent! If one were to include the "satellite" countries, then over two-thirds of those subjugated in the Soviet-Russian empire are non-Russians. This weapon is always being disregarded, even ignored by the US, and even more so by free Europe. For them there are 270 million Russians in the USSR, just as there are 35 million Persians in Iran!

The United States—the most powerful country in the world—is afraid to send weapons to the Afghan heroes who are fighting the onslaught of Russian tanks with bare hands! It must be stated that only Pakistan and China have been aiding the Afghan insurgents.

Why doesn't the U.S. take over Aden? Why doesn't President Carter proclaim a *Great Charter of National Liberation* of all the nations subjugated by Moscow in the USSR and the "satellite" countries, and initiate a holy war for the dissolution of the tyrannical godless Russian empire, a war for the idea of a nation, for liberation nationalism, a war for Islam and Christianity, both of which are united in the first front of the struggle. Liberation nationalism, heroic Christianity, and heroic Islam against the Russian barbarians, invaders, and atheists—this is the primary weapon! Why doesn't Washington strike at the USSR from within, when millions upon millions are waiting for the voice of America—not the voice of bureaucrats, but the voice of American dock workers whose working hands are embellished with callouses and who stand up for freedom for all nations rather than load the ships of the enemies of the United States and all the subjugated nations.

Washington ought to remember that the siege of its embassy in Tehran is no longer done by Moslem "fanatics" but by communist Russian agents. If Iran decides to send aid to the Afghan heroes (although this is improbable), then it will put Washington to shame, since Washington could have resolved the Tehran crisis within a matter of two months if a resolute stand were taken instead of postponing the issue prior to the Russian occupation of Afghanistan.

Washington ought to at least listen to the propositions of the statesmen of the subjugated nations, instead of being convinced that it has all the solutions to the problems of the empire, because—as experience has shown—it was not able to foresee the events in Czechoslovakia in 1968, nor Hungary in 1956, nor in Afghanistan in 1979, or in Cuba, in Angola, in Ethiopia, etc. Washington does not understand the larger strategic plan of Moscow, which was presented in depth by ABN spokesmen several years ago, and only now is becoming self-evident to everyone.

And finally, why was the development and production of the neutron bomb terminated at a time when it is so necessary? This is a secret, which we will not attempt to guess. How can one trust Moscow about the SALT II Pact, how can one recognize in Helsinki the territorial inviolability of the borders of the Soviet-Russian empire? Now is the time for Washington to show its strength. The ultimatum that Kennedy gave Khrushchev in Cuba forced him to run with his battleships.

The world is waiting for the implementation of the only successful weapon against Moscow: the dynamite of the subjugated nations in the empire!!

ABN Correspondence,
March-April 1980, pp. 1-3

In the Shadow of the Russian Military Intervention in Poland

Russian imperialist expansionist policy has recently been leaving its malignant mark on all areas of the world. The Free World, on the other hand, has not been able to galvanize any serious resistance to this Russian imperialist drive.

NATO is so deeply divided that it cannot even agree upon a common statement condemning the Russian military intervention in Poland, which was effectuated through Moscow's agent-puppet regime and the forcibly imposed system of a Russian way of life. This attests to the powerlessness of the free nations of the West divested of any patriotic idea, of a heroic morality, and of a will to fight.

The isolated efforts of the new American administration to, in the very least, pose some type of limited opposition attests to the paralysis of will prevalent in the commercialized part of Western Europe.

The Socialist International, headed by Willy Brandt, in view of the mass terror of the Russian invader against the Polish workers, has again reaffirmed the servile attitude of several of the leaders of this "International" towards Russian imperialism in its modest Communist form.

The policy of détente and balance of power has underscored the capitulation of the West with regard to the Russian aim of conquering the entire world. The so-called "Ostpolitik" of the Vatican has resulted in the complete demoralization of the Catholic Church in Hungary and Czechoslovakia. The ecumenical dialogue, which is being continued even by Pope John Paul II, has unilaterally benefited the imperialist, "Caesaropapal" Russian Church of Pimen.

The example of Afghanistan and the no less significant example of the struggle of the Polish nation should clarify once and for all to everyone who can think that détente and balance of power are only a well-orchestrated, deceitful Russian ruse intended to conceal their systematic drive to conquer the world. *Without an elementary agreement on common aims between partners—there can be no balance of power!* In view of Moscow's systematically effectuated plan to dominate the world, to pursue a policy of balance of power is absurd!

The nations subjugated in the Russian prison of nations—the USSR and the "satellite" countries—have been relegated by a concessionist-minded West to a Russian sphere of influence. As proof of this fact, we offer the following examples: the Ukrainian two-front war of liberation (1941-1951), the uprisings of prisoners in Russian concentration camps in the 1950s, the Berlin, Hungarian, and Poznan uprisings, the Czech and Slovak resistance—in not one of these cases did the West come to the aid of these fighters for freedom.

NATO, under the leadership of the United States, has not yet repudiated its conception of dividing the world, even though by adamantly adhering to this concept the West is forced to continuously redefine previously agreed-upon spheres of influence, according to each new Russian imperio-colonial conquest, whether it be in Africa, Asia, Latin America, or elsewhere. Furthermore, by signing the Helsinki Accords, the West cemented the indivisibility of the Russian empire and the inviolability of its borders, thereby reaffirming that the liberation of the subjugated nations does not yet figure in its political strategy. Any hopes that the subjugated nations, including Poland, may have had for obtaining aid from the NATO bloc in their liberation struggle have now become illusory and without content. It would not be so bad if the member-states of NATO in the very least decided not to assist the Russian imperialists in subjugating our nations with highly developed Western technology, electronics, grain, and even weaponry.

Our first demand with regard to a change in Western policy is the following: to declare the Helsinki Accords null and void; to terminate all forms of assistance to and trade relations with the Russian empire and its "satellites," through which the further subjugation of our nations is perpetrated; to cancel all agreements with the Russian imperialists which affirm Russia's subjugation of our nations according to the so-called concept of "spheres of influence"; to apply the UN Resolution on Decolonization—i.e., the dissolution of empires—to the USSR, as well as the UN Resolution on Namibia, dealing with the legality, from a viewpoint of international law, of rendering military aid to a subjugated nation in its struggle against an imposed colonial yoke (in this case against Russian imperio-colonial domination); to include the US Congregational Resolution on Captive Nations from 1959 as an integral component of US foreign policy vis-à-vis the Russian empire—the USSR and its "satellite" states; to overhaul the political content of the radio broadcasts of the "Voice of America" and "Radio Liberty" by proclaiming a *great charter of national independence* and to propagate this idea of independence and sovereignty for all nations subjugated in the USSR and the necessity of the dissolution of the Russian empire.

Only then will it be realistic to speak of the beginning of real assistance on the part of the USA and the Free World to the subjugated nations. Until that time, our slogan remains, "He who liberates himself will be free; he who is liberated will be led into slavery!"

We do not believe in "liberation," but in a common front of subjugated nations in the Russian empire which will topple this prison of nations from within through coordinated, simultaneous, and synchronized national-liberation uprisings, and erect on the ruins of this empire national and sovereign states, each within their ethnographical boundaries. *Freedom ex gratia is not freedom!* The revolutionary liberation front of subjugated nations strongly condemns the barbaric Russian military action against the Polish nation, achieved with the aid of Moscow's Communist lackeys. We completely support the Polish liberation struggle and call upon the Polish nation, its uncompromising, revolutionary, anti-Russian forces in particular, to unite with the common front of the Anti-Bolshevik Bloc of Nations (ABN) whose goal is the dissolution of the Russian empire and its Communist system of subjugation through simultaneous liberation revolutions and the *reestablishment of independent nation-states of the presently subjugated nations within their ethnographic territories.*

Our strength is in ourselves! The world only comes to the aid of the strong!

Without the dissolution of the Russian prison of nations in extenso—there can be no independence for Poland, or for any of the other subjugated natons!

ABN Correspondence,
May-June 1982, pp. 1-2

V

Russian Communism, Imperialism, and Oppression

International Communism or Russian Imperialism?

It was obvious to England when fighting against Napoleon's France that it was France and not the countries conquered by Napoleon which was England's enemy. Indeed, these countries were regarded by England as her allies. And the Duke of Wellington, for instance, said at Waterloo: "I wish it were night, or the Prussians would come." And together with Field Marshal Blücher he then defeated Napoleon. It was therefore obvious who the enemy was.

In World War II the Allies regarded Germany as their enemy, but France, Poland, Norway, Belgium, Holland, Serbia, and Greece were not considered to be enemies, but were treated like allies and friends. Only Germany was ruthlessly fought and bombed, and countless women and children there lost their lives. After the Allied victory the Hitler regime was abolished and the Nazi war-criminals were sentenced in Nuremberg. Just as the entire German people had previously been bombed during the war and had been fought with every means, now too it was obliged to bear the consequences of the war. Dismantling of works and factories, reparations, compulsory expulsion of 11 million Germans from the eastern and southern territories, severance of entire German territories, partition of Germany into four occupied zones, the occupation by the Russians even up to the present time of a third of Germany, the Morgenthau Plan, etc.—all this was directed not only against the Nazi regime, which no longer existed, and not only against the German militarists and imperialists, but also against the German people as a whole. Thus the German people were held responsible for German imperialism. Whether this was just or not is another question. We should merely like to state the plain facts at this point.

As regards the fight against Russia, however, matters are different. Actually the situation should be as follows: the enemy is Russia—just as in former times Germany was the enemy—and the allies of the West are the peoples subjugated by Russia. The fight should be directed solely against Russia, and the weapons of destruction against the Russian ethnographical territory, in exactly the same way as one dealt with Germany during the last war. But the countries subjugated by Russia should be excluded from the entire strategy of combat, for they are and remain the allies of the West, just as France and Belgium were during the last war.

Moreover, it was not only German imperialism that was attacked, but also the entire German people including women and children. And in Hiroshima it was not only Japanese militarism that was attacked, but even unborn children.

When it is a question of Russia, however, one desists from attacking the Russian empire. The blame for the Russian annexations, dreadful atrocities, and mass murders is thrust onto all the peoples languishing in the Russian sphere of influence. No mention whatever is made of the Russian imperialists and colonial rulers. One concentrates on so-called international Communism in order to exonerate the Russians. But where is the seat, the general staff, of so-called international Communism? Who is in command of the Communist Parties all over the world? Who sends out the conquering armies and equips them with arms? In whose empire have Turkestan, the Caucasus, Ukraine, Byelorussia, Bulgaria, Poland, and East Germany, etc., been incorporated? In the Russian empire! They are completely dependent on the orders issued by the Russian imperial headquarters in Moscow—which include compulsory Russification, national subjugation, and economic exploitation to the advantage of the militant Russian center. If the Western world only sees the enemy in international Communism, it will never be in a position to distinguish the main enemy. It will not know where to fight and whom to fight. But if one realizes that Russia is the enemy, the land that has bred Communism, which is organically in keeping with the nature of the Russian people, then one will also know where to look for the enemy.

The moment Russia is overthrown, Communism will cease to be a world danger. Actually, Communism, like anarchism, would have had no influence in the world if Russia had not adopted this idea as the most modern form of its imperialism. Incidentally, such Russian thinkers and writers as, for instance, Berdyaev and others have expressed the opinion quite openly that *Bolshevism-Communism is a peculiarity of the Russian mentality,* namely in the psycho-moral and sociological respect. Berdyaev analyzes this fact without beating about the bush in his works, in particular *The Meaning and Character of Russian Communism.* He admits that *Communism is a Russian messianistic idea,* just like Pan-Slavism, the defense of orthodoxy "with the idea of the Third Rome." And Dostoevsky prophesied the Bolshevik revolution as a typically Russian phenomenon. If Russian power were not behind Communism, each people would be able to deal with Communism itself.

Since Communism is an idea which is used in the service of Russia, a social-political system which is in keeping with the Russian character, a fact which is clearly proved by Dr. D. Donzov in his book *The Russian Mentality* and which Berdyaev also corroborated from the Russian point of view, its enforcement (even by Russian military means) is nothing but the enforcement of Russian alien rule on the subjugated countries. *It is therefore wrong to talk about "international Communism" as the main enemy, for the main enemy is Russian imperialism, which all the Communist parties in the world serve as henchmen.*

It is appalling to think how closely the forces of evil in the world are allied to each other. We are not by any means defenders of any kind of imperialism, since we ourselves are subjugated by imperialism; but in all fairness we feel bound to say that insults have been heaped on English, French, Japanese, Belgian, Dutch, German and Italian imperialism without any thought being given to the fact that the peoples in question might be offended. One never talks about monarchist English, republican French, or royal Belgian imperialism. But as soon as one talks about Russian imperialism, one inevitably uses the designation "tsarist or Soviet imperialism" so as not to offend the Russians in any way. And one purposely overlooks the fact that it was, of course, not only the tsars, for instance, who were responsible for Russia's imperialism.

In the Suez Canal Zone "the English and French imperialists tried to carry out a ruthless campaign of conquest," just as the Belgian imperialists did in the Congo, but in Hungary such a campaign was only carried out by the evil Communists, who are not organically connected with any people and probably dropped on Budapest from Mars! No one would dream of suggesting that those responsible for this campaign were Russian hordes who were lusting for conquest. In 1939 Poland was "invaded by German armies," but Berlin and East Germany, where German women were raped and children were murdered, were not overrun by Russian hordes but by "international Communists."

The following words appeared in Russian in *Pravda* of July 24, 1942:

> We do not want to speak. We do not want to be indignant. We want to kill. If you have not killed at least one German in the course of the day, then your day has been wasted.... When you have killed one German, kill a second. There is no sight more pleasing to us than German corpses. Do not count the miles. Only count the Germans whom you have killed.
>
> There is nothing innocent about the Germans, neither about the living nor about the unborn.... Crush the fascist beast in its den forever.... Break the racial arrogance of the Germanic women by force! Take them as your rightful booty! Courageous, advancing Red Army soldiers, kill, kill!

Nor were conditions any better in tsarist days. Slave labor, deportations, and sentences without trial were not invented in Russia by the Communists. These practices existed hundreds of years ago, as the French writer Marquis de Custine so fittingly points out in his book, in which he give an excellent account of these conditions.

Here and there in the West one is prepared to talk about "Moscow's imperialism" so as to lay the blame only on the central power. But one does not talk about London, Berlin, or Paris imperialism, but simply about English, German, or French imperialism. No one has any qualms about annoying the English people.

But the Russians must not be annoyed under any circumstances.

Nor is it correct to talk about "Soviet imperialism" instead of about Russian imperialism, or to use the designation "Soviets" for the Russians. This is actually nonsense, for the word Soviet in English means "council"; hence Soviet imperialism means "imperialism of the councils." And if one applies this designation to the state structure of the Soviet Union, then it is even more incorrect, for various subjugated peoples are incarcerated in the Soviet Union who have no connection whatever with imperialism and are, moreover, fighting a life-and-death struggle against Russian imperialism.

The British Commonwealth is above all a community of free nations, and no one dreams of talking about "Commonwealth imperialism." For it is obvious to everyone that the Greeks of Cyprus have nothing in common with any English imperialists. And as far as the British Empire is concerned, for example, how could one think of holding the Northern Irish responsible for any English imperialistic aims?

The Soviet Union is the most ruthless colonial empire of all time. How then can one possibly think of holding the nations incarcerated and subjugated in this empire, which calls itself the Soviet Union, responsible for the imperialism of the Russian colonial rulers! The designation "Soviet imperialism" is therefore merely another attempt to spare the Russians. It would be nonsense to talk about a "Union Française Imperialism," since in addition to the French there are also countless other peoples voluntarily united in the French Union—and, in any case, the Union Française cannot be compared to the Soviet Union. Thus, if one cannot talk about a Commonwealth or a Union Française imperialism, then even more obviously so, one cannot talk about a Soviet imperialism because the peoples have been forcibly incorporated and incarcerated in the Russian empire that is the Soviet Union. How could they share a common imperialistic cause with their subjugators, the Russian colonial rulers?

There is only Russian imperialism, and one should talk about it at least in the same way as one has hitherto talked about English or French imperialism, even though this is not a fitting comparison since one cannot relegate the civilized English and French people to the same level as the Russian barbarians.

If someone uses the designation "Soviet Russian imperialism," then he wants to define the actual Russian imperialism by this term, and similarly too, with the term "Russian Communist imperialism." We should like to point out that when talking about English or French imperialism, no such expressions are used in order to indicate a certain terminology. And the frequently used designation "Communist imperialism" also aims to divert attention from the main enemy. One does not talk about "democratic imperialism," even though France and England at the time of the expansion of their empires had a democratic system and spread this in their colonies in Africa and Asia. By analogy, therefore, one should talk about democratic imperialism in order to spare the feelings of the French and the English. But this is inappropriate, for fundamentally every idea can be used for imperialistic purposes.

In conclusion, we should like to stress that the enemy must be called by his right name—in this case historic Russian imperialism (combined with the messianistic attitude of the Russian mentality), which in various forms—as for instance Pan-Slavism, the idea of the Third Rome, "defense of orthodoxy," international Communism—is to bring about the realization of Russian conquest.

We preach neither racial hatred nor chauvinism. We make no objections to a Russian state in its ethnographical areas, nor do we object to the Russians if they withdraw from our national territories and keep to their own native soil.

But we definitely object to being held responsible for the Russian atrocities which have been committed in the course of centuries. The West has no right to try to thrust the list of crimes onto us, even though there may be certain guilty persons among our peoples. But among every people there are always some traitors and profiters who seek to further their own personal interests and place their services at the disposal of the Russian colonial rulers. The Norwegian people were not punished for Quisling, but Quisling himself was called to account.

The fact that the disintegration process of the empires (a typical phenomenon of the present era) is in progress must result in the universal and wholehearted support on the part of the freedom-loving world for the national liberation struggle of the peoples incarcerated in the Russian colonial empire, all the more so since the Russians are doing their utmost to overthrow the Western empires and to enter upon their heritage as the new colonial rulers. The disintegration of the Russian colonial empire, and the restoration of the independent democratic states of all the peoples subjugated by Russia—irrespective of the date when they became the victims—should be proclaimed as the aim of Western policy.

The Communist system, forcibly introduced by Russian armies in the countries subjugated by Russia in the Soviet Union and in the so-called satellite countries, is a form of modern Russian colonial rule.

Not an international Communism which has dropped from the skies or has been carried up out of hell rules over our peoples, but a perfectly concrete Russian Communism, that is to say, the most modern form of perpetual historic Russian imperialism and colonialism. Just as in tsarist times, perfectly concrete Russian armies, consisting of genuine Russians, with brutal force crushed and conquered our countries (and neither Peter I nor Catherine I was a Communist!), so too in Lenin's day perfectly real armies (and not phantom armies!), consisting of genuine Russians, massacred our peoples and forcibly introduced the Communist system in our countries.

Nicholas II, Kerensky, Lenin, Khrushchev, or the NTS chief—they all agree on one point, namely to preserve the Russian colonial empire by every possible means! "Better a poor dictator [Stalin!] than a dismembered living body of Russia [i.e., the Russia empire!] was the comment of Miliukov on one occasion, and *all* Russian parties from the extreme leftists to the extreme rightists agree with him on this point!

ABN Correspondence
November-December 1961, pp. 8-11

Transformation or Tactics?

It is a well-worn truism of our times that Soviet policy always endeavors to achieve its aims, which never change, by roundabout ways and means if its frontal advance proves unsuccessful. For this reason Moscow's "complacence" in the case of Austria, its deference in Belgrade, and its willingness to take part in the Four-Power Conference must be regarded most warily. Undoubtedly, this is the preparatory stage of a far-sighted tactical maneuver which aims to foster destructive forces in the West and undermine its defensive strength, in order to gain time and thus enable Moscow to surmount its own difficulties.

The present state of affairs in the USSR and the satellite countries compels the men in power in Moscow to postpone the final conflict for as long as possible. The fact that the Soviet economic system has failed as a result of the burden imposed on it by ever-increasing armaments is at present as indisputable as is the economic superiority of the Free World. In addition, there is also the so-called "Nationalities Problem" and the liberation movements of the many nations subjugated by Russia. These, as far as Moscow is concerned, are its chief worry and also provide the main motive for the present maneuvers of Soviet foreign policy.

And yet the Kremlin has every reason to be very satisfied with the well-tried tactical method it has applied so far. In the first place it starts aggressions in all those parts of the world where the West seems to be vulnerable and when, eventually, the Kremlin is prepared to be complacent, the whole world rejoices that the Soviets have once more adopted a "conciliatory" attitude, although in most cases the accomplished facts that have resulted from these aggressions can no longer be undone. These practices on the part of the Kremlin began with the blockade of Berlin and were repeated in Korea and Indochina, where the aggressions started by the Communists and their imaginary "conciliatory attitude" were even rewarded very considerably.

At present, the Russians are intent upon confusing and intimidating Germany. It is hardly to be assumed that they seriously believe that Germany can be neutralized. They would be quite satisfied with the exclusion of the Federal Republic from the Atlantic Pact, and would even be willing to make certain concessions if this would reduce Germany to the position it was in after the First World War.

But, for the first time in history, England, Germany, America, France, and several other countries are now united in the same camp against Russian aggression. It is not surprising that this unique situation is a most unpleasant nightmare for the Russians. The potential of this coalition, consolidated by cooperation with the subjugated nations, not only upsets Moscow's plans to rule the world, but might also destroy Soviet Russian despotism in the present sphere of power. And this is the sole reason why the Russians intend to try and tempt Germany with the status of a power which, it is true, would be armed but would not be allied to any other power. If it came to the worst, the Russians would prefer Germany without any alliances rather than the present situation created by Adenauer.

Another variation, as far as the aims of Soviet policy are concerned, might be an attempt on the part of the Russians to entertain relations with the Federal Republic, on the one hand, and with the so-called German Democratic Republic, on the other. The purpose in doing so would be to detach the Federal Republic, by degrees, from the Western bloc, by increasing economic relations with the Eastern bloc countries, or else to use the Federal Republic as an obstacle to America's policy with regard to Europe. It is assumed in Moscow that in this case German industrial circles in particular could be won over by a tempting export and import boom.

Howsoever that may be, the most important fact to bear in mind is that the Russians are still, as in the past, not in the least interested in a permanent world peace, and are not endeavoring to find a genuine solution for the German problem, but are merely seeking to gain time, so as to enable them to consolidate the Eastern bloc and ward off the noticeable pressure of the subjugated nations. And, having disposed of these problems, they could then start aggressions elsewhere, as soon as possible.

It is likewise perfectly obvious that the mission to Belgrade and the agreement with Yugoslovia were not intended to serve the cause of peace, but rather to strengthen the "neutralization policy," as conceived by Moscow, and, above all, to consolidate the Communist world as a whole, a fact which is quite in keeping with the Communist conceptions of the world in the future.

In any case, their previous experience with Russian negotiation tactics and political practices should have taught the Western statesmen such a lesson that there should be no danger of their being deceived by new maneuvers on the part of the crafty Bolsheviks.

ABN Correspondence,
July-September 1955, p. 3

Pan-Slavism, a Russian Idea

QUESTION: *What is your opinion of Pan-Slavism? Is there any possibility of a fusion of the Slav peoples into one family?*

ANSWER: Pan-Slavism is one of the various forms of Russian imperialism. Under the disguise of the "defense of the Orthodox Church," Russia in the past endeavored to extend her influence to the territory of Turkey. Russia pretended to be protecting the Slav peoples but in reality she was merely seeking to bring them all under her influence.

Communism is the most recent form of Russian imperialism. In the past Russian imperialism concentrated mainly on the idea of Pan-Slavism. This idea has still not been abandoned by Russia, and, according to her requirements, she plays either the idea of Pan-Slavism or of Communism or of the Third Rome as her trump card. Even the anti-colonial world movements are used by Russia in the interests of Russian imperialism.

I do not think there is any possibility of the Slav peoples ever being fused into one family. Not racial, but national factors and national interests are decisive among the peoples. Just as the Germanic peoples cannot form one family, but on the contrary have fought against each other in wars (as, for example, England and Germany) because national interests always come before racial relationship, so, too, no family can be formed of the Slav peoples.

QUESTION: *Under what circumstances can Pan-Slavism be realized?*

ANSWER: Pan-Slavism can never be realized. That is to say, a joint state union of the Slav peoples can never be formed on a *voluntary basis,* since national contrasts are too sharp and too profound and cannot be bridged solely on the strength of racial kinship. The individual Slav peoples have far more interests in common with non-Slav peoples. For example, Poland relied on her common interests with France. Ukraine joined forces with Turkey against Russia, and Bulgaria, Croatia, and Slovakia with Germany against Russia.

In any case, all the Slav peoples are now "united" in the Russian empire. Thus Pan-Slavism has already been realized in this respect. But all these peoples are longing for the day when the "big Slav brother," whether tsarist or Bolshevik, vanishes from their countries. And I also consider Titoist Yugoslavia in the present Russian sphere of influence.

QUESTION: *Do you at present at least see any "small beginnings" towards the formation of a community of Slav peoples?*

ANSWER: Russia at present includes in her sphere of influence not only all the Slav peoples—Czechs, Slovaks, Serbs, Croats, Slovenes, Ukrainians, Poles, Byelorussians, and Bulgarians—but also non-Slav peoples, as for example Germans, Turkestanians, Ugro-Finns, Mongols, Georgians, and Armenians, etc., and is seeking to form a Russian world empire. Russia has thus not only made "small beginnings" towards the formation of a community of the Slav peoples, but has already taken a huge leap towards forming a Russian world empire of slaves and not merely of Slavs!

The Ukrainian people have gained some extremely bitter experiences from living side by side with "other Slav peoples." And I think that the Poles, too, for instance, with their insurrections against the Russian oppressors, have gathered the same "experiences," just as have the Croats and Slovaks with other Slav peoples.

If one regards the Russians as belonging to the Slav peoples—I personally am of the opinion that, apart from their language, which is interspersed with numerous non-Slav words, the Russians have very few Slav characteristics—then it would be better for the Ukrainians, who for centuries have endured the most ruthless extermination campaign by the Russians, to forget that such a race as the Slav—not to mention the so-called community of Slav peoples—exists at all in the world!

QUESTION: *Do you think there can be any special form of a community of the Slav peoples at all?*

ANSWER: I am of the opinion that the same principles of cooperation hold good for the Slav peoples as for every people on this earth. I do not think there can be any special form of a community of the Slav peoples, because this question is in no way connected with racial kinship. On principle I am also opposed to the idea of including any racial elements as a decisive factor in the general world order and, in particular, in the European order.

Interview Published in the Bulgarian Exile
Paper *Svoboda*, No. 1, 1962

Europe and Russia

> *"We are as unknown, and yet well known; as dying, and behold, we live; as chastened, and not killed."*
>
> II. *Corinthians, 6:9.*

A discussion of this problem would be incomplete, were we not to designate the fundamental conflict which exists between the Occident and Russia as contradictory conceptions of the individual and, equally, of the community.

We are at present living in an age of great conflict between two forms of civilization, between two political, social, cultural, and religious ideals—the conflict between Europe and Russia.

Leibnitz and Renan, Napoleon and Hugo, Engels and Disraeli (Lord Beaconsfield) foresaw this conflict, and, stirred by feelings of revenge, Herzen and Leontev, Bakunin and Gorky conjured it up as a vision. It is completely erroneous to imagine that this conflict can be settled, for if ever something in the world was a question of blood and iron, then it is this!

In his *Journal of an Author*, Dostoevsky wrote as follows: "Why do practically nine-tenths of the Russians when travelling abroad always seek to establish contact with European radical leftist circles, who, as it were, disdain their own culture? Is this not an indication of the Russian soul, to whom European culture has always been something foreign? I personally am of this opinion. The Europeans, however, regard us, rather, as barbarians, who roam about Europe and are pleased to have found something which might still be destroyed, who carry out destruction for the sake of destroying and simply in order to enjoy seeing everything fall to pieces—just as the wild hordes did in the past, as for instance the Huns, who flooded ancient Rome and demolished holy shrines without knowing what great cultural treasures they were destroying."

Russian Messianism

And the Russian political emigrant Alexander Herzen cursed the Western world with the words "Long live chaos, vive la mort!"

We maintain that there is such a thing as Russian Messianism, which unchangeably fights against the West and is a thing apart from Bolshevism or tsarism; and that the entire ideology of Russian Communism and of Russian tsarism—and, incidentally, also of the present solidarism which is crystallizing under "White Russian" anti-Communist watchwords amongst the emigrants—represent nothing but various forms of the same entity, of the same historic phenomenon of a general character—that is to say, of Russian Messianism. Quite apart from the social, political regime which at present rules the Russian people, a deep mystical belief in the predestination, in the world mission of the Russian people remains characteristic of the Russian intellectual class. Russian intellectuals could paint their people in rosy colors, like the "national" Narodniki did, or could compare it to a herd of cattle, as for instance Chekhov did in his "Muzhiken," or they could kiss the hem of its stinking "caftan," as Leo Tolstoy did, or, in fear of its "unfathomable" nature, could appeal to the bayonet of the Tsar, like the liberal Struve did—it all comes to the same thing. Whether angel or devil, Apollo, or centaur, half man and half animal, the Russian people continued to be regarded by the Russian intellectual class as a "people chosen by God," and if it was an animal, then it was a sacred animal before which all other peoples should bow down in awe and reverence.

It was not Lenin, but the pope of the so-called Slavophiles, the tsarist Konstantin Leontev (who, incidentally, was the first to coin the word "tsarism"), who in the last century wrote in his book *The Orient, Russia, and the Slav Element* as follows: "I believed and I still believe that Russia, which must take the lead in a new formation of the Eastern states, is to give the world a new culture, too, and is to replace the decadent civilization of Romanic-Germanic Europe by this new Slavic-European civilization."

The above-mentioned Alexander Herzen—an opponent of Russian tsarism!—dreamt of the hoped-for decline of the West and waited for "new barbarians who will come to destroy it." In a similar way, the loyal tsarist Slavophile Yuri Samarin dreamt of the role which Russia was to play "in the whole world," whilst the anarchist Bakunin was firmly convinced that "the Russian people will introduce new fundamental ideas in history and will create a new civilization, new faith, new law, and new life...." Maxim Gorky "spits in the face of America" and of "lovely France" in the name of Moscow's proletarian rabble, and, finally, Lenin usurps the rank of an apostle of the socialist Church, by whose edicts the thrones of the wronged socialist idols in the Occident shall be reduced to dust and ashes. Fundamentally, however, it all comes to what the Russian aristocrat Chaadaev wrote a century ago: "Our task consists in disseminating a saving principle of order in the world, which has become a victim of anarchy. Russia must not refuse to fulfill this mission, which has been entrusted to her both by the heavenly and also by the earthly ruler." And precisely the same idea was expressed by the police chief of Tsar Nicholas I, Count von Benckendorff, when he affirmed: "Russia's past was amazing, her present is more than illustrious, and her future will surpass all that human imagination can conceive." (With these words the Count hit the nail on the head as far as the Bolsheviks are concerned!)

Russia's Fight for Supremacy over the West

There were ideological representatives of Russian Messianism who stressed the "healthy forms" of the Muscovite state structure which must save Europe; others wanted to cure the world by means of the Muscovite "Obshchina" (peasant community), or sought to define Russia's mission as identical with the liberation of the Slav peoples (the white internationalists) or with the liberation of the world proletariat (the red internationalists), or even as the theoretical ideal of a rebirth of human morals thanks to Russia. There were others who dreamt of Moscow as a third Rome ("the Tartar Rome"—to use the fitting expression coined by the French writer Madame de Stael), and others who saw in Moscow the seat of the Third International. The Tsars Ivan III and Ivan IV (the Terrible) had firmly believed that Moscow was the third Rome; Byzantium, the second Rome, was the heir of the first Rome, and the third Rome was to be the heir of the second Rome. This, incidentally, is a Russian belief which has nothing to do with either social or religious convictions.

It would be erroneous to try to understand Russia's foreign policy from the point of view of such conceptions as "revolution and reaction," "proletariat and bourgeoisie," etc.; the sole question at issue is the conflict between Russia and Europe. When the Bolsheviks play off the national, religious movements of the Orient against the West, they are appealing not to any class conflict, but to the national fight of the Orient against Europe; when they seek to curry favor with the King of Afghanistan, this is, of course, not an alliance with the "international revolution" against the "international reaction," nor an alliance with the "working masses," but an alliance between two states—namely, a commonplace "bourgeois" policy, the policy of national interests and of the fight for Russia's supremacy over the West.

The aforesaid "pope of the Slavophiles," the loyal tsarist Konstantin Leontev, in his above-mentioned work based his political theory on the following points: "In this vital, cultural meaning which I regard as so important, all the southern and western Slavs are nothing but a necessary evil, since all these peoples as far as their intellectual classes are concerned represent nothing more than the most ordinary and most commonplace European bourgeoisie in the history of the world..." (p. 108). "It is high time to put a stop to the development of the petty bourgeois, liberal progress..." (p. 384). "If the world has to cast aside bourgeois civilization in the near future, the new ideal of humanity will of necessity spring from Russia, from a people among whom bourgeois qualities are least developed..." (p. 415). Thus, the tsarist Leontev and Lenin both express the same formulas.

Conflict of Two Mentalities

And since France in the nineteenth century played the part of the chief herald of such "bourgeois culture," this tsarist Slavophile expressed the following opinion on the subject: "If it is necessary for the further independence of Eastern Russian thought from Romanic-Germanic thought and for the adoption of new cultural courses and state forms that the dignity of Romanic-Germanic civilization should be lowered in the eyes of the people of the East, if it is necessary that the judgment of values regarding that civilization should become violent prejudices against it as rapidly as possible, then it is to be desired that precisely that country which has taken the initiative in the present progress should compromise its genius as speedily and finally as possible." So much for France! And he wrote even more emphatically at the time of the Commune of Paris: "Would it be possible to imagine a victory and the rule of the Commune without vandalism, without the material destruction of buildings, cultural monuments, libraries, etc.? Surely not; and in view of the present means of destruction, it is much easier to reduce the greater part of Paris to dust and ashes than it was in ancient times to destroy other great centers of culture, as for instance Babylon, Nineveh, or ancient Rome. And this should be the wish of everyone who aims to introduce new forms of civilization." No, this is not a quotation taken from a leading article in the Moscow *Pravda*; these words were written by the apologist of tsarism Leontev; they expressed the profound opinion of a Muscovite patriot, conscious of the irreconcilable hostility of his country towards Europe. Naturally, his Pan-Slavism has as little to do with the actual national liberation of the Slav peoples as the Bolsheviks appeal to liberate the proletariat has to do with an actual liberation of the proletariat. In both cases it is merely a matter of kindling a world conflagration which should destroy European culture.

The same opinion is expressed by another ideologist of Muscovite Slavophilism, O. Miller, in his work, *The Slav Element and Europe* (1877): "If we were to support the national principle among the Slav peoples, we should have to stir up the whole of former Europe against us and precisely in Europe should have to seek an opposing counterweight to the latter—that is to say, a factor in close cooperation with its new forces" (that is, with the same "new forces" on which Lenin, too, later set his hopes). And the author expresses his opinion even more closely when he says: "It seems to me that it would be extremely important for Europe's attitude towards us if we were genuinely to renounce the policy which we pursued up to the Crimean War, if we were to abandon all traditions of legitimism and our fear of a revolution."

Tsarist Russia was thus ready to rely on the "revolutionary" elements of Europe and, with their aid, to pull down the entire structure of so-called "bourgeois" culture—that is, of European culture as such.

One could quote other Muscovite Slavophiles without end in this connection; the ideas they express will always be found to tally with Lenin's ideas. A toying with the idea of the proletarian revolution, a crusade against the bourgeoisie, the stirring up of anti-Western feeling in Asia, tirades, and attacks against the principle of legitimism—these ideas and methods are used equally by the Muscovite Slavophiles and by Lenin and in both cases pursue the same aim—namely, the destruction of "decadent Europe" *ad majorem Muscovite gloriam*. And herein lies the common character of both forms of Muscovite imperialism—the tsarist and the Bolshevik. As could already be seen from the political conflict of the year

1914, from the social conflict of 1917, and from the social and political conflict of the years 1941 to 1945, it is still a question of the conflict of two forms of culture, of two national ideals. The ideal cherished by Russia was always messianic, and every stage in her expansion—both prior to 1917 and under Bolshevik rule—was always regarded by Russia herself as a stage in her fight against Europe.

European Self-acting Society and Chief Traits of Russian Society

And what strikes one most when one compares these two worlds, the Russian world and the Greek-Romanic-Germanic world, to which the West Slavs, the South Slavs, and, above all, the Ukrainians also belong?

The multifariousness, a comprehensive historic standard, the mobility of the masses, the free play of political and cultural forces, the significant role of personalities, the predominance of justice and of logical thought—all these characteristics are to be found in the Occident.

One-sidedness, the suppression of personality, the colorlessness of historic events, the lack of differentiation of the masses, the exorbitantly important part played by the state—all these characteristics are typical of Russia. If we read the history of Europe, we become acquainted with the history of its peoples. But all we perceive if we read the history of Russia are the obscure masses who blindly obey their leaders and who move in one direction today and in another direction tomorrow. The important part played by individuals and their free grouping, a feeling of personal dignity, of one's own rights and duties, active participation in social organization—these are the chief traits of Western society. The suppression and passivity of the individual, the lack of a true conception of justice, the lack of an autonomous morale which is replaced by commands or sheer force—these are the chief traits of Russian society. And, hence, there is "self-government" in the widest sense of the word in the West, and chaos or despotism in Russia. This primitiveness, this lack of order in the structure of the Russian national organism is evidence of Russian life—both in the social and in the political and religious sphere, in the sphere of family life and in that of culture. The Russian "Obshchina" does not recognize any of the individual rights which are independent of society and are based on the work and achievements of the individual. "Our intellectual classes do not recognize any conceptions of rights which might discipline them from within; what we need is discipline from without"—this was what Lenin said in 1903 when the Russian Social-Democratic Party split up into Bolsheviks and Mensheviks.

Russia remains fundamentally hostile to Europe and is bound to fight the latter. The amorphous Russian masses can only be guided by despotism; European self-acting society, on the other hand, can only be guided by its own action. For this reason, Russia cannot permit the spreading of European ideas within Russian society, since the latter would thus be disintegrated. In addition, Russia is obliged to fight European ideas, since the latter oppose every form of totalitarianism, including Russian, which seeks to rule all continents in order to destroy precisely that spiritual affinity which in the West unites individuals in groups and classes. Russia is not fighting against the bourgeoisie as such, but against personal and human rights and against the recognition of the idea of justice, which, according to both Leontev and Lenin, is identical with "bourgeois ideology." Russia is not fighting against bourgeois morale, but against all ideas which are over and above the level of a ruthless totalitarianism. Russia is fighting against voluntary cooperation, against an organized community which is based on the principles of a highly developed individualism. It is not our concern to solve the question as to whether Russia will ever succeed in adopting European principles as her own, or whether Chaadaev was right when he affirmed in his *Letters on the Philosophy of History*: "We have something in our blood which rejects all genuine progress." One thing, however, is certain, and that is that all the attempts made by Russia in the course of her history to imitate the West have merely resulted in a caricature: instead of an enlightened absolutism—a "despotism tempered by assassination" (Rohrbach); instead of parliamentarism—something akin to the Persian Majlis or the Turkish sham parliament under the last sultans, and, of course, instead of socialism—a Red barracks-like regime. Russia is not a state which belongs to the cultural family of Western states; it is not a power whose internal, vital elements from time immemorial included the great moral forces that constituted the legacy of the West. On the contrary, it is a power which is possessed by the totalitarian spirit of destruction of all freedom-loving forms of life, the crushing of the subjugated, the annihilation of higher cultural values!

ABN Correspondence,
November-December 1957, pp. 5-6.

After the Fall of an Idol

What actually happened in the Kremlin a short time ago to make the whole world, as if under a spell, peruse the annals of the mass murders—or rather, the resolutions of the 20th Congress of the Communist Party of the Soviet Union and the speeches of Bulganin, Mikoyan, Khrushchev , and other tyrants—and try to discover something extraordinary, revolutionary, and epoch-making in them? Did Mikoyan's words, that this Congress was the most important one since Lenin's death, really have such an effect? Are the murderers in the Kremlin really going to succeed in deluding the Western world to such an extent that Togliatti's words (after his return from Moscow) might prove true: "The 20th Congress of the Communist Party of the Soviet Union will dominate the world stage for many years"? "Big Changes," "Consolidation of Collective Leadership," "People's Front in Sight," "Parliamentary Path to Power of the Communist Party," "Policy of Coexistence as Guide for the Future," "Stalin a Murderer in Opinion of Central Committee of Soviet Union Communist Party," "Decentralization in the Soviet Republic"—such are the headlines which appear again and again in the press.

What has actually happened?

On August 23, 1939, the USSR made a non-aggression pact and on September 28, 1939, a friendship pact with Hitler, despite the fact that only a short time previously Hitler had been described by the Soviet press as the greatest criminal in the history of the world and as the murderer of thousands of workers. But now the situation was suddenly quite different. "The extermination of Hitlerism"—so Moscow's official organ, *Izvestiya*, wrote on October 9, 1939— "has now become a fundamental demand [in the allied West]. This takes us back to the Dark Ages when religious wars, which ravaged entire countries, were waged in order to exterminate apostates and infidels.... It is a matter of taste whether one respects or despises Hitlerism...."

On November 30, 1939, Stalin stressed the following points in an interview published by the Moscow paper *Pravda*:

1) It is not true that Germany carried out a surprise attack on England and France, but exactly the opposite was the case;

2) After the outbreak of the war Germany made the British and French Governments an offer of peace negotiations, a step which was likewise supported by the USSR; but the British and French Governments rejected Germany's offer and the efforts of the USSR.

On October 7, 1939, the London Communist paper *Daily Worker* wrote, "This war is not a war of democracy against fascism." And the Communist Party of France addressed the following appeal to the population: "Let us unite to fight the imperialistic war...."

Did the clique in the Moscow Kremlin in those days not introduce some "revolutionary" changes? But was there actually any change at all? Moscow's aim continued to remain the same—namely, the conquest of the world. The chameleons of the Kremlin always manage to adapt themselves as circumstances demand, in order to deceive the Free World as to their true aims.

When Bulganin took Malenkov's place, a "continuous advance of the Army to power" was prophesied, and, in fact, even the assumption of power by a Muscovite Napoleon, as a means of safety for the West—just as if it were not all the same whether a military man like Zhukov, as a member of the Politburo, or a "civilian" like Khrushchev, likewise as a member of the same Politburo (or rather, Presidium, to use the present democratic designation) were to advance to the position of dictator and despot! We have not yet forgotten the fact that the word "democracy" was ridiculed in the 1920s by the Stalin clique. And what happened then? Stalin adopted it as a stock expression along with all the other favorite Communist catchwords and mottos, and actually affirmed that he himself was the greatest democrat, in fact, a genuine *people's* democrat. There was a "people's front" once before, at least in France, under Léon Blum. But did things change as a result of this front? Were fewer people murdered in the USSR in those days? In those happy days of a symbiosis between Socialism and Communism, Edouard Herriot visited Ukraine and denied that a famine was raging there, even though there were thousands of corpses lying in the streets of all the towns. A collective leadership existed in Lenin's day; and what, we may ask, is the fundamental difference between Lenin's and Stalin's regime? What would be the purpose of a "return to true Leninism"? By whom and when were the non-Russian nations, including Ukraine, subjugated? At whose command was the conquest march on Warsaw carried out? Is it possible that Lenin had no intention of conquering Poland and did not aim to make Germany or Hungary Communist by force? Of course, it is true that these aims were not achieved until twenty-five years later, by Stalin, thanks to Hitler's folly.

Why, then, has Stalin been criticized so severely? For having falsified history, for having failed to assess the crisis of capitalism rightly, for having spoilt Leninist collective leadership, as well as for having assumed sole power, for having been a dictator, an absolute ruler, a despot.... And what did his supporters do—as for instance, all the governors-general of Ukraine: Molotov, Kaganovich, and Khrushchev? Are not they, the present convinced democrats and champions of "humanity," the ones who, by their joint action, murdered millions of Ukrainians and enforced a ruthless collective system?

In condemning Stalin, have not the Muscovite rulers condemned their own assumption of power, headed by Stalin, in half of Europe and half of Asia? Have they withdrawn the Russian troops from the non-Russian countries? Have they allowed free elections to be held? Have they done away with concentration camps? Or have they abolished slave labor and forced labor, or given back the farmers their private property? Khrushchev himself is the inventor of the "agro-towns," the worst form of *kolkhoz* slavery, and of the satrap system, which has resulted in thousands of young Ukrainians being sent to cultivate foreign "new land." He is the oppressor who at present even abolished the small holdings system and stipulates that the farmers may not even keep a few sheep or a cow if they have not fulfilled their "quotas" in the collective system (or rather, have not fulfilled more than their quota). Little attention has been paid by the world press to this measure on the part of the collective leadership, the Central Committee of the Communist Party of the Soviet Union; but it is precisely this measure which implies a further and consistent consolidation of the *kolkhoz* slave system, since it stipulates that the size of the holdings (at the most 1 hectare) shall depend on the output per worker in the *kolkhoz*.

Such, therefore, are the "facilities" which have been granted to the rural population by the collective leaders—measures which, incidentally, were enforced after the 20th Party Congress.

Mikoyan affirmed that violent revolutions and civil wars are not absolutely necessary in order to enable the proletariat (that is, obviously, the Communist Party) to assume power, since this was achieved in Czechoslovakia, Poland, Rumania, and Bulgaria by other means—without bloodshed or civil war; and, according to Mikoyan, this proves that the proletariat is capable of assuming power by peaceful means.... Incidentally, he fails to mention an "accessory circumstance," the occupation of all these countries by the Soviet Russian invasion army.

With an unparalleled cynicism, Mikoyan offers the West European states precisely the same prospects, inasmuch as he maintains that the Communists would be able to assume power in these countries too by means of parliamentary elections, but he adds "provided that the ruling classes put up no powerful resistance" (that is to say, provided that they allow themselves to be slaughtered). It is obvious that such "free elections" are only conceivable *after* the occupation of the country in question by the Soviet Russian forces. In that case, the "proletariat" there actually no longer needs a civil war and not even the enforcement of violent measures. Marshal Konev will see to that!

The hangman of the Hungarian people, Bela Kun, was "liquidated" unjustly, so it is now said; the hangmen of the Ukrainian people, Antonov-Ovseyenko and Kosior, are likewise said to have been decent Communists who "disappeared" without deserving such a fate. But what advantage do we or the West get out of the fact that the Kremlin is now rehabilitating its former satraps who, together with Lenin and Stalin, subjugated us and, with the aid of the Cheka founded by Lenin, decimated our numbers? It is a well-known fact that Stalin adopted many of his ideas from Bukharin, Trotsky, and other persons, and to a considerable extent realized these ideas, but liquidated the originators. Were those whom he liquidated any better than he was?

Considered from the criminological aspect, all these Communist assertions are merely sensational and do not alter the essential facts; for the intrinisic nature of the cruel and barbarous Bolshevik Russian mentality cannot be altered and can, in fact, only be overpowered if its physical power is destroyed.

It is interesting to note that the 19th Congress made far more use of "revolutionary" catchwords (for export purposes) than the recent Congress did. In this connection we have only to recall Beria's speech on the national problem of the USSR, for instance! Beria, the people's hangman, who had already caused thousands of non-Russians to be murdered and millions of internees in concentration camps to die a wretched death because they had championed the cause of national freedom, on that occasion stressed the problem of the "nationalities" and their political claims.... And what about the 20th Congress? Nothing but hackneyed Communist phrases about the "crisis" of capitalism, the colonial peoples, the imminent "lawful" victory of socialism, the priority of the heavy industries—not a single idea or trend that was new! All the ideas expressed were either derived from the anti-imperialist ideology of the former colonial and semi-colonial nations or were merely a repetition of the hackneyed Marxist phrases used by Lenin and Stalin in former days.

Nor is the reconciliation with Yugoslavia sensational news. Had Stalin personally been more compliant, he would have settled up this old account in his lifetime, and, in fact, in exactly the same way as is now the case. Then the West would not have been duped and would not be setting false hopes on Tito's sham national Communism, which is as odious to the nations as "international Communism"; for either there is really no "genuine" nationalist in the world inasmuch as his Russian national Communism tallies with Soviet Red imperialism.

And the method adopted in order to destroy Stalin's halo is by no means a new and original one. It was Stalin who taught his clique how to blame one's own faults on people like Trotsky, Bukharin, or Tukhachevsky, and now Stalin's disciples are thrusting responsibility for the faults of their own "collective leadership" on the dead dictator. Malenkov assures his fellow countrymen that there will never be a repetition of absolute despotism; in which case a regime of collective despotism will prevail—and it is probably all the same to the victims whether they are hanged by one hangman or by several. But let us examine this "democracy" in the Party leadership more closely! The most significant feature is not so much the fact that the "collectivist" leader, Khrushchev, in his report on the activity of the Central Committee of the Communist Party of the Soviet Union, treated Malenkov and Molotov, both members of the Central Committee like himself, with considerable contempt as being fantasists and ignoramuses, but that there is no opposition whatsoever. There is no majority and no minority; all resolutions are unanimously accepted, just as in the days of Stalin's absolute despotism. And this is what is described as a "democratic revolution in the Party leadership" enforced from above!

No, the most important political events of the past months did not take place at the 20th Congress of the Communist Party of the Soviet Union, but somewhere quite different. And these events, which were actually reported by the Soviet press itself (as, for instance, by *Chervony Prapor*, the provincial newspaper of Rivne in Volhynia), were the armed resistance fights in the forests of Lithuania and Ukraine and in Turkestan; the resistance movements in Georgia, Armenia, and Azerbaidzhan, which had already increased in strength a long time before the 20th Congress of the Communist Party of the Soviet Union was held, are, of course, only to be regarded as a national fight for freedom against Soviet Russian tyranny, and not by any means as a measure to defend the allegedly "reverent memory" of Stalin, a measure which would, in any case, only be possible in the small clique of Stalin's accomplices and hirelings.

The heroic death of the five hundred Ukrainian women internees who, in July 1954, in the concentration camp at Kingiri in Central Asia (near Karaganda), allowed themselves to be crushed to death by Soviet tanks in order to protect their fellow countrymen in the camp who were fighting for the cause of human rights and national honor has now proved to be no exceptional case, but a significant indication of the ever-increasing willingness on the part of the peoples subjugated by Moscow to wage a life-and-death struggle against Communism and Russian imperialism!

The Ukrainian Review,
No. III, 1956, pp. 10-15

De-Stalinization as a Means of Stalinization

In the first place, it was necessary to make some sort of concessions to the national revolutionary liberation movements and to the anti-Communist opposition of the masses, and thus decieve the Free World by a fictitious new era of peaceful coexistence and peaceful competition between two systems. Stalin alone—not his co-workers—was to bear all the blame for the crimes which had been committed. The second reason lay in the fact that Khrushchev, in order to pave his way to power, was obliged to build up some sort of a legend regarding his own person: namely, that it was precisely he and none other who had unmasked Stalin. And in this connection one should always bear in mind the fact which is constantly overlooked by the Free World, that it is the aim of the Russian people to have one idol, a "Father of the people," an absolute ruler, a tyrant, but only one and not ten. The Russians have never known the meaning of freedom. What they need is one ruler and master, and he must be stern. Khrushchev is paving his way to despotic absolute rule by getting rid of his rivals as fast as he can; in the eyes of the Russians, despotic autocracy is justified by the fact that the Russian peoples' prison could only be preserved intact by means of ruthless terrorism. Every form of collective leadership leads to the weakening of terrorism, to a split in the central authority, to the importance of the regime. The Russians are endeavoring to introduce a new despotic autocracy such as has existed again and again in the history of Russia. Khrushchev talked about collective leadership, but in reality he is consolidating his own absolute rule; in unmasking the cult of the absolute ruler, Stalin, he is building up the cult of his own person.

The fact that five leading men have been expelled from the Presidium, men who had their own opinions and knew how to rule—quite apart from the question of whether they might have supported the former terrorist regime of Yezhov or Beria, or not—is already becoming the starting-point for a new Stalinist epoch.

It is most erroneous to imagine that the expulsion of these five men might strengthen the peace trend externally and further a "democratization" in Russia. That is hardly likely since the question at issue is the centralization of the Communist Party, the absolute rule of one of two of the most powerful tyrants—Khrushchev or, possibly Zhukov. Why should the Communist Party of the Soviet Union become weaker if its internal party disputes cease? Why should things look brighter for the West if Khrushchev no longer has any rivals in the Presidium? It is a sheer lie to affirm that the "hangmen of the war" have been thrown out and that Khrushchev is a peacemaker. Actually, they are all tarred with the same brush. Strange to say, the fact is overlooked that Malenkov was "relieved of his duties for this very reason that he wanted to expand the consumption-goods industry at the expense of heavy industry"; but it was Khrushchev, who had set his hopes on the heavy industry, who then won the game.

It is not a question of whether certain persons might be "hangmen of the war" and others not, or of what their attitude in public is towards Stalinism. In principle, all of them without exception are Stalinists, for they are all Russian Communists. Is there a single one among them who would like to liquidate the Bolshevik system or would not aim to bring about and prepare a Communist world revolution or an aggressive war of conquests? The whole situation is quite different: it is a case of who is to become the absolute ruler, in keeping with the laws of Russian history and the wishes of the Russian people, who need one single idol instead of ten.

The question at issue is how to preserve the Russian empire and how to crush the national resistance movements whether by a frontal attack (according to

Molotov and Kaganovich) or by the roundabout method of fictitious concessions (according to Khrushchev and Mikoyan). Khrushchev affirms that the structure of the empire has not been loosened by the "de-Stalinization" process and that the empire can be saved by cunning and terrorism; the others say the opposite, namely by terrorism and cunning. In principle they all revert to Lenin's so-called 'New Economic Policy,' for all his successors and descendants have learned lessons from him for all time—namely, that there are situations in which one should make a temporary retreat in order to attack with more force later on— "one step backward and then two steps forward."

In any case, there can be no denying the fact that, among the various reasons for the zigzag policy pursued by Khrushchev, there is one reason which at least plays an extremely important part, and that is the indomitable fight of the peoples enslaved by Russia for their national liberation. Whether it was Hungary, Poznan, or the Ukrainian riots in the concentration camps. Khrushchev always endeavored to postpone partial concessions. And, incidentally, the concessions referred exclusively to Communists (or to Communists who were dead and were to be rehabilitated), since Khrushchev hoped to have at least the Communists on his side if the peoples concerned were prepared to settle up with the system itself. Khrushchev in no way intends to change the system; on the contrary, he is endeavoring to preserve it by advocating illusory changes. The system is threatened by the peoples enslaved by Russia, but not by any means by Khrushchev's alleged de-Stalinization. Postyshev, who was recently rehabilitated by Khrushchev, and Khrushchev himself, Molotov, and Kaganovich were at various periods in their career Stalin's satraps in Ukraine and always sought to strengthen the Bolshevik terrorist regime there. The same thing also happened in other "national Soviet republics" of the USSR. Why should the non-Russian nations of the Soviet Union cherish any illusion, if one of these tyrants liquidates his rivals in the Kremlin?

The fact that the members of the alleged "anti-Party group" are accused of having sabotaged the strengthening of the "friendship between the Soviet peoples" and of having opposed "the extension of the economic, cultural, and legislative rights of the Soviet Republics" proves that Khrushchev's clique greatly fears the national liberation movements and, indeed, is even trying to curry favor with the latter. That it is only a case of trying to curry favor with them and nothing more can be seen from the national composition of the new Presidium, in which, of fifteen members, only three are non-Russians: Mikoyan, Kyrychenko, and Kuusinen. Of the "candidates" for the Presidium on the other hand, the majority are non-Russians—proof of the fact that Khrushchev's clique in this way wants to show sympathy for non-Russians, but are determined that the actual power shall remain in Russian hands, as usual. And, incidentally, the non-Russians amongst the "candidates" are vile traitors and yes-men who have nothing in common with their fellow countrymen. It is immaterial how many of them there are. Those chosen as "candidates" are men who have already betrayed their people or else are Russians in disguise with non-Russian names.

The same alleged "anti-Party group" is likewise reproached with having opposed the abolition of compulsory deliveries by collective farmers of part of the produce grown on their private plots. But who was it who, under Stalin's rule, proposed the much-propagated "agro-towns," a project which in principle was to do away with all private plots? It was Khrushchev himself, who would now like to make sure of the support of the farmers by resorting to the ever-prevalent custom in Russia of trying to cast his own blame on persons who have already been liquidated. He is quite right in assuming that the national problem and the agrarian problem are the two greatest dangers which confront the Kremlin; indeed, recent events in Poznan and Hungary and even in the Soviet concentration camps were determined by the anti-Moscow cooperation of workers and youth, including the youth of the farming class.

But the struggle of the rivals in the Kremlin is not yet over. It remains to be seen whether Khrushchev will really become a Red tsar, or whether this prize will be snatched from him at the last moment by Zhukov, who is held in such high esteem by the Red chauvinists. It would not make much difference for Zhukov would in this case not appear in the capacity of "Soviet Marshal" nor as a representative of "the Army" as such (for there is no such clearly defined conception in the Soviet Union), but as a Communist in uniform—that is to say, as a Party man supported by the Communist military administration.

But Zhukov's position, too, seems to be somewhat precarious, for it very much resembles the position of Marshal Tukhachevsky in Stalin's day; and it is not yet clear who in the end will "bite the dust." But someone or other will be obliged to do so, for such is the law of Russian history.

And the victors, whatever clique they belong to, will inevitably end up as the victims of the indomitable urge to freedom of the peoples subjugated by Russia.

ABN Correspondence,
July-August 1957, pp. 1-2

The Vital Problems of World Politics

No one will ever be rich enough to buy his enemies with concessions.
Bismarck

The Disarmament Bluff

We are of the opinion that all disarmament conferences are nothing but self-deception. And most probably, each of the partners is aware of the fact that disarmament is impossible as long as the Russian Bolshevik empire, the destroyer of world peace, continues to exist. And yet conferences are held and huge sums of money are spent on them, whereas even a small amount of this money, if it were used to support the anti-Bolshevik underground movements, would undoubtedly be more effective in causing Moscow to become compliant than all the endless tirades on the part of the Western delegates and all their assurances of goodwill. The real aim of all these conferences is to prevent any reproaches, on the part of the free nations, as regard lack of peaceableness or "provocation" of another war. Since Moscow is well aware that the West prefers peace, it suggests one conference after another in order to paralyze the defensive forces of the free nations in this way. Moscow likewise knows that the statements of the West, since they are obliged to consider the peaceful attitudes of their nations, cannot possibly turn down the idea of disarmament negotiations, and it therefore suggests one new project after another, all of which, however, merely serves propagandist purposes. For instance, it takes up some former suggestion made by one or other of the Western major powers, adds various important "amendments" to it, and then disseminates propaganda to the effect that it has accepted the Western suggestion, but that the West has now turned down the same, and that it is therefore obvious that Moscow is not the warmonger! Or else Moscow presents its own disarmament plan, knowing full well that it will never be accepted by the West. Such discussions go on and on, in a vicious circle and merely deter the will to act. It is regrettable that the West possesses no resolute elements, no political community with a definite program, which could determine the line of action to be taken in this respect and could venture to bear the responsibility involved. It is no good shirking the truth, namely, that there never will nor can be peace as long as the Russian-Bolshevik peoples' prison and the Communist regime continue to exist, as long as millions of people are forced to languish under this yoke. These millions are not interested in a graveyard peace. But Moscow is only interested in creating a temporary, sham peace, since its aim continues to be world conquest.

The way to achieve peace and to avoid a Third World War coincides with the policy of support for the national revolutionary liberation movements behind the Iron Curtain and the national revolutions, which the major Western powers, by their assistance, should prepare, allow to develop, and bring to a successful issue, even though this might involve a war—which would, however, in any case be localized once revolts have broken out in the enemy's hinterland. The Western powers should have the courage to admit the truth and to explain it to their own nations before it is too late. They should prepare for the decisive battle against the destructive forces of Russia, which, sooner or later, will launch an armed attack on the West. Indeed, this was hinted at by Mikoyan at the 20th Congress of the Communist Party of the Soviet Union, when he made the assertion that Communism had been victorious in Czechoslovakia, Bulgaria, and Poland without a civil war; the fact that Communism asserted itself in these countries by means of armed force by Soviet Russian divisions is, however, well-known. And Soviet Russian tanks will likewise bring Communism to Paris should the West refuse to abandon the disastrous policy of coexistence.

So far, two obstacles have prevented Moscow from launching a large-scale attack on the Free World—the superiority of the USA as regards atomic weapons and the imminent outbreak of revolts and revolutions within the USSR and its sphere of influence. Russia's superiority as far as traditional weapons are concerned is, as it were, a double-edged sword, insofar as about half the Soviet Army is made up of non-Russians and these weapons might therefore easily fall into the hands of the insurgents. Why, then, does the West not take advantage of this extremely favorable opportunity offered by the internal situation in the USSR?

The Vulnerable Spot of the USSR

The USSR is a Russian empire. And, as in every despotic empire, the national problem is its vulnerable spot. German, Belgian, and English ex-internees who have returned home from concentration camps in Siberia and Kazakhstan have brought back reports which are of far-reaching significance for the entire Free World; the power of the USSR is not only being undermined in the countries it has occupied by the non-Russian peoples, but also in the concentration camps, where about 15 million persons, who are being tormented and forced to do slave labor, have now overcome their fears and are carrying on an active fight against Russian tyranny. The heroic death of five hundred Ukrainian women in Kingiri (near Karaganda in Kazakhstan), who threw themselves in front of Russian tanks in order to protect their fellow internees, and let themselves be crushed to death, is the most significant event in the USSR during the past few decades. It is proof of the fact that there is internal ferment in the USSR and that the subjugated nations refuse to surrender to Soviet tyranny and even carry on their fight against the occupiers of their countries, in the concentration camps. And this is where the Western world should seize its opportunity, for the events which concern the subjugated nations are of far greater significance than the 20th Congress of the Communist Party. This Congress merely proves the internal weakness of Bolshevism; what is far more important is the cause of this weakness. The sole aim of the 20th Party Congress was to introduce illusory "facilities" and, in order to pacify the public, to give Stalin the blame for having been responsible for Bolshevik crimes. It is most imperative that the West should at this time, when national revolutionary processes are apparent in the USSR, take the initiative, for such action would destroy the Soviet Russian empire from within and localize the war of liberation in the Bolshevik sphere of influence.

The disintegration of this empire, the idea of national liberation, the idea of the freedom of man, of religion, and of social justice and equality, the unconditional abnegation of the Communist totalitarian system, recognition of the right to private property provided that it has been acquired by work, recognition of the sovereign rights of all nations and of their equality—these are the ideological principles by means of which Bolshevism can be conquered, for it will never be conquered by ideas which are akin to its own.

Russia's Offensive in Asia and Africa

The most characteristic feature of the present epoch is the national fight for freedom of the subjugated, colonial, and semi-colonial and other dependent nations—a fight which has now assumed universal significance. The twentieth century can, indeed, be described as the springtime of nations all over the world. The age of imperial realms is past; a new era of national states is dawning. Although Communism as a system means negation of the national idea, Soviet Russia in the name of Communism nevertheless seeks to establish contact with national liberation processes outside its own sphere of dominion and to win over the dependent and colonial peoples of Asia and Africa, by cunningly supporting their claims to sovereignty and fostering centrifugal trends within the rest of the Western empires. What is more, Soviet Russia offers to protect those nations of Asia and Africa which until recently were colonial dependencies of the Western empires, but have meanwhile, of their own free will, become independent. It is most certainly paradoxical that Russia, the advocate of the grimmest form of imperialism, should claim to be the protector of the national idea which is exactly the opposite of imperialism; in reality, it is a case of a conflict between two conceptions of world order; on the one hand, the forcible unification of the nations in one single nationless and anti-national world empire of the USSR and, on the other hand, the disintegration of empires into national states for the purpose of bringing about a world union and harmony of the nations based on the principle that the states of all the peoples of the world, be they great or small, shall be free and shall enjoy equal rights. An open frontal attack on the national idea would inevitably lead to Soviet Russia's immediate defeat. For opportunist reasons Soviet Russia is, therefore, obliged to establish contact with national liberation trends outside its own sphere of dominion, where it systematically exterminates such trends and endeavors to create one single "Soviet nation"— namely, in the Soviet Union.

In the first stage of its offensive, Soviet Russia does not produce a Communist social program, but a national, anti-feudal program, on condition that all reforms, however, are to be effected by the Communist Party, which, in this way, is to win the confidence of the masses and assume the leading role. Feudal landed property is divided up into holdings, which are distributed among the small farmers and peasants as "a present"; later on, once the Communist Party has consolidated its position, the farmers are deprived of their "present" and are forced to join the collective farming system. The nations concerned are thus, first of all, only "neutralized" and withdrawn from the sphere of Western political influence, which in itself represents a considerable success on the part of Soviet Russia, as well as being the first step to the gradual sovietization of such nations.

The Vital Problem of World Politics

The nations striving for complete independence include not only the enslaved nations in the Soviet Russian empire and sphere of influence, but also those colonial, semi-colonial, and other dependent peoples who are either still part of the remaining Western empires or who, though they may actually already be independent, as a result of their hardly justifiable fears and ill-feeling towards the West of today, allow themselves to be led and misled. The world policy of the major powers is constantly preoccupied with these national state problems—whether it is a question of oil in the Near East, Transcaucasia, or Romania, iron ore in Ukraine, or cotton in Turkestan.

Of all the major powers, the USSR, however, is the only one which consistently pursues a definite and unalterable aim—namely, to win over these Asian and African nations, to subjugate them by ideological and social subversion, and, after increasing its war potential correspondingly, to deal the major powers of the West a deadly blow in order to become the absolute ruler of the world. The Western major powers on the other hand, waver in their choice of policy between vague and confused ideas about a "federalist world government," a passive and inactive conservatism which does not intend to make any reforms until it is too late to do so, and even the idea of establishing contact with the national Communist trends and similar trends related to Bolshevism in intellectual circles of the dependent nations in question. And all this is overshadowed by the fatal illusion of "peaceful coexistence."

In his recent notorious interview, the French Prime Minister Guy Mollet expressed an idea which has long been the dream of many prominent political personalities of the West, that the "status quo" should be recognized and "disarmament" conducted on this basis. This would, of course, mean that Soviet Russia would be allowed to retain the inexhaustible production and natural resources of the nations which it has subjugated, as well as a huge human potential. The reunification of Germany "in peace and freedom" would, incidentally, be of little significance, since East Germany is not the vital problem of present world politics, but merely one of many problems. In any case, a reunited Germany would not be in a position to guarantee a world peace to the 280 million people still under Soviet Russian tyranny (not to mention the huge population of Red China). Even the setting up of the Russian empire within the frontiers of 1939 would be no guarantee that the Russian advance of 1939-1945 might not be repeated; the only guarantee in this respect would be the disintegration of the Russian empire into national states and the limitation of Russia to her ethnic boundaries.

Fear of an atomic war does not justify capitulation in the face of misdeeds. Even so, apart from this ethical point of view, it is obvious that atomic bombs of the modern type can only be produced in empires, and not in national states, which do not have economic potential high enough for this purpose and which, in any case, are hardly likely to be interested in imperialist conquests. The disintegration of the Russian empire into national states would thus relieve the world of the danger of an atomic war.

Liberation Policy as Disarmament Policy

If Russia is thus deprived of the main supports of her imperialistic policy—the economic and human potential of the nations subjugated by her—disarmament will be able to proceed practically automatically. What armed conflicts are likely to occur between Ukraine, Turkestan, Bulgaria, or Poland, and the USA and

Great Britain? The Bolshevik disarmament plans are intended to divert the attention of the West from the most vital factor which would render all negotiations on the disarmament question meaningless—namely, the liberation of the countries occupied by Russia. An integral precondition of disarmament is thus the liberation of all the nations subjugated by Bolshevism, and not merely the liberation of East Germany, as Bonn would believe. On the other hand, recognition of the status quo with regard to Germany's partition would, from the geopolitical point of view, be synoymous with a final renunciation on the part of the West of even broadening the question of the fate of the remaining satellite states; thus the German problem assumes the significance of a touchstone for Moscow's alleged "goodwill." All references to the withdrawal of the Soviets from Austria after the latter's "neutralization" are quite senseless, since there was no Communist Government in Austria.

By misusing the idea of the national and anti-feudal liberation movement in Asia and Africa, Soviet Russia is succeeding in overthrowing the remainder of the British and French colonial empire from within and incidentally, at the same time, is even being acclaimed as a liberator by the peoples concerned, despite the fact that it is inflicting a form of slavery on them which is very much worse than that which they endured under British or French rule. The strange thing is that the Western major powers—even if they have no definite liberation program— do not want to pay Russia back in her own coin. What could be simpler for one or other of the Western major powers than to support the national liberation movements in Ukraine, Georgia, or Turkestan and get its revenge in this way? At the Bandung Conference, for instance, the Sudan and even the Gold Coast were represented, so why not Turkestan? And should Moscow intervene in the question of the right of self-determination of Malaya or Algeria, one can but ask: what about the "sovereignty" of such ancient Christian nations as the Ukrainian or Georgian nation! If Soviet Russia aims to bring about the disintegration of the British or French empires, why should not London and Paris aim to bring about the disintegration of the Russian empire and, in fact, declare this to be the aim of their foreign policy! If the Soviet Union supports the Communist parties in the West, why should not the USA support the national liberation organizations behind the Iron Curtain, all the more so since these organizations enjoy the confidence of whole nations and, unlike the Western Communist parties, are not the agents of a foreign power! The West holds the dynamite in its hand with which it could blow up the USSR from within, but, for some reason or other it seems powerless to reach a decision.

Meanwhile, since Stalin's death, since Beria's fall, and since the 20th Party Congress, the Bolshevik empire has been undergoing an ever-increasing process of internal dissolution, despite the fact that the "collective" leaders are obviously doing their utmost to check this process by means of various tricks. Once again we exhort the Western world: Give the tyrants no breathing space! Give them no chance to consolidate their forces! Take the offensive! The subjugated nations have already begun to smash the peoples' prison. It only needs the active intervention of the West, and the tyrant's empire will burst into flames and turn into dust and ashes.

The USSR of today—like the Russian empire on various occasions in the past is a colossus with feet of clay. Prevent it from becoming a colossus with feet of iron! And this depends, entirely on the major powers of the West, and, above all, on the USA and Great Britain.

ABN Correspondence,
April-May 1956, pp. 5-6

I Accuse Khrushchev of Mass Murder
of the Ukrainian People

"Three-quarters of mankind may perish so that the rest may experience Communism!"

—Lenin

"I am a Russian and proud of my nation!" said Khrushchev during his visit to the Leipzig Fair in 1959, thus refuting the assertions made in the Free World that he was a Ukrainian.

The Ukrainians accuse Khrushchev of being one of the most ruthless mass murderers of their people in their tragic history. For many years Khrushchev held the post of Stalin's governor in Ukraine and on the strength of his cruelty and ruthlessness proved himself to be the most loyal henchman of his master. From the beginning of the Eastern campaign onwards, there was a man in the other camp who might have been his twin-brother—Hitler's governor in Ukraine, Erich Koch, an equally ruthless tyrant and servile toady. Two mass murderers in Ukraine, two representatives of the two most terrible totalitarian systems, which clashed in 1941.

We Accuse

We Ukrainians accuse Khrushchev of the mass murders of the Ukrainian people, whom—in his capacity as First Secretary of the Central Committee of the Communist Party of Ukraine from January 1938 until December 1947, as Prime Minister of Soviet Ukraine in 1947, and again as First Party Secretary from January 1948 to December 1949—he exterminated, in a most ruthless way.

We accuse him not only of the mass murders in Lviv in June 1941 and of having been responsible for other mass murders at that time in numerous towns and villages all over Ukraine, but also of the mass murders in Vinnytsa in 1938-40, where over 10,000 Ukrainians were massacred at his orders. Khrushchev is the most ruthless hangman of the Ukrainian people ever, and it is this policy of extermination pursued by him in Ukraine that has fitted him so ably for the post of hangman for the entire Soviet Union.

We accuse him of mass murders in Budapest, in Poznan, and in East Germany; we accuse him of ruthlessly crushing the riots of Ukrainian internees in the concentration camps during the years 1953 to 1956 (Vorkuta, Norylsk, Magadan, Mordovia, Tayashet, and Kingir) and in 1959 in Temir-Tau. At his orders 500 Ukrainian women internees in Kingir were crushed by Russian tanks when, singing Ukrainian patriotic songs, they tried to hold up the tanks in order to prevent a massacre in the concentration camp.

We accuse him of the mass deportation of young Ukrainians to Kazakhstan and Siberia. We accuse him of the treacherous Russification of Ukraine and of the perfidious persecution of Ukrainian freedom fighters.

We accuse him of the murder of the leader of the Ukrainian liberation movement, Stepan Bandera.

We accuse him of ruthlessly exterminating and fighting the Ukrainian Insurgent Army during and after the war when he held the office of Moscow's governor in Ukraine. We accuse him of ruthlessly crushing the Ukrainians' insurrection by the most perfidious methods, including the use of gas and bacteriological means.

We accuse him of the persecution of our Autocephalous Orthodox and Catholic Churches!...

We demand that an international court be formed, before which *we can bring forward the accusations against Khrushchev* and his hirelings regarding the mass murders in Lviv in June 1941, which he is trying to blame on German forces and Ukrainian nationalists, so that this blood-stained murderer will at least be condemned morally.

We demand the severance of all diplomatic, economic, and cultural relations with the Government of this hangman. We demand the exclusion of the Soviet Union and all its satellite Governments from all international organizations, as for instance from the UN.

We warn against the coexistence policy and against the pilgrimages of Western statesmen to Moscow, as well as against invitations to this criminal to visit the West, on which occasions these statesmen shake hands with this ruthless hangman whose hands are stained with the blood of millions of innocent men, women and children, and greet him as a "peacemaker"!

The so-called "Summit" conference did untold damage to the honor and conscience of the statesmen of the Western powers, who believe in God and respect human rights but tried to sit at the same table with the most ruthless of mass murderers, Khrushchev. He consistently pursues his aim, the recognition of the status quo by the West, a fact which is to provide the starting-point for his conquest of the world.

We warn the free world not to fall into the abyss!

Caveat Consules!

The Ukrainian Review,
No. I, 1960, pp. 3-19

Education—USSR

"Education—USSR," the traveling exhibit now on tour in the USA, must be scrutinized in terms of the wider plan of the Russian strategy to expand Communist influence and domination.

To Soviet Russia in the thermonuclear and ideological age a new type of warfare which is attuned to technological progress became imperative. This became necessary also because of Russian strivings to conquer the world and because of the national independence movements and anti-Communist resistance within the Russian sphere of power.

When the Western empires dissolved, the concept of national statehood was realized as a new principle of world order.

Why, then, should the greatest and most malignant empire of the world today—the Russian empire—be left intact? This empire holds in its tentacles nations with a thousand years of tradition and culture, like the Ukrainian or Georgian nations, while the Western empires gradually disappeared.

The creation of new states in place of the Western empires has an important influence upon the mobilization of the anti-Russian front among nations subjugated by Russian imperialism. A Ukrainian child might ask: why is it that Ukraine, a highly civilized country, has Russian occupation forces when Ghana or India are free from occupation?

The subjugated nations in her midst, including 50 million Ukrainians, are the Achilles' heel of the Russian-Communist empire. The decrepitude of the system was well demonstrated during the Hungarian uprisings in 1956, which would have been victorious had it not been for the West aiding Russia politically. The insurrection of Ukrainian, Baltic, and other inmates of concentration camps have also proven this point.

The national independence of the enslaved peoples and national liberation revolutions are the roads to *freeing* humanity from the fear of thermonuclear war as well as from Communism and Russian imperialism.

The Idea of Freedom Is Stronger than the Atomic Bomb!

The modern type of warfare in which we find ourselves and which is conducted by Russia and not the US includes the following elements:

1) An ideological and political offensive of Communism from within each country, coupled with the depreciation of all human values, traditions, patriotism, religion, and morals by introducing the relativism of all truths, a corruption of the spirit and morals of the nation, and attempts to create a complex of inferiority by artfully showing the so-called achievements of Communism with the "superiority" of the Russian race and its "genius";

2) Peripheral wars of "national liberation" and civil wars, engaging American manpower but not committing their own, in an attempt to extend the frontiers of the Russian Communist empire;

3) Being in a state of permanent war against the West and against the peoples subjugated by her, and creating fronts inside the free nations. Russia exploits other means to seize power from within. If, for instance, in the USA and in West Germany the workers are immune to Communism, Moscow places its bet on the intellectual elite, upon the students, and upon infiltration of the mass media. Thus Russia hopes to influence large masses of people so that—having brought the cultural elite under her control—she may conquer the United States from within.

This Plan Fits In with the Exhibition "Education—USSR"

As we so well know, "the best" always originates in Moscow. Moscow also discovered America. Americans must never forget that they are neighbors of the Russian empire across the Bering Strait. With the dissolution of the Russian empire into independent states, America could free herself from this dangerous neighbor. It would be interesting to know what the Russians were looking for in Alaska. Communism was non-existent then, but there surely existed the unchanging Russian imperialism. When we mention "Education—USSR," it is evident that we talk about the education of an aggressive atheist, Russian Communist imperialist! Is this educational ideal acceptable to those Catholic circles that recommended "peaceful co-existence" with Moscow? Uninterrupted ideological militancy against aggressive atheism and oppression of man—created in the image of God—is an obligation of a good Christian. Furthermore, if the Russian educational system is superior to the Western, then:

a) Why is there no freedom of creativity in the USSR? Creativity depends not on the perfect technical organization of upbringing, but in the IDEALS that guide that educational system.

b) Why are jails, concentration camps, and mental institutions filled with authors of cultural values, particularly in Ukraine and other enslaved countries? Why, are countless secret trials conducted against those whose sole aim is to be able to create freely in Ukraine and other subjugated countries?

c) Why are the patriotic Ukrainian educators silenced and many of them now in Siberia; why do the Russians play a dominant part in Ukrainian humanist and pedagogical sciences?

Our suggestions:

1) Let the Government of the United States of America, and the State Department in particular, which is the sponsor of this exhibition, assert themselves in achieving the following: to free from jails, concentration camps, and from mental institutions the SCIENTISTS AND EDUCATORS OF UKRAINE and other enslaved nations so that they can tell the West the TRUTH about "Education—USSR."

Let those who are jailed and suffering for the truth tell us what the real truth is.

2) Let the State Department, or for that matter the Council on World Affairs, with the objective of telling the truth to the American public and the intellectual and student elite in particular, initiate an exhibition on "Education—Ukraine"

and other oppressed peoples in the USSR and the "satellite" countries. The organizers of this can be: the Ukrainian Free University in Munich, Ukrainian Catholic University in Rome, Ukrainian Free Academy of Science in New York, the Shevchenko Scientific Society (New York-Toronto), and the Association of Ukrainian Cultural Workers (New York-Toronto). Instead of indoctrination by Moscow's propaganda, I urge Americans to learn the truth directly from those who chose the freedom so highly valued by the American people. Let the American public learn about the *IDEAS* that our young generation adheres to; the true situation of Ukrainian science, literature, art, education; about their fight for a Ukrainian set of ideals against enforced Russian system of ideals.

I, as a former inmate of Nazi concentration camps, sincerely urge the public opinion of America, in particular those who influence and educate, to portray—besides Nazi crimes against humanity—on TV and radio, in films, illustrated magazines, newspapers, and journals, the following:

a) the epic stories of martyrdom and heroic struggle of the UPA against both Russia and Nazi Germany;

b) the Bolshevik concentration camps, camps for forced labor, mental institutions where Russians incarcerate the spokesmen of the intellectual elite of Ukraine, as described by the writer Tarsis in his book *Ward 7*; secret trials of fighters for the freedom of creativity, for the freedom of nations and men;

c) the Moscow-organized famines in 1932-33, and 1945-46 in the granary of Europe—Ukraine—as the result of which millions died;

d) the Christian catacombs of the twentieth century: underground Churches, the Ukrainian Catholic and Ukrainian Autocephalous Orthodox Churches, and their hierarchy, priests, and thousands of faithful liquidated by atheistic Moscow;

e) the systematic extermination of the UPA fighters and of those who supported them in 1945-50, by chemical and bacteriological means; the raid of detachments of UPA into the West, crossing the "satellite" countries during 1948-49;

f) the uprisings of Ukrainian political prisoners in the concentration camps in 1953-59 and their liquidation by the Chekists; the mauling by tanks of 500 Ukrainian women who died with patriotic and religious songs on their lips as they tried to shield with their bodies other prisoners in Kingiri (Kazakhstan) in 1956. The West has living witnesses: American (such as the Jesuit Father Ciszek), British, Belgian, French, Japanese, Spanish, Italian, and German former prisoners and POWs;

g) strikes and disturbances of Ukrainian workers and youth (1959-67) in Ukrainian cities and towns against foreign occupation and exploitation, Russification and oppression; their fight for the rights of the individual and the nation.... This also applies to all other nations under the heel of Russia: Estonia, Lithuania, Latvia, Poland, Turkestan, Hungary, Georgia, Byelorussia, and all others sharing this dire fate.

Will this be told by those at "Education-USSR"?

Finally, we appeal in the name of the sacred rights of the individual and nations:

1) to the public opinion of the United States of America to condemn and stand up in defense and protest against the persecution of poets, artists, writers, scientists of Ukraine, and other captive nations. We appeal to the young cultural workers of the USA, especially those of the "Sixties" group, to defend those of the "Sixties" in Ukraine and other captive nations who with manly strength renewed the battle for the highest ideals—rights for men and nations; to help to free from jails, concentration camps, and mental institutions all freedom fighters; to liquidate all concentration and forced labor camps; we appeal to your Nobel Prize winners to stand up in defense of those who with their suffering and struggle defend their right to live free, those who with their sacrifice shield the Free World from the deluge of Communism;

2) to urge American youths, and students in particular, to lend their support to our students, who are forcibly indoctrinated in Russian culture and are denied the right to study their own history and culture in their native tongue and spirit;

3) to mobilize workers and trade unions to take steps in the defense of our workers, who lack the right to strike, the right to a decent living, the right to free national progress. The Soviet trade unions are mere functionaries of the Moscow dictatorship. The biggest cog in the trade union movement is now Shelepin, the former chief of the KGB, who gave orders to organize and carry out the murder of Stepan Bandera, who was the leader of the Ukrainian liberation movement;

4) to demand the withdrawal of the Russian occupational military forces as well as all means of aggression and oppression from Ukraine and other enslaved nations! When all empires are in ruins today, why does the Free World help to maintain the last tyrannical one?

HAVING PLANNED A WIDE COUNTER-OFFENSIVE, we ask: Why does the USA not support the national independence movements of the enslaved nations in order to disintegrate the Russian prison of nations from within, by way of national revolutions, bringing about the downfall of the Communist system and thus avoid the danger of an atomic war?

Press Statement, Buffalo,
N.Y., December 1967
(ABN Correspondence,
January-February 1968, pp. 22-24)

Scandalous Provocations of Russian Imperialists

The reason and circumstances leading to the shameful show trials which are being prepared by Brezhnev in Ukraine are known to everyone all too well. They are reminiscent of the twenties and, in particular, the Stalinist thirties—the years of terror of the Cheka, GPU, Dzerzhinsky, Menzhinsky, Yagoda, Yezhov, Vishinsky, and their followers. Brezhnev is steadfastly following in the footsteps of his master, Stalin. Even Shelepin, the murderer of the late Stepan Bandera, cannot compete with him. The cult of Brezhnev's personality, as an infallible leader of the empire, is systematically cultivated on the model of the cult of Stalin. A sly, typically Russian barbarian—treacherous, base, and brutal—Brezhnev is employing the same methods of extermination not only of the fighters for freedom and independence of the subjugated nations but also of the creators of the intellectual and cultural values who do not want to deny their national "I," their national traditions, but strive to foster the culture, the art, the literature, the folklore, and the traditions of their nation.

Obviously, it is of no significance for the Russian occupiers that the leaders and workers in the field of culture in Ukraine have unfolded their activity within the framework of the (paper) rights guaranteed to them in the so-called Constitutions of the USSR and the Ukrainian SSR and the Universal Declaration of Human Rights, which was signed by the USSR and the Ukrainian SSR as members of the UN. Every issue of *Ukrainskyi Visnyk* (The Ukrainian Herald) carried a note to the effect that the authors were taking advantage of the right guaranteed to them by the Constitution, and were writing and acting within its limits. However, in line with the practice of the Russian oppressors and occupiers, all the rights guaranteed by the USSR and the Ukrainian SSR Constitutions and the Universal Declaration of Human Rights of the UN in the Russian empire are destined only for export, for consumption abroad, as was expressed by a KGB officer in Mordovia. In the USSR, he said, the law of Stalin reigns, the law of violence and injustice.

The Organization of Ukrainian Nationalists has never recognized and still does not recognize either the Ukrainian SSR or the Constitutions of the USSR and the Ukrainian SSR, which it considers a bluff, a perfidious provocation in order to catch fish in muddy waters. The USSR Constitution is a Russian provocation, a means to expose the more courageous individuals, who wish to fight openly for its realization, so as to destroy them later or to confine them to prisons and concentration camps. Provocation and treachery, deception and terror—these are the roads and methods of Moscow's domination in Ukraine and in other countries subjugated by it.

The world press, including the *US News and World Report* of January 20, 1972, carried a report that, according to the information of Western intelligence sources, the leadership of the USSR decided at the end of last year to accelerate the solution of the problem of the Jews who want to leave the USSR, and to crush the activity of the intellectual elite of the subjugated nations—in particular, to liquidate the *Samvydav* (self-publications).

There is no doubt that Russia lost its duel with the Jews. Jewish power, which to a great extent, controls the mass media, has great material and technical means and a strong influence on the policy of the United States. Simultaneously, support of Jews in the USSR by Israel has forced Moscow to yield to the Jews in order to have a free hand in settling accounts with nations subjugated in the USSR—in particular, with unsubdued Ukraine—as the greatest threat to the Russian empire.

Suffering a defeat in its clash with the Jews, Russia is saving its prestige by taking a harder course against the nations subjugated in the USSR in order to show its "unconquerable might." The "concessions" to the Jews and the intensification of repressions toward the nations held captive in the USSR are also caused by the fact that an economic crisis is becoming more acute in the Russian empire. Ukraine faces a new famine. Hence, it is necessary to find "the enemies of the people" and to put all the blame on them, or at least to turn attention away from the real cause of the calamity.

Moscow is changing its course very rapidly. The Ukrainian nationalists whom it labelled "the killers of the Jews" are rapidly becoming "the partners of the Jews." Only yesterday Stepan Bandera had allegedly "issued orders" to annihilate hundreds of thousands of Jews; only yesterday the UDP (Ukrainian State Government) "had perpetrated" Jewish massacres in 1941, only yesterday "the candidate of history," a certain Kychko, published in Kyiv, under the auspices of the Academy of Sciences of the Ukrainian SSR, a diatribe on "the anti-Semitism of the Ukrainian," in particular the nationalists. Today the *Visti z Ukrainy* (*News from Ukraine*, a propaganda newspaper published by the Russian secret service for Ukrainians abroad), as well as other publications of the Ukrainian-language Soviet press, prints "revealing" articles by that same Kychko about "a bloc of Ukrainian nationalists and Zionists," about their joint, coordinated effort. The proof? Here it is: the ABN and EFC held an International Conference in Brussels, and immediately afterwards the Jews held their World Zionist Congress in that same Brussels. Thus, for Moscow's lackey Kychko, the "proof" is there. Allegedly the Ukrainian nationalists and the Jewish Zionists are inseparable friends and are "acting jointly" while Yaroslav Stetsko and the leaders of world Zionism are simply "Siamese twins." Yesterday Symon Petlura was "the killer of the Jews," while today, according to Kychko, he is a "sworn friend of Zhabotynsky."

What has happened? What has forced Moscow to take such dangerous turns in its policy? The Israeli-Arab conflict alone, in which Russia is conveniently using the Arabs to further its own interest, does not play a decisive role here. The Russian chieftains are also wary of the resurgent Jewish patriotism in the USSR itself, which is partially devastating their tried methods of utilizing Jews for their interests, as had been the case in the past with Trotsky, Zinovyev, and many other leaders and Cheka members of Jewish origin. They are aware of the fact that the growth of Jewish patriotism is directly reinforcing the anti-Russian front of the subjugated nations.

It is true that some Jews in the USSR hold prominent positions in industry, administration, technology, science, in the organization of culture and propaganda, even in the military. It is also true that the people of the countries subjugated by Russia, in particular of Ukraine, still remember the role played by the Kaganoviches, the Khatayeviches who razed their monasteries and churches, the Trotskys, the Litvinovs, the Radeks, Zinovyevs, Kamenyevs, and numerous other Jewish lackeys of Russian imperialism. Therefore, there is nothing strange in the fact that prejudice against such Jewish lackeys exists among the Russian-dominated nations. At present Moscow is counting on this very resentment, attempting to link the Ukrainian nationalists with the Zionists.

And so the Russian tactic of "catch the thief" is repeating itself. It is not the

Russians who are responsible for the subjugation and the exploitation of the Ukrainian people, for genocide in Ukraine, but the Jews.... The same tactic was applied in the past by the Russian tsars, and now it is being repeated by the Russian Communists. Russia is no longer able to conduct its destructive advance against the Ukrainian people under new propagandistic slogans which would conceal the real objective of its great-power chauvinism and imperio-colonialism. Therefore, it is searching for various pretexts for the persecution of Ukrainians on the one hand, and on the other is trying to evoke among the Ukrainian people an aversion for Ukrainian nationalists, as "allies of the Zionists" or Jews in general who have held in the past or are still holding prominent positions in the USSR.... Nevertheless, in this old, albeit tried, tactic, Russia is beginning to lose its balance and is in a state of confusion. The Trotskys, the Kaganoviches, and the Badeks were not Zionists, but Bolsheviks, lackeys of Moscow; they were also not "friends" of Petlura but of Lenin. They were destroying Ukrainians with fire and sword, together with the Russians, their employers.

The embarrassed Russian chieftains, having lost in their confrontation with world Jewry, want to salvage their "prestige" by demonstrating their power against the Zionists' "partners"—the Ukrainian nationalists. Ukrainians do not enjoy such a strong position in the world as the Jews. These are the prime reasons why the Politburo of the Communist Party of the Soviet Union resolved to make concessions to the Jews and at the same time to intensify its terror against the nations subjugated in the USSR, in particular Ukraine.

The anti-Semitic Russian chieftains are completely indifferent to the fact that their lie (as every lie) has short legs. They are taking advantage of the current situation. For this reason, the aforementioned Kychko, for instance, has completely "forgotten" to add Schwarzbart, the assassin of S. Petlura, who at the trial in Paris posed as a Zionist not as a Communist. In reality, Schwarzbart was a Russian agent. Still, after Schwarzbart's death, the Jews brought his remains to Israel, where they were buried. Thus, Schwarzbart's intelligence activities and his services to the Russian GPU, upon whose instructions he had assassinated Symon Petlura, were concealed. But the Jews officially took Schwarzbart's crime upon themselves—being a Zionist he killed Petlura, thus allegedly taking revenge for the massacre of the Jews. With the hands of a Jew, Schwarzbart, Russia murdered Symon Petlura, a symbol of the anti-Russian struggle, and at the same time made a fool of the Jews, because they themselves acknowledged Schwarzbart as a Zionist in spite of the fact that he was a Communist—an obvious agent of the GPU.

Russia no longer has enough strength to conduct an open ideological struggle with Ukraine, in particular with Ukrainian nationalist—revolutionaries. At first it attempted to present the Ukrainian nationalist-revolutionaries as German "collaborators," but this provocation fell through quickly, for even Khrushchev had to acknowledge the two-front war of the OUN-UPA. Then the OUN was showered with false accusations that it was cooperating with "the American capitalists" and "the British and American secret serivices." But this insinuation also dissipated, for the policy of the OUN is completely contradictory to the American policy of "peaceful coexistence" and negotiations with Moscow. When

Russia found itself in conflict with Israel (it was one of the first states to recognize Israel), it advanced a new provocation—"the alliance of Ukrainian nationalists with world Jewish capitalism," although world Jewry has not taken a positive stand on the concept of the dissolution of the Russian empire and the reestablishment on its ruins of independent national states, in particular of the Ukrainian state.

The very fact that individual Jews are favorably disposed to the renewal of the Ukrainian Independent United State and condemn the assassination of S. Petlura, executed by Schwarzbart upon the order of the GPU (for example, Alan Desroches, a French Jew, or Prof. Shuflinsky, a prisoner in a Russian concentration camp for expressing his admiration for Ukrainian political prisoners)—does not signify a change in the policy of world Jewry and Israel with regard to the Ukrainian liberation struggle. Of course, it would be of advantage if some Jewish groups of the Maoz type would assume a clear-cut anti-Russian stand and recognize the concept of the dismemberment of the Russian empire and the reestablishment of national states. Regrettably, reality is different. For instance, the center uniting all Jewish organizations in Canada disassociated itself from our anti-Russian demonstrations because its aims are different. A similar thing occurred in England, where only small individual Jewish student groups dared to put forward anti-Russian slogans.

Searching for ever new "guardians" for the Ukrainian nationalists, the Russian chieftains have become totally confused, themselves denying what they maintained earlier. Some new version appears every day, although the aim remains the same: to drum into the Ukrainian people the fact that the OUN is not orienting itself upon its own national forces and the front of nations subjugated in the USSR, but on some outside "anti-Soviet" power. They pin one label after another on the OUN: allegedly, it is always serving "foreign powers"—Polish, German, American, English, the Nationalist Chinese, and finally the Red Chinese and the Zionists. As it were, the nationalists are not counter-agents but agents, not partners but lackeys. In their drive against the "Ukrainian bourgeois nationalists", the Russian chieftains and their stooges go so far as to contradict themselves. Thus, for instance, the renewal of the Ukrainian state in 1941 was proclaimed by the nationalists, who were "German collaborators," while the government of the renewed Ukrainian state "was dispersed by the Germans." The UPA "was created by the Germans," while Khrushchev was forced to confirm that the UPA waged war against both the Germans and the Bolsheviks.

The very fact that Moscow is attempting to reduce the entire process of cultural renaissance of the Ukrainian nation to a provocative linkage with foreign "secret services" is proof of its greatest desperation. It is such an incredible and shameful provocation that a normal person could hardly conceive it. But at the same time it is a boomerang that will turn against Moscow itself. Can one imagine that the entire social labor movement of the past century was made up of agents? Can one equate the national liberation movement of formerly subjugated Poland, with Kosciuszko or Pilsudski at the head, with the action of foreign intelligence? Can one at present link, in any way, the creativity of Svitlychny, Dzyuba, Sverstyuk, Chornovil, Moroz, Stus, and many others with "intelligence services"? If so, then all people of great ideas, all of mankind's geniuses, all the creators of social and national concepts, all philosophers and ideologists should be considered as "lackeys" of some "foreign power," including such false prophets as Marx, Engels, and Lenin, who have become the idols of the Russian Communists. If, on the other hand, the works of an individual living in a country of despotism, where there is no freedom of speech, where terror and lawlessness reign, find their way abroad and are published against the will of the author and without his agreement, can this be considered a "crime" and the authors punished by harsh sentences and long-term imprisonment in prisons and concentration camps?

The realization of the Ukrainian cultural "I," the historic, traditional foundation of the Ukrainian nation, the attempt at free creativity, the effort to make use of the paper rights which are granted by the Constitutions of the USSR and the Ukrainian SSR and the Declaration of Human Rights, which the USSR and the so-called Ukrainian SSR had signed at the United Nations—these were the limits within which the presently imprisoned Ukrainian cultural leaders had acted. None of them had transgressed in their activity the rights guaranteed to them by the Constitution. When the Russian autocrats trample their own Constitution, this is not the fault of the Ukrainian cultural leaders. Not the cultural leaders, but the dictators and their stooges should be put on trial for violating human and national rights guaranteed by their own Constitution. The Russian "judges" fear that at an open "show trial" they will be unable to win a "dialogue" with the defendants on the question of who is violating the Constitution; the autocratic Government and the court, or the defendants? Therefore they attached to a fabricated "case" a comic pretext—a chance visit to Ukraine at the time by an innocent tourist, a student from Belgium, who is allegedly connected with the OUN (Bandera followers), and who is supposedly serving foreign "intelligence services." Such a fabricated accusation is particularly ludicrous and at the same time horrible. Creators and workers in the field of Ukrainian culture and...foreign "intelligence services"!

The charges against the Belgian student are an obvious provocation, as had already been authoritatively determined by the OUN Press Service. Instead of a Belgian student of Ukrainian descent, it could have been a tourist from Mars who appeared in the USSR on a "flying saucer" to spy for the "intelligence service of another planet." Upon orders from the Chekists, the "experts," the "brilliant" Russian scholars, would surely work out a whole version about the appearance of a "spy" from Mars and would link him too...the creators of Ukrainian culture. Proof? When the Russians could find "evidence" that America was not discovered by Columbus but by a "brilliant" Russian and therefore it should belong to the USSR, then they can fabricate "evidence" about the "espionage activites" of Y. Dobosh, regardless of whether he came from Belgium or Mars. Tukhachevsky, a USSR marshal and a faithful servant of the Red Russian empire, also "confessed" that he was a "German spy." At the SVU trial, the "witnesses" testified that SVU members were allegedly in the services of "Polish intelligence." It is not to be excluded that shortly the KGB will "authoritatively" confirm that Symon Petlura, the head of the Ukrainian State, was assassinated by Schwarzbart, not as an agent of the GPU, but as an agent of world Jewry. In 1926-30 the so-called industrial party was crushed in the USSR. Its members represented and "confessed" that they worked for "French intelligence."

In its subversive activity in the Free World, Moscow relies everywhere on espionage and corruption. Therefore, it imagines that with the aid of provocation it is possible to attribute...to "foreign intelligence" every national liberation movement in its empire and all the cultural processes of revival of an enslaved nation. Can we suppose that Mickiewicz and Slowacki, our Shevchenko, the Italian Mazzini, the Bulgarian Botev, the Hungarian Petöfi were dependent in their creativity on foreign "intelligence services"? Could anyone who is not in an insane asylum believe this? We do not know whether Brezhnev and Andropov belong in the category of the mentally ill, but we know that Hitler and Stalin showed traces of insanity toward the end of their lives....

Thus, time and again the contradiction between phrases and reality, between paper guarantees of human and national rights and a fruitless attempt to realize them can be witnessed in the USSR. Russia allegedly protects the rights of nations and individuals, refers to the UN Charter but only where it has an imperialist interest (Bangladesh, the Basques, Northern Ireland, and so forth). In reality, it not only violates national and human rights, but punishes in the most brutal way anyone who dares to demand respect of these rights, allegedly guaranteed by its Constitution. It is of no avail either that quite a few of the illegally imprisoned Ukrainian creators of culture have quoted Lenin and the Constitution in support of their rights.

Ivan Dzyuba wrote his work *Internationalism or Russification?* at the request of Shelest as documentation of injustice in Ukraine. This work, like similar works of other authors, was not written from the standpoint of the revolutionary OUN, but on the basis of the Constitutions of the USSR and the Ukrainian SSR and the deceptive theses of Lenin. And for this alone the authors are confined to prisons and concentration camps, expelled from the writers' and artists' union, persecuted and harassed for "subversive anti-Soviet activity," and provocatively linked with the OUN center abroad and foreign "intelligence services."

Yet none of the arrested and the convicted are to blame for the fact that the Constitutions of the USSR and the Ukrainain SSR are a shameful deception. They had not drafted them, nor had they written the false Leninist theses, but were only trying to put into life that which is allegedly guaranteed by the Constitution. It is not their fault that the Russian hypocrites defend the rights of even such foreign Communist terrorists as Angela Davis who helped to kill people. Today, she is free (in the country of "capitalist hyenas") and can write and say what she wishes. The creators of Ukrainian culture, on the other hand, who only wished to make use of the paper rights of the Constitutions of the USSR and the Ukrainian SSR, which allegedly guarantee freedom of thought and speech, found themselves behind bars. Can they be tried for the fact that the Marxist dialectic itself exposes the hypocrisy of the Russian Bolshevik system and that they are calling to it the attention of the "judges" who are trying them?

Finding themselves in a blind alley of contradictions between theory and practice, for they are already harshly punishing innocent cultural creativity which is unfolding within the framework of the Constitutions of the USSR and the Ukrainian SSR, the Russian occupants of Ukraine have no other choice but to revert to the tsarist formula: "There never was [any Ukraine], there is not and there cannot be." There is only one nation, "one and indivisible Russia," a Russian super-nation, a unique phenomenon in world history, while the entire world is to be its fertilizer.

The growth of the resistance movement and the national forces of the nations subjugated in the USSR has become a moral danger for the Russian empire, for it can lead to its downfall. And the Russian imperialists and chauvinists have found themselves in a blind alley—they can neither go forwards nor backwards; the provocative bomb directed against Ukraine is exploding in their own hands. Their endeavors to accuse the Ukrainian cultural leaders and workers of activities "contrary to the Constitution" has come to nought because the so-called Constitution of the USSR even contains an article (17) about possible secession "of the sovereign Soviet republics" from the USSR. Therefore, the Russian occupants are attempting to link the defendant with the OUN, which does not recognize any Russian Bolshevik Constitutions, any occupation laws, any puppet states such as the Ukrainian SSR or any imperialistic structures such as the USSR. The so-called Ukrainian SSR is considered by it as a mere colony of the despotic Russian empire. It neither takes advantage of, nor bases its arguments on, the paper Constitutions of the USSR and the Ukrainian SSR. The deceptive articles of the USSR and the Ukrainian SSR's Constitutions are considered by the OUN as a vile trap for those who are trying to implement them openly, albeit within the minimal limits of freedom of speech.

The OUN respects every leader and patriot of Ukraine who strives to serve his nation by whatever means he considers appropriate under the existing conditions. But the OUN has no links to any known formations or people in Ukraine who are acting within the Constitutional framework. It has an entirely different concept of national revival and Ukraine's liberation from the Russian Bolshevik occupation. The KGB attempts to link Ukraine's cultural leaders with the OUN, to ascribe to them connections with a revolutionary underground, regardless of the fact that the OUN fully negates not only the Russian Communist system in Ukraine, but also the Russian *gauleiters* and governors-general, to whom the arrested turn, pointing to the lawlessness from the standpoint of human and national rights guaranteed by the Constitution. Ivan Dzyuba, for instance, wrote his documentation for Shelest. This the OUN has never done and will never do. Nevertheless it considers all the Ukrainian patriots in Ukraine, including those under arrest and those harassed, as noble, brave, and morally excellent people who are serving their nation in their own way. But their concept is not the OUN's concept. As a matter of principle, the OUN does not dispatch any couriers to the cultural leaders in Ukraine who are acting publicly within the framework of the Constitution because its concept of liberation does not recognize any appeals to the laws and the constitution of the occupants.

Of course, various Philbys and Felfs can assist the KGB in preparing still another provocation at the trial of the arrested leaders of Ukrainian culture. Dzhugalo never had anything to do with the OUN but nevertheless "testified" about "OUN's lackeyism to foreign intelligence." This "testimony" was fabricated in advance by the KGB organs. However, in Ukraine nobody believes anymore in the revolutionary OUN's services to foreign powers, for it has the reputation of an uncompromising fighter for freedom and national rights. It will do the Russian occupants no good to link the Ukrainian cultural leaders with casual tourists to whom fantastic missions are attributed. Khrushchev himself had at one time exposed Stalin's terrorist methods, including the circumstances surrounding the preparation of court proceedings against the Kremlin doctors who "upon orders of foreign intelligence" were alleged to have poisoned the Russian chieftains. Later these doctors were "rehabilitated" and those who prepared the provocation were annihilated. Hence, they destroyed some in order to save other Russian despots. The convicted Ostap Vyshnya was also "rehabilitated," but now those who are popularizing his works are being sentenced.

It is simply impossible to enumerate all those who were found guilty by the Russian Stalinist courts of "espionage," "subversive activity," "high treason," and so forth, and who were "rehabilitated" after Stalin's death. They were convicted, executed, or exterminated in prisons and concentration camps, and then..."rehabilitated."

Brezhnev and Kosygin with their *gauleiter* Shcherbytsky are following in the footsteps of Lenin, Stalin, Dzerzhynsky, Yezhov. Russia has prepared a great provocation against the Ukrainian nations, in particular against its cultural élite. It is our duty to expose before the whole world the horrible provocation of the KGB, which aims to destroy the Ukrainian creative intelligentsia which, under conditions of shocking terror, attempts to serve its subjugated nations selflessly. We must mobilize all the freedom-loving forces of the world, its cultural elite, in defense of those arrested and persecuted, and of the entire Ukrainian nation in order to condemn and put an end to the barbarity of the Russian tyrants.

The Ukrainian Review,
No. III, 1972, pp. 71-81

Russification and National Genocide

The new Constitution of the USSR is a constitution of an empire which is a prison of nations and people—not a constitution of a multinational society. It guarantees only the rights of the imperial, ruling nation (the Russians); the rights of the totalitarian Communist Party; the rights of the General Procurator of the USSR.

The new constitution legalizes the sovereign rights of the fictitious "Soviet people" to avoid mentioning by name the Russian people as the backbone of the empire. It officially sanctions terror as a governing system, investing the General Procurator of the USSR (i.e., the KGB) with uncontested rights to appoint, or approve the appointments of, the prosecuta on the so-called "republican" level, who are also KGB candidates. The Politburo in Moscow has absolute control over all the Communist Party branches in the so-called "republics." Not one of the "sovereign republics" has its own Communist Party. The Governments of the "republics" have, on the basis of their paper Constitutions, fewer rights than a county administration in any free nation of the world. The USSR is not even constitutionally a multinational state, but the state of a "super-nation"—the Russian—under the name of the "Soviet people."

Not a single "republic" has even a paper right to secede from the USSR, because the fictional article about "voluntary secession" is neutralized by the unlimited sovereign rights given to the "Soviet people" (i.e., the Russians), the Communist Party centralized in the Politburo, the centralized KGB, the office of the General Procurator, the centralized Soviet armed forces commanded by the Politburo, and the totally centralized state bureaucracy commanded by the all-Union Government. The latter holds in its hands all the vital aspects and functions of the State, leaving to the so-called "republican" governments trivial administrative tasks of a colonial nature.

There are no safeguards whatsoever of the rights of a nation (even in theory)—that is impossible in an empire, and, therefore, the human rights of a person who belongs to a subjugated nation also cannot be guaranteed. The general preamble and the preambles to the relevant articles of the Constitution reject in principle all national and human rights when they state that those rights are subordinate to the interest of the "Soviet people," the Communist Party, the "working class," and the USSR. Moreover, the Constitution is interpreted by the General Procurator of the USSR (i.e, the KGB).

A logical outcome of the "new" imperial Constitution is the strengthening of the Russification processes of the subjugated nations. The introduction into the Constitution of a new element—the "Soviet people" as a euphemism for a Russian super-nation—has resulted in a bold and pressing Russification policy on the part of Moscow. The Russian language has been given the status of a privileged language—"the language of Lenin, indispensable in the relations among peoples and as a means of access to the achievements of world culture." In reality this makes the Russian language a tool of the denationalization and assimilation of the non-Russian nations. With the complete bankruptcy of Communism as a system of life, Moscow has now totally disclosed its imperialistic policies both in theory and practice.

If any of the subjugated nations wished to practice Communism, then logically, it could best be preached in the mother tongue of a given people. But since Moscow can no longer rely on an ideology that is dead in the occupied countries, it openly stirs the chauvinistic instincts of the Russian masses in order to mobilize them for the campaign to russify the subjugated nations.

In Georgia and Armenia Moscow tried to eliminate from the "republican" Constitutions the native tongue as the official language of the "republic," but the people demonstrated in the streets and Moscow had to retreat. The offensive on Byelorussia has escalated drastically and Russification is already celebrating its pogroms. Because of Russian colonialism in Kazakhstan, Latvia, Lithuania, and Estonia, ethnocide and genocide continue. Russification is not only a forced implementation of the Russian language, but it is simultaneously a type of colonization by the Russians of the occupied territories—a cultural, ethnic, religious, and physical destruction of entire nations. The forced deportation of North Caucasians, Crimean Tartars, Volga Germans, Kalmyks, and Don Cossacks, and the simultaneous mass importation of Russians into those territories to replace the native populations, is a contemptible form of Russification. The mass importation of Russians into the Ukrainian regions of Donbas, Kharkiv, etc.—that is also Russification. The privileged status of the Russian language in the educational system of the occupied countries, the compulsory nature of the teaching of Russian culture, history, and literature, the promotion of the cult of the Russian tsars, military leaders, writers—all are paths to Russification.

The struggle for a national culture, a national environment in the schools, national spirituality in literature and the arts, and, finally, the struggle for the preservation of the mother tongue, are tasks of prime importance in our respective homelands, which demand our full support from abroad.

The newspaper *Soviet Education* (Nov. 11, 1978) published a decree of the Russian colonial Government in Ukraine which paves the way for Russification of the entire Ukrainian educational system on all levels. The decree calls for: the teaching of the Russian language to Ukrainian children *en masse* from the first grade; the improvement of the teaching methods of Russian to the privileged status enjoyed by foreign languages, which means teaching in smaller groups with the exclusive use of Russian in all subjects of study; increasing the number of Russian teachers in the Ukrainian educational system; the creation in Ukraine of more centers of specialization in the field of Russian language and literature; the holding of "language olympiads" in Russian language and literature on all levels of the public school system—from the regional to the "republican."

The struggle for the national cultures (by content and language) and the battle against the policies of total Russification have become an issue of prime concern in the countries occupied by the Russian imperialists. We, as spokesmen for the subjugated nations, and our entire diaspora must join in this struggle with all the means at our disposal.

Against the current onslaught of Russian imperialism and chauvinism it is necessary to rise in massive protestations, emphasizing in particular the Russian occupation (national, political, economic, and cultural) of numerous countries. The main objective of such occupation is Russification, which consists of a whole array of methods and means of annihilation of the ethno-national, cultural and religious, ideological and philosophical, folkloric, traditional, and linguistic substance of the subjugated nations. The mother tongue is a particularly important factor for the preservation of the intrinsic national cultural spirituality. *THE STRUGGLE FOR THE MOTHER TONGUE IS AN ELEMENTARY FACTOR IN THE STRUGGLE FOR THE SOUL OF A NATION!*

It is the duty of the political leadership of the diaspora of the subjugated nations to call for and organize joint massive actions of all types against Russification and in this manner strengthen the battle for the national culture and language in their respective homelands. Community, academic, cultural, youth, women's, veterans', and other organizations must also join the growing anti-Russification front. It is also imperative to mobilize analogous organizations of the nations among which lives the diaspora of the subjugated nations. This struggle in defense of the national language and culture of the subjugated nations is, in its essence, a struggle against the barbarization of life, against the cultural impoverishment of mankind. World geniuses thrive and create when nourished by their own national spiritual, cultural, and linguistic environment. HE WHO KILLS THE LANGUAGE OF A NATION KILLS THE SOUL OF THAT NATION, which, in turn, leads to the de-spiritualization of the life of mankind because world culture is, in its essence, a mosaic of national cultures.

It is imperative in the Free World to document the Russification policies and practices before government, parliamentary, academic and cultural forums, as well as in the mass media, and urge their intervention in order to force Moscow to stop its ethnic, cultural, linguistic, and biological destruction of the subjugated nations. The current wave of Russian chauvinism must be turned into a subject of concern and action at all international political conferences and academic and professional meetings of a local, national, and international character. Those Russian nationals WHO OPPOSE Moscow's policies of imperialism and chauvinism have now yet another opportunity to declare their anti-imperialistic stand with concrete actions which would be useful for the establishment of good relations between them and the subjugated nations.

The representatives of the subjugated nations in the Free World must, by all possible means, supply their respective countries with information about the actions taken against Russification and in support of the reestablishment of independent national states in place of the Russian empire. Such information is vital in order to strengthen the embattled nations morally, spiritually, and ideologically in their struggle against the Russian invader.

Special efforts must be channelled into a continued defense of the cultural activists of the subjugated nations, who were the first to join in the battle against Russification—a gallant stand for which they paid with long terms of confinement in prisons and concentration camps—some of them even with the lives.

The defense of the nationalist-revolutionaries currently incarcerated in the "Gulag" is our constant duty, because they embody the ideal of national sovereignty and independence, which is the key to the realization of all the national and human rights in our homeland. Our actions cannot be limited to "armchair protests." We must bring out into the streets masses of people to protest and put pressure on Soviet Russian embassies, consulates, and other representatives of the invader in the Free World, and, at the same time, urge and demand intervention on the part of the Free World to assist our nations battling now for their very survival.

The Ukrainian Review,
No. II, 1979, pp. 3-6

We Accuse Moscow and Remind the Free World

October 15 marks the 20th year since the assassination of the leader of the Ukrainian liberation struggle, Stepan Bandera, the head of the OUN. Stepan Bandera was murdered by an agent of the KGB, Bohdan Stashynsky, on the territory of the German Federal Republic by means of a poison gun. The murder was carried out at the instigation of the Soviet Russian Government of N. Khrushchev and on the explicit order of the KGB chief, Alexander Shelepin, who was approved by the head of the Supreme Soviet, K. Voroshilov. *We accuse the government of the USSR, the Central Committee, and the Politburo of CPSU of genocide and murder, a policy and practice which is being conducted systematically to this day.*

A similar assassination, also planned and ordered by the Soviet government took place in 1957 when the Ukrainian exile political and academician Prof. D. Lev Rebet was murdered, also by Stashynsky. According to the testimony of Stashynsky before the German Federal Court in Karlsruhe, an assassination attempt was also to be carried out against the former Ukrainian Prime Minister and current head of the OUN and the ABN—Yaroslav Stetsko.

The German Supreme Court in October 1962 sentenced the assassin Stashynsky to eight years imprisonment for his complicity in the murder, *but the actual guilt for the assassination was ascribed to the Soviet Russian Government, specifically to Alexander Shelepin, the former head of the Committee for State Security (KGB).* Such criminal methods, liquidating leading members of the liberation movements of the captive nations on orders of the Soviet Russian Government, have not changed to this day, neither on the territory of the so-called USSR nor in her satellites, where the security services are under the direct control of the KGB. The same applies to the persecution and liquidation of other leaders in the Free World who oppose Russia's colonial rule. A recent example of this was the assassination of the Bulgarian author Georgi Markov, by the KGB-controlled Bulgarian secret service. The murder weapon was a poisoned needle at the tip of an umbrella. In 1962 Bandera's assassin, Stashynsky, told of assassination plans of precisely this nature when he testified about the potential assassination of Yaroslav Stetsko. He said: "We may well have used a poisoned needle released from a device by air pressure which would leave no trace behind."

The recent kidnapping of the Lithuanian sportsman Vladislavas Cessiunas, who sought political asylum in Germany, is a stark reminder of the impunity with which the KGB continues its operations on the territory of sovereign Western states. Yet it appears that the German Government is more interested in helping the Kremlin to cover up this sordid affair.

Assassinations Continue

In the last several years the KGB was involved in the murders of the following Ukrainian activists: the artist Alla Horska, R. Paleckiy, two Ukrainian Catholic priests Luckiy and Luchkiw, and the composer V. Ivasiuk were hanged; the author H. Snehirov was murdered in a hospital; a member of the leadership of the Organization of Ukrainian Nationalists, M. Soroka, was murdered on the eve of his release from twenty-five years imprisonment. There are hundreds of other unknown persons.

Most recently, members of the Ukrainian Helsinki monitoring group in Kyiv— Lev Lukianenko, M. Rudenko, O. Tykhy, M. Marynowych, V. Ovsienko, and others—have been sentenced to terms of up to fifteen years imprisonment and exile by Russian occupational courts.

Hundreds of Ukrainian authors, artists, and scientists were sentenced to brutal terms of imprisonment of twelve to fifteen years in 1972 on the sole grounds that their works contained Ukrainian patriotic and Christian elements. Among these were: I. Svitlychny, I. Hel, I. Kalynets, E. Sverstiuk, V. Stus, S. Karavanskiy, and many others who still languish in prisons, concentration camps, and psychiatric asylums.

Unprecedented is the persecution of Y. Shukhevych, the son of the commander-in-chief of the UPA. Shukhevych has been sentenced several times for a total of thirty years imprisonment because he refused to denounce the legacy of ideals for which his father fought and died. Numerous members of the OUN are routinely sentenced in secret trials for up to fifteen years in high-security prisons, while some of them have been secretly executed.

Genocide Through Russification

The 25th Congress of the CPSU passed a resolution regarding "further improvements in the education and training of students in public schools" which in fact directed that all schools in the non-Russian republics are to increase the teaching of the Russian language as the "language of friendship and brotherly relations of the peoples of the USSR." As a result of this resolution, the colonial Ministry of Education of the Ukrainian SSR decided in November 1978 that in the period 1979-85 the Russification processes will be intensified and "upcoming generations are to have a complete knowledge of the Russian language." Consequently, beginning in 1980, the Russian language will be introduced in the first grades of all public schools in Ukraine. This move has alarmed the population of Ukraine and calls for the maintenance of the mother tongue have already been issued. Among many protests, it was pointed out that in the next school year the Russian language will assume a dominating position not only in the public schools but also in the kindergartens at the cost of Ukrainian-language instruction. This situation is already compounded by the fact that in the larger centers in Ukraine most schools already provide instruction exclusively in the Russian language.

It has become clear that the current leadership of the USSR is in fact continuing and intensifying the Russification and assimilation policies of the former Russian tsars. Today, the policy objectives of the tsarist Minister of Education, D. Tolstoy, are being realized. Tolstoy had stated in 1879 that "our goal in the education of the non-Russian peoples...is their Russification and assimilation with the Russian nation." Further proof that the policy of assimilating the non-Russian peoples is being stepped-up systematically was offered this May at an academic conference in Tashkent, Turkestan, where the Minister of Education of the Soviet Union presented in his speech precise party directives concerning an increased Russification program, beginning at the kindergarten level.

Millions in Concentration Camps

According to a recent document signed by Ukrainian political prisoners M. Matusevych, Z. Antoniuk, and V. Marchenko and the Russian dissident Yu. Orlov, there are currently five million citizens (two percent of the Soviet population) in Soviet Russian prisons and labor camps and in exile. In the document written in April 1979 in a Perm concentration camp, Yu. Orlov stated the following: "The nationality policy being conducted by the USSR is reflected in the composition of the inmates of the camps. Accordingly the inmates of the camps in the Urals and Mordovia are composed of forty percent Ukrainians, up to thirty percent Balts, and about thirty percent other nationalists. The major burden of the struggle against the arbitrariness in the camps today, as in the Stalinist camps, falls upon the shoulders of Ukrainians. If the sea of unemployed is considered to be a typical evil of the capitalist system, then the equally strong contingent of human beings who are condemned to forced labor must be considered as a typical evil of the totalitarian socialist system."

Olympic Coins Made in Gulag

One of the most shameful moments of this century must surely be the consent of the Free World to hold the Olympic Games in Moscow—the center of horrible genocide and murder, the capital of the largest and most brutal colonial empire in the world, and the administrative center of concentration camps, psychiatric asylums, and Russification policies. To add to this sad spectacle, it has become evident that the medals and souvenirs of these Olympic Games are being produced by the forced labor of political prisoners whose work norms are being increased through punitive isolation, torture, and lower food rations. The sale of these Olympic items to Western tourists will provide the USSR with lucrative profits. Facts concerning this were revealed at the International Sakharov Hearings in Washington this September by M. Sharygin, a recently released Ukrainian political prisoner whose ten-year imprisonment provided him with insights into the production of these items.

We appeal to the Free World, for the sake of its own honor and dignity, to take the following position concerning the Moscow Olympics: as long as human beings are being imprisoned in Russian prisons, concentration camps, and psychiatric asylums or exiled for their political or religious beliefs, as long as the assimilation of the captive nations robs them of their national, linguistic, ethnic, and cultural identity, and as long as priests, artists, writers, and freedom fighters are being murdered and hanged, no athlete of the Free World should set foot in Moscow's Olympic stadiums.

A Spiritual Revival

Today we are witnessing in Ukraine, as in other subjugated nations, a spiritual and ideological renaissance of the young generation in a national and religious sense. The ideas of materialism, Marxism, and Leninism are dead. The young strive for the ideals of God, of their nation and fatherland, for spiritual values, for an understanding of the great epochs and personalities of their nation's past. *"Back to our traditions"* is the revolutionary slogan of the current struggle, a slogan which is not only confined to Ukraine.

The self-realization of a nation's traditional, spiritual, cultural, ethical, social, and political values, and the spontaneous struggle for them in all spheres of life in opposition to the forced foreign Bolshevik concepts are typical of the current phase of our liberation struggle. This is a struggle between two world-views, two philosophies, two opposing concepts of the natural order, two conflicting concepts of culture, a fight between differing concepts of social and economic order, where the idea of nation is opposed to the philosophy of imperialism, religion against atheism, individualism against collectivism, heroic humanism against barbarism and terror, the idea of man as a God-created being versus hatred and the trampling of human dignity.

As freedom fighters behind the Iron Curtain have stated, we live in the age of liberation and nationalism, which is diametrically opposed to imperialism, chauvinism, racism, and totalitarianism. In view of this, the ideals of national liberation and demands for the dissolution of the Russian empire must become an integral part of the foreign policies of the West, just as Marxism-Leninism has become an integral component of the foreign policies of the Soviet Union.

Statement at the press conference on October 11, 1979 in Munich, Germany before the International Press Regional Television.
ABN Correspondence,
November-December 1979, pp. 1-4.

In a State of War with Russia

Mr. Chairman, Reverend Fathers, Distinguished Guests, Ladies and Gentlemen!

It gives me genuine pleasure to be with you today. May I first of all take this opportunity to extend to all of you my sincere greetings on behalf of the Central

Committee of the Anti-Bolshevik Bloc of Nations, the European Freedom Council, and the Ukrainian Revolutionary Liberation Movement, the OUN.

I wish that this tenth observance of Captive Nations Week would afford your American community a greater understanding of the subjugated nations' plight and liberation struggle, for this struggle is also aimed at the preservation of freedoms in the countries still free, since it calls for a change of policy of the free governments of the world towards the Russian empire!

Our peoples, oppressed in the USSR and the satellite countries, will never reconcile themselves with Russian and Communist enslavement, and will continue their struggle for national independence and the rights of individuals no matter what the attitude of the Free World may be! But this world must understand that its fate is being decided in that very struggle. Whoever helps us helps himself!

We came from our homelands not to beg someone's help in our struggle; we came to the free nations of the world to inform them of the fact that once we fall in battle against the Russian aggressor, the fate of the peoples now free will be in greater danger.

We know from Russian history what Peter I exclaimed: "Keep the Russian nation in a constant state of war." He said further: "In the interests of the expansion of development of Russia, war must serve peace and peace must serve war."

The most important methods of Russian imperialism are the following: gradual conquest of the lands neighboring on Russia under the motto of securing Russian interests; furthering unrest among nations whose conquest is planned in order to create preconditions for military occupation; political, economic, and diplomatic pressure on the free governments or even threats against them in order to make them pliable towards Russia.

During the time of the so-called peaceful coexistence Russia expanded her influence to new countries, and after the rescue of the Lebanese Government from Communist subversion by American Marines, and after the Cuban failure, they built up their navy to a level which is today second only to that of the United States. The Russian fleet has nowadays become a powerful instrument of political pressure on the Free World—360 submarines (55 of these powered by atomic energy), 17 cruisers, 25 destroyers—all equipped with rockets. In 1967, a few days before the outbreak of the war in the Middle East, the Russians brought their navy for the first time to the Mediterranean Sea. Since that time the Russian men-of-war have not left the waters between Gibraltar and the Bosphorus, thus observing every move of the American fleet in the Mediterranean which for two decades was regarded as an "American sea."

In November 1968, the Secretary General of NATO, Brozzio, stated that, "the strengthened Soviet actions and influence in the Mediterranean basin and the Middle East are a very serious matter." Although the British Minister of Defense, D. Healey, said that "in the eventuality of war the Soviet fleet would be sunk in a few minutes," the Chief of Staff of the U.S. Navy, Admiral Moorer, stated that "they are becoming constantly more aggressive.... The USSR is striving, according to plan, to become a leading sea power..." and asked President

Nixon for approximately three billion dollars for building new warships....
Furthermore, NATO decided to introduce a naval fire-guard against the threat
of the Russian fleet!

The dreams of the tsars thus became reality: Russia in the Mediterranean Sea,
penetrating the Near East, the Indian Ocean, and Africa and threatening what is
left of free Europe from the South.

I am asking you, does not all this threaten the interests and safety of this very
country? And how about the Russian influence in Latin America? Catherine II
meddled in the internal affairs of Venezuela. And what was Russia looking for in
Alaska during the tsarist era? How the Latin Americans—subverted by the
Russians—"greeted" the Governor of New York is well known. Is it possible to
remain silent? Russia through Cuba is knocking on the doors of your city, New
York, and she is already within your city as a fifth column. "You will never be
victorious if you do not expel the agents, if you do not fight them within the walls
of your city"; thus Demosthenes used to warn the Athenians before the threat of
Philip of Macedonia.

I wish to remind you of the following facts which are ignored by the news
media: the American continent borders on the Russian empire across the Bering
Straits. Russian submarines frequently appear in American waters! Alaska
belonged to Russia once, and Russia may yet claim that piece of American land!

Dear Friends in the struggle for Freedom:

It is necessary for us to realize clearly that our enemy is Russian imperialism
and Communism, the Russian system of life imposed on our peoples.

Who are our friends? All those patriotic and religious forces in the world that
stand for freedom and real peace with justice, and therefore for the disintegration of the Russian empire, for the outlawing of Communism, for the disintegration of all artificial state structures like Yugoslavia or Czechoslovakia, for active
support, including military help, or the revolutionary liberation struggle of our
enslaved nations!

What then are our paths, our concepts of victory? These are: national liberation revolutions, armed uprisings of the enslaved nations against Russia, synchronized and coordinated, supported politically and morally by the freedom-
loving forces of the Free World. For that reason our duty is to organize all the
freedom-loving peoples into one common world front based on the national
principle. It would be directed against any imperialist principle, against any trend
toward world government which would allow the large states to dominate the
smaller nations, and which would allow the Russian empire to promote its ideas.

Our appeal: don't compromise with one tyranny against another! Don't regard
Russia as a friend in the conflict with Peking, but do stand against Russia as *THE
MAIN ENEMY*. Join a common front with the enslaved peoples against all
tyranny and for liberty, independence, and justice for *ALL NATIONS* suppressed
by imperialist domination!

The upheaval of the enslaved nations makes a nuclear war impossible, and
would dissolve the Russian empire and the Communist system from within! The
Russian empire is a giant with feet of clay. The revolutionary upheavals of the
enslaved nations are beginning to stir and will inevitably lead to a definite

dissolution of the Russian empire! The Russian empire exists not because of strength, but because of the weakness of the ideo-political offensive of the West, and the lack of heroic and aggressive spirit within the Western societies!

The ABN has a clear and solid conception of liberation—a revolutionary, political, armed path, an all-national upheaval! The revolutionary does not know any compromise, does not know any "evolutionary" path of liberation, "legal-isms," "liberation by stages," or appeals to the Constitution of the USSR; he does not know any compromise either with Moscow or with Communism!

The enslaved nations are in a state of war with Russia. Between these warring sides no compromises are possible. There are no appeals to the laws of the invader. Between our peoples on the one hand and Russia on the other there is a sea of blood and where blood is being shed there cannot be any compromising.

Russia is quite aware that the independence of our people will mark the end of her position as a major power. For that reason, my friends, the oppressed peoples believe that only blood and steel will be the judges between them and the Russians, as nothing else can move Russia. Moscow may tolerate "protests," "revisionists," and "reformists," but will never tolerate nationalists—rev-olutionaries! Moscow will never tolerate the ABN or willingly accept our ideas! The ABN fights for the dissolution of the Russian empire, so that nothing should remain to remind us of slavery. We do not fight for the Russians to become better disposed toward us, we fight for their expulsion from our lands! For us Brezhnev is a tyrant of the same type as were Lenin, Stalin, Catherine II, and Peter I.

We call people to arms—this is the secret of success of the ABN! Moscow and Communism feel a panicky fear because of our ideas and actions! For that reason ten years ago Moscow murdered the leader of the OUN, Stepan Bandera. Furthermore, not long ago the Communist plotters murdered Croatian national-ist leaders in Western Europe; and before that, Slovak, Byelorussian, Turkestan-ian, and Azerbaidzhani patriots met a similar fate. The Bulgarian King, Borys, was poisoned by Russian agents.

ABN is against the CPSU and the Communist parties—the slave drivers of scores of nations!

ABN is the vanguard of the enslaved nations: the CPSU is the vanguard of the nation that enslaves!

The question of captive nations in the Soviet Russian bloc is a problem of an explosive colonial crisis. In all non-Russian countries, and particularly in Ukraine, the struggle for national independence is breaking out into the open at last. But this is only the beginning. The same "winds of change" that destroyed colonialism in Africa are blowing from Vladivostok to Berlin.

The Russian barbarians, together with their Communist agents in various countries, proclaimed not long ago in Moscow a common anti-imperialist front, condemning the freedom-loving American nation. A nation that has never had any intentions of enslaving anybody! If Moscow and its international clique can be "anti," why can't we? For that reason we must fearlessly and offensively proclaim that we are ANTI-Bolshevik, ANTI-Communist, ANTI-Russian! Not only what we are for, but what and who we are against. We have to decide who is for preservation of the empire and who is for its fall! We severely condemn the imprisonment of our intellectual, cultural workers, fighters for freedom of speech, thought, conscience, and national and human rights of all nations enslaved by Moscow and Peking! Just recently another crime was committed by Russia, as confirmed by news that the Ukrainian Catholic Archbishop Vasily Velychkovsky died in a Russian prison. The Free World should urge the immediate release of all the imprisoned priests, Orthodox and Catholic, Protestant ministers, Moslems, Jewish clergy, and of all prisoners—fighters for freedom and independence. The Free World should demand the abolition of all concentration camps in the Russian empire and its satellites!

We condemn the Russification of the subjugated peoples, the destruction and burning by the Russians of cultural, historical, and religious monuments, of archives, museums, churches—as, for example, the Vydubetsky Monastery in Kyiv and the library of the Academy of Sciences of the Ukrainian SSR or the destruction of the Synagogue in Odessa, which contained valuable archives. We urge His Holiness the Pope, President Nixon, and the leaders of all nations of the Free World to condemn the USSR and its satellites.

After the latest assault of Russia on Czechoslovakia the expulsion of Russia and her satellites from the UN and the breaking of all relations with the empire are highly appropriate.

We call on the world to stage a patriotic crusade against Russian tyrants and Communist despots!

One American, one Jewish, and three German prisoners from concentration camps in Mordovia have been exchanged. They contacted us and suggested that a campaign should be initiated in favor of the release of political prisoners, and especially of a Ukrainian lawyer, Dr. Volodymyr Horbovy. He has been confined to prisons and concentration camps for twenty-five years because he does not want to give up his convictions. His imprisonment has been repeatedly prolonged although he never had a trial in court; only the KGB decides in his case, and such cases are in the millions.

To sum up I should like to say that one should keep in mind the following facts:

The armed Soviet intervention against the independence endeavors of the Czech and Slovak nations.

The Russian threat to Southern Europe and Northern Africa via the Mediterranean.

Russian imperialistic attempts to establish bases on the Indian Ocean in order to dominate the new continents.

Russian efforts to gain influence in Northern Europe.

The Russian inspiration of civil wars in Latin American with the aim of establishing Communist governments dependent on Russia and thus dominating Latin America.

The Russian effort to undermine the social order in Western Europe and North America by means of general demoralization and student revolts.

The subversive actions of Moscow in Africa in order to dominate this continent.

The Russian and Red Chinese aggression against the independence and reunification of a free Vietnam, by means of armed support for North Vietnam and the Vietcong.

The national, social, and cultural oppression of all the nations subjugated by Russian imperialism in the USSR and so-called satellite countries, which are fighting for their national independence, social justice, and human rights.

We would like to sound a note of warning to the United States against a compromise with the Communists in Vietnam, for this will be a capitulation before tyrants and a threat to Southeast Asia! Our aim is dissolution of the Russian colonial empire, into national, independent states, the restoration of national independence to the peoples of CSSR and Yugoslavia, as well as the reunification in freedom of Germany, Vietnam and Korea and the liberation of mainland China. The young people in our countries have great faith in their nations.

Let us remember: Not peace, but the sword! Only arms will judge us and the Russians.

Let us keep that in mind, friends! Let us revive the idea of independent states of all nations enslaved by Russian imperialism and Communism in our hearts.

Let us help those people and the governments who seem to fail to see our point of view to understand our ideas on this Tenth Anniversary of Captive Nations Week.

Our strength lies within ourselves! And God helps only those who are strong!

Speech delivered at Captive Nations Week
Celebrations in New York, July 13, 1969.
ABN Correspondence,
July-August 1969, pp. 5-9

The Russian Empire is Not Invincible

We have frequently pointed out that the free world overestimates the strength of the USSR since it forgets that Russia's power lies in the weakness of the West, and above all in the West's ideological, ethical, and political weakness. It is Moscow that, by means of its propaganda, which has assumed proportions hitherto unknown in the world, endeavors to convince the free peoples of the world that it is invincible. In reality, however, the USSR is not a monolith, but a Russian empire which rules over many nations. Even if one assumes that the Russians number more than 90 million instead of 80 million, there are still over 100 million non-Russians in the Soviet Union; and if one adds a further 90 million (the population of the satellite countries), then the Russians constitute less than one-third of the peoples ruled by Moscow; and for a ruling nation this figure in itself is certainly too small to guarantee its complete predominance.

On the other hand, the population of the NATO countries numbers 250 million, without taking Spain, Finland, Sweden, or Switzerland into account.

And whereas the peoples in the USSR who have been subjugated by Moscow are only waiting for the day of their liberation, the free peoples of the West—should they be forced into a desperate situation—will always wage a war in order to save their own freedom.

If one also takes into account the 15 to 20 million present and former concentration camp internees, deportees, and other persons who are most definitely opposed to the Soviet regime, then it becomes obvious that the human potential on which Moscow has to rely is extremely uncertain. The myth about Moscow's inexhaustible human reserves is, after all, nothing but a myth.

But what is of primary importance is not the number of people, but the infiltration of ideas, the *political factor*. The hearts and minds of the subjugated peoples can be won over, and the arms which they have been forced to bear by their arch-enemy can be used for the cause of freedom. The great task of the West consists precisely in neutralizing human hearts and minds, and what is more, in winning them over to its side. Regarded from this point of view, the *purport* of the psychological war seems of primordial significance in this final contest for the sympathy of the subjugated peoples and nations; and it is precisely for this reason that Taiwan must never be left to its fate by the USA. The Chinese masses are not Communist-minded and can never be so. Deeply rooted national traditions and a way of life which is five thousand years old can never be obliterated by several decades of terrorist rule, nor can Marx replace Confucius, nor Lenin, Sun Yat-sen.

Japan, too , has not yet had its final say, but in any case, it will never become Communist. India, spiritually misled by Nehru, will sooner or later find its way back to its own great and individual spiritual world, which is the very antithesis of anti-human Communism with its dialectical and historical materialism, with its militant atheism, which is so alien to the Indian mentality.

Moreover, the ethical, ideological, and political weakness of the Soviet Russian empire internally will compel it to continue to carry on the colossal psychological war which is becoming more and more costly and which aims more and more at the disintegration of the West—that is to say, there will be an even more intensive activity by the Communist parties and other Fifth Columns in the West; for Moscow's strength lies in the psychological weakness of the Free World. In reality, Moscow is a giant with feet of clay. Ethically, ideologically, and politically, the West is in a position to deal Russia a serious blow—indeed, the revolution of Budapest already dealt it an ideological blow which was without precedent—and need not fear Russia's military strength, for the soldiers who bear arms in this case are persons whose hearts and minds the West can and should win over for itself.

Let us now, however, consider the actual military aspect of the problem. According to NATO experts, the Soviet army consists of 175 divisions, of which 75 are tank units. The satellite states have about 65 divisions, which makes a total of 240 divisions. In the event of war, the USSR would be able to set up 300 divisions within a short time. Within the Soviet Union the Bolsheviks can combine the national detachments of their armies as needed, since, in principle, there are no national troops there; but this does not mean that the percentage of non-Russians in the Soviet army is decreased. On the other hand, a similar national element in the satellite armies will always be the overwhelming majority, and these armies will always be an unreliable factor in the calculations of the Kremlin.

Thus, in the ideological and political respect, the Bolsheviks can rely neither on the Soviet army as a whole nor on the satellite armies, and only the Russians themselves will fight for their empire out of conviction. But what is the position as regards Soviet military science? Military science is making more and more progress from year to year, and what was ultra-modern five years ago is now completely out of date. The military equipment of the 175 Soviet divisions, which has remained unchanged for years, is nowadays no longer of great significance; it is adequate for guerrilla warfare, but not for a clash with the modern divisions of the West. Moscow, however, has neither the financial means nor the industrial capacity to modernize the military equipment of these 175 divisions. And this is hardly surprising in view of the fact that the USSR probably only produces 75,000 cars a year. Moreover, Moscow is not in a position to develop the technique of precision rapidly, which today is the basis of a war industry.

If, however, Moscow were to equip the 240 divisions at its disposal with modern weapons, it would need 180 billion dollars to do so. In 1957, Khrushchev himself affirmed that the Free World was spending 60 billion dollars a year on armaments—and this figure is certainly not too low; what it means in practice can be seen from the fact that the entire armament of Nazi Germany (up to the outbreak of World War II) did not cost more than 15 billion dollars. In the same year, however, the USSR spent 100 billion rubles on armaments, which at the most can only equal the purchasing power of 10 billion dollars, but actually fluctuates between 6 and 7 billion dollars.

It is true that, apart from its land forces, Moscow is also equipping huge naval and air forces. But it is precisely in this field that Moscow is finding it increasingly difficult to keep up with the modernization of military science. Who knows, for instance, whether fighter planes will not be replaced by long-range rockets tomorrow? And, in any case, the huge progress of military science can only continue with the free productive activity of man. Whether slave labor can compete with the latter for any length of time is extremely doubtful. It is true that one can let slaves build canals, railways, and mines under the whip of the overseers, and that "sputniks" can be constructed by a highly qualified team which is limited in number; but science today demands the willing productive activity of large masses, as well as the advancement—unhampered by political motives—of the best elements among thousands of millions of people working in freedom. The completely centralized, ideologically totalitarian, excessively bureaucratized, and terrorized Soviet industry is not in a position to produce the substantial elite which would be necessary in order to keep pace with the productive activity of the free peoples.

NATO experts assume that the USSR at present has at its disposal over 20,000 planes of its own, which could be used immediately for the purpose of war, as well as over 2,500 military planes belonging to the satellite states.

It is obvious from the statistics that the economic capacity of the USSR in almost every sector is only equal to a proportion of the capacity of Europe which is still free, not to mention the USA. As regards the production of motor vehicles, free Germany alone surpasses the entire Soviet Union, and the same also applies in the case of the engineering and electrical industries. It is true that the satellite states modify these figures in favor of the countries of the Communist bloc, but not decisively. Red China, on the other hand, as far as population figures are concerned, surpasses all the European and American countries, but as regards the economic aspect needs as much external help in order to be able to develop further as, say, Africa. Red China, incidentally, also subjugates other peoples who also long for independence.

Even so, the West can only gain a decisive political superiority over the Communist bloc by means of a better *idea*—namely, by putting its trust in the revolutionary national forces of the peoples subjugated by Russia; otherwise, its superiority in military, financial, economic, and technical potential will not be of any advantage.

The Free World must realize that the 175 Soviet divisions are allowed to continue to exist in their partly out-of-date form because Moscow needs them to crush possible internal insurrections. For this purpose the Kremlin does not consider it necessary to have modern weapons—atomic bombs and long-range rockets cannot, of course, be used in street fighting or in guerrilla warfare. Thus, the purpose of these 175 Soviet divisions is not only to make naïve persons in the West fear the "invincible" forces of the Soviet Union, but also to protect the present Russian empire against the national liberation movements of the peoples subjugated by Russia.

These out-of-date weapons, however —of which the West has no need since national revolts which would have to be crushed by tanks are unthinkable in the Federal Republic of Germany, in Great Britain, or in the USA—are also needed by Russia for the "local" wars it carries on (although it does so with foreign cannon-fodder). It was precisely with such weapons that war was fought in Korea, Vietnam, the Near East, and in Africa by the partisans. In other words, Moscow needs such weapons for the civil wars which it instigates either directly or indirectly, and with the help of which it aims to expand its rule. But the time is not yet ripe for a Third World War, and time is not always on Moscow's side, least of all as regards the technical sector. As far as military science is concerned, the West will always have the advantage over Moscow, provided that Moscow does not succeed in subverting the West from the *moral* point of view. Incidentally, the West is apt to overlook an important point with regard to the "inexhaustible" masses of Soviet cannon-fodder: the huge loss of human lives in World War II, which after all, ended only fourteen years ago, has by no means been overcome in the Soviet Union, and it will take almost a whole generation before normal conditions in age-groups prevail once more.

For this reason, the Cold War is at present of the greatest significance: internal differences and the ethical decay of the West are today more important for Moscow than a hundred divisions, and the Fifth Columns, the pacifists, and the "neutralists," the instigators of the fear of atomic war, are far more important than any military science. And it is for this reason that further foreign policy diversions, "peaceful" attacks and political subversion of the West on the part of Moscow can be expected in the near future. The Kremlin will do everything in its power to effect a recognition of the status quo of the territories which it has conquered, and in this way will seek to intensify the distrust of the subjugated peoples towards the West. Of course, there will also be some rattling of sabers, but for the time being Moscow will not venture to start a world war: whenever it encounters determined resistance, it will hurriedly withdraw. On the other hand, it will in every way support the campaign conducted by naïve pacifists and blind Russophiles against atomic weapons, in particular against the arming of the Free World and free Germany with such weapons. In this respect a *one-sided* disarmament or non-armament will, naturally, only increase the deadly danger of a Russian invasion immeasurably; for it is only a country equipped with atomic weapons that does not tempt the Russians, precisely because it is not weak and can carry out a surprise attack. In any case, the West must always take into account the possibility of a Kremlin ruler deciding to start a nuclear world war if he sees no other means of retaining his position—even if only for a short time: in such a "borderline case" the Kremlin ruler in question will not have any scruples about staking the life of all human beings on earth. Moscow, however, will never agree to an effective control of atomic armaments, a fact which has already been proved often enough in the course of the completely futile conferences held in Geneva. One must bear in mind in this connection that never in the history of the world has a totalitarian dictatorship submitted to an effective control of its actions.

Instead of continuing to experiment (and there is no other way of defining the vague and hesitant policy of the West towards Moscow) with "peaceful coexistence" without the least success, the West should endeavor to counter-balance the weakness of its world strategy by recognizing and supporting the national liberation movements behind the Iron Curtain, which are directed against *every form of Russian rule*. Since the West cannot hope to equal the quantitative superiority of the Soviet Union and Red China as regards the human potential, it should endeavor to influence the psychic quality of the armed "Soviet subjects"—above all, that of the non-Russians, who are most certainly not in the least interested in preserving and expanding the Russian imperialist prison of peoples.

The Ukrainian Review,
No. I, 1959, pp. 3-9

Communism Behind the Iron Curtain in Crisis

While Communist parties within the Free World have recently obtained some substantial gains (in European countries like Italy and France, or in African countries such as Angola), within the countries behind the Iron Curtain, enslaved by the Communist totalitarian system Communism, as far as ideological, socio-political, and economical matters are concerned, is bankrupt. This situation calls for a somewhat paradoxical diagnosis: should the nations presently enslaved within the USSR free themselves through national revolutions? They could in the future, after their own liberation, come to the assistance of some Western countries and help to free *them* from the Communist yoke by which these countries are now directly endangered.

How is it that Communism is in crisis within the countries controlled by it and what are the means to get rid of the Communist menace?

The Communist system did not grow organically out of the life of the peoples in their own countries. The enslaved nations neither selected the Communist way of life by free will, nor by democratic election, nor by civil wars within their boundaries. Not one single subjugated nation within the USSR nor of the satellites established Communism by its own desire and efforts. Communism was imparted to them by Russian bayonets and maintained by the force of the occupying troops.

During 1918, and a short time after, independent states of Ukraine, Byelorussia, Turkestan, Georgia, and others (some even with Socialist governments) were reestablished by the will of the peoples. The "advent" of Lenin was a clear masking of the messianic, imperialist Russian Communist ideology by which the new Russian chauvinistic mafia tried to save the empire by replacing the corrupt tsarist elite with a Bolshevik one. New slogans took over the old. Instead of the old messianic ideology of the tsarist regime in defense of the "orthodoxy" and Pan-Slavism—there was a new ideology, more perfidious and deceitful, yet just as messianic, preaching proletarian, international Communism and aiming at "proletarian revolutions" throughout the world. Such "ideas" had been stated before.

The tsarist ideology, and system, therefore, became the *modern*, Communist, Russian, *neo*-Imperialist, and *neo*-Colonial ideology and system. Lenin had Marxism applied to Russian realities, to the collective mentality and sociological needs of the broad Russian masses. Russians were already used to a collective way of life, having their *mir*, the *obshchina*, their "collective" tilling of the land. Yet, Karl Marx had meant his doctrines for the industrially developed nations and had excluded any possibility of their taking root in Imperial Russia.

First Element of the Crisis

The first element of the crisis the Communist system is undergoing now in the countries behind the Iron Curtain is caused by the fact that Communism has taken on the modern form of Russian *neo*-Colonialism and *neo*-Imperialism. The *Union* of the Soviet Socialist Republics (USSR), with all the satellites, *is not* and *does not* represent a voluntary union of sovereign nations. It is a "union" under a totalitarian system making up the new Communist Russian empire, enforced by Russian arms and terror, of cultural nations, some with more than one thousand years of heritage. *The Achilles heel of every empire was and is any enslaved nation held within it by force.* The national liberation struggle of any enslaved people destroys an empire from within.

During times when the contemporary development of world affairs is characterized by disintegration and decolonization processes, such processes *cannot* terminate after reaching the present borderlines of the Communist Russian empire. Membership in the United Nations has quadrupled since the inception of this organization. At the same time Russian imperialists, under the cover of Communism, proclaimed the creation of a new, unheard of, phenomenon: under Brezhnev's leadership, one *Soviet people*, with one *Russian* language is to be molded in the USSR. On February 13, 1976, during the 25th Communist Party Congress of Ukraine, the first secretary, Shcherbitsky, delivered his address in *Russian* rather than in Ukrainian. The official language of the congress, held in the Ukrainian capital, Kyiv, was also Russian. There was no doubt that the Communist Party of Ukraine was directly *subordinated* to the Central Committee in Moscow, the Politburo, the General-Secretariate of the Central Committee.

In the Soviet Constitution we read that the USSR is a state of workers, peasants, and working intelligentsia, and not a union of separate nations, states, and republics.

Proletarian internationalism, Communism and Marxism *deny*, in principle, the *nation* concept and by ethno-, geno-, and linguicide try to destroy it.

The *nation*, however, is a natural phenomenon, with God-given rights, everlasting and indestructible, while the *Soviet people* is an artificial, enforced phenomenon created by the Russians.

Distribution of Power—Two to One

The collision between the concept of *empire* with that of a *nation* within the territorial space overpowered by Communism only contributes to the peculiar crisis of Communism behind the Iron Curtain. The distribution of power within this theater of operations is in the ratio of two to one, if we put the population of the enslaved nations and the satellites of the USSR on one side and the Russian nationals on the other. The more numerous the nations are that are swallowed up—the stronger become the possibilities of destroying Russian Communist oppression from within, by a coordinated effort of national revolutions. The *domino* theory not only can but must work also in reverse. The Russians suffocate in their own controversies more and more. To deny the existence of various nations and nationalities within the USSR, to deny their inalienable right to be sovereign, with all its attributes, and, at the same time, to defend the rights of Angola and all its prerogatives for sovereignty, must be regarded as a slap in the face in Georgia, Turkestan, Ukraine, or Lithuania even by schoolchildren. To say that these nations are disappearing from the face of the earth and are melting into one *Soviet people*, while the Uganda of Idi Amin has inalienable rights for absolute sovereignty, is absurd. Uganda certainly does have its inalienable rights to exist, but let's not be hypocritical about it—so do all the other nations on this earth. If Russian *realpolitik* is to be valid, should not then, looking from such a perspective, *the whole world* be composed only of one "great" *Soviet people*? Should not all of mankind merge?

In the Russian language the word "Soviet" means "council." What a strange, if not macabre, nation the whole world would then become: *council people*! All speaking *Russian*, of course!

What kind of prospective world would the *council people* make? During the 25th All-Union Communist Party Congress Brezhnev said: "To deny ourselves the conception of proletarian internationalism would mean to take proven arms out of the hand of Communist parties and labor movements throughout the world." Brezhnev emphasized the "interests of the working class" and said nothing about the fact that there are still national states. The proletarian class makes up only a part of the population in these states. More than half of the world's population is marching today under the banner of nationalism.

The Alternative to Communist Internationalism

The alternative to Communist internationalism is national freedom and independence of individual states. The choice is clear. Communist internationalism, proletarian internationalism, and Soviet unnatural "patriotism" of the non-existing "Soviet people"—all bring about the total barbarization of life. There is no culture without traditions. All the cultures of contemporary nations are based on centuries-old religious and social traditions. Without the mosaic of national cultures there is no heritage for world civilization, only automatic thoughtlessness. *If you know how to drive an automobile that does not mean that you know how to make one.* The world's most famous inventors (Edison), philosophers (Plato, Confucius), writers (Shakespeare, Shevchenko, Goethe)—all became part of the world's civilization by first being national geniuses, the pride of their nations. There is no such thing as a *synthetic* genius. Denationalization, or "Sovietization,"—robs people of their cultural heroes and ends in the vulgarization of life, an *anti-hero* cultism of pseudo-international ignorance in a mob of faceless mongrels. National cultures did not appear overnight and they cannot be *forced* to appear. They are a part of centuries-old processes. There is no such thing as a "cultural revolution." Only national-political revolutions can take place. They are anti-imperialist by nature and make it possible for the cultural development of the involved nation to continue while preserving a centuries-old cultural heritage, not destroying it. "Back to traditions," "back to the original principles of Christianity," "back to Confucianism"—these are the revolutionary slogans in the epoch of struggle against barbaric Communist proletarian internationalism. Maoist "cultural revolutions" are destroying more than five thousand years of Chinese culture by importing into the Chinese spirit anti-Chinese *Stalinist, Leninist, and Marxist* elements, all foreign to the Chinese heritage.

Some peoples have *Christian*, others *Hebraic* or *Islamic*, still others *Buddhist*, *Confucian*, or *Shinto* cultures. Neither "Marxism-Leninism-Stalinism-Brezhnevism" nor "Maoism" can be accepted, all of a sudden, as the basis for one universal monoculture. Enforced indoctrination by such unnatural, anti-religious, and anti-national elements in the long run must end in spiritual emptiness, the animalization of humans, and the creation of people without roots. Peoples can grow and develop only if supported by centuries of national heritage. The same goes for the human being; a person must have a sense of belonging, must have national identity. Marxist theories are robbing mankind of its national roots.

Integral Imperialism

Such an aim creates a crisis. The integral difference between Russian Communist imperialism and Western imperialism (as once practiced by such powers as Britain, France, and Spain) is that Russian imperialism is not limited to strategic, military, and economic aspects. It attempts to enforce upon the overpowered nations as well as upon individuals its own conceptions about what life is, enforcing its own ways from ontology to philosophy, from atheism to collective farming and "Socialist Realism" in culture. For two thousand years Christianity and other religions have tried to change human nature. So how can it be possible for "dialectical materialism," the diabolical Communist system, to change what two thousand years of religious preaching could not? In the very root of Bolshevism lies the beginning of its own crisis and eventual downfall.

The Thief of Ideas

At the beginning of "war Communism" there was rape, terror, the *Cheka* (today the KGB), and the law of the gun. From the beginning there was deceit. Never did Communism obtain a victory, by its own ideology; it always used stolen ideas. Lenin issued slogans about giving all land to the peasants, all factories to the workers; he promised independence, self-determination— including separation of national states from the claws of "Mother Russia." Not one of these slogans is of Communist origin, nor was any of them ever fulfilled. What Communism brought peasants and workers was enforced collectivization of farms, rejection and denial of private ownership, the takeover of factories by thieving party bureaucrats, and national enslavement rather that national sovereignty. A one-party state, collectivism, state-capitalism, party dictatorship, Politburo cliques, enforced colonialism, Russification, religious persecution— this is the true face of the Communist system in the USSR. No other version of a "Communist system" was ever demonstrated there, nor anywhere else. The anti-natural ideology cannot thrive in any other way but by enforcement through terror. The very conception of "dictatorship of the proletariat" implies dictatorship of a one-party system, which means, by the way, the close circle of the party's Central Committee, subordinated to an even closer circle of the Politburo, subordinated to the unlimited power accumulated in the hands of the "Secretary General"—with terror down the line. There was never a *democratic* empire on this earth and never shall be. Parliamentary democracy always was metropolitan. But in the "colonies," or enslaved nations, there has always been a reign of terror supported by military occupation.

Without Rights for Nations No Human Rights Can Be Had

Human rights cannot be gained, nor respected, in any empire. The fundamental prerequisite for human rights is maintenance and respect of the peoples' rights in sovereign states. It is ridiculous to talk about "democratization," or "Communism with a human face," with the borders of an empire, and even more ridiculous to imagine any human rights in the Russian Communist state. The downfall of the empire must come before any human rights can be had there, for only the downfall and dismemberment of an empire can automatically assure the inalienable rights of every nation, including that of the former oppressor.

Let us not forget; terror and deceit are the cornerstones of the Russian Communist empire. The accompanying chorus for its formula of "Communist internationalism" consists of: a) dialectical materialism; b) historical materialism; c) classocratism (with a special recipe for dictatorship of the proletariat); d) militant atheism; e) anti-nationalism; f) an international anti-natural union of proletarians with misfits of all kinds; g) an active demonstration of Russian imperialism as a cover-up for the *neo*-colonialism elsewhere, such as *Titoism* (Europe), *Maoism* (Asia), *Castroism* (Latin America), all bound to the *personality cult*, in a "worthy" tradition. It remains to be seen what new "personalities" will appear in "united and liberated" Vietnam and in Angola.

Can human rights be gained and respected under such circumstances? Not under terror and deceit. Both are significant elements of the crisis and bankruptcy of Communism as such.

Communist Hermaphroditism

Liberating nationalism is striking into the fundamentals of Russian *neo*-imperialism and *neo*-colonialism in every phase of life. Proletarian internationalism has degenerated into the enforced pouncing upon the enslaved nations of reactionary Russian traditionalism, with the cult of grasping tsars and feudal marshals such as Suvorov or Brusilov.

The escape into national-communist heresy by some satellites is also a clear indicator of crisis for it is a hermaphroditic phenomenon. Such a political, ideological, philosophical, or even socio-political combination does not exist. Communism can only be internationalist, never national.

Efforts at national Communism are only transitory attempts for a compromise between Communism and some antipodal tendencies in certain aspects of life, since the Communist doctrine is dependent exclusively upon Moscow's bayonets within the enslaved nations and within the satellites—that is, dependent exclusively upon Russian military intervention (examples: the Berlin uprising of 1953, Hungary 1956, the CSSR in 1968).

With the downfall of Bolshevism within the enslaved nations and dismemberment of the empire, regimes like those of Husak, Gierek, and even Ceausescu collapse. They can only exist as long as a Russian Communist empire does. The analogy could be extended to include Tito's Yugoslavia. Therefore, at a decisive

moment, all Giereks, Husaks, Ceausescus, Castros, even Titos must find themselves on the side of rescuers of the Russian Communist empire, fully conscious
of the fact that, were it not for Moscow's powerful presence, their own peoples
would wipe them off the face of the earth. Every hybrid is a harbinger of a crisis.
Therefore the national Communist conception must be as well.

Renaissance in Facts and Figures

The collision between the Russian Communist mode of life on one side and the
organic desires of liberty intrinsic to every enslaved nation on the other results in
a lasting, difficult struggle of these two opposite worlds. One of them shall be
victorious. Resistance and tensions systematically increase. From 1942 to 1953
massive, organized liberation wars (directed first against Nazi and after 1944
against Russian occupation) took place in Ukraine and Lithuania. Between 1953
and 1959 massive strikes and uprisings by Ukrainian, Turkestanian, Lithuanian,
Caucasian, and other inmates (it is estimated that over 17 million inmates were
involved) took place in concentration camps located in every corner of the
Russian Communist empire. In 1962 there were uprisings in Novcherkassk, in
Temirtau in 1959, and others in Vorkuta, and Kingiri. Violent demonstrations in
Dniprodzerzhinsk and in Dnipropetrovks in 1972, massive demonstrations of
students in Kyiv, Lviv, Odessa, Kaunas, Erivan, and Tbilisi, workers' demonstrations in Donbas and Nalchyk during the sixties as well as the seventies—all make
up an impressive record. Just like the uprisings in Berlin (1953), Hungary and
Poland (1956), the CSSR (1968), and again in Poland (1971), they were motivated
by a desire for sovereignty and independence, justice, and human rights, in
defense of national cultures. It is indicative, for instance, that the Ukrainian
inmates in the Vorkuta concentration camp complex appealed to the Western
world demanding help, arms, and medicine to be dropped to them by a massive
airlift so that they could destroy the empire and Communism. It is equally
important to know that during the Temirtau, Novocherkassk, and Kingiri uprisings the regular army units had to be withdrawn and the crushing of the
uprisings had to be done by the special units of the KGB-MVD forces. Both in the
Hungary and CSSR uprisings regular army units had to be withdrawn as well.
This fact signifies that oppression is maintained mainly by the KGB-MVD special
forces and that regular army units cannot be trusted, for regular army units are
drafted mainly from the population reserves of the enslaved nations which hate
the Communist system and imperialist greed.

It is people who bear arms. The value and power of the arms depend upon the
value of the people. What if the people serving in the Russian Communist
occupying army turn the arms against the oppressor? The most modern arms
will not save the empire should the soldiers of its army turn against it. More than
half of the regular Soviet army units are composed of non-Russian nationalities;
if we take into account the satellite countries, the proportion of non-Russian to
Russian soldiers is two to one in favor of the non-Russians. It should be realized
by the Western world that psychological warfare for the soul of the non-Russian

soldier is of the utmost importance and should be conducted systematically. It is Brezhnev who consistently reminds the Western world that *detente* does not and never shall exclude *ideological warfare*. Let the Western world remember that.

Let me repeat; Communism as *neo*-Colonialism, *neo*-Imperialism, is a totalitarian, monoparty, anti-natural system; a sheep-like, collective way of life which denounces the human being and individuality and cultivates faceless conformity. Communism, by its materialistic manipulations, has antagonized and mobilized for open warfare all national-liberating, democratic, anti-collective, anti-materialistic, theistic, and freedom-loving forces. During the sixties and early seventies there began the miracle of national renaissance among the young generation within the enslaved nations in a national, traditional, theistic, anti-materialistic, anti-Communist spirit. This miracle is a deadly blow to Communism and Russian imperialism.

Various underground publications in the USSR, literary works voicing what was stated above, the revival of the Church in the catacombs, massive protests by writers, poets, and artists, activities of the younger generation in every walk of life, demonstrations, strikes, protests, assaults against "Socialist Realism," sabotage in manufacturing and collective farming, massive stealing of goods, shortages caused by bureaucratic indifference, massive deportations to the far corners of the empire—all these symptoms indicate crisis and bankruptcy.

Economic Bankruptcy

Communism, as an economic system, negates the principle of private ownership. The cultivation of official state capitalism is maintained by force. A human being can only be free if the freedom is extended to include economic enterprises. With the enslaved nations in the USSR the principle of private ownership is inherent, especially where the soil is concerned, while for the Russian people it is not specific. The richest soil in Europe belongs to Ukraine. Ukraine was always regarded as a granary by other European nations, yet there is famine in Ukraine today. Here are the figures resulting from the after-effects of the enforced collectivism; out of the 215.7 million tons of grain planned by the USSR for the year 1975, only 135 million tons were reaped. This is some 35 percent less than the figure necessary for the empire to maintain its equilibrium. And even the admitted figures are probably manipulated.

During the ninth five-year plan in the USSR the capital investment in agriculture throughout the imperial complex was increased some 75 percent over the figures of the eighth five-year plan, yet the average grain production increased only 10-13 percent. It seems that under the collective system the soil does not want to yield crops; its productivity in comparison with the capital investment is relatively small. And out of all the industrialized countries in the world the USSR shows the lowest productivity of labor. As the folk saying goes: "Life is great on the collective farm—one man works, another hundred charm." Two thousand peasants in the Dniester region (Ukraine), where initiative still thrives because collective farming was introduced only after the Second World War, succeeded in covering with plastics some 735 acres of cucumbers and saved their crop from frost, while all the collective farms of the region covered only 7 acres of cucumbers. Private initiative does not accept collective thinking. "Collective responsiblity" is cruel, robs the individual of his or her initiative, makes robots of people.

Brezhnev stressed during the 25th All-Union Communist Party Congress the difficulties encountered in strategically important production sectors and postponed any consideration of consumer needs. He admitted that billions of rubles were wasted because of organic defects within the system. During the 25th Communist Party Congress of Ukraine Shcherbytsky said that the capital investment in Ukraine during the recent five-year plan had been 500 billion rubles. Sixty percent of the entire production resulting from this capital investment was taken away by Moscow, mainly for the production of Russian tanks, rockets, and naval vessels, including atomic submarines. Should a direct conflict arise, all this naval hardware would be vulnerable facing the Western fleets for lack of supply routes and naval bases. Is not that the true reason why Russians show so much interest in Somalia and Angola, supplying arms and millions of rubles daily for Cuba and North Vietnam?

In the meantime, the *lumpenproletariat* is on the increase in the USSR. The wild "state-planned" economy cannot supply work for qualified workers in their fields.

Billions of rubles in gold are being spent to buy needed goods and consumer products from, as Brezhnev puts it, "decadent capitalist Western countries." Now 30 million tons of grain later another 30 million tons. During the next five-year plan Moscow wants to take from Ukraine alone 235 billion kilowatts of electrical energy, three times the amount needed by Ukraine by 1980. Plans are approved to take out of Ukraine by 1980: 229 million tons of coal, 54.6 million tons of iron ore, 61 million tons of steel, 61 million tons of readied blooms, 6.9 tons of steel pipeline, 50 million tons of grain. In return, some million sets of *Collective Works* by Lenin are to be delivered to Ukraine. Ukraine, its national economy, is being geared to become a raw-material producer to feed industrial complexes and production centers located outside Ukrainian territories.

The tenth five-year plan aims to increase heavy industry in Ukraine by 35 to 39 percent and agricultural enterprises by 14 to 17 percent. Nothing is said about light industry and production of articles for everyday needs. The promised "paradise to come" is still, somewhere in the distant and hazy future. Scherbytsky attacked the "bourgeois nationalists" and Zionists for trying to ruin "the spirit of Helsinki" instead.

Acute Aspects of the Crisis

By citing facts and figures on Ukraine we have given an example of the proportions of exploitation the national states are subjected to in the USSR, and proved what a vital and acute role such national states are made to perform for the empire and for its arms race with the Western world. With the liberation and independence of Ukraine alone the world could breathe more easily, the natural resources and ores in rich abundance would no longer be available for imperial disposition. At the present time Ukraine is forced to contribute 60 percent of the arms for the empire. The national liberation struggle, growing and expanding in Ukraine, makes the crisis of Communism in the USSR an acute problem. To aid this national liberation struggle means driving a wooden peg into the heart of the Russian imperialist vampire; it means bringing the acute crisis to its final stage, the actual downfall of Russian Communism. Strategically, Ukraine holds the key position in the national liberation struggle, with all its human revolutionary potential, its geopolitical position on the world's map, its economic capacity, and almost 50 million people, most of them conscious of their national-political destiny.

Ukraine and other enslaved nations are the political factors of the future with immense importance for the fate of the entire world. With their independence the political maps of Europe, Asia, and Africa will change, for Russia would lose the seaways to warm oceans. The independence of the Caucasus, Turkestan, Byelorussia, and the Baltic states, as well as all present satellites, would then make the domino theory work in reverse.

So it must be clear to all where the Achilles' heel of the Russian empire and the Communist system lies.

Leading Crisis

The Communist leadership is corrupt, morally decadent, degenerate. It failed to create the classless society; instead it transformed itself into a privileged class. The gap between Communist leaders on one side and the broad masses on the other is immense. In practice Communism is responsible for a system of exploitation worse than any capitalist system ever could be. Between 70 and 80 million people fell victim to and perished because of this system. Most of the victims were non-Russians of the enslaved nations or of the satellite countries. How acute the crisis of Communism must be if it must turn to geno- and ethnocide over and over again in order to survive. Internationalism indeed! From 70 to 80 million international victims! Such degeneration of humanity, such cruelty there never was. Nazi Germany was only a grade-school pupil in comparison. The horrors of concentration camps, the massive extermination of nations (Northern Caucasus), the starving to death of seven million Ukrainian peasants (including women and children) by the artificially created famine in 1932-1933, to using slave labor to construct canals (e.g., the White Sea Canal in 1933 and Moscow-Volga Canal from 1933 to 1937), causing thousands to perish, using chemical and germ warfare against the UPA, criminal abuse of inmates by prison and concentration camp guards—all is evidence of a deep crisis and the total bankruptcy of Communism in practice.

As Communism denies the immortality of the human soul and the existence of any form of transcendental life, as Communism only depends upon the impetus of force backed up by materalistic, economic, and classocratic factors in its historic development—then it must end in the animalization of mankind. Ethics without a transcendental basis degenerates into absolute egoism and mortal self-consumption. Dechristianization as practiced by Nazis brought about the gas chambers. The total denial of religion by Bolsheviks brought concentration camps and slaughter of more than 70 million men, women, and children, within fifty-eight years.

"Humane" Communism is just as impossible as "humane" gangsterism. For that reason more and more party members let their children be baptized, which proves that they themselves have little faith in Communist dogmas. The spread of religious faith by churches in catacombs, especially among the young, even the reluctant tolerance of the Russian Orthodox Church shows that Communism is capitulating in confrontation with transcendental values. The fact that the Russian Orthodox Church is doing all it can to appease the regime is only one side of the coin. The other side is the faith in transcendental life which means the total collapse of Communist ontology. Controversies continue. If religion is the "opium" of the peoples, then why tolerate the Russian Orthodox Church and wag one's tail at the Vatican? Real religious faith, no matter of what denomination, destroys the very foundation of Communism and does not conform to either dialectical or philosophical materialism.

Contradictions That Cannot Be Resolved

The Russian Communist empire slyly finances and supports with arms national liberation wars outside its own domain. This is a contradiction that cannot be resolved, for here the Communist class conception collides with the conception of *national independence*. Communist doctrine regards *nation* and *national* as "bourgeois inventions." At the same time a monstrosity like the "Soviet nation," which in itself is a contradiction, is replacing another monstrosity just as contradictory. National liberation wars outside the countries behind the Iron Curtain naturally connect mentally to similar wars in the Communist sphere of influence. In order to survive, "proletarian internationalism" just like imperialism must expand, must go on frightening people about fictitious "aggressions and assaults" and "capitalist aggressive forces," about atrocities awaiting the class of "peasants and workers," other nonsensical slogans about dangers that simply do not exist. By frightening the naïve and by using speculators and opportunists, "proletarian internationalism" expands, furthering Russian Communism and its imperialist interests by taking over more and more countries. All these "takeovers" also contribute to the crisis of Communism behind the Iron Curtain, for they antagonize more and more people, foes and friends alike. Nobody believes in Communist ideas anymore; they have become rather transparent, revealing the true face of Russian *neo*-Imperialism hiding behind them.

The Kremlin clique creates the core of the Russian Communist imperial center. Should a member of the Politburo be a Latvian, a Finn, an Armenian, a Georgian, a Jew, or a Ukrainian—it is of no importance. What is important is whom they serve. If comparison is to be allowed, then Admiral Mountbatten (Battenberg in the German language) was one of Great Britain's foremost strategists, and General Renekampf headed Russian armies during the battle of Tannenberg against Marshal Hindenberg. Trotsky, when he choked the young Ukrainian National Republic to death together with Russian Commissar Muraviov, was not serving the Jewish cause, but the Russian imperial cause. So was the former Georgian seminarist Dzhugashvili (Stalin) as well as the members of Politburo Pelshe (a Latvian) and Kuusinen (a Finn). Is it in the interests of the world's "international proletariat" or of world Communism to rob small Finland of some of its territory and create from it the Karelian SSR, which lasted from 1940 to 1956—to russify it during that period and then reduce it, with Kuusinen's help, to an "autonomous region" within the Russian Soviet Federative Socialist Republic? Does the "world Communist revolution" require enforced deportation of Ukrainians, Byelorussians, Lithuanians, Latvians, and others to Kazakhstan, where Russian settlers are busy denationalizing Kazakh and Turkestani people? What does all this have to do with the *theory of Communism*? All this is not just a problem; it is a crisis that causes the bankruptcy of Russian Communism and of its doctrines behind the Iron Curtain.

Conclusion

The intellectuals of the enslaved nations are presenting an alternative to Russian power. Freedom-fighters of the enslaved nations are no *dissidents*. They do not fight to "heal" the Russian Communist system and save the empire. They are a revolutionary force that strives for the downfall and disintegration of imperial Communist Russia. The unlikely "healers" and "savers" of the empire are, paradoxically, some countries of the Western world.

The Helsinki agreement not only confirmed the status quo of the Russian empire, but, as the Kremlin interprets it, gave Moscow a free hand to actively intervene, in Angolan internal affairs today, or tomorrow in the internal affairs of Northern Ireland, Scotland, Wales, Brittany, the Sahara, Puerto Rico, Panama, and elsewhere.

The Western world should finally realize that the Achilles heel of the Russian Communist empire is the enslaved nations. The strategy of the Western world should be exactly the opposite of the policies adopted in Helsinki. The Western world should renew the ideological, psychological, political, and if necessary, guerrilla warfare, against the Russian Communist empire. It should pursue exactly the same policies as the Russians adopt towards the West.

Instead, in constant fear of a possible atomic holocaust, the Western countries try to appease the Russians in every possible way. They help, therefore, to strengthen the bankrupt Russian system. Why are the Russians not afraid of the atomic holocaust and why do they inflict subversion after subversion upon the West? The answer is that they know quite well that nobody is insane enough to start using atomic weapons because this would mean the end of the world.

What could be easier than to recall to active validity the United Nations

Declaration of December 14, 1960 dealing with the "granting of independence to colonial countries and peoples" (reconfirmed in 1972), the United Nations Charter about the "rights to independence of every nation in the world," the *law* passed by the Congress of the United States of America in 1959 in "support of independence and sovereignty of the enslaved nations in the USSR and in the sphere of Russian Communist influence"? These items should be considered as preconditional for *every* agreement, *every* treaty, and *any economic dealing* with Russians!

What could help to deepen the crisis of Communism and neo-imperialism behind the Iron Curtain more than such a principal stand by the Western world? What could be more desirable for the well-being of the West than active support by the Western nations of the national liberation struggles taking place in the nations enslaved by Russian imperialism?

There should be one unified stand of all Western states, all freedom-loving forces threatened by the Communist menace.

There should be one united stand, one solid front, of all monolithic religions of the world against the deadliest of all enemies of religion.

There should be bravery instead of cowardice.

The way things are, the "savers" and "healers" of Russian neo-Imperialism are mostly in the West. Will the West ever awake?

The Ukrainian Review,
No. I, 1976, pp. 3-20

VI
The Anti-Bolshevik Bloc of Nations (ABN)

Ten Years of the ABN

In the late autumn of the year 1943, in the middle of the Second World War, there arose in Ukraine, out of the ruins, a spiritual light. Armed representatives from thirteen subjugated nations met together on the night of November 21st and 22nd in the forest of Zhytomir, for a general conference of underground movements and revolutionary alliances to declare a common war upon Bolshevism and Nazism. It was characteristic that immediately afterwards there was a fight between these champions of freedom, under a Georgian major, and the Gestapo. That memorable conference's resolution on a common struggle and brotherhood between the nations was at once put to the test. It is also characteristic that the initiator of this first conference, General Taras Chuprynka, was killed seven years later while commanding the Ukrainian Insurgent Army (UPA) in a battle against MVD units near Lviv in Ukraine. During these seven years he had directed a most bitter underground struggle.

During the war years this underground struggle was waged on two fronts. At that time two imperialisms were in collision, Russian Bolshevism and German Nazism. The subjugated nations, inspired with the ideal of national and individual liberty, had to oppose them both. They were fighting for national liberation, social justice, and true democracy. Even then the slogan of these fighters was *"Liberty for nations—liberty for individuals!"* They appealed to the world with the cry *"Liberty-loving peoples of the world, unite in the struggle against tyranny!"*

The representatives of the subjugated nations in the East united in the ABN and proclaimed their solidarity with the war aims of the West in a common, coordinated fight against tyranny and totalitarian dictatorships of every kind. At the same time, however, they warned the democracies of the dangers of making common cause with Bolshevism, which, as World Enemy Number One, puts Nazism far in the shade.

The Western world, at that time still an ally of Moscow, disregarded our warning. It spoke only of "unconditional surrender," which, in its ultimate effect, was to mean capitulation to Bolshevism. It could not see the woods for the trees. What was then predicted, however, has been fulfilled. Bolshevism already presents a deadly threat to the entire world. Teheran, Yalta, Potsdam were the milestones of this fatal progress. Subjugated territories are now more extensive. The enslaved countries of the Soviet Union have been joined by the so-called "satellites." Today they extend so far that the whole world is divided into two parts. It consists only of nations already enslaved and those threatened with enslavement.

For ten years the ABN has warned against every concession to Bolshevism. From the cellars of the underground, from chapels in the catacombs, from the graves of fallen fighters for liberty, a warning light streams out into the Free World. It leads us on to the construction of a new world, which can be founded only upon those high principles for which our peoples have long fought against fearful odds.

For centuries, two conceptions have opposed each other in the East—the ideal of national and personal liberty of the non-Russian peoples, and the Russian despotic system of imperialism. The idea of equality of rights for all nations and their right to liberty and independence has always to be defended against Russian conquest.

The solidarity of the subjugated nations and the conception of a united fight against tyranny, which have found their expression since 1943 in the ABN, had their beginnings in the great coalition planned by the Ukrainian Hetman Orlyk in the 19th century, which has been written about by Taras Shevchenko in his epic poem, *Caucasus*, and also in the initiative of President Hrushevsky, who, in 1917, convened a general conference of the subjugated peoples in Kyiv, and also in the combined committee of representatives of seven subjugated nations which, in 1941, on the initiative of the Ukrainian revolutionaries, published the journal *Our Front* in five languages and circulated it in the USSR.

Experience has shown that the sense and urge for justice is more deeply rooted in a subjugated nation and is more strongly in evidence than in the nations of the Free World. The loathing of injustice and inequality is more intense and more explosive there than here. A prisoner longs even more for liberty than for bread. In this very fact lies the key to understanding the enslaved peoples.

This should be the pivot of Western policy towards our nations. Today, when, in view of the critical atmosphere in the Soviet sphere of domination, the hopes of the subjugated peoples in the East have sharply risen, it is all the more necessary that the West should understand the temperament of our people. The Kremlin should not be given the chance to convince our people that they have been deserted by the West and are only used as currency in shady bartering with Moscow. For, should the hope of these nations that the Free World is prepared to stand by them in the desperate struggle for freedom be extinguished, the game in the East would be decided in favor of Moscow and the effect upon the world situation would be incalculable.

In this conflict of two philosophies, the victory of the West, as the champion of liberty, can only be attained on the basis of a total rejection of tyranny. It allows neither compromise nor partial solutions. Success requires unconditional acknowledgment of the high ethical value of liberty, equality, national independence, social justice, and religion, to which our nations have long dedicated themselves in their fight against Russian-Bolshevik despotism. In this revolutionary age, one must be unconditionally loyal to this modern ideal. Should the West, however, turn its back upon the fulfillment of these aims of our struggle, in favor of the expedient and futile purposes of a short-term policy or of egoistic self interest, this would be tantamount to the abandonment of ethical principles in politics and would make smooth the way of Bolshevik nihilism, allowing the world to drift to certain ruin.

The power of the herd instinct is on the increase in our times. The difficulty of building a just international and social order is one that gives rise to a dangerous growth of skepticism. Mankind thirsts after a clear ideal in which are to be found values and precepts which seem capable of guaranteeing to the individual as well as the nation a secure and dignified existence. Military means alone are not enough to overcome the Bolshevik world-peril of today. That can be achieved only by the sacred code of a spiritual revolution which must form the foundation of our faith in a new and better future.

Reactionary ideas must have no place in the conception of the West, least of all plans for preserving the structure and systems which have been the very cause of the rise of Bolshevism in the past. The worst of these evil institutions is the Muscovite Empire, which could only be held together by means of a despotic system of government and thus was bound to become the breeding ground of Bolshevism.

Bolshevism's destructive influence was from the first directed against national and personal liberty, social justice and faith in God. For the renewal of our world, consequently, the West must not confirm anew this destructive influence in the East, but rather must it adhere to the basic principles of freedom and humanity.

Bolshevism has not merely preserved the despotism of Russian imperialism but has in fact renewed and consolidated it. Therefore the revolution of our times has to make the dissolution of this despotic empire and the restoration of the overthrown national states its first objective. Bolshevism has carried Russian domination as far as Berlin and Vienna, and has conquered Asia for Russia. Therefore the revolution must primarily reestablish liberty here and must restore national independence to all the enslaved peoples.

The ABN is waging war *against* Communistic despotism and dictatorship in every form, against the exploitation of men by the state or their fellowmen, against godlessness, against imperialism; *for* spiritual and religious rebirth, for national independence, for private ownership of land and property, for the development of native industries, for free competition and individual initiative within the framework of social justice, for the promotion of ethical values, for national traditions, for free development of the creative powers of all nations through the abolition of artificially imposed state systems based on force.

On the tenth anniversary of the foundation of the ABN, these simple ideas must be repeated, for they do not seem to be sufficiently appreciated by many people and nations in the West living in freedom and well-being and enjoying a worthy human existence, which our peoples still vainly long for while it is taken for granted in the West.

Today more than ever we persist in our conception of the individuality of freedom. The world stands at the crossroads; either our ideas will make an end, once and for all, of Russian despotism and lust for world conquest, or there will remain this disastrous conflict between the Free World and the miscreants of Russian Bolshevik tyranny. Then the world cannot escape the disaster that is sure to come sooner or later.

During these ten long years of our struggle, in the enslaved homeland at the point of the gun and in the free West with pen in hand, undiverted by the blandishments of Moscow or the temptations of compromise, we have uttered our warnings. Today, at the beginning of the second decade of the ABN, we again preface our activities with a warning to the West against making any kind of ideological, political, or tactical compromise with Russian imperialism.

Two worlds are in the throes of a mortal struggle. One of them must inevitably go under if the other is to survive.

ABN Correspondence,
November-December 1953, pp. 1-2

The Perspective of Our Campaign

We often hear Western circles inquire about our number, the extent of our power, the sacrifices of our struggle, the possibility of our self-deliverance and when the revolution against the Russian Bolshevik domination is to begin.

A single spark may kindle a conflagration. Nobody foresaw the destruction of the Bastille and its result, the rule of Napoleon. The strength of our revolution lies in the idea of deliverance, in the conception of the national revolutionary fight and in the mental constitution and strength of character of our subjugated peoples. Oppressed people have a stronger sense of truth and justice than free ones. We fight in all domains of life: in the sphere of agriculture, labor, industry, administration, culture, religion, and especially in national politics. The more invisible this fight is to the outer world, the more penetrating is its effect.

The Character of the Resistance Movements

The underground war leaves its evidence in "legal" literature. The Bolsheviks try to find national deviation in it, as, for example, in Turkestan: "The party organization of Uzbekistan is to fight ruthlessly against the symptoms of bourgeois nationalism and disclose the reactionary character of Pan-Turkestanism" (*Pravda*, 28. 9. 1952); or in Georgia: "The literary critic has insufficiently disclosed ideological perversion and been lax in combatting relapses into bourgeoisie nationalism" (*Pravda*, 20. 9. 1952); or in Ukraine: "The deficiency in ideological work is not in the least made good...serious ideological perversions in arts and literature are even now not eradicated" (*Pravda*, 19. 9. 1952); in Poland: "As to the Polish people, it must be stated that its resistance against the Bolshevik system is still stronger nowadays than it was even against Germany...." (*Die Weltwoche*, 9. 1. 1953).

Another important factor of Bolshevism is its struggle against the Church, which entailed the obliteration of the Ukrainian Autocephalous Orthodox Church, with its Metropolitan, Vasyl Lypkivsky, as well as the entire Ukrainian Catholic Church with its episcopacy and its Archbishop, Joseph Slipy. They were sent, with thousands of priests, to concentration camps in Siberia. In spite of the dual persecution, both Churches are now functioning underground. It is the same with the Baltic states, with Byelorussia, Bulgaria, Hungary, Romania, Bohemia, etc. The basic attitude of our peoples as a whole contrasts with Bolshevism and the Russian conception of life. Thus insurgent military troops came into being as symbols of national sovereignty, the most substantial of which has always been and still is the army.

The political resistance movements carry on and organize the fight of our peoples. The sacrifices to be borne are very heavy, especially among the leading members. Terrorism, blockades, provocation, deportations are everyday events. But the fight still goes on. The resistance movements make use of the consistency of the brutal subjugation of the peoples within the Iron Curtain and the lying propaganda about the liberation of the peoples on this side of the Iron Curtain. Those deported to Siberia work also against the regime.

Our Sources of Strength

The strength of our national ideal of liberation and the uneasiness it induces in the Bolshevik despots may be clearly judged by the fact that this problem was the central theme of the 19th Party Congress in Moscow.

The main force of the ABN conception lies in the fact that we stress this decisive role of our native countries and the assistance of the emigrants in the Western world in our fight. It is most important, aside from the necessity of maintaining connections between national emigrants and the home countries—which may be interrupted at times—for us and our peoples to stand out as bearers of ideas which coincide with those at home. We must assist those peoples and defend their aspirations here.

The ideas of national deliverance, of social justice, of liberty and freedom of religion are now the pregnant ideas behind the Iron Curtain. Thus we must find kindred elements in the West, mobilize them for the common cause, and closely cooperate with them.

The conception of the ABN (independence of each people in a national state of its own and liberty for every individual) and the Russian and Communist subjugation of nations are now encountering each other. The scale is slowly inclining to our side.

It is no accident that President Eisenhower, Senator Wiley as Chairman of the Commission for Foreign Affairs, and State Secretary Dulles have expressed the thought that Bolshevism must be fought from ideological positions by confronting Communism with Christendom in the West, with Islam in the Near East, with Confucianism, Buddhism, and Shintoism in the Far East. Another characteristic symptom may be seen in the fact that nations now want their fate in the hands of firm and responsible characters. Or why is it that in the majority of nations the power has been taken over by military persons (USA, Egypt, part of South America, Greece)? The army has always been a symbol of resistance against corruption as has been proven by Ukraine, Byelorussia, and Turkestan.

The ethnographical principle and the recognition of the claim of all displaced persons to return home will give us a just clue to the solution of borderline problems. The allies may choose between our ideas and the further oppression which makes up the program of the Russian imperialists and Communists. It is symptomatic that we hear now in the West: "ABN conception," "ABN people think otherwise." It is not always inquired of which people the ABN consists, but is simply said "ABN people"; that is to say, people of a certain character and of a different, certain, clear objective.

The recent joint action against CSR, the united step of all Ukrainian factors against CCAC and the common declaration of the national-political centers and organization of non-Russian peoples against CCAC now issued by ABN are a telling witness for the truth of our persuasion. Recently a politician wrote to us: "The Americans are telling the Russians: ABN unites nations, while you, the Russians, disunite them."

International Problems

We must show a solid and uniform attitude. Our conception is opposed by the Russian, the Yugoslavian and the CSR conception. The point of our common interest is that whoever sympathizes with the "Green International" is sympathizing with an indivisible Russian Empire. And on the other hand, when the Russian empire falls, Tito's Communism will have to fall with it. Consequently every adversary of the Russian empire must oppose Tito's Communism, too. In reality, the frontline runs through the nations in the west. There is no unity in France, Italy, or the USA. Fifth columns there defend Moscow's interests. Thus the interests of the western patriots coincide more with the actions of the ABN than with those of their compatriots serving Moscow. We have stated that the ideas of the West in their development are gradually inclining to our side; thus our work has not been in vain. May it remain equally clear, unwavering, and uncompromising! True, we have no funds, but a true ideal will win, sooner or later, even with such very small means as ours, and untruth cannot prevail, even by means of its millions. Furthermore, we must not forget the important role of the Islamic peoples in the Orient and the perils awaiting them from the cunning tactics of the Bolshevik and from anti-Semitism, which will only strengthen the insane neutralism of some nations in the Near East. We must also focus our attention on the Mediterranean as an essential field in a possible war against Bolshevism.

Prospect and Prognosis

The friendly feelings the West entertains for us may be a consequence of our strength and the manifestation of our inner unity. The ABN itself is the means, not the end. There exist only the interests of each nation and these are the interests of the ABN, which is not an international organization but a coordination center. The stress is laid by design on the political tendency of the West against Bolshevism: the war waged is an ideological, political, and even a religious one. If the West aims seriously at the dissolution of the Russian prison of peoples, its strategy must be to separate the subjugated nations from the enemy and to attack only Russian territory in the case of actual war. This war is not to be waged against our peoples but in common with them against Russian imperialism. Only a united front of subjugated nations, including Germany, can be victorious. The die will be cast in the years 1953 and 1954. The fate of the world will be determined then for centuries. Therefore our part in the war is of particular importance.

The USA, with Great Britain, can make a substantial contribution to a favorable solution if, as nations of wide political experience, they support our ideas.

Come what may, we are determined to keep the initiative in our own hands and to appear upon the world stage with the claim that our peoples, as a potential factor in the present world crisis, are a power in themselves. In the tenth year of the existence of the Anti-Bolshevik Bloc, we have every reason to gaze confidently into the future.

> Speech at the Plenary Meeting of the Council of Nations and the Central Committee of the ABN on January 25, 1953. ABN Correspondence, March-April 1953, pp. 1-10.

The Light of Freedom from the Forests of Ukraine

The guiding idea and principle of the ABN—the disintegration of the Russian empire into national independent states of all the peoples subjugated by Moscow by means of national liberation revolutions—is also the liberation idea of the Ukrainian nation. Its genesis dates from the days of Hetmans Mazepa and Orlyk. Hetman Orlyk formed an anti-Russian coalition headed by Turkey, and in this way continued the noble work of one of the most famous figures in the history of

Ukraine, Hetman Ivan Mazepa. Hetman Orlyk left us a valuable legacy in the form of an unparalleled example of an untiring and consistent campaign abroad in behalf of the liberation of his people by revolutionary methods. In his works, in particular in his profoundly stirring epic poem *The Caucasus*, Taras Shevchenko, the great Ukrainian poet, laid the ideological foundations for a common front of all the peoples enslaved by the Russian tyrants. "Fight and you will be victorious, for God will help you"—this is the appeal which Shevchenko addressed to all the peoples who are languishing in the Russian peoples' prison.

The freedom aims of S. Petlura, the Ukrainian national hero and head of the Ukrainian state, who also continued his fight for the liberation of his country abroad; the campaign of the founder and organizer of the UVO and OUN Colonel Evhen Konovalets; the freedom manifesto of the OUN in 1940; and, lastly, the formation of the Committee of Subjugated Peoples—which, thanks to the initiative of the OUN and of the UPA and in particular of General Taras Chuprynka, was realized at the conference held in the forest of Zhytomyr, Ukraine, on November 21 and 22, 1943—all these events are stages in the organic and political development of the ABN, which during the past twenty years has become an anti-Russian and anti-Communist force of global dimensions.

In the midst of dreadful chaos and a two-front war against the most powerful war-machines in the world at that time—the German and the Russian—the revolutionary nationalists of the peoples, subjugated by both forms of tyranny defined and established in the forest of Zhytomyr the ideological, political, and military principles and methods of the liberation of these enslaved peoples from the tyrants. From the technical and material point of view these revolutionary nationalist forces were much weaker than those of the German and Russian tyrants, but they were spurred on and inspired by the idea of freedom, by a vision of the future, by their moral strength and their belief in eternal ethical values to such an extent that they could have moved mountains. In their manifesto these revolutionary nationalists appealed to the subjugated peoples of East and Central Europe to form a joint front against Russia and Germany and to initiate and conduct a coordinated revolutionary liberation war by insurgent movements against the imperialist powers. It was stressed that one should beware of "liberating" the countries occupied by Germany by resorting to assistance of the new Russian occupants. The allies were exhorted to assist the subjugated peoples in their fight against Nazi Germany and not to join forces with the foul fiend Moscow. Former soldiers of the Soviet Army who deserted to the side of the insurgents also attended the secret conference in Zhytomyr—a fact which incidentally clearly showed the vulnerability of the Russian empire, which is composed of the subjugated peoples, and also emphasized that the USSR would merely be a colossus with feet of clay if the West adopted the political principles of the subjugated peoples and actively supported them. The conference warned the Western World of the grave danger which would threaten the whole world if Russia were to win the war, for by 1943 it was already perfectly obvious that the Germans had lost the war.

The fact that the German Nazis designated the Ukrainian and other insurgents who opposed the German invasion as "Stalin's lackeys" and that the Red

Russians, on the other hand, designated them as "Hitler's lackeys" is clear proof that these insurgents were fighting against both forms of tyranny and that in doing so they were obliged to rely entirely on their own forces. It therefore seems appropriate to mention the fact that the Polish insurgents in Warsaw were sadly mistaken in believing that the advancing Russian armies would help them to repulse the Germans. *Ukraine and the peoples allied with it at that time did not count on any help from either Berlin or Moscow.* What was more, the splendid fight which was put up by the 200,000 men of the Ukrainian Insurgent Army (UPA) was ignored and passed over in silence by the Western allies out of "loyalty to Moscow." Even their fight against the Germans was passed over in silence by the Western allies so as not to "offend" Stalin, since the UPA together with its allied insurgents from other subjugated peoples was also fighting against Stalin. In this connection we should like to point out that there were also various other national units of subjugated peoples, under their own commanders, in the Ukrainian Insurgent Army. The secret conference in Zhytomyr in November 1943, for instance, was guarded by Georgian units under the command of a Georgian major. Even though the hostile major powers directed their attacks against *Ukraine, this country was not obliged to rely entirely on its own strength. A large-scale front of the enslaved peoples against the tyrants was being set up. It was the front of the struggle for the national idea,* a symbol of our day, which promises to be victorious on all continents.

In the forests of Ukraine in November 1943 the spark of a great fire, the inextinguished conflagration of coordinated national liberation revolutions, which can destroy the Russian empire from within, was kindled. This is the first front of freedom-loving mankind against the menace of Russian imperialism and of Communism, which is the instrument of this imperialism.

The arrogant forecasts of Hitler, according to which a few German bombers would be able to crush all resistance on the part of the subjugated peoples, did not by any means come true. The national insurgents of these peoples played an active and decisive part in bringing about the collapse of Hitler's hitherto invincible armies.

The fundamental idea of the ABN as a reality of our day and the armed fight which was put up twenty years ago may serve as a two-fold guide for freedom-loving mankind—that is to say, as both a political and a military strategic guide.

The national liberation idea and the nationalism which aims to achieve national liberation must be regarded as the driving forces in the fight against the Russian empire and prison of peoples. And this implies the acceleration of the disintegration of the Russian empire, its complete annihilation as well as the support, furtherance, and recognition of the national peculiarities of the individual peoples, of their traditions and of their intellectual and spiritual life, of which inherent qualities are religious idealism and faith in God. Hence the slogans of every nation in its fight against militant Russian atheism and the enslavement of peoples are: God and the fatherland.

The national wars of liberation—that is to say, a series of insurrections—can bring about the destruction of the USSR from within; it is imperative that such insurrections be given active and wholehearted support by the Free World, since the Russian danger is not confined solely to the peoples who are already subjugated but also threatens the entire Free World. As long as Bolshevism, the modern form of Russian imperialism, is not annihilated by the disintegration of the Russian empire, the Free World will be constantly threatened by the Russians.

And since the West, by helping the subjugated peoples, is helping itself, we take the occasion of the twentieth anniversary of the ABN to appeal to the West to give the insurgent peoples its military aid if it wishes to prevent a thermo-nuclear war.

The West should proclaim the aims of the ABN as the aims of an anti-Russian and anti-Communist crusade on the part of all freedom-loving mankind. The destruction of the Russian empire should be inscribed as a slogan on the banners of all free individuals and peoples.

Russia is at present more or less in a state of war with the West, a tension which is being aggravated by various ways and means but which the leaders of the Free World, strange to say, refuse to realize. This state of war must be countered by warlike means and methods. The subjugated peoples are also in a state of war, directly or indirectly, with Russia, and this fact cannot be concealed. War in this atomic age can assume various forms, especially as Russia, by means of its extremely powerful fifth columns, Communist parties, diversionary maneuvers, subversive campaigns, and warlike operations on the peripheries, is constantly extending the boundaries of its empire and is working its way further and further into the territories of the Free World. The Communist parties and their subsidiary organizations must be proscribed as parties of traitors, as parties of the enemy in the heart of every nation. The policy of coexistence must be ended for all time, since it is only advantageous to the tyrants. The Russian prison of peoples must be isolated and blockaded. An offensive policy must be adopted. The morale of the Free World must be strengthened by the severance of all relations with Russia, and the subjugated peoples must be encouraged by the support given to them by a world front of freedom-loving individuals and peoples, for the cause of the subjugated peoples is the cause of all mankind. One should above all appeal to the subjugated peoples and not to the tyrants. The Russian despots would certainly be alarmed if, instead of the endless tirades in the Russian language in the broadcast programs of the world, the free countries were to speak solely in the language and in the spirit of the subjugated peoples!

The slogan of the ABN—"Freedom for nations! Freedom for individuals!"—should become the guiding principle of the psychological war of the Free World, but in its true interpretation, the national independence of the subjugated peoples and not in the sense of a non-predetermined act or a plebiscite. The precondition of the freedom of the individual is the sovereignty of the nation.

Five years ago Stepan Bandera, the leader of the OUN, said at the grave of Colonel Konovalets, who was murdered by a Russian agent in 1938: "Ukraine will have to fulfill an important and great mission which concerns other peoples too, inasmuch as it will realize and defend the universal slogan: Freedom for nations! Freedom for individuals!"

On page 11 of his work *Russia Is Not Invincible* General J.F.C. Fuller, the famous British military theoretician, says of the ABN:

"Because in the Atlantic Pact—however defective it may be—is to be found the only potential first front against the Soviet Union, so in the ABN—however lacking in organization it still is—is to be found the only potential second front. Together the two should constitute the grand strategic instrument of the Western Powers, the one being as essential as the other, for neither without the other can achieve what should be the Western aim, not the containment of Communism, but the complete elimination of Bolshevism, without which there can be no peace in the world. From the value of the ABN as a disruptive instrument, I will next turn to its ability economically to strangle the USSR in another way."

This is General Fuller's opinion of the ABN. It is thus erroneous to assume that the ABN is solely an emigrants' organization or an instrument of foreign policy. The main emphasis of the ideas and the liberation policy of the ABN is concentrated behind the Iron Curtain. Without a common front of the subjugated peoples and without coordinated revolutionary insurrections which pursue the same aims, the liberation of Ukraine is impossible. For the question of Ukraine is a revolutionary world problem, and the restoration of Ukraine's state independence will fundamentally change the present distribution of power in the world, since in that case what is today the largest empire in the world will cease to exist. The activity of the ABN in the Free World is solely one sector of the fight. Because of its uncompromising attitude in the fight against all trends and forces which seek to preserve the Russian empire and because of its refusal to reach any compromise with the enemy, the ABN in the Free World has become the symbol of national, freedom-loving, anti-imperialist and anti-Communist, anti-Russian revolutionary forces, which will never reach any kind of agreement or unity with the forces of the Russian Communist evil. This applies to the entire international sector, to all the subjugated peoples. Similarly, in its national aspect the revolutionary OUN has become the symbol of courage and fearlessness in the fight against the enemy. Individual persons may weaken or fail, but the ideas and the organization of the OUN remain constant and unswerving; hence the three letters OUN have become legendary in Ukrainian reality. The organization which coordinates the national revolutionary forces of the individual subjugated peoples (who are fighting for the disintegration of the Russian empire and the victory of the national idea), the ABN—which has mobilized, on a global scale, all those elements and forces that support the same idea and are akin in their revolutionary attitude—is becoming a deadly danger to the Russian tyrants. It is the foremost task of the ABN to give an impetus to the coordination of the actions of those forces of the various nations which think alike in political and ideological respects, to create a new class of leaders in the Free World, who will reject all compromises and agreements with the Russian Antichrist and oppressors of peoples and individuals, and to form a new order of national fighters and crusaders (an order which should play a decisive part in organizing a crusade against tyranny and atheism). The ABN constantly, systematically, and uncompromisingly endeavors to set up such a world front, wherever and whenever it has an opportunity. Numerous international conferences in Taipei, Saigon, Bangkok, Manila, Tokyo, Mexico, New York, Rome, Malta, Frankfurt, Edinburgh, Escorial, Bolzano, Guatemala, Toronto, and Sydney, and campaigns in various capitals of the world—this is the sphere of the struggle and of the political victories of the representatives of the ABN. The US Congress Resolution on "Captive Nations Week," which supports the idea of the disintegration of the Russian empire, and the historical speech of the former Canadian Premier John Diefenbaker before the United Nations are both measures which are in keeping with the fundamental ideas and principles of the ABN. The task which was begun twenty years ago in the forests of Zhytomyr has in the meantime become a symbol of a new world order which is diametrically opposed to the present reality. The noble idea of this new order, which was initiated by the unforgettable Commander-in-Chief of the UPA, Taras Chuprynka, and by the revolutionaries of other subjugated peoples who took part in the conference of Zhytomyr, whose names in many cases are unknown and who laid down their lives for their nations and for one common idea, is gaining more and more advocates in the world.

The ABN is not the creation of an individual, of a group, or of an organization, but of the entire world. What is more, it is the common property of all the peoples subjugated by the Russian tyrants.

From the Ukrainian point of view the ABN is an historical conception of the liberation of the Ukrainian nation, a conception which has developed out of the geopolitical and other demands of the Ukrainian nation. For this reason substitute organizations of the ABN are set up here and there as part of the common front. The imitators of the ABN are, however, forced to adapt themselves by the policy of the governments of certain major powers. This is indeed proof that one cannot get away from the truth of this conception even though one may try to falsify it (as, for instance, the Paris Bloc, ACEN, etc.).

On the eve of the conference of Zhytomyr in 1943 the insurgents of Ukraine, Georgia, Turkestan, and Byelorussia were engaged in a fierce combat against the Nazi invaders. The freedom fighters of these nations defended a forest which was to become of historical and decisive significance. This anniversary is hallowed by the sacrifice of countless of our fellow countrymen who laid down their lives on this occasion.

The greatest revolutionary insurgent strategist of our day, General Taras Chuprynka, who initiated the conference of Zhytomyr, was killed in action in Ukraine in March 1950 while fighting against the Russian occupants. He gave his life for the realization of a noble and patriotic ideal. In venerating his memory we see in him the symbol of all the heroes and martyrs who have sacrificed their lives for our ideals, for the ideals of God. Whatever may be decided in the palaces of Fifth Avenue in New York will most certainly be annulled by the swords of our freedom fighters if it is not compatible with the ideas and resolutions of the revolutionaries in the forests of Zhytomyr twenty years ago.

And however much the Russian tyrants may endeavor to eradicate the longing for freedom and national independence in the hearts and souls of the subjugated peoples, they will never succeed in doing so. For our truth and our idea will in the end be victorious, thanks to our faith and our indomitable will and as a result of our fight, which will never accept any compromises. The idea of freedom has always been stronger than the power of tyrants. In this fight for Christ and the fatherland, God is on our side and will help us.

The Ukrainian Review,
No. I, 1964, pp. 53-59

VII
The Ukrainian Insurgent Army

The Ukrainian Insurgent Army
(Part One)

Introduction to the Ukrainian Problem

The Ukrainian problem, one of the most complicated in the whole of modern Europe, is superbly simple if the idea is once accepted that the Ukrainians are a separate people, distinct from the Russians.

Nationally, the USSR is not a homogeneous entity, as many "specialists" on East European affairs would lead the world to believe, but a diverse multiplicity of races and peoples subjugated by Moscow. Thus, Ukraine is nationally and culturally a distinct and a separate nation, the most easterly stronghold of Western civilization in Eastern Europe. Modern research in anthropology and archeology in Eastern Europe makes it plain that these two distinct national ethnic types, the Russian and Ukrainian, existed long before the Tatar invasions of Eastern Europe in the 13th century. The Ukrainian language is quite different from the Russian. Ukrainian manners and customs, national art, and historical traditions; all these external characteristics distinctly set the Ukrainian people apart from the Russians. But the deepest cleavage between the two peoples is found in the Ukrainian mentality and Ukrainian idealism, which are completely at variance with the mentality of the Russians. A Ukrainian is an individualist and a Russian exactly the opposite. By nature, the Ukrainians are democrats and opponents of all forms of dictatorship and tyranny. The contrary is true of the

Russians, who have a natural inclination to accept an absolute government imposed by force and remain subservient to it. As William C. Bullit writes in *The Great Globe Itself*: "From the time of the Mongol until today, the Russians have been inured to living in a totalitarian state under the tyranny of an absolute dictator" (p. 28), and Soviet dictatorship is similar to the barbaric despotism of the autocracies of Ivan the Terrible, Peter I, and Catherine II.

Ukrainians, in contrast to Russians, are decidedly Western in outlook. They have always regarded themselves as independent and free citizens and placed the highest value on freedom, to which they are devoted wholeheartedly. Ukraine was influenced by all the cultural movements of Western Europe. The Crusades, the Magdeburg Law, humanism, the Reformation and the Baroque penetrated to Ukraine where they were analogous to the trends in the West. The culture of the French Enlightenment became the source of the national regeneration of Ukraine in the 19th century. Likewise, contemporary Ukraine seeks inspiration in the creative culture of Western Europe, whereas Russia has evolved its own way of life, its own world, hostile to the West.

In the spring of 1945, the Ukrainian Soviet Socialist Republic was formally accepted at the Conference in San Francisco as a member of the United Nations. This could not satisfy the aspirations of the forty million Ukrainians suffering under the Communist yoke, but it did bring prominently before the public opinion of the world the fact that Ukraine is not the creation of propagandists, not the result of "German intrigue," but a nation with its own geographical areas, its own population, and its own history.

The Struggle for the Liberation of Ukraine

The history of Ukraine throughout the ages is a tragic story of a great people who have been doomed to suffer every form of oppression that the mind of man can create. However, the Ukrainians have clung to their own land, language, and traditions. Every time there has been an upheaval in Europe, the Ukrainians have responded and have sought to secure the right to determine their own national destiny.

The struggle of the UPA is a continuation of that centuries-old struggle which the Ukrainian people have been waging to win their national freedom. The independence of Ukraine and the union of all Ukrainian lands into ONE NATIONAL STATE has been the ideal of the Ukrainian people for centuries. This ideal has its origin in the national memory of independence and feeling of fraternal unity enjoyed during the periods of the great and progressive Ukrainian Kyivan State of Volodymyr the Great (981-1015) and Yaroslav the Wise (1018-1054). This ideal was foremost in the careers of the Ukrainian "Cromwell," Bohdan Khmelnytsky (1648-1657), and the great patriot Ivan Mazepa (1686-1709). It almost saw its realization during World War I (1914-1918).

In the period between the First and Second World Wars, the struggle of the Ukrainians for liberation went through different phases depending upon existing circumstances. World War II created favorable circumstances for the strengthening of the Ukrainian struggle for liberation. Manifesting its aspirations for freedom under the German occupation, the Ukrainian Resistance Movement created its armed resistance groups in 1942, and by 1943 those were united into a large and powerful UPA under one supreme command. Through its activities the UPA, supported by the entire Ukrainian people, greatly contributed to the destruction of the German armed forces in Ukraine.

When the Soviet forces reoccupied Ukraine, the Ukrainian Resistance Movement with its UPA met them fully prepared for the political and military struggle. For this struggle it mobilized not only hundreds of thousands of Ukrainians but also other peoples whose countries were subjugated by the Bolsheviks. It proudly offered stern opposition to the powerful Soviet Union, whose excellently trained detachments of the political police were not quite capable of coping with it. This struggle, spreading from Ukraine to other countries, received great publicity throughout the world.

The Standard Technique of Bolhsevizing a Nation

At the close of World War I, and especially after the fall of the tsarist Russian prison of peoples, the Ukrainians proclaimed the Ukrainian Independent State— on January 22, 1918. This proclamation was the expression of the will of the Ukrainian people. The reborn Ukrainian state had a democratic-socialist government and its first President was the famous Ukrainian historian and archaelogist Professor Michael Hrushevsky. For a while it seemed as if a final solution regarding the future of Ukraine had been reached.

But then, for the first time, the standard technique of bolshevizing a nation was adopted in Ukraine. The same technique was later used in many other countries: 1920 in Armenia and Azerbaidzhan: 1921 in Georgia; 1923 in the Far Eastern Republic and Outer Mongolia; 1939-1940 in Western Ukraine and Western Byelorussia, Estonia, Latvia, and Lithuania; and 1944-46 in Bulgaria, Yugoslavia, Albania, Romania, Hungary, Czechoslovakia, Poland, East Germany, North Korea, etc. The action against Ukraine was then directed by the Russian Commissar of Nationalities, Joseph Stalin. He induced the Executive Committee of the local Kyiv Soviet of Peasants, Workers, and Soldiers to call an All-Ukrainian Convention of Soviets. This was to precede the election for the Ukrainian Constituent Assembly in order to produce a *coup d'etat*, to overthrow the Ukrainian democratic government, and to proclaim the Government of the Soviets in Ukraine. But this meeting proved clearly that Bolshevism in Ukraine was a foreign intrigue of the Russian Government against the independence of Ukraine. Of the 2,000 delegates, only 150 (and the majority of them were non-Ukrainians) took a stand against the Ukrainian Government. The overwhelming majority proclaimed their full loyalty to the Ukrainian Government and the meeting became an enthusiastic demonstration for the independence of Ukraine.

The small minority, about 150 delegates, led by the Russian Sergiev (Artem), left Kyiv and moved to Kharkiv, close to the border of Red Russia, and there opened their own conference of Soviets and proclaimed Ukraine a "Soviet Republic." They named themselves the "Soviet Government of Ukraine" and applied to the Soviet Russian Government for aid.

In order to Sovietize Ukraine the Red Army marched in, and the Ukrainian War of Independence (1918-1921) began. The defensive war of Ukraine lasted four years and the Ukrainian Army was compelled to conduct an unequal struggle against Red and White Russians, Poles, and Romanians. Because the enemy forces were numerically superior, the Ukrainian Independent State fell after years of desperate fighting. Ukraine was conquered by the Bolsheviks and became the Ukrainian Soviet Socialist Republic. Western Ukraine was divided among Poland (Galicia and Volhynia), Romania (northern Bukovina and Bessarabia), and Czechoslovakia (Carpatho-Ukraine).

For the Ukrainians there was little consolation in the fact that they saved Europe by their prolonged resistance against the Bolsheviks in this war, because they themselves fell victim to the most ruthless oppression under the Soviet regime. Unfortunately, the Ukrainian fight for freedom had found no sympathetic understanding in the democratic world. Attempts to obtain consideration for the claims of Ukrainian independence abroad were not successful. There was little knowledge of the historical side of the Ukrainian question among the representatives of the leading powers. France was committed to the idea of a "strong Poland," the United States was comparatively uninterested in Eastern Europe, and Great Britain wavered between the aggressively anti-Bolshevik policy of Winston Churchill, then Secretary of War, who aided the Russian White leaders (Kolchak and Denikin) with arms, munitions, and supplies, and the inclination of Prime Minister Lloyd George to seek a basis of agreement with the Soviet regime. Instead of aiding the Ukrainians in their fight against the Bolsheviks, the Allies had decided to back Denikin, the enemy of Ukraine, who simultaneously fought the Ukrainians using British war materiel. This devious policy meant that any attempt to establish a stable government in Ukraine was doomed to failure and would lead to anarchy. In the end the Ukrainian Army was demoralized by a terrible blockade. Even food and medical supplies were not allowed to enter the territory occupied by the Ukrainian Army. Moreover, typhus broke out, which took the lives of thousands of Ukrainian soldiers and civilians because of the lack of medicines.

The Ukrainian Resistance Movement between the Two Wars

Several years after the War of Independence, many Ukrainian armed groups of partisans became active against the Soviet regime, and eventually were transformed into an underground political organization resisting the Russians. There were also attempts to oppose the Soviet regime by such means as opposition within the Communist Party of Ukraine and the Ukrainian Soviet Government. Two representatives of this tendency in the twenties were O. Shumsky, who was for a time Commissar for Education, and M. Volobuyev, a famous journalist and economist. Shumsky defended the Ukrainian national position in the Communist Party and tried to take advantage of the cultural Ukrainization ordered by the Communist Party to strengthen the Ukrainian national spirit (1926). Volobuyev exposed in his articles the "colonization tendencies of Soviet economic policy in Ukraine" (1928).

Another rebel among the Ukrainian Communists was the popular writer Mykola Khvylovy. He vindicated the right of Ukraine to maintain cultural contacts with the West—as an indirect form of resisting domination from Moscow. The Russian Communists regarded Khvylovy and his friends as Ukrainian nationalists. Moscow became truly alarmed when Khvylovy issued his "Literary Manifesto" in which he called upon Ukrainian writers not to imitate Russian literary trends and not to seek inspiration in Russian culture because, as he said, "it lacks healthy elements." Instead, he recommended that they should turn away from Moscow and face Western Europe. As early as 1929 Stalin himself made the following reference to Khvylovy: "If we had nothing else but these discussions about Khvylovy, which have become so wide and heated in Ukraine, there would be sufficient cause for profound alarm." Khyylovy committed suicide in May 1933, probably because he foresaw his arrest and execution as a "nationalist."

The attack of the Communist Party and its agencies on Ukrainian culture began in the early thirties and grew to tremendous dimensions. Between 1933 and 1938 widespread purges took place which were especially felt by Ukrainian intellectuals and men of science and culture who opposed the Soviet attempt to destroy Ukrainian national culture and supplant it with a Russianized Communist culture alien to the spirit and soul of the Ukrainian people. In these years the Bolsheviks annihilated scholars, writers, artists, military men, political leaders, and thousands of thinking people. Among these tortured leaders of Ukrainian art, literature, and science, there were many great names and talents, known and honored not only in Ukraine, but throughout the world (e.g., Prof. Michael Hrushevsky, a famous historian and archaeologist, and Prof. Stepan Rudnytsky, a famous geographer). Among twenty-eight authors and scientists executed by Soviet firing squads in December 1934 were such talented Ukrainians as Hryhory Kosynka, Kost Bureviy, Oleksa Vlyzko, and Dmytro Falkivsky. Many others were exiled: Mykola Kulish (the great Ukrainian dramatist), Valerian Pidmohylny, Borys Antonenko-Davydovych, Volodymyr Gzhytsky (well-known novelists), Mykola Zerov (poet and professor of Ukrainian literature at the University of Kyiv), Pavlo Filipovyh, Mykhailo Dray-Khmara, Evhen Pluzhnyk (poets), and Ostap Vyshnya (a very popular satirist). Many scientists and professors, such as Yeremiv, Doroshkevych, Slabchenko, and Hanstov, the artists Padalka, Boychuk, and Les Kurbas, and army officers Tyutyunnyk and Dubovy also perished.

The Ukrainian peasantry strongly opposed the economic policy of the Soviet Government, as exemplified by its forced collectivization of Ukrainian agriculture. The peasants had been as turbulent in Ukraine as anywhere else in rebelling against the forced Stalinist collectivization. Crushed by the famine created artificially for political purposes in 1932, they gave up the struggle for individual landholdings and entered the collective farms. It seems clear that at least twenty percent of the population of Ukraine starved to death during this famine. There has probably been no disaster of comparable magnitude in history that received so little international attention.

After the period of mass anti-Bolshevik risings in Ukraine (1921-1924) the Ukrainian Resistance Movement assumed the form of secret political organizations. In 1930 an organization called "Union for the Liberation of Ukraine" was discovered in Ukraine and a group of alleged members were brought to trial. Forty-five Ukrainian intellectuals were tried in Kharkiv in 1930: All were condemned to slave labor, including Serhiy Yefremiv, Vice-President of the Academy of Sciences; Volodymyr Chekhivsky, head of the Ukrainian Autocephalous Orthodox Church; and Andrew Nikovsky, former Minister of the Ukrainian National Republic. The same year witnessed the discovery of SUM (Union of the Ukrainian Youth) and some 20,000 alleged members of this organization were executed in Ukraine. In 1931 the discovery of a Ukrainian organization known as the "Nationalist Center" was announced, and in connection with this a number of political leaders who had formerly been associated with the Ukrainian democratic Government, including Holubovych, Shershel, and Mazurenko, were executed. In 1933 the ever-active GPU announced the discovery of a Ukrainian Military Organization (UVO), and among the prominent individuals who were shot in connection with this was Yuri Kotsiubinsky, the former Vice-President of the Council of People's Commissars. The same year, 1933, witnessed the suicide of a veteran Ukrainian Communist and friend of Lenin, Mykola Skrypnyk, who was Vice-President of the Council of People's Commissars and acting Commissar of Education. In 1934, another "nationalist organization" was discovered, and in connection with the assassination of Kirov many prominent Ukrainians were shot in retaliation.

During the next few years the purges continued. For reasons which can never be fully clarified, the men who showed the greatest energy in stamping out Ukrainian nationalism often fell victim to the purge themselves. This was the case with Postyshev, Stalin's principal lieutenant in Ukraine in the thirties and Kosior, who at the same time occupied the post of Secretary of the Communist Party in Ukraine. In 1937, Moscow sent Lazar Kaganovich to Ukraine with the purpose of liquidating the Ukrainian opposition. Under his pressure another prominent Ukrainian Communist, Panas Lubchenko, President of the Council of the People's Commissars of Ukraine, after once boasting that Ukrainian nationalism had been eliminated by the firm policy of the Communist Party, apparently became suspected of nationalism himself and committed suicide rather than face a trial in which the result was a foregone conclusion. Still another Prime Minister, Bondarenko, vanished mysteriously from the political scene and was presumed dead or in exile. Thus, all Prime Ministers of the Ukrainian SSR from Rakovsky to Bondarenko were liquidated by the Russians.

Still another important current in the Ukrainian nationalist movement was represented by the OUN. It emerged from the UVO and accepted a regular plan of action based on firm ideological foundations aiming at the political, spiritual, and social liberation of the Ukrainian people from foreign rule. The OUN was a strongly disciplined revolutionary anti-Soviet and anti-Polish force which created a number of illegal groups armed as far as was possible. The leading

figure in the OUN and perhaps the most militant figure in the Ukrainian nation-
alist movement after the murder of Gen. Simon Petlura in Paris (1926) was Col.
Evhen Konovalets. He met his death in 1938 when a Soviet agent in a cafe in
Rotterdam handed him a bomb which exploded.

The Ukrainian reaction to Polish rule in Western Ukraine took various forms.
Historically the relation between the Poles and the Ukrainians had never been
cordial. The proclamation of the Republic of Western Ukraine on November 1,
1918 and the resulting Polish-Ukrainian war in Eastern Galicia only increased
the bitterness which had developed historically. From the first days of the
existence of the Republic of Western Ukraine the Ukrainians had to defend
themselves against Poland and Romania. By the summer of 1919 Polish military
control had been extended over the whole of Western Ukraine. The 100,000-man
Ukrainian Galician Army passed into Eastern Ukraine and joined the Ukrainian
forces under Gen. Simon Petlura's command which fought against the Bolshevik invaders. The brilliant offensive of the combined Ukrainian forces caused the
total defeat of the Bolshevik forces in Ukraine and led to the seizure of the
Ukrainian capital, Kyiv, on Aug. 31, 1919, where the Ukrainian armies were
insidiously attacked by the advancing White Russian army of General Denikin.

On June 25, 1919, the Allied Supreme Council authorized the Poles to occupy
Eastern Galicia up to the line of the river Zbruch, the old frontier between
Austria-Hungary and Russia. Finally, the Treaty of Riga (1921) secured from the
Soviet Union recognition of the Polish control over Western Ukraine. For a time
the Allied powers refused to recognize the Polish occupation of Western
Ukraine, but there was no desire to challenge it by armed force. The situation
was complicated, and the Polish Parliament passed a law in the autumn of 1922
establishing autonomy for Eastern Galicia. This paved the way for the recognition of Poland's possession of Eastern Galicia by the Conference of Ambassadors
on March 14, 1923, over the articulate protests of the Ukrainian people. Unfortunately, steps were never taken to fulfill the unilateral promises contained in
the autonomy law of September 1922, and Eastern Galicia was always governed
from Warsaw.

From year to year the Ukrainian Resistance Movement in Poland changed its
form as various measures were put into effect by the Polish Government to
break the Ukrainians. The opposition represented by the legal political parties
(the Ukrainian National-Democratic Union, the Ukrainian Radical-Socialist
Party, and the Ukrainian Socialist-Democratic Party) advocated a policy of trying
to obtain maximum rights for Ukrainians within the Polish state, and at the same
time stressed the right of all Ukrainians to unite in a sovereign and democratic
Ukraine within Ukrainian ethnographic boundaries. The clandestine opposition
represented by the UVO and the OUN organized surprise attacks on individual
Polish officials who were held responsible for oppressive acts of the Government. Such an attack was the assassination of the Polish Minister of the Interior,
Pieracki, in Warsaw in 1934. He had been responsible for the "pacification" of the
Ukrainians in the autumn of 1930. This "pacification," as it was offically and
euphemistically termed, was quite widely reported in the American press at the
time. After the statement of Minister Pieracki that "the Ukrainians must be

burned out with white-hot steel, and for every act of the Ukrainian revolutionary organizations Poland must continue to punish the entire population according to the principle of collective responsibility," brutal reprisals were inflicted relatively indiscriminately on the Ukrainian population by Polish troops and police. Libraries and cooperatives were destroyed, Boy Scout organizations were dissolved, Ukrainian high schools and institutions of every kind were closed, and concentration camps were established. Several thousand Ukrainians were held in prisons or in camps, and the majority of arrested Ukrainians remained in jail, without any charge being preferred against them, while the police hunted for evidence.

The cultural and economic methods of suppression were demonstrated in the Polish campaign to abolish Ukrainian schools, churches, cooperatives, and cultural and sports organizations. For example, the Ukrainian Encyclopedia estimated that there were only 134 Ukrainian schools left in Western Ukraine in 1930. In 1924 there had been 2,417, and under Austria-Hungary there had been 3,414 primary schools. In the summer of 1938 alone the Polish Government destroyed at least 112 Orthodox churches belonging to Ukrainians, on the pretext that they had once been Uniate (i.e., united with Rome as Catholics of the Eastern Rite). Such an act, which drew the protest of the Catholic Metropolitan of Lviv, Count A. Sheptytsky, only succeeded in antagonizing both the Uniates (Greek Catholics) and the Orthodox against the Poles and in bringing the two religious groups closer together.

The *Service d'Information Ukrainiennes* of Paris estimated that, in the period after 1921, 914 political trials of Ukrainians were held, excluding those of Communists, and that 65 percent were against persons accused of activity on behalf of the UVO and OUN. Of a total of 3,777 persons tried 2,520 were found guilty, 17 were sentenced to death, 27 were sentenced to life imprisonment, and the others to a total of 5,870 years of imprisonment. In 1939 alone, the arrests, convictions, and years of imprisonment meted out surpassed the totals of all those from 1921-1939. For example, in August alone, the month before the Nazi invasion, 111 Ukrainians were tried on political charges and 75 were found guilty. These were given sentences totalling 132 and one half years imprisonment. Most were charged with membership in the OUN.

It must not be thought that the Ukrainians did nothing but revolt. Even during the years of oppression, the Ukrainians continued to consolidate their position in the state. They tried to build up a life of their own and created organizations for assisting education, spreading Ukrainian culture, and improving agriculture. Their cooperative organizations increased in numbers, in capital, and in membership. Thus the number of cooperatives belonging to the Ukrainian Auditing Association in Lviv was only 1029 at the beginning of 1925, but grew to 3337 by 1934. By 1939 the Ukrainians of the West were in a much better position than they had been before and constituted a kind of "state within a state."

The Soviet Government always regarded the Ukrainian nationalist movement in Western Ukraine as a dangerous enemy. One of the reasons Stalin was insistent on annexing Poland's former eastern provinces stems from his desire to bring all the Ukrainians under his rule and to stamp out all traces of non-

Communist Ukrainian nationalism. It is significant that, in spite of the constant struggle of the Ukrainians against Polish oppression, the Western Ukrainians remained bitterly and steadfastly anti-Communist and considered themselves champions of Ukrainian independence and the unification of all Ukrainian lands into one sovereign Ukrainian state. There was hardly another country in Europe where anti-Communist feelings were stronger than in the semi-proletarian Western Ukraine. The signing of the Ribbentrop-Molotov non-aggression pact on August 23, 1939 rendered possible the realization of Stalin's plans of annexing Western Ukraine. On September 17, 1939, the Soviet Army invaded Western Ukraine despite various treaties with Poland, on the grounds that the Polish Republic had ceased to exist as an organized state, and occupied the whole of Western Ukraine giving as its aim the "liberation" and "protection" of its Ukrainian "brethren." On June 28, 1940, the Russian Bolsheviks "liberated" other parts of Western Ukraine which in 1918-1919 had been seized by Romania—northern Bukovina, with its capital of Chernivtsi, and parts of Bessarabia. These were incorporated into the Ukrainian Soviet Socialist Republic.

We are more than certain that the fate of Eastern Europe could have been much different had the restored Poland and Romania acted more wisely and with a sense of historical responsibility in regard to Ukraine. Instead of being guided by political reason they apparently fell under the spell of chauvinistic blindness and political greatness. Newly-created Poland, largely supported by the Allies, committed an unpardonable crime by attacking the Ukrainians, who, like Poland herself, after the fall of the Russian and Austro-Hungarian Empires, had sought freedom and independence. This attack was timed with the onslaughts of the Russian Bolsheviks who invaded the Ukrainian National Republic from the north and east. It is already a matter of history how the Poles deceived the Allies by claiming that all help provided was being used against the Russian Bolsheviks, whereas the fact is that whatever aid the Poles obtained in 1919 was directed against the Ukrainians. Thus, Poland helped the Russian Bolsheviks to establish their control over Ukraine, securing for itself part of the Ukrainian lands.

It is interesting to note that the very first opposition to Hitler's plans was offered by the Ukrainian Resistance Movement in Carpatho-Ukraine, a small mountainous country which had been a part of Czechoslovakia since 1919. When in the autumn of 1938 Czechoslovakia was restructured along federal lines, Carpatho-Ukraine gained autonomy. In March 1939, Hacha, the President of Czechoslovakia, surrendered the freedom of his State and the Czech army did not fire a single shot in defense of its lands. The freedom-loving Ukrainians, however, not in the habit of bowing to aggressors, organized a bitter armed resistance against the Hungarians and Hitler when Hitler let his puppet Hungarian Army march against Carpatho-Ukraine. It was the first shot fired against the so-called Nazi "New Order" in Europe and this shot was fired by the Ukrainian Resistance Movement. The small country of Carpatho-Ukraine won the sympathy and admiration of the world.

Today Carpatho-Ukraine is also a part of the Ukrainian Soviet Socialist Republic. The first President of Carpatho-Ukraine, Msgr. Augustine Voloshyn, was arrested by the Russians and died in a Soviet prison. Thus, Stalin succeeded in uniting all the Ukrainian lands under his rule.

The Ukrainian Resistance Movement versus German Nazism (1941-1944)

Poland was partitioned between the Soviet Union and Nazi Germany according to the Ribbentrop-Molotov pact in the autumn of 1939. Eastern Galicia and Volhynia with their large Ukrainian populations were incorporated into Soviet Ukraine. Elections were held in Western Ukraine after the Soviet occupation. In keeping with the usual Communist practice, a "Provisional Popular Assembly" made up of Communists and of individuals who were regarded as politically reliable voted on October 27, 1939 for union with Soviet Ukraine. By a decree of August 2, 1940, Northern Bukovina and parts of Bessarabia were also absorbed into Soviet Ukraine.

Active Ukrainian opponents of Soviet Russian rule remained in the country and worked out plans for the development of the Ukrainian Resistance Movement in the whole of Ukraine. They succeeded in organizing cells of the Ukrainian Resistance Movement in Donbas (in the Donets coal basin) and in all large cities of Ukraine (Dnipropetrovsk, Kharkiv, Odessa). Aiding this was the fact that many members of the Ukrainian Resistance Movement were transferred there, having volunteered to work in the factories and mines of the Ukrainian industrial regions.

When the Germans attacked the Soviet Union, on June 22, 1941, Ukrainian resistance forces took advantage of the confusion and demoralization in the Soviet-occupied regions and seized control of many places (Buchach, Tovmach, etc.).

From June 24th to June 26th, street fighting took place in Lviv, the largest city of Western Ukraine. Soviet troops were overcome by a tremendous panic. Soviet tanks bombarded the churches of this city, naively believing them to be the centers of the revolt. On June 27, 1941, Soviet troops succeeded in restoring order. On this day the NKVD troops massacred Ukrainians in the prisons of Lviv, which literally had become filled with the corpses of the murdered Ukrainians. The same scenes were repeated in the cities and towns of Western and Eastern Ukraine—in Sambir, Stry, Stanyslaviv, Zolochiv, Ternopil, Dubno, Lutsk, Rivno, Berdychiv, Zhytomir, Vinnytsia, Dnipropetrovsk, Kyiv, Poltava, Kharkiv, and many others. In some prisons (Sambir) the prisoners revolted and succeeded in escaping their fate.

However, on the night of June 30, 1941, Ukrainian underground forces took possession of the radio station in Lviv and proclaimed the reestablishment of the Ukrainian Independent State. This proclamation was a clear challenge to the German Government to declare its policy, all the more since the Germans in their first appeals promised Ukraine heaven and earth trying to win their favor.

Had the Germans been willing to cooperate with the Ukrainian Resistance Movement in its fight for Ukrainian independence and not to interfere with internal problems of the Ukrainian Independent State, a good deal of Ukrainian-German cooperation might have been expected. The Germans might have won the war in Eastern Europe if they had fully exploited the power of the Ukrainian Resistance Movement and of other subjugated nations. Ukraine would have been able to raise an army of 3 to 4 million men and immense resources for this fight.

However, the Germans came not as liberators but as conquerors. They made no effort to consult the wishes of the subjugated peoples of the Soviet Union and establish national independent states in Eastern Europe. The Nazi leadership, overcome with power and success, chose to follow a policy of unilateral conquest, domination, and enslavement. The Germans did not want allies in Eastern Europe, but slaves. They sought only "quislings" who would consent as German collaborators to push the people into a definitely subordinate position as a subject race. Long before they lost their war strategically, the Germans had lost it politically. They played into Stalin's hands chiefly by their backward policy in Eastern Europe. Today there is no doubt that the chief reason for Hitler's debacle in the East stemmed from his blundering policy, especially in Ukraine.

The reaction of the Gestapo to the Ukrainian proclamation of June 30, 1941 came very swiftly. The Ukrainian Government was liquidated and prominent Ukrainian patriots were shot or imprisoned. During the opening weeks of the campaign in the East, Ukrainians deserted from the Soviet armies by the hundreds of thousands. They expected to take part in the liberation of their country, but Hitler sent them to camps to die of hunger. He flatly rejected all plans to draw the Ukrainian people and the other peoples of the Soviet territories into the struggle against the Bolsheviks. He ordered the seizure of several million Ukrainians, both men and women, and had them sent to Germany as slave-laborers, in order to prevent a Ukrainian mass movement. And he ordered a systematic pillaging of the countryside for the benefit of Germany, which chronically lacked foodstuffs.

It should be kept in mind that Ukrainian guerrilla warfare against the Germans was launched at the time when German power was at its peak and when Nazi Germany was celebrating her greatest military victories. Guerrilla warfare flared up at a time when, other nations were receiving aid from their Governments-in-exile and the support of Western Allies, the formation of a guerrilla army was merely an idea awaiting concrete measures. Thus, the Ukrainian people started their fight against the Nazi invaders at a time when corresponding movements in Western Europe had not yet been born (1942). The UPA was, along with the Polish Home Army, one of the first underground armies which operated on a large scale against Nazi Germany. This struggle cost Ukraine hundreds of thousands of casualties and brought it unbelievable destruction. What was once a land of proud beauty became one of the most desolate places in the whole of Eastern Europe.

The Ukrainians also fought Nazi Germany in the ranks of the Soviet Army (1st, 2nd, 3rd and 4th Ukrainian armies) and in the ranks of the French resistance (Ukrainian battalions under Ukrainian command). The Ukrainian population, including old men, women, and children who helped to organize guerrilla warfare, effectively disrupted German communications, wrecked their supplies, lines, and depots, and otherwise demonstrated their full support of the UPA. Owing to this action and the favorable terrain, the UPA was able to accomplish a feat impossible for the underground forces in Western Europe—the clearing of the enemy out of large regions, which then became administered by the government of the Ukrainian Resistance Movement. In the second half of 1943 and in the first of 1944, the situation in Eastern Europe was such that the Germans could only hold on to main roads and larger urban centers. They were unable to occupy the broad expanses of the country. This territory was controlled and administered by the UPA. The UPA was the only underground army in Eastern Europe, having under arms about 200,000 people including men and women, the old and young, workers and farmers, intellectuals and clergymen. It was equipped with arms seized from the Germans and the Russians. It had numerous supply centers at its disposal as well as training camps and field hospitals, which were well camouflaged and guarded in the mountains, forests, and marshlands. The soldiers of the UPA were well-fed and clothed, the wounded nursed. Ukrainian and Jewish doctors, pharmacists, nurses, specialists, and social workers were recruited in the UPA, which thus became an armed organization of the whole Ukrainian people. Such guerrilla warfare was only possible because it had the whole hearted approval of the Ukrainian people.

The Nazis fought the Ukrainian Resistance Movement by launching offensives against it and by conducting a campaign of terror unheard of in recent history against the Ukrainian population and, especially against Ukrainian intellectuals. Three times during the German occupation (April-May 1943, July-October 1943, and February-March 1944) Nazi Germans launched their offensives against the UPA. The entire campaign was fierce and bitter. The Germans used aircraft, artillery, and tanks, followed by infantry and police units. Several attacks against the UPA were repulsed with heavy losses for the enemy. The Nazi offensives were broken and the Germans were defeated. They then limited themselves to the bombardment of Ukrainian villages and towns and to the murder of political prisoners and the non-combatant population in the vicinity of the large towns. On July 24, 1943, three Ukrainian villages—Tolychiv, Lityn, and Radovych—were destroyed by the German police and several hundred defenseless people were murdered. On July 14, 1943, a terrible slaughter of the Ukrainian and Czech population took place in the village of Melyn in the province of Dubno in Volhynia. The people were driven by force into the wooden village church and burned alive. Similar incidents took place in the village of Hubkiv in the province of Kostopil on July 2, 1943, and in many other villages of Ukraine. The Germans also organized mass executions of political prisoners (in Rivne, Kremyanets, Kyiv, Chortkiv, and Lviv) and of prominent Ukrainian intellectuals taken as hostages (in Drohobych, Kovel, Kremyanets, Kryvy Rih, and Kremynchuk).

The troops of the UPA did not restrict themselves to defense. They attacked and disarmed detachments of the German army and police, captured war matériel and food from German convoys, and freed workers being transported to forced labor in Germany. The UPA detachments organized ambushes on principal roads. In May 1943, Victor Lutze, Commander-in-Chief of the Nazi SA, was killed on the highways from Kovel to Brest-Litovsk in an ambush. In August 1943, another detachment of the UPA surrounded the concentration camp in Dubyne, near Skole in the Carpathian Mountains, and set free all political prisoners and killed the camp guards. Still another detachment of the UPA seized the prison in Dubno, Volhynia, and set free all the political prisoners.

After several months of hard battles, the Germans were forced to retire to large towns protected by strong garrisons. The rest of the country was exclusively dominated by the UPA and administered by Ukrainian authorities. Meanwhile, agriculture and industry were developing normally, and agrarian commissions appointed by the Supreme Command of the UPA were dividing up large estates among poor peasants. Schools and cultural institutions operated normally. The civilian and military police of the UPA kept order. The Ukrainian youth enlisted in the UPA and was trained in its camps and officer schools operating in Volhynia and in the Carpathian Mountains. Some Dutch officers, delivered from German captivity, passed several weeks in one of the UPA's training camps in the Carpathian Mountains. With the help of the Ukrainian Resistance Movement they succeeded in escaping to Budapest, from which they returned safely to Holland. French and Serbian prisoners of war and German and Italian deserters served with the UPA.

Thus, the UPA became the third largest military and political power in Eastern Europe and the champion of all revolutionary forces, representing not only the resistance movement of Ukraine but of all the subjugated peoples of Eastern Europe, the Caucasus, and Central Asia. As a result of the well-planned and directed propaganda of the Supreme UPA Command, German military units composed of former war prisoners taken on the Eastern Front began to disintegrate and their members began to filter into the ranks of the UPA. A constantly increasing number of Byelorussians, Georgians, Armenians, Uzbeks, Tatars, Azerbaidzhanis, and Cossacks led to the organization of separate national legions of those peoples within the UPA. The net result of this process was the convening on November 21 and 22, 1943, in the territories then under the control of the UPA, of a conference of representatives of Soviet-enslaved peoples of Eastern Europe and Asia, attended by thirty-nine delegates. The conference drew up a platform of common aims of the enslaved nationalities and adopted a common slogan: "Freedom to the peoples, freedom for the individual!" Thus, the Anti-Bolshevik Bloc of Nations (ABN) came into being.

The propaganda of the UPA succeeded in estranging the allies of the Germans. One day all the so-called Ukrainian police of Volhynia went with their arms to the UPA. Hungarian, Romanian, Slovak, French, and Belgian troops stationed in Ukraine had been used in the expeditions against Ukrainians. Gradually, however, the commands of these troops agreed with the Supreme Command of UPA and observed neutrality during the Ukraino-German hostilities. A special agreement was concluded with the representatives of the Hungarian High Command in the Carpathian Mountains, and friendly neutrality between Hungarian troops operating in the Carpathian Mountains and the UPA was observed during the operations of the Hungarian Army in Eastern Galicia. This agreement came after heavy blows dealt to the Hungarians, who had initially tried to fight the Ukrainian guerrillas. It became the basis of collaboration between the Ukrainian and Hungarian resistance movements.

The Germans violently denounced the UPA in their propaganda. They stated in their leaflets that the UPA was led by "Bolshevik emissaries." They tried to demonstrate to the Ukrainians that their resistance was of no consequence and hoped by propaganda to weaken, to corrupt, and to break the fighting morale of the Ukrainian people. "Everybody who knows the gangsters," wrote the Nazi Commissioner-General of Volhynia and Podolia to the "working and peaceful Ukrainian population" in July 1943, "and does not denounce them to the German authorities will be severely punished. To save yourselves, your children, your country, and your countrymen from disaster, report any gangster, or any Bandera partisan, to the German authorities. The German police will protect you against their vengeance...."

But the German police could not protect their hirelings against the vengeance of the Ukrainian people and the UPA. On Sept. 11, 1943, the chief agent of the German Gestapo, Michael Tarnavsky—who was at the same time an *agent provocateur* of the NKVD—was captured and court-martialed by the UPA. He was tried and condemned to death. There were many examples of Nazi-Soviet collaboration in combatting the UPA during that time.

The terror and propaganda of the German occupation authorities in Ukraine could not break the spirit of the fighting Ukrainian people. Having survived many hard blows in the past, they rose again against the ruthless Nazi invaders. In the beginning the Ukrainian civilian population suffered heavy losses, because it was quite defenseless. Later, the major part of the townspeople fled to the regions under the UPA's control, and in these regions a system of signalmen protected the population against German motorized expeditions. As before in the ancient times of Tatar incursions in Ukraine, the Ukrainian population signalled to one another by means of bonfires. UPA detachments were ready and met the enemy, which incurred heavy losses. On October 8, 1943, on the road between Refalivsk and Volodymyrets, detachments of the UPA encircled and annihilated a German punitive expedition, killed 300 men, and captured a tank. On January 9, 1944, near the village of Lysohirky in the province of Kamyanets Podilsky, in a battle against another expedition, a detachment of the UPA captured 3 motor cars, 7 machine guns, 2 mortars, 30,000 rounds of ammunition, and other war matériel. The attack against the "Black Forest" near Stanyslaviv in the Carpathian Mountains was repulsed with very high losses for the Germans.

The Germans lost their fight against the UPA. During the last months of 1943 and in the first months of 1944, when the Soviet counteroffensive began to roll nearer to Western Ukraine, the UPA consisted of four large groups: (1) UPA-North operating in Polissia and Northern Volhynia, (2) UPA-West in Eastern Galicia and in the province of Kholm, (3) UPA-South in Northern Bukovina and in the provinces of Kamyanets Podilsy and Vinnytsia and (4) UPA-East in the wooded sector north of Kyiv and Zhytomyr in the area of Bazar—the battlefield of a famous Ukrainian anti-Bolshevik uprisings in 1921. These four groups comprised more than 200,000 armed Ukrainian guerrillas, which were united under one command—the Supreme Command of the UPA. In addition, the Ukrainian Resistance Movement organized underground combat groups in the Donets Basin, Dnipropetrovsk, Dniprodzerhynsk, Kryvyi Rih, Odessa, Kremenchuk, Kyiv, Uman, and other towns of Ukraine and the peninsula of Crimea. The chief of the Ukrainian Resistance Movement at that time was Maxym Ruban, succeeding Stepan Bandera, who was then in the concentration camp of Sachsenhausen. The Supreme Commander of the UPA was Col. Roman Kliachkivsky (Klym Savur); his chief of staff was Gen. Anathol Stupnytsky (Honcharenko). Both officers fell in the fight against the Bolsheviks. General Stupnytsky, a former colonel of the Ukrainian Army (1918-1921) and the hero of an anti-Bolshevik uprising in 1921, was chiefly responsible for the development of the military strength of the UPA. He and his colleagues-in-arms indefatigably worked to build the organization of the UPA, its training, and supplies, and led its operations.

The growth of the UPA went hand-in-hand with the growth of the OUN, the only important political organization in Ukraine during the German occupation and at present. But the second occupation of Ukraine by the Russians raised the apprehension that this occupation would turn out to be of long duration. The general strategy of the Ukrainian Resistance Movement had, therefore, to be broadened and developed accordingly. First of all, however, full national unity had to be secured. It became evident that the Supreme Command of the Ukrainian struggle for liberation could not rest in the hands of only one party. This conclusion was reached as a result of the developments in Ukraine during the German occupation. In a very short time the UPA lost the appearance of a guerrilla organization of one political party and became truly national in its character. The ranks of the UPA were swollen with Ukrainian peasants, workers, and intellectuals who were not members of the OUN. Thus, the UPA became an armed organization of the whole Ukrainian people, common to all, in which the whole people participated and took pride. Even the most indifferent obeyed the orders of the UPA, regarding it as the true Ukrainian authority. Thus, the general consolidation of the Ukrainian people into one military camp was brought about.

The necessity arose to give an outward expression to this internal consolidation by the formation of a supreme directing body. It was necessary that a supreme political and state organ should crown the national struggle, in which all forces and elements taking part would be represented. In July 1944, a Ukrainian National Congress was summoned in the territory occupied by the UPA. This Congress gave birth to the Supreme Liberation Council (UHVR), as the supreme state organ of the Ukrainian nation for the duration of its struggle for freedom and sovereignty. This Council was built on democratic principles. Its executive is the General Secretariat. At the head of each department there is a General Secretary. The aim and purposes of the Council are expressed in its Constitution and in its Proclamation to the Ukrainian people. Some extracts of this Proclamation are quoted below:

Ukrainian People!

...It is not in the cause of your freedom that the imperialistic aggrandizers are waging this bloody and cruel war. For you they bring only ruin, enslavement, and death. You did not allow yourselves to become enslaved but demonstrated an unyielding determination to live in independent statehood on your native land. On guard over your freedom, you have set up—from the Carpathian peaks and beyond the Don to the Caucasus—armed cadres of your sons—the Ukrainian Insurgent Army....

In order to unite all national liberation elements of the Ukrainian people, in order to direct their struggle for freedom from one common center, in order to represent their political will before the world...the Supreme Ukrainian Liberation Council has been brought into being....

The Supreme Ukrainian Liberation Council swears before you, the Ukrainian people, that:

It will fight to make you the sole master of your land,

For a just social order without oppression and exploitation,

For the destruction of serfdom,

For free enterprise of the peasant on his own land,

For free enterprise for the worker,

For wide initiative of the working people in all branches of the economic order,

For the widest possible development of the Ukrainian national culture....

The Supreme Ukrainian Liberation Council greets the struggle of enslaved peoples for their liberation. The Ukrainian people desire to live with them, particularly with their neighbors, in neighborly friendship and to collaborate with them in the struggle against common enemies....

Our liberation struggle demands heroism and sacrifices, and above all an unshakable faith in our own truth....

The heroic struggle of your ancestors and the memory of their knightly death in the cause of Ukrainian statehood are a dictate to you.

We therefore call upon you: Rise and fight for your freedom and for your nation. Unite yourself in the struggle, and strengthen your spirit.

SUPREME UKRAINIAN LIBERATION COUNCIL

Headquarters, June 1944

(Note: The Supreme Ukrainian Liberation Council met in the Carpathian Mountains on July 7-14, 1944, on territory under control of the Ukrainian Insurgent Army. Of thirty-six elected members, twenty Ukrainian political leaders appeared and participated in this meeting. They represented all Ukrainian lands, faiths, and parties which stood on the principle of the underground revolutionary fight against both invaders of Ukraine. For reasons of secrecy all documents of the First Meeting of the Supreme Ukrainian Liberation Council are dated June 1944.)

In addition to this declaration and its Constitution the Council worked out a political program for the entire Ukrainian Resistance Movement. It envisages a democratic government in a free Ukraine, and reserves for the Ukrainian people the right to choose their own form of government, the form of their social-economic order, and the form of local government by a Constituent Assembly which is to be convoked after the overthrow of Russian Bolshevism in Ukraine.

"The present Communist system," states the program, "alien to Ukrainian tradition and repugnant to the spirit of the people, is to be replaced by a system of cooperatives, which have proven themselves very popular in Ukraine."

The Supreme Ukrainian Liberation Council chose the members of the General Secretariat and delegated to the President of the General Secretariat, General Taras Chuprynka, the responsiblity for all operations of the UPA. In addition, the Supreme Ukrainian Liberation Council made provision for its administrative organs and the method of their election. According to its Constitution the center of the Supreme Ukrainian Liberation Council always must be in Ukraine and only its delegations are sent abroad. At the present time the Foreign Representation of the Supreme Ukrainian Liberation Council consists of twelve members.

Soviet propaganda claims that the Ukrainian revolutionaries (UHVR, UPA, OUN) were tools of the Nazis. They have never explained why these Nazi tools fought long after the Germans had gone and long before the Germans came. The lie that the Ukrainians were working with the Nazis is disproved by the reports in the captured German archives showing the trouble the Germans had with the Ukrainian Resistance Movement and its UPA. It is disproved by the order of the day issued by General Taras Chuprynka, Commander-in-Chief of the UPA on VE Day. The original text of General Chuprynka's Order appeared in a UPA underground journal *Povstanets* (The Insurgent), No. 5-6, April-May 1945. In addressing his men, he spoke for practically the entire Ukrainian nation and for the world:

Fighting Men and Commanders of the Ukrainian Insurgent Army!
 Hitler's Germany has found its final and irrevocable destruction.
 The Ukrainian people will no longer fear death in gas chambers or liquidation of their entire villages by the Gestapo. No more will the German smite the freedom-loving Ukrainian peasant in the face, nor take his land in order to turn him into a slave for the German master. No longer will the Germans be able to drive thousands and tens of thousands of peasants and workers into modern slavery in Germany. Nor will the Ukrainian intellectual worker have to wait his turn to be liquidated because he always has been a menace to the invader. The barbarian from the West no longer will dominate the Ukrainian land.
 A great contribution toward the victory over Germany was made by you, Ukrainian insurgents. You prevented the German from freely exploiting Ukrainian soil and using its fruits for his aggressive designs. You prohibited his pillaging of Ukrainian villages, you fought the forced deportations to Germany. Your retributive hand repaid the German for the mass executions and burning of villages. In the struggle against Germany our Ukrainian Insurgent Army was first organized and received its battle training.
 But with the defeat and collapse of Germany an even worse invader has come back to Ukraine—Russia. For centuries enslaving Ukraine, Russia, whether ruled by the tsars or by the "most democratic regime in the world," has always had sinister and imperialistic designs upon our country. This so-called "socialist republic" finally decided to put an end to the aspirations of the Ukrainian people for liberty and independence. Having enchained all its people in a new social system of state capitalism, the ruling clique has created such unbearable economic conditions that under it the freedom-loving man has become perpetually hungry. Having introduced a new culture, "national in form, but socialist in content," the Soviet

Government, with the help of such terrorized Ukrainian slaves as Pavlo Tychyna, Mykola Bazhan, Ostap Vyshnia, and Mykhailo Vozniak, forcibly injects Russian culture into Ukraine. To mislead still further the Ukrainian people, the Soviet Government has even created the Commmissariat of Defense and that of Foreign Affairs, which have no other tasks or duties but to glorify Stalin. By the most inhuman terror mankind has ever known and by insidious provocations, it attempts to "cook" the Ukrainian people in a Russian "pot," so that the Ukrainians would forget that they were once free and independent, and that they would accept without protest the status of permanent slaves of the "big brother"—of the new and powerful Russia. Those who reject this Russian culture are rewarded with the Siberian taigas, the Solovetski Islands, mass executions, the burning of villages, state-instigated famine, and other "modern methods of education."

But the Ukrainian people have not and will not ever capitulate before the enemy. In 1943 they gave you, Ukrainian insurgents, weapons with the explicit command to defend to the last the ideal of Ukrainian freedom and independence. With superb determination and heroism, with unheard of faith and devotion, you have been fighting for this ideal for more than two years. Neither hunger nor privation nor terror applied to your families has shaken your intrepidity and your belief in the final victory. In reply to the deceitful approaches and addresses of the "Government of the Ukrainian Soviet Socialist Republic," you have strengthened your effort. You remember only too well that by such methods Russia tried to demoralize and weaken the brave soldiers of Mazepa; the same insidious propaganda was used in the years 1920-1943 by the Russians in order to entice those from among us who were naïve enough to believe them. All those who trusted the Russians were "rewarded" by being sent to slave-labor camps or executed as soon as their usefulness to Russia came to an end. When you embarked upon the struggle with the Stalinist regime, you knew that we could not capitulate because the enemy that menaces the very existence of the nation must be fought until victory or death comes. I am certain that the weapons given to you by your people will not be covered with dishonor, and you will leave your names covered with immortal glory for posterity.

Ukrainian Insurgents!

The world has no peace as yet. The revolutionary movements of the oppressed peoples as well as the antagonism between the Western democracies and the USSR will increase. People the world over will become increasingly aware what the "dictatorship of the proletariat," formulated in and propagated by the Kremlin, means to humanity. In the struggle against the Kremlin you are by no means alone. The brave Serbs and Croats continue to fight Tito, who is nothing but a tool of Moscow; the Bulgarians also are rebelling against the bloody terror brought to the country by the "allied" USSR. The mountains of Transylvania are overcrowded with those Russians who have refused to submit to Russia. Even little Slovakia conducts regular guerrilla warfare against the invader. The Polish patriots by constant sabotage and armed struggle fight all the attempts of Stalin to enslave them. The ranks of fighters against the Oriental satrap are increasing daily. All this, of course, creates favorable conditions for continuing our struggle and brings nearer the moment of downfall for the USSR.

To be able to survive to that moment with weapons in your hands and to give leadership to all those fighting Stalin—this is your sacred duty. I have a firm belief that you will fulfill it with honor and determination as you have fulfilled all your previous tasks and duties. By using the new methods of struggle, adaptable to the new conditions, you will give a resolute answer to the challenging enemy.

Onward with unshakable faith!
Long live the Independent and Sovereign Ukrainian State!
Glory be to those who fall fighting the invader!

Glory to Ukraine!
Taras Chuprynka, General
Commander-in-Chief of the

Headquarters, May 1945   Ukrainian Insurgent Army

Such was the Ukrainian Resistance Movement at the time of the German occupation of Ukraine and such was the Ukrainian Underground Government which came into being on the eve of Soviet reoccupation of Ukraine. For the greater part of the Ukrainian people it is now a true Ukrainian Government opposed to the "quisling" Soviet-Ukrainian Government of Khrushchev, Manuilsky, etc. It is recognized as such by the UPA and by the broad masses of the Ukrainian population. The best proof that this statement is no exaggeration is the fact that the Ukrainian people, united in the revolutionary UPA and under the leadership of the Supreme Ukrainian Liberation Council, proudly offered stern opposition to the powerful Soviet Union for forty years after the end of military operations in Europe. The Ukrainian Resistance Movement spread all over Ukraine and beyond the borders of Ukraine, appearing from time to time in Poland, Czechoslovakia, Yugoslavia, and Byelorussia. Its aim was to coordinate the underground action of the other peoples enslaved by the Russians and it succeeded in doing so, because in their fight of long duration the Ukrainian Resistance Movement was alone able to develop the best methods and to create the most convincing ideology for the struggle against Bolshevik totalitarianism. This fact places the Ukrainian Resistance Movement in a *prominent position* among the enslaved nations of Eastern Europe and Central Asia and the "satellite" nations.

The rulers of the Kremlin are fully aware of the danger from the Ukrainian Resistance Movement. At the 16th Ukrainian Communist Party Congress in Kyiv (January 1949) Mr. Dmytro Manuilsky, Foreign Minister of the Ukrainian SSR, called on the delegates for constant vigilance against "nationalist distortions" on the Ukrainian home front. He spoke in the course of a general discussion following the main report delivered the previous day by Ukrainian Communist Party Secretary General Nikita Khrushchev. Mr. Khrushchev had called on the delegates to intensify the struggle against the "Ukrainian bourgeois nationalism" which had not ceased to exist after thirty-one years of Soviet rule in Ukraine. The Free World must realize that this "Ukrainian nationalism" is a very concrete factor in Eastern European affairs and that it will become once more "a grave danger" for the seemingly powerful Soviet Union.

The Ukrainian Resistance Movement versus the Kremlin (1944-1949)

By the spring of 1944, after the collapse of the German front in Ukraine, the German commanders in Ukraine had hastened to make contact with the troops of the UPA and proposed an anti-Bolshevik alliance with them. But any negotiations with the Germans were interdicted by the Supreme UPA Command. By the autumn of 1944, when nearly all of the territory of Ukraine was occupied by the

Soviet army, the German policy had changed entirely: the German press was full of praises of the UPA for its anti-Bolshevik successes and the UPA Fighters were now called "Ukrainian fighters for freedom" (although some months before the same press had called them "Ukrainian national brigands"). The leader of the German-sponsored Russian "Vlasov Army," in his interview given to international journalists which was printed in *Völkischer Besbachter* on December 7, 1944, confirmed the army in it fight against the Bolsheviks. But it was already too late.

When the Soviet armies began launching their offensives against the Germans, and the Germans began rolling back from Ukraine, the UPA utilized the German retreat to gather as many weapons as possible for its own use. The troops of the UPA attacked and disarmed the retreating detachments of the German and Hungarian army and police, capturing weapons, vehicles, clothing, footwear, and other war matériel, and seizing stores of arms and ammunition. When the Soviet war machines began to roll over the territory occupied by the UPA, the UPA could meet the new enemy fully prepared and well-armed for the struggle

It must be emphasized that at this time the UPA detachments did not fight against the Red Army, which in this area consisted chiefly of Ukrainians (i.e., the armies of the 1st, 2nd, 3rd, and 4th Ukrainian fronts). They only defended themselves, preferring to circulate and distribute leaflets among the Red soldiers, by the hundred of thousands, which called on the soldiers of the Red Army to turn their arms against Hitler and Stalin. The activity of the UPA was also directed against the restoration of Soviet military and civilian authorities. The UPA systematically opposed the mobilization of Ukrainians into the Red Army. It routed NKVD units by sudden raids on administration centers which caused heavy personnel losses for the new occupants. This action was taken against the local Red spies and collaborators, as well as agents of the NKVD among the local population. Simultaneously, the UPA opposed the restoration of the collective farms and the exportation of Ukrainian wheat and other foodstuffs, the deportation of the Ukrainian population into semi-slave labor camps in the Donbas (the Donets Basin) or farther north and east.

At the time, when the Soviet war machine was engaged in the fight against the Nazis, the Russians could not organize a serious military action against the UPA. Several times the Soviet Government presented an ultimatum to the UPA ordering the Ukrainian insurgents to surrender and promising an amnesty. Soon the Russians realized that the only way they could crush the UPA would be to exile the whole of the Western Ukrainian population to Siberia and to replace it with Russians. By spring and summer, the Russians had begun their famous deportations of the Ukrainian population to Siberia and Kazakhstan. The UPA was forced to resort to arms. At this time, its activities reached the scale of an all-out war. To counter the activity of the UPA, the Russians organized and launched their first great offensive against the UPA which was personally led by Premier Khrushchev and "Ukrainian" Minister of the NKVD, Lt. Gen. Ryassny. This offensive, called the "Khrushchev-Ryassny" offensive, lasted from spring to autumn of 1945. The Russians used airplanes, artillery, tanks, and blocked villages, roads, and forests. They tried to encircle groups of the Ukrainian insurgents and annihilate them. The latter defended themselves by mining roads, railway tracks, natural crossroads, and even stream-beds. Several battles took place in the forests of the Subcarpathian region and in the Carpathian Mountains.

The great offensive led by Khrushchev and Ryassny could not break the resistance of the UPA. The battalions and companies of the UPA withdrew to the Carpathian Mountains and from there continued their fight against the Communist oppressors. Small groups of fighters remained in the country. Having hidden in the underground bunkers and shelters, they made sudden raids on the administrative centers and NKVD posts or ambushed military transportation facilities, columns, and convoys. Railway trains were destroyed by exploding the roadbed or removing trackage. Before an attack all telephone communications were usually destroyed.

The Ukrainian Review,
No. II, 1982, pp. 3-26

The Ukrainian Insurgent Army
(Part Two)

By October 1945, this offensive against the UPA had ended. The Bolsheviks were taken aback by the strength of the UPA and by the support given it by the Ukrainian population. They were surprised by the slight success of the general amnesty they proclaimed in the country, and by the insignificant success of their extensive action against the UPA. But mostly they were surprised by the behavior of the units of the Red Army which were used in this action. And this behavior was the chief reason for the sudden halting of this action in the autumn of 1945.

When the Russians planned their action against the UPA, they decided to employ in this action the units of the Red Army which were being transferred from west to east after Germany's defeat. In connection with that, the Russians developed a special route through Western Ukraine. The most trusted troops were lodged for a long time throughout the country with the task of helping the "interior" police troops (NKVD-MGB) break the resistance of the Ukrainian population. In executing this plan, however, the Russians did not succeed. The UPA opposed them not only with passionate armed defense, but also with an uncommonly strong political campaign which began to influence the Red Army's troops garrisoned in Ukraine. The revolutionary, progressive slogans of the UPA program, which disclosed all the falseness and evil of the Bolshevik totalitarian dictatorship, found a broad, lively response among the Red Army's soldiers, who had just returned from the front. They themselves had seen in Europe quite another reality from the Soviet one, and now attentively listened to the voice of the UPA. The Red Army's soldiers—and very often a whole red Army detachment—were not willing to take part in persecution and terrorist actions directed against the UPA and the Ukrainian population. And whenever they were obliged to take part in such actions, they very often did so only perfunctorily, endeavoring to avoid the UPA formations so as not to fight them, and even very often aided them with information and weapons.

The Russians, dismayed by these facts, were obliged to withdraw the Red

Army troops from any direct actions against the UPA and never used them again. They had to withdraw the demoralized troops of the Red Army from Ukraine and replace them with more disciplined and trustworthy troops. From all parts of the Soviet Union they brought fresh divisions of the MVD-MGB security police into Western Ukraine. The best units of the MVD-MGB troops were selected in the Far Eastern region, from Siberia, and the Leningrad area, and after passing a special course of training were thrown into the fight against the UPA. At least fifteen divisions of MVD-MGB troops were concentrated in the Subcarpathian area and in Volhynia with the purpose of annihilating the UPA. These units were composed of young fanatics who were told that they were going to fight the "remnants" of German "fascists," SS-men, members of the most hated "Vlasov Army," and other criminal elements which were hiding in the Carpathian Mountains. They were asked to fight the "people's enemies" without any respect to sex, age, etc. Most barbarous methods were permitted: pillaging the country, murdering the population, and raping the womenfolk.

The "Ukrainian" Minister of the Interior, Lt. Gen. Ryassny, took responsibility for carrying out the new action, and Col. Gen. Moskalenko was appointed chief commander of the MVD-MGB troops assigned for it. The second large action against the UPA began in the middle of December 1945, and lasted till the end of June 1946. It was called the Ryassny-Moskalenko offensive.

Meanwhile, the Ukrainian Resistance Movement made preparations for the "electoral" campaign for the Supreme Soviet of the USSR. In order to show the Ukrainian people that the Ukrainian Resistance Movement had not been liquidated by the action of Khrushchev and Ryassny in 1945, the battalions of the UPA made a sudden raid on the provincial center of Stanyslaviv (120,000 inhabitants) in the Subcarpathian area, on October 31, 1945, and seized it, having delivered a severe blow to the Soviet occupiers. This attack was conducted by five UPA battalions at night, caused a panic among the Bolsheviks, and brought great satisfaction to the Ukrainian population.

Knowing the character of Soviet "elections," the Supreme Ukrainian Liberation Council decided to boycott the elections to the Supreme Soviet of the USSR and called on the Ukrainian people not to take part in these elections. The Ukrainian Resistance Movement started an anti-electoral campaign, with the result that the Ukrainians of the Western Ukraine did not go to vote.

The Soviet "electoral" campaign had nothing in common with a democratic electoral campaign. As there is in the USSR only one official party, the Soviet "electoral" campaign is only a planned maneuver of the official Communist Party to strengthen and fortify its psychological pressure on the masses of the population and to terrorize them both psychologically and physically. The official electoral propaganda campaign has the task of terrifying, hypnotizing, and mobilizing the masses of the population and, in this way, making them flexible, dumb, and obedient instruments in the hands of the official party clique.

As it is forbidden to put forward non-official candidates, no anti-electoral propaganda is allowed. Such propaganda was possible only in the form of an active, persistent, and organized mass struggle, including the armed resistance of the UPA. It had as its purpose to defend the citizens against the terrorism of the state police and of the special troops, which had the task of forcing them to participate in the elections. Thus, the boycott of the Soviet elections proclaimed by the Supreme Ukrainian Liberation Council soon was transformed into the wide and very persistent fight of the Ukrainian people against the Soviet occupiers.

This fight began in the middle of December 1945, and developed into an ardent struggle. The MVD-MGB troops of Ryassny-Moskalenko were already concentrated in Western Ukraine, and they began to fight on December 18, 1945.

For a month before the beginning of this action an "order" of Lt. Gen. Ryassny was distributed in the country. It is reproduced here in full. Of course, there were not many people in Ukraine so naïve as to be deluded by it.

ORDER

of People's Commissar of Internal Affairs of the Ukrainian SSR
November 15, 1945

A great number of partisans have recently come voluntarily to the organs of NKVD and have said that they could not arrive before the 20th of July this year, which had been fixed as the last term by the government of the Ukrainian SSR.

One of the chief reasons that the people could not arrive on time, they state, was the fact that, although they wanted to break with the partisans and apply to the organs of the Soviet administration, they were not able to do so.

In addition to the partisans, a great number of Red Army deserters are arriving to join the organs of NKVD.

Consequently I declare that:

All members of partisan bands who have ceased their partisan activities and who could not arrive only because of the above-mentioned conditions, as well as those who have avoided mobilization into the Red Army, will not be subjected to any reprisals and will be directed immediately to their places of residence.

People's Commissar of Internal Affairs
of Ukrainian SSR
(signed) Lt. Gen. V. Ryassny

After December 18, 1945, military detachments of the interior police, troops of MVD-MGB, and special selected troops of the Red Army continued to be garrisoned in every locality of Western Ukraine, in every village and even in the smallest hamlets. The number of troops ranged from 10 men in the smallest hamlets to 300-500 in larger localities. The only duty of these police-military troops was to spread violence and terror. In the woods and forests incessant searches for the Ukrainian insurgents took place. The prisons were being filled with prisoners, often arrested for suspected anti-official attitudes. Under such conditions, the Ukrainian anti-electoral campaign was carried out successfully by means of: (a) secret talks and small secret meetings; (b) clandestine spreading of proclamations, short written instructions, and calls; (c) whispered propaganda; (d) posting in visible places of manifestos and appeals of the Supreme Ukrainian Liberation Council and of the UPA; (e) open mass meetings, speeches, and open distribution of manifestos and appeals under the protection of the detachments of the UPA; (f) breaking up of official meetings and transforming them into anti-official ones.

During the period of the "electoral campaign" 1500 battles and engagements against Red troops were fought by the UPA. Five thousand officers and soldiers of the UPA were killed and wounded in action. The Bolsheviks lost at least 15,000 men killed and wounded, but the Ukrainian people did not go to vote!

In the majority of the villages, especially in the western provinces of Ukraine, few went to the elections. Because of this the Bolshevik occupiers retaliated with acts of terrorism. The soldiers of the garrisoned military-police troops used force against the people to compel them to enter electoral halls and throw the electoral slips into urns. They shot at fleeing people and killed many Ukrainians. They set on fire the houses of the opponents. Finally, they themselves put as many electoral slips as they wanted into the urns. We are in possession of many protocols about thousands of cases of maltreatment and many hundreds of murders perpetrated against the Ukrainian people who were not willing to take part in the "elections."

The Ukrainian people used the day of "elections" as a demonstration against the Soviet totalitarian dictatorship. They showed that they were not willing to take part in these elections because they were striving for liberty and freedom in their own independent state. The Ukrainians boycotted the elections in order to protest against the suppression of Ukraine and other subjugated peoples, and against the reign of terror and violence. One anti-election appeal read: "Communists lie all over the world that the Ukrainian Soviet Socialist Republic is a free and independent nation. We shall reply to this common lie with a general boycott of the elections. We are obliged to tell the world that we are against dictatorship and tyranny. Long live true democracy! Long live free elections in a United Ukrainian Independent State!"

The occupiers falsified the election returns, stating that 99 percent of the voters participated in the elections. In the *rayon* of Woynyliv, the province of Stanyslaviv, 10,672 persons were eligible to vote. Of this number only 176 voted voluntarily, 599 were forced to vote, and 9897 did not vote at all. Nevertheless, the authorities proclaimed a great "election victory" in this *rayon* and reported a 99.8 percent vote in this area.

One of the principal actions of the Ukrainian Resistance Movement which took place after the "elections" was the opposition to the forced reunion of the Ukrainian Catholic Church with the Russian Orthodox Church, as announced by Moscow on March 17, 1946. Ukrainian Catholics in Western Ukraine were being deported, imprisoned, subjected to forced labor, or killed if they refused to join the Orthodox Church. In connection with this persecution a proclamation of the Supreme Liberation Council stated: "Neither the Red divisions which stood against the UPA nor the bloody terror of the Russian Gestapo-NKVD could break the Ukrainian resistance. We are convinced that Russian Orthodoxy under the leadership of the Russian NKVD police will not subjugate the spirit of the Ukrainian resistance. Suppression of religion, and the introduction of Orthodoxy by means of force, will only strengthen the front of our struggle and will widen its perspective...." Of course, the Supreme Ukrainian Liberation Council issued orders forbidding the forced apostasy and asking the priests and faithful to oppose the Bolshevik pogrom against the Ukrainian Catholic Church.

This pogrom began as early as 1945, when the Catholic Church was denounced in the press in Kyiv and Lviv and other Ukrainian cities. The Pope's Christmas message on "True and False Democracy" was bitterly attacked, and the Pope was labelled an "abetter of fascism." In April 1945, an article entitled "With the Cross and the Knife" by Volodymyr Rosevych appeared in Soviet-Ukrainian newspapers in Lviv and Kyiv. The article attacked the late Metropolitan Sheptytsky as the "servant of reactionary Rome." Rosevych asserted that the Ukrainian Catholic Church and its clergy, in league with the Vatican, were supporting the Ukrainian Resistance Movement against the Soviet system, and therefore could not be tolerated.

Following these verbal sallies actual physical attacks began. We reproduce here eyewitness reports printed in the publication *For an Independent State* (No. 9-10), which appeared clandestinely in Ukraine:

> On April 11, 1945, a special detachment of NKVD troops surrounded the Cathedral of St. George in Lviv. After a thorough search, according to the best methods of the NKVD, the following were arrested: Metropolitan Joseph Slipy; Bishop Nykyta Budka; Bishop Nicholas Charnetsky; the prelates Rev. O. Kovalsky and Rev. L. Kunytsky; Reverends Gorchynsky, Beley, and Sampara (Rector of the Theological Seminary); Reverend Bilyk (Director of a Catholic School), and Reverend Hodunko—who after brutal tortures died a few days after his arrest. The students of the Theological Seminary were rounded up and put in a camp on Pieracki Street. All the professors of the Theological Seminary were herded into a meeting organized by the NKVD and informed that the Ukrainian Catholic Church had ceased to exist, that its Metropolitan had been arrested, and the Cathedral of St. George would be taken over by the Orthodox bishop appointed by the Soviet authorities. During the search the NKVD conducted itself in a brutal manner and took all gold and silver objects, liturgical wine, etc.

These raids were carried on throughout Western Ukraine. All Ukrainian Catholic bishops were arrested. In Stanislaviv, the NKVD arrested Bishop Gregory Khomyshyn and his auxiliary, Bishop Latishevsky. In Peremyshl, which nominally does not belong to the Ukrainian SSR but rather to Poland, the NKVD arrested Bishop Josephat Kotsylovsky, together with his auxiliary, Bishop Gregory Lakota. Of these Ukrainian Catholic prelates at least two, Bishop Khomyshyn and Kotsylovsky, were reported dead in Soviet dungeons, while others were forced to work under the strict supervision of the MVD in the Vorkuta coal mines in the Soviet subarctic region. In the autumn of 1947 the last Catholic Bishop of Ukraine, Bishop Romzha of Carpatho-Ukraine, met his tragic death in an "accident" involving a Soviet army tank.

After the pogrom against the Ukrainian Catholic hierarchy, the Russians went on to liquidate the lesser clergy. But out of a total of 3600 Ukrainian Catholic priests only 42 had submitted to the apostasy by the end of June 1945. Finally, on March 8, 1946, a "synod" was convened in Lviv. It was headed by those Ukrainian priests who submitted to the apostasy and "officially" proclaimed the "reunion" of the Ukrainian Catholic Church with the Russian Orthodox Church. But the Supreme Ukrainian Liberation Council stated that this "synod" was illegal and its decisions invalid, because, according to canon law, only bishops had the right to convene such ecclesiastic meetings. Reports stated at the time that, among 216 "priests" attending this "synod" the majority were Russian NKVD agents disguised as Catholic priests.

In connection with this pogrom against the Ukrainian Catholic Church, the Supreme Ukrainian Liberation Council submitted to the Holy See a memorandum regarding the persecution of the Ukrainian Catholic Church in Ukraine and requesting the Holy See (1) to designate an exarch for the Ukrainian Catholic Church in western parts of Ukraine until all bishops and priests were released from Soviet prisons, (2) to make every effort for the liberation of Ukrainian bishops and priests from Soviet prisons, (3) to take a canonical stand in regard to the so-called "reunion" of the Ukrainian Catholic Church with the Russian Orthodox Church, (4) to ask the United Nations to send a mixed commission to investigate the "voluntary" transfer of the Ukrainian Catholic Church to the Russian Orthodox Church, and (5) to nominate a Field Bishop for the Ukrainian Insurgent Army (UPA).

Here we must point out that the mock trial of Cardinal Mindszenty, in which the venerable prelate was condemned to life imprisonment on trumped-up charges by Stalin's Communist puppets then in power in Budapest, was an exact replica of the so-called "purge" trials long in operation in Soviet Russia. Only after tortures and the forced administration of drugs, which were commonplace practices under Soviet Russia's judicial system, was Cardinal Mindszenty allowed to appear before the court as a morally and physically broken man. The trials against the Ukrainian Catholic bishops were announced by the Russians but the bishops themselves did not appear before the court because no tortures or drugs could break their spirit—and they did not confess to the crimes they had not committed. We can only be surprised at the fact that the whole world remained calm and silent when the Bolsheviks imprisoned all the Ukrainian Catholic bishops because they had refused to abandon their faith, and when the Ukrainian clergy and the faithful were persecuted and arrested because they had refused to be separated from their true Mother Church. The New York Times of August 5, 1949 printed a letter by Most Rev. Ivan Buchko, D.D., Apostolic Visitator for the Ukrainians in Western Europe, about the largest persecution of clergy and laity in Ukraine by the Soviet authorities. The letter, sent from Rome and dated July 20, 1949, read:

> For some time I have been reading editorials of The New York Times and other American newspapers that reach me about the persecution of the Catholic Church and her hierarchy by the Soviets and their satellites. I am surprised and deeply regret that nothing has been mentioned of the liquidation of the Ukrainian Catholic Church in Western Ukraine and Carpatho-Ukraine, which had been persecuted for so long.
>
> The tragic fate of Cardinal Mindszenty and of Archbishop Stepaniac is well known, as well as the recent persecution of Archbishop Joseph Beran of Prague. But

hardly anything is known of the fact that the entire Ukrainian Catholic hierarchy has been completely liquidated. Some bishops are dead, others are still suffering in the Soviet camps, where they are assigned to hard labor.

The cruel hand of the Soviet fell upon them during the night of April 11, 1945. All of them had long been singled out as Church leaders and patriots, firmly believing in the cause of Ukrainian national independence. All were arrested on the same night, and within a short time—hundreds of priests and faithful as well. Convenient tools were soon found who dissolved the Ukrainian Catholic Church as such and made it a part of the Russian Orthodox Church under the leadership of the Kremlin-dominated Patriarch of Moscow.

His Holiness, Pope Pius, in his famous encyclical "Orientales Omnes," called the attention of the world to the martyrdom of the Ukrainian Catholic Church under the Soviet regime and appealed to all Christians to pray for the Ukrainian Catholics.

The Ukrainian Catholic Church was the first, but not the last, to fall victim to the Muscovite war against Rome. Nonetheless according to reports that still reach us here, the religious spirit of the Ukrainians and their national fervor burn brighter than ever before.

Under the protection of the Ukrainian Resistance Movement the free Ukrainian Catholic Church continues to exist in Western Ukraine. It went underground and in this way fulfills the religious needs of the Ukrainian population.

Meanwhile the large Ryassny-Moskalenko offensive spread to the Subcarpathian areas with the purpose of totally annihilating the UPA. By the spring of 1946, all the forest of Western Ukraine, such as the Tsumansky Forest near Kovel, the Yaniv Forest near Lviv, and the Black Forest near Stanislav, were burnt down in order to deprive the Ukrainian insurgents of their natural bases. The devastation was immense. In order to infect the populations the Soviets sold serums of typhus and other bacteria on the black market where the medicines for the UPA were bought despite the fact that bacteriological warfare was outlawed by international treaties. Even the Nazis did not use such methods in combatting the UPA.

On May 3, 1946, Col. Gen. Moskalenko, a colonel, and two majors were shot in an armored car near the railway station of Tyshiv, in the province of Stanyslaviv, by an UPA subdetachment of "Avengers." Secret informers had told the UPA detachment of the exact time of the departure of the commander-in-chief of the anti-UPA movement and his staff officers to go from Stanislaviv to Stry. The armored car was hit in an ambush at close range by missiles from an insurgent bazooka. The UPA subdetachment was attacked by the convoy of the NKVD general and was forced to withdraw to the nearest forest. This incident was reported only by the illegal journal of the Supreme Ukrainian Liberation Council, *Samostiynist* (Independence), in the Summer 1946 issue (p. 159).

About the end of June 1946, the garrisons of MVD-MGB troops withdrew from the country. As usual the Soviets announced their "great victory" over the "remnants" of "Ukrainian-German" nationalists and proclaimed the "definite liquidation" of the "Ukrainian partisan bands." But the Soviet leader responsible for this action, Lt. Gen. Ryassny, got neither the Kutuzov nor the Suvorov medal for this "victory." He was relieved of his post as Minister of the Interior of the

Ukrainian SSR and replaced by Gen. Kruglov, former Minister of the Interior of the USSR. This was the best proof that the Ryassny "victory" was no victory at all. The MVD-MGB detachments "succeeded" in killing many Ukrainian civilians, and in devastating the country, but it was a very hypothetical "victory." It caused only an unlimited hatred of the Ukrainian people for the Soviet-Russian methods of combatting the UPA. And these methods were worthy of their masters. All the horrors of the times of Ivan the Terrible or Peter the Great were revived in Western Ukraine.

The Ukrainian Resistance Movement survived the terrible offensive of the Ryassny-Moskalenko forces and showed Ukraine and the world that there are limits to terror. It showed that determined people are able to withstand the pressure of overwhelming enemy forces who know no mercy. It showed the world that such people are even able to win their fight since they know what they are fighting for.

The significance of the survival of the Ukrainian Resistance Movement was immense. By its survival it showed that an underground revolutionary-political fight against the Soviet "colossus" is possible. Its armed groups not only protected the Ukrainian population from the terror of the Soviet secret police, but also paralyzed all efforts of the oppressors to carry out their occupation policies. Through solidarity, sacrifices, and the fanatical heroism of its fighters, the Ukrainian Resistance Movement gained the admiration of the whole Ukrainian people and even of its opponents, and succeeded in calling the whole Ukrainian people to the struggle against the bloody usurpers.

Nevertheless the Ukrainian Resistance Movement became aware that it had to change its methods of organization from a mass underground to an individual conspiracy. It had to replace the breadth of the movement with depth, extensiveness with intensity, quantity with quality. The Ukrainian Resistance Movement had to become a body with clockwork precision. It had to liquidate all second-rate sectors and replace them with more tightly organized political, economic, and propaganda sectors. Then, it had to widen its activities in Eastern Ukraine to win over the people of the eastern provinces to the struggle. It had also to expand beyond the borders of Ukraine and summon others of the subjugated peoples, especially in the satellite countries, to the struggle against the Bolshevik occupiers, showing them the Ukrainian experience in this uneven fight.

The Ukrainian Resistance Movement reorganized its forces according to the principles mentioned above in the second half of 1946. Preparations for this reorganization were made as early as 1945 soon after the war came to an end, as we can see from a document entitled "Instructions of the Central Directing Body of the OUN concerning the conclusion of World War II." The large insurgent units (battalions and companies) were disbanded and their fighters were used to strengthen the units of the territorial network. Instead of disorganized units, small units of armed Ukrainian insurgents were organized, each with its own area of activity to which it was confined except in rare cases as necessary. The detachments were divided into "subdetachments" and all had their numbers and names. The dislocation of the detachments and subdetachments was planned by the Supreme Command in such a manner that they could easily be mobilized for special actions in case of emergency. At the same time, the mobilization order to the affiliated "Youth Organization" was issued, and young boys and girls between sixteen and eighteen years of age joined the armed detachments to bring them to full strength, and also to get their training, both political-ideological and military. Finally, the Propaganda and Information Center was organized: its chief task was to reorganize the material base for the continuation of propaganda activities.

The Russians were very surprised at the vitality of the Ukrainian Resistance Movement in the second half of 1946. Having publicly announced their "total" victory over the UPA, they were dismayed that these forces were being reactivated. Their disappointment was complete when they learned that clandestinely printed journals of the Ukrainian Resistance Movement had appeared with articles by well-known underground writers such as Poltava, Hornovy, Kuzhil, and Honcharuk.

Having destroyed the chief base of the Ukrainian underground propaganda during the time of the Ryassny-Moskalenko offensive, the Russians could hardly expect such a regeneration in so short a time. A clandestine journal of the Supreme Ukrainian Liberation Council, *Independence*, had appeared as well as *Idea and Action* (No. 10), the ideological journal of the OUN, and many others, as well as thousands of leaflets which found their way all over the Soviet Union.

The first issue of *The Independence* (1946) contained an excellent article entitled "Shame of the Twentieth Century" which described the Bolshevik methods of combatting the Ukrainian Resistance Movement during the time of the Ryassny-Moskalenko offensive. *Idea and Action* (No. 10, 1946) contained many interesting articles, one of which was by Poltava, the leading underground writer, entitled "The Ideological Principles of Ukrainian Nationalism."

In the autumn of 1946 the Ukrainian Resistance Movement began to fight against the forced collectivization of agriculture as practiced in Western Ukraine, and this became its principal activity in Ukraine during the following years.

To this day in the West, there still persists the belief that the collectivization of agriculture, as practiced in the Soviet Union, despite the inhuman methods used for its enforcement, is an economic measure calculated to increase production. Actually, however, in Western Ukraine and other subjugated countries, collectivization is a political act and is enforced in spite of the fact that it is ruinous economically. Lenin himself said that if the peasants are allowed to keep their land, they will continue endlessly to produce capitalist elements which, from the countryside, will penetrate the towns, trade, industry, and the administration. In short, the existence of a peasant class based on private property enables capitalism to reproduce itself perpetually, making Communism impossible.

In order to ensure the existence of their regime, the Communists instituted the collectivization of agriculture. Needless to say, they met with a desperate resistance on the part of the peasants, especially in Ukraine and in the Cossack lands. Soviet terrorism triumphed, however, and millions of peasants either perished in the famine of 1932-33 or were deported for forced labor in Siberia.

The collectivation of Ukraine's agriculture proved most eloquently and conclusively that the *kolkhozes* had nothing to boast of with regard to productivity of labor or economy of production. The Bolshevik system needed *kolkhozes* to ruin the individual farmers as a class. As is well known, farmers all over the world are the staunchest patriots and the most stubborn fighters for individual freedom and private initiative. Only by means of *kolkhozes* was it possible to reduce the Ukrainian farmers to the level of slave laborers, and their real income to the level demanded by the exploitation current in the Soviet Union.

Immediately after the reoccupation of Western Ukraine the Russians made haste to prepare the ground for collectivization. Their success was almost nil, for the Ukrainian Resistance Movement frustrated all their attempts. The Russians were, therefore, eager to make Western Ukraine ripe for collectivization. They decided that the best method to achieve this end was to make the life of the individual farmers as intolerable as possible. These measures were calculated to ruin the farmers and to make them willing to abandon their land. All the farmers who were not partisans of the new order were declared "kulaks'" and "enemies of the people" and burdened with exorbitant taxes. They were threatened with deportation and imprisonment if they did not pay. The individual farmers had to pay an income tax which was three to four times higher than that which the *kolkhoz* farmers had to pay on their private incomes. Individual farmers owning horses, moreover, had to pay a heavy tax in order to compel them to sell the animals sooner or later. The *kolkhozes*, however, paid no taxes at all in their first years.

The individual farmers were, moreover, burdened with oppressive statutory labor. They had to cut lumber, cart firewood and timber out of the forests, mend roads, and do public transport service. The farmers failing to comply with all these obligations risked a sentence of hard labor coupled with the confiscation of all their property.

The individual farmers had to deliver to the state a certain amount of various products every year: grain, hay, milk, meat, wool, potatoes, flax, sugar beets, etc. The state paid ridiculously low prices for these products. Fodder and fertilizers, on the other hand, were reserved exclusively for the *kolkhozes*.

It is evident that, under these circumstances, to be an individual farmer in the USSR was far from pleasant. The individual farmers had only one choice if they wished to avoid deportation to Siberia: to join a *kolkhoz*.

As long as the Ukrainian Resistance Movement continues to be strong, the realization of the Soviet programs will continue to encounter difficulties. Although they came from every class of the population, a great proportion of the Ukrainian insurgents were sons of farmers and enjoyed the complete and unstinting support of the whole of the Ukrainian peasantry in combatting the hated and unpopular *kolkhoz* system.

Owing to the vigorous resistance, the Russians made their first attempt to collectivize in the autumn of 1946, when they thought the Ukrainian Resistance Movement had already been destroyed by the Ryassny-Moskalenko offensive. They organized some fifty *kolkhozes* in Western Ukraine and provided them with an armed guard of NKVD troops.

Summoned by the Ukrainian Resistance Movement, farmers all over the country reacted to the rumors of imminent collectivization with large-scale sabotage. They sold their livestock, keeping only one cow each. Grain was hidden in the woods and pigsties were erected in the most unlikely places, as had been done during the German occupation. The farmers hid their animals or slaughtered them clandestinely.

Counter-propaganda against collectivization brought on riots in various parts of the country. The existing tractors were wrecked on all these occasions for fear of subsequent collectivization. In various places the Communists agitating for collectivization among the farmers were either assassinated or harassed.

The Ukrainian Resistance Movement did not confine itself to the distribution of countless leaflets among the farmers explaining the consequences of their joining the *kolkhozes*. One night in November 1946, armed groups of Ukrainian insurgents suddenly attacked the MTS (agricultural machinery stations), the backbone of the *kolkhoz* system, and demolished them. Again they attacked the *kolkhoz* estates and burned them down. Both these attacks were made simultaneously throughout the country and Russians suffered a major blow frustrating their attempts to collectivize farming in Western Ukraine.

Of course, the authorities did not give up their efforts to enforce collectivization. In the spring of 1947, they organized new *kolkhozes* and brought more armed MVD-MGB troops. But the struggle against forced collectivization lasted the whole year and the Russians could not boast of any great success. Even in 1949, Kyiv Radio broadcast the following figures from a report of the Secretary General of the Ukrainian Communist Party, N.S. Khrushchev, on the progress of agricultural collectivization in the West Ukrainian provinces: Volhynia—80 percent, Drohobych—79 percent, Ternopil—34 percent, Lviv—34 percent, and Stanyslaviv—17 percent. By his report Khrushchev indirectly confirmed the success of the Ukrainian Resistance Movement in vigorously opposing collectivization.

The Russians soon realized that as long as the Ukrainian Resistance Movement existed, their drive for enforced collectivization would not succeed. They began, therefore to study the Ukrainian Resistance Movement in order to learn the best measures for combatting it. A center aiming at the liquidation of the Ukrainian Resistance Movement was organized under the jurisdiction of the Ministry of State Security (MGB). It is significant that this "internal" Soviet-Ukrainian problem was put under the control of an All-Union authority in Moscow, and this is one more proof that the Ukrainian Resistance Movement had become a "grave danger."

The anti-collectivization struggle of the Ukrainian Resistance Movement in 1947 gave it a big chance to spread all over Ukraine. In Eastern Ukraine, climatic conditions were unfavorable in 1946 and in 1947. The meager harvest of 1946, combined with the usual requisitions of grain and other foodstuffs, caused widespread starvation among the Ukrainian *kolkhozniks* of Eastern Ukraine. On the contrary, climatic conditions in Western Ukraine were extraordinarily good and the harvest there was above average. In the spring and summer of 1947, Western Ukraine was, therefore, crowded with groups of starved *kolkhozniks* from as far as Kharkiv and Voronezh provinces who had been attracted by rumors that Western Ukraine abounded in food and goods. As the peasant in the USSR lives mainly on the proceeds of his small private garden lot of 0.25-1 hectares, crowds of *kolkhozniks* came into Western Ukraine to beg for grain and other foodstuffs. The authorities persecuted them in all possible ways, but their movements to Western Ukraine was unchecked. It is estimated that more than 1 million *kolkhozniks* visited Western Ukraine, taking at least 200,000 quintals of grain and other foodstuffs.

This was a big opportunity for the Ukrainian Resistance Movement. It issued a proclamation to the "Brethren of Eastern Ukraine" asking them "whether they know why they are starving although they are the owners of the richest soil in the world." This proclamation explained the aims of the Ukrainian Resistance Movement and called the Ukrainian *kolkhozniks* to the common struggle against the Bolsheviks. It stressed that the West Ukrainians had plenty of food and other goods because they systematically opposed the *kolkhoz system* and fought against Bolshevism as the most ruthless exploiter of the Ukrainian people. It asked the *kolkhozniks* of Eastern Ukraine to follow their example and fight against the barbarous Bolshevik system for an independent Ukraine. The West Ukrainian population was asked to aid the brethren of Eastern Ukraine and assist them in all possible ways. The slogan "A quarter of grain to the starving brethren from the East!" was circulated everywhere. The Ukrainian insurgents often held meetings with the *kolkhozniks* to explain to them the hypocrisy of the Bolshevik system and to advise them how to fight it at home. The success of this propaganda can be judged from press statements from Eastern Ukraine showing how the *kolkhozniks* became passive resisters against the Bolshevik system, hiding foodstuffs and sabotaging the orders of the Communist Party. Of course, the rumors of Ukrainian armed resistance in Western Ukraine spread throughout the Soviet Union.

It is an open question whether the teachers in the West are fully able to envisage what their colleagues behind the "Iron Curtain" must feel when forced to teach their trusting pupils arrant lies and an ideology of hate. Directives from Moscow require, for instance, that Russian culture and Russian achievements be regarded as the first and oldest in the world and that Western culture be regarded only as a derivative of the Russian. The origin of the Ukrainian State must be explained "from the point of view of present Soviet historiography"—i.e., intentionally falsified. In the same way, in all courses in Ukrainian literature and history it is necessary to emphasize the national peculiarity, originality, and greatness of Russian thinkers, writers, and scholars and their "great influence" on the Ukrainian people. The pupils must be acquainted with the Soviet system and convinced of its "immeasurable superiority" to bourgeois ways. All this the Ukrainian teachers are compelled to inculcate in the defenseless children, contrary to their own knowledge that Ukrainian culture was already highly developed when Russia was still a vast forest peopled by wandering tribes of nomadic barbarians. However, the tasks of the unhappy teachers are not confined to teaching in the schools. They must be "enlighteners of the people" in the broadest sense. In schools and out of school the teacher has to be not only a champion of Communism but an active fighter against his own people, Western culture, etc. "The sacred duty of the Soviet teacher is to be the engineer of the growing mind, to combat the effects of the drugs of capitalism, political neutrality, ideological slackness, bourgeois objectivism, bourgeois Ukrainian nationalism and religious relics which poison the mind of our youth," wrote a Ukrainian school dignitary. Everything Western is poisonous and degenerate, everything Eastern vigorous and excellent. Every day and every hour the consciousness of the power of the Soviet state must be drummed into the minds of the young.

In order to combat the danger of such an "education" for young Ukrainian people, the Ukrainian Resistance Movement decided to start its own school action. It issued directives to Ukrainian teachers requiring that Ukrainian culture and its achievements be regarded as the principal aim of education. The detailed instructions of the Ukrainian Resistance Movement asked the teachers to teach Ukrainian literature, Ukrainian history, and geography from the point of view of Ukrainian nationalism. They forbade any anti-religious activity in the schools, as Ukrainian religious feelings are predominant in everyday life. The pupils had to be acquainted with the achievements of Western culture, and the relation of Ukrainian culture to Western culture had to be stressed. Finally, the pupils had to know what is meant by Soviet exploitation, what the situation of the peasant and workers in the USSR is as compared with that of the capitalist countries, and what the essence of Russian imperialism is. Simultaneously with the directives to the Ukrainian teachers, the Ukrainian Resistance Movement issued a proclamation to young Ukrainian people asking them to facilitate the difficult task of their teachers.

In connection with this it is interesting to note that as early as 1945 almost 6,000 teachers were brought from Eastern into Western Ukraine with the aim of liquidating nationalistic tendencies in the teaching of history and literature, and of heightening the standard of ideological and political training. The West Ukrainian teachers were said to be under the influence of Ukrainian nationalism. Most of the arriving teachers were young girls, often members of Komsomol (the Communist youth organization). They were, without doubt, under the strong influence of Bolshevik propaganda, which denounced the Ukrainian insurgents as "bandits," "murderers," "fascists," and the like. The fear of the "Ukrainian-German nationalists" was so great that the girls refused to take food and to speak to the people in the villages of Western Ukraine. But the authorities could not secure satisfactory living conditions for them. The lodgings assigned to them were insufficient and out of repair, food was short and of inferior quality, and they had no money to have their clothes and shoes repaired. As they got salaries from 130 to 240 rubles a month, they were not able to buy anything at the time when 1 kg of butter on the black market cost nearly 300 rubles.

The Ukrainian Resistance Movement soon made use of the chance their arrival provided to spread its ideas among the Eastern Ukrainian population, and to make these teachers instrumental in a planned fight for Ukrainian independence all over Ukraine. It ordered its members and sympathizers to observe the girls in their everyday lives and to support with food and clothing those who, without any doubt, were good Ukrainians. Moreover, it ordered its members to inform these girls about the concepts of Ukrainian nationalism. The girls had a chance to see at close hand the Ukrainian insurgents in their fight against the Russians and observe the fanatic heroism of the Ukrainian boys and girls. Soon they became acquainted with the aims of the Ukrainian Resistance Movement and understood the situation as it developed in Western Ukraine. In many cases they became enthusiastic followers of the Ukrainian Resistance Movement and contributed much to the spreading of its ideas in Eastern Ukraine. According to reports from the country, 75 percent of them followed the directives of the Ukrainian Resistance Movement as regards teaching in the schools. Many were arrested and deported and other became active fighters for the Ukrainian cause. In November 1948, one of the teachers, a former Komsomol member from Eastern Ukraine named Tamara Lushchenko, was killed in the streets of a Subcarpathian town while executing an order of the Ukrainian Resistance Movement to assassinate an *agent provocateur*. She mortally wounded him, but in his last spasm he succeeded in shooting her down with his submachine gun.

Simultaneously with its school action, the Ukrainian Resistance Movement opposed the conscription of Ukrainian youth into FZU schools (trade and craft schools), which were notorious as center of ruthless slave labor. FZU schools were chiefly located in Russia. The students were uniformed and were subject to strong military discipline. They attended schools which were, in fact, factories producing war matériel.

Among other things, the Ukrainian Resistance Movement carried out a strong propaganda campaign among the veterans of the war. In many of the towns in Western Ukraine and in the whole of the Soviet Union disabled war veterans could be seen sitting and begging at every street corner. Those who had lost both legs propelled themselves in boxes which moved not on wheels, but on old discarded ball-bearings. These people always wore their orders and medals and abused the Government openly. The Ukrainian Resistance Movement issued a special leaflet directed to them in order to strengthen their anti-Soviet feelings, considering them a significant factor in the anti-Bolshevik struggle of the Ukrainian people.

Among the chief activities of the Ukrainian Resistance Movement were the UPA raids in Eastern and Central Europe. The operations of the UPA in the territories of Central Europe found an echo in the press of Western Europe and of the United States, because many foreign correspondents in Czechoslovakia and in Poland reported on them.

The first raid of the UPA in Central Europe began as early as 1945. In the summer of 1945, UPA forces made extensive propaganda raids into the territories of Carpatho-Ukraine, Hungary, Romania, Slovakia, Byelorussia, and Lithuania. The success of these operations was great. They had excellent results, consolidating the population for the fight against the common foe. At the same time they showed the true fighting spirit of the military personnel waging war for an independent Ukrainian State.

UPA raids into Slovakia became especially famous. In their march through Eastern Slovakia, the Ukrainian insurgents crossed the districts of Stropkov, Oiraltovce, Presov, Sabinov, Bardyjov, Snina, and Humenne. In all settlements they passed, they called together the local population and arranged discussion evenings about current topics. They distributed leaflets in the Slovak language and registered a considerable number of volunteers who wished to join the UPA forces.

On August 28, 1945, in the village of Dispalovce, the commander of the raiding group, First Lt. Andrienko, split the raiding group into three parts after having received instructions from the home base. One part of the raiding group went into Carpatho-Ukraine, the other into southeastern Poland, and the third group, under Second Lt. Myron, turned south.

When this group approached Preshov, the Czech authorities brought in heavy concentrations to surround the woods. All the roads were full of moving troops, heavy equipment, and dispatchers. But in spite of all this, the raiders peacefully passed through the villages of Cerbenice, Huviz, and Lysecek towards the west. In many villages the Ukrainian insurgents (they were members of the First insurgent Officer School and mostly students of universities or of high schools) gave vocal concerts. They took leave of the hospitable Slovak territory by giving an evening of dancing which was well attended by the local population in Tspelovce, eight kilometers from the Slovak-Polish boundary.

UPA raids deep into Slovakian territory in the spring of 1946 became world famous. This raid was well prepared. Participating troops were aware of the importance of this operation. The raid was preceded by a sudden attack of the Insurgent battalion of Capt. Didyk on the railway station and town of Lukiv in southeastern Poland. The Polish garrison fled in panic into the Slovak territory and was disarmed and interned by the Czechoslovakian authorities. The fact became known all over the world and the correspondents of different English-language press organs went to the spot to gather reliable information. In this way the first reports on the UPA appeared in the world press. The UPA was described by these correspondents as a force of 20,000 Ukrainians fighting against Red Army detachments, well-clothed and armed, well-fed and wearing the national insignia on their caps. Further information was added by Homer Biggart, a *New York Herald-Tribune* reporter, in a dispatch of April 18, 1946. He detailed the UPA activities and stressed the fact that the insurgents behaved well towards the civilian population. He pointed out that because they fought for an independent Ukraine they were both anti-Russian and anti-Polish.

The raid of the UPA in Slovakia, in the spring and summer of 1946, was a march of triumph. Everywhere the raiders were met with enthusiasm, and the Slovaks were delighted that their local Communist bosses had been humiliated. The raiding detachments crossed the Ukrainian-Slovak boundary in complete secrecy so as not to alert Polish and Czechoslovakia forces. Abundant literature was distributed in this raid, which reached nearly all districts of Eastern Slovakia.

Another battle of the UPA developed in Slovakia in the spring and summer of 1947. In May 1947, the Czechslovakian Government proclaimed a state of emergency in all of Slovakia. As in time of war, people were forbidden to move freely between populated areas. In the evening one was not allowed to leave one's house. The military detachments of the Slovaks which had been sent against the UPA went over to the side of the Ukrainians without offering any battle. Young people began to join the ranks of the UPA. A detachment of the UPA, forced out of Slovakia by the Czech armed forces, retreated in separate groups across Moravia and Czechia. Small groups of Ukrainian insurgents appeared in the Sadzhava Woods. The route of some detachments of the UPA led obviously towards Bavaria, where they expected to surrender their arms to the Americans. Some of them even crossed the Danube south of Lake Balaton in Hungary and reached Yugoslav territory to join "chetniks" and "kursari."

The same story was repeated in spring and summer of 1948. The Czechoslovak Ministries of War and of the Interior published a joint communiqué which said: "Czech army and police troops are fighting against UPA units which hold positions and fortifications from World War II in Slovakia." It went on to say that, after several days' fighting, police troops had taken a bunker whose defenders (three UPA soldiers and a Red Cross nurse) had fought to their last breath with knives and bayonets after they exhausted their ammunition.

The battle of the UPA on the territory of Slovakia was mentioned several times in the Czech Parliament. During the first phase of the UPA raid, in 1947, the Czech Vice-Minister of Military Affairs, Gen. Ferencik, gave the names of the detachments of the UPA and explained to the members of Parliament the political background of the UPA. During the second phase of the raid, which took place on the territory of Czechia itself, the Minister of Military Affairs, Gen. Svoboda, addressed Parliament regarding the battles with the UPA detachments. He gave the exact number of casualties on both the Ukrainian and Czech sides, and described the UPA as "an excellently trained and perfectly organized military force. Its battle equipment was good," he said.

Tvorba, the organ of the Communist Party in Czechoslovakia, wrote in June 1948 that "small but exceedingly well-equipped and well-disciplined UPA units have again broken into Czechoslovakia," and that it was "most alarming that numerous Czech and Slovak rebels have joined them and begun to liquidate Communists and People's Democrats." It sharply reproached the Soviet-Polish-Czech high command in Slovakia for its failure to liquidate the UPA, which, "by its activities, is said to have turned the military forces of the above-mentioned three powers into a laughingstock. The very existence of the UPA is encouraging the anti-Communist elements in all of the East European countries." *Tvorba* blamed the united high command for failing to issue constructive slogans to counteract the ideas of the UPA and command the sympathies of the Czechs and Slovaks.

A further development which arose out of the UPA raid in Czechoslovakia was the trial of members of the UPA which took place in the capital of Slovakia, Bratislava. It began on November 19 and ended on November 28, 1948, with the death sentence being imposed on the four Ukrainian defendants. On the first day of the trial the presiding judge, Dr. Karol Berdna, began to refer to the defendants as "bandits" and "killers." To the astonishment of the court, Ivan Klisch, one of the defendants, rose to protest immediately after the reading of the charges. "We are soldiers of the Ukrainian Insurgent Army," the defendant declared. "As such, we swore to obey the orders of the Command of our armed forces; therefore, we strongly protest against the court's reference to us as bandits and killers." He went on to demand that they should be referred to as "soldiers of the Ukrainian Insurgent Army," and stated that, if their army uniforms and insignia were not returned, they would not answer the questions put by the court. The defiant attitude of the defendants in spite of their long struggle against both the

Nazis and the Bolsheviks, and the tortures they suffered in the Communist prisons of Czechoslovakia, appeared to confuse the court. A recess was called, and after several hours of deliberation the court ruled that their uniforms should be returned. For the remainder of the proceedings, the Ukrainian underground was referred to as the Ukrainian Insurgent Army. The trial received much publicity in the Czechoslovakian press.

Details of the UPA raid into Eastern Ukraine are known from firsthand reports by participants in these raids. The first raid, under the command of Col. Eney of the UPA-North, was organized in the autumn of 1946. It started in Northern Volhynia, which was the operations base of the UPA-North, and finished near the River Dnieper in the region of Kyiv. The raiding group traveled more than 400 kilometers and had twenty-one encounters on the way. It was divided into small raiding detachments which worked simultaneously, while in Eastern Ukraine the raiding units often changed their field of operations in order to carry out a given task, to secure supplies, or to evade discovery and prevent encirclement. Strict discipline on the march was maintained. Marches were generally at night, by routes known only to the local population. Small insurgent units synchronized their moves over a large terrain marching thirty to forty miles daily. Everywhere the raiding units found the full support of the Eastern Ukrainian population, which supplied them with food and gave them shelter.

Another raid under the command of Major Khmara was organized in the spring of 1947. It was organized by UPA-South. The raiding detachments crossed Bukovina, Moldavia and Bessarabia and reached Odessa. The raid covered more than 1,000 kilometers and was made in about 100 days. The raiding detachments made contact with many local insurgent groups in Moldavia and Bessarabia and got the full support of the villagers when the raiding detachments demolished the granaries and distributed grain among the population.

As early as 1945, the UPA made several raids into Poland. It made contact with WIN (Freedom and Independence), a Polish underground army in Central Poland, and with NSZ (National Armed Forces), a Polish underground army in Western Poland. The Ukrainian insurgents went as far as Wroclaw (Breslau) and established liason with WRN (Liberty, Equality, Independence), another Polish underground organization. The Ukrainian insurgents not only established contact with the Polish underground, but also concluded an agreement of mutual support and assistance. According to this agreement, which was concluded on May 18, 1946, the combined Polish-Ukrainian underground forces attacked the town of Hrubieszow on May 27-28, 1946, inflicting heavy casualties on the NKVD troops and the Polish militia.

With the assistance of the Polish underground, Ukrainian insurgents raided the Bialowieza wilderness (in 1945, with the battalion of "Wolves" under the command of Major Chernyk), in Central and Western Poland (in 1946), and eastern Prussia (in 1947 under the command of Cpl. Prirva). The enforced colonization of East Prussia mainly with Ukrainians from the Ukrainian territories west of the Curzon Line provided the UPA with an opportunity to extend its activities to the Baltic Sea and to make contact with the well-organized and strong Lithuanian Liberation Movement. The aim of the last raid was to visit the

Ukrainian population in Eastern Prussia, to organize an underground network covering this province and the Danzig area, and to establish contacts with the Lithuanian Resistance Movement (the BDPS, the National Democratic Resistance Movement). The contacts were established and the Ukrainian insurgents observed the strength and the perfect underground organization of the BDPS.

At the same time the UPA group which operated in the westernmost regions of Ukraine was concentrating all its efforts on preventing the Red Polish Government from forcibly transferring the Ukrainian population from the territories west of the Curzon Line into the Soviet Union. In accordance with the Soviet-Polish Treaty of August 16, 1945, a Polish-Soviet state boundary was established. The Red Polish authorities announced officially that all Ukrainians had to leave Poland and move to the Soviet Union. It must be emphasized that this transfer action was carried out by the Red Poles with great terror and violence. The Red Polish security troops (UB) and the Red Polish Army, under Soviet command, destroyed whole Ukrainian villages, setting fire to them, plundering, and murdering the inhabitants. On January 24, 1946, at 9:00 a.m., units of the Red Polish Army surrounded the village of Zawadka Morochivska. These units were from the First Battalion of the 34th Regiment stationed in Sianok. The headquarters of the regiment, under the command of Col. Pluto, was in the village of Mokre. The Red Polish soldiers murdered fifty-six persons who were in the village and set fire to the buildings. The soldiers committed many atrocities, torturing their victims before killing them. Not even children and infants were spared, nor did the aged escape a fearful fate. Stomachs of the children were cut open and their eyes pierced, and women suffered the loss of their breasts and their tongues which were cut off by the sadists. Several persons were thrown into the flames. The whole village was completely plundered. The Red Polish troops seized seventeen horses, thirty-four cows, and other livestock. On March 28, 1946, the same village was again seized by the same battalion of the Red Polish Army. The battalion commander addressed the people gathered in the village square near the schoolhouse, and declared that he would have everyone shot who refused to leave for the USSR. Then he chose eleven men and ordered them to be shot before the eyes of the crowd. The third assault on the same village was made on April 13, 1946, and further inhabitants were shot while fleeing to the woods. Finally, on April 30, 1946, the whole population of this village was forcibly evicted and brought to the railway station at Zahiria to be transported to the USSR. Such was the sad story of one Ukrainian village in this area, and such was the story of many other villages west of the Curzon Line.

It is evident that the UPA was forced to defend the population. Reinforcements came from Ukraine and the fighting became fierce in this area. On March 29, 1948, one of the leading Red Polish generals, Vice-Minister of War Gen. Walter Swierczewski, fell in the fight with the Ukrainian insurgents. He was inspecting the Red Polish troops in the area of the Soviet-Polish frontier and was killed in an ambush near the town of Baligrod. The assassination of Gen. Swierczewski was an indication that the activities of the UPA had increased to such a degree that they were becoming dangerous for the Soviet Union and its satellites.

At this point it is important to note that Gen. Walter Swierczewski was the

fourth prominent enemy leader killed in action with the UPA. The first was the
SA commander Lutze; the second was Soviet Marshal Vatutin, who was mortally
wounded in an UPA ambush in Northern Volhynia in 1944; and the third was
Col. Gen. Moskalenko, who was killed in 1946.

The assassination forced the Soviet Union, Poland, and Czechoslovakia to
conclude a tripartite pact on May 12, 1947, aiming by mutual aid to wipe out
UPA-West, which operated in regions near the borders of these countries.
Special forces were brought into action against the Ukrainian insurgents, but
they could not break the resistance of the UPA. The Supreme Command of the
UPA elaborated its own plan and accordingly divided the UPA-West into small
detachments. The main forces of the UPA-West broke the encirclement and
passed into Ukraine to continue their fight against Communist oppression.
Other detachments were ordered to raid Czechoslovakia, Hungary, and the
Balkans with the purpose of mobilizing the forces of the other subjugated
peoples in a united fight against Bolshevism. The complete removal of the
Ukrainian population either to the Soviet Union or to Eastern Prussia finally
forced the rest of the UPA detachments to abandon Southeastern Poland and to
transfer their action to Poland or Slovakia, where they found a sympathetic
element among the population. On the territory west of the Curzon Line only
small detachments were left for special purposes. They stayed out the winter
and, by the summer of 1949, had forced their way across Poland and Czechoslovakia into the US Zone of Germany.

On the occasion of the 5th Anniversary of the UPA, Gen. Taras Chuprynka,
the Commander-in-Chief of the UPA, issued an order which we give here in full:

FIGHTERS AND COMMANDERS OF THE UPA!
MEMBERS OF THE URM!

Five years have passed since Ostap, a member of the OUN, began setting up
armed groups for the struggle against the occupiers of Ukraine. These small groups,
fighting simultaneously against the Nazi Germans and the Red Partisans, founded a
new form of struggle—a liberating revolutionary movement—the Ukrainian Insurgent Army (UPA). In a few months this movement spread to the whole of Polissia,
Volhynia, Galicia, and Pravoberezzhia. The year of 1943 and the first half of 1944
are marked by the struggle of the UPA on two fronts. On the anti-Nazi front the
UPA stopped the mass deportation of the Ukrainians for slave labor to Germany and
made impossible the economic plundering of the people. On the anti-Bolshevik
front the UPA prevented infiltration of Red partisan units into Ukrainian territory.
It was the UPA that, in a series of victorious battles, defeated the hordes of Stalinist
Huns that were sweeping in from the Northeast to conquer Europe.

Dauntless commanders and fighters of the UPA have inscribed on their banners a
series of feats of arms that will be entered in golden letters in the annals of the
Ukrainian Army. Repeatedly the units of the UPA stormed the enemy administration centers, forced their way into provincial centers, and by far-reaching raids
ranged through their own and foreign territories. They harassed the enemies by
ambushes and invasions and prevented them from realizing their plans of exterminating the Ukrainian people. The names of Hrehit-Rizun, Yastrub, Yasen, Stor-

chan, Prut, Konyk, Peremoha, and Khrin have spread the glory of Ukrainian arms beyond the borders of Ukraine.

But in the field of politics, the UPA also achieved great results. Acting according to the slogan "liberty to peoples, freedom to the individual" it organized, as early as 1944, national units of Azerbaidzhanis, Georgians, Turkestanis, and other peoples subjugated by Moscow, for the struggle to overthrow the Kremlin to establish independent states of all these nations in the East. On its initiatives, the Conference of the Enslaved Nations was called in November 1943. On the initiative of the UPA all Ukrainian independent parties united and established the Supreme Ukrainian Liberation Council that, since 1944, directs the whole struggle at home and abroad for the Independent United Ukrainian State. The UPA raids in Poland and in Slovakia filled the ranks with new allies from among the Poles and Slovaks.

The successes achieved by the UPA have surpassed the goals set for it by the Supreme Ukrainian Liberation Council and the whole Ukrainian nation. These successes have been achieved by the UPA under the most trying conditions.

Fighters and Commanders of the UPA!

You who today fight in the armed units against the Bolsheviks and you who have swelled the ranks of the liberation-revolutionary underground! Be aware that the five years of the heroic struggle of the UPA and of the liberation-revolutionary underground is the most heroic period of Ukrainian history. The history of mankind does not know such an heroic epoch. New Ukrainian generations will be taught about the heroism of the UPA and the liberation-revolutionary underground. The UPA fighter, the Ukrainian revolutionary, will replace the manly Spartan in the history of mankind. Be conscious, therefore, of the great epoch in which you live and do not put to shame the glory of the Ukrainian insurgent as they did not who have already fallen in the fight.

On today's festive day of the UPA, proudly look upon the past five years and remember with veneration all those who, by sacrificing their lives, have forged the New Epoch. On today's festive day look with Victory!

Long live the Supreme Ukrainian Liberation Council!

Eternal Glory to the Heroes who have given their lives for Ukraine!

> (Signed) Gen. Taras Chuprynka
> Commander-in-Chief
> Ukrainian Insurgent Army (UPA)

(This order is translated from the Ukrainian original which was reprinted in the pamphlet of the UPA Group "Bug" published in October 1947. Commander Ostap, mentioned in the order, a leading figure in the Ukrainian Insurgent Army (UPA), was reported killed in November 1948, in a battle with the Soviet MVD troops near Torchyn in the province of Volhynia.)

On September 25, 1947, in order to offset efforts of various Ukrainian political groups abroad claiming a preferred status in the Ukrainian Insurgent Army (UPA), Taras Chuprynka issued a declaration, published in the bulletin of the Central Propaganda and Information Center, in which he emphasized that the UPA was not associated with any political party, although the OUN headed by Stepan Bandera was most active in its formation. Gen. Chuprynka declared that the soldiers of the UPA were soldiers only, and were fighting for the abolition of foreign rule over the Ukrainians. The political arm of the UPA was the Supreme Ukrainian Liberation Council which has a membership of varied political directions.

The last major action of the Ukrainian Resistance Movement in Ukraine about which we know from original UPA reports was the action against large-scale deportations of Ukrainians which took place in October 1947 and in March-April 1949. Deportation is one of the most efficient methods in the practice of genocide by Soviet Russia. It was legally established in February 1930, when the Council of Peoples' Commissars authorized the local soviets to "take all necessary steps in the fight with the kulaks, including the confiscation of their property and their deportation from the region or district." Millions of Ukrainians were affected by this measure. In his latest book, *The Rape of Poland*, S. Mikolajczyk estimates the number of Ukrainians deported to various parts of the Soviet Union at around 10,000,000 people.

In order to understand the UPA anti-deportation measures, it is necessary to discuss the characteristics of the deportation and its techniques. First of all, the people were entered on the deportation lists. Then the villages were surrounded and the people arrested and taken to the assembly points and to the railway stations where the cattle trains were waiting for them. The people who in various ways avoided arrest were not troubled any further and were safe until the next deportation. The whole action took twenty-four hours. No information was given to the deportees about their destination.

Bearing this in mind, the Ukrainian Resistance Movement, with all its affiliates, realized the necessity of intensive intelligence work so that successful anti-deportation measures could be taken. Long before the planned deportations systematic observation by the security service (SS) were made at railway stations and information was disseminated and exchanged by various affiliations of the Ukrainian Resistance Movement. In addition, intensive intelligence work preceding the deportation was carried out by UPA scouts and informers within the rank-and-file of the Soviet administration.

The Ukrainian Resistance Movement divided the measures to be adopted against deportation into offensive action and passive defensive measures. The tasks of the offensive action were as follows: (a) demolition of bridges, roads, and railway tracks; (b) destruction of wire communications; (c) terrorization of Soviet collaborators and locally recruited Soviet auxiliary personnel; (d) surprise raids connected with freeing deportees and ambushing trains, columns, convoys, assembly and resting places, etc. Passive measures were designed to make the people avoid deportation by warning the people threatened and by hiding them in underground shelters prepared weeks in advance in woods and forests. In June 1948, the Ukrainian Resistance Movement issued an instruction telling the people how to behave in case of a large-scale deportation.

A report by Hanson W. Baldwin in *The New York Times* (May 15, 1949) disclosed that two divisions of Soviet troops in Ukraine and two in the Caucasus were aiding local police to combat anti-Communist guerrillas. From Ukrainian sources we know that the "guerrillas" made raids from mountain and forest hideouts to resist the large-scale deportations which took place in the spring of 1949. It is highly significant that the actions of the Ukrainian insurgents still required military countermeasures by the Soviets.

The activities of the UPA, despite the determined efforts of the Soviet Union and her subservient satellites to combat them, were formidable and strongly detrimental to Communism. The UPA constantly developed new guerrilla techniques; its detachments often changed their field of operation in order to carry out a given task, to secure supplies, or to evade discovery and prevent encirclements. Strict discipline on the march was maintained. Marches were generally at night, by routes known only to the local people, and from these routes they made their raids so that, before the Soviets could strike back, they had already returned to the forest. In their bases they not only had foxholes, but their deep bunkers were painstakingly built, four to ten meters underground, with storerooms, first aid stations, and shelters. Special troops of NKVD-MGB did not succeed. The insurgents had a splendid news and communication system. What happened one day somewhere in the country was known the next day in the distant headquarters in the forest bases. Collectives went up in flames with all their supplies and machines; the transports of the deportees were frequently attacked and the slave laborers set free. The Russian secret police was not in complete control, even on its own territory.

The Ukrainian Resistance Movement, in its seventh year, still kept steadfast to the same goal in its fight: *an independent, united Ukraine.*

The Ukrainian Review,
No. III, 1982, pp. 3-28

The Ukrainian Insurgent Army
(Part Three)

Ukrainians in their Struggle for Freedom

The Ukrainian Resistance Movement has manifested itself most markedly and powerfully during and since the last war. The fact that just after war had ended in West Europe there were several armed groups of the UPA operating under Bolshevik occupation attests to the determination of the Ukrainian people to fight against all forms of Russian aggression and persecution. The social and economic system imposed upon the freedom-loving Ukrainian people is naturally totally alien and abhorrent to them. Traditionally individualistic by nature and consequently opposed to Communism the Ukrainian has fought that system with all his might and power. Moreover, he rightly sees Bolshevism for what it actually is, just another facet of traditional Russian imperialism. For him freedom from Moscow and freedom from Communism are synonymous. And that is why the Soviet rule of terror and intimidation manifests itself most markedly in

Ukraine and why the Soviet policy follows closely the line of the old Russian imperialism in regard to Ukraine. Such a "solution" of the Ukrainian problem by the Russian has considerably inflamed anti-Russian feeling among the Ukrainians, and Soviet abuses and crimes inflicted upon the Ukrainian people have burned into their soul a hatred of the Bolsheviks and have made them irreconcilable enemies of Soviet Russia. The wholehearted support the UPA has received from all classes of the Ukrainian people is the best proof of such an attitude.

Simultaneously with the armed struggle, well-organized anti-Soviet action is being conducted in various sectors of life with one purpose: to undermine the Soviet system and its regime. The only way to the liberation of the Ukrainian people is the national liberation and anti-Bolshevik revolution of the whole Ukrainian nation in a common front with other nations enslaved by Bolshevism. This can only be reached by the revolutionary liberation struggle of the widest popular masses, by the intensifying and deepening of the revolutionary process with its final aim of a national uprising. Three hundred years ago such a revolutionary process among the Ukrainian masses led to the victorious uprising of the Ukrainian people against Polish rule. The Ukrainian "Cromwell"—Hetman Bohdan Khmelnytsky—was to establish a Ukrainian Cossack Republic (1648)! According to this line of thinking the revolutionary process has to saturate all spheres of life and counteract the hostile goals and efforts of Bolshevism with the ideals and aims of the liberation revolution and its principles of national-political, social-economic, and spiritual-cultural freedom of the people. This conception of liberty through revolution has been represented by the Ukrainian Resistance Movement since the very beginning of its existence and realized consistently in all situations. The basic element in this conception is the stress laid upon the struggle of the whole nation, of its broadest popular masses, and not solely upon its organized forces (OUN, UPA, UHVR), which are only the pioneers and directing force behind the revolutionary process. The degree of ripeness for the national liberation revolution depends, in the first place, on the degree to which it is possible to permeate the popular masses with revolutionary sentiments, on the enthusiasm of the masses for the cause of liberation, and finally on their willingness to fight actively against their oppressors.

The internal situation in the USSR was influenced by the imminence of renewed conflict with the Western bloc and the concrete possibility of a new war. The preparation for this new war in the USSR, which meant ever increasing military expenditures, led to poverty and to an unheard-of exploitation of the popular masses. In this context the regime increased its terror so that hatred and anti-Soviet feelings grew from day to day among the enslaved nations.

This dissatisfaction of the people, their extremely hostile attitude to Bolshevism, to the Government, and to the Party, as well as to its economic system and totalitarian order, has been growing steadily since the end of the last war. Many reasons have brought about this situation. Above all Bolshevik propaganda cannot claim that in countries surrounding the USSR people are suffering poverty, because the soldiers of the Red Army had the chance to see with their own eyes the true state of things and were able to spread this information all over the USSR. Furthermore, the ordinary population of the USSR expected that with the end of the war there would come changes, a greater freedom would be allowed, and living standards would rise. Bolshevik propaganda during the war encouraged these hopes and promised all kinds of marvels. Instead of "changes" for the better, however, loomed bitter disappointments. New five-year plans, new state loans, new social competitive campaigns—all signs that economic development was geared toward the preparation of a new war. The expected "evolution" of the regime has bogged down and what has resulted is the new privileged position of the Party and of the new Soviet aristocracy (generals, writers, engineers, etc.) along with the worst pauperization and exploitation of the broad masses. The communist doctrine has lost all credit in the eyes of the people.

The only way in which the Bolshevik system has been able to combat the solidarity of the non-Russian peoples has been through the use of unbridled terror campaigns involving unheard-of atrocities and a spy system which permeates all levels of life: the whole governmental setup, industry, the army, education, even family life and the Church. Spies and police agents are evil features of the Soviet state which give it its satanical strength. The first aim of the fight for national liberation has been to break the Soviet system of terror, as other factors of Soviet power are only the derivative products and branches of the terror and spy system. To combat the terrorist Soviet system and to change the hatred and passive hostility of the population into an active fight against the oppressors—in short, to destroy Bolshevism as a terrorist system—has been the chief aim of the Ukrainian Resistance Movement. Now, looking back after years of fighting against Bolshevism, we can say that it has had some success. The Ukrainian Resistance Movement has overcome the influence of Bolshevik terror and propaganda and made the Ukrainian masses conscious of their strength. Instead of just hating Bolshevism and waiting for its fall, the Ukrainian people have started fighting it with all their might to accelerate the revolutionary process.

It would be an utter fallacy to suppose that through social slogans alone the Russian people can be stirred to rebellion against their Communist regime. Bolshevism as a social phenomenon is deeply rooted in the mentality, social structure, and national tradition of the Russian people. Therefore, it is not surprising that within the span of thirty years of Soviet rule there was no mass resistance by the Russian people against their despotic government. Facts are stubborn things and once we rid ourselves of the myth of the homogeneity of the inhabitants of the Soviet Russian Empire, we clearly see that uprisings against the Soviet regime have been made by non-Russian peoples, notably by Ukrainians, Lithuanians, and by the peoples of the Caucasus and Turkestan—never by Russians.

Since the last war the dissatisfaction of the Ukrainian people and other enslaved peoples with Bolshevism has intensified on a national scale. The Bolshevik system has become more and more chauvinistic and has openly praised the "superiority" of the Russian people, to recall only Stalin's famous toast to the "Russian people" at a Kremlin banquet in May 1945, when he singled out "the Russian people" as the "most outstanding nation of the Soviet Union." The campaign for the russification of the non-Russian peoples has become more brutal. Bolshevik imperialism has become merely the latest and most virulent form of Russian imperialism. The last war has shown clearly that Ukraine as well as other non-Russian populations are hostile towards Bolshevism. Having the experience of the last war, Bolshevism is openly striving to strengthen Russian imperialism. For Ukraine and other non-Russian countries, this means the russi-fication of all sectors of life. Such a policy generates a great hatred towards Moscow among the enslaved peoples which is self-perpetuating. But this hatred is also the natural breeding ground for the development of the struggle for national liberation within the USSR.

Thus, the real goals of the UPA campaigns in Soviet-dominated Europe go far beyond the borders of Ukraine. Soviet totalitarian practices compel the enslaved peoples to fight the Soviet regime in underground organizations, because non-clandestine methods of opposing the Soviet regime under Soviet conditions are unthinkable. This truth was realized long ago by the Ukrainians, who have been fighting Bolshevik imperialism for the last thirty years. But this truth is just beginning to be realized by many other enslaved peoples, especially by the "satellite" countries and by the Baltic states. Ukraine, as the champion of the anti-Soviet fight, has thus gained many valuable allies behind the "Iron Curtain." The UPA, which during the war called on the peoples of the Soviet Union to fight with arms in their hands both against Hitler and Stalin, now finds support everywhere behind the "Iron Curtain," in Poland and in Slovakia, in Lithuania and Byelorussia, in East Prussia and in the Crimea. Following the historic tradi-tion of Ukrainian revolutionaries, it tries to organize a league of peoples oppressed by Soviet tyranny and to form a wide front of national underground armies fighting against Moscow. It is important always to remember that this is a struggle of ideas and that the nationalist movements among the enslaved peoples of the USSR constitute a most dynamic force. Therefore, the idea of national liberation is the most powerful weapon in the hand of these opponents of Soviet Russia. Surprisingly enough the democratic press of the Free World has given little—if any—attention to this significant fact.

On December 8, 1948, the International Press Bureau released a lengthy article dealing with the future map of Europe, which, according to the infor-mants of the Bureau, is being charted now by the oppressed peoples of Eastern Europe. The aspirations of many peoples are closely tied to the plans, accredited to General Taras Chuprynka, commander-in-chief of the UPA. This plan, which is said to be widely circulated inside the Soviet Union, aims at the transformation of the Soviet empire into a series of national independent states. What is known as the "Chuprynka Plan" is a far-reaching blueprint for the reorganization of Eastern Europe and Asia based on national self-determination of the enslaved peoples within the Soviet Union and the "satellite" states as the first and most important prerequisite of the "world of tomorrow..." which will be followed by the establishment of four principal state units as follows: (1) Siberia, (2) the Caucasus, (3) Turkestan, and (4) the Black Sea Unit. The importance of the latter for the "world of tomorrow" cannot be overemphasized. Economically, it would be a precious pearl in a future "United Europe." The cornerstone of the

Scandanavian-Black Sea Bloc—Ukraine—is the world's third largest producer of iron, fourth of coal, eighth of oil, and has the largest manganese mines in the world. It is a veritable "granary of Europe," and for generations has been a breadbasket for all Europe. And it is in Ukraine that a powerful anti-Soviet underground army, the UPA, waged a gallant fight for the realization of these ideas.

The Political Program of the Ukrainian Resistance Movement

The history of every people of the world reveals continuous efforts in seeking national self-determination and freedom. Many a bitter battle has been fought to free a given people from encroachment upon its human, economic, and political rights by more aggressive and stronger nations. In like manner, at the end of the First World War, the Russian Empire of the tsars was forced internally by her subjugated peoples to permit the creation of a series of national states on its ruins. In the throes of the civil war, the Russian Revolution (1917), various disenfranchised peoples declared in quick succession their national independence from Russian political domination and oppression. Democratic, free national states of Finland, Estonia, Latvia, Lithuania, Poland, Ukraine, Byelorussia, Georgia, Armenia, Azerbaidzhan, Siberia, and Turkestan, Cossacks of Don and Kuban, mountain people of Northern Caucasus, Tatars and Bashkirs of Idel-Ural—all declared themselves sovereign states, completely independent from Russia. It must be stressed here that during the Revolution the claim for freedom by subjugated and stateless people was repeatedly guaranteed and affirmed by the present regime of Soviet Russia.

Thus, nearly thirty years ago, a free Ukrainian state came into being, creating an independent state for a Slavic nation almost as large as France. This Ukrainian National Republic was recognized *de facto* by Great Britain and France, and *de jure* by Germany, Austro-Hungary, Bulgaria, Turkey, the Republic of the Don Cossacks, the Republic of the Kuban Cossacks, the Republic of the Northern Caucasian Mountaineers, Byelorussia, Georgia, the Russian Soviet Federated Socialist Republic, and Poland. When the freedom of this Ukrainian Republic was threatened by the Bolsheviks, the Ukrainian government under Otaman (Commander-in-Chief) Symon Petlura appealed in vain to the Western democracies for help, and Ukraine again fell under the iron rule of Moscow. The Baltic States, Finland, and Poland succeeded, with the aid of the Allies, in retaining their independence. Ukraine, the largest nation without statehood in Europe, with other smaller subjugated nations of Western Europe became in effect Russian colonies.

Again and again during the past thirty years the advocates of Ukrainian independence and the martyrs for Ukrainian freedom have brought to the world's attention the character of the intruding despotism that has wiped out every phase of Ukrainian liberty, murdered its leaders, starved its peasants by the millions, and deported millions of others to die in the Far East and North. In the face of all these tragic events the Western world has remained passive, silent, and indifferent.

Thus, the principal aim of the Ukrainian Resistance Movement is the overthrow of Bolshevism and the establishment of the new order in Central and Eastern Europe and Soviet Asia, based on the principle of self-determination of peoples, on independence and sovereignty of national states within their own borders, and on the idea of social justice and prosperity of the popular masses. The realization of this aim entails: (a) the partition of the USSR into national states established on their ethnic territories; (b) the restitution of national sovereignty to the "vassal" states of the USSR which were deprived of their sovereignty in the course of and after the Second World War. Furthermore, the realization of these aims calls for: (1) complete democratization of state and social life of nations, liberated from the Bolshevik yoke, (2) free choice of forms of government and of social and economic structures, and (3) assurance of free spiritual and cultural development for the peoples in question.

Such a solution alone can settle the rightful demands of all the nations concerned, can bring order to Central Europe and Eastern Europe and Soviet Asia, and help maintain peace in the entire world. Otherwise the entire political and economic structure of Europe and the world will again be based on fragile foundations, producing unrest among the peoples and inviting future invaders and "liberators" to disrupt the economic and political security of the world and endanger the durability of peace.

Fighting for the elimination of the totalitarian Stalinist government, for the overthrow of Bolshevism, for the extermination of the clique of Stalinist satraps, and for a truly progressive order in the whole of Central and Eastern Europe and Soviet Asia, the Ukrainian Resistance Movement realizes that a just social-economic order covering the interest of the broadest masses of population has the greatest importance for the realization of its aims in the future. The historical experience of our times shows that an unstable political order, shaky social-economic system, and low living standard of the population undermine the structure of any state and society. Therefore, the Ukrainian Resistance Movement fights for a Ukrainian State without exploiters or exploited, for a full participation of all citizens in civil liberties, and for all efforts of the government to be directed towards the raising of living standards. Economic democracy is clearly envisaged in the political program of the Ukrainian Resistance Movement. The best way to show it is to quote one of the proclamations widely spread throughout Ukraine by the Ukrainian Resistance Movement during the campaign against the Soviet elections of 1946. Here we reproduce it in its entirety translated from Ukrainian.

UKRAINIANS! AWAY WITH STALIN'S IMPERIALIST
TYRANNY!
Away with Stalin's imperialist tyranny!
Away with Stalin's compulsory election!
We will not go to vote for terrorism, plunder, imperialism, slavery, and tyranny, for hunger and misery!

We will go to democratic elections in a free and independent Ukrainian State!

UKRAINIANS! We will not go to vote for Stalin and his dictatorial party! We will not go to vote for the new Red bourgeoisie, for party exploiters, for the leeches of people's blood!

We will not go to vote for compulsory work for hunger pay, for Stakhanovization that wrings sweat and blood from the worker!

We will not go to vote for *kolkhozes*, for slavish work of the peasants, for the unheard-of exploitation and plunder of property, work, and blood of the workers and peasants!

We will not go to work for imprisonment, for concentration camps, for deportations to Siberia, for the burning of our villages by savage NKVD police guns, for maltreatment of the masses, or for the murders perpetrated daily by Stalin's police!

We will not go to vote for Moscow's sway over Ukraine. We will not go to vote for Moscow's sway over Byelorussia, Lithuania, Latvia, Finland, Poland, Romania, Bulgaria, and many other countries of Europe and Asia which have been occupied, by violence, through Red Muscovite imperialism!

We will not go to vote for new imperialist wars which bloody Stalinist imperialists are preparing!

We will not go to vote for those who betrayed and annihilated the ideals of the French Revolution concerning the rights of man, who betrayed and ruined Christian culture, who have been faithless to any ideals of Socialism!

Away with bloody Red Fascism—blood brother of German Nazism and terrorism!

Long live the freedom of human thought, religion, and speech! Long live freedom of the press, literature, art, and science, denied and ravaged by the totalitarian system of Bolshevism!

Long live freedom of assembly, freedom of criticism, freedom of political and parliamentary representatives of the peoples! Long live freedom of political, social, and professional organizations!

Long live free elections and democratic parliamentary governments, pushed aside and soiled under the Bolshevik regime!

Long live freedom of work! Long live the right of all workers to the products of their own work! Long live social justice, welfare, and happiness for all men!

Long live the Independent Sovereign Ukrainian State! Long live the Free States of all nations in a mutual alliance, friendship, and fraternity!

FREEDOM TO NATIONS! FREEDOM TO THE INDIVIDUAL! DEATH TO TYRANNY!

February, 1946

Ukrainian Insurgents.

Such is, in short, the political program of the Ukrainian Resistance Movement. In any case, it is certain that a democratic Ukraine will be able to cope more adequately with the problems of social, economic, political, and cultural needs for the benefit of her people than could any imaginable occupier ruling her by force. And, therefore, the Ukrainian Resistance Movement is fighting with all its might to destroy this force and to free the Ukrainian people from the yoke imposed on them by the foreign invaders.

The Territory of Ukraine under the Control of
the Ukrainian Resistance Movement

As a result of the Second World War almost all Ukrainian lands came under Soviet rule. Only little strips of Ukrainian territory remained in Poland, Slovakia, and Romania. The Ukrainian territory under Soviet rule in Europe comprised 330,000 square miles with a population according to the census of 1939 of 50,000,000. The Ukrainian Soviet Socialist Republic is only a part of Ukraine, ethnographically speaking. It has an area of 220,000 square miles with a population of 40,000,000 (in 1939). Situated in the southwest of the USSR, bordered in the south by the north coasts of the Black Sea and Azov Sea, on the east by the region which adjoins the Don River, and on the west by the northeastern slopes of the Carpathian Mountains and by the San River, it merges almost imperceptibly into Russia on the north. Ukraine has a fertile soil, a mild, humid climate, and rich mineral deposits such as coal, iron ore, manganese, salts, and oil. During World War II the problem of drawing Ukraine's western frontier arose and was discussed at the Conference of Teheran (November 1943). At the Crimea (Yalta) Conference (February 1945) Roosevelt, Churchill, and Stalin agreed that "Poland's eastern frontier should be based on the Curzon Line, with qualifications in her [Poland's] favor." This was a slight sacrifice of territory from the Russian-German (Molotov-Ribbentrop) partition of 1939. As a result, more than 1,000,000 Ukrainians found themselves under Polish rule. On August 15, 1945, Russia and Poland signed a boundary agreement in which Russia conceded to Poland modifications of from three to five miles east of the Curzon Line in some areas. Another agreement provided for exchanges of population between Poland and Ukraine.

The Ukrainian Soviet Socialist Republic, which in the spring of 1945 was formally accepted at the Conference in San Francisco as a member of the United Nations, is theoretically an independent state within the framework of the Soviet Union. Although it is called a separate republic, Ukraine does not enjoy liberty of action, because the most important political, economic, and cultural decisions concerning Ukraine and other constituent Soviet republics as well as so-called "satellite" states are invariably made by the authorities in the central Moscow administration.

As might be expected, over such a large area as Ukraine one finds a considerable variety of scenery and of climatic conditions. Apart from the ramparts of the Carpathians in the west and the Crimean Mountains in the south, Ukraine is a level country, gently rolling in some provinces. In the east and south there is a predominance of the open steppe type of landscape, reminiscent of many stretches in the Middle West of the United States. Ukraine is poor in forests (12 percent) and for that reason presents extremely disadvantageous conditions for guerrilla warfare, but regions more suitable for such purposes lie in Western Ukraine—the marshy forest of Polissia and of northern Volhynia, north of Kyiv and Zhytomyr and in the Carpathian Mountains. However, the Carpathian Mountains, with their gentle slopes, broad valleys, and thin forests cannot be compared with the natural "fortresses" of the Alps. Occupied by Russian tsarist troops in 1914, and by the Red Army in 1944, the Carpathian Mountains do not represent any serious obstacle to a great army. Moreover, these mountains are quite accessible to light troops directed against guerrillas.

At its peak, the Ukrainian Resistance Movement controlled an area of nearly 100,000 square miles, with a population of more than 15,000,000 inhabitants. In this area the Russians were forced to retire leaving strong garrisons in large towns and administrative centers of the *rayons* (subdivisions of a province). The network of the Ukrainian Resistance Movement embraced all the urban and rural places of this territory, with its resistance groups and armed UPA units in each region. The underground had its own system of administration protected by armed guerrillas, its own security service with secret informers in the ranks of the Soviet army and police, and numerous other varieties of resistance cells. It included the area of Polissia (the province of Pinsk, Byelorussian Soviet Socialist Republic), Volhynia (the provinces of Rivne and Volhynia), the Subcarpathian area (the provinces of Ivano-Frankivske and Drohobych) and Bukovyna (the province of Chernivtsi). The Ukrainian Resistance Movement had partly spread over Carpatho-Ukraine, Galicia (the province of Lviv), Podilia (the provinces of Ternopil, Kaminets-Podilsky, Vynnytsia), and the province of Zhytomyr. UPA activities also spread to the mountains of the Crimea. The woods and forests north of Kyiv and in the district of Chernihiv at one stage were reported to be full of Red Army deserters and other anti-Bolshevik elements. The wilderness of Bialowieza, in the frontier region of Poland, Lithuania, Byelorussia, and Ukraine, is the spot where more than once meetings of guerrilla groups of different underground armies were held. On Ukrainian territories to the west of the Curzon Line UPA activities were carried out up to the middle of 1947.

The Ukrainian Resistance Movement tried persistently to expand its activities to include all of Eastern Ukraine with its unfavorable terrain for guerrilla activities. The area comprises a belt of steppes, wide expanses of level, rolling country completely deforested, with a very sparse population. There, the Ukrainian Resistance Movement constantly tried to organize underground resistance cells in the urban industrial centers. It succeeded in establishing its groups in this area, because many young West Ukrainians were recruited to work in the Donets coal mines and Zaporizhia iron works. Banishment to forced labor has all too often been the fate of Ukrainians, but this latest drive was a big opportunity for the Ukrainian Resistance Movement, which sent many of its members to this area as labor "volunteers." As a result, the Ukrainian Resistance Movement established strong cells in Donetsk, Makiyivk, Dnipropetrovsk, Nikopol, Dniprodzerzhynsk, Zaporizhia, Mykolayiv, Kryvy Rih, and Odessa. Along with resistance cells, underground religious communities were organized in this area, and "God's underground" is widely spreading all over Ukraine. Among the local population of this industrial area the Ukrainian Resistance Movement received wholehearted support and gained devoted and enthusiastic followers.

Ukrainian insurgents operating in Ukraine and launching raids into neighboring countries were the only insurgents in Europe who did not receive supplies from the air. They could get their arms and ammunition only from their enemies by disarming enemy detachments and by assaulting enemy military transports. The only support the Ukrainian partisans have ever had in their fight is the full support of the whole Ukrainian population. This support far exceeds any haphazard type of aid. It is no exaggeration to say that because of this support, the Ukrainian Resistance Movement was repeatedly able to survive all the offensives, raids, and blockades of the Bolsheviks during large-scale actions against the UPA after the end of the last war.

The Forces of the Ukrainian Resistance Movement and their Organizations

It would be an utter fallacy to think of the Ukrainian Resistance Movement as if it were only the armed battle groups of the UPA. In fact, the Ukrainian Resistance Movement consists of diverse units and forms a widespread underground organization, based chiefly on the political network of the OUN.

The Ukrainian nationalist underground has existed on Ukrainian soil for over fifty years. In spite of the fact that the Russians and Nazis referred to the OUN as a "fascist" or "terrorist" organization, or even a "subversive movement," because its existence threatened the fruition of their plans, it is a political and military organization of Ukrainian patriots who strive for the liberation of Ukraine and for Ukrainian statehood. If it uses "subversive" methods, it is for the sole reason that there are no possible legal methods by which a struggle for independence can be conducted in Russia. As a clandestine organization it must operate according to the best principles of conspiracy and adopt military procedure within its organization.

The OUN was born long before "fascism" or "Hitlerism" appeared in Europe. The OUN's first predecessor was the Revolutionary Ukrainian Party (RUP), an underground Ukrainian political organization which was founded by an ardent Ukrainian patriot, Mykola Mikhnovsky, in 1902. Its successor was the Ukrainian Military Organization (UVO), which came into being after the fall of the Ukrainian National Republic in 1921. The UVO was founded by the officers and soldiers of the Ukrainian Army who decided to continue to struggle for independence. Headed by the late Col. Evhen Konovalets, a former Ukrainian army corps commander, it gradually changed its character from that of a military organization and widened its activities, becoming an illegal political organization. At the First Congress of Ukrainian Nationalists in Prague in 1929, the Organization of the Ukrainian Nationalists came into being, the successor of the UVO. It was led by Col. Konovalets until the day of his death in 1938.

Faithful to the motto of OUN—"You will secure Ukrainian statehood, or die fighting for it"—the Ukrainian patriots who joined the OUN declared war on the enemies of the Ukrainian independence. It was the OUN which organized the first serious opposition to Hitler's plans in Eastern Europe. As early as 1939, the OUN put up a stern opposition to the advancing Hungarian army in Carpatho-Ukraine. In 1941, the OUN gave birth to the UPA, which in the beginning consisted only of the combat groups of the OUN. Because it was the sole political organization of the Ukrainian people which was active under German and Russian occupation of Ukraine, it appealed to the Ukrainian people to join the struggle for independence against the German and Russian occupiers. The Ukrainian people answered the appeal of the OUN and the ranks of the UPA swelled with Ukrainian peasants, workers, and intellectuals who took up arms to rid Ukraine of Germans and Russians. In this manner, the UPA became the armed organization of the whole Ukrainian people.

Since it consisted of true Ukrainian patriots, the OUN in Ukraine never had any monopolistic tendencies, and when, as a result of the widening revolutionary process in Ukraine, the UHVR came into being in 1944, the OUN participated in its creation by sending a delegation to the Ukrainian National Congress. The OUN subordinated its activities to the direction of the elected Council and General Secretariat of UHVR and follows its directives. Within the Ukrainian Resistance Movement the OUN holds the responsibility for special branches and services and is a unit of the Movement in Ukraine.

Besides its political activities, the OUN became the quartermaster of the Ukrainian Resistance Movement, responsible for the regular delivery of required supplies to all units at stipulated times and places. It supplied the Ukrainian Resistance Movement not only with money, food, clothing, war matériel, and other supplies, but also with trained men. It was responsible for all communications to headquarters and other units on a similar level. It looked for the necessary contacts between the different units of the Ukrainian Resistance Movement and prepared shelters and underground bunkers for the winter quarters of the resistance fighters as well as underground shelters for special purposes. It supplied combat troops with all the ordnance stores that they may have required, and recovered and repaired their equipment. It also had the responsibility for the provision of laundry service, for decontamination of clothing, and for protecting the units and installations of the Ukrainian Resistance Movement from enemy attack. It maintained depots, workshops, ammunition depots, and small factories for soap, leather, tanneries, etc. It provided for the transportation of the supplies needed by different units of the Ukrainian Resistance Movement. It was concerned with personnel, which included recruiting, training (political and ideological), organization, administration, discipline, and welfare.

The political credo of the OUN remains the same as it was during the Nazi occupation. It is fighting for a free and democratic, independent Ukrainian state, for the destruction of Bolshevik exploitation and the slave labor system, for the liberation of the Ukrainian peasant, worker, and intellectual from political and social-economic slavery, for freedom of the press, of expression, of religion, and for free cultural progress unhampered by Stalinist dictatorship. Through its tireless counterpropaganda the OUN explained to the peasants, workers, and professional intelligentsia the unbridgeable chasm between the ideals propagated by the Bolsheviks and their application under existing Soviet conditions. It trained Ukrainians in anti-Soviet methods and reminded the Ukrainians by propaganda in the underground press and by word of mouth of the nature of Bolshevism and its aim towards Ukraine and towards the rest of the world. It tried to unite all the oppressed peoples of Eastern Europe in a common front against Bolshevism and to prepare them for an all-out anti-Russian and anti-Communist uprising when the opportune time would arrive.

The widening scope of these activities was possible because the OUN had a widespread underground organization of its own in the country for years. Long after the war was finished in Europe, the widely dispersed and well-concealed network of the OUN still existed in close cooperation with the UPA and embraced wide territories in Ukraine.

In addition to the territorial organization of the OUN, the Ukrainian Resistance Movement controlled such important services as the "Security Service" (SB), "Ukrainian Red Cross" (UCK), "Propaganda Service," and "Technical Service" (TZ) which had an autonomy of their own within the framework of the Ukrainian Resistance Movement.

The Security Service of the Ukrainian Resistance Movement (SB) was the most effective service and was composed of the best underground fighters. It was very well organized and did the Soviets much harm by its activities. It succeeded in organizing a network of its collaborators among Soviet officials as well as among Soviet army and police forces. It was the sector of the Ukrainian Resistance Movement which was most hated by the Soviet occupation administration. This is evident in an article entitled "Nationalist Phantoms" published on August 14, 1946, in the Soviet-Ukrainian official newspaper *Radyanska Ukraina* ("Soviet Ukraine"). The author of this article stated frankly that the fight against Ukrainian nationalists was very difficult, because the latter were "masters of masquerade" and had a "security service" of their own which consisted of the most experienced "bandits." In addition, they had their own "propaganda" based on the ideology of publications of Professors Mykhailo Hrushevsky and Serhiy Yefremov (Ukrainian scholars "liquidated" by the Soviets).

Another statement concerning the Ukrainian SB was included in the "manifesto" of Premier Khrushchev and NKVD General Ryassny to the Ukrainian Insurgents and SB men. They stated that the "criminal" and "dangerous" SB held the troops and civilian population in strong control. Another statement was included in the secret order of the chief of the MGB (political police) of the province of Drohobych (Western Ukraine), General Saburov. He stated that the SB was "a very dangerous organization," that it had adopted the "Hitlerite methods of provocation" and tried "to fight insubordination and desertion with all its forces." Gen. Saburov asked for the "constant vigilance" of his subalterns and instructed them as to the "methods of combatting SB activities."

The "Ukrainian Red Cross" provided the medical service in the Ukrainian Resistance Movement. Under its jurisdiction were the various nursing services, the evacuation, care, and treatment of sick or injured resistance fighters, advice on measures to insure the health of troops and population, supply and replenishment of medical equipment, and supply and organization of field ambulances for the UPA. It mobilized girls and trained them as nurses for the UPA, organized the underground hospitals and cared for wounded and sick soldiers of the UPA. The underground hospitals of the UPA became famous throughout the world. The Red Polish newspaper *Glos Ludu* ("People's Voice") wrote about one of these hospitals in June 1947: "Recently an underground hospital was discovered in a forest. There was nothing seen on the surface but trees and grass. Ten meters under the ground there was a hospital with corridors, operating rooms, infirmaries, beds, and medical equipment. When the hospital was discovered, the doctors and the nurses defended themselves heroically and committed suicide when their ammunition came to an end." The correspondent of the Polish Communist newspaper ended his article by saying: "Nobody on the surface heard anything of this underground tragedy of men and women...who showed a ferocious fanaticism and strange heroism." Another description of such a hospital we find in *Le Phare* (Brussels) in the issue of July 10/11, 1948, and in the *Times* (London) of June 20, 1947. The role of Jewish doctors must be emphasized here. During the German occupation of Ukraine, the Ukrainian Resistance Movement mobilized many Jewish doctors, pharmacists, and nurses into its service, in this way saving their lives. When the Bolsheviks reoccupied Ukraine, Jewish doctors and nurses continued to serve with the Ukrainian Resistance Movement. Many Jewish doctors and nurses sacrificed their lives in the fight against the Nazi and Soviet occupiers of Ukraine. A Jewish doctor called Kum died as a hero in the defense of the field hospital which had been in his care for more than two years, in Trukhaniv in the Carpathians (1945). Another Jewish doctor, Maksymovich, committed suicide when facing the destruction of his field ambulance in the Carpathians.

The Ukrainian Resistance Movement had developed a very good propaganda service of its own. Every detachment of the UPA, as well as each unit of the territorial organization, had its own propagandist who was responsible for the propaganda service and propaganda activities in the area where it operated. All those propagandists followed the directives of the "Propaganda Center," which was located somewhere in Ukraine. The "Propaganda Center" had its printing presses where the press organs, periodicals, and leaflets were printed. There were many underground periodicals in Ukraine. The leading journal of the Organization of the Ukrainian Nationalists was *Ideya i Chyn* ("Idea and Action"). Others included the journal of the UPA, *Povstanets* ("The Insurgent"); the journal of the UHVR, *Samostiynist* ("Independence"); the humorous bulletin *Perets* ("Pepper"); the popular information bulletin *Informaciini Visti* ("Information News"); and *Lisovyk* ("The Man of the Forest"). It is interesting to note that Ostap Vyshnya, once the outstanding Ukrainian satirist and author of *Usmishky* ("Smiles"), who was banished to Siberia in the thirties, was brought back in 1945 to Ukraine to combat the widespread Ukrainian underground satirical pamphleteering. Because the Ukrainian illegal satirical magazine *Pepper* was very popular in Ukraine, the Soviet Government founded a magazine called *The Red Pepper* in Kyiv and Vyshnya was put in charge of it. Apparently, he did not justify Communist Party hopes, since the Union of Ukrainian Writers, an official Soviet organization, upon the order of the Poltiburo, charged that *Red Pepper* was "substituting spite and vulgarity for popular humor."

The underground propaganda network quickly disseminated all available information by means of a whispered propaganda technique which was used frequently. In addition, letters, newspapers, bulletins, poster slogans, and pamphlets were printed and distributed chiefly in urban centers where military garrisons were stationed. Propaganda to the Soviet Army was considered especially important. Material which was small in size and easily distributed was used when the Soviet Army units carried out roundups and blockades against the UPA. Slogans like "Do you want to go on starving?", "Do you know what the fight is for?" or "Down with Stalin's tyranny" were used, and had a strong influence upon the morale of Soviet Army soldiers. The Ukrainian Resistance Movement published thousands of leaflets calling Soviet Army officers and soldiers to a common struggle against Stalin's tyranny. It spoke to them with a profound knowledge of the terrible conditions of life under the Soviet regime. "With the overthrow of Hitler," wrote the UPA in its proclamation to the Red Army in 1946, "only dictator-imperialists have changed their positions. Nothing has changed in the conditions of the people, of the working masses. Oppression, exploitation, and terror go on." After this statement the UPA concluded: "Your fight for the victory of justice has not ended yet. You will end it if you overthrow the dictatorial-terroristic exploitive system of the greatest foe of the people, Stalin's Government, and his gang of exploiters, the Communist Party. Let us undermine the Stalinist system from within...."

A book by Mykola Lebed which was published in Ukrainian about the origin, growth, and activity of the UPA reprinted the texts of various appeals which were addressed to the Georgians, Armenians, Cossacks, Volga Tatars, and other non-Russian nationalities. Each text was adapted to the grievances and historical background of the people concerned. Some leaflets were printed in Russian, others in the original language of the people concerned, using appropriate type faces. During raids in Poland or Czechoslovakia, leaflets in the Polish, Czech, and Slovak languages were issued by the thousands, summoning the peoples to fight against the common oppressors. The appeals concluded: "We shall fight for the Ukrainian independent state and for the independent states of all the peoples whom the Bolshevik hangmen have enslaved.... The peoples of Europe do not want Hitlerism or Stalinism.... Long live the revolution of the oppressed peoples! Long live the sovereign states of all peoples! Long live peace and friendship of peoples!"

There were different methods of distributing propaganda material. In the urban centers propaganda material reduced in size was put into letter boxes or into coats or other garments in restaurants and cafes, and into books and magazines in public libraries. Other material of a similar small size was sent by post. In some cases Soviet officials were taken prisoner and then set free after being given intensive orientation and having been provided with propaganda literature. Other persons from the Soviet administration were selected and approached individually. In some cases meetings for the population were organized, and different points of the Soviet propaganda line were attacked. Theater performances and concerts for the Ukrainian population were organized by a special propaganda group called the "Flying Stage" under the protection of the UPA.

The revolutionary formations of the UPA and OUN paid very great attention to the fight in the economic sector. Slogans against Stalin's Five-Year Plan were spread everywhere in Ukraine and the anti-democratic and parasitical character of it was shown. The slogans of the Ukrainian Resistance Movement called for the fight against the exploitation of the peasants and workers, for social justice, for higher living standards, and for independence. Here we quote some appeals of the Ukrainian Resistance Movement:

"Working People! In the fourth Five-Year Plan the Stalinist parasites have made only airplanes, guns, and tanks, but nothing you may need in your daily life! Make no preparation for war! Fight for real peace and a higher standard of living! Down with Stalin's imperialism!"

"Working People! Down with the inverted declarations of Stalin about the transition to Communism! We do not want to be deceived by boasting about the construction of socialism. We want a free and good life! We want to fight against the Bolshevik exploitation! Down with Stalin's parasites!"

"Workers! Stalin's parasites ordered the Trade Unions to organize a new socialistic Stakhanovite contest! Down with the Stalinist Trade Unions! Down with this tool in the hands of the Stalin clique to exploit the working class! Death to the commissars of the Stalin Trade Unions! Let the real workers be the leaders of the Trade Unions! We want to fight for real democracy in the Trade Unions!"

"Farmers of the *kolkhozes*! The Stalinist parasites enjoy life by means of your products, while you suffer from starvation! Take the products for yourselves, for you are the producers. Take your own bread! Chase away the guards of the *kolkhoz* grain! Kill the active agents of the NKVD and their spies!"

"Workers of Ukraine! The fourth Five-Year Plan is a preparation for a new war aimed at the suppression of other peoples of the world! We do not want to die for Stalin's imperialistic interests! Fight all of Stalin's plans wherever you can! The sooner that the Stalinist empire collapses the better for you! Long live the fight of the Ukrainian people for their independent state! Long live the freedom of the peoples and the freedom of the individual!"

The leaflets of the Ukrainian Resistance Movement were spread all over the Soviet Union. Often they were printed on field-presses with handmade wooden type. Often they had artistic engravings which conveyed more than the contents of the leaflets.

The propaganda of the Ukrainian Resistance Movement classified it not only as a "subversive organization" but also as a most important political force behind the Iron Curtain.

The Technical Service (TZ) operated the underground presses, prepared leaflets, printed materials, stored explosives, mined terrain, and carried out the demolition of bridges, railway tracks, buildings, and railway trains carrying supplies and war matériel, and, at the time of the German occupation, operated the underground radio stations. It directed the famous "Insurgents V1," which so brilliantly demolished the garrisons of the Russian NKVD and Polish UB in the battle of Hrubeshiv, on May 27 and 28, 1946. This was a joint Polish-Ukrainian underground action in which the troops of VIN (Freedom and Independence), the Polish underground organization, participated alongside the troops of the UPA. The action ended with the seizure of Hrubeshiv. As we said, the Ukrainian "Insurgent V1" completely demolished the buildings where the Soviet NKVD and Polish UB troops were garrisoned, causing many casualties.

This "Insurgent V1" was simply a 28/32 cm. wooden rocket launcher of the German Army which could fire high-explosive 28-mm. rockets or incendiary 320-mm. rockets. This rocket launcher and more than a hundred rockets were captured during the retreat of the German Army from Ukraine. Among the other duties of the Technical Service was the preparation of false documents and other identification papers.

Having the territorial organization of the OUN as its chief base, the UPA carried out its operations throughout Ukraine and far beyond its borders. The troops of the UPA were organized into operative groups with group commanders and their staffs. The groups were divided into sectors with sector commanders and staffs. The sectors were divided into detachments, the detachments into subdetachments, and the subdetachments into squads. Each detachment had its own area of activity and the borders of its territory were crossed only in exceptional cases and only on the order of the group or sector command.

The strength of UPA forces was a secret and it is impossible to give its numerical strength. Alfred Berzins, a former public affairs minister of Latvia, and former President of the Anti-Bolshevik Bloc of Nations (ABN), estimated it in the Washington *Times Herald*, July 18, 1949, at 20,000 armed men, at the same time estimating the strength of the partisans operating in the Baltic states of Estonia, Latvia, and Lithuania at 8,000 men. In due course, however, the number and strength of the UPA detachments was reduced to a minimum, while the strength of the territorial organization of the OUN was increased. The main stress was then laid upon the expansion of the Ukrainian Resistance Movement to the East and upon propaganda activities, which absorbed most of the personnel. Once more the character of the Ukrainian Resistance Movement changed, losing its military character and becoming more political. Nowadays politics is the chief focus of the fight of the Ukrainian Resistance Movement.

All UPA activities were planned by the Supreme Command of the UPA. The Supreme Command was the main advisory body to the Supreme Commander on operations, intelligence, organization, supply, and general matters of UPA policy. It basically consisted of separate branches which covered all the proper staff and planning functions and which were groups under senior staff officers acting under supervision of a Chief of Staff.

The Ukrainian Review,
No. V, 1982, pp. 54-72

The Ukrainian Insurgent Army
(Part Four)

The Soviet Methods of Combatting the Ukrainian Resistance Movement

In the Soviet methods of fighting the Ukrainian Resistance Movement we must distinguish two factors: (a) an ideological-political fight against Ukrainian "nationalism" which gave birth to the Ukrainian Resistance Movement, and (b) an armed terrorist fight against the Ukrainian Resistance Movement itself.

In their ideological-political fight against Ukrainian nationalism, the Bolsheviks widely use (1) misinterpretation of historical facts concerning Ukrainian history and their unscientific explanation; (2) liquidation of all free centers of Ukrainian science by means of arrests, tortures, shootings, and deportation of scientific workers; (3) suppression of whole series of scholarly works that had already been published and destruction of works which were ready for publication; (4) terrorization of the Ukrainian scientific institutes and their workers.

In consequence of such measures, scientific and academic work in Ukraine lost its objectivity and its value and assumed the character of a pseudo-scientific service to aid political propaganda and governmental designs.

This is especially true of research in Ukrainian history. As early as 1930, Professor M. Hrushevsky, the head of the Department of History at the Ukrainian Academy of Science in Kyiv, and the creator of the modern historical school, was exiled. At the same time, many renowned historians, such as Slabchenko, Vasylenko, Hermaize, and Ponomarenko, were liquidated. After the reoccupation of Western Ukraine, such West Ukraine historians as Krypiakevych, Korduba, Terletsky, and many others were forced to make retractions and to say that they had been led onto "false nationalist paths" by Michael Hrushevsky. Ukrainian history is now to be written and taught according to Stalin's prescriptions of 1932, "How to write the history of the Soviet people." This new history of Ukraine has two characteristics. The first is its slanting of national affairs to the political line of the Communist Government of the Soviets. The second is adjusting this history to Marxist dialectics; it becomes interwoven with quotations from Marx, Engels, Lenin and Stalin. Thus, any historical work becomes simplified Communist literature, without any scientific value.

Because of this slant Soviet-Ukrainian historical books sharply diverge from the fundamental ideology of Ukrainian historians, outside the Soviet Union. Just as in the days of tsarist Russia, the Kyivan period of Ukrainian history now has to be treated as a period common to both Ukrainian and Russian history, although it is a historical fact that the Russians first made their appearance as a national entity during the 12th century, in the form of the embryonic Suzdal-Rostov principality, on the vast colonial stretches of the ancient Ukrainian Kyivan state. Ukrainian relations with Russia are presented either one-sidedly, or completely ignored if they are inimical and impossible to explain. The Treaty of Pereyaslav, 1654, concluded by Hetman Bohdan Khmelnytsky, is interpreted as one of "allegiance to the Muscovite Tsar," whereas in fact Khmelnytsky concluded a treaty of alliance with Muscovy with the provision that Ukraine retain her full independence in all internal and external affairs. Also, as during tsarist times, Ukrainian historical personages who endeavored to free Ukraine, such as the hetmans Vyhovsky, Doroshenko, and especially Mazepa, are politically anathematized. Hetman Ivan Mazepa, the nationalist who declared war against Russia, is regarded as a traitor and an enemy of the Ukrainian people. The same is said of *Otaman* Symon Petlura, the leader of the Ukrainian national forces in the Ukrainian War of Independence (1918-1921), and the Ukrainian struggle for independence is presented as the work of bourgeois elements opposing the interests of the workmen and peasants of Ukraine, although exactly the contrary was the case. The entire interpretation of Ukrainian history aims to show the paths along which Ukraine has been brought closer to Russia, under the tutelage of the Russians, playing the role of the "big brother" among the enslaved peoples—i.e., to the further enslavement of Ukraine.

After the reoccupation of Western Ukraine the Russians disbanded the Shevchenko Scientific Society at Lviv (which is now celebrating its seventy-fifth anniversary in emigration). For three-quarters of a century, since its foundation in 1873, it has been the outstanding center of Ukrainian scientific and scholarly work.

As to the Ukrainian language, Stalin was willing to allow its existence, but he made clear that all articles written in this language were to be approved by the "big brother" of the Ukrainians, the Russian people, and by the Supreme Politburo of the Communist Party sitting in Moscow and dictating the destiny of the entire Soviet Union. He made it clear that the culture of Ukraine was to be Communist-Russian culture, though expressed in Ukrainian.

Russian Communism is trying to attack the very soul of Ukraine. It is attacking not only the leaders but also the masses. It is trying to eradicate all those principles under which the Ukrainians, like other Christian peoples, have lived for nearly one thousand years. Yet the attack is failing for, apart from physical extermination, the spirit of the Ukrainians is unquenchable.

The attack of the Communist Party and its agencies on Ukrainian literature grew to tremendous proportions. It began with the distortion of the classics of Ukrainian literature. The fate of Shevchenko, the greatest national poet of Ukraine (1814-1861), is typical: with monotonous regularity, the Soviet critics stress his friendship with the Russian radicals of his day. They ignore his great works which emphasize the cultural differences and historical diversity of Russia and Ukraine. Such works as the *Rozryta mohyla* ("The Plundered Grave"), in which the poet dealt with the past of Ukraine and her relations with Russia, are entirely omitted and the poet is only shown as a foe of the old tsarist order, not a foe of Russian imperialism. The attack of the Russian Communists on Ukrainian literature culminated in the physical extermination of Ukrainian writers and critics. Ruthless terror conducted against Ukrainian literature from 1932 to 1939 and after the Second World War caused the death of hundreds of Ukrainian authors and critics. Among the Ukrainian writers executed we find talents honored and known not only in Ukraine, but throughout Europe.

At the 17th Congress of the Ukrainian Communist Party, Prime Minister

Khrushchev charged that Ukrainian Communists had failed "to organize widespread criticism of the hostile Ukrainian bourgeois nationalist ideology in literature and the press." He complained that "owing to this, there have been ideological mistakes and distortions, attempts to allow rebirth of the bourgeois nationalist concepts of the historian Hrushevsky and his school in some books and newspapers." At the meetings of the Union of Ukrainian Writers in Kyiv, several writers and editors were criticized and censured for spreading theories tainted with Ukrainian nationalism. They were accused of "propagating Ukrainian nationalist ideas alien to the Soviet ideology," according to the opinion of the Politboro. Furthermore, it was charged that in their books they had "ignored progressive leaders in Soviet literature, exaggerated the influence of Western European literature, and failed to emphasize the ties between Russian and Ukrainian literature." Several writers and poets were denounced for "forgetting fundamental ideological demands of the Party." L. Smiliansky was accused because he "openly contrasted the Ukrainian people and culture to the Russian people and culture." Another writer, A. Kundzich, was charged with spreading the idea of the "patriarchal self-generating origins of Ukraine's people and its culture." A woman writer, V. Cherednychenko, "idealized the remote past and distorted the life of the Soviet people." L. Kovalenko, I. Pilhuk, G. Lazarevsky, and Ostap Vyshnya, all critics, were severely criticized for "distorting" the actual conditions of Soviet life.

Premier Khrushchev's revelations, as well as all the criticisms and self-criticisms at the meetings of the Ukrainian writers and critics, show that, despite the policy of persecution and mass deportation, Ukrainians remain bitterly opposed to Stalin's regime and do not cease fighting for their liberation.

Another subversive tool of the ideological and political fight against the Ukrainian Resistance Movement is slander of it and its leaders throughout the Soviet Union and the whole world. By this means, the Russians aim to undermine the confidence of the Ukrainian people and the whole world in the Ukrainian Resistance Movement. In their written and oral propaganda against the Ukrainian Resistance Movement, the Bolsheviks speak of an "independent" Ukraine as a "German" or an "Austrian" intrigue to divide "indivisible Russia." Therefore, they speak of "Ukrainian-German" nationalists as Nazi-German "collaborators" and "traitors" who "sold Ukraine to Germans." In speaking to the Western world the Bolsheviks maintain that the UPA is composed of "armed terrorist gangs which raid and pillage the villages and murder their population," or that they are "fascists," "Red Army deserters," a "Vlasov army," or other "criminal elements." Even the Minister of the Ukrainian SSR, Mr. D. Manuilsky, in his address delivered at the Conference of teachers of Western Ukraine on January 6, 1945 (i.e., on Christmas Eve according to the Greek-Catholic rite!) maintained that the UPA had "staged massacres of the Ukrainian population, committed atrocious crimes, tortures, and murders, forced Ukrainians into German slavery, and had deceived the Ukrainian people by saying that they had gone underground to struggle against the Germans."

The UPA and the Ukrainian Resistance Movement are now no longer called the "hirelings of German Nazi fascists" but rather "spies" and "diversionists" either of the Vatican or of "American warmongers." The term "Ukrainian-German" nationalists has disappeared from the Soviet press and, gradually, has changed to "Ukrainian-American" nationalists. The Soviets are attempting to convince the population at large that the UPA has entered the "service of American fascists." In January 1948, at the celebration of the "Thirtieth Anniversary" of their bloody and barbarous conquest of Ukraine, Premier Khrushchev delivered a lengthy harangue against the Ukrainian Resistance Movement, and, of course, against the United States and Great Britain in the presence of Molotov who himself had been dispatched by the Kremlin to deliver "a message of friendship" to the Ukrainian people from Stalin. Khrushchev claimed that the USA and Great Britain were actively supporting the Ukrainian underground. After admitting that the Ukrainian Resistance Movement had been giving some serious trouble to the MVD-MGB and the entire Soviet administration in Ukraine, Khrushchev called upon the Ukrainians themselves to "exterminate" the Ukrainian nationalist elements, "lackeys of the Anglo-Saxon powers, the worst enemies of democracy and humanity."

The last appellation—"lackeys of the Anglo-Saxon powers"—is significant because of the time as well as the linking of the USA and Great Britain with the Ukrainian underground. First, it becomes evident that the opposition against the totalitarian power of Soviet Russia in Ukraine was not negligible; second, the Russians apparently intended to identify the Ukrainian Resistance Movement with the United States and Great Britain, which had become their leading enemies in the Russian hate campaign against the West.

It is extremely disturbing to note the degree to which the Russians have succeeded with their propaganda. Ukrainian insurgents, these ordinary people, akin to American Revolutionary heroes, have been accepted as "bandits," "fascist hirelings," "SS-members," etc., by certain organs of the Western democratic press. In this case the Western pressmen have swallowed not only the Red baited hook, but also the line and sinker.

The truth is one and it is "indivisible." The truth is, the Ukrainians are now fighting for those ideals which are common to the whole Western civilized world and this is the chief reason for such hate propaganda against them by the Soviet "super-democrats" of Moscow.

In their armed, terroristic fight against the Ukrainian Resistance Movement and its armed branches, the UPA, the Bolsheviks applied the following measures: (a) broad actions carried out by the army and police troops supported by artillery, tanks, and airplanes against the UPA units; (b) the garrisoning and prolonged blockading of villages and woods in the insurgent territories; (c) sudden round-ups in villages and woods; (d) the deforestation of the country by the burning of the forests; (e) the use of bacteriological warfare; (f) the planned starvation of the Ukrainian population; (g) the public torturing and murdering of the Ukrainian insurgents and their relatives, as well as the murdering of the Ukrainian population; (h) the organization of a spy system and of a network of *agents-provocateurs*: (i) the organization of special gangs for fighting the UPA; (j) the forcible deportation of the population to Siberian and Kazakh deserts; (k) the economic pillaging of the population; (l) the amnesty and propaganda campaigns against the Ukrainian Resistance Movement.

During the spring and summer of 1944, the Red Army began advancing into insurgent territory. The Soviet commanders decided that they were sufficiently strong to deliver one sweeping *coup de grâce* to the Ukrainian Insurgent Army (UPA). Consequently, the Red commanders worked out an almost brilliant plan for combatting the UPA-North operating in Volhynia and Polissia. They aimed to divide it into two parts, separating it at the same time from the UPA-West and South. The Russians decided to start their first action against the UPA-North in April 1944, just after seizing this territory from the Germans. The Red Command thought that if one force could pin the UPA forces in the Polissia marshes, and the other could sweep around their left flank in the Kovel area, the chief mobile force consisting of 30,000 elite troops, largely cavalry and tanks, would encircle the main forces of the UPA-North in the Kremyanets area and capture or destroy them. The plan was carried out.

The proceedings of this action, which became a model for all future actions against the UPA, were as follows: First, the insurgent territory was saturated with spies weeks in advance. Then the troops were concentrated in the villages and woods in the vicinity of the targets. Strong reconnaissance troops were sent to find out the position of the enemy. The heavy equipment was moved up and the attack was opened. The woods and villages were advanced upon by the troops in skirmish line. The insurgent positions were attacked and the insurgents were pushed back into the waiting arms of the blocking forces called "bags."

The first action against the UPA-North began in April 1944 by blocking the Kovel area in Western Volhynia. Here two Red Army divisions were used in combatting the UPA and cutting it off from the front rear area. Another expedition force started blocking the access to the Polissia marshes in the north. Here another two divisions were used. The chief mobile force, consisting of three divisions supported from the air and two tank brigades, encircled the Kremyanets area in southern Volhynia in April 1944, aiming at the destruction of the main forces of the UPA-North, which had their base in this area. The action ended with a big battle at Hurby, on April 24, 1944. This battle ended with a partial victory for the Ukrainian insurgents. Around 5,000 UPA fighters were able to escape from the encirclement, inflicting on the attacking Soviet forces heavy casualties (at least 33 percent of the total strength of the Red infantry). However, the Ukrainian casualties were also very high. Many Ukrainians were either killed or wounded—for instance, Gen. A. Stupnytsky, chief of staff of the UPA, fell in this battle.

The UPA survived many actions of this kind. The first action against the UPA base in the Carpathians, the "Black Forest," was carried out by the same scheme using two Red divisions between the 1st and 4th of November, 1944. This attack was forced back by forces of the "Black Forest" base causing the attackers heavy casualties. Immediately all *rayon* centers in the vicinity of the "Black Forest" were attacked by the advancing insurgent units. Also unsuccessful was the attack of one Red Army division and of numerous police troops against the so-called

"Hutsul Republic" in the "Black Mountains" (in the southeastern part of the Carpathians). This started the Khrushchev-Ryassny offensive of April 1945. Concerning this operation, the commander of the UPA group "Hoverlia" stated in his report of June 30, 1945: "The battalions of my group pushed back the attack of the 271st Red Rifle Division supported by many NKVD troops, and raided eight administrative centers. The death toll of the enemy in these incidents was 3,975 persons, including 6 majors, 10 captains, 30 lieutenants, 17 NKVD officers and party leaders, and 1,385 persons wounded; 21 truckloads and 5 locomotives were destroyed; 9 bridges were blown up; and 22 machine guns, 103 submachine guns, 29 automatic rifles, 321 rifles, 38 pistols, and ammunition were captured. Our losses: 215 killed and 129 wounded fighters; 20 fighters blew themselves to pieces with hand grenades in order not to be captured alive by the enemy."

Further actions of the same nature were: (1) the attack on the forest block Yaniv-Zhovkva-Yavoriv to the northwest of Lviv, in June 1945, carried out by two divisions supported by tanks and airplanes; (2) the simultaneous attack of three divisions of the forest Lopatyn-Hrycevola-Toporiv-Triyca northeast of Lviv in June and July of 1945; (3) the second operation against the "Black Forest" in July 1945, carried out by three Red divisions with the support of the air forces and NKVD troops; (4) the operations against the Zavadivsky forest between Kovel and Volodymyr Volynsky in July 1945. All these operations aimed at the total destruction of the UPA and were part of the major Khrushchev-Ryassny offensive in 1945 in which three army corps and many divisions of NKVD troops were used against the UPA in the provinces Ivano-Frankivske, Drohobych, Lviv, and Volhynia (Lutsk). This offensive had to be halted because the Red Army units used in it showed themselves to be rather unreliable in the fight against the UPA.

The next major Ryassny-Moskalenko offensive against the UPA started in December 1945, and lasted until June 1946. It was preceded by the attack against the UPA mountain positions of Hoverlia and Chornohora in October and November 1945. This time three elite NKVD divisions could not succeed in ejecting the Ukrainian insurgents from the Carpathian Mountains. The NKVD troops waged a campaign of terror unheard of before against the mountain people (Hutsuls) and tried to annihilate the population of the mountain *rayons* by a terrible blockade which caused hunger and typhus among the civilian population. The UPA carried out a general inoculation against typhus and shipped large quantities of food from Romania and Hungary into the *rayons* threatened by starvation.

The Ryassny-Moskalenko offensive against the UPA practically ended with the death of Col. Gen. Moskalenko. Even this offensive could not prevent the Ukrainian population from boycotting the February 1946 elections to the Supreme Soviet, and could not succeed in liquidating the Ukrainian Resistance Movement.

The last major action of this kind was the Swierczewski offensive against UPA-West from February to July 1947. Gen. Swierczewski was killed during this offensive, on March 27, 1947. Following his death a tripartite pact between

Soviet Russia, Poland, and Czechoslovakia was concluded aiming at the total destruction of UPA-West. Large enemy forces were thrown into action. According to this anti-partisan pact, Poland brought into action one motorized infantry corps of three divisions, the Soviet Command of the Sub-Carpathian Military Area at Lviv brought one tank division and special anti-partisan units, and Czechoslovakia brought one mountain brigade. All these troops were supported by the Soviet and Polish air forces. Fierce fighting continued in a large area during that spring and summer. The center of this anti-partisan activity was the Likso district in southeastern Poland. A Soviet tank brigade passed the Soviet-Polish frontier and advanced against the main insurgent force. With the help of Polish troops, it tried to encircle the insurgents, but the latter succeeded in escaping southwards and reached Slovakia and Carpatho-Ukraine. Another group of Ukrainian insurgents crossed the river Sian and reached Ukrainian territory, concealing itself in the forests north of Lviv. Still another group of the UPA escaped northwards in the direction of the Polissia marshes. The insurgent group under the command of Major Bayda crossed into Slovakia and reached the US zone of occupation in Germany in September 1947, after a march of 1500 km. across Czechoslovakia and Austria.

At the time of these major operations the Bolsheviks did not cease systematically to harass the UPA. They blockaded or raided villages and woods in the insurgent territory. They tried to interfere with UPA preparations to create suitable winter quarters and acquire clothing and other goods. The garrisoning of soldiers in the insurgent territory lasted for the duration of the Ryassny-Moskalenko offensive in 1946. This assignment was given by the Soviets to the special NKVD-KGB troops, allowing them to murder any Ukrainian they pleased. They were allowed to rape women and to pillage houses. The Ukrainian Resistance Movement could, in fact, fill a big "Black Book" with all these despicable acts of violence, atrocious crimes, tortures, and murders committed by the NKVD—a book no less terrifying than the accusations drawn up by the peoples of Europe against the German Nazis. They ravaged like ferocious beasts, and tortured the population in order to intimidate the Ukrainian people. The terror was unparalleled even in the history of Muscovy, including the "Oprichina" of Ivan the Terrible and the "okhranka" of the tsars. But it did not succeed in breaking the spirit of the Ukrainian people.

During the major Ryassny-Moskalenko offensive against the UPA the Bolsheviks carried out a large-scale deforestation of the country at each UPA concentration. As usual, the forests were burned down. This deforestation was usually limited to the area actually known to be held by partisans. The targeted area was encircled by NKVD troops and their circling lines were supposed to prevent the insurgents from escaping the burning forest. On a given signal airplanes threw incendiary bombs in the forest. If the insurgents were in the area, they were supposed to be burnt alive or to disperse. There were many actions of this kind in Western Ukraine. By spring 1946, all pine woods in the Kovel area (Volhynia) were completely burned down. By summer 1946, this action embraced the whole of the Black Forest and the Hrycevola-Lopatyn Forest in the province of Lviv. The material losses caused by such a "deforestation" were tremendous. Between only Toporiv and Triyca in the northeastern part of the province of Lviv, nearly 5,000 hectares of forest were completely burned down.

Despite the fact that bacteriological warfare is forbidden by international treaties, the Bolsheviks used it in the fight against the UPA. The Ukrainian Resistance Movement has many records in its archives that such methods were used both against the UPA and against the Ukrainian civilian population. The Bolsheviks knew that the UPA was buying anti-toxin on the market, so, in 1946, the Soviet agents began to sell poisoned injections in large quantities. The victims of these injections died in extreme pain. Soon the trick was discovered and the UPA ceased buying medicine from the local black market and began buying them in Poland, Czechoslovakia, and even in Germany. The UPA had to overcome great difficulty in mastering this situation. It organized whole expeditions to buy medicines in West Cracow, Katowice, Budapest and Bratislava, Vienna and Prague, and to bring them back to its bases in the Carpathian mountains. This is a true story of the supreme heroism of Ukrainian men and women in their fight against the vile and contemptibly low methods of the "most democratic state in the world".

We have already mentioned the planned starvation of the mountainous population in the Carpathians. By mounting a strict blockade of the *rayons*, the Soviet forces aimed to deprive the UPA of its natural bases by the same methods as applied in the marshy *rayons* of Polissia, which had another natural base for the UPA. In this area the Ukrainian people were not allowed to move from village to village and no food was brought by the cooperatives. Intensive fishing in the Prypriat river and in its tributary ordered by the UPA was the sole possible means of survival. The population of the Carpathians was saved by large quantities of food brought by the armed UPA expeditions from Hungary and Romania. Under the protection of armed detachments of the UPA, the Ukrainian mountain people in the threatened *rayons*, went to Hungary and Romania and brought back the necessary quantities of food to replenish the stores in the last weeks before the new harvest.

Alarming news which came to the West in 1948 from Carpatho-Ukraine confirmed earlier rumors that large-scale hunger and starvation had broken out that year. Famine raged in such traditionally rich and fertile areas as the districts of Uzhorod, Mukachiv, and Berehovo. The most likely reason was that the authorities had confiscated the bulk of the crop in order to force Ukrainian peasants into the much-hated collective farms.

The Soviet-sponsored famine is not a new instrument in attaining their economic and political ends. In the years 1932-1933 millions of Ukrainian peasants died from starvation. Moscow used the same device again in Western Ukraine and in Carpatho-Ukraine, and it not only succeeded in introducing collectivization, but in exterminating the recalcitrant Ukrainians as well.

It is impossbile to speak without a feeling of boundless anger and indignation at the savageries committed by the Ryassny-Moskalenko troops during their big offensive against the UPA and the peace-loving Ukrainian population. All these methods are a brazen mockery of the phrase "Freedom from Fear." "The function of compulsion inside the country has ceased, has withered away," Stalin announced in 1939. "The exploiters are no more and there is no one to suppress any more." Why, if "there is no one to suppress any more," was it necessary to apply such sadistic methods of extermination against the Ukrainian people in 1946? Why was it necessary to cut off heads with axes, to saw the bodies of captured insurgents in two, to strangle them with ropes, and to burn them in locked houses, to bury them alive, and to slaughter whole families including small children? Why was it necessary to execute all this torture in public? In the village squares of Western Ukraine captured insurgents were boiled and roasted alive, girls were violated in public, the wounded were summarily executed, and the whole population of the "insurgent villages" were slaughtered systematically until but a few were left in the ruins of their villages. All of this, in order to "edify" the citizens and to compel them to obey the Bolshevik criminals.

The atrocities which were committed in the name of the "people" were not accidental abuses by the Ryassny-Moskalenko special troops. The "Red terror" was a recognized and integral element in the process of subjugating the nation to the Bolshevik will. Lenin himself declared, "No dictatorship of the proletariat is to be thought of without terror and violence." And this terror and violence was applied *en masse* in Western Ukraine during the sorrowful days of spring and summer in 1946. Even the corpses and graves of the dead insurgents were desecrated by the Bolshevik beasts in uniform.

Five hundred years ago, Ivan the Terrible, tsar from 1544 to 1584, introduced into Russian life a peculiar institution which has continued to exist until the present day: the secret political police. Ivan called the directing organ of this police the *Oprichina* and its members the *Oprichniki*. Their duty was to ferret out disloyalty to the tsar and to punish it with the most severe cruelty. Ivan the Terrible's *Oprichina* became the *Prikaz* of Peter the "Great" and the *Okhrana* of the tsars, then Lenin's Cheka, then Stalin's GPU, then his NKVD, MVD, and MGB. Its name changed, but its task remained unchanged: to sniff out and sweep away ruthlessly all opposition to the dictator. Its ear was everywhere. The NKVD-MGB-MVD developed spying to a fine art and made it the dominant factor in Russian life. In every establishment, school, and institution there was a *spetsotdiel*, a branch of the MVD-MGB, which openly spied on every worker, every pupil, every employee. Beside the "special department" there were hundreds of thousands of *secsots* (secret spies) bought with money or coerced by fear.

In the first days after their arrival in Western Ukraine the Bolsheviks tried to organize a network of *secsots* among the Ukrainian population. For this purpose, they arrested the Ukrainian youth *en masse* and afterwards turned them loose. This complicated the task of the UPA because it was known that among these boys and girls hundreds had been pressed into the services of the NKVD. The UPA and SB had to check all persons set free to find out whether they were *secsots* or not. This required much effort on the part of the UPA and SB, but they preferred to do that than "liquidate" all suspects, as was intended by the NKVD.

Having had no success in building up a *secsot* network among the Ukrainian population, the Bolsheviks laid special stress on placing their agents in the UPA and OUN and attempting to disorganize them from the inside. Thus, initially, they set free all prisoners taken in battles in order to mislead the counter-agents of the UPA and SB. Of course, it was a hard task to determine who had volunteered for the job of an *agent-provocateur* and who had not. The recruited *agents-provocateurs* tried to infiltrate the ranks of the UPA and report on its proceedings. To dispel any possible doubts the NKVD created situations which would clear their agents from any suspicion. It organized "break-outs" from prisons, "flights" from detention camps, etc. But the UPA and SB knew that the odds were great that such a freed prisoner could be a stooge. Therefore, all those who returned had to pass through a careful screening and observation before they were again admitted to positions of importance. Having once been in Bolshevik hands created the highest suspicion. Such an *agent-provocateur* could sit in the underground bunker for months doing nothing suspicious and behaving normally. The Bolsheviks did not rush such agents into action knowing that the more their man had slipped into the confidence of the UPA the more he could achieve.

A certain number of Ukrainian insurgents, softened up by the Soviet amnesty, came out of the woods, and took up residence in the Bolshevik-controlled areas. To encourage this the Bolsheviks let the first groups go free. Some of them were afterwards selected for acts of provocation. They were used in the assassination of underground leaders, and to disclose the underground shelters and stores. The Bolsheviks expected the Ukrainian SB to act indiscriminately and to kill the pardoned fighters, thus creating a tension among the population. But the SB proceeded cautiously and acted promptly only in verified cases. Victims who agreed to cooperate with the NKVD found themselves trapped in the cross-fire between the two sides, and sometimes committed suicide or tried to hide themselves.

Another method was to send "rats" to the UPA. Red army and police officers with an excellent knowledge of the Ukrainian language or sometimes without (if they were Georgians, Uzbeks, or the like) approached the UPA, presented themselves as anti-Bolsheviks, and offered their services. They tried to gain the confidence of the UPA and did not refuse any means to achieve it. A Georgian, a major of the NKVD and an *agent-provocateur* on a large scale, was admitted for service in the UPA. Trying to get the full confidence of the command he uncovered the network of minor Bolsheviks and executed the death sentence, hanging them with his own hands after the trial. Of course, he was allowed to do that by the all-powerful NKVD in order to achieve in this way a higher position in the ranks of the UPA and its full confidence. In 1947, NKVD Captain Chereshukin ordered an *agent-provocateur* to kill NKVD Major Nosov, the chief of MGB in the *rayon* administration and a former Red partisan, in order to get the full confidence of the dangerous insurgent group in this *rayon*, which had not been willing to admit the *agent-provocateur* into its ranks. The shocking story of this assassination was told in UPA leaflets under the heading "Why was Comrade Nosov Killed?" and retold by the newspaper *Ukrainian Tribune* in its coverage of June 30, 1949. Another fact illustrating Bolshevik methods in placing their *agents-provocateurs* within the ranks of the UPA was told in the reports of the Ukrainian Resistance Movement. One day, in 1946, a "political prisoner" was brought into a village office near Lviv. He was under the guard of two NKVD officers and four NKVD men. The population of this village was called into the office and asked to "recognize" the man. Nobody knew him. Asked about his name the "prisoner" did not answer the questions at all, and was severely beaten. During the questioning, one of the NKVD officers put his pistol on the table. Suddenly the "prisoner" seized the pistol from the table, shot another officer of the NKVD who was in his way, and ran from the room. The ordered "chase" brought no results. The "prisoner" could not be found because the local population gave him protection. He told the man who gave him shelter that he was an officer of the UPA and asked him to contact the nearest group of the UPA. It was done. But there, despite the staging of the shooting, he was held under suspicion, and was soon disclosed as an officer of the NKVD sent to the UPA with a special job. The shooting in a village office had been organized by NKVD in order to gain the confidence of the local population. The dead officer was a political prisoner dressed up as an officer of the NKVD.

The main efforts of the NKVD in combatting the Ukrainian Resistance Movement were directed towards setting up a network of *agents-provocateurs* within the ranks of the UPA and affiliated organizations. But many of these efforts, according to the secret instructions of Gen. Saburov, chief of MGB in the province of Drohobych, failed because of excellent countermeasures by the Ukrainian SB.

In their war against the Ukrainian Resistance Movement, the Bolsheviks used false bands of supposed Ukrainian insurgents. These Bolsheviks, disguised as Ukrainian insurgents, raided Ukrainian villages and pillaged them in order to provoke the opposition of the population to the Ukrainian Resistance Movement. In other cases such "insurgents" sought shelter and help in order to find out which people sympathized with the UPA. At the beginning of the struggle against the Soviets, such a masquerade was very dangerous and caused much harm, as the Ukrainian population showed an open sympathy to every manifestation of the Ukrainian Resistance Movement. But later such methods became very well known all over Ukraine and, therefore, did not meet with any success. The alleged "insurgents" who came to the village without contacts with the local representatives of the Ukrainian Resistance Movement received no aid and support from the Ukrainian population.

The bands recruited from former insurgents and from low characters called *istrebiteli* were also very dangerous. They knew the local conditions and the language very well. Extreme effort had to be used to neutralize them. They were exterminated without pity. Later, their ranks became considerably thinned out and they limited their activity to guarding warehouses and administrative buildings.

In order to combat the Ukrainian Resistance Movement the Russians ordered the registration of the Ukrainian population. All inhabitants had to be registered in the local Soviet office and the lists of the present population had to be stuck on the door. By February 1946, the Bolsheviks began to confiscate the property of the Ukrainians whose relatives were with the UPA. When a shot was fired in the village, the Soviets used to burn down the section of the houses from which the shot came and murder on the spot the people of the section. In the village of

Berlohy, County Kalush, the Bolsheviks murdered fifty-three innocent peasants as a reprisal for the murdering of only one Bolshevik. Many incidents of public torture, murder, and pillage directed against Ukrainians were reported from all parts of Ukraine.

Soon the Bolsheviks realized that the only means of exterminating the Ukrainian Resistance Movement was to deport the Ukrainian people who gave their full support to the Ukrainian Resistance Movement. As early as 1945, the Bolsheviks started their infamous deportations to Siberia and Kazakhstan. The Bolsheviks then picked out some UPA sympathizers in order to intimidate the remaining population. In 1946, they started a mass deportation, which continues even now. On the night of October 20-21, 1947, the Bolsheviks started to deport people in unprecedented numbers; between 500,000 to 800,000, or one-fifth to one-fourth of the population of Western Ukraine were uprooted.

A month before the operation, the MVD collected barred cattle cars at all the railway stations. Units of the MVD-MGB forces, *istrebiteli* (destruction battalions), and units of the Soviet Army were billeted all over the countryside under the pretext of operations against resistance groups.

Most locally prominent people were placed on the deportation lists on charges of contact with the Ukrainian Resistance Movement, of having relatives abroad, of having "collaborated" with the Germans, etc.

After the preparations, the villages were surrounded and the deportees arrested. The whole action took twenty-four hours. The deportees were allowed to take with them only the luggage they were able to carry, and no information was vouchsafed on their ultimate destination. Later it was learned that the majority had been taken to Kazakhstan.

Those who managed to weather the fatal twenty-four hours in hiding were not troubled later, and remained safe until the next deportation.

Large deportations took place in March and April 1949, from the southern part of former East Galicia and the Kyiv province. In many parts of Ukraine the population was in a state of panic for fear of deportation. Often the MVD dragged people directly from their places of work to the deportation trains. The general spirit was one of revolt, and partisan activities sprang up with renewed vigor, especially in the Eastern Carpathians and Volhynia. The Soviet authorities combatted the Ukrainian Resistance Movement by deporting the inhabitants of whole villages as soon as any inhabitant was suspected of helping the partisans.

That the deportation was a really large-scale action is substantiated by the fact that two regular divisions of the Soviet Army were transferred to Ukraine from Turkestan to help the MVD.

Foreseeing the deportations, the Ukrainian Resistance Movement issued printed instructions on how to behave in case of deportation. They ordered the Ukrainian population to organize an active and passive resistance against the deportation, to hide themselves in the woods and forests and to erect special underground shelters and hiding places in order to avoid deportations. Of course, the UPA detachments stood in defense of the deportees with all their forces. Here we give a report of a person who escaped the deportation: "In the spring of 1948 the Bolsheviks began a forcible collectivization in the districts of

Zhovkva and Rava. Many peasants were arrested, among them the escapees. They were accused of campaigning against collectivization. All arrested were transferred to the infamous Brygidky prison in Lviv, where at least 400 other Ukrainians were detained. Most of them were peasant youths, including children between the years of ten and fourteen who were arrested for putting wreaths on the graves of UPA fighters killed in action. On June 24, 1948, all the arrested were taken from the Brygidky prison and put on a cattle train destined for the central parts of the Soviet Union. The transport had fifty wagons, each containing fifty men. Leaving Lviv at night, the train was stopped a few kilometers outside the city by a raiding party. The cars were broken open and their occupants freed. One of the attackers identified the raiding party as the UPA and advised the released Ukrainian youths to hide from the Bolsheviks for 'very soon we will need all able-bodied men for an important task.' The MVD guards were either killed or taken away by the insurgents." (From *Ukrainian Word*, a Ukrainian newspaper in the British zone of Germany, Dec. 5, 1948).

The population obeyed the orders of the Ukrainian Resistance Movement, and thus the Bolsheviks could deport only 150,000 men and women instead of 500,000. The rest remained in the country. Settlers from Russia who were resettled on the farms of the deportees were ordered to leave, and, in case of resistance, were forcibly evicted. Only Ukrainians from other provinces were allowed to settle on the farms of the deportees.

The amnesty and propaganda campaigns were an attempt by the Communist Party and the Soviet Government of Ukraine to break down the morale of the Ukrainian Resistance Movement. To strengthen their appeals, the Soviets carried out blockades of the insurgents' territory with massed troops, and then tried to whitewash their actions by blaming the underground for hardships on the population caused by their countermeasures against the UPA. They also forced innocent people to sign surrender applications and afterwards boasted of the great number of illegal partisans who allegedly gave up.

Before July 1945, there were three appeals to the Ukrainian insurgents issued with huge fanfare: September 1944, December 1944, and May 1945. In their last appeal, the Russians boasted of their victory over Germany and threatened that this would be the last appeal and that it would be followed by a merciless destruction of the Ukrainian Resistance Movement. In January 1945, the Minister for Foreign Affairs of the Ukrainian SSR, D. Manuilsky, delivered a great speech before the teachers' convention in Lviv. His harangue was entirely devoted to the Ukrainian Resistance Movement and he promised in the name of the Soviet Government to "pardon" all who would cease their anti-Soviet activities. Anti-Soviet activities increased considerably after this speech however, and elections to the Supreme Soviet were boycotted everywhere in Western Ukraine.

One of the last "siren songs" was sung by the Ukrainian Minister of the NKVD, Gen. V. Ryassny, on November 15, 1945, and has already been quoted. It was distributed in the country in the spring and summer of 1946. There were not many that obeyed this order. Often the surrendering came from "holers," unorganized partisans and Red Army deserters who carried on a warfare of their own. The insurgents organized in the UPA seldom participated in such amnesty schemes. One of their rules was that no one should be captured alive and this rule was consistently observed by the men and women of the UPA.

Following the well-tested methods of the Russian MVD, the Czech Minister of the Interior issued an appeal to the "members of the UPA in Czechoslovakia." In it, the Czech Communist appealed to the Ukrainians as follows: "Kill your comrades, throw away your weapons and report to the NB" (the Czech Security Police). It concluded: "Surrender! You will live and work! The Slav truth will win!"

There was no doubt that the fight against the Bolsheviks was very hard and difficult. But the Ukrainian Resistance Movement waged an implacable war against the Soviet forces. It was very efficient in fighting Soviet forces despite the fact that the occupation army and police forces had heavy weapons while the Ukrainian Resistance Movement had none. Everything had to be seized, including munitions, because the Ukrainian fighters were not supplied by the West. Yet even now the might of Soviet Russia has still not wiped out the indefatigable spirit of those years of armed struggle....

The Ukrainian Review,
No. 1, 1983, pp. 68-84

VIII
Insurgent Ukraine

The Liberation Struggle of Ukraine on Two Fronts

Forty years ago, on June 30, 1941, on the initiative of the OUN, the Ukrainian nation proclaimed the Reestablishment of Ukrainian Statehood in the city of Lviv. June 30, 1941 marks the beginning of a period in our history known as that of the Ukrainian Underground State, which lasted well into the 1950s, when the military units of the OUŃ and the UPA were still leading an armed struggle in defense of Ukrainian independence and statehood.

As a result of this proclamation the Ukrainian nation launched a war of liberation fought on two fronts against both Nazi Germany and Bolshevik Russia—two of the largest imperialistic, totalitarian, and military powers of the twentieth century.

The Ukrainian Government that was created by the Proclamation of Independence included not only members of the OUN under the leadership of Stepan Bandera, but also national democrats, socialists, social revolutionaries, and individuals not affiliated with any political party. The Government was recognized by and received the full support of both the Ukrainian Catholic and the Ukrainian Autocephalous Orthodox Churches. A parliamentary body was formed with Metropolitan Archbishop Andreas Count Sheptytsky as its honorary President and Dr. Konstantyn Levytsky, the leader of the National Democrats, as its Chairman. The parliament was made up of representatives from various Ukrainian political parties and currents. The new Ukrainian Government enjoyed the full support and loyalty of all strata of the Ukrainian nation.

The ideological and political foundation upon which Ukrainian statehood was

321

restored in 1941 was contained in a Manifesto issued in 1940 by the Organization of Ukrainian Nationalists. From this Manifesto we quote the following:

"The complete destruction of the Russian empire through a Ukrainian national revolution and armed uprisings of all subjugated nations is the only means for achieving an independent Ukrainian state and the liberation of all nations subjugated by Moscow."

The political principles and concepts articulated in this Manifesto were later to serve as the basis of the ABN, which was founded in the autumn of 1943 in the forests of Zhytomyr (Western Ukraine) at a Conference of Subjugated Nations.

The newly founded Ukrainian Government had the support of the Ukrainian Nationalist Military Formation and of numerous insurgent units throughout Ukraine fighting against the invading Russian Red Army. Having secured the main radio station in Lviv, the Revolutionary Government informed the nation of the restoration of Ukrainian statehood. Upon learning of these momentous developments, the Ukrainian population openly and enthusiastically endorsed the new Government at mass assemblies in towns and villages throughout the country.

The contemporary international situation is particularly grave. The expansion of Russian imperialism is well known to us all. Policies of friendship, appeasement, containment, convergence, and détente have proven to be useless in stemming the brazen centuries-old Russian imperialism which aims at complete world domination.

While we applaud the current US Administration's resolve, under the leadership of President Ronald Reagan, to bolster its military readiness, both in the area of nuclear and conventional armaments, and finally to stand up to Russian racism and imperialism, we are nonetheless appalled by the contemptible and immoral defeatist policies of appeasement pursued by several Western European nations, most notably West Germany. The Governments of these countries must remember that in Europe the United States is *primarily* defending *their* interests over its own, in light of the everpresent and more acute threat of Russian imperialism to Western Europe. Chancellor Helmut Schmidt's token gesture of opposition to the recent 50,000-strong, violent, pro-Russian demonstration in Berlin against US Secretary of State Alexander Haig—staged by the youth wing of the party of which Chancellor Schmidt is the actual leader—was indeed a heavy-handed slap at Germany's most loyal ally, the United States, upon which depends the future fate of all of Europe. In light of the increasingly anti-American attitude in Western Europe, we would propose that the United States should place greater trust in its natural, albeit neglected, allies against the threat of Russian expansionist imperialism—the nations subjugated by Russian imperialism and Communism, which threaten to tear asunder internally the Russian prison of nations, thereby forever extricating the world from the imperialist threat.

The West must realize that within the Russian empire there exists a new ideological and political revolutionary superpower—the subjugated nations—which is destroying the empire from within. The processes of the disintegration of the Russian empire are at different stages in the various subjugated nations: Afghanistan, Ukraine, Poland, Lithuania, Turkestan, among others.

Taking this factor into consideration, we urge that the following points be included in Western political and military strategy:

1. The Free World should engage Soviet Russia in the struggle of ideas and ideologies by recognizing the liberation movements of the subjugated nations as the legitimate representatives of these countries at all international forums, including the United Nations;

2. The West should provide the national liberation movements with access to the various forms of mass media to facilitate communication with their countrymen behind the Iron Curtain on a mass scale;

3. Assistance should also be provided in the form of military training as well as other political, material and technological means of support;

4. All of the nations of the Free World should proclaim A GREAT CHARTER OF INDEPENDENCE for all of the nations subjugated by Russian imperialism and communism;

5a. The United States should *establish a radio broadcasting station* at the disposal of the Organization of Ukrainian Nationalists (OUN), through which we can freely propagate our national ideals and concept of liberation, independent of the détente-oriented policy of NATO;

b. The content and political aims of the Ukrainian radio broadcasts of Radio Liberty ought to be changed in accordance with the needs and exigencies of the revolutionary national-liberation struggle;

6. The United States, as the champion of freedom and justice, should establish a World Freedom Academy, as a counterpart to the Moscow Lumumba University, which trains imported terrorists for the implementation of Russia's imperio-colonial policies throughout the world;

7. A Department of Insurgent-Liberation Warfare should be established within the Pentagon and/or Headquarters of the NATO alliance.

The liberation struggles of Ukraine, Afghanistan or Poland are proof of the internal weaknesses of the Russian prison of nations—this colossus on clay feet. Millions of soldiers of the Red Army deserted to Germany's side during World War II, not because their sentiments were pro-German, but, rather, because they did not believe that the West could have engendered such a brutal, cruel and inhumanly barbaric system as National Socialism. The soldiers were destroying the empire from within. Presently, the situation is similar, particularly in that the majority of the Soviet army is non-Russian and is predominantly made up of members of the subjugated nations, who are also in a majority as far as the population of the entire empire is concerned. The might of a subjugated nation in its struggle against a foreign imperialist invader is exemplified by Afghanistan, where soldiers of the Red Army refuse to fight against a freedom-loving people. Poland is proof that a nation, even without arms, can, nevertheless, through various revolutionary means, render impossible a military intervention on the part of a nuclear superpower because the consequences may lead to an expansion of the armed resistance of the subjugated nations throughout the entire empire. The atomic superpower is helpless in suppressing the will to freedom of the smaller Polish nation. An intervention of new Russian forces may lead to a cataclysm throughout all of the empire. Non-intervention, on the other hand, may lead to a systematic burgeoning of the revolutionary liberation processes in Poland and their expansion to all of the subjugated nations in the empire bringing nearer the day of the empire's collapse. If Moscow will not succeed in undermining Solidarity from within, then military intervention will become an absolute necessity, regardless of all the risks that this may entail.

The Russian empire, which is needlessly feared by America, is being checkmated by the subjugated nations. Yet the West actually helps to subjugate these nations through its policy of détente and economic and military aid to the empire (technology, electronics, grain, etc.). Hence, our first demand is the following: at least cease in helping to subjugate us, if you do not wish to help us liberate ourselves?

Moscow, not being able to mobilize the working classes against their nations, created a center of international terrorism, as a means of destroying the free societies of the West.

The danger of a nuclear holocaust cannot be negotiated away. Soviet Russia has skillfully exploited western fears of nuclear war by blackmailing the West into meekly acquiescing to its ever-increasing conquests. Our strategic alternative is based on the knowledge that the subjugated nations within the Russian empire represent a vast untapped force, which in a common front with the nations of the Free World provides the strategic raison d'etre for defeating the last remaining empire. A political and military strategy, based on synchronized national liberation revolutions within the Russian colonial empire is the only alternative to thermo-nuclear war.

In conclusion, I would like to quote an unforgettable personal friend of mine and an outstanding British military thinker—Major General J.F.C. Fuller, who once wrote: "Only the unity of the western nations and their agreement with the national liberation movements behind the Iron Curtain can ensure final victory.... The reason should be obvious. It is that the Kremlin is living on a volcano, and it knows that the most explosive force in the world is not to be found in the hydrogen bomb, but in the hearts of the subjugated peoples crushed under its iron heel..."

Ukraine Review,
No. 1. Spring 1982, pp. 3-8.

The Status and Role of Ukraine
in the World
(Part One)

Revolutionary Factor

Ukraine is an immediate, revolutionary world problem. Its independence in the national and political sense would create an entirely new constellation of international power, for, as a result of the restoration of Ukrainian national state independence, the Russian peoples' prison would disintegrate into independent states of all the subjugated nations. On the Eurasian continent a number of states would come into being or would be restored and they would decide their international relations of their own free will. Thus a completely new relationship of the international political factors would ensue. As a Black Sea power, Ukraine would tend to belong to an entirely different geopolitical bloc. And the same would apply in the case of the Turkestanian and Caucasian countries.

Ukrainian statehood is likewise a revolution from the international political aspect. The fact that the largest and most ruthless empire in the world would be liquidated, a liquidation which would be synonymous with the restoration of the sovereign, integrated Ukrainian state, would have a far-reaching and lasting influence on the establishment of interstate relations in Asia and Europe and thus in the whole world—all the more so since Russia in this way would be prevented from continuing the various efforts which it at present undertakes on a large scale.

With the restoration of the independence of Ukraine, other relations between individuals and peoples would be realized on the Eurasian continent. Hence the fight for Ukraine's national state independence is at the same time a fight for a completely different world of ideas—a world which is entirely different from that in which the subjugated peoples are forced to languish. Kyiv is the symbol of a different ideological, political, cultural, social, and religious system of values, the opposite pole to Moscow, which, in the name of its conceptions of the life of the individual and of the whole of mankind, ruthlessly aims to conquer the world in order to force its own Russian order on the world.

The Ideological Position of Ukraine in the World

The fight which is developing before our very eyes on a huge scale is not exclusively a political fight. It also involves the deepest inner values of human nature, the most vital problems of human existence. With the realization of the political independence of Ukraine and of other peoples subjugated by Moscow, an entirely different aspect of the life and existence of the individual and of the nation would be realized. Some decades ago the fight between the major imperial powers had not yet assumed the character of a struggle for the victory and triumph of the eternal truths of human existence—it was merely a struggle for the division and demarcation of political spheres of interests, of economic or cultural influences. There were no diametrically opposed differences between the worlds of ideas of Paris or London, Madrid or Rome. Nowadays it is a question not only of the realization of a political order in the whole world dictated by Moscow, or of the expansion of the Russian empire to the dimension of a global USSR, but also of the realization of the Russian conception of life in all its phenomena, from aggressive atheism, the negation and denial of human dignity, individuality, freedom, the idea of justice and moral principles, to the extermination of the nation as an historical and natural phenomenon.

The fate and destiny of Ukraine in bordering on two worlds imposes certain demands on it and on us, its sons. Ukraine upholds and personifies these different ideas, the ideas of the world that is opposed to Russia. Our fight and our struggle for national state independence bear the features of a fight for the victory of eternal values which are common to all men: for God, for the individual, for the nation—as an organic human community and for the family—as an organic part of the nation.

The national liberation fight of a people has never been characterized by such universal human elements, nor has it ever personified as many eternal ideas as the present liberation fight of the Ukrainian people. Never in the whole of history did the fate and future of countless peoples and individuals depend so largely on the victorious fight of one nation as in our day.

Two conceptions of life—the Ukrainian and the Russian—clash in every sphere. Their fight against each other is the confrontation of two national organisms in every form and sphere of life: culture, religion, social institutions, moral principle, economy, political views, and national traditions.

On the Russian side, aggressive atheism—on the Ukrainian side, militant Christianity. The Antichrist against Christ!

On the Russian side, the collectivist conception of social and economic life—on the Ukrainian side, the national conception which stresses the personality of the individual and regards man as a being created in the image of God; the subjugation of the individual versus the general development and furthering of his creative powers; the theft of property and expropriation versus respect of the other person's property; lies and deception versus the truth; lawlessness versus honesty and uprightness; and injustice versus justice.

On the Russian side, the enforced imperialistic principle for the construction of the world; on the Ukrainian side, the national principle of shaping the free life of the people and of the individual; the empire, the peoples' prison versus free national states; imperialism and colonialism which aim at world conquest versus nationalism, which aims at liberation; the class struggle, which holds the individual in contempt, and mutual extermination versus the solidarity and the mutual help of all classes of the nation; disparagement of the family versus recognition of the family as the natural cell of the people, as the preserver of the moral and biological health of the people.

On the Russian side—tyranny, exploitation, murder, slavery, and contempt for the individual; on the Ukrainian side—the idea of social justice, human dignity, recognition of the independence of other peoples and of the organic order of the world, which is based on national elements and constitutes the spiritual unity of the human heart.

For these reasons there can be no possibility of creating a synthesis of the values of two worlds out of the principles and ideas of national Christian Ukraine and the opposing principles and ideas of anti-national, anti-Christian, and imperialistic Russia. For it is not a question of effecting a harmonious union between good and evil, but of destroying evil so that good can reign, of extirpating injustice so that justice can be victorious, of destroying tyranny so that freedom can triumph, of crushing the Antichrist so that Christ can rule over the world, and of overthrowing the empire so that the idea of free nations can gain the upper hand. Where Russian "truth" rules, there is no room for divine and human truth.

Opposition to Russian Bolshevik Mendacity

But here and there a bargain is made with truth. The icon of the Holy Virgin, which is set up at the entrance door of the churches in the West in order to exhort the free peoples "to pray for Russia," is a Ukrainian icon stolen from Kyiv by Andrew Bogolyubsky. Since time immemorial, theft and mendacity have been typical Russian phenomena.

The Russian Bolsheviks have a slogan: "Rob what has been robbed!" But the Ukrainians say: "Let us not disgrace the Ukrainian soil, for we shall lay down our lives here, and the dead know neither dishonor nor disgrace"; "To liberate our brothers is to gain honor and fame"; and "For the orthodox faith and for our native country."

Centuries have passed but nothing has changed, and the Russians have remained the same as they always were. In former times they conquered and pillaged neighboring foreign countries; now they try to grasp the whole world. In former times they lived collectively in communities (obshchina), now they live in kolkhozes. The Russian sects, for instance the Dukhobory, Molokany, Byeguny, Stranniki, and Nemolaki—paved the way for Communism, and they supported it long before the advent of Bolshevism. Even the Russian philosopher Berdyaev admits that Bolshevism is an organic creation of the Russian mind and a typically national Russian phenomenon. The gifted Ukrainian painter Maria Bashkirtsev, who died eighty years ago at the age of twenty-four, prophesied the advent of Communism in Russia and characterized the Russians as a people who were susceptible to Communism. The Ukrainian historian Kostomarov stressed the superficial religiosity of the Russians, their religious atheism, their nihilism, and the corruption prevalent in the theological colleges. The Frenchman A. de Custine wrote that the majority of the sons of the Russian clergy were anti-religious organizers. Atheists such as Dobrolyubov and Chernyshevsky came from Russian clerical families. In 1620 the Swede Botwin raised the question as to whether the Russians were Christians at all. Peter I threatened to punish his officials if they did not go to church. Byelinsky wrote to Gogol that his, Gogol's opinion that the Russians were Christians was wrong—the Russians, he said, were a godless people. Gogol, who was a Ukrainian, could not believe that man could be so mendacious. Stepniak and Bulgakov, both of them Russians, affirmed that the atheism of the Russians was a form of religion; and Stepniak stressed that the Russians believe in the Devil as the co-worker and fellow conspirator of God.

The opinion that the Russians began to persecute religion ruthlessly because Marxist theory demanded this is false. Long before Marx their character and nature were exactly the same as they are today. Although Marx negated religion, he did not demand that religion should be forcibly destroyed by Bolshevik methods. This is only the privilege of the Russians and their pupils for whom the Kremlin is a Mecca.

The Russian attitude to spiritual things is in every way entirely the opposite of our attitude, and the fight for the human soul which is being waged behind the Iron Curtain is not of recent date. It is constantly and consistently decided in our favor—that is to say, in favor of the eternal values and ideas for the sake of which man exists. The young people in particular are searching for the divine truth and want to believe in eternal, transcendent values that do not belong to this world. They are rebelling, for they have had enough of skepticism and nihilism. And the doubts which they express on occasion are an accusation against the Russian Bolshevik system: "Today I no longer believe in anything; I do not trust my own eyes, I do not trust my own ears. Everything is propaganda, the whole world is propaganda...." But youth is refusing to be servile and skeptical any longer.

It was not thanks to the so-called "de-Stalinization" that the young people were enlightened? On the contrary! The fiction of "de-Stalinization" was in the first place the result of the revolt of the young freedom-loving sons and daughters of the subjugated peoples. The riots in the concentration camps, the magnificent creative work of young thinkers, poets, writers, and sculptors, and, in fact, the indestructible creativity and productivity of the entire nation in all their forms—all these things are proof of the indestructible spirit of the nation. Only the conceited and arrogant Russians dare to affirm that in the course of forty years they have succeeded in "re-molding" the soul of the individual and "re-educating" him in the Communist spirit. Christianity, created by God, has been educating and making man more perfect for the past two thousand years—without, however, affirming that it has turned man into an "angel"; indeed, it has set itself no such task. Man fights against his inclination to evil, and if he falls, then he gets up again and resumes his efforts and his struggle, and this will be repeated again and again until the end of the world. The life of man and of mankind develops quite differently from and in defiance of Russian blindness and boasting.

Idealism of Youth

Youth in the Russian peoples' prison is striving for justice and is seeking the true ideals which corroborate man's mission on earth in accordance with the will of the Creator. The young people there scoff at Khrushchev's prophecies to the effect that Communism will allegedly be "realized" by 1980. They ask themselves: What then? Can Communism really be the highest ideal of mankind? They negate this question and endeavor to find another idea; they try to ascertain what the purpose of life is; they ponder over religious, metaphysical, ethical, and moral questions; they seek truth, for which it is worth sacrificing one's life. Their search and their efforts are centered on man as an individual and not on Communism, and their attitude in this respect is so determined that Khrushchev is obliged to change his Communist slogans and introduce the lying slogan "Everything in the name of the individual, everything for the good of the individual," in the new program of the Communist Party of the Soviet Union. This Russian deception is obviously a contradiction of the ideology of Marxist collectivism. For it should really say: "Everything for the proletariat. Everything for the commune. Everything in the name of Russia."

The silence which reigned during the Stalinist epoch has been broken in several spheres. The absolute Russian rulers realized that the moment of explosion was approaching for the people and above all the youth were striving to attain absolute ideals—both human and national. Khrushchev endeavored to save what in his opinion could be saved, but his efforts were in vain, for empty words cannot appease the unrest in the human soul, an unrest which affects everyone and which rouses the urge to fight for higher ideals.

Double-dealing Nikita, the greatest phrase-maker of our century, will not be able to conceal from the world, by means of his trite speeches about the "construction of Communism" and the training of "a new Communist individual," the revolt of the human soul and the national aspirations in the concentration camps, in Berlin, Poznan, and Budapest, the insurrection of the young people, their thoughts and their loud protests against the standardization, collectivism, and alien values forced on them by terrorism. The individual, degraded to the level of a slave, is "to construct Communism" in a senseless, vacuous state of drunkenness. On an average 70 liters of alcohol per head are consumed per year by the male population in the USSR. People drink in order to forget their unhappy fate on the "joyful" path to Communism.

Some time ago, things were simpler in Moscow. Anyone who opposed Moscow's rule and its system was an "enemy of the people." Nowadays matters are more complicated, for the activity of those who refuse to submit to Moscow's rule has assumed various forms. Hence Moscow is obliged to combat them by various means. Moscow directs its attacks above all against the "bourgeois nationalists" whose activity is apparent in every sphere of life. Moscow is obliged to fight against manifold forms of resistance to its system and its rule. Thus it endeavors to combat the *tuneyadtsy* (parasites and profiteers), *khuligany*, (antipatriots), "nihilists," "living apostles," "sellers of Christ" (sellers of crosses and pictures of saints), "anonymous persons," "*nibochos*" ("*ni do Boha, ni do chorta*"—that is, those "belonging neither to God nor to the Devil," persons who have been completely disappointed by the regime), "political vagabonds," and "protesting citizens." Action is also taken against the "enemies of the people"; the internal Russian problem of "enemies of the Party" is an established fact. All these designations for "hostile elements" are obvious enough in their meaning and clearly illustrate the manifold nature of the resistance against the Russian Bolshevik system.

The fight for the freedom of the intellectual development of the individual and the nation is constantly assuming greater proportions. Open attacks and action on the part of the subjugated non-Russian peoples in the USSR against the Russian Bolshevik system, against colonialism, imperialism, and subjugation, are constantly increasing in number, while the Russians merely protect and defend the empire and its system. It is thus hardly surprising that the youth of the subjugated people in the USSR shows more interest in Hemingway and Orwell, for instance, than in Gorky and Tolstoy. And this fact in itself is typical and significant.

Khrushchev is hoping in vain if he thinks that he can win over the young people of the subjugated peoples with the deceptive phantom of Communism and promises of better food supplies; the young people have long since seen through and exposed the deception of Russian colonialism, which hides under the guise of Communism. They are striving to attain a free, universal creativity within their own nation and to develop their own abilities as free citizens of a free people.

In July of this year the *Frankfurter Zeitung* published an interesting report from Moscow which gave the reader an idea of what the young people in the USSR discuss and think and which problems occupy their attention and interest. The attitude of the participants in the discussion from Kyiv, seventeen and eighteen-year old boys and girls, was particularly interesting. They said quite frankly: "I want to be an individual"; "School should teach us to get to know all that is new and beautiful"; "I object to being sent to the regions which are being opened up for cultivation"; "In our country they always talk about the good influence of the collective, but in reality people sit about there inactively, waiting to be retrained"; "We are opposed to skepticism and also to illusions." Scoffing at the illusion of "the commune beyond the mountains," these boys and girls affirmed that Communism would only be possible when general prosperity and comfort existed. One schoolgirl emphatically demanded not only aestheticism as regards objects, but also aestheticism as regards human beings and the desire to attain self-perfection, ethical and moral integrity, and ideals. In this way youth censures Khrushchev.

Spirit of Ukraine Not Crushed

The wishes, aspirations, and ideas which are expressed in countless songs of the UPA and in the poems and prose writings of the underground fighters continue to stir the hearts of the people, burst the fetters of Russian censorship and of the stereotyped style that has been enforced, and are forcibly revealed in the creative strength of the people. These ideas and aspirations are: God, the fatherland, freedom, fame and honor, truth and justice, human dignity, and the power of the people in their own country; in addition, religion, the respect and honor due to one's mother, family ties, the glorification of the graves "in which our freedom sleeps," love of tradition, and admiration and veneration of the noble heroes of Ukraine.

The Russian terrorist regime has failed to crush the spirit and sincere attitude of the people. How powerful this fundamental strength of the people must be—how firmly rooted in the broad masses, if the Russian rulers are obliged to retreat before it again and again! How universal, how stirring and how invincible must be the national ideas which inspire the people if the occupant is forced to "allow" and tolerate the memories, in songs and poems, of "old Kyiv," of the graves of heroes in the vicinity of that city, of the longing for past ages, of those who are forced to leave their native country and go to the far-off mountains of the Pamirs.

The Russian occupant is forced to officially "allow" the Ukrainian people to express their yearning and their indignation at least in sentimental songs and poems. True, they are not revolutionary songs, but songs full of yearning and sadness; but at least they prove that Moscow has not succeeded in eradicating either the "old Kyiv," the graves of illustrious ancestors, of the love of one's parents and one's family from the soul of the people. Even the "Song about the Embroidered Towel," a profoundly sentimental and, in fact, depressing song (which has been sanctioned by the censorship), clearly shows that Bolshevik Moscow has not succeeded in destroying the moral status of the mother in the Ukrainian family. On the contrary, it reveals—even though only in a symbolic way—the Russian terrorist regime which prevails in Ukraine, for where is the son going who says goodbye to his mother, while she sadly and yearningly gives him an embroidered towel as a parting gift to remind him of home! He is, of course, setting out on a "long journey" to distant, foreign lands—to Russian exile, for no mother says goodbye to her son in this way if he is only going into the countryside or on an excursion.... A mother only bids her son farewell like this if she has no hope of ever seeing him again once he has been exiled to Siberia.

What has Bolshevik Russia achieved during its forty years' rule in Ukraine? Ukraine continues to speak the same language that its people spoke fifty years ago. And the characteristic features of the Ukrainian mentality have proved to be invincible, for, even though they have been trampled under foot and crushed again and again, they have always arisen. The Ukrainians have preserved their own spirit and mental attitude, and there continues to be a fierce protest in their hearts—for "the spark of the great fire" cannot be extinguished. The Ukrainians live in a world of ideas that is diametrically opposed to the Russian system of ideas; and they endeavor to apply these ideas in all spheres of practical life and to realize them in the fight against the Russian system of life which has been forced on Ukraine.

Stirrings in Literature

Bolshevik Russia had hoped that in the course of its forty years' rule over Ukraine, it would have succeeded, by means of physical and spiritual terrorism, in destroying the way of life and the ideas of the Ukrainian people and in forcing the Russian collectivist ideology on them. But Moscow's hopes and expectations in this respect have proved in vain, for now, after forty years of terrorism, "my father had decided to plant an orchard," as a young author writes. "Vigorously he pushed the spade into the soil and laughed about the weals on his hands, and I suddenly felt that here was one person at least, on this lovely day, who had thought about life seriously and who realized that he was growing old, and for this reason wanted to lay out a garden...." Merely a garden—and not a kolkhoz garden, but his own garden—surrounding his house. This man does not want to leave any trace of himself either in the kolkhoz or in the machine-tractor station—he wants to lay out his own garden.

Nature is to some extent eternal. And the soil has always been part of the Ukrainian nation, for on it the fame and greatness of our ancestors thrived, and it is steeped in their sweat and blood and strewn with the graves of those who have defended it. The Ukrainian soil, which has become a battlefield, has been trampled on and violated by the enemy, but, as expressed by the Ukrainian writer of mysticism, Stefanyk, and in the folksongs of Ukraine, it heals the wounds, the heart, and the soul of the Ukrainian people and inspires them with courage for a new, productive life.

And, as in the poems of Shevchenko, the graves in this Ukrainian soil are remembered and venerated anew: "Gray graves in a green field, drops of dew fall from the gray grave, the corn sways in the breeze, the moon shines over the plains.... Why are there so many graves? They have defended my Ukraine...."

There is no mention of politics in these lines, but only of the Ukrainian soul; they express profound feeling—and though it is perhaps only a subconscious feeling, it comes from the very heart of the Ukrainian people.

Could there be anything more powerful, more sacred, and more sincere than these lines: "And I have united my blood with yours, like the corn is united with the soil in the spring, and then you become mine, my fatherland, and in the dawn I became yours, and my eyes were opened by you...." "And one can already hear the soil turning, and, together with it, Ukraine...." And the status and role of Ukraine in the world: "I love you through the universe and through mankind, and through the golden sunflower...and through gray-haired scholars and thinkers, and through the flowers of the field amidst the stubble...." "No, my fatherland, I am not only yours in sorrow and joy!"

And the truth? "One has to pay for me with life. And I shall bring you unhappiness and misery.... Poetry is my very own sister, and human truth is our mother." "And whatever may befall me, I have no claim to the fate which I have chosen myself."

The younger generation seeks an answer to the most complicated questions of life. Those who think more profoundly and are not content with a superficial knowledge, but seek the profound values and purpose of human life and exist-ence, regard dialectical materialism as outmoded. "In the universe and in the world everything is in constant, perpetual motion, and only the graves remain constantly in their place." In view of this great striving to find eternal values and truths, what can the promise of the Communist party of the Soviet Union in its new program offer man? "That the present generation of the so-called Soviet people will live in an epoch of Communism"—that is to say, allegedly in an epoch "of peace, work, freedom, equality, brotherhood, and happiness for all peoples"—according to the preamble to the program of the Communist Party of the Soviet Union. But there is not a single new and original idea contained in this program, for all the points mentioned therein are already contained in the French declaration on human rights and in the Declaration of Independence of the United States—with the sole difference, however, that neither of these declarations was as mendacious and as false as that of the Russians. Both revolutions took as their motto and championed the idea of national independence, which Russian Bolshevism negates and ruthlessly combats.

Bankruptcy of Communist Ideas

The program of the Communist Party of the Soviet Union stresses in conclusion: "Under the well-tried and experienced leadership of the Communist Party, under the banner of Marxism-Leninism, the Soviet people have constructed socialism...." In practice this socialism means the setting up of slave-labor camps, genocide, slavery, poverty, starvation, injustice—in short, the greatest evil in the entire history of mankind. The only difference between the epoch of Communism and Russian Bolshevik socialism will be that the former is characterized by even greater slavery and starvation and by an even more intensive Russification.

It took Lenin fourteen years to realize the dictatorship of the proletariat as decreed in the first Bolshevik program of 1903. In the second program, which was drawn up at the 8th Party Congress in 1919, the Russian Bolsheviks decided "to build socialism." They realized this "construction" by means of a genocide hitherto unheard of in the entire history of mankind; in order to introduce collectivism, an artificial famine was created in 1932-33, by means of which million of Ukrainian farmers were exterminated. Such was the nature of the realization of socialism!

The third program of the Communist Party of the Soviet Union promises the final construction of Communism, which is to be completed by 1980. This would mean that it has taken as many as fifty years (from 1932 to 1980) to "realize Communism." But just as the picture of the "socialist future," which has been realized before our very eyes as a hell on earth, has failed to rouse the enthusiasm of serious-minded and honest persons, so, too, the picture of the "Communist future" will fail to inspire those who have been disillusioned, deceived, and terrorized. To win over someone for the "vision of the commune" is equivalent to breaking his backbone and maiming his human soul. One only needs to read the "works" of P. Tychyna and M. Rylsky to gain an idea of the way in which Moscow exploits these writers and forces them to write in keeping with its own aims and intentions. "Rejoice, O Ukraine—for we have arisen. We shall only proceed on the straight path. For we have been one with Russia since time immemorial...." these and similar dithyrambs and agitatory "poems," which might have been composed by any schoolboy, characterize the present "poetic creativeness" of Tychyna.

Or another example: "Our life is wonderful. And in the near future it will become incomparably more wonderful, clearer, richer, and more exalted." So writes Rylsky in an editorial (in *Dnipro*, No. 12, 1961), in which he glorifies "the entire multinational Soviet people who are united in work and brotherhood." Formerly talented writers, Rylsky and Tychyna have been transformed by Moscow into its servile agitators, and their spirit has been broken and their character corrupted.

Revival of Nations

Khvylovy—who was oriented to Europe—showed far more character when he voiced his courageous slogan: "Away from Moscow!" Moscow has never forgiven him for this. His name will probably never be posthumously "rehabilitated," but that is not necessary, for one is bound to admire his courage. Just as it is erroneous to regard Khvylovy as one of the foremost champions of the Ukrainian nation, which he incidentally never was, so, too, it is equally erroneous to underestimate his anti-Russian attitude during the last years of his life, especially when we compare him with those who capitulated to Moscow and have not the courage to censure and condemn Russian colonial policy in Ukraine, at least in the manner in which the Montenegrin M. Djilas does.

Orientation to Europe and the slogan "Away from Moscow" undoubtedly sum up the historical Russo-Ukrainian conflict. The intellectual status and role of Ukraine lie in eternal opposition to Russian ideas. A free evolution of Ukrainian ideas on Ukrainian territory as well as in East Europe and in those parts of Asia subjugated by Russia. An Asiatic renaissance will only be possible after the overthrow of the Russian empire and after the liberation of the Asian peoples who are subjugated in the Russian Communist sphere of influence. The renaissance of Asia will not be affected as a result of the withdrawal of the European powers from Asia, but in consequence of the overthrow of the Russian empire and after the liquidation of Communism. In Asia, too, the European powers have created the preconditions for a national rebirth. The ideas of liberation nationalism are European ideas, and Ukraine is the most powerful champion of these ideas in the Russian empire. And it is precisely these ideas which will disintegrate and burst asunder the Russian peoples' prison from within.

The national liberation idea, the idea of human dignity, freedom, and justice, the ancient Greek and Roman ideals, and heroic Christianity determine the intellectual and spiritual status and role of Ukraine in the world of today. And this status and role are characterized by Ukraine's leading role in the fight against the Russian empire for the realization of the Ukrainian conception of the life and existence of the nation and the individual, and these same principles and ideas constitute the essential elements of a new world order which will rise up out of the ruins of the Russian empire.

The national liberation of Ukraine is the precondition for the realization of a new order and of a universal evolution of the creative powers of individuals and peoples. In our ideas on a new world order emphasis is on the national individual, for at the height of his evolution no individual is supra-national or extra-national.

The idea of liberation nationalism has become the characteristic feature and signpost of the present epoch; this idea was tenaciously defended by Ukraine in the most difficult period in its history, during the fight against German and Russian colonialism. Hence Ukraine at present occupies the foremost position in the fight for justice and freedom.

If the Allies during World War II, instead of supporting the Antichrist against the Devil, had supported the national liberation movements of the peoples subjugated by both tyrants, the world would today be free of fear, and freedom and not slavery would reign in a territory which is inhabited by a thousand million persons. The political and ideological position of Ukraine at that time, which was expounded at the conference of subjugated peoples held in the forests of Zhytomyr in 1943, indicated the only course which would lead to a universal victory. The appeal to form a common front of the peoples subjugated by national socialism and Russian Bolshevism for the purpose of fighting against both occupants indicated the only course which would lead to the realization of the idea of freedom of the individual and independence of the peoples. As a result of having disregarded and scorned these ideas the major Western powers have forfeited their empires, which nevertheless in some respects constructively and creatively helped the development of their colonies, while the Russian empire, which—in contrast to the major Western powers—has subjugated civilized and cultured peoples, has expanded and has become a menace to the entire Free World.

In an article in the well-known English periodical *The Royal United Service Institution Journal*, of May 1962, Major-General J.F.C. Fuller rightly says that Hitler had already lost the war the moment he hoisted the swastikas in Kyiv instead of the Ukrainian flag.

Against Any Imperialism

We advocate and support the national, as opposed to the imperial, principle as the ideological factor in the organization of the world. But it would be erroneous to assume that at the same time we join the so-called front of subjugated peoples all over the world. We accord to all peoples who are fighting for their freedom our sympathy and our moral support, but for manifold reasons we cannot join such common fronts. The national principle has been abused by the Bolsheviks (before the United Nations they recently demanded "independence" for an island with a population of 24,000 which belongs to Australia), or has been identified by some Western states with the frontiers of their former colonies as administrative units. The same can also be said of the so-called "Arab nation," which the imperialist Nasser is endeavoring to create or to "unite"; there is no such nation, but only an Egyptian, Sudanese, or Moroccan people. Similar methods are adopted by Sukarno, who, in the name of a "united Indonesian nation," is trying to subject foreign territories to his rule, and these too are the methods of Nehru, who likewise subjugates foreign peoples. In all these cases it is therefore not a question of the realization of the national principle, but of imperialist wishes and aims of petty chiefs who have recently come into power; they are allegedly fulfilling their mission of making the world happy on the ruins of the British, French, Dutch, and Belgian colonial empires, by which they were not merely exploited but from which they also derived benefits.

There have also been similar petty imperialist chiefs in Europe—as, for instance, General Anders, General Sosnokowski, Zenki, certain Hungarian imperialists who have still not gotten over the fact that they have been deprived of their rule in Carpatho-Ukraine, and certain Romanian reactionaries who aim to bring about the incorporation of Bukovina. If colonialism has even come to an end in Africa, how can one aim to set up colonies in Europe? One must indeed be bereft of one's senses if one now tries to deprive Ukraine of its western regions with Lviv, of Carpatho-Ukraine or Bukovina. The Ukrainian people are willing to be friends with anyone who aims to set up a common front against the Russian empire, but never at the expense of their own national territories; the Ukrainians will evict all new conquerors from their territories. We ourselves have no desire to conquer or subjugate foreign territories, for we want to live and cooperate in peace with our neighbors. Anyone who attempts to seize Lviv, Uzhorod, or Chernivtsi will meet with a determined resistance on the part of the Ukrainian people. There can be no common front with anyone who attempts to claim Ukrainian ethnographical territory.

Combatting "Neutralism"

Nor can we form any common front with those liberated peoples and newly founded states of Africa and Asia that veer towards the so-called bloc of neutralists, for in this way they are strengthening the Russian Bolshevik front. We are, for instance, interested in the independence of Algeria provided that the latter joins de Gaulle's anti-Bolshevik front. But if Ben Bella, after having seized power, introduces collectivization of Algeria's agriculture and orients himself to Moscow, then such Algerian "independence" will be detrimental to freedom, since it would favor and promote tyranny in the world and pave the way for the subjugation of Algeria by the Bolsheviks. And Ben Bella would thus not be a freedom fighter but a tool of the Russian colonial imperialists in North Africa.

All the newly founded states which have developed out of the complex of colonies of the Western states and which are now oriented to Moscow are consolidating the most ruthless colonial power in the world, the greatest enemy of the national idea, and are paving the way for the victory of the largest colonial empire—the so-called USSR (that is to say, the Russian empire), and, moreover, are becoming the supporters and representatives of the Russian colonial conception of conquest and domination of the whole world. Thus their independence— from the moral point of view a positive factor—from the political point of view becomes a disadvantage, for the question at issue is the overthrow of the Russian Bolshevik empire and its ideas, whereas some newly founded states are placing their territories at the disposal of the Russian imperialists for setting up military bases or bridgeheads to spread Russian influence. For this reason it is the duty of the anti-Bolshevik circles of all new states to do their utmost to insure that the political orientation of these states becomes anti-Bolshevik and anti-Russian, for only then will their independence have both a moral and a political value. In any case, collaboration with the Russian imperialists undermines the moral independence of the people in question, and this moral depreciation eventually leads to the collapse of the independence of the state. It is moral prostitution on the part of the newly founded states to accept money both from the Russian imperialists and from the USA and other Western states and then to play off the one against the other.

And no less a danger is the "policy" of the West in granting financial support to the so-called "neutral states," which are, as it were, milking two cows at the same time. The West must definitely refuse further support to such "neutral" states and must concentrate on only supporting those states which are wholeheartedly and genuinely on the side of the West. Turkey, Pakistan, Free China, South Korea, Vietnam, the Philippines, and Thailand must be given support, and not Nehru, who is flirting with Moscow and buying arms there, and not Indonesia, Burma, or Yugoslavia.

Is it not strange that Tito financed the Belgrade Conference of the "neutral states" with money from the American aid fund, yet the Conference condemned the USA and praised and supported Khrushchev! The idea of such a conference of "neutrals" in all probability originated in the brain of the American Ambassador to Yugoslavia, Kennan; Tito carried this idea out and the American taxpayers paid for it. With the money that he had received from the USA Tito supported certain African states and forced them into the camp of the "neutrals," a fact which is entirely in keeping with Khrushchev's wishes.

In such a situation we should always support, for example, anti-Bolshevik France and not presumably "neutral" Algeria, anti-Bolshevik Holland and not pro-Communist Indonesia, Great Britain and not "neutral" India, and also such anti-Communist states as Pakistan, Free China, the Philippines, Korea, and Vietnam.

If the West ceases to support the "neutrals" it will undermine their influence and in this way will accelerate internal upheavals by sound national forces that will liquidate the pro-Russian or pro-Communist course of their countries. Khrushchev is not in a position to help his friends, the "neutrals," effectively, but the United States and other Western powers give them loans and with the aid of these loans the pro-Communist Governments of these countries are consolidated, which means that the pro-Western forces there are weakened and deprived of the possibility of successfully applying their political orientation in practice. If the "neutrals" practice "moral prostitution" in their own policy and accept American and Russian help at one and the same time, then they are also demoralizing their own people and undermining their national strength. It is an established fact that the Russian imperialists have their own peculiar method of "granting aid" to the developing countries. In the first place their help consists of vitiating the country in question with Communist agents and agitators whom they have either sneaked in or hired. If the Americans, for instance, then send wheat or foodstuffs to the Asian or African country in question to be distributed free of charge among the needy, the Communists, when unloading these supplies, tip them into sacks containing the words "Made in USSR" in the national language of the country. When the supplies are distributed among the population the Communist functionaries point to the words on the sacks and praise the Russians for their helping spirit and, at the same time, condemn the Americans who refuse to help the needy population. Similarly, when Moscow builds schools or hospitals in any African or Asian country, it always does so in the capital so as to to be able to boast of its "philanthropy" more effectively later on. The United States builds countless schools and hospitals, but it does so where these institutions are needed most, in the rural areas. Communist teachers even teach in these schools, and medical personnel trained in Moscow works in these hospitals.

Thus the Americans give real and effective aid, while the Russians send agents and agitators to the countries in question, and these same agents and agitators then make use of the financial aid of the Americans and disseminate Communism. As far as the West is concerned, the situation is indeed a paradox. The only way out of this situation for the Western states is to break off relations with all the "neutralists" and cease all aid to them, a fact which will eventually lead to internal changes that will result in the national, anti-Communist forces coming to the fore. Only when this has been achieved will the moral recovery and the internal rebirth begin, and the pro-Communist "ministers" of Ghana or other states will no longer be able to build palaces, and their wives will no longer be able to buy gold beds worth thousands of pounds.

Moscow's Ideological Capitulation to the National Idea

The ideological status and role of Ukraine—the signpost for the freedom-loving peoples and for their vanguard—is on the side of the morally and politically uncompromising forces of the world, which are based on national and theistical principles and on unswerving social and moral principles, as well as on social justice and on internal national solidarity—that is to say, the solidarity of the social classes of the people. Uncompromising Ukraine, with its ideas of the regeneration of mankind, ideas which are radiated by the national and religious underground, with its fight for human and divine values, is a cornerstone of the new spiritual and political order in the world. Treacherous Moscow is well aware of this world-significant revolutionary role of Ukraine; for this reason it is endeavoring to silence Ukraine, or else to pose as the "defender" of the national liberation idea itself—always on this side of the Iron Curtain.

Hence the new program of the Communist Party of the Soviet Union is in itself an ironic capitulation when it affirms that there is a "nationalism of the *subjugated* nations" and a "nationalism of the *subjugating* nations"; there is no longer any mention of the "class of capitalists," but only of the nation. The new Party program designates the nationalism of the subjugated people as "nationalism with a general democratic purport, which is directed against subjugation," and it supports this nationalism since it "can be justified historically in the present stage."

The nationalism of the Russian people, which subjugated other peoples, is reactionary and barbarous—such is the logical conclusion reached by every Ukrainian behind the Iron Curtain who is forbidden to express himself creatively in the Ukrainian spirit and in the Ukrainian language. The Russian imperialists are inevitably digging their own grave. The entire fourth section—"The National Liberation Movement"—of the program of the Communist Party of the Soviet Union is a capitulation on the part of Moscow before the national idea, before the sovereignty of the peoples, which on an ideological basis is defended by Ukraine for all peoples of the world. Ukraine endeavors to put these ideas into practice against Russian Bolshevik slavery and subjugation in order to set up a political and moral front against Bolshevism, which is a synthesis of Russian imperialism and Communism. The mendacity of the Russian imperialists is being exposed to an ever-increasing extent, for it is in this case a question of concealing and disguising colonialism in its worst form. At the same time the iron encirclement of the Russian empire is steadily becoming tighter, while colonialism is limited to its sphere of influence. The fact that there is an outcry on the part of the Russian imperialists about the colonialism of the Western powers, which incidentally no longer exists, clearly shows how anxious the Russian imperialists are to conceal their own colonialism.

> The world is experiencing the stormy epoch of the national liberation revolutions.... The main condition for the solution of all national problems is the consistent fight against imperialism [namely Russian imperialism]; the liberation movement of the peoples who have become nationally conscious is in many countries conducted under the motto of nationalism.... By new methods and in new forms the imperialists [namely, the Russian imperialists] are applying every means—colonial wars, military blocs, alliances, terrorism, subversive activity, economic pressure, bribery—in order to keep the countries under their rule.... Nationalism manifests itself in the efforts of the subjugated peoples to achieve their liberation from the imperialistic [namely, Russian] yoke, their national independence, and their national rebirth.... The mighty wave of the national liberation revolutions is sweeping away the colonial system and is undermining imperialism. Former colonies and semi-colonies have become and are becoming young independent states.... The peoples have risen up as new creators of a new life, as active participants in international politics, and as a revolutionary force which is destroying imperialism.... Peoples who are to outward appearance independent, but in practice are still politically and economically dependent, are rising up against imperialism [namely, Russian imperialism] and against the reactionary imperialist regime [namely, the national Communist regime].... A heroic fight is being conducted against the foreign [namely, the Russian] oppressors by peoples who are still fettered by the chains of colonial slavery.... Political independence can only be consolidated by a people who had fought for its democratic rights and its freedom and who takes part in the leadership and administration of the state....

Blunders of US Policy

We have purposely quoted some passages from the new program of the Communist Party of the Soviet Union (section IV/1) in which the national liberation movements of the world are mentioned in particular, in order to show the extent to which Russian Communism is forced to capitulate before national-ism in order to be able to assert itself with its propaganda in the Afro-Asian states. If we add the words "Russian" to "imperialism" and "colonialism" and "in the Russian peoples' prison" to the "colonial or dependent peoples," we would have a true picture of the present situation in the world. The United States is indeed an "advocate of colonialism," not of its own but of Russian colonialism, if it allows Mr. Dean Rusk to affirm that Ukraine, Georgia, and Armenia are "integral, traditional parts of the historical state of the USSR," or if it gives aid to the Russians, Poland, pro-Russian Yugoslavia, Ghana, Nasser, and other politi-cians and states that are oriented to Moscow. Indeed American policy is directed towards the preservation of imperialism—namely, Russian imperialism! Unfor-tunately Khrushchev did not mention this fact in the new program of the Communist Party of the Soviet Union. In the statement that the liberation fight of the peoples is being conducted under the motto of nationalism and not socialism, Khrushchev admits the bankruptcy of socialism. Fifty years ago Pil-sudski led the liberation fight as head of the Polish Socialist Party.... And in this respect the program of the Communist Party of the Soviet Union also admits the bankruptcy of socialism, which Russian colonialism all over the world has brought into disrepute and discredit.

Ukraine—Vanguard of the Fight

Let us imagine that a serious-minded and thoughtful young Ukrainian at home reads this chapter of the program of the Communist Party of the Soviet Union and compares it with the true conditions in Ukraine. He is aware of the ever-increasing Russification (for instance, at Kyiv University lectures in Ukrainian are only held in two faculties, that of philosophy and of journalism, while in all the other twelve faculties lectures are only held in Russian—and that in the capital of Ukraine!). He is aware of the economic colonial exploitation of Ukraine by Russia; he knows that the Russian KGB deports citizens of the "independent" Ukrainian SSR to other "independent" Soviet republics, sends people to the slave-labor camps, and executes, exterminates, and persecutes innocent persons *en masse*. He knows that "independent" Ukraine possesses no army of its own and has no diplomatic representatives abroad, and, similarly, that there are no for-eign diplomatic missions in Kyiv, and that there are no free elections in Ukraine. He knows that Ukraine is in every respect dependent on the Central Govern-ment in Moscow, and is deprived of all the characteristic features of national, political, and economic independence, he is only too well aware of the mendacity of "self-determination without secession," and he comes to the conclusion that all these factors are characteristic not of an independent but of a subjugated country, which, in the stormy epoch of national liberation revolutions, is still fettered by the chains of colonial slavery—in the peoples' prison, in the Russian empire. All that is said in the new program of the Communist Party of the Soviet Union about national liberation movements, about colonialism and imperialism, is characteristic of the conditions which prevail in the Russian imperium—that is to say, in the USSR and the satellite states. In this way Khrushchev is sawing through the bough on which he himself is sitting. The wave of national liberation revolutions is indeed and inevitably approaching—namely, in the Russian empire itself.

Our place—the place of Ukraine—is in the vanguard of these anti-Russian, anti-Communist, anti-imperialist, national, and social revolutions of peoples and individuals.

The fourth section of the program of the Communist Party of the Soviet Union is a corroboration of the ideological and intellectual ignorance and mendacity of the Russian imperialists, who are trying to save their empire by a new deception, inasmuch as they suddenly resurrect values and slogans which only yesterday they condemned. The fact must above all be stressed that Khrushchev, who is endeavoring to assert himself for some time to come on the surface of world politics—in particular in the Afro-Asian world—is obliged to steal the ideas and slogans of the Ukrainian revolution with which the latter is undermining the Russian empire from within and, after having slightly altered them to his own advantage, is presenting them as his own ideas and slogans to the peoples on this side of the Iron Curtain.

The ideas of the Ukrainian revolution are not confined solely to Ukraine, but pertain to the entire peoples' prison and to all peoples, for they are based on the principle of independence for all peoples and the freedom of the individual, an aim which can, however, only be achieved by crushing the Russian empire, and destroying Communism, the most ruthless colonial system of all time.

Ukraine, which in the spiritual and intellectual conflict holds the foremost, the most important, and most responsible position, is standing in the vanguard of the fight against the center of evil and barbarity and for the realization of the just ideas of our epoch.

The Ukrainian Review,
No. IV, 1962, pp. 49-69

The Status and Role of Ukraine in the World
(Part Two)

At the Turning Point of Epochs and Worlds

The chief problem which at present occupies our world is the threat of an atomic war. And the questions connected with this problem make other matters, which are no less important and concern the majority of mankind, appear insignificant by comparison. In any case, the danger of an atomic war determines the policy of the major Western powers. But, in addition to this undoubtedly many-sided and complicated problem, other equally important matters confront all mankind, and though they leave their mark on the world more noticeably than events in any other epoch of the history of the world, they are assiduously avoided as if they did not exist. The problem of the subjugated peoples in the Russian and Communist sphere of influence as a whole is the key problem of world politics at present. In practice world politics hinge on this problem, although this fact is not admitted. Are not Berlin, East Germany, Laos, and the Chinese mainland, all of which have been subjugated under the Communist system introduced from Russia, part of the complex whole of subjugated peoples, as a special, decisive third force which determines the aspect of the world today? The problem of Ukraine, which, in view of the human fighting potential of that country, its geopolitical position, its natural reserves, and its role as an intellectual center in the fight against Russian tyranny, is a most vital problem, belongs to the category of questions about which world politics keep silent.

At present a number of trends are in evidence which aim at a solution of the complicated problems that confront mankind. But intellectual and political chaos—the ideological crisis of the Free World, the crisis of religious faith, still continue to prevail; it would, however, be wrong to assume that there are no longer any sound ideas in the Free World and that they are all in some way or other out of date and old-fashioned. The ideas have not been used up, but man has misused them. The ideas of Europe have not stagnated, but the people of Western Europe have become disloyal to them. The characteristic feature of Europe is heterogeneity and not homogeneity (uniformity)—nationalisms and not internationalisms. The strength of European ideas always lay in advance and progress—in the firm conviction that these ideas were superior to other ideas, in a willingness to fight in the spirit of the ancient conquerors on the part of the champions of these ideas. But what of our day? Western Europe has grown indifferent. It has ceased to show enthusiasm for any ideas. Politics and, to an even greater extent, foreign policy are nowadays more an art than a science. One must be able to comprehend the most important problems, to unravel and understand the main trends in the development of the world and the central ideas which determine the present process in the world's history. What is needed are great statesmen, politicians, and historians, who are capable of comprehending and of orienting themselves to what is happening all around us. What is needed are men who have the great gift and the courage to make decisions, and to reorganize the concatenation of the events that are happening in the world. They need not necessarily be highly erudite, but they must above all be personalities with a sound common sense, political courage, instinct, and farsightedness.

The present state of the world is due to many causes. During the past 500 years there were fewer far-reaching and momentous revolutionary events than during the past 50 years, if one takes into account the conglomeration of upheavals occasioned by revolutionary events during this relatively short period. True, the discovery of America was the first and most unique event of its kind and it brought about an upheaval in the world and left its mark on the past 500 years of history. Thanks to the spirit of discovery new continents, countries, and peoples were discovered and opened up. In this way different cultures, religions, ideas, ways of living, and social conceptions were able to meet. The European discoverers and conquerors entered new continents and countries; they discovered new peoples, who then became acquainted with each other. True, abuses occurred, but the essence and purpose of all these efforts was a creative one—man's wish and longing for what was new and his search for what was still undiscovered drove the restless spirit of Europe into the unknown. This spirit was the champion and herald of the ideas of Europe, of its religious faith and its way of living, and not solely of colonial rule. It was very different from the Russian spirit of ruin and destruction.

In the meantime the revolutionizing events of the past fifty years have led to the downfall of many idols. Since Western Europe did not remain loyal to its ideals but surrendered its integral eastern territory to the barbarous Russian Eurasians, it was bound to forfeit its political position in the world sooner or later, for it was now divided.

Betrayal of the National Idea

Had Western Europe comprehended the ideas and plans of Charles XII and Mazepa and thus prevented the defeat at Poltava in 1709, it would not have paved the way in Europe and the rest of the world for Russia. Had Western Europe in 1918 supported the national state independence of Ukraine and of the other nations liberated from the tsarist yoke, it would now occupy a stable and powerful position in the world. The armies of the Russian barbarians would not at present occupy the very heart of Europe, and Russia would not be the dominating force in Asia. The Western statesmen failed to comprehend the great historical process—the rebirth of the nations, above all after the disintegration of the peoples' prison in 1917-18.

Hitler and the National Socialists did not in the least realize the course which the development of the world was taking; they wanted to turn back the wheel of history. Nor did Churchill and Roosevelt, the former ally of Stalin, comprehend the nature and meaning of the development of mankind, the significance of the historic hour. In place of the empire, national states began to appear on the scene of history. Hence, from the aspect of culture, freedom, and justice, it was erroneous to ally oneself with gangsters against criminals. In any case, the historical process during the first decades of this century already indicated the direction in which the future development would proceed. Japan won the war against Russia in 1905 thanks to an internal revolution in the Russian empire. The Russians lost the war owing to national liberation revolutions within the Russian empire. As a result of the First World War three empires collapsed: Imperial Germany, Austria-Hungary, and Turkey. But in spite of the grim struggle, new forces matured, and the main trends of future development were already clearly apparent. In order to play off their partners against each other and to justify their own aims, the empires that remained created "miniature empires" as they infected the Serbs, Poles, and Czechs with moribund imperialism; they created Yugoslavia, which was not a creation of the Serbs but of the French. Millions of Ukrainians, Byelorussians, Lithuanians, and Germans were forced under Polish rule; Slovaks and Ukrainians were handed over to the Czechs, and Ukrainians, Hungarians, and Bulgarians were abandoned to the Romanians.

Even in those days the Western powers betrayed Europe by forcing one European people under the rule of another. In this way they made Russia, a non-European and anti-European power, the arbitrator in Europe. The Czechs, the Serbs, and the Polish national democrats set their hopes on Russia, with whose aid they hoped to be able to preserve their "miniature empires." The statesmen of Europe failed to realize that Russia, once she had intervened in European affairs, would always emerge out of each dispute as the victor, for close relatives who quarrel usually hate each other afterwards. Neither Poincaré nor Clemenceau regarded Ukraine as a problem. Neither of them saw beyond Versailles, and neither of them wanted to take the development of historical events into account.

Instead of realizing the idea of national states in Europe forty-five years ago, the West did something most improbable and absurd. It supported the Russian Bolshevik empire; it supported Deniken, Wrangel, Kolchak, and Kerensky in order to prevent the independent states of Ukraine, Georgia, and Turkestan from being restored. To its own disadvantage it held up the process of development in the East that would have been most expedient for itself.

Changes in the Balance of Power

As a result of World War II all the "victorious" empires in the world which had existed until that time, above all the British, French, Dutch, and Belgian empires, made their exit from the world stage. The most significant and portentous event of the postwar period is the disintegration of the British Empire, hitherto the greatest world empire in history. The fading of this power within so short a time had disoriented many people. The picture of the world as they conceived it has been disturbed and confused. The largest fleet in the world no longer rules the oceans; the power which could prevent any other power from ruling the world is no more. New powers have come into being to which the world has not yet accustomed itself, and whose abilities and intentions as regards the world order are little known. India, with her neutralism and her vague and constantly veering course, and other, similar members of the Commonwealth do not occupy a clearly defined and stable position in the political power conflict. The fact that the African and Asian continents have ceased to be dependent on European powers, the creation of a number of independent states out of former colonies, the defeat of Germany, the loss of her position in Europe, and the occupation of one-third of her territory by Russia have led to a shift in the distribution of power. The increase in power of the largest and only existing empire, the Russian empire, which—since the European world powers made their exit—has extended its sphere of influence to huge territories and is aiming to rule the whole world, including the mother countries of the former European colonial empires, has changed the entire appearance of the world.

On the other hand, as a result of the two world wars, and above all as a result of

World War II, an extra-European state, the United States, has become the strongest power in the world, and the Asian aspect is as important to it as the European. The Russian empire, which ranks next to the USA in the technical and material sense, is likewise an extra-European power, but it is above all an anti-European power, whereas the USA in its ideology adheres to the European idea of freedom and of the independence of peoples. The Russian empire has achieved a hitherto unparalleled expansion, inasmuch as it has taken advantage of the erroneous policy of the Western powers, in particular of the USA, to occupy vast territories of Central Europe. But the West overlooks the internal weakness of this empire, its vulnerable spot the subjugated peoples. It is a colossus with feet of clay. But it is an undeniable fact that the British Empire and other vanished empires of the West have been supplanted by new forces—the world-embracing imperial, barbarian Russian power and the American power—with the newly created national states which are caught between two powers.

In Africa there are no longer any colonies, but there are now colonies in Europe. At present 17 million Germans, members of a people whose leaders not so very long ago strove to rule the world, are colonial slaves. The most political nation of the world, England, which until recently possessed the greatest empire in the history of the world, is in danger of becoming a colonial dependent of the most barbarous power in the world, Russia.

Never before in history has a large proportion of a people threatened by a foreign attack served the potential aggressor by betraying their own country, as, for instance, the Communist parties in Italy or France and their supporters are now doing. Never before have people who were threatened ignored to such an extent peoples subjugated by the same enemy as possible allies, and thus undermined all means of self-defense.

All this is the result of the chaos of ideas and of man's disorientation as regards the trends of the development of mankind and of a lack of faith in the truth of these trends. In former times it would have been unthinkable for England or France, for instance, to have permitted Nazi ideas or those of the French revolution—that is to say, ideas of the enemy—to exist side by side with the English or French way of thought, as is now the case at the universities in Great Britain and in France.

China, which is ruled by the Russian idea, will also cause considerable trouble if the politicians of the West, who overlook the fact that the ideas of freedom are stronger than Communist terrorism, do not take the initiative and resort to countermeasures on a political level.

The fact that France has confined itself to the European continent and the alliance of those two sworn enemies Germany and France, undoubtedly an event of historical significance for Europe, are two factors which are expedient, inasmuch as they defeat any intentions on the part of either of these states to make an ally of Russia. The lost war of the Western victors, who have joined forces with defeated Germany and Japan, and the inclusion of the states that were conquered in the camp of allies against the former "friend" Russia have rapidly changed the entire distribution of power.

Revolutionized Strategy

If one takes into account the great revolutionary changes and progress in the technique of warfare—nuclear weapons and the destructive power which they represent, the rapid increase in technical achievements, and at the same time the decay of moral values and the discrepancy between the intellectual, moral processes and the civilizing, technical processes which run counter to each other, one is bound to recognize the ever-growing dangers that threaten the world.

The increasing religious indifference and atheism in the Free World—as can be seen from the alarming example of the USA, where religion has been banned as a subject of instruction in the schools—and the degeneration of the moral principles of individuals and peoples lead to a life of chaos and result in a people becoming an amorphous mass without spiritual leadership, without energy, and without a noble aim.

In addition to the revolutionizing changes in the technique of arms, the significance of the armed people, of insurgent partisan units, and of insurgent tactics and strategy is steadily growing, much to the surprise of all technocrats. Atomic weapons are countered by the weapons of the intellect and of ideas, of partisans and underground tactics and strategy, a fact which was recently acknowledged by the President of the United States. Twenty years after it was founded, the UPA and its ideas are now becoming the salvation of mankind and also the salvation from the atomic threat. The strategy at present adopted by Russia is something unprecedented—a combination of aggression with internal civil and peripheral wars, the aim of which is the achievement of world domination by means of so-called "salami tactics"—that is to say, step by step—in which the opportunism of the West, which maintains that it is not worth risking a war on account of such trivial matters, is used to advantage by Russia. The result has been the loss of Laos, Vietnam, and Korea, and the "Wall" in Berlin. The fact that the West does not follow a clearly defined political principle and course in the present conflict, which has assumed global dimensions, and Moscow's orientation towards the peripheral regions for the purpose of diverting the attention of the West from the inevitably of an attack on the starting-point of the evil are resulting in the West concentrating on fronts that are of secondary importance. Africa is certainly a continent of strategic importance; but the decisive battle will be fought not in Africa but in the steppes of Ukraine, in the world of the subjugated peoples, in the Russian peoples' prison.

The main issue lies in reducing the human potential of the Russian Communist bloc by winning over and rousing the enthusiasm of the subjugated peoples for new ideas and by supporting and defending these peoples. For it is precisely such measures which will augment and strengthen the insurgent partisan forces, which will be the deciding factor in any future cataclysm. As long as the West fails to realize that a new world is about to emerge from the interior of the Russian empire, it will continue to steer towards its downfall. As long as the West fails to encourage the new constructive order of national independent states on the ruins of the Russian empire and does not recognize this revolutionary

order—irrespective of whether it desires this order or not, it will continue to feel
that it is threatened by approaching danger.

Ukraine's Key Role

New forces are at work in the catacombs of the Russian peoples' prison. And
the West must set its hopes on these forces. The light of the rebirth of the peoples
and of the idea of national, Christian, and human freedom shines forth from the
underground movement in Ukraine. The greatest bulwark against every
menace—whether it is a yellow, a red, an existing, or a non-existing menace—
must not be based on injustice and coercion, but always on free individuals and
peoples who defend freedom and not slavery and who would die rather than
submit to enslavement. Any general and politician who is a man of moral
principles will prefer to defend a fortress with free individuals rather than with
prisoners.

Thus the key position in the fight against evil, the center of which is Moscow,
is held by the subjected peoples. And it is time the West realized this fact. It must
drastically wipe out the treachery in its own ranks. For this reason the Communist Parties must be prohibited as parties of treachery and parties of the enemy.
The dissemination of the ideas of the enemy, of ideas of treachery, at the
universities must likewise be prohibited.

The freedom-loving world possesses a huge intellectual potential. But its
vulnerable spots are a lack of faith in its own values; defeatism; an overestima-
tion of material values as compared to spiritual values, duty to God, human
dignity, moral values, self-sacrifice; and further, worship of the golden calf,
egoism, self-complacency, and indifference to the fate of the subjugated peoples.
It is senseless to hope that vital human problems can be solved by Utopian
dreams, for *the world is a planet of strife and of work, of tears and suffering, of sweat and blood,
of self-sacrifice and heroism, of eternal striving to attain an ideal which mankind will never
achieve. At the point of divergence of epochs and worlds* the same truths are binding for us
which the Christian faith taught mankind 2000 years ago. And we must continue
to fight for these same truths, always bearing in mind that we shall never find a
nobler ideal than self-sacrifice for our "neighbor." The answer to all the doubts
which assail the world at this point of divergence and to the dread of destruction
by nuclear weapons is: those who, in spite of all the troubles and misery of this
world, fight for the Truth of God on earth, for justice, for freedom, against
injustice, against godlessness, and for their own fatherland, will never be the
object of destruction. If it has been decided by Divine Providence that this planet
is doomed to decay, then it is better to lay down one's life in the fight for freedom
rather than to capitulate before evil. We have many guiding signs in our life and
our fight. The conception of the world which is propounded by Ukraine is a
realization of the ideas of the independence of peoples, of justices and of freedom
of the individual.

In the chaos of ideas and principles the great historical course of Ukraine
stands out clearly marked and defined. Although the reality of this world is

complicated and burdened by many factors, the main trends of its development have assumed a definite shape, and one is to some extent justified in hoping that the freedom-loving world will eventually find the right path which Ukraine has been following for the past fifty years.

The Ukrainian Review,
No. III, 1963, pp. 31-37

Ideology and Program of the New Ukraine
(Part One)

The dynamic Ukrainian nation, fully conscious of its destiny, indomitable and invincible, full of spirited initiative and rich in economic resources, fulfills its historical mission in the fight against Bolshevism. Chronologically, Ukraine stands with the vanguard in the battle for the destruction of the Russian empire and the Communist system. In conjunction with the achievement of Ukrainian sovereignty in a state separated from Russia, following the disintegration of the Russian empire and the total destruction of Bolshevism as the synthesis of Russian imperialism and Communism, the political map of the whole world will undergo fundamental changes.

In view of the ideological, political, cultural, and religious crises, as well as the crisis in the social institutions of the West and particularly of the Russian and Communist world, it must be emphasized that militant Ukraine is determined to bring back into current idealistic human values and eternal divine truths, respect for the concepts of human dignity, fatherland, heroic humanism, and liberating nationalism, to restore the ideals of full national sovereignty and independence, and to uphold the right to sovereignty of every nation. At the same time, militant Ukraine condemns a priori imperialism and colonialism as manifestations diametrically opposed to nationalism, and regards as the main purpose of every political and social measure that it should provide a real guarantee for the universal rights of man and for the establishment of social justice, in accordance with the basic nationalist ideal of harmony and cooperation within and among nations.

Ukraine is fighting for a truly spiritual and idealistic revolution of mankind which will sweep away materialism, internationalism, and hedonism, and will ensure the triumph of a heroic conception of life. A moral victory of this kind is the prerequisite for the success of a political, military, and insurgent offensive— supported by a revitalized Free World—against Russian and Communist tyranny, imperialism and colonialism, these anachronisms in the present era of new ideas and thermonuclear power in which ideological controversy, insurgency, guerrilla fighting, liberation struggles, and civil war are imminent.

Life in our time has been subjected to the barbarities of Bolshevism and Nazism as a result of the process of dehumanization and de-Christianization which in those two phenomena reached their climax. We live in an age of cynicism and nihilism, of constant fear and the impending threat of total annihilation, an age in which for a number of people worship of the Golden Calf and pure hedonism constitute the sole purpose of life. At a time like this, the idea of willingly sacrificing one's life for a great cause, for eternal values, for freedom, justice, truth, honor, for fatherland and God, may to many appear paradoxical.

Yet, in spite of that, the Ukrainian people are firm in their determination to fight for these eternal, true values, to bring about the spiritual and moral regeneration of mankind, and to restore men's faith in God and fatherland. They are fighting for their belief in the divine essence of Man, for "true faith and homeland," for "honor and glory, and the liberation of our brothers" (as the Cossack maxims say). They act true to the ancient saying of Prince Sviatoslav: "We shall not disgrace our Ukrainian land, but rather die here. The dead cannot be a shame to the country." This is an attitude in sharp contrast to the Russian "Rob what was robbed," the German demand for *Lebensraum*, and the modern standard of value—the dollar.

In her battles against Russia, Ukraine has been inspired by the old yet forever valid world of ideas, which is a synthesis of the ancient Greek, Roman, and Christian conception of life, diametrically opposed to the Russian view of human beings as members of a herd rather than individuals.

Moral courage, high ethical standards, and the determination to fight to the last for the values of the true faith, for human rights and universal justice, these are the qualities urgently needed for the salvation not only of Ukraine.

Truth does not triumph by its virtue; it can only triumph if its supporters are resolved to win and are prepared to fight to the death if need be.

An objective view of developments in the world, with its crumbling empires and the rise of independent nation-states, confirms the correctness of the subjective attitude of the Ukrainian nation, consistent with its character, and its determination to crush the Russian empire and to reestablish its own sovereignty. A sovereign, united Ukrainian state will thus be wholly in line with progressive developments in the world.

The Ukrainian nation's accumulated wealth of ideas embraces the most progressive thought of our time. By contrast, the Russian empire has become the chief obstacle in the process of the development of mankind as envisaged by all freedom-loving nations and individuals. This process of development makes for the differentiation between peoples into sovereign nation states and not for their compulsory incorporation into artificially constructed political combinations of an anti-national, supranational, or a-national nature.

When moral values and virtues, which ought to strengthen and keep the spiritual side of man in proper balance with material progress, are corroded, then the quality of life is bound to deteriorate into barbarism and hedonism.

Modern technology and the discovery of the secrets of atomic energy prove in a deeper sense, and no less convincingly than the researches of natural philosophy in the past, the existence of the greatest of all mysteries of the universe: the absolute—i.e., God. For anyone with a belief in spiritual forces beyond the visible world, the fear of the all-destroying power of nuclear weapons becomes irrelevant, since it cannot be in God's design that those who heed His commandments should be destroyed or that the decision over the existence or non-existence of half a billion people should rest with criminals and mass murderers. The very attempt to solve the most complicated problems of life by the methods of pragmatism and empiricism is the main factor in the world crisis, and that at a time when technological and sociological advances have long ago broken through the narrow limits of pragmatic thinking. It is an attempt to use the fire brigade for fighting a by-now-uncontrollable world-wide conflagration—the world of ideas.

Without idealism the problems of mankind cannot be solved. A solution can only come from the new elite of the ideological—that is to say, from that elite whose members combine clear ideological visions, not connected with exclusively earthly things, with a great faith and a willingness to die for the object of their faith. Besides, whoever denies idealistic values will also materially be the loser!

The main question facing mankind today is how to avoid nuclear war. This problem cannot be solved without a faith in higher values and absolute truth and the resolution even to lay down one's life for such convictions, knowing that in this way we fulfill our destiny on earth. Only a renewal of religious belief and obedience to its laws and a revival of true patriotism can prevent the world from plunging into hedonism or despair. Only a spiritual revolution of this kind can provide a solution to the terrible problem of untamed nuclear energy in the hands of criminals.

The organization of political, social, and cultural life in our own state must, of course, take into account every aspect of the latest technological achievements, the results of human ingenuity, and the discoveries in the world of science, and this is what we intend to do. But we shall have to bear in mind that even a most perfect and scientifically planned material culture is not enough to fire the people's imagination. Only a great vision can arouse the enthusiasm of a nation, an idea permeating the whole program of state-building, so that this program itself reflects the unique and traditional elements of the people's soul, the nation's state of mind and its idealistic conception of society, its ardent desire to attain national, cultural, and moral greatness, and its respect for human dignity. That vision, I believe, can be expressed in the simple formula:

Kyiv Versus Moscow!

In this age of conflict between diametrically opposed concepts of faith, ideologies, political and social ideas, of the new forms of psychological and nuclear warfare, there is on the one side: Kyiv—the personification and symbol of the forces of good, the pioneer for human and national rights, the exponent of heroic humanism, Christianity, belief in God, truth, justice, tradition, and the moral progress of Man; and on the other side: Moscow—the embodiment of evil, of retrogression, and of all the forces opposed to the Kyivan values.

The main theater of the struggle between these opponents is the territory of the Russian empire, that prison of nations and individuals. Yet the contest is not restricted to that area alone, as in a wider sense it involves the whole world.

Kyiv and Moscow are in every respect poles apart. The spiritual, ideological, cultural, religious, social, and national positions of Ukraine are the exact opposite of those held by Moscow. It is a battle not merely between two political concepts, but between two civilizations antagonistic to each other.

The prerequisite for establishing the identity of those two antipodean centers is the awakening of a strong faith in our own values which represent divine truths on earth. This faith is absolutely essential if the victory is to be ours.

Sadly characteristic of many Christians in our day is their reluctance to fight for their faith. The reason for this lack of militancy must be ascribed to a crisis of a personal and ethical nature in some representatives of the Christian idea. Further contributing factors are latitude of interpretation and the tendency—by the Vatican, for instance—to allow Christian concepts to be adapted to the "modern" way of life—in other words, a permissive attitude which treats human weakness far more leniently than in the past, thus aiding and abetting complete secularization of human life in some sectors of Western society. Yet it was the very strictness of Christian morality, the militant affirmation of its values and of national ideals, that in days gone by made Western society great and caused its standards to spread beyond the frontiers of Europe.

On the other hand, the Russian Orthodox Church has made Christianity the servant of the Bolshevik political system, the essence of which is militant atheism, genocide, misanthropy, and insatiable Russian imperialism and expansionism.

Finally, there are the simultaneous efforts of the Western Churches to try to find a modus vivendi with the sworn enemies of every religion, with the murderers of the faithful of every denomination and of the millions of fighters for freedom, truth, "the orthodox faith and the fatherland" (as the Ukrainian Cossacks say). "A good tree cannot bring forth evil fruit, neither can a corrupt tree bring forth good fruit." (Matthew VII, 18.)

In the circumstances described above, the Ukrainian metropolis, Kyiv, clearly has to perform these tasks: to deepen and expand that vision of Christianity which was nourished in our cave-monasteries of St. Anthony and St. Theodosius and which inspired life throughout the noble, princely epoch of our history; to honor the Kyiv-Mohyla tradition, emulate the moral austerity of our monks and the example set by the Christian Cossacks' republic—unique in the Orthodox East—of the Zaporozhian Sich, modelled on strict, medieval Christian Orders: and, generally, to follow the traditions of our Cossack era with its Hetmans and the Zaporozhian Sich and their undying slogan "For the Orthodox faith and the fatherland."

It is the further duty of Kyiv to cultivate the spirit of nationhood which prevailed in 1918 and the years following: to uphold the traditions of the UPA, in which national and Christian concepts were fused into one idea; and, above all, to foster the spirit of resistance, which in the period of terrible Bolshevik persecution enabled the Ukrainian Christians to stand fast. Witnesses to our triumph in those days were such figures as the Metropolitans Lypkivsky and Sheptytsky and other martyrs without number, all of whom displayed the greatest heroism in their uncompromising fight against the atheist regime of the Russian tyrants.

Arrayed on the ideological battlefield are St. Sophia and all the righteous of Christian Ukraine, their bodies buried in unknown graves, against the mummi-fied symbol of aggressive atheism and genocide, the Russian Lenin in his mausoleum—the "temple" of Moscow.

The ideals of our sacred and immortal metropolis, Kyiv, the ideals rooted in our Ukrainian native soil—sometimes identical with the concept of the State, as in the days of Sviatoslav the Brave—these are the sources of our spirituality.

For the Ukrainian nation the native soil assumes a mystic quality. On Ukrain-ian soil our ancestors won fame and glory, the earth is soaked with their blood and sweat, and the graves of our heroes cover it.

The Ukrainian soil, which became a battlefield and was trampled on and desecrated by our enemies, is returning to life again, showing once more the qualities extolled in the works of Stefanyk and Shevchenko and by our folksongs.

The attitudes which have for a long time now been evident in Ukraine can be outlined as follows: from the philosophical point of view, the greatest importance is attached to the unification of Christianity, with Ukrainian patriotism—and here the young Ukrainians have found their model in "our first intellectual giant," the Christian philosopher Skovoroda—and to a faithful adherence to the age-old traditions of Kyiv, with which the call "Away from Moscow" is closely associated, as well as the orientation towards "psychological Europe," the old Europe of noble spirit, morals, and idealism. Finally, there is the admiration for the renaissance in Asia, in the sense of Asiatic nations gaining their independ-ence, a fact which has not only political but also ideological repercussions on the ever increasing anti-Russian resistance of Ukraine. These attitudes do not imply a sentimental, "folksy" Ukrainianism of the Kvitka-Osnovyanenko type, but represent a conscious and purposeful process in the nation's determined effort to fulfill its historic mission in the world-wide confrontation: *Kyiv against Moscow*.

From the ideological, political, social, and cultural point of view, the central problem before the Ukrainian elite and their aspirations is that of actual government—i.e., the exercise of power.

If the Ukrainian nation is to enjoy genuine health and happiness, then not only the ideals of freedom and justice must be realized, but the ideal of government, of the exercise of power by Ukrainians over Ukrainian territory, must become reality. When that condition is made the focus of cultural creativity then there is not room for purely superficial and popular educational preoccupations.

It is not only liberty, not only justice we demand!

The idealistic concepts of authority, of power, of the nation as an organic unit in human society are forcefully expressed in the work of our poet Symonenko. "My people lives! And it will live forever! No one can erase it from the earth! All renegades and worthless vagabonds will perish, and routed will be the invader's hordes! You, bastards of torturers and devils! You, fiends, remember this: my people lives, and the hot blood of Cossacks pulses through its body!"

Or: "Tremble you murderers! Repent, you toadies; life spews you out, you cancerous brood!"

What profound mysticism—the immorality of the nation—is expressed in the brave words of this unique poet!

Then there is the motto "Away from Moscow!" of the unrehabilitated writer Khyvlovy, who went astray until under the blows of Moscow he found his way back.

A mighty nation—that is the cause the young generation of Ukrainians have espoused. Power in the hands of their own nation, which will drive out the invaders, that is what young Ukrainians are demanding openly, clearly, and without fear. In the national idea they are the dominant influence of our time, and that idea means to them the fully sovereign political and cultural life of the Ukrainian nation and its contribution to the common weal of the world.

In their opinion, the national idea does not supplant the great ideals of humanity as a whole, but rather acts on them as a catalyst. The very absorption in nationalist ideology and devotion to the national idea makes for a deeper understanding of the social and spiritual needs of others. The new Ukraine certainly feels the close kinship that exists between the national idea and the national value common to all mankind, the concepts of human divinity, honor, conscience, and justice, of personal and social morality. It is precisely these concepts of dignity, responsibility, and justice which lead the young generation towards the national idea and to a new consciousness of their mother country, Ukraine. There can be no harmony in the world, nor a true community of men, if the achievement of those aims should make even the slightest injustice towards a single nation necessary. In this way the national question is intricately connected with the most important matters of the human conscience. A lofty conception of the national idea can therefore induce in every creator of cultural values a profound feeling for the aspirations common to all mankind and the pathos of self-sacrifice. There are in history periods when grave issues are decided by a society's moral and civil spirit and behavior, when even rudimentary human dignity will resist brutal pressure and develop into a potent revolutionary force.

We are living in such a period now, and nothing is of greater importance at present than civic morality and conduct of the highest standard. What men need most are examples of a heroic attitude, since these will reassure them that even in our time heroic action is possible and by no means futile. Now as in the past "the madness of the brave" is equated with "the wisdom of life," and young Ukrainians keep repeating: "Even today, and perhaps just today rather than later, it is possible and necessary to fight."

The traditions of the old, heroic Ukraine are coming to life again. The phrase "only our heroes' graves cannot be removed" (i.e., by the Russian enemy) expresses the feeling of the immortality of our nation.

Everything now happening around us has taken on a significance which men did not foresee. Side by side with the growth of the most modern techniques of war the fight of a people armed with conventional weapons has gained more and more importance. Without any planning, this development was brought about by the thermonuclear threat itself. In this age of ideological conflict nuclear weapons have not only lost their exclusive power, but in spite of their technical perfection have been rendered practically worthless.

Warfare on the line of insurgency and guerrilla tactics, as initiated and practiced by our UPA and OUN, has in our time become predominant. (One example of this is Vietnam.) National revolutions are an example of how the nations enslaved by Russia can achieve their liberation, and at the same time they emphasized the fact that atomic weapons are already outmoded, since by now their use cuts both ways. In essence, the new strategy consists of waging war on the territory controlled by the enemy. National wars of liberation assuming the character of revolution must today be regarded as the most up-to-date form of war. They are also typical of our age, in which ideological differences tend to result in civil wars. In this era of the disintegration of empires—above all the Russian—when the subjugated nations rise against the foreign armies of occupation and their rule of terror, the new type of warfare becomes of prime importance; all the more so as in these foreign armies there are the sons of captive nations, who from within can turn against the enemy of their own countries. The Western powers have pulled out of their imperial positions without recourse to atomic weapons and, apart from a few exceptions, even without using any armed force against the population of their non-European colonies. This in itself supports the view that in our time it is no longer the imperial, but the national idea which presents the driving and controlling force.

In employing armed force against rebelling captive nations Russia cannot make use of nuclear weapons, since these are double-edged and essentially suicidal. Moreover, the sons of subjugated nations serving in the Soviet army also have access to such weapons. Russian attempts to suppress with conventional arms carefully planned and synchronized national revolutions will fail in the end because of the ideological, political, qualitative, and quantitative superiority of the subjugated nations, and above all because the process of the disintegration of empires is irresistible as the gaining of independence by more and more nations, and even by African tribes, goes to show. By that same process the Russians are driven into a position of disadvantage where they can no longer disguise their chauvinism and racism, their belief in a Russian master race, and their brutal imperialism.

In these circumstances the principles of the ABN acquire decisive importance. According to these, the first front consists of the national revolutions for liberation in the countries concerned, while the second front—supporting the first—is formed by the joint forces of emigrants from all the suppressed nations and by mobilizing the anti-Russian element among the free nations.

One of the causes for the moral and ideological crisis in the dechristianized West, the fear of nuclear war, does not exist in militant Ukraine, which sees the alternative solution in a national, revolutionary war of liberation, which by its very nature makes it impossible to employ the nuclear bomb, as a self-defeating weapon, against our homelands.

Another factor preventing for all practical purposes the use of atomic weapons is the stalemate resulting from more than one of the Great Powers possessing the bomb, a position similar to that which in the past led to the renunciation of chemical and bacteriological warfare.

Let us now recapitulate as follows: there is no religious, ideological, socio-political, or military crisis in the underground Ukraine, which is fighting for Christ, for the strengthening of the national idea, for human dignity, and self-respect, for honor and freedom from slavery, for national independence, for the inviolability of the nation as the basis of world order and for the inexhaustible human spirit. The battle-cry of that underground Ukraine exhorts men to stand by their own nation and in the defense of its cause to seek and find their purpose in life.

The new light emanates from Ukraine's ancient sources of light. It shines forth from the Orient, but this time from the national and Christian Ukrainian East; from the Lavra cave monastery of St. Antonious and St. Theodosius; from the ideas and the way of life of the great monk Ivan Vyshensky; from the suffering of the indomitable princes of the Church, Lypkivsky, Sheptytsky, and Slipy; from our cathedral of St. Sophia; from the prisons and labor camps in Siberia and elsewhere; from the heroic battles of Bazar and Kruty; from the deeds of our UPA, OUN, SVU, and SUM; from the works of the young generations of present-day Ukraine; from the invincible city of Odessa and its freedom-loving people, who long for national and social liberty and have nothing but loathing for the Russian "pharaohs" who took away their freedom; from Odessa, the city representing Ukrainian-Hellenic tradition at its best, which could become the Ukrainian Budapest, as the history of its underground movement during World War II demonstrates; from our Donbas, saturated with the blood of Ukrainian workers; from Novocherkassk; from our Cherkassy, the hometown of the poet Symonenko; from the blood that flowed for freedom and independence during the mass demonstrations against Russia by our youth and workers in many Ukrainian towns in recent years.

From these luminous sources shines forth the new light, the reflection of eternal Truth.

Ex Oriente Lux—but from the underground East! Our new, militant Ukraine knows no crisis!

The Ukrainian Review,
No. II, 1968, pp. 2-14

Ideology and Program of the New Ukraine
(Part Two)

The Well-Being of the Nation Is Man's Highest Aim on Earth

The basis of our political philosophy is the Ukrainian nation as a natural category of the first importance.

The nation is the highest form of an organic and spiritual community which, as a result of certain historical, geographical, cultural, religious, economic, and social conditions, took shape, grew, and developed into a living organism of a well-defined character. It is a biological and social reality, as well as a cultural unit, in which the irrational and the subconscious are essential components.

The individual Ukrainian is an inseparable part of the Ukrainian nation. The well-being of the national community is man's highest aim on earth. There is no such thing as abstract a-national Man: there is only concrete Man with his roots in the nation.

The idea of freedom and the determination to fight for it are innate in Man; so is the social instinct. Together these form the basic elements of human nature. Man is a social creature. By nature he is an inwardly free being whose own conscience holds him responsible for fulfilling the aims of the society to which he belongs.

The creative freedom of Man, the well-being of the community, and social justice, these are the absolute values in this life on earth. Any limitation of freedom can only be justified if there is a danger of its abuse and when restraint becomes imperative in order to safeguard and strengthen freedom itself for the benefit of the community, as well as of the individual, whose freedom has its limits there where it is contrary to the common good and to justice. Modern man plays his role in this world through and within the framework of the national community.

The family, as the living cell of the national organism, tending and guaranteeing the moral and physical health of the individual and the community, stands at the very center of our efforts to foster the well-being of the nation as a whole.

Nation, family, individual—that is the hierarchy of society. The synthesis of these three categories, with priority freely conceded to the common good over egoism, to national over personal interests, makes up the substance of our concept of Man.

The variety of professions, the type of goods produced or services rendered, divides society in a natural way into vertical groupings. Any horizontal stratification within these vertical structures brought about within the framework of social justice as a result of individual creative initiative, must be kept within well-defined limits in order to prevent exploitation of any kind.

Our social philosophy rests on a conception of Man which accepts the values of the nation, the family, of creative and social diversity, and, finally, of the individual as a responsible member of society.

Metaphysical philosophy and human morality, two subjects which by themselves lack the drive of an ideology or of a social-political movement, are fully covered by the Christian faith.

Above the nation and above Man there are the absolute values of the Universe, whose creator is God, to whom both nation and individual, as the creations of his omnipotent will, are subordinate.

The Ukrainian nationalist ideology, of which one aspect is the belief in heroic humanism, springs from the spirituality and social sense of the Ukrainian nation, shaped by a thousand years of Christianity, and is fully in harmony with Christian morality and the Christian philosophy of life. Ukrainian nationalist ideas and

Christian ideas form a complex whole. The Ukrainian fight for national reality is at the same time the fight for Christian reality.

We are today in the thick of the struggle of the world of theism, the exponents of national ideology, of human dignity and freedom, of social justice, against the world of militant atheism, the exponents of aggression and imperialism, of the persistent contempt for human values, of enmity between people in their own country raised to the principle of the class struggle, of dialectical and historical materialism as a further means in the ideological conflict between the Russian nation and the Ukrainian and other nations. In this confrontation of radically different views the ideological and political position of Ukraine is of decisive importance.

The world of ideas of our Christian, national, sacred, and immortal Ukrainian metropolis, Kyiv, fighting for the inalienable rights of man and nations, today stands facing the ideological world of Moscow, metropolis of atheism, with its thirst for conquest and its hatred of men, the personification of everything evil and destructive. This means a collision of two opposing worlds whose feud is a matter of life and death.

Historically and with a view to the future, the motto of the OUN, "Freedom for Nations—Freedom for Man," has its complement in this further motto: "Kyiv against Moscow."

For a Ukrainian the most precious thing on earth is the Ukrainian nation. The goal of all endeavor and action of every Ukrainian must be the power, well-being, and spiritual growth of the Ukrainian nation.

The highest form of existence, the translation into reality of a nation's will, and the continued development of a nation can only be achieved and guaranteed in a nation-state. Thus the existence and development of the Ukrainian nation depend on the creation of an entirely independent, sovereign, all-Ukrainian nation-state, and it becomes the highest duty of every Ukrainian of our time "to win or to die in the battle for the Ukrainian state."

Freedom and Justice Are the Highest Ideals of Mankind

Freedom and justice are the ideals which all individuals and peoples, ever since the beginnings of mankind, have ardently desired and fought for. All the epoch-making events in the life of mankind, of individual nations and men, all revolutions and cataclysms, have been motivated and characterized by these ideals.

At the present stage in the development of the human race, the realization of the ideals of freedom and justice means national and political self-determination—i.e., political independence for all nations irrespective of race, creed, wealth, or size, and personal freedom for all men, guaranteed by a politically and socially just and lawful State.

The Ukrainian slogan "Freedom for Nations—Freedom for Man" assumes universal significance, since the fight of the Ukrainian people for national and political independence and for a just social order in a state of their own is at the same time a fight for the victory of freedom and justice everywhere in the world.

Freedom of the nation implies a sovereign nation-state, dependent upon no one, and embracing the whole of the people within its ethnographic frontiers.

The freedom of Man implies the individual's unhindered enjoyment of civil liberty, his direct share in the ownership of economic wealth through his own work and through inheritance from his parents, as well as the right to use his earned income within his own country as he pleases.

The present era is marked, more than any other in the history of mankind, by the fight for human dignity and self-respect, for honor and conscience, for freedom and justice. Nowhere and never before have the most sacred ideals of humanity been so brutally trampled underfoot as they are today in the country that embodies everything evil and retrograde, in the totalitarian Russian empire, in which nations and individuals are cruelly imprisoned.

The reconstruction of the world is undertaken by combating every form of enslavement, exploitation, and degradation of nations and men. In the course of the revolutionary renaissance, the first step towards satisfying historical justice is the restoration of the sovereign Ukrainian state.

To the Ukrainian People and the Ukrainian Individual Ukrainian Revolutionary Nationalism Has Become the Exponent of the Ideas of Freedom and Justice

Modern Ukrainian nationalism grew out of the fight for the spiritual, national, political, and social liberation of the Ukrainian people and is the synthesis and embodiment of a desire for life, which throughout the ages inspired the Ukrainian people as an indivisible national community. Ukrainian nationalism denotes the striving after freedom and justice for the Ukrainian people, after personal liberty and the well-being of the community, and after unlimited freedom for the cultural creativity of the Ukrainian individual.

Ukrainian nationalism started as a movement of an active and heroic minority. It aroused the enthusiasm of the mass of the people and with their support grew into an all-embracing national movement.

Ukrainian nationalism means the realization of a society from which parasitic elements are excluded and in which oppression has no place. It repudiates internationalism, totalitarianism of any kind, the preponderance of state bureaucracy over the creative individual, and, finally, class warfare, which according to Marxism is the whole meaning of history.

Ukrainian nationalism condemns every exploitation of men by the State—i.e., by other men—since internal relationships in the Ukrainian state must be based on the recognition that the interests of the community are identical with those of the individual.

Ukrainian nationalism means the realization of government by the people and of human liberty; it provides the link with historical Ukrainian democratic traditions and satisfies the needs of the Ukrainian people, who have become the exponents and defenders of the national idea. It also means an extension of the democratic basis, so that government rests not with one group, one social stratum or class, but with the people at large, the nation.

Ukrainian nationalism does not view the nation as the sum total of a number of unconnected individuals, but as an organic whole, an indissoluble unity formed by the nation's past, present, and future. It rejects the class character of an obsolete type of democracy and substitutes for it direct participation in the country's government by the people as a whole through their freely elected representatives from all walks of life, with due regard to the interests of the various territories. Ukrainian nationalism insures the freedom of the individual, his share in the country's economic wealth and the means of production, and his right to dispose freely of the product of his labor.

The Ukrainian Review,
No. III, 1968, pp. 20-24

Ideology and Program
of the New Ukraine
(Part Three)

Ukrainian nationalism aims at constructing a sociopolitical order which is based on the Ukrainian people's concepts of truth and justice and on a harmonious relationship between the aspirations of the individual and the needs of the community. For their ideas and ideals of the social order in the Ukrainian state, the exponents of Ukrainian nationalism do not draw on alien liberal or socialist doctrines and speculative theories, but on the fundamental qualities of the Ukrainian people, their spirituality and way of life, their aspirations and needs.

Ukrainian nationalism relies on the positive and creative aspects of Ukrainian tradition, as well as on the Ukrainian people's innate conception of an ideal society. At the center of that desired social order stands the creative and productive individual, linked by the ties of nature to his family and the traditions of his ancestors, whose value has been and always will be judged by his personal contribution to the common good.

On the strength of Ukraine's creative energy and of the present liberation struggle, Ukrainian nationalism embodies the future of Ukraine in all spheres of life: a complete and organic Ukrainian system of life and work. The Ukrainian system embraces all that human ingenuity has ever achieved. In contrast to liberal capitalism or Marxist socialism, Ukrainian nationalism represents a broadly based and enduring system, free from internal contradictions—analogous to the Ukrainian nation itself. While rejecting both liberal capitalism and Marxist socialism as dominant systems, Ukrainian nationalism contains in its own, totally different system everything that practical experience has shown to be useful or justified. Rooted in the hearts and minds of the Ukrainian people, Ukrainian nationalism offers the solution to every one of the nation's problems.

Ukrainian nationalism provides a system of democracy in the true sense of the word, a system which solves the problems of life by taking into account not only the interests of the living generation, but also the interests of generations to come, of the entire nation's present and future. It is a rule *by* the nation *for* the nation. Based on its nationalist ideals, the genuine democracy of the liberated nation will therefore have the future very much in mind. Its measures in the different spheres of life will be designed to further the well-being not only of our people now living, but of the nation in the future; not only of a class, but of the people as a whole; not only of the family, but of continuing generations. Under Ukrainian nationalism the people's full participation in the government will not be a mere promise, but will be guaranteed by absolutely free and direct elections, by the freedom to establish political organizations which are not in principle hostile to the independent Ukrainian state, by the freedom to form professional associations, and the unimpeded use of every other means of free expression. There have been those, compatriots and foreigners alike, who made great promises to the Ukrainian people; but credibility must be achieved by guarantees, and these can only consist of measures which insure the people's participation in the government of the nation. The basic principles of our social and political order contain these vital guarantees.

Harmony and Solidarity within the Nation

The guiding principle in building up the sociopolitical order of our country is to bring into full harmony the well-being of individual, family, society, and nation.

In our social measures, attention is focused on the Ukrainian people—as a unit of all the creative forces and as the representative and defender of the nationalist idea in our time—as well as on the Ukrainian individual.

The purpose of these measures is to de-proletarianize man by allocating to as many Ukrainians as possible a personal share in the means of production and by insuring the right of the individual freely to choose his place of work and to dispose of his earned income as he pleases. The further aim is to de-collectivize— that is, to raise him from the depersonalized status which has been forced upon him, to give scope to his aspirations and stimulate his creativity. Appropriate legislation will guarantee unfettered freedom for the creative genius of our people, in sharp contrast to the collectivization principle by which man is deprived of his dignity and creative activity is made impossible.

An economic system based on capitalism which encourages irresponsibility and the uncontrolled play of market forces must be seen as historically obsolete, since the economy is not a game but an important and basic factor of human life. Ideologically and politically the national concept must permeate the entire life of the nation and the idea of the class struggle must be eliminated. After the abolition of the Communist system every citizen must be able to hold private property, and the work he does will be the legal criterion for the acquisition of property. This would make a return to capitalist finance in the economy impossible. The *kolkhoz* system must be abolished and private ownership of land—within a given minimum and maximum—reestablished. The right of inheritance and the best use of the land under modern methods of cultivation must be safeguarded. There can be no recurrence of large-landed estates.

Absolutely indispensable means of production shall be the property of the state as and when this is in the public interest. The nationalization of any means of production will be approached empirically. Certain forms of transport are to be nationalized.

Attention is to be given to the development of cooperative societies and other voluntary forms of organization in certain production and marketing sectors. Constructive planning is to aim at the prosperity of the nation as a whole without destroying any incentives from individual effort and enterprise. In the entire economy the principle of private ownership has priority over that of state ownership. Work as the source of private property must be free from all exploitation and the right of inheritance must be respected.

It is essential that the nation should act and administer itself through the organs of its choice on the principle of local concentration, not on the principle of a mechanical centralization which destroys every creative impulse. At the top of the political system the creative individual carries out the task of government, with proper regard to the interests of the various territories, drawing on the assistance of the peoples' representatives from all walks of life, of socially valuable institutions, and of political organizations whose representatives have been chosen by universal, free, secret, and direct vote.

Specific rights must be conceded to the family as a socially and politically most valuable institution. After the political as well as social and economic revolution, the state must also insure the rights of those who participated in the fight for freedom and independence, of the prisoners and deportees and their families, and of the victims of enemy occupations.

The dignity of the human being is sacrosanct and it is the duty of the powers that be to respect and defend it together with the civil and political rights of man.

To the Sources of Ukrainian Spirituality and the Ukrainian Sense of Justice

Ukrainian nationalism rejects as alien and hostile to our way of thinking the historical and dialectical materialism of the Marxist doctrine and sets against it Christianity and a Ukrainian nationalist philosophy of life with its own sociopolitical and economic doctrine of which the Ukrainian individual and the Ukrainian nation are the cornerstone.

Ukrainian nationalism insures the development of a national culture, growing organically out of the soul of the people and their creative genius.

The motivating ideas of our cultural, creative work are the ideas of God, Motherland, Glory, Truth, Justice, Freedom, and Power—in the Ukrainian form. The spiritual make-up of a nation can most clearly be seen from its spontaneous creative work. Collections of Ukrainian folklore offer an inexhaustible source. In particular the spirit of a nation speaks through its songs and popular sayings.

Militant Christianity, liberation nationalism, the heroic humanism of Shevchenko, the mission of Kyiv, the holy city of Ukraine, in the age-old struggle against the city of blasphemy, tyranny, slavery, and violence—Moscow—must be put in the center of our ideas of cultural, creative work.

Kyiv's mission is to carry on the age-old struggle with Moscow. Kyiv is to symbolize the world of ideas completely different from those symbolized by Moscow. Ideas which are to save mankind from destruction by Moscow are to be centered around Kyiv.

Soldiers always followed poets. The struggle of cultures, as a political fight, as the struggle between two world outlooks, two conceptions of life, is unfolding itself in Ukraine. Communism's alternative to man is a collective, its alternative to individuality is a herd. If man is to be saved, the world must be individualized, must free itself from the idle mass of the soulless who know only their stomach. The mass returns man to a herd of human apes. When socially noble personalities are formed, life becomes worthy of man. Art begins where general norms are broken.

We have to show the ideological bankruptcy of Bolshevism and the great danger of a new Russia which may replace it and again deceive the world with ideas such as those of Berdyaev and the NTS. We must never give up the concept of the struggle of two cultures—those of Russia and the Occident, two opposing worlds. For otherwise Russia will again deceive us and the West and will again realize her world, hidden from the eyes of the West, the world of the herd, the slave, and the tyrant.

Our program is to give a direction in the worldwide struggle in the cultural field, showing what we are for and what we are against.

The Ukrainian National Revolution will outline the paths along which the revolutionary legal order should develop. Lawlessness is an inherent feature of the Russian regime in Ukraine. To restore legality, or rather to introduce it, is the central, moral problem of the revolution.

At the basis of any order should be put Man as a social being, who grows up and develops in the community and for the community, in the family and in the nation. Such an understanding does not deny the concept of the nation, a quality higher than an individual; nor of the family, which an individual should also serve.

Nationalism, as a great movement of spiritual, ideological, and ethical renovation of the individual, introduces a new understanding of the duties and rights of the individual, starting from higher categories—the interests of the nation and the family.

Nationalist legality and Ukrainian traditional legality are founded on the old Ukrainian legal codes. Ukrainian common law offers many elements for Ukrainian juridical reforms. The Christian concept of legality is always nearer to Ukrainian mentality than the positivist-liberal one.

The Russian legal system has been disintegrating the family and the national community—i.e., organic cells—in the name of a crowd, ostensibly in the name of the proletariat, but in fact in the interests of the Russian occupation power, hostile to Ukraine. It has split the Ukrainian farmers as a class, as a social-economic stratum, as a bastion of the biological and moral health of the nation, as the protector of the traditions of the nation.

The entire Russian legal system in Ukraine must be changed. Russian legal institutions are diametrically opposed to the Ukrainian ones, which are Western-oriented, close to Roman law. The Russian form of imperialism is a form of total domination over the enslaved, not only over their bodies, but also over their souls. Therefore, the Russian legal system in Ukraine, all jurisdiction, legislation, administration of justice, must be revised.

The spirit of a nation, her legal concepts, and moral feelings reveal themselves in folklore. The collections of Ukrainian folklore provide a host of original ideas for Ukrainian law.

Montesquieu's tripartition of power has been justified. One of the guarantees of legality is the separation of each of these three main kinds of power.

Ukrainian nationalism is for a bold negation of the existing order and for a clear enumeration of what will be absent under the new order. The Russian code of laws will cease to be valid in Ukraine immediately in all those areas which reflect a class approach to the administration of justice, and Russian occupation interests in Ukraine, which contradict the freedom of man, restrict his liberties, freedom of speech, conscience, association, and gatherings and contradict private property and the interests of the family. Laws which concern such crimes as murder, robbery, theft, etc., can remain temporarily.

The equality of all before the law will be particularly and firmly upheld. However, in the aspect of private law (concerning property) particular care will be extended to the families of soldiers of the revolution, deportees, war invalids, prisoners, etc.

During the transitional period special attention will be devoted to appointing judges from the people whom professional judges will advise. Methods of appointing such judges and of selecting candidates will have to be worked out well beforehand, in order to prevent lynch trials. Two elements—conscience and a guarantee of legality and professionality—will have to be synthesized. In many cases the dispensation of justice will have to be left to the people until a normal legal system is set up. It should be remembered that inhabitants of a village know best who is guilty and who is innocent there, and the same goes for workers in a factory.

All concentration camps in a free Ukraine will be abolished and all inmates will be released, with the exception of common criminals. As regards those sentenced for theft, it should be ascertained what the circumstances were of the crime. If a collective farmer stole from a collective farm, then this is justice and not a crime, for he took that which had been taken away from him.

Secret political police will be abolished in the Ukrainian State. Internal defense of the State will be taken over by courts of justice and ordinary police. Apart from this, special legal norms will be introduced for exceptional circumstances which would not require secret police.

Courts-martial will have to exist and be applied with regard to internal enemies, Russian and pro-Russian, and in general enemy subversion, for high treason and subversive anti-State, anti-Ukrainian activities, and punishment by death will have to be retained as the highest measure of punishment.

The rights of police will be restricted by law, and Western European—in particular Anglo-Saxon—experience will be followed to a great extent.

The struggle for rights and for justice is the greatest stimulus of a revolution.

The National Idea—a Universal Idea

A world organized on the national principle—i.e., a separate statehood and independence for every nation, respect for the freedom, dignity, and rights of man, his well-being—these are the objectives of the nationalist liberation movement.

Revolutionary nationalism strives to attain sovereignty, freedom, and justice for our people. It opposes every kind of slavery and its cause, imperialism. A characteristic feature of the history of mankind is the struggle of nations against empires and imperialism, as well as the strife between the imperialist powers themselves.

Every subjugated nation best fulfills its universal mission when on the basis of the national principle it fights for its own independence and sovereignty. By freeing itself from slavery, that nation most effectively furthers the victory of freedom and justice all over the world.

The nationalist liberation movement condemns internationalism, the deceptive doctrine of certain Great Powers, in the knowledge that never in history has internationalism helped the suppressed nations towards freedom; it has always been the idea of national liberation that made them succeed in their fight for independence.

While rejecting internationalism as an idea hostile to nationalism and, in fact, only another form of imperialism, the national liberation movement favors many kinds of international relations and international institutions, ethical and social causes transcending the borders of individual nations (e.g., religion, among others), which help to eliminate wars and enmity and instead promote friendships, cooperation, and mutual assistance among the countries and nations of the world.

The nationalist liberation movement gives support to such international institutions as accept the principle of equality among nations, respect the sovereignty of each nation, do not lend themselves as instruments of any imperialist power, and do not attempt the setting up of an anti-national world government, a world state—in short, a world empire. It supports international institutions which advance cooperation and mutual assistance among free and sovereign nations, those very nations which by their joint efforts strive to eliminate the causes of enmity and wars and to remedy national and social distress and injustice. It backs those international bodies which are prepared to give aid to the poorer nations without attaching any strings, which have the freedom and prosperity of all mankind at heart, and which further the exchange of technical and cultural achievements. It is in favor of any international institution which provides a forum, not for mutual betrayal, but for mutual respect, not for contests between the great powers supported by their respective satellites, but for understanding and cooperation amongst nations.

The highest aim and purpose of Ukrainian nationalism in the political sphere is to attain full independence for the Ukrainian nation within the ethnic frontiers of its own sovereign Ukrainian nation-state, to the benefit of the country's entire population and regardless of creed, language, nationality or race. This is to be achieved by breaking up the Russian empire into its ethnographic parts and establishing these as sovereign nation-states and by abolishing once and for all the Communist system of slavery and tyranny in all its manifestations.

As the revolutionary liberation movement of the subjugated Ukrainian people, Ukrainian nationalism respects the right of every nation to sovereignty within its ethnographic borders and denounces, condemns, and in international relations entirely disassociates itself from imperialism as the enemy of freedom and justice.

Nationalism is the symbol of freedom, imperialism is the symbol of slavery and chauvinism.

Harmony within and among nations, a world free from war, poverty, fear, and slavery—that is the ideal inspiring Ukrainian revolutionary nationalism.

For this reason Ukrainian nationalism condemns any possible imperialistic deviation in Ukrainian political thought.

Ukrainian nationalism is insistent in its view that federations, coalitions, or alliances among nations and states are feasible only if those participating can act and are treated as free and equal partners. It is convinced, therefore, that its aim of world unity—that is to say, unity through harmony of the peoples of the world—can only be achieved by differentiation among peoples, their existence in independent nation-states on an equal footing with each other. Only by the defeat of imperialism and totalitarianism through an anti-Russian and anti-Communist war of liberation can just and lasting peace be obtained. World peace is only possible when the ideals of freedom and justice and self-determination are finally realized in the form of independent statehood for each nation.

Nation-states lacking imperialistic ambitions for the conquest of other countries are more likely to guarantee the peace of the world than the multinational empires of Great Powers, often the instigators of devastating wars.

Even in a nation-state the growth of imperialist tendencies cannot be ruled out, as the past has frequently shown. The best safeguard against this contingency is "old-fashioned" defense agreements, which represent the real interests of the concluding parties and protect the peace far more effectively than "modern" international organizations, which are by no means the last word in the history of progress, but often are—as we know from past experience—an instrument of imperialism. However, Ukrainian nationalism does not reject out of hand the possibilities of international affiliation, but the choice of organization and adherence to it depend, of course, on the precondition that the nations concerned—and this applies above all to the countries now under Russian or Communist rule—have become truly sovereign and independent states and their peoples are able freely to express their will in all respects, and in particular about any associations of an international nature.

At the same time Ukrainian nationalism absolutely rules out, for the present as well as the future, any ties between Ukraine—or other nations subjugated by

Moscow—and Russia. This refusal is grounded on the dire experiences of the past and the unchangeable Russian tradition of genocide. The entire history of Russia's relations with the peoples enslaved by her is characterized by the continuous struggle of the victims against their murderous Russian oppressor.

Ukrainian nationalism is of the opinion that Russia will never voluntarily confine herself to her own ethnic borders. For this reason it considers it imperative that the liberated peoples, once they have attained sovereignty, and the nations now under threat should enter into agreements and form alliances against Russia, whatever its political hue may be at the time.

There can be no change in this now dogmatic Ukrainian attitude unless there is tangible proof over a considerable length of time that such a defensive stand is no longer necessary.

Ukrainian nationalism affirms the right of the Russian people in an independent state of their own, strictly within the ethnic frontiers of the Russian nation.

Rooted in the creed and ethics of Christianity and a heroic conception of life, Ukrainian nationalism condemns and rejects genocide as an act of revenge against the Russian people. However, it insists that the Russian state should make amends to the Ukrainian and other subjugated nations for the wrongs and damages the Russian nation has inflicted upon them throughout the long and terrible period of oppression.

For the crimes of the Nazi regime the entire German people have had to pay, even with the loss of ethnically German territory, and this despite the fact that the principle of collective responsibility had been explicitly rejected by the World Powers.

In the view of Ukrainian nationalism it is absolutely necessary that the nations likely to be threatened in the future by Russia or other imperialists should, as equal partners, conclude among themselves a defense agreement which would guarantee their freedom and ours. Ukrainian nationalism is opposed to any future association, whatever its shape, between the hitherto subjugated nations and Russia. We will have no truck with any federations, unions, or confederacies, with a "Union of Three Russias," "United States of Eastern Europe," "Eurasian Peoples' Union," "Pan-Russia—Eurasia," or any other schemes of that sort, since they are essentially nothing but variants of one and the same thing, Russian imperialism.

Ukrainian nationalism is resolute in its opposition to the USSR—that prison of nations and individuals—and to any concept of a Russian Empire in one form or another. It sets against it the separation of peoples in nation-states and their full independence; equality among these free national states, regardless of their size or wealth; mutual assistance and harmonious cooperation between them; the freedom and well-being of every individual in his own nation-state.

Correlative with Ukrainian revolutionary nationalism are all those national liberation movements which strive for the independence of the peoples they represent and for the establishment of a just socio-political order of national traditions that rejects imperialism and the exploitation of man by other men or the state.

Ukrainian nationalism rejects and combats every form of totalitarianism as the means of enslaving both the individual and the nation.

One international body whose purpose it is to coordinate the national revolutionary liberation movements and their fight for the destruction of the Russian Empire and its puppet regimes, the eradication of Communism, the establishment of a new and just social order, and the creation of free and sovereign states for every one of the hitherto captive nations, is the ABN.

The ABN stands for the liberation of the subjugated peoples through national revolutions.

The ABN stands for concerted action in the field of foreign policy by all the nationalist elements of the suppressed nations now living in exile.

The ABN represents the anti-Russian, anti-imperialist, and anti-Communist front of the freedom-loving, national, and theistic forces of the world, who set themselves against every form of tyranny and strive for social justice, the freedom of the individual and the independence of nations.

The aim of the ABN is the complete dissolution of the Soviet Empire into its ethnographical parts and the establishment of each part as a sovereign nation. The ABN is, therefore, opposed to any form of Russian imperialism, whether tsarist, Socialist Democratic, Republican, or Bolshevik. Nor will it tolerate any form of Russian federation, because it fears that, whatever form it may take, it will inevitably lead to the reestablishment of Russian hegemony.

The driving force and one of the main factors making for the strength of ABN can be said to be the Organization of Ukrainian Nationalists (OUN), whose political aims and revolutionary methods of liberation coincide in principle with the concept of the ABN.

Address to the Fourth Congress of the Organization of Ukrainian Nationalists
The Ukrainian Review,
No. II, 1969, pp. 13-23

Our Ideas on the Offensive

There is an unprecedented process of ideological, moral, and political decay in the Russian empire—the power of the present rulers is visibly disintegrating. In the past, the tsarist aristocracy failed through its own decadence and was replaced by a clique of Bolshevik leaders who at the time saved the Russian empire through their mendacious ideology and ruthless aggressive practices. But this ruling class is in turn decaying and is doomed to failure. Former ideals are fading, self-confidence is on the wane, imperial and messianic ideologies are perilously shaking in their foundation. Elements of sybaritism and hedonism are becoming prevalent and the leaders behave like satiated tyrants. The men at the top today stake almost everything on one card, on the Russian people and—quite openly—on their notorious, brutal chauvinism, without taking into account the clear indications, perceptible in every sphere of social life, that their chances of success are poor indeed. The ideology has completely lost its power of attraction inside the Bolshevik paradise and survives only outside the Russian empire, in the Free World, in the minds of snobs and misguided and deluded workers in the West. We many well be faced with the paradoxical situation that Russian Bolshevism and the Russian empire will be wiped out by internal, centrifugal, national forces and by theistic and Christian thinking, while a modified Bolshevism will continue to exist in our present Free World. What makes the latter event possible is the fact that the Free World has largely lost its sense of values, its faith in the eternal truths, in God and Fatherland. Its main concern is with the petty, materialistic and transient things of life. The West has turned away from spiritual values and overrates the importance of the ephemeral.

But above this disorder voices can be heard from the concentration camps in the tundras and taigas of Siberia proclaiming the resurrection of everlasting ideals; the imprisoned Ukrainian insurgents have once more taken up the fight for Christ and Fatherland. The revolutionary liberation struggle has taken on new forms and entered a fresh phase in massive confrontations with the enemy. Clear proof of this are the events at Novocherkassk, Donbas, and Dnipropetrovsk, where in street demonstrations Ukrainian crowds were in open collision with enemy forces. Below the surface beat the waves of Ukrainian revolution, and as the temper increases there are here and there flashes of lightning and rolls of thunder.

Young Ukrainians are reverting to ancient ways of thinking and ancient esteem for their country. They reject the alien and deceitful ideology and the strange mode of life which have been imposed by force upon the Ukrainian nation. The Ukrainian people are becoming aware that they are not leading a life of their own, that they are not pursuing their own ends and are not putting into practice their own ideology, but are reduced by force to vegetate in the manner of the occupier and are made to swallow his lies. Unexpectedly and, it seems, all of a sudden there has risen, like the phoenix from the ashes, a new elite of poets, writers, and critics who give expression to wholly non-Russian—in fact to Ukrainian—ideas. How strong and powerful must the political world of ideas of the Ukrainian nationalist underground movement and that other hidden Ukraine really be in its entirety, if one small sector could bring forth so characteristic a phenomenon as the poet Vasyl Symonenko! And this is only a beginning. Ukrainian ideas and the Ukrainian revolutionary potential in every corner of the empire have by no means come fully into action so far. The new Hetman Khmelnytsky era is still to come. But the early signs of the rising storm can already be seen today.

In his book *Christians in the USSR* the French writer of Russian descent, Professor N. Struve, points out that Ukraine must be regarded as the reservoir of the priesthood and thus of Christianity in the USSR.

In the Swiss press and even in the reports of the usually anti-Ukrainian German press there are explicit statements to the effect that Ukrainian nationalism is on the increase and determines the direction not only of its own resistance movement, but even that of other nations. *Pravda* raises the alarm with an article by Malanchuk, and *Robitnycha Gazeta*, the organ of the Central Committee of the Communist Party of the Ukrainian SSR, devotes whole columns to the dangerous ideology and activity of the ABN. The Swiss paper *Weltwoche* confirms that in Moscow's restaurants national groups are coming into evidence that disassociate themselves from their Russian environment and lay stress on their national distinctiveness and superiority. The ideological offensive of Ukrainian, Georgian, Turkestani, Byelorussian, and Lithuanian nationalists is gathering momentum.

In Siberia, and wherever Ukrainians are living, the Ukrainian national liberation movement is also active. Its ideology knows no frontiers; it is opposed to imperialism and the Soviet regime. More than that, its ideology is an important, salutary factor in the process of the world's regeneration, since the ideas of nation and fatherland, the heroic conception of life, the respect for tradition, the view of man as a being created in God's image embody the principle of social justice. All this offers a mighty and triumphant alternative to the false doctrine of Marxism and Leninism.

According to the Bolsheviks, a "return to Leninism" is to be the salvation. But no honest man in Ukraine can ever be deceived by that false dogma. Was not Lenin the creator of the Cheka, and his right hand in the mass murders the degenerate henchman and Cheka chief Dierzhinski? The glorification of the Cheka is a glorification of genocide and criminal lawlessness, which were no different from the genocide and lawlessness of Yezhov's and Stalin's GPU and NKVD agents.

The younger Russian generation—with the former KGB chief Shelepin at the top—Brezhnev, Kosygin and the lot are all trying to save the Russian empire from ruin with the same old ideas, with the same principles and the same terrorist system of government as before. They have completely lost their heads; they experiment but are beset by dissensions and rivalries, they squabble amongst themselves and settle personal accounts, they make promises and break them—just as in the past. But there is this difference: never before were these gangsters with their predatory instincts, these rabid criminals with their diabolic designs and their lust after world power, in such a state of demoralization as they are today. Formerly, Stalin, in his frenzied attempts to impose the Russian way of life, had by his bloody purges seen to it that his gangster rivals were eliminated or at least brought to heel. But those days are over.

A new competitor has entered the arena of the USSR. A mighty resistance movement has sent forth its fighters for other ideals, for the noble aspirations of the subjugated peoples, and the influence of their ideals has spread far and wide in all directions. The war which the UPA has waged for decades has conquered the paralyzing fear. The peoples, freed from their dread of the devils incarnate, are marching into battle for Christ and Nation.

Ukraine has entered the arena to fight for the realization of the ideals and visions, the ancient principles of justice of the eternal metropolis of Kyiv; in all spheres of life Ukraine has taken up the fight to make her own conception of life come true.

The Kyiv of the underground, the national, Christian, traditional, eternal Kyiv has risen against Moscow!

From now on the battle cry is: *Kyiv against Moscow* in every field and in every respect!

The conflict is spreading in ever-widening circles. The "white" Russians are well aware of this: they want to appropriate our trident; they would even consent to Kyiv becoming the metropolis of the new empire.

Many students from Ukraine, Georgia, Turkestan, and other countries of the USSR, encountering difficulties with their studies at home, or for various other reasons, go to study in Moscow, the center of the empire. To them must be ascribed the initiative in the different kinds of demonstrations there, which are joined by the dissatisfied elements among Russian students.

Sinyavsky has called the Russians a nation of "drunkards and thieves" and therefore one of the charges against him is that of insulting the Russian people. It is quite possible that one purpose of his trial was to strengthen Russian chauvinistic, if not anti-Semitic, sentiments, apart from the general aim of terrorizing into silence the intellectual elite. Certain Western observers are sure to point out that there is no sign in Ukrainian lands of similar resistance and that a trial like this does not take place in Kyiv—in short, that the center of resistance is obviously in Moscow. But a trial like that of Sinyavsky and Daniel in Moscow would not be held in Kyiv; there one deals with such people by liquidating them, as in the past, with a shot in the neck. In Kyiv one does not show consideration for anything or anybody. In the capital of spiritual resistance, the headquarters of the ideological campaign with its mystic symbols, there reigns unabated the Shelepin terror as in the days of Maluta Skuratov. This kind of trial is unknown in Kyiv, not because there is no ideological and political resistance, but because accounts with courageous opponents are settled there in a different manner.

But let us examine the Moscow trial and the simultaneous departure of Tarsis for the West. Some people see it this way: in their confusion the Moscow tyrants had decided on repressive action against the writers, but they had not reckoned with the reaction of the snobbish and leftist intellectual circles in the West, where there is growing disbelief in the genuineness of "de-Stalinization." The Italian Communist boss, Longo, is said even to have threatened Suslov with a public protest of the Italian Communist Party if the writers in Moscow were convicted. The granting of the exit permit to Tarsis was to smooth over and neutralize any unfavorable reaction in the West to the conviction of the other writers. The conviction itself was designed to intimidate writers all over the USSR and to put a stop to their ideological resistance. While Tarsis's journey to the West was to create the impression there that the other two writers had justly been brought to account for the actual crimes of insulting the people and treasonably undermining the Soviet state. This was made to look even more plausible by the fact that Tarsis, before his departure, had expressed disapproval of the defendants, either from a personal grudge against Sinyavsky and Daniel for not liking his work or, perhaps, as recompense to the authorities for his own travel permit. At the same time, the Bolsheviks try to brand Tarsis as a paranoiac and megalomaniac.

There can be no doubt that the Russians have utterly lost control of the situation since they destroyed the Caligula-Stalin cult and rocked the "faith" in their dogmas. Brezhnev's star is fading, and now one prepares the way for Shelepin.... It is questionable, however, whether the genuine Russians, who are truly Russian in soul and mind, are actually playing the leading role among the dissenters. We are not denying that in the political sense Tarsis is a Russian, but by descent he is Greek on the paternal side, a Russified Greek, and his mother was a Ukrainian whose maiden name was Prykhodko, a typically Ukrainian surname. If a comparison is permissible, one might say that Tarsis is in many respects a Hohol (Russian: Gogol) in miniature. In the political sense Hohol had also suffered sometimes from a Russian complex, but ideologically and culturally he was in essence a Ukrainian. As the Ukrainian writer E. Malaniuk quite rightly says, Hohol had his revenge on the Russian empire by sowing through some of his works (as, for instance, *Dead Souls*) the seeds of destruction among the imperial intellectual elite.

The ideological basis of Tarsis's creative power, his philosophy and the values he affirms, is entirely un-Russian, especially in his book *Ward Seven*. He speaks out openly against the concept of human society as a herd and firmly stands up for the principle of individualism. He is an admirer of Nietzschean ideas and his cultural-political vision is anti-Russian. In *Ward Seven*, for instance, he speaks of the absolute necessity of freedom for all nations.... His tragedy lies in the fact that, by the criteria of culture, ideology and philosophy he belongs to the Hellenistic-Ukrainian world of thought, which is diametrically opposed to Russian thinking, while at the same time he considers himself a Russian in the political sense. This dichotomy makes for his personal dilemma and probably accounts for his ideological and political balancing acts. He might well, with Goethe, say of himself: "Two souls, alas, dwell in my breast!"

For the same reason the serious misconception may arise in the West that it is the Russians who are leading the protest movements and that the West must therefore put its main stake on the Russians as an anti-Bolshevik force, rather than on the subjugated nations. The Russophiles, at any rates, those who support the idea of a single, indivisible Russian empire, feel justified in making the misleading statement that Russian writers are the vanguard in the anti-Communist struggle. But Tarsis's ideological creative power shows no signs of a Russian mentality, just as Hohol's never did. Tarsis's ideas are strange to the Russian mind and therefore will not stir the Russian masses.

The only correct course of action is to back the peoples subjugated by Russia— i.e., to support their national-political aspirations, which accord with the ideological and cultural anti-Russian way of thinking.

In the meantime one can only welcome the fact that ideas proper to a way of life other than the Russian, ideas which have for long been dominant in Ukraine, are beginning to storm the human fortress of the national unconscious, causing or increasing internal conflicts, raising doubts, carrying confusion and dissensions into the enemy lines. There is no doubt that our ideas are on the offensive in various ways.

But a warning is necessary here: we must never accommodate ourselves to the style and strategy of those content with half-measures; we must not attempt to compromise and make common cause with them. We must, rather, deal uncompromisingly with every question and insist on the solution of all problems on national-political lines, the only basis on which cooperation is possible.

We can join hands only with those whose aims are the same as ours, the dismemberment of the Russian empire and the creation of national states. For the ultimate purposes of our struggle is and always will be the dissolution of the empire and thereby the eradication of Bolshevism—not merely the abolition of Communism, with the empire remaining intact!

While we consider useful all ways and means which contribute to the disintegration and overthrow of the Soviet regime, we cannot join forces in action with anyone who is not at the same time for the destruction of the empire.

Ukraine is more than an opponent of the regime, she is in the vanguard of the anti-imperialist and anti-Soviet revolutionary struggle for the liberation of suppressed nations!

Kyiv against Moscow! That battle-cry stands for national independence versus imperialism, and it implies another world of ideas, another way of life, and other values than Russia has to offer.

The truths of Kyiv are not the truths of Moscow! Our cathedral of St. Sophia is not a Kremlin.

ABN Correspondence,
July-August 1966, pp. 5-10

Cultural Elite Fights Back

Ideological and political processes with far-reaching implications are taking place in Ukraine. Neither the cultural elite nor the nation as a whole is yielding to Moscow's unrelenting pressure. It seems the fear of terror has been finally overcome. Entangled in its own contradictions, characteristic of a large multi-national power, the Russian Communist empire is swaying on its foundations. This process is speeded up by the inordinate efforts of the dominant Russian nation to impose its own concept and way of life in its manifold forms on the captive nations with the aim of completely subjugating them and transforming their spiritual outlook in accordance with the Russian pattern and its content. The final goal of this unnatural desire is to create a greater Russian nation, under the misleading formula of a "multinational Soviet people." Moreover, this ambition is pursued not only by the Russian Communists, but by the Russian non-Communists as well. In the program of the Russian emigré organization NTS of 1959, the plan and conception of the present Russian ruling faction were merely reshaped. The idea of the Russian nation, for instance, was defined there as follows: "In its construction the Russian nation is unique; it is a family of peoples and nations which in the course of the centuries of common historical destinies have been historically united and have formed a self-awareness as a community of national, cultural, and economic interests.... The political and cultural development, the national consciousness and national traditions of some peoples which are part of Russia can be listed in the category of Peoples-Nations, but this does not deprive them of their organic attachment to a higher entity—i.e., the Russian nation" (p. 14).

The NTS program contains the following with respect to the Russian language: "Since the Russian language is the language of the Russian culture and State and since it is understood by the entire population of Russia, it is recognized as a unifying, general State language..." (p. 51).

This should be a sufficient proof of the complete identity of aims of the Red and White Russian imperialists, who, both in form and in essence, hold the same position with regard to the question of dominance over other nations and the exclusiveness of the Russian nation as a secular, characteristic, unique, and mystical phenomenon which unifies the peoples and nations in a single whole. The Russian philosopher Berdyaev goes a step further. He wants to transform this anti-Christian nation, which persecutes the Christian faith, into a God-seeking nation of chosen people, which, purified, as it were, by genocide, is to demonstrate how a nation which has enthusiastically entrusted its destinies to criminals, man-hunters, and mass-murderers can become a world-renewing nation, in the sense of the Christian religion.

It is in the face of the new wave of terror against the intellectual elite in Ukraine that we bring up this subject, so that everyone should realize that the policies of the present Russian regime in Ukraine are being justified and supported by the elite class of Russia, including that part of it which is in opposition to those now in power and which wants to dethrone the present leaders. This is precisely the attitude of the Russian nation as a whole with regard to Ukraine; hence we cannot cherish any illusion. Two nations, it must be realized, are engaged in a fierce struggle, two nations representing diametrically opposed cultures, a diametrically opposed mentality, diametrically opposed views of life; two rival centers of authority—that of Kyiv, which functions illegally and underground, and that of Moscow. The volcano which is raging in the depths of the Ukrainian soil is beginning to shake the empire. The prospects of a joyous fiftieth anniversary in 1967 do not at all look promising for Moscow. For the moment, the waves of the spontaneous elementary Ukrainian forces do not appear too strong. Protest is relatively mild. But the storm is gathering. Who can foresee the extent of its explosion? Symonenko is only a symptom and by no means the most articulate expression of this spontaneous, elementary Ukrainian force. Svitlychny and Dzyuba are merely more or less conscious indicators of what is raging beneath the surface. Neither the poet Vinhranovsky nor the poet Lina Kostenko are typical harbingers or true spokesmen of this elementary force, the explosion of which Moscow is not capable of preventing. What purpose does it serve that Moscow has silenced them?

How could there not be tensions in Ukraine in the light of the following paradox? The poets, say, of the Ivory Coast are not forbidden to write songs similar in spirit to Sosyura's famous poem "Love Ukraine" (about their own country, of course), but it is precisely for writing this poem that Sosyura had to do penance. A great poet of Ukraine was forbidden to write what freedom-loving Negroes under "a reactionary capitalist yoke" were permitted. How are the Russians to ward off the stormy winds of freedom that are blowing from the African jungle and Europe or, for that matter, to shut the door to the influence of the ideas inspiring the Vietcong struggle, be it even in their own distorted interpretation? And even if they should succeed in silencing the poet, in taking away the brush from the painter, or in breaking the chisel of the sculptor—would it be of any value, in the long run? Ideas are duty free, and the deepest longings of the human soul, to freely reveal itself in a creative form, cannot be suffocated. The new wave of terror directed against the intellectual elite of Ukraine does not at all mean the strangling of Ukraine's revolutionary elite, which is using other forms and methods to bring about the total annihilation of the empire and the regime.

Moscow has arrested those men who openly, indeed within the permitted limits of the fictitious Constitution, fought for the most elementary rights of Ukraine, for the preservation of Ukrainian culture, and the Ukrainian language, for the elementary freedom of creative expression, which has become an inviolable human right, even of African Negro peoples.

Such human rights, which are vouchsafed to an uneducated native of an African country, are not ceded to the creators of the high values of one of the oldest and culturally most highly developed nations, namely Ukraine. This is proved by the arrest and condemnation of such men as Svitlychny, the critic Dzyuba, and the recently sentenced Ukrainian scientists, poets, artists, writers, and students, who were not only forbidden to express themselves in the Ukrainian spirit, but even to write cultural works in Ukrainian. And in the face of this, there are peoples in the West who regard this colony of Russia called the Ukrainian Soviet Socialist Republic as a "Ukrainian state." In this "Ukrainian state"—as we learn—the accused requested to have their indictment read in Ukrainian instead of Russian. Must not such autonomy be regarded as an insult?

It wasn't too long ago that we received the news that a group of Ukrainian lawyers, relying on the provisions of the articles of the State Constitutions of the USSR and the Ukrainian SSR, planned to submit a motion to the Supreme Soviet of the Ukrainian SSR calling for the separation of the Ukrainian SSR from the USSR. This plan was betrayed to the KGB, however, and on the day before the sitting of the Supreme Soviet of the Ukrainian SSR, the KGB arrested all those who had taken part in this plan—as a matter of fact, all those who had knowledge of this plan, both lawyers and non-lawyers. The arrested have not been heard of since that day. The information concerning this matter is sparse; however, it is reported that a number of the arrested have already been shot, while others have been confined to mental institutions. The rest are said to be confined in a highly secret concentration camp in the vicinity of Potma in the Mordova Autonomous Republic. The world has never received any news from this concentration camp in which the men who have not yet been liquidated are imprisoned. This should be a lesson to those who are of the opinion that, through so-called liberalization of the tyranny, controlled by the tyrants themselves—a contradiction in itself, by the way—lies a possible path to liberation.

However, it would be false to dispute the personal courage of the Kyiv lawyers, for they were certainly well aware of the risk they were incurring. Notwithstanding their excellent knowledge of the complete mendacity of the Russian "law," they dared, at least in this form, to proclaim the will to a separate life and the right of the nation to such a life.

Here abroad, in any case, it is our duty to defend the right of our people to a sovereign life, and especially to defend the right of our cultural workers and our creators of cultural values to express themselves freely. Man has been fighting for this right for centuries and it has always been a measure of his development. As a being created in God's image, this has been given to Man as his most holy right. Without this right, Man simply cannot exist, and it is precisely this eminence that Moscow wants to destroy.

> Your croft alone still spoils our view:
> Why does it stand upon your land
> Without our leave? Why can we not
> Throw you your bannocks as to dogs?
> Why don't you, when all's said and done
> Pay excise duty on the sun?
> That's all we ask!....

> (T. Shevchenko, *The Caucasus*
> Translated by Vera Rich.)

Such were the tsars and their accomplices; such was and such is Russia today, essentially unchangeable, tyrannical. The Bolsheviks, those alleged enemies of tsardom, follow in the footsteps of their predecessors—"Painting and writing is prohibited!" The restrictions they impose on our creative writers today are the same as those imposed by the tsars—indeed, much worse.... Mental institutions for people who seek truth in a scientific or artistic form—that is an Orenburg or Orsk fortress (where Shevchenko was imprisoned). The inspired poet and painter Taras Shevchenko was punished by ten years' service as a soldier in a convict company. Today, in the language of the Muscovite instigators, his "crimes" would mean the Mordovian concentration camp or Ward Number 7 of an insane asylum. In a letter, Tarsis called upon the world to direct its special attention to the cultural and artistic creators who are presently being confined in large numbers in the insane asylums of the USSR. Imprisonment in the asylums was an invention of that darling of Western progressives—Nikita Khrushchev!

On the one hand, the criminal policies of the Muscovite tyrants with respect to the present cultural workers in Ukraine and all the other subjugated peoples should be analyzed and held up to public scorn; on the other hand, widespread and far-reaching mass protest actions on the part of the Ukrainian community and the other subjugated peoples in emigration, and above all of the intellectual and political circles of the Free World, must be initiated. The broad possibilities of such actions were recently set forth in an ABN protest resolution, with particular reference to the strengthening of the cultural-political front. This plan must now be realized step by step. It is especially imperative that scientific, cultural, and artistic institutions in the West work out a protest declaration, which should be signed by them and by hundreds of intellectuals of the Free World. The solidarity with the aspirations of the Ukrainian creators of cultural values, as well as of the creative people of other subjugated nations, for complete freedom of creative expression, must be stressed in this declaration.

It is absolutely necessary that the avant-garde writers among the free peoples declare their solidarity with the aspirations of their colleagues in Ukraine, denounce terror in Ukraine and in other countries, and condemn Russification. An appeal of our cultural workers in the Free World to the defenders of Ukrainian culture is also of supreme importance. The appeal should be not addressed to men like Korotych and Tychyna, however, but to those cultural creators who do not submit, to give moral support to their strivings for cultural values.

In this protest appeal it is also absolutely necessary to have the signatures of the most outstanding Western scientists, artists, writers, poets, and cultural workers. And this protest memorandum should be submitted to the proper international organizations, but especially to the United Nations and the International Jurist Commission in Geneva, with the intent of prompting these organizations to investigate and denounce these illegal practices. Student organizations must enlighten the students of the Free World concerning the men and women in Ukraine who are fighting for the most sacred rights of individuals and nations. In this matter youth organizations must speak up against Soviet practices, either separately or jointly. It is also imperative that Ukrainian political parties in the Free World take part in this action. It is also of the utmost importance that our entire Ukrainian community and our youth organize street demonstrations with protest placards, especially before Bolshevik diplomatic missions. They must also appeal to wide circles of Western society with appropriate calls for support. This was done with great success by the Ukrainian community in Canada, on the initiative of the League for the Liberation of Ukraine in Ottawa, and by the Ukrainian community in Great Britain on the occasion of Kosygin's visit in February 1967.

The successful action of the Shevchenko Scientific Society in Canada and the United States, as well as of the Association of Ukrainian Cultural Workers of North America, must be praised. This action was initiated by Professor Dr. Vertyporoch, Dr. M. Kushnir, Dr. B. Stebelsky, and Dr. S. Halamay.

The Union of Ukrainians in France has initiated a laudable action in collecting signatures of prominent people in Western Europe under an appeal in defense of Ukraine's rights.

It is to be hoped that the widest circles of the Western intellectual world will come to the defense of the persecuted and imprisoned fighters for Ukrainian national independence and Ukrainian culture, for in this way they defend their own national heritage.

The Ukrainian Review,
No. I, 1967, pp. 11-16

Russian Defeatism and Ukrainian "Madness of the Courageous"

G. Lauter, one of the most recent Russian emigrants, who came to the West in 1972, provides us with a very characteristic example of Russian defeatism. He, in his own words, is a philosopher by profession and a Christian by conviction. In fact, he is a political capitulant, a totally resigned pessimist, when one speaks about chances of any struggle within the USSR. In his opinion, "all demands put to the Soviet leaders in the sphere of political freedoms are totally unsuccessful, useless, leading to an even greater oppression of an individual." Therefore, he suggests urging only "the extension of freedom" in the sphere of humanistic culture which has no connection with politics, as well as the "softening of the ban on religion, for it is impossible to lift it [the ban] completely." In brief, to raise the least possible demands and to fight for minimal concessions from the regime.

One should not demand freedom to criticize either, for this is unrealistic. One should limit oneself to demanding that "legality" be preserved with respect to those who are "guilty" in a political sense. In Lauter's opinion, the West should launch a campaign in defense of humanistic culture, spiritual freedom, spiritual life, and those persecuted in the USSR—in particular Bukovsky (whom he calls "our conscience")—and this only with the help of petitions to the Central Committee of the Communist Party of the Soviet Union from churches and political and cultural leaders, as well as intervention of the Human Rights Commission at the United Nations. The Church in the West, in particular the Pope, should defend the Church and humaneness in the USSR. On the other hand, he justified the Church's silence about the events in Hungary or Czechoslovakia or the political trials in the USSR of Sinyavsky and Daniel and other dissidents, for this is allegedly politics. He also makes excuses for Pimen, for the latter is allegedly a "captive."

Thus, although Lauter rightly criticizes the Vatican for its silence and the Western churches and governments for their inertia, he puts forward to the West demands which could be called completely defeatist and minimal and which could hardly be considered a blow of any kind for the USSR. "The sole thing," he says, "which could be done to lessen the threat of Communism is to achieve limited humanization in the sphere of spiritual culture and the preservation of legality" in the USSR. This is all! For him there is only "Russia and Eastern Europe"— i.e., Russia and her satellites. On the other hand, he entirely fails to see the nations subjugated within the USSR. When there are no subjugated nations, the national problem will not exist either. There are only oppressed individuals in "Russia and Eastern Europe." The force of terror and the power of Communism are so great that it is nonsense to be at odds with them; to reach for the sun with a hoe are dreams of "silly children."

Thus, Lauter, a supporter of "the one and individual Russia," suggests that the West capitulate in the face of Communism, advising the nations of "Russia and Eastern Europe" to reject all attempts of fighting for their national liberation. At the same time Valentyn Moroz, a Ukrainian, hurls a slogan at the tyrants worthy of Homer's ancient heroes: "Well then, we shall fight!"

As if in reply to the Russian capitulants one of the unyielding Ukrainians writes:

"The madness of the courageous is a song which must be created [composed] by everyone in the best moments of life. Otherwise, life will be long and boring—without holy days.... Heroic individualism and the Don Quixotes are one of the old tales, long forgotten in our cybernetic world of great organisms, systems, and sub-systems. Your truth is so small that it is not suited for export, for one can only export great truth, which has power, an aim. But why do you deny that besides the portative realists there are internally strong, fine people? They are spattered with mud, but tomorrow they will become pure again, and their eyes will shine with the beauty inherent in them, which you are attempting to reduce to hallucinations. Train them to subordinate themselves to you as much as you will, but they will again walk in their full stature with their own gait. Why do you fail to see them?... Legends are created by a Don Quixote, gazing with a fiery look beyond the pinnacle of life. And the reckless Don Quixotes of this world become heroes of folk tales and folk history.... Great figures are great first of all by their faith, their love and their ignoring of the Sunday-school truths. Their scale is determined first and foremost by the merciless, highest man.... History makes great romantics part of the basis of spiritual culture and creates a foundation from their fervent visions and prophecies. It places Shevchenko high above Kulish, Franko above Drahomaniv, Lesya [Ukrainka] above Vynnychenko.... And on the Black Sea in their light canoes and with a brazen song, the Zaporizhians, of whom only a small fraction will emerge victorious, sail to the shores of Turkey in the face of storms."

Here we have two examples of two representatives of two totally different nations—Russian and Ukrainian. The first of these is in the Free World, but he preaches defeatism and capitulation; the second, harassed and persecuted in his native land, preaches "madness of the courageous." Two contrasting figures, two opposing viewpoints—Tolstoy-like toleration of evil and the dynamic posture of the Cossack "Don Quixote."

Therefore, it is not astonishing that Lauter was readily permitted to leave the USSR for the Free World, for here he confirms the myth about the legendary indestructibility of the colossus on clay feet. His concept is totally in line with the policy of so-called peaceful coexistence, the gradual, peaceful (by way of petitions, requests, and appeals to the "humanity" of the tyrants) "rebirth" of the USSR, for, in his opinion, only thus can the chains be made lighter, can Communism be "humanized" according to the Dubcek model. On the other hand, the Ukrainian fighters do not strive for the "humanization of Communism." They want to break Russian chains. Moroz and Lauter! One says: "We shall fight!" The other: "We must beg!" Moroz and Pomerants! Kosmach and Babylon! Kyiv and Babylon!

For Moroz Kosmach is a symbol of the nation's millenial tradition, a symbol of national order in the world. The Soviet society is a Babylonian mixture of peoples. It is a nationless and therefore a cultureless world society. There is no international world culture or literature, for world culture and literature do not exist beyond nations. Shakespeare is an English world treasure, Goethe a German, Shevchenko a Ukrainian world figure and treasure. What is the meaning of the phrase, "knowledge of world literature"? Are not Shevchenko, Franko, Lesia Urkainka, Moroz, Sverstyuk, Lina Kostenko, and Kalynets component parts of it?

The essential breakthrough in the spirituality of the Ukrainian nation occurred as the result of the actions of the Ukrainian Insurgent Army (UPA) and the Organization of Ukrainian Nationalists (OUN) and the struggle for liberation of the subjugated nations during and after World War II is first of all the overcoming of fear. Hence the great crisis in the countries subjugated within the Russian empire is already known to the whole world. And so now, when the unsubdued are at odds with the tyrants, the so-called third Russian emigration released by Moscow into the Free World begins to unearth the old myth about the impossibility of resistance in the USSR, about the unconquerable fear among the subjugated nations, about the stability of the Bolshevik Government, about the only correct road of making demands—through "petitions" and appeals to the "humanity" of the Kremlin beasts. Apparently, it is necessary to cover up facts of active, even armed struggle for liberation in the Russian empire—the USSR and its satellite countries (Budapest, Berlin, Poznan, the concentration camps, Novocherkassk, Donetsk, Dnipropetriovsk, and so forth)—and to propagate again the view about the impossibility to overcome terror stemming from Stalinist times. Thus Lauter and Agruzov and their counterparts in the West—whether they want it or not—are performing a service for the Kremlin through their defeatism.

They might be right when speaking about the Russian people, who do not rebel, do not resist their regime. But this characteristic cannot be transferred from the nation-oppressor to the subjugated nations, in particular Ukraine. As proved by concrete facts, Ukraine, Lithuania, Turkestan, Estonia, Georgia, and other subjugated nations are already on the brink of a revolutionary guerrilla struggle against Russia—the occupant. Their fear has been conquered. Now a struggle is being waged not for the improvement of the occupant's system, but for the toppling of the hated empire. The subjugated nations' liberation movement has become a popular movement.

First of all, we would like to point to the absolutely false thesis of the Ossete Avtorkhanov, who declared the following at the NTS conference in November 1972: "Russia is our common fatherland, a union of peoples of various religions and various races, but sharing the same fate. Our road leads through Moscow, and as long as the regime in Moscow is not toppled, we shall neither see a [free] Tashkent, nor Tiflis, nor Kyiv...."

We have already mentioned that any hopes of revolution in Russia, in particular of dissolution of the empire through Russian forces of opposition, are futile and naïve. The Russian opposition movement has absolutely no support from the Russian people. Yuriy Yofe—an emigrant from the USSR to Israel—stated at the same NTS conference: "The Democratic Movement [in Russia] is a purely intellectual phenomenon which was never as popular as, for instance, the Zionist, the Crimean Tatar, the Ukrainian Nationalist movement...." Therefore, there is little wonder, Yofe writes further, that when Bukovsky was tried, a "female patriot from the public" said in agitation: "Why should the likes of him be tried? They should be strangled without any trial!" This is the attitude of the "public" in Russia!

And what about Ukraine? The people tossed flowers under the prisoners' feet in court, and even in the streets; when they were led by KGB agents, they covered their path with flowers.

The NTS concepts are rejected not only by the subjugated peoples, but also by anti-Communists in free countries. N.B. Shyrokova, an NTS activist in Sweden, was forced to admit the following: "In Sweden, the youth which fights Communism and uses NTS materials for that [purpose] has a hostile attitude towards NTS...." And this means that the age of imperialism has passed and that honest people do not defend it anywhere.

A.E. Chemesova of the NTS also emphasizes that today the liberation movement in Russia is a "movement of the intelligentsia.... In the present stage, the liberation movement in Russia does not enjoy the support of the people." And further: "An agreement of the intelligentsia and the common people is reached only where the national interests of individual nationalities or religious freedom is at stake...."

V.A. Kapshytser, a recent Jewish emigrant from the USSR to Israel, writes: "One of the major questions facing us is the national question.... The national forces are breaking the Communist empire apart...."

We are quoting foreigners not because they reveal something new to us, but because they confirm the things we have been writing about for many years. Apparently, we have evaluated correctly the situation in the present-day Russian empire and made correct diagnoses and prognoses. Hence, we have been and are on the right track. And there is much evidence as to the mighty force of the national liberation movements in the Russian empire. Take, for instance, the revolts and disturbances in various countries subjugated by the USSR, and the heroic sacrifices for the national idea: Makukh, Bereslavsky, Palach, Kalanta, Soroka, Olynyuk, Moroz, Horska, and countless others!

We have evaluated correctly, too, Russian chauvinism and imperialism. Thus, the NTS leader R. Redlikh, at the NTS conference in November 1972, openly stated: "For me the national question—our relations with Latvians , Estonians, Georgians, Uzbeks, and Ukrainians—is a question of secondary importance. It must be examined as part of the scheme of interrelations among nations on a global scale...." He allegedly has forgotten that the present "interrelations" among nations on a global scale appear as follows: all empires of the world (with the exception of the Russian) have been liquidated; the fifty nation-state members of the UN have been joined by almost 100 new nation-states, which have rid themselves of colonial domination.

"And for me," says Redlikh, "there is no non-Russian fate, I am first and foremost a Russian.... I can feel this much more strongly than the concern for the fate of humanity or democracy...."

Thus, everything is clear. A Russian confirms the things about which a Ukrainian, M. Lado, writes from the Vladimir prison in an essay, "Stalin's Death": "We fully depend upon the Russian nation [says Stalin].... It willingly annexed, in spite of sacrifices, other nations to its state.... We call the Russian nation a nation-internationalist, a nation-liberator. We call it this, but we are aware that it is far from being this; we know first of all that it is a nation-chauvinist, a nation-imperialist.... Our state...is a barrel, made from many staves, which is holding together only thanks to the hoops which were put on it. When the hoops break, the staves will fall apart, the barrel will disappear. This barrel should have disintegrated in '17, and only through unbelievable efforts, at the price of huge [amounts of] blood, we, the Bolsheviks, managed to preserve it, to put new hoops on it.... And what will happen today?... Ukraine, the largest peasant country...the largest untrustworthy nation...."

Both Redlikh and Stalin in principle think the same way. But both of them are forgetting the great truth, which was expressed by another author in Ukraine referring to the role of Shevchenko: "And so the coffin of the greatest enemy of the Russian empire is transported to Ukraine with the permission of the Russian emperor.... The imperial state wisdom had always known one general line—to kill. It was afraid of everything living. It closed the "personal files" of the dead with relief and no longer feared them. Naïve, it differentiated between the living and the dead through the signs of visibility.... Meanwhile, says a folk legend, our tsars had not died, but only pretended to be dead. The nation felt that real life, both its and the poet's, had not begun yet...."

What a totally different world is that of young Ukrainian authors of subjugated Ukraine—philosophers, sociologists, historians, poets—from the world of Lauter or Agruzov! Lauter opposes even the dissemination of leaflets, for, allegedly, only "extravagant personalities" get caught in the noose.

"But let's look at national history," writes one young historian in Ukraine, "had not those become its heroes who with a child's smile have passed over the abysses and who have raised the highest the spirit of national immortality? Had not the practical, the down-to-earth, and the well-adjusted been lost anonymously? ...those who ridiculed the Don Quixotes, because they do not have a cause of their own, but are concerned with everything..."

Yes, heroes and giants are concerned with everything, for they are the movers of the nation, of progress, justice, truth, goodness, freedom. The content and the "practical" are ignored by national memory, are passed over by legend. But it does not pass over heroes, inspired with the ideals of truth and justice. "The people collect into a legend the traces of great, often futile, efforts of a Don Quixote, and sing a song to the madness of the courageous," stresses a young author of reborn Ukraine.

It is for this reason that the national liberation movement of Ukraine and other subjugated nations has become a nationwide movement. The case is different in Russia. Gleb Rar (also from NTS) writes in the newspaper *Die Welt* of February 2, 1973, that no more than three to five thousand people participated in the actions of the Russian democrats. All of them were intellectuals. The "liberals" are again dreaming about and expecting a "thaw." Others plan to search for contacts with the workers who are keeping aloof from the movement of the intellectuals. These are the so-called scientific socialists. Rar acknowledges that "the most natural and the most real are the ties between the elite and the people in the national republics where all are strongly united by the threatened national culture, nationalism."

Yuriy Glazov, an Orientalist from Moscow University, in July 1972 referred to the following eight Russian opposition groups: the neo-Communists, who are active within the Communist Party of the Soviet Union as an opposition to the top echelon, propagating "humane Communism" of the Dubcek type (for some reason he included Gen. Hryhorenko in this group, although the latter was active on the national front in regard to the Tatars); the constitutionalists, who believe that the dominance of the party and official ideology can be overcome by internal corrections of the system and the application of legality (in this group he includes Sakharov); the neo-Slavists (or rather neo-Slavophiles), who refer to historic traditions and openly propagate the primacy of the Russians, with traces of anti-Semitism; the *liberals*, who defend personal freedom and oppose collectivism; the *Christian socialists*, who propagate Christian socialism, as in tsarist times; the *Christian democrats*, who favor the democratization of the system; the *Jews*, who defend their right to emigrate to Israel; and the "action group for human rights," in which, from an ideological point of view, one can include Solzhenitsyn.

In spite of the fact that all these groups, with the exception of the Jews perhaps, are not of very great importance in the USSR, they are widely publicized in the West. On the other hand, the national liberation movements are concealed, although the Jews and even the Russians are forced to acknowledge that they alone have deep links with the people and are nationwide movements.

Not one of the representatives of the national liberation movements was permitted by Moscow to go abroad. On the other hand, it lets its own "dissidents" go to the Free World—as, for instance, Aleksander Yessyenin-Volpin, a mathematician; Yuriy Igtavnov, a well-known movie producer; A.P. Fedosyev, doctor of technical science, a specialist in military electronics twice-decorated with the Order of Lenin, a laureate of the Lenin Prize, hero of "Socialist labor," and so forth. All this is particularly significant.

In conclusion, with respect to Russian opposition or semi-opposition groups, it must be emphasized that all of them favor the preservation of the Russian empire and totally disregard the national aspirations of the subjugated nations.

1) They demand a relative liberalization of the system, but within such limits as to preserve the indivisibility of the empire and not to shake its foundations. Their tendencies are manifested in the loyal opposition to "His Royal Highness" Leonid I, in an attempt to correct and democratize the party from above or by pressure from below, but without the use of force.

2) In principle they reject revolutionary methods of struggle and the revolutionary way of removing the present system, the basis of which the majority tries to leave intact, imposing on it a "Dubcek" character. All Russian opposition groups—with the exception of the All-Russian Christian Social Union for People's Liberation, crushed in 1968—reject and condemn armed struggle. The latter was considered to be a chauvinist and anti-Semitic group.

3) They—as groups of intelligentsia—restrict themselves to professional affairs, struggling within these or other limits for freedom of speech and religion or human rights, but disregarding the socio-political aspects of life, the situation

of the peasants and workers, and failing to raise the question of the socio-political system and socio-economic oppression.

4) Nowhere do they stand up in defense of national or human rights in the countries subjugated by the Russians, nor do they even mention them in their petitions and memorials, although it is generally known that, for instance, about eighty percent of all political prisoners and those persecuted on political grounds are Ukrainians.

5) They do not propose any alternative to the Communist Government, but only wish to "correct" it and partially "democratize" the regime.

In the event of an action which would hasten the fall of the empire, all of them would rally to the side of the regime in line with the theses of Milyukov and Kerensky who said that it is better to have a tyrant and a tyranny than "the lacerated living body of Russia." From this stems their very restrained pressure on the regime, including the proposals (Sakharov, Osypov) for a joint introduction of reforms from above so as not to shake the empire and the system which is the basis of the empire's existence.

Therefore, one should not wonder that Moscow permitted some Russian dissidents to go to the West. It prefers to have them in the Free World, where they play the part of defenders of the empire and focus the attention of Western society on secondary matters—the various "alleviations" which can allegedly be achieved in the USSR. Hence, they are saving the Russian empire from dismemberment into national states.

All the demands put forth by Sakharov, Osypov, Agruzov, or Lauter to the regime seem like a farce of those begging for scraps from Brezhnev's table.

A Gun Is Powerless against Ideas

Thus, unnoticeably it would seem, Brezhnev's neo-Stalinism—approved by Nixon and Pompidou—emerged on the horizon of the Russian empire. Even in Stalin's time some captured insurgents were sentenced to twenty-five years in prison, while now the "liberal de-Stalinizer" Brezhnev punishes wives with long prison terms in order to break their husbands. Yurko Shukhevych was sentenced to another fifteen years only because he refused to denounce his father, while Ukrainian intellectuals are sentenced to fifteen years in prison or confined for life in insane asylums (Plushch, Hryhorenko). Brezhnev, using modern methods, surpasses Stalin in brutality.

But no barbaric methods can break the spirit of the nation, or destroy its ideas. A gun is powerless against an idea.

Liberation nationalism is the mightiest and the sole force which can destroy the prison of nations. Moscow is particularly afraid of unity between the Christian and the national idea. *Robitnycha Nazeta* of March 13, 1973 writes: "Priests and former Uniate monks, who have not joined [the official Russian Orthodox Church], attempt to conduct illegal religious activities.... Joseph Slipy, who headed the Uniate Church abroad, together with the former criminal Stetsko, took pains to revive the Berest Union on the territory of Soviet Ukraine...."

Having driven the Ukrainian Autocephalous Orthodox Church into the catacombs by terror, the Russian tyrants also attempt to liquidate the Ukrainian Greek Catholic Church in Ukraine, which has a Ukrainian national character. Therefore, this propaganda sheet in Ukrainian is very much alarmed because:

> As of late, the activity of former Uniate clergy who conduct illegal agitation for the reestablishment of the Uniate Church has also risen considerably in individual regions of Ukraine. These priests...project themselves in the eyes of the faithful in the role of martyrs for the faith, disseminate among former members of the Uniate Church religious leaflets, small calendars, and prayer-books with anti-Soviet and anti-Communist contents, which are delivered with the aid of tourists." One of the most repulsive variants of Uniatism is the so-called Penitentialism. [The "Penitents"—stemming from the word "penance"—sharply denounce the pro-Russian politics of the Vatican.] Penitentialism's organizers—former Uniate priests Soltys, Potochnyak, Syretsky, and others—staged the miracle of the appearance of the Mother of God near a spring on the Serednyany Mountain on December 22, 1954. In their instructions the chieftains of the Penitents urge the faithful not to work in Soviet institutions, refuse to accept passports, military cards, and other Soviet documents which allegedly bear the stamp of the devil....

Here we still have another proof that Moscow fears Christ and the national idea. But the ideological bankruptcy of Communism and tyranny is obvious to the point that even terror and persecution of Ukrainian national Churches and their faithful will no longer save the Russian empire.

Christianity and the national ideas have already penetrated the broad popular masses, as an invincible force. The Russian empire and its atheist Communist system find themselves on the verge of collapse and will be destroyed under the blows of the national liberation forces of the subjugated nations.

ABN Correspondence,
July-August 1973, pp. 15

Invincible Urge to Realize National and Human Rights

The most important feature of the recent decade is the growth of the realization among the non-Russian nations subjugated in the USSR that the national idea is the most potent force able to arouse men for the struggle against a totalitarian regime and for the rights of man.

The aims of the liberation movements of the enslaved nations are conditioned by: a) the traditional background of revolutionary struggle and the desire to realize the great tradition, historical and cultural, and the invincible will of each nation to live its own independent life; b) the worldwide victory of the national idea and disintegration of almost all the empires of the world, which mobilizes morally and ideologically the nations enslaved within the Russian empire; c) the insurmountable contradictions within the Russian empire.

The deceptive expectation that it is possible to realize human rights in the Russian empire in the form of a proposed Union of Democratic Republics advocated by the self-styled Democratic Movement of the USSR (claiming to have the support of Ukrainians, Balts, and others), has also dissipated. The clandestine publication "Ukrainian Herald" (No. 3), underground organ of the nationally minded and democratic circles of Ukrainian intellectuals, denies that any Ukrainians have had anything to do with the "Democratic Movement of the Soviet Union" or with the elaboration of its program. This is also true of the Estonian, Lithuanian, and Latvian intellectuals, who will certainly not give up the right of the republics to sovereignty in favor of a future Russian non-Communist empire under the disguise of a Union of Democratic Republics.

In the pamphlet "To Expect or to Act?" written by members of the technical intelligentsia of Estonia, criticizing the programmatic positions of academician Sakharov, which owe a lot to Marx and Lenin, the Estonians defend spiritual, Christian values and show the bankruptcy of Marxism and dialectical materialism. They make precise the aims of the Baltic nations: a) sovereignty; b) the primacy of spiritual, Christian values; c) liberation through revolutionary armed struggle and not evolution of Communism towards democracy or "humane Communism."

A section of the opposition in the national republics makes an attempt to base its demands on the ambiguous clauses of the legally existing Constitution of the USSR and of the Union Republics, thus trying to minimize the risks of cruel reprisals by the regime.

Thus, for instance, in Ukraine, a group of lawyers which founded the underground Ukrainian Workers' and Peasants' Union in 1960 tried to mobilize the Ukrainian public for demanding the secession of the Ukrainian SSR from the Soviet Union by utilizing the appropriate abstract and perfidious articles of the Constitutions of the USSR and Ukrainian SSR. They had planned to make a motion for the secession of Ukraine from the USSR at a session of the Supreme Soviet of Ukraine.

The Ukrainian Workers' and Peasants' Union headed by the lawyers L. Lukyanenko and I. Kandyba and propagandist S. Virun, was discovered by the KGB in 1961 and liquidated—seven of its members were convicted, two of them condemned to death, though the death sentences were later commuted to fifteen years of imprisonment. One of the members of this group suggested action among the Soviet Army and preparation of an armed struggle. The aim of this group was also to gain independence for Ukraine.

"The Ukrainian National Front" was an avowed revolutionary organization, ideologically akin to the old Organization of Ukrainian Nationalists (OUN), and during the years 1964-66 published an underground journal, "Freedom and Fatherland." In fifteen issues this journal reprinted many publications of the OUN and the Ukrainian Insurgent Army from the years 1947 to 1949. In 1967 this group was arrested and at a trial in Ivano-Frankivsk three of its leaders—D. Kvetsko, Z. Kraivsky, and M. Dyak—were sentenced to death. Later the sentence was commuted to twelve to fifteen years of imprisonment. Others were sentenced to shorter terms.

"The Ukrainian National Committee" which was liquidated in December 1961, was a revolutionary nationalist organization. Two of its leaders—Ivan Koval and Bohdan Hrytsyna, workers from Lviv—were shot. The death sentences of two other people were commuted to fifteen years of imprisonment; and sixteen other young workers and students also received long sentences.

In 1958-59 students and workers in Ivano-Frankivsk founded the "United Party of the Liberation of Ukraine." Its aim was the sovereignty and independence of Ukraine. At the secret trial in March 1959 they were sentenced to terms of imprisonment ranging from seven to ten years. Their leaders were Bohdan Harmatiuk, Yarema Tkachuk, and Bohdan Tymkiv.

Apart from these, there were many less well-known groups, some of them with a more radical revolutionary platform, as for example, the Ukrainian group from Novorosiysk, which advocated partisan struggle for independence and rejected the tactics of pseudo-legal struggle on the basis of the Constitution of the USSR.

Similar centers of organized struggle exist or are in the process of formation in other countries enslaved in the USSR and in the satellite states. There is widespread opposition to policies of Russification by Moscow. And it is not by chance that the Byelorussian writer Bykov criticized "great power assimilators" at the Congress of Byelorussian Writers: the same was done by Abashidze at the Georgian congress.

In Byelorussia, Georgia, Turkestan, Azerbaidzhan, North Caucasus, Lithuania, Latvia, Armenia, and Estonia as well as in Bulgaria, Hungary, Slovakia, Czechia, East Germany, Romania, and especially in Croatia, the national liberation struggle is growing in strength on the basis of traditional national and religious ideas.

A powerful stimulus to the national liberation struggle was given by the young poets and writers in the early 1960s, the so-called "poets of the sixties," especially in Ukraine, where one of their leading lights was Vasyl Symonenko (born 1935, died 1963). In his strongly-worded, invigorating poetry there was condemnation of the entire hypocritical, dictatorial, and oppressive system in the USSR and the policy of Russian domination. This movement even penetrated the ranks of the Communist Party and Komsomol in Ukraine and threatened to engulf the Russian colonial domination. A whole underground literature began to spread like wildfire in Ukraine.

In 1965 the regime dealt a blow in retaliation. Over twenty of the most active Ukrainian intellectuals, including the critics I. Svitlychny and I. Dzyuba, were arrested. And although these two were released and punished only by dismissal from their jobs, the others were sentenced to several years of imprisonment each. Voluminous material about their writings, arrests, secret trials, and KGB persecutions was collected by the journalists Vyacheslav Chornovil and published in the West (Chornovil Papers, McGraw-Hill). A brilliant work by Ivan Dzyuba, entitled Internationalism or Russification? circulated in Ukraine clandestinely, and was published in the West (Weidenfeld and Nicholson). Chornovil himself was sentenced at a secret trial in November 1967 to three years' imprisonment, later commuted to eighteen months. But even after completing his sentence, he continued to sign protest statements against the persecution of Ukrainian intellectuals, secret trials, and suppression of human rights in the USSR. Many Ukrainian intellectuals and students helped the former Canadian Ukrainian Communist Party member John Kolasky to collect documentary material about the Russian colonial policies in Ukraine, which were published on his return to Canada in two books (*Education in Soviet Ukraine* and *Two Years in Soviet Ukraine*). The savagery of the sentences meted out to Ukrainian intellectuals in the trials in 1966—the historian Valentyn Moroz (four years), the painter O. Zalyvakha (five years), the poet and translator S. Karavansky (the remaining nine years of his previous twenty-five-year sentence which had been interrupted in 1960 after sixteen years of imprisonment)—shocked Ukraine. Far from intimidating the nationally minded Ukrainians, it encouraged them to new acts of civic courage. Reports about arrests and sentences for "Ukrainian nationalist propaganda and agitation" multiplied over the second half of the 1960s, coming not only from Kyiv, Lviv, Ivano-Frankivsk, and Lutsk, but also from Donbas, Dnipropetrovsk, Chernihiv, and many other cities of Ukraine, and even from Ukrainian settlements in Kazakhstan.

The chairman of the Union of Writers of Ukraine, Oles Honchar, wrote a novel, *The Cathedral*, which tried to show the conflict between those who wished to preserve the spiritual heritage of the Ukrainian people and those who, out of servility to the occupying power, worked to destroy that heritage. The novel evoked great commotion in Ukraine and the authorities took it out of circulation, condemned it, and persecuted those who spoke up in favor of it. Particularly vicious persecution took place in 1969 in Dnipropetrovsk, where several writers and critics were imprisoned, including the poet Sokulsky, who was sentenced to four and a half years of imprisonment in January 1970.

A deep philosophical commentary on the ideas expressed in Honchar's novel *The Cathedral* is contained in a pamphlet written by the young critic Yevhen Sverstyuk under the title "Cathedral in Scaffolding" and circulated widely in Ukraine and also published in the West. Sverstyuk asked the Communists: "What have you created for your people to replace the insidious propaganda against religious faith and rites, old customs, traditions, and feasts—i.e., all that which a foreigner had to respect in the past if he wanted to show his respect towards the people?" Seeing the barbarity of the present-day Russian occupants of Ukraine, he exclaimed: "How much did it cost our forefathers to instill in their children humane ideals, faith, selfless love of truth, and respect for the God of their ancestors!"

In 1970 the first issue of the clandestine journal *Ukrainian Herald* appeared in Ukraine and was republished in the West. Since that time four more issues have come out. This journal republishes material circulating among Ukrainian intellectuals, especially dealing with the regime's suppression of national and human rights in Ukraine.

Having come out of prison in September 1969, the Ukrainian historian Valentyn Moroz did not give up his views and his public activities. He again wrote articles which could not be published in the Communist press, but were circulated among his friends and acquaintances. In these articles, especially "Report from the Beria Reserve," "Chronicle of Resistance," and "In the Midst of the Snows" he scathingly unmasked KGB terror, the arbitrariness of the Russian occupation regime, and Russian colonialism in Ukraine. In his most recent work, "In the Midst of the Snows," Moroz writes: "No spiritual revolution has yet taken place without its apostles. The present-day rebirth is also impossible without them.... One can have great spiritual treasures but they will remain unnoticed if an inspired person does not get hold of them and does not melt them in the hearth of his inspiration." He speaks against skepticism, opportunism, "realism," in favor of what he calls inspiration with a great idea of spiritual renovation and Ukrainian national rebirth. He calls for a tremendous civic courage against all the threats, reprisals, and persecutions of the lawless regime of Russian oppressors.

Arrested again on June 1, 1970, Moroz was sentenced in November to fourteen years' imprisonment and exile in Russia and Siberia, far from Ukraine. He refused to testify at the trial, declaring all secret trials illegal, and refused to beg for pardon. All the witnesses refused to testify against Moroz. The unheard-of sentence called forth a wave of protests not only in Ukraine, but throughout the Free World.

The leading force of the Ukrainian resistance is the OUN, followers of the late Stepan Bandera, assassinated by a Soviet agent in Munich in 1959. Although the network of the OUN in Ukraine has suffered tremendous losses in the post-World War II years (thousands of its heroic fighters fell in the course of the struggle), the ideas which it has sown are sprouting in multifarious forms in the most unexpected places and the trend towards the crystallization of the organized liberation movement is becoming ever more apparent.

All indications reveal that, at the present time, there is taking place a spontaneous eruption of a spiritual force enveloping all the subjugated nations—an elemental volcanic force of traditional spiritual values, faith in God, and belief in national destinies, an invincible urge to realize profound human aspirations of freedom, justice, honesty, truth, and national and individual rights and obligations. This elemental force cannot be halted by any prohibitions and persecutions by the rigid, rotten regime, built on lies, compulsion and terror. Sooner or later an armed revolutionary struggle for independence of nations and freedom of individuals will erupt. Our task is to hasten the victory of this struggle by giving it every assistance from the Free World.

ABN Correspondence,
September-October 1981, pp. 11-14

Soviet Russian Colonialism and the Current Situation in Ukraine

Russia and the Free World

The present international scene is dominated by several problems, chief of which is the intensified arms race of the superpowers and the continuous struggle between the Russian Communist imperialists and their subjugated nations. The arms race is being accelerated primarily by Russian efforts to achieve military superiority, which will be used by Moscow for blackmail of the free nations and for further conquests and suppressions of the national liberation movements of the nations under Russia's yoke. Moscow's development of intercontinental ballistic missiles with multiple warheads further endangers the Free World's liberty and security. At the same time, with oil shortages and inflation looming over the Free World, Russia strives to achieve economic supremacy. It attempts to make at least some nations economically dependent upon it and this in turn is followed by political and military domination.

Russia and the Subjugated Nations

At the same time, Russia tightens her colonial and totalitarian grip on the many nations she holds captive in the Soviet Union. For Russia does not only want to secure her ethnographic borders; she also wants to maintain control over Ukraine, Byelorussia, Turkestan, the Baltic States, the Caucasian nations, and other countries that are in her sphere of influence. It is through these countries that Russia has the status of a "superpower," since it is by being in control of these countries that Russia has access to the Mediterranean, the Near and Middle East, and Africa. It is also because of these countries that Russia plays a key role on the Asian continent. At the same time, while Russia extends its sphere of influence at the expense of the Free World, explosive national liberation movements take place inside the Russian empire and systematically weaken it. This struggle for independence inside the empire goes on in every domain of life; it is economic, political, national, cultural, religious, anti-Russian, and anti-Communist. If the West wishes to be victorious in its confrontation with Russian imperialism and if it wishes to avoid nuclear war on its own territories, it must actively support the struggle for national liberation of the subjugated nations within the Russian empire; for the aim of these nations is the dissolution of the empire into national independent states and the consequent destruction of the Communist system.

The Situation in Ukraine

The reestablishment of a sovereign and independent Ukrainian State through the liquidation of the Russian empire and its transformation into national and democratic states would result in revolutionary changes in the political map of the world. The geopolitical situation created by an independent Ukraine would be of exceptional significance for a new arrangement of world political forces. The revolutionary anti-Russian and anti-Bolshevik concepts propagated by Ukraine and the indestructible human potential and natural resources of Ukraine are component elements of the exclusive position enjoyed by Ukraine at present and in the future. Today, as in the past, there exists a strong desire in Ukraine to be rid of the Russian yoke. This was manifested, in modern times, by the establishment of an independent Ukrainian State formally proclaimed on January 22, 1918. This Ukrainian State, however, was destroyed by Russian Communist invaders in the course of the war of 1918-1920. Then, at the outbreak of the Second World War, the Ukrainian National Liberation Movements proclaimed the reestablishment of independent statehood by the formal act of June 30, 1941. This act proclaimed a national Government, which was subsequently liquidated by the Nazis with its Prime Minister and cabinet thrown into concentration camps.

Russian Persecution of Ukrainian Intellectuals

Today the Ukrainians are continuing their struggle for national independence, while the present Moscow rulers are intensifying their brutal and anti-social campaign of stifling the very existence of the Ukrainian nation and its struggle for national liberation. Russian racist and colonial policies in Ukraine continue to rage:

a) A recent appeal was made by the Ukrainian National Defense Front against the persecution of hundreds of prominent Ukrainians from all walks of life who are exposed to the most brutal treatment by the Soviet secret police and whose lives are being systematically shortened by modern and refined means in Russian prisons and concentration camps.

b) Eyewitness reports from the Soviet Union and Ukraine reveal that the Russians treat the Ukrainian population perhaps even more brutally than the Nazi regime treated the Jews because swift execution is not as brutal as long-term torture and psychological terror directed against the religious beliefs, civil rights, patriotic sentiments, and the language and cultural traditions of the native population.

c) Outstanding Ukrainian fighters for national and human rights, such as Yuriy Shukhevych, Sviatoslav Karavansky, Ivan Svitlychny, Vyacheslav Chornovil, Leonid Plyushch, and many others are cruelly imprisoned and subjected to physical, chemical, medical, and psychiatric abuse as a means of breaking their will power. The case of Valentyn Moroz deserves particular mention as an example of this. Moroz, a Ukrainian historian and scholar, is serving a long prison sentence, completely unjust and illegal even according to Soviet law. He is a courageous freedom fighter whose many writings have exposed the Russification of Ukrainian language and culture and the lawlessness of the Soviet state. Moroz recently announced a hunger strike until death if his conditions in prison are not improved.

Appeal to the Governments of the Western Countries

In the common interest of the Free World and of the nations enslaved by Russian imperialism and Communism, we appeal to the Governments of the Western countries:

1) To adopt a policy of liberation of all nations subjugated in the USSR and in the satellite countries and to aim at the disintegration of the Russian empire into independent national states;

2) To put on the agenda of the United Nations the acts of national, cultural, and linguistic genocide as applied by Russian imperialists against Ukraine and other nations, and, furthermore, to condemn Russian chauvinism, colonialism, and the attempt to create a so-called "Soviet nation" by force and by so-called "merging" of nationalities;

3) To brand the persecuting, imprisoning, and sentencing to long years of prison and concentration camps of fighters for national and human rights—as, for example, Zynoviy, Krasivsky, Osyp Terelya, Anatol Lupynis, and others; to condemn the sentencing to harsh prison terms of women and cultural leaders—as, for example, Iryna Kalynets, Nadia Svitlychna, Stephania Shabatura, and others; to condemn the confinement of political prisoners for terms of up to twenty-five years and longer—as, for example, Maria Palchak (twenty-five years), Ivan Ilchuk (twenty-five years), Oleksa Bilsky (thirty-seven years), Svyatoslav Karavansky (thirty years), and others, and to condemn the use of chemical and medical means of torturing political prisoners and interning them in insane asylums;

4) To refuse any economic and technological cooperation with the Russians and to abstain from participating with them in any negotiation or conference that would tend to perpetuate the status quo of the Russian colonial empire;

5) To defend all persecuted and imprisoned freedom fighters, intellectuals, and cultural workers in the Russian empire and the satellite countries, and especially demand from the Soviet Russian Government that it free Ukrainian historian Valentyn Moroz, sentenced to fourteen years imprisonment and exile and slowly tortured for his defense of Ukrainian culture and national and human rights.

Appeal to the Conference

In view of these alarming reports, we ask the conference:

1) To urge the liquidation of all concentration camps!

2) To demand the release of all prisoners condemned and imprisoned for their national, political, and religious convictions!

3) To demand the termination of the application of chemical and medical means of breaking the will power of political and religious prisoners in order to extort statements of repentance from them!

4) To vigorously denounce the practice of confining fighters for national and human rights in insane asylums!

5) To demand an end to persecution of believers in God and cultural leaders who defend the spirituality of their nation, without which a nation perishes!

6) To demand the withdrawal of Russian occupation forces and the Communist terror apparatus from Ukraine and other Russian-subjugated nations within the USSR and its satellites.

7) To demand a return of national sovereignty to Ukraine and all the nations subjugated by Russian communism and imperialism in the USSR and the satellite states.

The Ukrainian Review,
No. IV, 1974, pp. 18-21

Fear of One's Own Strength

The Course of Antitheses

The national world-freedom movement is a powerful ideological and political force of our day. Freedom-loving nationalism, which does not degenerate into imperialism and which recognizes the same rights for foreign nations that it desires for its own nation, is also an important constructive power of the present times. Inspired in the Christian world by heroic Christian critics and based on the philosophy and the metaphysics of Christianity, it opens up grand perspectives for the human race.

As a permanent feature of the social program of the national liberation movement of Ukraine we constantly stress the principle of private property for the working class and, above all, for the Ukrainian peasantry. We regard the demand for a complete liquidation of the collectives—namely, by revolutionary means—as an important element of the revolutionization of the masses. Only a complete rejection of everything that originates from Russia can bring our salvation!

Moscow represents militant godlessness, while Kyiv represents militant Christianity. Moscow stands for lust of conquest, imperialism, and colonialism, while Kyiv stands for liberation nationalism. Moscow stands for a collective, social economic herd-system, while Kyiv is the protector and defender of private property—a private property acquired by the work of the individual and constantly expanded, and in this respect the mass use of means of production is of decisive importance. And these means of production will only be nationalized to such an extent as is deemed imperative on the grounds of actual practice and experience. Moscow is in favor of collectivization, "nationalization," totalization of all human life in economic, social, and intellectual respects, whereas Kyiv advocates de-collectivization, the reestablishment of private property, and creative freedom for the individual in every respect. Moscow favors the total enslavement of the individual, in order to subjugate the whole nation; Kyiv, on the other hand, advocates the liberation of all the creative powers of the individual, his freedom, and his rights. Moscow supports internationalism as a camouflage for Russian imperialism, while Kyiv supports nationalism as a universal idea, as the right of every people to its independence and sovereignty. Moscow advocates a Russian world empire of tyranny and slavery, a "World Union of Soviet Socialist Republics"; Kyiv advocates the national statehood of all peoples without discrimination of race, religion, wealth, and size; it advocates the same rights for all peoples and individuals, not only in theory but in practice.

Seen from this aspect, the fight for the restoration of a sovereign and united Ukrainian state is the highest commandment for every Ukrainian of our day. This fight will help the realization of the slogan "freedom for peoples" (that is, state independence) and freedom for individuals (that is, the recognition of human rights) to the universally victorious.

Moscow regards the individual as a tool of the entire state apparatus, according to the motto "we have sufficient human material"; Kyiv, on the other hand, believes in the dignity of man as a being created in God's image, who sees his purpose in life in serving God by serving the nation. Accordingly, nationalism aims to make possible the self-realization of all the creative faculties of the individual as a being who is organically part of the national, collective body and who was created in God's image, since in the words of a philosopher, "People are God's thoughts."

Moscow advocates the "happiness" of all peoples of the world, inasmuch as it seeks to force tyranny and enslavement on them; Kyiv has no ambition to "make people happy," nor does it propagate a specifically Ukrainian "messianism," for the path to eternal happiness was shown mankind by the Messiah Christ. By the realization of the idea of the state independence of Ukraine, Kyiv, since it is fighting for this cause in a united front with other enslaved peoples and under the banner of Christ, is furthering the realization of truth, freedom, and justice among individuals and peoples in the whole world. If each people respects its rights and likewise the rights of the individual within the framework of its state in keeping with the higher ideals of life and fights for these rights, then it will in this way fulfill the mission for which it has been chosen by God in a global plan.

Moscow pursues its plans and machinations by arousing criminal instincts in the individual with the aid of slogans such as: "Berlin, with its women and girls, its wealth and dazzling pleasures of the bourgeoisie, will be yours, soldier of the Red Army, as soon as we have conquered it!"

Kyiv's aims, on the other hand, are noble: "We will fight for the glory of the Orthodox faith by liberating our brothers," or "For truth, freedom, honor, and glory—for God!" (the slogan of Bohdan Khmelnytsky in the Cossack revolution), or "We shall in no way cause our old Ukrainian country to blush for shame, but all of us will sacrifice our life, for the dead are not ashamed!" (Sviatoslav the Brave, in the 9th century).

The Russian motto is "Rob the robbers," with the prospect of violating the womenfolk and murdering the people as one of the fruits of victory.

The Ukrainian motto, on the other hand, consists of noble words, the courageous words of Sviatoslav the Brave, the high ideals of the soldiers of the old Cossack units and of the Ukrainian Insurgent Army (UPA).

The world-famous Cathedral of St. Sophia in Kyiv and the Moscow Kremlin are two entirely opposite worlds, and one of them is bound to collapse at the first collision. This reminds us of one of the two symbolic walls of the great Hetman Bohdan Khmelnytsky, who fought for the Christian faith, for the freedom and glory of Ukraine. The world of Kyiv, the famous Petcherska Lavra Monastery there with its saints, Antonious and Theodosius—Kyiv, the city of the apostle St. Andrew (just as Rome is the city of St. Peter), on the one hand, and, on the other hand, the world of Moscow and of the Kremlin, with the mausoleums of Lenin and Stalin, with its persecutors of the Christian faith and ruthless murderers of whole peoples. Anyone who still believes in the possibility of an understanding between these two worlds has obviously no conception of the profundity of the historical world process, for this is essentially a problem that concerns the whole world.

Ukrainian nationalism uncompromisingly defends all those ideals which are diametrically opposed to godless Russian imperialism. And because of their magnetic force, these ideals not only triumph behind the Iron Curtain, but also elsewhere.

The West Lacks Faith in Its Own Ideals

Russian Bolshevism is doing its utmost to eradicate the desire to possess private property. This wish is above all typical of the character of the Ukrainians and is in no way connected with egoism, but must be regarded as an essential quality of free human will. For it is a fact that man is capable of making a free decision that elevates him above the beings that have no soul.

The eternal conflict of the human soul, of human moral principles, between good and evil, and the constant struggle between these two powers determine the vital struggle of mankind from the very outset. The one-sided Calvinistic theory of predestination implies a certain irresolute acceptance of evil as such. This attitude is to a certain extent also a typically Russian psychological and moral phenomenon, which is also characteristic of Russian Orthodoxy, but is completely alien not only to Ukrainian Catholicism but also to Ukrainian Orthodoxy.

Both branches of Ukrainian Christianity, seen in the light of the great reformative work of the Kyiv Mohylian Academy, are closely related to each other. The entire Christian underground movement of Ukraine is waging an uncompromising fight against militant godless Moscow. This Russian atheism can be traced back in its origin to the era of Russian autocratic papism, which developed out of Russian Christianity, a fact which is so aptly expressed in Tolstoy's philosophy of life. Bolshevism by no means has its roots in Marxism; even the Russian philosopher Berdyaev admits this. It was not Marxism that produced Bolshevism, but Bolshevism that adopted Marxism, which would have remained one of the less dangerous and more insignificant doctrines in the world.

ABN Correspondence,
July-August, 1961, p. 8

The International Situation and the Liberation Struggle

The Ukrainian Liberation Struggle in the Perspective of World History

The characteristic feature of the present historical period is the disintegration of empires and the triumph of the idea of the nation-state. A differentiation of the world's population on the natural basis of national organism is universally in process, although at the same time attempts are being made by some powers to identify, for the sake of their economic and other interests, former colonial administrative divisions with the frontiers of emerging nation-states.

The victory which the idea of national independence has won in the world this side of the Iron Curtain confirms the essential correctness and progressive character of the Ukrainian revolutionary liberation struggle, which aims at the destruction of the Russian empire and its dissolution into national states. This victory also demonstrates the fact that Ukrainian aspirations are in full accord with historical development in the world at large.

World harmony can only be achieved by the differentation of mankind into separate national organisms and by respecting the sovereignty of these individual nations.

Kiev against Moscow

In its ideological aspect the Ukrainian problem has become the revolutionary problem of the world. In this respect it is neither "peripheral" nor "sectional" nor "East European" but a problem of universal significance. With its ideological, geopolitical, and human revolutionary potentialities of advancing the just and progressive ideas of a new world based on the elimination of all forms of imperialism and colonialism, and on the recognition of the national principle of world organization, the Ukrainian problem is truly capable of revolutionizing the world.

Principles of Our Policy

Our international policy is based, now and in the future, on the following unalterable principles:

The idea of sovereignty and the idea of the Ukrainian nation, which embraces all Ukrainian lands, to be upheld without compromise in the face of all suggestions of supra-, extra-, or anti-national regional substitutes for national sovereignty;

the fight against every form of Russian imperialism and the preservation of the integrity of all Ukrainian ethnic territories within a united sovereign state;

the pan-Ukrainian concept as opposed to territorial grouping and particularism;

the upholding of the national idea against the ideas of imperialism, whose main champions are Russia and Red China and, in the West, certain advocates of a supra-national "world-government" with powers of veto for a few;

a common front of all peoples subjugated by Russian imperialism and Communism, in alliance with those elements in the world which are ideologically and politically friendly towards us and hostile towards Russian imperialism and Communism;

the reaffirmation of the revolutionary importance of the solution of the Ukrainian problem in the context of international affairs with regard to its ideological and political significance, the country's human potential as a fighting factor, and its geopolitical position in the future pattern of the grouping of international forces once the Russian empire has been dismembered;

no isolation and no disassociation of the Ukrainian fight for freedom from the liberation struggle of other nations under the Bolshevik yoke;

no reliance on liberation through extraneous factors, but dependence on the nation's own strength. This conception is based on the fight in the homeland and the revolutionary processes in the country, as well as action by the Ukrainians in exile who are ideologically and politically in close connection with the home base.

The liberation concept translated into action, the anti-Russian, anti-imperial, and anti-Communist revolution taking place simultaneously in Ukraine and other subjugated countries, offers a possible alternative to nuclear war.

United Front of the Enslaved Peoples

Taking this into consideration, it is certainly right and proper to talk at international gatherings not only of the independence of Ukraine, but also of the dissolution of the Russian colonial empire, of the resolute desire of the Ukrainian people for complete separation from Russia. It is stern necessity dictated by the exigencies of the present world situation.

The goal which the ABN strives to attain is the disintegration of the Russian empire into national, independent, democratic states of all subjugated peoples. Three forms of its present activities are (a) coordinated and directed, principally simultaneous, revolutionary actions in the subjugated countries of the USSR and the so-called "satellites" of the USSR; (b) political actions by the representatives of the ABN nations in exile, advocating the dissolution of the Russian colonial empire and destruction of Communism, among the nations of the Free World; (c) mobilization of the Second Front of the national forces of the Free World, opposed to Russian imperialism and Communism, for the support of ABN ideas and against the policies of coexistence, appeasement of Moscow, and capitulation before the advance of Communism. Such a mobilization is now more pressing than ever.

Yaroslav Stetsko (ninth from right) with members of the United States Congress in the offices of Speaker of the House Tip O'Neill commemorating the fortieth anniversary of the reestablishment of Ukrainian Statehood. (July 15, 1981).

Yaroslav Stetsko (left) at the reception held in Congress on the fortieth anniversary of the reestablishment of Ukrainian independence with (second from left to right) Congressman Philip Crane (R-Illinois), Congressman Daniel Crane (R-Illinois), and Professor Lev Dobriansky (Chairperson of the Ukrainian Congress Committee). (July 15, 1981).

(Left to right:) Professor Lev Dobriansky, Yaroslav Stetsko, Congressman Eldon Rudd (R-Arizona) and Mrs. Slava Stetsko at the fortieth anniversary party hosted by Congress. (July 15, 1981).

Two Aspects of the ABN Concept

The idea embodied in the ABN is not only an important aspect of external politics in connection with the revolt of a subjugated nation, whose liberation cannot come about without the disintegration of the empire, but is also a strong factor in the internal liberation struggle, aiming at a simultaneous rising of all the enslaved peoples—a point that was confirmed and stressed twenty years ago at the First Conference of Captive Nations, held in Ukraine in November 1943.

Relying on her own strength and on the concerted action by all subjugated nations, Ukraine will foil any tendencies to turn her territory into a pseudo-democratic international marketplace and to exploit the Ukrainian economic and human potential for purposes other than her own. Ukraine will make common cause with all those who oppose every attempt at imperialism and international-ism and will work together with the national forces of the independent countries in the West and the freedom-loving world as a whole menaced by Moscow and the international circles. In short, Ukraine will join forces with all those who uphold the ideals of independence, of Christian civilization and of Western traditions, and who stand for the preservation of a nation's characteristic culture and of the spirit of its people.

The mobilization of anti-Russian and anti-Communist forces in the world in support of the fight for freedom and the revolutionary strategy of accomplished facts in the homeland—these are the two aspects of ABN action.

The attempt to detach the Ukrainian problem from the complex whole of the peoples imprisoned in the USSR and include it in the so-called satellite complex would not serve a useful purpose. On the contrary, it would reduce the charac-teristic value of Ukraine, weaken the common front, and cause the loss of vital allies, as a consequence of reliance on extraneous forces. However, to treat the Ukrainian problem exclusively in connection with the USSR would diminish the fundamental importance of Ukraine in the universal anti-Russian and anti-Communist struggle.

What really matters is to recognize that the destinies of all the enslaved peoples in the USSR and in the satellite countries are inextricably linked and that there is only one chance of an integral—and not piecemeal—process of liberation, that brought about by simultaneous revolt everywhere.

Who Are Our Allies?

Among other factors in the present international situation, the conflict between Moscow and Peking should find a special emphasis here. On the psycho-logical side, this conflict may be welcome as it tends to weaken the monopolistic position of Moscow in the Communist camp and strengthens the revolutionary potential of the enslaved peoples. However, on the political side it may lead to confusion, as it may call forth unfounded hopes of liberation with Red Peking's help. No liberation can be achieved with the help of Chinese Communism, the essence of which is no less aggressively imperialist than that of Hitlerism or Stalinism. From this point of view our policy should be only to exploit existing antagonisms and to determine our position regarding the potential foe and his probable designs. The experience of those non-Germans who tried to collaborate with German Nazism for the liberation of their countries has certainly taught people a lesson which should be taken into consideration by all advocates of collaboration with Chinese Communists for similar purposes.

The Ukrainians and other enslaved nations can expect help neither from anti-Communist but pro-Russian defenders of the Russian colonial empire in the West, nor from anti-Russian Communists in Peking. Neither can be true allies of the nations carrying on the struggle for liberation because both are for the continuation of enslavement in a new form.

Besides, collaboration with Peking would alienate all the truly democratic forces in the world which detest Communism, recognize the national idea, advocate the annihilation of Russian colonialism, stand for a moral renewal of the world, and combat internationalist plots and schemes. In the Free World today these forces are legion.

Only the truly democratic forces in the Free World can be our real allies in the struggle against both tyrannies. Neither tyranny can be our ally and struggle against both of them is necessary. In this, we Ukrainians follow the strategy of our great leader, General Roman Shukhevych-Taras Chuprynka, who led the struggle of the UPA and OUN against both Nazi Germany and Red Russia in a two-front war. His strategy of a common front of enslaved nations against both Nazi Germany and Red Russia found no understanding in the West, which favored Red Moscow and let the Russian Bolsheviks seize Berlin and, by abandoning its Chinese ally, surrendered China to the Communists.

Coexistence or Support of Resistance?

At present, two conceptions of the policies towards Russia have been discernible in the West.

The *first* conception suggests a policy of peaceful coexistence, appeasement, and virtual capitulation. The protagonists of such a policy disregard the fact that bitter reality refutes their wishful thinking. Despite the Free World's attempts at coexistence the flames of war are burning high in Vietnam, the Congo, Laos, etc.

The *second* conception rejects "peaceful" coexistence in the form just described and demands the encouragement of the resistance movements in the USSR and the satellite countries, and their moral support by the Free World. Such a conception comes close to our conception of the struggle against Moscow and Communism.

Contradiction in the US Foreign Policy

(a) The foreign policy of the USA is double-tracked. One group of US politicians, who have considerable influence over the present US Government, pay attention only to the factors of material power, accept for the present the division of the world into two, and, with a view to the future, promote the idea of a world government. This group is strongly influenced by concealed pro-Russian elements and negates the dynamic force of the nationalist liberation effort.

The other group of US politicians strives for a policy that holds the nation supreme—starting from the principle that America is a nation, despite the mixture of ethnic ingredients. This group is represented by the Congress and bases itself on moral principles of the kind that prevented for more than ten years the recognition by the USA of the USSR and is still preventing that of Red China. This group favors the idea of the dissolution of the Russian empire and its division into nation-states, and advocates the support of the national liberation struggle.

However, to the detriment of America, the Free World, and the enslaved nations, the US Administration actually pursues a policy which runs counter to the directives enacted by the Legislature with regard to the peoples subjugated by Moscow.

(b) The policy of this Administration is also followed by various so-called private institutions, such as the American Committee for Liberation (ACL), Radio "Liberty," the Institute for the Study of the USSR in Munich, as well as the official "Voice of America." This policy does not treat Ukraine, or the enslaved nations in general, as parties to a contract. Nor does it oppose Communism on principle, but adapts itself to the state of Russo-American relations at any given time, thereby devaluing the policy completely, since the issue of the liberation of enslaved peoples must not be allowed to become the object of a bargain or a tactical game.

(c) Regarding the idea of a so-called "Common Front against Communism"—which overlooks Ukrainian national aims and therefore means the fight against one form of tyranny in order to impose another—the idea of the Ukrainian sovereign state must never be substituted for by such concepts as a federation, a union of East European states, a plebiscite, or non-predetermination, since there is for the Ukrainian nation, besides God, no idea more sacred than that of independent statehood.

(d) The promotion of national forms of Communism, as alternatives to Russian Communism (e.g. Titoism or Gomulkaism), is equivalent to a weakening of the national, pro-Western, revolutionary forces and, through the so-called "positive neutrality" of such states, serves to strengthen the Russian position in the world. The attempt to detach the non-Russian countries from Russia, not by the action of the national revolutionary forces, but by supporting national Communist regimes, is based on an illusion, since these regimes will stand up against Russia only for so long as they do not need her might against the resistance of their own people. Any antagonism against Russia would also collapse when the chances of a victory of the West over Russia increased, because these Communist regimes can only survive with the help of Russia's superior strength. The economic aid given to such countries does not therefore benefit the peoples concerned, but indirectly benefits Russia.

Victory can be achieved not through experiments of this kind—i.e., pro-Russian ideas and forces—but through those which in essence and form are the opposite.

"Cultural Exchange" Mirage

The so-called "cultural exchange" in vogue at present has been a result of an agreement between Washington and Moscow. Its advocates want to prove their thesis of evolutionary liberalization of the Communist regime through, among other things, "cultural exchange" between Communist and democratic States. Their thesis can hardly be proved, because Communist regimes are not able to evolve, and the incitement of some minor Ukrainian groups in the USA to engage in "cultural contacts" with the oppressors of the Ukrainian people is, to be sure, like a new Yalta in miniature.

The Vatican and Ukraine

In the fight for freedom of the Ukrainian people the national idea is inseparably linked with the Christian idea. This makes the Ukrainian people extremely sensitive to any changes in the attitude of the Christian world from against the militant atheism which, in all its forms and variants, is inherent in Communism. The Russian Orthodox Church, which allied itself with the Kremlin, shares the responsibility for the liquidation of both Ukrainian Churches. It is a conscious tool in the hands of the atheist Government. Each and every Communist government has exterminated and is exterminating religion by all possible means, for there is no room for religion in a system which is based on the totalitarian Communist ideology. When against this background attempts are being made by the Vatican to come to terms with the Kremlin-controlled Russian Orthodox Church and the Communist regimes, such a course is bound to be in conflict with the notions of our freedom fighters about the role of the Church. In our opinion the Church is to be the vanguard in the war against atheism and injustice.

The members of the two Ukrainian Churches, now underground, will never consent to collaborate with the caesaropapist Kremlin Church, the instrument of the imperialist, atheist regime. For the genuine Church, it is better to be persecuted than to be protected. Concerted action by the real Churches is most important; they must be united in their spiritual and ideological crusade against militant atheism, against injustice and slavery, against the trampling down of the dignity of man, who was created in God's image, and against the disenfranchisement of nations, which are "thoughts of God"; they must be united in their crusade for the embodiment of Christ's teaching in all aspects of our life. They must join forces for the protection of the genuine, clandestine Christians, their Churches and their martyrs, who in our day fight and suffer for the truth and for justice among men and nations. A Church reborn, its priests and faithful, must once more imitate the life of the followers of the true faith, the neophytes, and appreciate the spiritual strength which lies in martyrdom and in the persistent fight against all evil.

We consider it to be a grave error that the aim now being pursued is no more than to reach a compromise with the imperialist, atheist regime and its tool, the caesaropapist Church, in exchange for ephemeral concessions to the faithful in the outward practice of their religion, while at the same time the existence of the atheist regime, the archenemy of Church and Man, is being prolonged.

The imperialist atheist regime is incapable of improvement; it must be brought down and destroyed. The Church must become and remain the strongest and very last bulwark in the defense of the truth; it must have no truck with the center of evil and must not allow the distinction between good and evil to become blurred. In its fight for the good and the truth the Church must never make compromises, regardless of the victims who fall for the sake of eternal life.

By their courageous protests against the presence at the Vatican Council of observers from the Kremlin Church and against a policy of accommodation with the Communist regime, the Ukrainian Catholic bishops have rendered a great service to the cause of Christianity and of Ukraine.

The Ukrainian community expects our Orthodox Church abroad to lodge with the competent international authorities a strong protest against, and condemn the impertinence of, any attempts by the Kremlin-sponsored emissaries of the Russian Orthodox Church to figure as the representatives of Ukrainian Orthodox believers.

The Ukrainian revolutionary liberation movement protests vehemently against the endeavor of the Russian Church to speak on behalf of Ukrainian Orthodox Christians, whose Ukrainian Autocephalous Orthodox Church has been persecuted and driven into the catacombs by the Russian imperialist atheist regime with the help of the Russian Church.

The Intercontinental Aspect of Cooperation by Treaty

(a) According to the treaties concluded, and on the basis of the ABN platform adopted at the 1958 conference in Mexico, ABN cooperates with the Asian Peoples' Anti-Communist League, Nationalist China, the Inter-American Confederation for the Defense of the Continent (ICDC), and with the anti-Communist organizations in Latin America and in sixty-five countries of the world. As the result of such ABN activity, the liberation of the subjugated peoples in the USSR and satellite countries is very much a live issue with all the treaty partners, as well as at numerous international and intercontinental conferences. In certain circumstances it leads even now to a direct partnership between the national liberation organizations and official or semi-official bodies in the Free World for the planning of liberation actions, and it provides for such partnership in the future on the basis of the ABN platform.

(b) Considering the basic significance of the revolutionary liberation struggle of Ukraine and the oppressed peoples in general, as well as the great changes to be expected in the future composition and grouping of world forces after liberation, it is evident—and the global discussions on the subject confirm this view—that the problem of Ukraine and other enslaved nations has become an inescapable, permanent, and essential element of the world crisis, which can never be resolved unless the Russian empire is broken up and divided into nation-states.

(c) Turkey, Iran, and other states bordering on the USSR are, in accordance with their own vital interests, Ukraine's natural allies on the anti-Russian and anti-Communist front. At the decisive moment they could become in the international forum the advocates of the dissolution of the empire.

(d) Japan, who has lost some of her ethnic territory to Russia after World War II, can also be counted among the natural allies of Ukraine.

(e) Owing to the geographical isolation of Australia and the danger of Chinese Communist aggression, the universally valid concept of the Ukrainian struggle for liberation has a political partner in Australia, too.

(f) The countries of Africa and Latin America should be made aware of the vital issue of Ukrainian liberation. In the moral and political sense, the importance of the smaller states in the international arena is steadily increasing, a process directly related to the growing strength of anti-colonial, national liberation movements.

(g) The political importance of smaller countries is often far greater than their military or economic importance. This applies also to the countries of the Atlantic complex (e.g., Holland). With their support, therefore, we shall have a chance of getting our political ideas onto a wider and more authoritative international platform.

(h) In countries which have won their fight against Russia and Communism (e.g., Spain) and which cherish the national idea, we are able to carry on our activities (e.g., radio broadcasts) with propaganda to Ukraine and behind the Iron Curtain in general, without being hampered by restrictions.

(i) Canada, a country of economic and military strength and with a large, nationally conscious Ukrainian element in its population, could make a valuable contribution towards expounding the Ukrainian cause within the Commonwealth. On the wider, international forum, the historic initiative taken by Mr. Diefenbaker, who was the first head of government in the Western world to put the Ukrainian problem on the agenda of the world institution, the UN, should serve as an example.

The Common Front of White and Red Russian Imperialists

There is no Russian political group which takes up an anti-imperialist position and which would declare itself for a Russian state limited to Russian ethnic territory. There is, on the contrary, a common front of the Russian nation against the Ukrainian nation, and White and Red Russians aid each other in their fight against Ukraine, despite all their socio-political differences of opinion and regardless of the sociological conflict between the rising generation of new leaders and the old and out-of-date ones whom they seek to replace.

Particularly dangerous is the White Russian imperialist NTS group, which (following the example of the CPSU) not only tries to speak for the Russians themselves, but has deceitfully and hypocritically appropriated Ukrainian symbols of independence—e.g., the Tryzub (Trident)—and Ukrainian social and political ideals, and thus has caused confusion in the international forum. It is trying to do the same inside Ukraine through its radio transmissions. Financially, NTS is dependent on certain Western interests.

The Ukrainian nation must prepare itself for a war on two fronts: against the Red as well as the White Russian imperialists, since the latter may conceivably receive support from Polish imperialists and, perhaps, from some anti-national circles in the West.

The Attitude of Polish Exile Groups

The policy of the more important exile groups invariably insists on the restoration of the eastern frontiers of the Polish state as they stood in 1939 and does not advocate the disintegration of the Russian empire into national states. It thus makes itself in effect an ally of the Russian imperialists and an anachronistic defender of colonialism in Europe, and that at a time when even in Africa colonialism is being abolished.

This policy separates Poland from the common revolutionary front of enslaved nations and turns the Polish liberation concept into a policy of intervention, even in relation to other, now subjugated nations. With the help of foreign bayonets, even in alliance with the White Russian imperialists, Poland hopes to restore in the East her frontiers of the year 1939 and, at the same time, to preserve the present state of her frontiers in the West. This policy utterly destroys the cooperation, initiated in the forties, between the Polish and Ukrainian underground movements in their fight against the common enemy at home, and it causes subversion in the front of free and captive nations in the anti-Russian and anti-Communist campaign.

The Jewish Problem

(a) The Ukrainian revolutionary liberation movement, in full agreement with all Ukrainian political groups, stands firmly for the equality, in principle and in practice, of all citizens of Ukraine without regard to race, religion, or national extraction. On this basis all Ukrainian citizens of foreign descent, and therefore also Jewish citizens, are offered full scope for their development in every direction (without, however, allowing any minority ascendancy or special privileges). This equality presupposes, of course, the positive attitude of the minorities towards the idea of Ukrainian independence and their active support in this respect.

(b) In accordance with Christian and humanitarian principles and from a sense of justice and national dignity, the Ukrainian liberation movement condemns and combats anti-Jewish excesses and pogroms, which are inspired, organized, and carried out by the enemies of Ukraine in an attempt to bring the Ukrainian liberation struggle into disrepute.

(c) We stress the fact that Ukrainians, and especially members of the Ukrainian liberation movement, have, under directions from their leadership, exposed their own lives and their own freedom to the gravest risks in order to succor and save Jews hunted by the Nazis.

(d) We call attention to the harm done to the Ukrainian people by those Jewish elements which, as members of the Bolshevik occupation authority, and in rank and number second only to the Russians themselves, ruthlessly destroyed the national potential of Ukraine together with the country's cultural monuments and churches. We further point out that in the past centuries the majority of influential Jews have always supported the enemy occupation of Ukraine.

(e) The Ukrainian revolutionary movement calls on the Jewish citizens of Ukraine to support the national fight for liberation and the idea of an independent Ukrainian state. It also appeals to them to use their influence in the appropriate quarters of world Jewry in order to bring about a change in the negative attitude of the latter towards the reestablishment of the Ukrainian independent state, so that favorable conditions are created for cooperation and friendly relations between all the inhabitants of Ukraine.

Growth of Anti-Communist Forces

Anti-Communist and anti-colonialist forces in the Free World have been growing from day to day and their steady increase bears witness to the fact that a powerful movement for a moral and ideological renewal has begun in the Free World, with its ideas of patriotism, heroism and ABN action in the Scandinavian countries at the time of Khrushchev's visit there. Mass participation of the Scandinavian youth in our action must be stressed;

—unanimous support for the ABN conception at the 10th and 11th International Conference of the Asian People's Anti-Communist League (APACL) in Taipei and Manila, in which representatives of over fifty nations took part;

—staunch support for ABN ideas and conceptions by leading American legislators of both parties;

—resolute support for the ABN conceptions by leading Australian politicians, especially those who realize the imminent threat of Communist aggression to their Commonwealth;

—massive support (twenty-seven million votes) for the new and revolutionary platform advanced by Barry Goldwater. It is true that the Republican Party was defeated in the US elections, but we can speak only of the success of the platform, which was advanced in this form for the first time and assembled such a large vote in the elections;

—emphasizing of the national idea and national sovereignty by De Gaulle;

—growth of the national liberation movements in the world and their victorious march to independence;

—the beginning of a fundamental change in the public opinion of the world, evidenced by the growing demand for our information services in different circles. On the other hand, public opinion has been resolutely turning against various circles sponsoring utopian internationalist and anti-national schemes. The fact that the technological basis of the nuclear age has been creating favorable conditions for "separatism" has been acknowledged even by theoreticians of federalism, and the ultimate destruction of imperialism and colonialism in the course of the next decades has been prophesied....

"The Principles of Ukrainian Foreign Policy,"
London: Ukrainian Information Service, n.d.,
pp. 8-28

IX
Nationalism and Nationalist Ideology

The Forgotten Superpower

The Primacy of the Spiritual and National Element

Let us recall some of the major principles of the ABN's liberation policy which we have been stressing continuously:

1) In the organization of the world, the concepts of national liberation and the establishment of nation-states have become the general tendency as opposed to the idea of forming larger units. The national principle—nationalism—is the predominant feature of the present era.

2) The two superpowers, the USA and the USSR, whose power position was determined by the possession of the atomic or hydrogen bomb, were later joined by a third superpower, Red China; and today one can almost say that there are five of them if one takes into consideration Japan and Western Europe, whose economic complex is now being joined by Great Britain with her economic "club" of smaller states (EFTA).

We can see here the continuous process of the division of the world. The rapid development of technology does not prevent the emancipation of nations and thermonuclear arms are incapable of arresting the triumphant march of the national idea and its realization, which is tantamount to the dissolution of empires. The very formula of "thermonuclear stalemate" among the superpowers signifies the self-neutralization of the nuclear threat. Thus, the theory which we expounded for years is being confirmed—namely, that thermonuclear war is an anachronistic concept, alien to the spirit of the time. On the other hand, the

concept of an armed people, of national liberation revolutions, of guerrilla warfare has become characteristic of our age. Hand in hand with the development of
military technology comes an increase in the significance of man as a spiritual
being and of human communities as free nations. And although in the Western
world technological progress does not always correspond to the ethical and moral
perfection of man, to a Christian and spiritual way of life and the eradication of
materialism and hedonism, we can discern in the countries behind the Iron
Curtain, a subjugated spiritual renaissance of the individual and of the nation. As
in the past, so today, it is those deprived of freedom, the persecuted and
oppressed, those who suffer and are ready to make sacrifices in defense of
national and human rights and freedom, who in the day-to-day struggle realize
the heroic concept of life, are more strongly inspired by national ideas than men
who are free, content, and self-satisfied.

Today, thermonuclear weapons "neutralize" themselves, and all the more so
from the moment when their possessions extended from the "club of two" to the
"club of five." Technological progress facilitates the cheap production of thermonuclear arms, which in turn means that in time thermonuclear weapons can be
produced by smaller states as well. The utilization of the atomic bomb at the end
of World War II (Hiroshima and Nagasaki) was possible only because at the time
the USA had a monopoly. But later, neither in Korea nor in Vietnam was it
possible to employ thermonuclear arms for victory over the adversary. The
Russian empire now finds itself in an analogous position. It cannot use thermonuclear weapons against an uprising of the subjugated nations, for instance,
because it would destroy itself in the process.

Thus, in conformity with established principles, everything continues to
remain within God's Providence, which cannot be changed by any human force.
The annihilation of mankind does not depend on the will of man, but on a Higher
Power which guides the whole world. The universe is governed by unalterable
laws and man is incapable of guessing the plan of his Creator. Here is the source
of our great, unshakable belief that a nation which fulfills the mission designed
for it by God cannot be the object of destruction.

It can be seen quite clearly that in subjugated Ukraine, spiritual and godly
values are dominant today. The Russian executioners have exterminated Soroka, have murdered Alla Horska, have condemned Valentyn Moroz to hard
labor; but spiritual grandeur radiates from the life of those who refuse to submit
and from the death of those who fall in battle. How very wrong are the pragmatists and the skeptics who define the role of Ukraine in technical and material
terms alone—i.e., compare the economic and technical potential of Ukraine with
that of the Russian empire, the USA, or Red China.

Spiritual values are eternal. Faith in truth, faith in ideals, in victory of spirit
over matter, is of decisive importance for a subjugated nation, for otherwise it
will be overcome by lack of confidence in itself and by underestimating its own
strength in relation to the mighty, technical, material power of the adversary—
the occupying power. Therefore the theory that "inevitably" the liberation
struggle and politics will function without an ideological basis is a knife in the
back of every liberation movement. Even the Marxists, the greatest materialists

in the philosophical sense, had to become idealists in their psychology and ethics when they wanted to dominate the masses of workers and lead them to the barricades. Even in the struggle for an eight-hour workday, a vision of a different social order was concealed. Here the major stimulus was the sense of wrong as an ethical phenomenon. And none, even from among the "proletarian revolutionaries," would go to die on the barricades for some petty, material benefit alone, if he did not see in the struggle itself a more profound spiritual meaning, a great vision of an idealistic character. It is the contradictions between the philosophical materialism and ethical idealism in the struggle for a different world which have driven the Communist movement into a blind alley, into a dead-end street from which there is no way out. Obviously, there are other reasons as well which are responsible for the bankruptcy of Communism, but they are beyond the subject under discussion.

To deprive a subjugated nation of the ideology of its struggle is tantamount to disarming it, to robbing it of its symbols of truth and faith, to forcing it to forget that man does not live by bread alone. A sense of justice is particularly developed in a subjugated nation. Therefore, it has at the same time a very strong sense of wrong. And the sense of justice and the feeling of wrong do not belong to the material but to the spiritual and ethical sphere. There is not a single nation in the world which does not have its great visions which are based on its ideology.

Those who are searching for reasons why the contemporary Free World has found itself in a hopeless situation will see that first and foremost it is a consequence of the spiritual crisis. Today, in particular, spiritual revival is essential. Great statesmen, men of vision, ideologists, and leaders are needed who unconditionally believe in great truths and pass their faith on to others.

Our age is not only the thermonuclear age, but also the age of ideology. Those who flee from ideals, from the system of ideas which determines our relationship to the surrounding world and to the potential world, are perplexed by the chaos of relativism, skepticism, and disbelief, and this in turn leads to the "vision" of the world of hippies and drug addicts. Those who in this day and age say that our liberation struggle must do without ideology have failed to comprehend the lofty process of the spiritual revival in contemporary Ukraine. There, in Ukraine, are the cult of the Golden Gates, the cult of the Cathedrals, the cult of the Zaporozhian Sich—in its time the only Orthodox Christian order of knights comparable to the Knights of Malta. All this is neither material nor pragmatic nor "real" under present conditions, and he who is a "realist" will never be a Ukrainian. Present-day Ukraine is "a flower in the midst of the snows." Is this perhaps "reality" or "pragmatism"? No, here faith comes into play first of all, and faith above all. When Ukraine's renaissance, its struggle, is "de-ideologized," only skeptics, pragmatists, relativists remain.

Symbols in the External Liberation Policy

Does all this have any relation to the foreign policy of a subjugated nation? Yes, because its own forces are the basis of its foreign policy; they develop and grow stronger only when they have a definite, clear motivation. No nation, especially no subjugated nation, can remain without a helm and sails. It must draw its strength from the spring of eternal values and fight for them, if it is striving for victory. This was so in the past, when Ukraine regenerated itself and our Zaporozhian knights fought "for Christian faith and fatherland" and marched "to liberate brethren—to win glory."

Ukraine has its own world of ideas and in our age this is what makes us different from the Russian world. Among all people there exists a national egoism and dominant national interests. National egoism exists among us as well, but it has never assumed the genocidal character of Russian chauvinism. Therefore the path followed by Ukrainian nationalism is in no way identical with the road of chauvinist Russian nationalism. We are not advocating a struggle for the sake of struggle, only a struggle for the victory of certain national and universal human values. The ideals of Shevchenko, Skovoroda, Lesya Ukrainka, and Franko, and in our day those of Moroz or Sverstyuk, are completely different from the ideals of Gorky or Dostoyevsky, from the Russian ideals in which the sin of Sodom is intermingled with the immaculacy of the Madonna, fratricide with the crocodile tears of a penitent, tyranny with slavery. Our ideals stem from the millennial tradition of the Ukrainian nation. They became a projection of the just order in the world, built on the national principle. Russia rejects the national principle recognizing only the imperialist principle and attempting to create a "nationless society," to merge all nations and to drown them in the "Russian sea." This means in effect the total destruction of culture among the nations of the world because culture only grows on organic national soil. The disappearance of culture and nationhood leads to the loss of the heroic element in life, while dechristianization results in the destruction of the traditional national structures, in the elimination of spiritual values in life, which then loses the aspect of eternity, the immortality of spirit, both of the individual and of the nation as a society of the living, the dead, and the unborn. The ideals of Kyiv are in direct opposition to those of Moscow and of every modern Babylon, deprived of spirit and traditions, in opposition to the pseudo-industrialized society which is used as a camouflage by those who attempt to liquidate nations because they, allegedly, do not fit in the contemporary atomic age, although in reality the atomic age is no less favorable to the development of nations than the Middle Ages were.

Just as in the past Christianity grew out of the catacombs, so today the spiritual revival comes from the catacombs of Ukraine, from the underground, from the concentration camps, from St. Sophia in Kyiv. At a time when a considerable part of the Free World is being Bolshevized, in Ukraine and in other countries subjugated by the Russian imperialists, Bolshevism—Communism—is becoming bankrupt. Despite the fact that our age is also an ideological age, in the Free World thermonuclear power alone is being stressed as a dominant force, while the more important, the spiritual, the ideological force is "forgotten" completely. This is the result of the fact that statesmen have become pragmatists-empiricists. Our age requires new Richard Lionhearteds, new men like Cromwell, Volodymyr the Great, Khmelnytsky, Cato, Leonidas, and Mucius Scevolli. But instead of anti-Lenins it has brought forth only Brandts; instead of a Moses who led his people through seas and deserts to the promised land, it has produced Pierre Trudeau; instead of the Crusader-Popes, we have Popes who engage in "dialogues" with the enemies of Christ, the perpetrators of homicide and genocide. Instead of the cross and the sword, a combination of the cross and the hammer and sickle is now being suggested. Instead of a new Churchill who would oppose Moscow and Bolshevism with the same firmness with which he opposed Hitler and Nazism, we have a Nixon, who is balancing between the beast and the dragon. Instead of the cult of ancestors and the standards of morality which were instituted by Confucius, instead of the national principles of Sun Yat-Sen, there came Mao Tse-Tung—an imitator of a world alien to the Chinese nation, a pupil of Marx and Lenin. None of these statesmen, including Pompidou, has the courage to repeat Cato's words: *Ceterum censeo Cartaginem delendem esse!*— "Carthage [Moscow] must be destroyed!"

In the Free World, a lack of understanding of the essence of our epoch can be sensed, and along with it, a light-hearted attitude towards the Russian-Bolshevik threat to nations and individuals. In the world a contest is in progress not for the expansion of the geographic boundaries of this or that empire, as was the case in the past, but for the preservation of nations and free men, because imperialistic Russia attempts to dominate the whole world and to force upon it its way of life. And mistaken are those who consider democracy as the sole instrument against all types of evil, both national and personal, because democracy as such is only the framework into which the essence of life must be instilled. The idea of freedom also loses its meaning without the appropriate content. Freedom provides an opportunity to choose ideas and the substance of life, and having selected them, to put them into effect. The Free World enjoys freedom; yet the quality of its ideas and the content of its life are a different matter. First of all, freedom is not an end in itself. Those enjoying freedom must have a higher purpose for which to live and work. For those who have such a goal, the service to God and the nation, the lofty ideals of justice and truth come first; while for the hedonist, selfishness, their own interest, and self-gratification are of prime importance. For them national heroism and martyrdom for great ideals become the object of ridicule. Thus, they take advantage of freedom and demoralize society.

In Ukraine, the concept of freedom has a different meaning. There, a struggle is being waged for the great spiritual values, for Ukraine's ideological position in the world. Yuriy Lypa wrote: "Forward, Ukraine! You have heavy feet. Burning houses are smoking beneath them. Neither Russia nor Europe is destined to understand your sons!"

At a time when the Free World, impoverished ideologically and ethnically, is relying exclusively on technological and material power, when thermonuclear arms and the number of human robots are considered of decisive importance, we must recall the "forgotten," different world which forms a component part of this contemporary age we live in, which is atomic and ideological at the same time. What we have in mind is the individual, ideas, and the subjugated nations. General J.F.C. Fuller wrote that ideals are stronger than atomic bombs. Therefore the guerrilla-partisan war of an armed nation is an alternative to the nuclear war. When today one speaks about five superpowers, it is impossible to pass over in silence the sixth one—the subjugated nations, headed by Ukraine. In the future, this sixth superpower will be decisive for it enjoys superiority over the others by virtue of its noble and just ideas and cultivates the heroic concept of life, which elevates the dignity of man and nation. In addition to this, the sons of the subjugated nations who are serving in the army of the Russian occupying power have weapons in their hands; hence they also have technology at their disposal.

The Concept of the "Balance of Power"

The United States, the greatest power in the Western World, employs the concept of the "balance of power" among the superpowers in its world policy, having completely disregarded the nations subjugated in the USSR. In its very basis such a concept is erroneous and results in ruin. It does not lead to victory, but to the defeat of the Free World. In the past, Napoleon lost the war with the Russian empire because he failed to see the potential power of subjugated Ukraine, which was striving to liberate itself from the Russian yoke. Hitler not only ignored the subjugated nations, but wanted to transform Ukraine and other nations into his colonies. Today the US is making a similar mistake and this will also lead to tragic consequences. Why does the US ignore a power (the subjugated nations) which at a critical moment can alone save the USA and the Free World from disaster?

The first reason is that the Americans do not understand the meaning of an ideological force. They define the elements of a superpower in terms of yesterday and fail to grasp the essence of the age in which they live. They pay no attention to the fact that today wars are won first in the hearts of men and then on the battlefields. Nixon's policy is influenced by Kissinger, a great admirer of Metternich and an expert on the age of the "Holy Alliance." Kissinger transferred Metternich's concept (to play the European powers of the time against each other, thus assuring a leading position for the Austrian empire) to today's world politics. This was also the old British concept of the "balance of power" in Europe, which was often also advantageous for smaller nations—as, for instance, for Poland, Belgium, and others. But the application of Metternich's and London's concept to our age is a complete anachronism. When the "spring" of European nations came in 1848, Metternich lost in a confrontation with Kossuth, and the "Holy Alliance" of empires left the world political stage with Metternich. Today is the age of the downfall of empires and the triumph of the national idea on a universal scale. The concept of the "balance of power" is an entirely useless relic in world policy. Outdated concepts are most damaging when they are transferred from a time long past into a completely different age. Can an oil lamp compete with electricity? Can the prison of nations compete with the idea of the construction of the Free World upon a national principle?

The United States is living by the ideas of yesterday. Thermonuclear arms, as the world's decisive power, also belong to yesterday. Of course, neither science nor technology is an anachronism, but only a manifestation of the progress of human inventiveness, provided that the spiritual development of nations and individuals is being perfected at the same time. Besides technology and civilization, there exists culture and above all the spirit, the human soul, the moral, ethical, national, and religious values. There are no contradictions between technology and culture, between technology and the spiritual values, but technology is the product of the human spirit and not vice versa. It is impossible to cultivate civilization while forgetting the world's Creator. What would the world be like if destructive weapons, which could make all nations and individuals tremble, were concentrated in the hands of a few homunculus intellects? What would become of man's will, of his soul, of nations as the highest forms of human society? However, people and nations are God's creations, and this should not be forgotten.

Pragmatists and empiricists, "realists" and skeptics, relativists and disbelievers may say that we are introducing mysticism into national politics instead of concrete factors. But every rejuvenation of a nation and every liberation movement must have its own mystique in order to return to the almost forgotten eternal truths of nation and man, which are the substance of their existence. And in a time like ours, when the world stage is occupied either by crusaders or by emissaries of the devil, by the champions of nationhood or the perpetrators of genocide, by those who regard man as an individual or those who see him as a cog, by those possessed by eternal truth or by eternal evil—the "realists" and disbelievers will find a place neither for Ukraine nor for the Ukrainian people. Only the inspired can "cultivate a flower in the midst of the snows," states Moroz.

The forgotten superpower itself, which is composed of the subjugated nations, is not only a mystical force, but also an immense human potential. These dozens of nations possess wealth above and underground, vast areas, unusually important from the military and geopolitical point of view, and a huge accumulation of explosive force within the Russian empire, which can topple it and remove it from the face of the earth.

At one time, the official Jewish and Roman world did not accept Christ with His new world of ideas. But in spite of the fact that Ananias and Caiphas, Pilate and Herod, Nero and Diocletian officially did not recognize either Christ or the Christians, a new world superpower was born—Christianity. In spite of the fact that Russia and the other "powerful of this world" do not recognize nations and nationalism, but consider them as "relics"—nationalism has become the outstanding characteristic of our epoch, the most just and progressive idea. Nietzsche said that "God is dead" and was quite wrong. Hand in hand with the development of civilization and the exploration of the universe, the belief that God lives is confirmed.

Together with the development of human societies and civilizations, the national principle becomes a cornerstone of just law and order in the world. Therefore, when we speak of a forgotten superpower (nations subjugated under a tyrannical regime, in particular the Russian), we are not projecting the problem of empires as the sign of the epoch, but the significance of the nation as the standard of our age. In particular, we emphasize the importance of national liberation with its noble ideas, which become the basis for the reconstruction of the world.

In his interview of last year, published in *Life*, President Nixon, as the "man of the year," declared that the time had come to do what neither Eisenhower nor Kennedy was able to do—to establish a lasting peace on the basis of the "balance of power" among the superpowers. It is this "balance," based on Metternich's formula, which would constitute the "peace of the dead" for the subjugated nations, because for Nixon the world of subjugated nations does not exist. With that aim in mind, Nixon set out for the "forbidden city" of Mao Tse-Tung, and later for the den of the Russian chieftains, in order to reach an agreement with the greatest enemies of mankind and of God about a "lasting peace" on the basis of the "balance of power" and the division of the world into spheres of influence. The naïve know-alls consider Nixon's trip to Peking as a consolidation of the anti-Russian front, but in reality it is only a "balancing act." Nixon is walking a tightrope between the bear and the dragon. In line with the outdated concept of Metternich, he wants to maintain "the balance of power" with the help of separate treaties about "peaceful coexistence" with Peking and Moscow. Therefore, the political innocents, who, having seen new prospects, think that Peking or Washington is going to bring us liberty, are cheering prematurely. Freedom guaranteed by foreign bayonets is the freedom of those who bring it and not of those who receive it. It is one thing to take advantage of every conflict encountered by Moscow, including that with Peking, and quite another to place one's reliance on liberation by a foreign power.

Our Prognoses Are Justifying Themselves

The invasion by the Communist armies of North Vietnam of the territory of South Vietnam is also a consequence of the "balance of power" politics. At the time when Nixon was negotiating his visits to Peking and Moscow, the Russians supplied the Vietnamese Communists with the most modern weapons, while the Red Chinese assisted. With Russian and Red Chinese weapons, the Vietnamese Communists are killing American troops. And here we can see the greatest paradox of our time—Nixon is shaking hands with chieftains whose weapons kill the flower of the American nation.

Our political activity in Asia has justified itself completely, for its primary aim was to show the Asian peoples that for them, too, the main enemy is Russia. For many this seemed unbelievable, but facts have convinced them and the subsequent course of events confirmed the correctness of our political predictions.

Ukraine is the revolutionary problem of the world. Together with other subjugated nations, it is the forgotten superpower. The detractors and skeptics are accustomed to treating Ukraine as an appendix to something "great" and "important." Therefore for them, as Moroz puts it, there is always Pushkin *and*

Shevchenko, Nekrasov *and* Lesya Ukrainka, and never Shevchenko *and* Pushkin. Orientation toward Peking means the Ukrainian SSR is tending to become a Maoist satellite, as a manifestation of the remnants of a spiritual Little-Russianism. We are not going to join one side or another; we have our own liberation concept and orient ourselves on the subjugated people's own forces, on the national liberation revolutions. Hence, we are combatting at the same time both Russian imperialism and the Communist system, which was forced upon Ukraine and the other subjugated nations by Russia as a way of life and a means of subjugating other nations.

Our liberation revolution is simultaneously a national and a social revolution. He who advocates national revolution alone and ignores the social one fails to understand the meaning of the national liberation revolution, which encompasses all phases of life of a subjugated nation. He who rejects a social revolution in Ukraine will consequently arrive at national Communism, at the preservation of the contemporary collectivist Russian system imposed on our people by force. Social revolution goes hand in hand with national revolution, as essential components of the anti-Russian revolution. National revolution must bring basic changes in all spheres of life of the nation, weed out everything Russian, everything alien and hostile to Ukrainian spirituality. These same views are held in Ukraine itself, where it is emphasized that dechristianization, collectivization, industrialization at the cost of the destruction of the spiritual values of a people, forced migration from the village to the city, and the ruining of the traditional Ukrainian structures are most tragic for Ukraine.

Ukraine has its own spiritual values. It believes in itself and unfolds an anti-Russian and anti-Communist front across the world, fights for the liquidation of the Russian empire and for the reestablishment on its ruins of national states with their own social order. Every sovereign nation should build its own state according to its own will and adopt a system of government which is most suitable for it.

First of all, it is necessary to answer the major question: What other reasons exist for the conflict between Moscow and Peking, aside from the competition for the leading position in the Communist world? It is above all a clash of two imperialist powers over the so-called frontier strips which were taken by the Russians from the Chinese, hence a struggle for colonies. Red China wants to regain territories which are not its own, which are now occupied by Russia but which are not Russian either. Why should parts of Siberia, West Turkestan, or other frontier regions belong to China? Why should Vladivostok, the Green and the Gray Wedges, be under Chinese occupation? It is obvious that here only a change of the occupant is at stake—from the Russian to the Chinese. All these lands are neither Russian nor Chinese. The Chinese imperialists are laying claim to the non-Chinese lands which were conquered by the Russian imperialists. Hitler also launched an attack against the Russian imperialists with similar claims in mind. He wanted to take Ukraine and turn it into his colony, for in the past Normans or Germans and other mercenaries of Ukrainian rulers allegedly lived there. What right does China have to Tibet, Manchuria, Inner Mongolia?

Red Peking wants to exploit Ukraine for its own imperialistic interests. Its aim is not, for instance, independence for Siberia or the unification of the two parts of Turkestan—the western, now under Russian occupation, and the eastern (Sinkiang), which is under Chinese occupation. The "Maoists" make no mention of the fact that Red China subjugates the non-Chinese peoples and puts forward its imperialist claims to other territories as well. They, on the other hand, criticize us for cooperating with Spain, which subjugates the Basques, with Great Britain, which rules in Northern Ireland. And what about Tibet, Manchuria, Mongolia? The Chinese rule over them. What about the Croats, the Slovenes, the Macedonians? They are ruled by the national Communist, Tito. Hence, for the "Maoists," Communist domination over other nations is an obvious "taboo." Therefore, some people find it possible to cooperate with the Communists and to look up to them as the "liberators" of Ukraine.

To the phrase-mongers who attack us with regard to the Basques we reply: We are building a world anti-Russian front, not a world front opposing every nation which contains a national minority. The Basques are not interested in Russian imperialism, have not recognized the right of the Ukrainian people to their sovereign national state, nor are they supporting the anti-Russian front of nations subjugated in the USSR. From the moral aspect, we recognize the right of all nations to their independence. This is our principle for the construction of a new world on a just basis. From the purely Ukrainian point of view, we center our attention on the interest of Ukraine, on its liberation struggle for freedom from Russian occupation. Therefore, we do not deem it expedient to oppose all states of the world, to organize a front against them and thus turn them against Ukraine, its people, and its liberation struggle. We are not going to fight against Spain for the Basques, against Italy for Southern Tirol, against Portugal for the African colonies, against Great Britain for Northern Ireland, against the USA for Negroes, Indians, and so forth. This question of Northern Ireland is first of all a question for the Irish themselves. After all, it is also an internal religious conflict among the Irish of two denominations, both inhabiting Northern Ireland. We are neither organizing nor supporting religious wars, for we consider them an anachronism in our time. What do the critics want from us? To create a front against Great Britain, France, Italy, Turkey, Iran, Iraq, Spain, Portugal, Canada, the USA, and so on allegedly for the sake of liberating "the subjugated"? Hence, we "liberate" everyone except ourselves?! One of the saboteurs and demagogues has made yet another "revelation": "the people of Formosa" are oppressed by Chiang Kai-Shek.... The critics and saboteurs must really have lost their senses, or they are counting on the naïveté of the readers of the poison they write. The idea of a struggle on all fronts, instead of a concentration of forces against the prime enemy (Russia), is a subversive anti-Ukrainian concept, planted by adversaries of Ukrainian statehood. We put forward our principle of world order, the national principle versus the imperialisitic. This means that from the moral point of view we uphold everywhere and always the idea of national liberty and national independence. However, in order to liberate Ukraine we organize a political and military front throughout the entire world against the Russian imperialists and conquerors, and he who is at that front for the dissolution of the

Russian empire and the construction on its ruins of sovereign national states, will also be supported by us within the framework of our guidelines based on principle.

The dissolution of the Russian empire is in the interest of all the subjugated nations, even of those in the Western sphere of influence. Russian imperialism expands continuously and threatens all nations, in particular those which are liberating themselves from colonial dependence on the great Western powers. Russia promises them support, "bearing Greek gifts" for which they must pay very dearly, for they fall under her influence and subsequently into her slavery, far worse than the one from which they have liberated themselves. The enemy of freedom is the one most to be feared, even at a time when, for instance, he gives the Basques weapons for their "liberation."

Today, only one empire—the Russian empire—remains in the world, the most infamous and barbaric. The British empire granted independence to dozens of nations. It even considers the unification of Northern Ireland with the Irish Republic, although against the will of the Protestants of Northern Ireland. And what about the Russian and the Red Chinese empires? To whom have they granted freedom and state independence? Great Britain and France are giving up colonies, while Moscow and Peking are acquiring new ones. In this, we can see a basic difference. In the West, the empires are falling apart, while in the East a forcible integration into the imperial structures is taking place. Each year Great Britain grants independence to some of its last colonies, while Russian crushed with tanks the Hungarian revolution and the emancipation of the Czechs and Slovaks, and brutally avenges itself on every freedom-loving movements both in the so-called USSR and in the lands of its satellites.

We do not defend any imperialists, for our concept is national and hence anti-imperial, but we do point out how deceptive and harmful is the "suggestion" of various saboteurs and critics about creating fronts against those states which themselves are surrendering their imperialistic positions, instead of concentrating our forces against Ukraine's oppressor—the Russian empire.

No less nonsensical are the "suggestions" about abandoning our anti-Communist positions in order to take advantage of the conflict between Moscow and Peking. We have already mentioned that our world of ideas is quite the opposite of the Russian world, with its *obshchina* (commune) and Communism. Therefore to fight only for formal Ukrainian statehood, while denying the spirit which should inspire it, means to capitulate and to accept a system alien and hostile to Ukraine. To deprive the national revolution of its ideological content and to strip it down to only one objective—to take over the government with the help of national Communists or Maoists—is tantamount to the establishment of the Ukrainian "Socialist Republic" as a colony of Peking, instead of a colony of Russia.

Of course, every conflict between Moscow and any other power or state is of benefit for it weakens our enemy and assists in the psychological and moral mobilization of revolutionary forces in the Russian empire. But this does not mean that freedom and statehood will be brought to us by foreign forces on their bayonets. We have still not forgotten that German bayonets only brought us new slavery. Therefore, taking advantage of every conflict between Russia and other states, we must remember that we cannot repay any potential "ally" by accommodating ourselves to his political, social, and ideological system, for we should then become a colony of the new "liberator."

Ukraine, together with other nations subjugated by Russia, is for the time being the forgotten superpower of our age. But its lofty ideals are not fading. On the contrary, they are shining ever brighter and pointing to the only road to be followed by those who search for a way from the blind alley of the world's political, ideological, social, and even religious crisis.

The Ukrainian Review,
No. III, 1972, pp 3-15

Peace is National Independence, Freedom, and Justice For All

Common to all of us are fear, hope, and the endeavor to find some way out of the critical situation in which subjugated nations in the Russian Empire and others have found themselves.

I am speaking not only about problems concerning one part of the world but about people and nations who are both subjugated and free! It is said that humanity is confronted with the possibility of being destroyed by thermonuclear war. Does such a danger really exist? Is there no way out other than capitulation before the tyrants or appeasement and detente at the cost of hundreds of millions of the subjugated peoples, and dozens of the subjugated nations accepting their slavery and the rule of the Russian tyrants?

Do we not have another superpower not so much in material and technological terms as in spiritual, ideological, and political values—whose existence has gone unnoticed, but which plays a decisive role in the developments that are irrevocably coming upon us?

Shall the world crisis be solved by detente with tyrannies and balance of power on a worldwide scale—i.e., capitulation before tyrants—or by reliance upon the eternal spiritual values of man and nations?

Besides the technological assets of superpowers, especially the thermonuclear, there is another which is more important: the spiritual asset.

The spiritual superpower is that of the subjugated people and nations in the Russian Empire and under the Communist yoke, who are ready to sacrifice everything, even their own lives, to obtain freedom and justice.

Why should the process of the disintegration of empires stop at the frontiers of the Russian prison of nations?

The way in which this Russian empire imposes on the subjugated people and nations its own way of life, from metaphysical doctrine down to the kolkhoz system, is something unprecedented in the entire history of empires. Why should this empire not finally break up, instead of being preserved as a "new world system of ideas and values"?

The spiritual and political superpower of our epoch—consisting of hundreds of millions of human beings and dozens of subjugated nations in the Russian empire and under the Communist yoke—is the real factor of world politics which will decide the future of mankind.

Is there, besides the USA, a second superpower in the world? The so-called superpower made up of the Russian prison of nations is a "colossus with feet of clay."

General Fuller, writing about Russia, quotes Theodor Mommsen: "The Russian Empire is a dustbin that is held together by the rusty hoop of czardom." And General Fuller writes, "Break that hoop and its empire is at an end."

It is not sufficient to have the most modern type of weaponry and military technology; it is also necessary to possess the sympathy of people and of nations.

Does Russia or Communism possess on her side the souls of Ukrainians, Turkestani, Georgians, Azerbaidzhani, Byelorussians, Lithuanians, Latvians, Estonians, Bulgarians, Hungarians, Poles, Czechs, Slovakians, North Caucasians, Jews, Tatars, Romanians, Croats, Albanians, Don Cossacks, and Germans? Even Professor Sakharov (a Russian) has to acknowledge the mighty (disruptive) power of the national liberation idea although he is fighting for human rights only, not for the rights of nations.

In his book *Statement* Prof. Sakharov writes, "Those who fill the concentration camps and are the most persecuted are those most faithful to God and the representatives of national minorities" (not minorities but subjugated nations).

We raise as the central problem the right of nations to liberation nationalism, because never have the human rights of a subjugated nation been realized unless the precondition of national independence was first realized, and above all of a democratic sovereign state. We support the movement for human rights but the ideas of this movement will not be realized in the nationally subjugated countries in the empire.

In order to realize human rights, George Washington had to gain national independence for America. There does not exist any other individual in the world without a concrete national imprint and there are no human rights realized without the realization of rights of the nation to which the human being belongs. And what of the democratic empires? Did they guarantee human rights in the countries they subjugated in the past?

The slogans of our epoch: independence versus empires! Nations versus the prison of nations! Human rights as the consequence of the realization of a nation's independence and democratic order! Self-determination is not a revolutionary slogan of our epoch. Lenin proclaimed a far more advanced slogan, "Self-determination including separation," and he deceived the people.

Not a plebiscite by ballots but a plebiscite of blood, starting a thousand years ago and constantly renewed through liberation and defensive wars and revolutions against the aggressors—of Ukraine, Georgia, Lithuania, Turkestan, Bulgaria, Latvia, Estonia, Hungary, etc.—self-determined these people with their ancient traditions as nation-states!

The power relationship in the Russian Empire, including the satellites, is one to two to the advantage of the subjugated nations. Not only the occupiers but also the subjugated are in possession of weaponry. Democratic order and modern techniques make it practically impossible to wage the classical type of war in the style of Clausewitz. Modern techniques are superseded by partisan insurgent warfare.

General Fuller wrote: "If the West is to gain the sympathies of the enslaved peoples, it must inspire them. To think in terms of the atomic bomb is autocratic; to think in terms of liberation is democratic. Though the atomic bomb has its uses, it must be weighed against the psychological effects it is likely to produce. To use this weapon indiscriminately is to repeat Hitler's blunder, and the way in which it is used will determine whether the millions of enslaved people in Europe and the USSR are to be the allies of the West or the unwilling defenders of Moscow. What they seek is liberation and not obliteration—let the Western nations remember this."

In the *International Herald Tribune* of March 3, 1974, we read: "Alexander Solzhenitsyn, the Russian dissident writer, has addressed a long letter to the Soviet leaders asking them to abandon Communism as an alien, unworkable political philosophy, dismantle the Soviet Union, and focus on developing Russian proper as a separate state.

"In addition to abandoning the Soviet sway over the countries of Eastern Europe, the Kremlin would also be expected by the author to drop its control over the Soviet Union's fourteen non-Russian Republics.

"They are Estonia, Latvia, and Lithuania in the Baltic; Armenia, Azerbaidzhan, and Georgia in Transcaucasia; Kazakhstan, Kirghizia, Tadzikistan, Turkmenia, and Uzbekistan in Central Asia; Ukraine and two republics not mentioned by Mr. Solzhenitsyn—Byelorussia and Moldavia. All have strong nationalist sentiments."

"Nationalism," writes Solzhenitsyn in the well-known letter to the Soviet leaders, "was declared by your ideology dead in 1848. But is it possible to find today a greater power in the world than nationalism?"

Frightened by the growth of the nationalist movement inside the Russian Empire, one Bolshevik historical journal (*Ukrainian Istorychnyi Zhurnal* in Kyiv, No. 3, 1973) writes: "The ideologists of anti-Communism openly maintain that nationalism is a type of 'explosive against Communism' and that allegedly, at long last, Communism can capitulate before nationalism on the global scale...."

And Brezhnev, in a speech on the 50th anniversary of the USSR, said that "Nationalist superstition is an unusually vital phenomena which has a firm grip on people's psychology." He also stated that "it must not be forgotten that nationalist prejudices are also a very vital phenomenon rooted in people's psychology. One must also take into consideration that manifestations of nationalist tendencies are often interwoven with local patriotism that in turn is associated with nationalism."

Liberation nationalism—opposed to imperialism—has become the symbol and banner of our age. "Without nationalism," write the fighters in our native lands, "there is no progress; without nationalism there is no nation." Under the banner of nationalism, a national liberation movement in the whole world is taking place. More than half of humanity considers it its own banner.

Remarks at the 7th World
Anti-Communist League Conference
Tuesday, April 9, 1974
The Ukrainian Review,
No. III, 1974, pp. 13-16

One Other Superpower

We are all here united by the common ties of fear, hope, and the struggle to liberate our respective subjugated nations from the rule of the Russian Empire. Skeptics do not believe that this is possible; they think that the only alternative to thermonuclear war is capitulation before the tyrants or appeasement or detente. They do not take into account and are not concerned with the fate of hundreds of millions of people or the fate of the subjugated nations.

Is there not a superpower in the world that will stand up against this Russian tyranny like David against Goliath? Yes, there is! Although the existence of this superpower has gone unnoticed so far, because it is not rich in terms of material and technological achievements, have no doubt that this superpower exists. It exists and it is growing because it is strong in spiritual, ideological, and political values, and it will soon play a decisive role in the developments that are irrevocably upon us.

This spiritual superpower consists of all the subjugated nations within the Russian Empire and under the Communist rule which are desirous of freedom and justice and will sacrifice everything to achieve this goal. They do not want to have imposed upon them the Russian way of life and Russian thinking, beginning with metaphysical doctrines and ending with the kolkhoz system. The Ukrainians, Turkestans, Georgians, Azerbajdzhani, Byelorussians, Lithuanians, Latvians, Estonians, Bulgarians, Hungarians, Poles, Czechs, Slovaks, Jews, Tatars, Romanians, Croats, Albanians, Don Cossacks, and Germans are not Russians and they all want their national independence and their own sovereign states.

This idea of nationalism, which seems so repulsive to the Kremlin leaders, has been eagerly embraced by the young generation in all the subjugated nations, a young generation brought up in the philosophy of Marxism-Leninism. Is it possible that the young people have seen for themselves the discrepancies between Communist slogans and Communist reality? Is it possible that the young people want to believe in something deeper, something more meaningful, something more real than the empty slogans chanted on each anniversary of the Bolshevik Revolution? The answer to that question can only be yes. Moroz, a Ukrainian, wrote that:

The national idea encompasses countless other ideas common to mankind...and the dedication to it leads at the same time into the most secret depths of other social and spiritual needs.... The national question is knitted together by thousands of the finest threads with the most essential question of human conscience.... An individual who respects, knows, and loves the history of his nation lives not only his own lifetime but as long as his people, his land.... The nation is immortal, it will live.... Know yourself in your people.

If these are the ideas by which the young generation in the subjugated nations lives, is it any wonder that the struggle between nationalism and Russian imperialism rages with such intensity within the Soviet Union? This struggle is embodied in concrete actions in the concentration camps, in street revolts and disturbances in Dnipropetrovsk and Dniprodzerzhynsk in 1972, the armed clashes of Georgian nationalists with the Russian occupation detachments in Tiflis, armed clashes in Erivan in Armenia, self-immolations in Lithuania, student disturbances in Hungary in 1973, and countless other examples from each of the subjugated nations showing the growth and the strength of the struggle against Russian imperialism.

The national liberation movements of the subjugated nations are popular movements, in which students, intellectuals, workers, and peasants take an active part. It is a struggle of nationwide scope that is a direct response to the total Communist offensive upon the way of life of the subjugated nations. The struggle encompasses the farmer's right to private ownership of land, the worker's right not to be exploited, the artist's right to freely express his creativity, the right of each citizen to worship, the right of each student to explore many and diverse ideas. All the various strata within the subjugated nations have joined this struggle for national liberation, for they see that all their goals can only be accomplished within a sovereign and independent national state. This is a total struggle, a clash of different national organisms of the captors and the captives, of the exploiters and those exploited, not only for their birthright but for their national soul and spirituality. The greatest achievement of this struggle and the best guarantee of our victory is the fact that it was taken up by the young generation, born of parents that have grown up under the Bolshevik occupation, a generation which has never seen the Free World, but, on the contrary, was reared in an atmosphere totally hostile to everything that they are fighting for now. The banner of freedom and independence for the subjugated nations was raised and is being carried by the generation of the sixties and the seventies, by the sons and daughters not only of prison and concentration camp inmates but by the sons and daughters of workers, peasants, and technocrats.

This ideological, spiritual, moral, and political revolution is a precondition of the armed revolution that will undoubtedly come, for the young generation has a clear national state. This can only be accomplished, in the era of thermonuclear weapons, by well-planned and coordinated revolutionary uprisings within each and every nation within the Soviet Union and behind the Iron Curtain. The tactics that will best serve in these types of uprisings will be those of guerrilla warfare, for this "primitive type of warfare" is extremely effective against an army that possesses a high degree of technology and sophisticated weapons. An excellent example of the success of guerrilla warfare against a technologically equipped opponent was observed in the Vietnam War.

This path of simultaneous revolutions and of guerrilla warfare in the country-side and in the city is the only path that is open to us. None of the Western powers has expressed any desire to help us or support us in our struggle for national liberation. Only a few people in the West have raised their voices in the defense of human rights, religious freedom, and cultural creativity for the subjugated people. On the whole, neither the press nor the politicians nor the governments nor the churches nor the Vatican nor any of the numerous humanitarian and judiciary institutions have issued any protests or statements against the tortures, imprisonments, and persecutions that are daily occurrences within the Russian empire. They all remain silent and mute and are afraid to say "J'accuse" to the Kremlin tyrants. It is sad and tragic to witness this decline of the West. This continued indifference to the fate of millions of people and of the subjugated nations will sooner or later destroy all support for the West among the subjugated nations. General Fuller wrote: "If the West is to gain the sympathies of the enslaved people, it must inspire them." If no one in the West will help the subjugated nations in their struggle, then we will have to rely upon our own forces, but we must warn the West that if national rights and freedom of individuals, of creativity, and of religion are defended only by us, who are suffering persecutions and cruel treatment, and not by the entire civilized world, then a massive and intensive terror will gain the upper hand in the whole world, for the expansion of the Russian empire will not come to a standstill and Communism will not be satisfied with what it has already conquered. We call upon the workers, writers, artists, scholars, students, women, religious leaders, and all people of good will to demand the immediate abolition of chemical and medical methods—including the malpractice of psychiatry—for suppressing opposition to the Soviet regime, the release of all political and religious prisoners, the liquidation of concentration camps, the end of Russification, and the realization of national independence for the nations subjugated in the Soviet Union in accordance with the UN Charter and the Universal Declaration of Human Rights.

In view of the reports that come almost daily from the Soviet Union about the treatment of fighters for national rights, about the brutal use of terror and torture, about the use of chemical and medical devices for breaking man's will, about the application of national and cultural genocide, I respectfully ask the Conference:

To severely condemn the existence of the concentration camps and urge their liquidation.

To demand the release of all prisoners condemned and imprisoned for their national, political, and religious convictions.

To demand the termination of the application of chemical and medical means for breaking the willpower of political and religious prisoners in order to extort statements of repentance from them.

To vigorously denounce the practice of confining fighters for national and human rights in insane asylums.

To demand an end to the persecution of believers in God and cultural leaders who defend the essence and spirituality of their own nation, without which a nation perishes.

To demand the withdrawal of Russian occupation forces and the Communist terror apparatus from the subjugated nations within the USSR and its satellites.

To demand a return of national sovereignty to all the nations subjugated by Russian imperialism and Communism in the USSR and the satellites, as well as those nations enslaved in the artificial state of Yugoslavia.

Without national culture there is no world culture.

If you do not want to see KGB terror and Moscow's oppression prevail in the world, fight for humanism and morality based on religion and tradition.

We ask you to join us in the protest against Russian and Communist crimes and in the defense of the imprisoned and persecuted fighters for human and national rights.

ABN Correspondence,
1974, pp. 29-32

X
Criticisms of Policies of the West toward the USSR

The West on the Wrong Course

Friends! Fighters for the freedom of your peoples! Friends from the Free World!

In this epoch, full of dangers and great events, we, the representatives of the peoples subjugated by Russia, decided once more to appeal to public opinion in the Western countries, because the trend in the policy of the Western powers, especially that of the USA, is making us uneasy. We raise our voices in the name of the oppressed, and especially in the name of their underground liberation movements.

We hope that our protest, our demands, our warnings will be heard, above all in the West where the decisions as to the policy of the Western powers are made. We particularly want the truth of the indivisibility of freedom to be understood and grasped.

Today, happily, there is no need to warn the West of the menace of Bolshevism because, aside from a few incorrigibles, the fact has become clear to all.

Now, however, comes the question of how the West is to act in order to accomplish its task. It is no longer a matter of preserving peace—that has gone already—but of securing victory. The answer from official quarters, up to now, fills us with misgivings. There is a serious danger of the same inexcusable mistakes being repeated in certain official quarters, expressed in the attitude of the Western powers to the Russians.

Over the whole earth, wherever there is no real state independence or national sovereignty, irresistible liberation movements are at work. India, Pakistan,

Indonesia, the Philippines, and many other lands have joined the ranks of the free peoples. It is still seething in Morocco, Indochina, and elsewhere, but gradually the Western World is yielding to those countries. The countries this side of the Iron Curtain which do not yet have sovereign rights, are approaching independence.

And behind the Iron Curtain?

The national liberation movements behind the Iron Curtain are still more vigorous, though the circumstances are much harder in a totalitarian state. In spite of all the persecution by the Bolsheviks these peoples never cease their fight.

It is hardly six months since the news echoed around the world of the death of the Commander-in-Chief of the UPA, General Taras Chuprynka, the leader of the revolution in Ukraine, killed fighting against an MVD division. But at the same time another piece of news reached us, that the fight was going on under another leader. The men fall, but the fight continues without a break.

A year ago *Pravda* reported fierce fights with the insurgents of Osman Batus in Turkestan, and alleged that they had been overcome. Yet recently information reached us from Pamir that the fight was going on, just as in the Caucasus. The other day *Pravda* announced that the Supreme Council of the Soviets had bestowed decorations and awards on members of the MVD for work against "political bandits"—i.e., members of the underground.

Even the sham republics set up by the Bolsheviks confirm the fact that mighty national movements exist in the USSR which the Russian Bolshevik imperialists are trying to neutralize, both by their unheard-of terrorism and the smoke screens of the so-called "independent federal states" which, in reality, are nothing but Moscow's colonies. It was not by accident that Bolshevism in 1917 took up the slogan of "self-determination of nations, including the right of secession." The very fact that it did so is clear evidence that deceit was required in addition to terrorism to enslave the people. It is not the Russian people with its other so-called "tribes" which forms the Empire, but different nations which have been forced into this Empire.

There is no united, indivisible Russian Empire; there is, for example, only a united and indivisible Turkestan, Georgia, Azerbaidzhan, Armenia, North Caucasus, Ukraine, and Byelorussia, and there is also a national ethnographical Russia—but the Empire must be broken up. Whether the leading circles in the West like it or not, the process of bursting the USSR by the national anti-Bolshevik liberation revolution has already begun and sooner or later will be achieved!

The third, independent power within the Soviet Union is at work—the subjugated nations. It is not a question of so-called insignificant "minorities," but of ancient, highly developed States, whose capital cities existed when some of the present Western metropolises were not on the map.

We are not fighting for the creation but for the reestablishment of states which have existed for hundreds, in some cases thousands of years. In the struggle to recover our independence our people behind the Iron Curtain have made the greatest sacrifices. Does the West intend to stand in our way and attempt to force upon us another Russian dungeon of nations?

The Age of Nations

The world is not developing into an enforced Union or World Empire—that is to say, a "World Union of Soviet Socialist Republics"—but rather into independent states whose consolidation is based on equality and freedom without distinction of race, size, wealth, or any other peculiarity. The free nations and those still to be liberated will, by reason of their national, independent democratic forms and mutual respect of rights and liberties, combine in world institutions for mutual aid and cooperation and there, without any "right of veto" and the like, they will discuss and settle their affairs in harmony.

War as the means of settling international disputes will only cease when there are no more superior and inferior nations, no masters and slaves; when certain people in every nation cease their robbing; when each individual is content with what he has and gives up coveting from his neighbor what he has not; when all chauvinism and international hatred have ceased.

The greatest enemy of truth, freedom, justice, and harmony among men and nations is the Russian empire, no matter what hue it may take—red, pink, green, or white. Its present name is Bolshevism. It no longer fights for a division of spheres of influence, but solely for its exclusive, total, and absolute domination of the world—i.e., for a Moscow World Empire! There is no end to its covetousness. Wherever in the world there is a small nook where speech is free, there Bolshevism stretches its tentacles. That is its law. Yet the idea of liberty, no matter how remote, might send its rays into the Russian dungeon.

The ABN comprises the Mongolian, Slav, Ugro-Finnish, and other races, all of whom face Russian imperialism in a common front. We reject and oppose Pan-Slavism as a form of Russian junkerdom. The Russian state must be confined to its own ethnic borders to prevent the pressing of its "order" on other people.

The conception of a World Empire is alien to the national liberation idea. *Only with the latter can victory be gained, not by half measures.*

Therefore the efforts of imperialist circles among the Russian emigrants, which are aimed at upholding the Russian empire, if only within the frontier of 1941, are indirectly an advantage for the Bolsheviks for they disintegrate our common front and discredit the Western world in the eyes of our subjugated people as accomplices in setting up a new kind of serfdom.

Condition for National Liberty

Real freedom of the individual is the basis of national liberty. The ABN is fighting against Russian imperialism, against serfdom, but not against those

Russians who stand aloof from the oppressors. We call upon the Russian masses to shake off imperialism and be content with a state within their ethnic borders. We do not protest against the collaboration of the West with Russian anti-Bolshevik circles when they speak on behalf of their own people but we do protest against the collaboration of the West with Muscovite imperialists, we protest against all assistance given to any new form of serfdom planned for us, even if it is called "white" this time.

For us every Russian imperialist, even though he calls himself a democrat, is a Bolshevik tool. And it is the same with those who have collaborated with Bolshevism, for they demoralize the anti-Bolshevisk front; they confuse the minds of the subjugated nations in their notion of the West, thus strengthening Bolshevik supremacy. If the West supports such elements it means that the fate and the real freedom of nations are a matter of indifference. We on our part are ready to cooperate with such circles as lay no claims to our countries and are content with their own ethnic territory. That is our one condition.

We here publicly accuse the White Russian imperialists and their friends in certain Western circles of undermining the united anti-Bolshevik front, fostering chauvinism, and confusing the objectives in that they harm the Russian-Muscovite people proper.

We blame them for their indirect support of Bolshevism because they ignore the most important factor in liberation: the national ideal. What should our people fight for in common with the West? Only to change their fetters? Why will those chauvinists and new totalitarians not recognize the greatest truth of our time—namely, national and personal freedom for every individual? Some people in the West look upon them as democrats and our liberation movement as undemocratic. Where does the truth lie? Is the man who fights for freedom a fascist, while he who seeks to enslave him a "democrat"? Since when have these terms been confused in the West?

No one can openly go against our ideals. It is also an error *when some Western people believe that we, in propagandizing our ideas, are driving the Russian people into Bolshevism.*

The West has not to choose between us and Russia as a nation. The West has rather to choose between the ideas of a future order—i.e., between the idea of national liberation or further enslavement. If it chooses the former it will have our peoples and the Russian people proper behind it—that is to say, of course, if the sound element among the Russians stands aloof from its imperialist compatriots. Should the West choose enslavement, then our people will be against it. *That is not lightly said! It is a considered opinion!*

The explosive power of the national idea can be seen by its effect, when its greatest enemy, Moscow, uses it as a means to stir up the colonial peoples of Asia and Africa. Why does the West not support this idea *behind* the Iron Curtain with honest intentions, when the Bolsheviks do so much *this side* with treacherous intent?

No Hatred for Russians

And another thing. Not long ago, the Bolsheviks decried the fight of the Ukrainians, Turkestani, Azerbaidzhani, Byelorussians, the people of Idel-Ural, Siberia, and others as anti-Russian. Today, in the exhilaration of their chauvinism and Russification policy, it is the fight of Bulgarians, Poles, Hungarians, East Germans, etc., that is anti-Russian, and tomorrow it will be the turn of France or Italy if we do not all conform to their way of thinking.

Any people attempting to shake off Moscow's chains is regarded by the Russian despots as hostile. Moscow alone allegedly knows no hatred of other nations. Shall we defame Bulgarian, Hungarian, Romanian, Croatian, Czech, Slovakian, Latvian, Lithuanian, Siberian, Cossack, Georgian, or North Caucasian fighters for independence as chaunivists or Nazis, although we neither claim foreign territory nor hate any other nation?

We want the Russian people to enjoy freedom; we seek Russia's friendship, just as we want the friendship of all other nations who respect our rights, on the basis of freedom and equality. We regard the readiness of the West to break up the dungeon of nations and restore full sovereignty to all nations on the basis of their national ethnic borders as the first condition for a victory over Bolshevism.

Our Appeal to the World

We appeal to the Western world to leave the decision as to our future to us. Do not, if you are really democrats, as we are from the bottom of our hearts, hang more chains around our necks. Treat us as you treat other Western nations upon whom you have no wish to force your will. Do not forget that our peoples have demonstrated their will to freedom, not in paper plebiscites but with their blood. If Bolshevism should once rule over your countries and you had to fight against it, would you think it necessary to hold a plebsicite to decide whether your people should be free after the victory?

Measure our peoples by the same rule you claim for yourselves. Do not forget that, just as you have collaborators with Bolshevism in your lands and deny them the right to speak in the name of your people, our people too despise them because they have contributed to strengthening tyranny in the subjugated countries. Do not repeat the mistakes of the past.

Our National States a Guarantee of Peace!

Would there be any Bolshevik menace if the Western countries in 1917 had not helped to maintain the dungeon of nations? Should one have to fear a Russian atomic bomb? None of our national states would have been in a position materially to produce it. The Soviet Union is so placed because all the wealth of various peoples and countries is at its disposal. Was it not in your children's interest to destroy this horror then? Would a Georgia with 3 million inhabitants, a Byelorussia, or a Turkestan have been able to produce that weapon today when aside from USSR and USA, even Great Britain is not able to do so? Were the Moscow despots deprived of the mineral oil of Azerbaidzhan, the bread, iron, and coal of Ukraine, the cotton of Turkestan, the wood of Byelorussia, and the riches of other countries, would they be in a position to threaten the world and finance a world revolution? Only the national States can guarantee world peace, for they cannot pile up war matériel and reserves of manpower singly. They therefore are really a guarantee for peace, progress, and humanity.

Military Strategy

Ladies and gentlemen!

Strategy depends on the political conception of a war. The political conception of the dissolution of the Russian dungeon of nations demands, of course, a strategic conception of the war. If this dungeon is to be left in some form or other, the cooperation of the subjugated peoples will be excluded. For a strategic conception of the war the constitutional anti-Bolshevik attitude of the West is not sufficient. It must be based on a positive idea: the dismemberment of the Russian empire as the dungeon of nations, national liberation of the peoples subjugated by Moscow.

It is time that the West made some decision in this direction. In making these demands today we are not acting from our own egoistic interest, but because it is high time to prepare effective counteraction.

The Subjugated Peoples—Second Front

The victory of the West is only to be gained if there is an adequate second front behind the Iron Curtain.

National revolutions are necessary and for them favorable conditions must be created, in order to assure cooperation with the Free World.

The West cannot count on success without coordinating and bringing the operations of the West into line with the front of the subjugated peoples. Such coordination is only possible if the West recognizes and supports the political platform of the subjugated peoples. That is, *the conception of the dissolution of the Russian dungeon of nations and recognition of the sovereignty of the liberated States therein.*

Bolshevism is preparing, and, in some places waging, a two-front war: aggression from outside and civil war within. It draws the West into peripheral wars, such as Korea, China, Indochina, for the purpose of attrition and to bring the West into conflict with the other nations. So the bastion of tyranny must be attacked in conjunction with the subjugated peoples—i.e., the second front. The real core of Bolshevism, ethnographic Russia, must be overpowered, for only then will its forces in the whole world break down. The moment the West makes a counterattack on the bastion of evil, on Moscow itself, the real ethnographic Russia, the subjugated peoples with some help from the West would not find it hard to settle accounts with the Russian Bolshevik occupation troops in their countries.

Possibilities Not Fully Used

Conclusions should be drawn, now, from the fact that the Soviet army is made up of soldiers of different nationalities. It is known, for instance, that the Far East divisions, stationed near Korea, are for the most part men belonging to our nations. Would it not be advisable to start a political offensive now by broadcasts, etc., so that our ideas penetrate from all sides into the USSR? Why does the West not make it possible for the broadcasting stations in Europe, Asia, and the Near East to appeal to the subjugated peoples in our names and with our representatives? Why do not uncompromising fighters against Bolshevism broadcast from the stations available to the West? And why are broadcasts not composed in the spirit of national freedom? Why are these important factors not in the hands of approved anti-Bolsheviks who have never had any dealings with Bolshevism?

Our Idea Is Advancing

The subjugated peoples are a supreme power. They are not a "fifth column" of the West, but an equal partner and a valuable potential ally. In contrast to Bolshevism, which can only attract a certain type of person in the West, the West could win whole nations behind the Iron Curtain on one condition, *support of the national idea*.

It is necessary and high time to bring the two great plans of the Free World and the subjugated peoples to a common denominator.

Slowly our conception is advancing from its previous isolation. The sooner it penetrates into competent quarters the better it will be, not only for us, but for the whole freedom-loving world.

Finally, we shall never cease our cry: the Russian empire, of whatever color, must be broken up into national independent States among which there also should be a Russian state within its ethnic borders.

Those are the conditions for victory and for enduring peace in the world, a peace for which we all long, but we place freedom above peace and life.

Long live freedom and justice for all!

ABN Correspondence,
June-July 1951, pp. 3-5

A Time For Firmness

In the forum of international politics the year 1954 ended on a sad and dismal note. A wave of faith in "coexistence" with Bolshevism is sweeping the Western world, and, unfortunately, even men like Dulles, Eisenhower, and Churchill, who are acquainted with the essence of Bolshevism, are beginning to be full of enthusiasm for the fanciful idea of the coexistence of the world of slavery with that of freedom. It is disheartening to think that, in the face of of this disease which is taking hold of the Western world, many bold men who perceive it as such are forced into silence. While preparing to launch its next attack on the world which is still free, Bolshevism makes good use of the coexistence obsession at present prevailing in Western Europe and America; it pretends it is willing to exist peacefully side by side with the "capitalist" world, its aim being to subjugate Asia first of all according to a far-seeing plan and then to deal America and the rest of Europe a deadly blow. For instance, the pestilential wave of Bolshevism is now threatening to inundate the rest of of Indochina. Asia is indeed far away from the banks of the Seine, the Rhine, and the Tiber, although even Nicholas II and Lenin realized that the way to Paris is via Peking.

This policy of coexistence—that is to say, of an externally camouflaged capitulation to the Kremlin—is also advocated by the so-called "Third Bloc" of classical supporters of coexistence, a bloc that is being welded together by Tito and Nehru. All the world knows that Tito's Yugoslavia can only continue to exist under coexistence conditions. A victory over the USSR would inevitably result in the democratization of Yugoslavia, in its dissolution into national states, and in Tito's downfall. For this reason Tito is making every effort to prevent a conflict between the West and Soviet Russia. Those who are farsighted enough will realize that Tito's break with the Kremlin is extremely advantageous to the latter, since the conflict between the West and Bolshevism has been and will be postponed. The conjecture which is now spreading in the West, that Tito went to Asia on the instructions of West European political circles in order to dissuade Nehru from pursuing his pro-Communist policy and from further support to Mao Tse-tung, is actually unfounded, especially as Tito himself has always supported Mao, and delegations from his own country have constantly voted for the admission of Red China to the United Nations. And it was not just a coincidence that Malenkov recently proposed a toast to Tito's Yugoslavia. Tito's former quarrel with the Kremlin has not made him friendlier towards the West, but it has thrown the entire policy of the West into confusion and has given it a false trend. The ensuing ideological and political mistakes on the part of the West as regards the peoples subjugated by Bolshevism may, if continued and intensified, have catastrophic results.

It is a well-known fact that official circles in the West have for some time now—and precisely because of the alleged "exemplary" clash between Tito's country and Soviet Russia—been looking for salvation in national Communist and other "leftist" political trends. The entire anti-Bolshevik struggle is thus being diverted from its true course, and confidence is placed in the Slanskys and the Gomulkas. But no court revolutions are likely to put an end to Soviet Russia; this can only be accomplished by national freedom insurrections and wars, which, as regards the ideology by which they are prompted, must oppose every form of Communism. The result of the conception which has originated from Tito's revolt is that the official and semi-official policy of the Western world, including American Republicans and British Conservatives, is tending to support "leftist" elements—namely, those groups among the peoples subjugated by Moscow which most closely approach Titoism. For instance, it is no mere coincidence that Nagy, Dimitrov, Rybka, Zenkl, Lettrich, the Russian NTS organization, and many of the "leftist representatives" of the subjugated non-Russian peoples in the Soviet Union enjoy the goodwill and confidence of certain official and semi-official political circles, among them right-wing circles, in the West; this is logically in keeping with that general trend which builds its hopes upon Titoism and upon a possible revolution on the part of the "provincial governors" who by the grace of Moscow have advanced to power in the political life of their countries and who will allegedly revolt against this same Moscow in times to come and who will break with it, just as Tito has done. And the same attitude is adopted with regard to Mao and the European satellites.

Further, the confidence placed by Radio Liberty on alleged experts on "Soviet life," in those persons who "know how to speak to the Soviet people" (just as if they were not ordinary persons at all, not as normal as the people in the West with normal aims and needs and an immortal soul!), is nothing other than the same "leftist action"; and in this connection neither nationalist nor anti-Marxist representatives of even the most recent emigrant groups are allowed to count as "experts"; on the other hand, a Marxist, even if he has never read a single paper printed in the Soviet Union in all his life, is still an "expert," inasmuch as his mentality is in keeping with the Communist mentality. The Ukrainian underground publications and those of the OUN, the UPA, and the UHVR, which are compiled and published by men who have experienced "Soviet reality" and are fighting this same reality, are, for instance, not acknowledged as valid, since they are also directed against the Moscow provincial governors. It is true that in one of his recent speeches Dulles, in addition to expressing some peculiar ideas on coexistence, did reveal a certain perceptive faculty when he mentioned attempts to burst the USSR asunder from within. Such an idea is right and appropriate; but it is perhaps after all nothing but a plaster on a deep-seated coexistence boil—"ut aliquid fecisse videatur" (to make it appear that something was being done in the matter). And, in any case, who would support an attempt to burst the USSR asunder from within? The "American Committee," Radio Liberty, or possibly the pro-Russian "Research Institute"?

Is there any central anti-Bolshevik organization in the West which would unite forces with the national underground movements and support them? Where, indeed, can we find a united staff for the "first front," for the front that lies behind the Iron Curtain?

In a series of talks with a well-known war theorist of the West, General Fuller, the present writer had an opportunity to discuss in detail with him the question of the possible cooperation and mutual support of the free West and the nations subjugated by Moscow. The result of these talks was a pamphlet published by the Scottish League for European Freedom, "For What Type of War Should the West Prepare." General Fuller formulated his strategic conception of both World Wars in advance, and it would be very regrettable as far as the West is concerned if his present ideas were ignored, as was previously the case. No prophet is accepted in his own country, and Fuller's theories were first adopted and put into practice by men of other countries who had recognized the essential factors of modern warfare in time—for instance, Guderian and Zhukov—before they were at last accepted by the Allies. The strategic conception of the Third World War, as Fuller foresees it, is already being put into practice by the Bolsheviks, while official circles in the West look on calmly. How long, one may ask, do they intend to look on?

In any case, the fundamental neutrality of Yugoslavia's strategic position, which can be forecast for some time to come, is a weak spot in Western policy, all the more so as the support given to Tito by the West—namely, the support given to national Communism and thus the denial of the cause of the anti-Communist national liberation movements—is arousing bitter feelings against the West among the nations subjugated by Soviet Russia. The fact that Ukrainian underground circles have informed us that the Ukrainian nation no longer has any faith in a war and does not believe that such an event, even if it should occur, would in any way aid the Ukrainian struggle for freedom is indeed most significant. And it should be a warning to the West. It is quite possible that anti-Bolshevik camps—one consisting of the free West, the other of the countries subjugated by Bolshevism—might be set up, their activities running parallel but not coordinated and perhaps even partially in conflict. In our day, when wars are based on ideologies, this might lead to tragic consequences, inasmuch as the entire bloc of nations subjugated by Communism and the bloc of Western powers, who are ill-disposed towards us, would be confronted by the ruthless fanaticism of a united Communist camp led by Soviet Russian Bolsheviks.

The responsibility as regards such a sequence of events rests exclusively with the statesmen of the West. America has every chance of becoming a standard-bearer in the cause of national and social justice in the West, but only providing that the Americans themselves take an active part in America's Eastern policy and ignore the opinions expressed by naturalized "experts" of Eastern origin, who are pursuing anything but an American policy.

In view of the deadly Bolshevik menace to the whole world it is both sad and deeply humiliating to watch some statesmen of the West dilly-dallying over the problem of Germany's rearmament. Geneva's capitulation to Moscow and Peking; the surrender of Indochina, strategically and politically invaluable, to the Communists; France's misgivings as to Germany's rearmament, although France herself is not even in a position to protect her own country against the pernicious influence of Communism; the fact that the French Government, acting under Communist pressure, issued a decree forbidding the activity of the ABN in France; all kinds of obstacles placed in Spain's way to prevent her from assuming a fitting role in present world political affairs; the evident delay in dealing with the question of Japan's rearmament—all these thing are unpleasant

indications of a defeatism which emanates from the politicians who are responsible for the fate of the world which at present is still free.

As far as Japan is concerned, it is no mere coincidence that the Government
there is at present being taken over by men who have been imprisoned in Allied
camps. This is the result of Japanese feelings in the face of the Bolshevik menace.
Instead of ignoring Japan's feelings and trying to introduce certain ideas and
pernicious changes in Japanese ways of living, it would have been wiser to treat
the Japanese nation with a certain amount of tact, to avoid arousing bitterness
towards the West.

All the other peoples who were defeated in the last war and who at that time
fought against Soviet Russia, even if they did so under the wrong leaders and
under the wrong mottoes, should be restored without delay. The nations subjugated by Bolshevism, with Ukraine at their head, and Japan, Germany, Spain, and
Turkey are the forces which, together with the USA and Great Britain, will play a
decisive part in the clash which is inevitable. If they do not unite forces and
cooperate, it will be extremely difficult to overcome Bolshevik tyranny. The year
1955 sees the USA and Great Britain confronted by an exceedingly important
task—namely, the setting up of a united anti-Communist front of the Free World
and the subjugated world, on the strength of the equality of rights of all the
participators, and the respecting of national and individual freedom.

It is quite possible that the current problem of the liberation of the peoples
subjugated by Soviet Russia may be taken into consideration once the Paris
Agreements on West Germany's sovereignty and rearmament have been rati-
fied. It is quite possible that the future idea of holding another Four Power
conference may be abandoned, without the Western world compromising itself
once more in the eyes of the nations subjugated by Bolshevism, at whose expense
the conference was to reach a "successful" conclusion. But it is likewise quite
possible that the deadly disease of the coexistence idea may spread even further,
in which case the West will forfeit its chances, while the subjugated nations, for
their part, will continue to wage their wars for freedom on their own initiative
and according to their own plans, without taking the special and exclusive
interests of the West, erroneously presupposed by the latter, into account.

The Ukranian Review,
No. II, 1955, pp. 3-8

The Situation in the Middle East and the West

Today, the Soviet Union emerges as a "protector" of the Islamic and Arab
peoples of the Middle East and seeks steadily, through infiltration and indirect
aggression, to subvert the peoples of Asia and Africa under the slogans of
"liberation from Western colonialism." How much different the situation in the
Middle East would look today if the nations enslaved in the USSR and the
satellite countries were confident that the United States was on their side, and

stood for their liberation! Regrettably, such is not the case. The United States has failed to realize and to support the forces which stirred the Near and Middle East and which aspired to genuine national independence and social reforms, while being opposed to old style feudalism and colonialism. It is also lamentable that the United States, in its dealings with the countries of the Middle East, should have limited itself to the owners of oil fields and wealthy potentates; it has largely ignored the common people. And yet what was needed was support for the ideals of national independence propagated by the various nationalist anti-Communist movements. The United States could have implemented this policy successfully, had it taken into account the fact that in the Soviet Union there are about 30 million Moslems who religiously, culturally, racially, and historically are kin of the peoples of Iran, Turkey, Pakistan, Afghanistan, and the like. The Moslem peoples of the USSR have a sizeable political emigration on this side of the Iron Curtain which comprises several liberation groups and organizations interested in liberating their native lands from the Russian Communist yoke. Had the enlightened campaign in the Middle East—that is, the psychological warfare campaign against Russian Communism and colonialism—been conducted by the representatives of the nations enslaved by Moscow, especially the Moslem emigrant leaders, this anti-Russian propaganda assuredly would have enjoyed considerable success. But the United States has not only failed to recognize these new forces, but in actuality has placed various obstacles in the way of realization of the ideals of independence of the enslaved nations. How, for instance, can the National Turkestani Unity Committee carry out a successful propaganda action among the Moslems of the Middle and Near East against Communist Russia when the United States forbids the propagation of Turkestani independence through its propaganda media? How can anyone be certain of the sincerity of American support in regard to the independence of the nations of the Middle East if the United States does not support the aspirations for independence of the nations enslaved in the Soviet Union? As long as the Americans hesitate to stand up in outright defense of the independence of the nations subjugated by Communist Russia, they will pursue a losing course among the Asian and African nations.

The recent situation in the Middle East, with American and British troops in Lebanon and Jordan respectively, could not have occurred had the Americans and other Western powers carried out a policy of liberation, a policy of lending support and assistance to the nations aspiring to their full freedom and independence.

If we look back into the past, we can readily see that the United States has never accorded any support to the nations enslaved by Russia, as in the case of Hungary a few years ago or in the case of Ukraine, Turkestan, and other nations forty years ago. Moreover, "the Voice of America" is rigidly censoring its broadcasts to the countries behind the Iron Curtain, eliminating any reference to the matter of independence of the non-Russian nations. Under these circumstances, how can any Arab leader trust the United States? By playing down the aspiration of the non-Russian nations in the USSR, including the Moslem nations, the United States inadvertently confirms the Moscow-propagated view that Ukraine,

Byelorussia, the countries of Turkestan, and the Caucasus are all truly enjoying "Soviet independence," inasmuch as the United States refuses to underline the colonial oppression of the non-Russian nations. Although the United States rightly supported the emancipation of the peoples of the former British, French, and Dutch empires, it refuses to do so in the case of the Soviet Russian empire.

Thus the peoples of Asia and Africa are led into believing that:

a) the Soviet Union is not a colonial empire held together through sheer force of police terror and persecution;

b) the so-called "Soviet Republics" are in fact free and independent, and the Soviet Union is in truth a "voluntary" commonwealth of peoples.

By so doing, the United States is undermining its own propaganda against Communism in Asia, wherein it accuses Communist Russia of intending to enslave the Asian and African nations, since at the same time it omits mention of the enslavement of Ukraine, Byelorussia, Turkestan, and the Caucasus by Moscow. Hence, how can we expect the Arabs to believe the assertions of the United States that Russia does not desire Arab independence when assertions by Moscow that the Caucasian and Turkestani Republics are independent are not controverted by American propaganda? Moreover, it even seems that the United States does not desire true independence for these countries, inasmuch as the Voice of America and Radio Liberty are expressly forbidden to discuss in their broadcasts the matter of independence of these non-Russian countries.

This situation in turn creates suspicions in the Arab world that the United States is aiming at the enslavement of the Arab countries. While Moscow is propagating the independence of the "Union Republics" of the USSR, the United States is, in fact, denying their rights to independence by conducting a psychological warfare campaign which indirectly is favoring the preservation of the Russian empire (although under a somewhat different regime). As a result, it seems to the Arabs that the United States approves of colonial systems in general and that it wishes to become a new colonial power in Eastern Europe and Asia as soon as Communism is liquidated. Whether the United States recognizes it or not, its failure to come out openly against Russian colonialism as a whole creates unavoidably the impression that it does not fight against colonialism, but merely against Communism as such.

It is a pity that the Western powers permitted the present conflict in the Middle East to develop into an explosive international situation. Lacking proper ideological and political comprehension of the conflict, the United States had to intervene in Lebanon. Unfortunately, America is not regarded by the Middle Eastern peoples as a defender of their national independence. Instead, Moscow has taken over the mantle of the "liberator" and "protector" of these peoples.

We must not forget that the coming war will be a war in which political factors will play an essential part. It is not possible to defeat Russia without gaining a political advantage over her. It is possible to wrest this advantage if the United States truly and genuinely applies the principles of the liberation policy. These principles are no less relevant today than they were yesteryear. Perhaps they are even more pertinent today with the danger of a world conflict looming on the horizon. The form and content of psychological warfare cannot be ignored; it would be, in fact, a catastrophic mistake to neglect the political and psychological nature of the conflict. Not atom bombs, but ideas, will decide the final issue. Accordingly, my attention is devoted precisely to those seemingly abstract problems which, at bottom, furnish the driving forces of our present-day world.

Now, when a new world conflict is threatening to erupt, it is doubly necessary to study these problems and to draw the necessary conclusions.

First of all, it would be advisable to create, on the bases and concepts advanced by the ABN, a coordinating center together with the competent authorities of the Free World, and especially the United States, for insuring a successful conduct of the psychological warfare and for coordinating practical activities both behind the Iron Curtain and in the Free World. It is necessary at this point to provide practical opportunities and possibilities for activities of the national liberation movements and organizations that are members of the ABN, which could extend behind the Iron Curtain, to the Middle East, as well as to Asia and the Far East. These activities should be stimulated by radio broadcasts by the ABN around the borders of the Communist Russian and Red Chinese spheres of domination. They should manifest themselves in practical operations, such as penetration and infiltration behind the Iron Curtain both in Europe and Asia.

As long as the United States does not consider the national liberation revolutionary organizations as its partners and allies, but only as mere servants of certain US agencies, little success, if any, is to be expected. These activities should be conducted through the representatives of the enslaved nations in various countries bordering on the USSR and Red China, such as Turkey, Iran, Pakistan, Korea, and the like.

The Caucasus, Turkestan, and some parts of Siberia are situated near the countries from which such intensive action could be conducted. Moslem exiles from the USSR should be able to stir the Moslems of the Middle East and Near East against Communist Russia, while the anti-Communist nationalists, opposed to Russian Communist domination of their countries in the USSR and the satellites, ought to encourage the activities of nationalists in the Asian countries and in the Middle East, explaining to them the real essence and nature of Communism as an instrument of Russian colonialism. I believe that such practical and political activities should be launched from Taiwan, Vietnam, and Korea, where the representatives of the enslaved nations, specifically the nationalist liberation leaders from the USSR and the so-called satellite countries, should be included. Communist Russia attacks on a global plane, not locally; therefore, she must be combatted on a similar scale.

The resolute and decisive attempt to counteract Russian penetration into the Middle East with American troops landing in Lebanon and British troops descending upon Jordan was a first manifestation of this needed positive approach to the problem. However, this action contained certain elements of indecision. A compromise, even to the point of a division of influence with Communist Russia in this area, was being sought by certain Western leaders. Such a wavering attitude implied that the United States and Great Britain were unwilling to continue their resolute action to the end. The pro-Western governments ought to be supported; at the same time, however, their true sovereignty should be maintained and preserved. Such Western influence as is exerted there should be directed towards effecting social reforms, and not towards the strengthening of the feudal order. The nationalist, anti-Communist, and anti-feudal elements in those countries should be supported.

There is no reason to fear the outbreak of an atomic war, for Russia cannot afford such a war at present. The West can safely carry out its plans in the Middle and Near East, for Russia will not allow herself to become directly involved. Furthermore, she lacks satellites there which she could send to fight for her interests.

Thus, complete elimination of the Russian influence from the Middle East is possible now, on the condition that this policy be resolutely carried through to the end. Russia will not intervene, she will not dare to occupy Iran, if the United States holds steadfast; otherwise it would mean the beginning of a world war. Knowing that the United States, lacking conventional weapons, might use atomic weapons, in which field the USSR is far behind the United States, Moscow will not risk a conflict. She is vulnerable because of the presence of the millions of non-Russian peoples in the USSR, a factor which regrettably enough is not being sufficiently and effectively exploited by the West. Russian brandishment of a possible dispatch of "Soviet volunteers" to the Middle East is a double-edged weapon. In the fall of 1956, during the Hungarian uprising, many Soviet soldiers, principally Ukrainians, Georgians, Balts, and Byelorussians, deserted the Soviet troops and joined the Hungarian freedom fighters. The same thing, only on a larger scale, might happen if Khrushchev were foolish enough to send "volunteers" to face the US and British troops in the Middle East.

The argument of sheer physical force is the only one Communist Russia is likely to understand. The more force the United States exerts, the sooner Russia will retreat. Her propaganda boasting and threatening is designed primarily to cover up her internal weaknesses and anxieties.

The greatest weakness of the foreign policy of the United States and of the Free World in general is, its timidity and indecision. It is a lack of courage to pursue to the end its political objectives, which at times are bold and effective. I believe that this indecision generates confusion and causes the loss of friends and allies all over the world. The United States and Great Britain should not only not compromise with Moscow in the matter of Lebanon and Jordan, but should try to eliminate Russian influence at all costs from that vital and strategic area. It seems now, with Western leaders stampeded by Khrushchev into a UN "summit" conference, that the actions taken in Lebanon and Jordan might be "half-actions" after all. Such a "half-action" does not impress the Arab nations, but it will benefit Communist Russia, which will become a great power in the Middle East.

Thus the principal aim of the United States foreign policy in the Middle East should be a total elimination of the influence of Russia and then an amicable understanding with the Arab nations. The Arabs would respect only those who are determined and consistent in their political moves. The United States should make it known that it will support the legitimate aspirations of the Arab nations, that it will sustain nationalist, but anti-feudal and anti-Communist, movements. The Arabs must be told in no uncertain terms that while the United States supports their nationalist and anti-feudal movement, it will not tolerate any flirting with Moscow, nor will it countenance any Russian political and economic infiltration in their countries. Through such a policy a relative peace can be achieved in the Middle East. The United States could support the internal social and political reforms in the Arab countries and thus help them sustain themselves economically and socially. It would be disastrous for the United States to support the rich and feudal circles in the Arab countries, rather than the enlightened Arab nationalist movements, for such a policy would of necessity lead again to the dangerous pro-Russian orientation of the Arab countries.

A turn of events in favor of the United States and the Free World can come only when the United States finally declares itself in favor of nationalism and the liberation movements of the enslaved nations in the USSR, which are against Russian imperialism and colonialism.

ABN Correspondence,
September 1959, pp. 18-22

The Somnolent Western Elite

European ideas are penetrating to new continents, and a new world revolution is taking place before our very eyes. The first great European revolution on a global scale occurred 500 years ago, when European explorers conquered new continents, and peoples, races, religions, and cultures met. European ideas remained victorious, for the European mind was inspired by the immanent spirit of European expansion, its creative boom, its faith in its cultural mission, and by the crusades with "cross and sword." Now, however, Western Europe is steadily losing the prestige of its world position, for it has betrayed its ideals. The old ideals of the Occident are experiencing a rebirth in other parts of Europe and on other continents.

Western Europe of former times is atrophying in intellectual and political respects before our very eyes; it puts the ideals of cosmopolitanism, of the "little man," of materialism and hedonism, and personal interests before the common good, and the comfort of civilization before creative, cultural activity. It is turning its back on its former ideals, those ideals which are often reborn amidst hardships, suffering, hunger, and need.

The present ideals of Western Europe are, for instance, expressed in such slogans as: "Better a living coward than a dead hero," "Better Red than dead," etc. The Occident is in danger of losing its freedom. For there can be no freedom if it is not defended courageously. Cowardice is a renunciation of experiencing and defending this freedom in keeping with one's own human dignity. The courageous enjoy more freedom since they risk more for it. But, unfortunately, the courageous have become rare in the free Europe of today. Nowadays little effort is made to elevate one's own nation and to see the purpose and pleasure of our life in work and creative activity. On the contrary, the general idea is to work as little as possible. No one has ever died for the cause of a "six-hour working day" or an afternoon rest ("siesta"). But thousands and millions have died for the noble idea of their native country, or for the victory of Christian and religious truth on earth, or for social justice.

Life on this earth begins to get boring when one reflects that the aim in life of the individual is the latest model in motor cars, the latest furniture, the latest type of television set, a monthly rise in wages, extra pay for holidays, or an extra month's wage at the end of the year. Yes, life is boring if there is no pleasure in creative work, but only an effort on the part of the present "citizen" of the Free World to acquire material profit and to lead a life of comfort and ease.

On account of their horrors, wars no doubt seem to mankind to be a doom and a damnation. But wars in the old days of chivalry were always a trial by fire (and they will continue to be so) in which character was molded and which brought forth heroes; the ideal overcomes the material, the everlasting the transitory, and the feeling of community overcomes egoism. And in this way myth and legends are created about persons of superhuman greatness—that is to say, not about the "little" or average man, but about outstanding persons. In pursuit of a higher standard of living and greater comforts of life, people are so dazzled by wealth that they forget that the sword of Damocles is hanging over their heads; the Antichrist of Moscow is attacking the world. In ancient times the Crusaders of the Occident headed by Richard Coeur-de-Lion, conducted their campaigns against the unbelieving, and Peter the Hermit of Amiens exhorted all Europe to defend the Christian faith. Today, the European "knights" are even afraid to designate the enemy by his name; indeed, they even prefer a coexistence of the Christian faith with the Antichrist in order to avoid any risk to their hedonistic way of life. Times and people have changed....

True patriotism and a fervent and enlightened freedom-loving nationalism stirred the people to great deeds and set the spirit of self-sacrifice and the fundamental principle of the common good above egoism. Priests and patriots, as, for instance, Cardinal Mercier, gave the soldiers their blessing when they marched against the invader: they exhorted them to fight under the banner of Christ against the enemies of their native country. Nor did this fighting spirit degenerate in any way when the national and the religious ideas were linked together and when man was regarded as being created in God's divine image. The degeneration which occurred during the Nazi era, which was the result of the negation of Christianity, and its principles in the life of the individual and of the peoples, enabled the forces of evil to demoralize the Occident and to degrade the sincerest idea of our day—the national-liberation idea, the idea of enlightened, freedom-loving nationalism.

Thanks to its loyalty to national and Christian traditions, the Occident remained steadfast. But the forces of evil are endeavoring to replace both the national and the Christian idea by cosmopolitanism and religious indifference. In this connection they seek to depreciate freedom-loving nationalism, which is based on Christianity, as a reactionary and untimely phenomenon. The Occident has allegedly survived the historical stage of nationalism as an unavoidable evil, and for this reason it is now time to pay homage to the "higher" supranational and extra-national ideals, the "united Europe of Cudenhove-Calergi." And, in Calergi's opinion, Europe ends where, at a favorable opportunity, the invasion of the barbarous Russian occupants comes to a halt, so that—heaven forbid—Moscow should not be annoyed by a possible shifting of the frontiers of Europe—for example, as far as the Caucasus. From the point of view of the forces of evil, it is not worthwhile sacrificing one's life for such a "reactionary" ideal as the fatherland, and patriotism resulting from one's service to God and faith in higher, spiritual ideals should be regarded solely as an indication of backwardness, religious faith, enthusiasm, productive ardor, the sensual pleasures—every apotheosis of the heroic fight for God and the fatherland is ridiculed by these forces. Heroic deeds, the mysticism of life and the fight, the training of the younger generation according to the ideals and in the spirit of the Cossack and UPA fighters in Ukraine, in the spirit of the immortal Ukrainian heroes Shcherbak or Danylyshyn, General Chuprynka, or the Ukrainian Head of State S. Petlura, according to the ideals of the Ukrainian Archbishops, the martyrs Lypkivsky and Sheptytsky, and the famous Ukrainian freedom fighter and literary scholar S. Yefermov, and many others, are allegedly nothing but a sign of hopeless backwardness. On the other hand, the mysticism of Communism, of the "great Russian people who crushed Hitler's hordes," the mysticism of the Red partisans, of the "last decisive battle," of the "daring deeds" of the soldiers of the Red Army in the "wars of the fatherland," of the Red spies and agents, the mysticism of the militant atheists who even defy God, the apotheosis of that child Judas Pavlik Morozov, who denounced his own father, the "martyrdom" of Lumumba, of Rosenberg, and of other Abels, the blackening of Mobutu's courage as "brigandism"—all this is allegedly a sign of progressiveness, which is worthy of enthusiasm and emulation since it is a vision of the future of our world.

In the meantime, however, distant continents, numerous newly founded states and regenerated peoples, races, and cultures are being inspired by the revolutionary ideas of the Occident. World-embracing, freedom-loving, enlightened nationalism is becoming the banner of our day and the most truly progressive and just idea of the present. In the West religious indifference prevails, while behind the Iron Curtain a militant Christianity is becoming the idea of the intellectual, moral, and national rebirth of millions of subjugated persons. The vanguard of this rebirth movement by no means consists of the aged, but, on the contrary, of young persons, of the revolutionary youth—a youth that "has seen nothing but Communism," for it was born in the darkest age in the history of the world, under Bolshevism, in the Red Russian prison of peoples. And yet it has by no means lost its conception of what is eternal, everlasting, and divine.

"Liberty, equality, and fraternity"—these were the ideals of French democratic nationalism, which kindled the great French Revolution and with the help of which Napoleon was victorious on many battlefields in numerous countries. The ideas of "la patrie" of Robespierre and Saint-Just, who were both "Incourruptibles," and the idea of the equality of all individuals inspired all those who, as natives of the French colonies, learned the essence of the conception "la patrie" and of the slogans of the French Revolution at the Sorbonne in Paris. The French empire was disintegrated by Rousseau, by the Encyclopedists, by Danton, Marat, Robespierre, Saint-Just, and Napoleon, since the French Revolution disarmed French imperialism ideologically. For, according to their ideas, the inhabitants of the Ivory Coast, Algeria, or Madagascar had the same right to freedom and independence as the inhabitants of "eternal France."

The impact of two opposite ideas—the imperial idea, which in essence discriminates between individuals (since it even discriminates in the case of the subjugated nation), and the national patriotic ideas—led to a victory of the latter in the "Union Française," as a result of the universal aspect of human rights which was stressed by the French Revolution. The Union became a community of free peoples with equal rights. And hence the convulsion which the empire is undergoing....

Congolese General Mobutu is rendering "eternal Europe" a far greater service than the white traitor to Europe Thorez, or the coexistentialist B. Russell, inasmuch as Mobutu is attacking the Russian Fifth Column in a grim fight.

The aristocratic, democratic, and traditional nationalism of Albion, which in Oxford, Cambridge, and all its other universities trained the elite for its colonies in the spirit of British universal ideas, made the evolution from a colonial empire to a "Commonwealth" of free peoples with equal rights an almost painless affair, and in fact carried this out with admirable skill. We witnessed a triumph of the ideas of the Occident in what was yesterday the greatest empire in the world, with the help of the political elite of the liberated peoples, an elite that was trained according to Western example.

Western Europe abdicated from its position as a world power. But its successor (as far as fulfilling the same function is concerned), the United States of America—or, to be more exact, that part of the political and cultural elite of the USA which has remained faithful to the ideals of ancient and Christian Europe—defends the eternal ideals of the Occident. Hence the frontiers of Europe are not geographical in character, but extend as far as men sacrifice their lives for the victory of European ideas, venerate these ideas, and serve them. Thus the Australians, the Mobutus in the dark continent are defending European ideals when they set up a front against Bolshevism, whereas white men such as Cyrus Eaton, Sartre, Picasso, Togliatti, and many others betray these ideals.

In the concentration camps of Kingiri, Vorkuta, in the taigas and tundras of Siberia, the self-sacrifice of the insurgent Ukrainian prisoners represents a far greater service to Europe than the activity of some of the European parliaments, which are so fond of imitating Khrushchev's coexistence smile. The ideas of militant, freedom-loving, enlightened nationalism are far more comprehensible to the New World, for, although these ideas originated in the Old World, the latter has renounced them and thus itself. The ideas of freedom-loving nationalism are taking whole continents and the countries of the future, America, Eastern Europe, Asia, and Africa, by storm. Meanwhile, in the official West—as regards the peoples subjugated by Russia—respect for the individual and for human dignity, the freedom of the spirit of enterprise, the creativeness of the individual, dynamic Christianity, and liberation nationalism as European revolutionary and anti-Communist factors behind the Iron Curtain are ignored or disparaged in a reprehensible way.

The Ukrainian Review,
No. II, 1961, pp. 24-28

The Quid Pro Quo of Western Anti-Bolshevik Policy

In the social and economic respect, Marxism has not gained the upper hand anywhere in the West; and at present it has no chance whatever of being victorious either in Germany or in Great Britain, and least of all in the United States of America—that is to say, in the most industrialized countries of the world. The precondition for the victory of Marxism is not so much the economic position of the country in question, the extent of the development of its industry, but rather the morale of the leading class, the stability of the ideas propagated by the intellectual elite, and the moral principles of the broad masses.

The American capitalist Cyrus Eaton is not pro-Communist because he lacks money, but because he has lost faith in Western ideals, in Christ, and in the nation, and because his individual and national morale is not stimulated by a transcendent faith but by earthly, transient values. Certain of the French intellectuals have been caught up in dialectical materialism and Communism not because they were stirred by pity for the social and economic misery of the working classes; not one of them (including Eaton) has become an ascetic and has distributed part of his possessions amongst the poor, as did those who in ancient times proved their faith by their deeds. These persons have only been swept along by the current of Communism because they abandoned the traditions of their native soil, the traditions of their native country and its ideals, and thus landed on shores which are foreign to their people from the ideological point of view.

The psychological warfare of the West is characterized not so much by theorists of its own, which are opposed to the Bolshevik theories, but, rather, by analogical "corrected" theories.

Militant, freedom-loving, world nationalism will be victorious in all countries, including the Western empires. In spite of this, however, the West does not adopt the ideas of a new order established on the ruins of Bolshevism (such as the national liberation idea, or the disintegration of the Russian empire, etc.) as the basis of its propaganda in its psychological warfare, but solely endeavors to correct the Bolshevik "theories" in favor of the empire by the NTS or Kerensky. In the Western countries socialism ceases to be a class doctrine unrelated to reality. It changes into a national party which not only unites proletarians but also employees, peasants and the petty bourgeoisie, and rejects Marxism as a theory which is outmoded. These socialist parties of the Western countries (Germany, Austria, and Great Britain) reject the principle of the total socialization of the means of production. They now make the nationalization of the branch of production in question exclusively dependent on practical expediency. They have decided to replace the former doctrinaire principle of integral nationalization and socialization by a kind of national solidarity and another social economic policy, and above all by a participation of the broad masses in the means of production from the point of view of private property. In the social respect the realization of this theory guarantees the victory of the idea of the social solidarity of the producing classes against the class-struggle theory and does away with socialist totalitarianism. But the official policy of the West in no way takes into account the social, economic, and national political processes behind the Iron Curtain. In its sham political war against Bolshevism (by means of such broadcasting stations as the Voice of America, Radio Free Europe, the BBC, and Radio Liberty), the West propagates the old socialism or Titoism for precisely those countries which are obliged to live under the most abominable form of totalitarian socialism.

And this at a time when the Marxist parties in the West under the conditions of a free democratic life are forced to admit the ideological and political shipwreck of Marxism. Hence the West propagates a Marxism that has already fallen into disrepute in a partially "corrected" national Communist or "democratic socialist" form—for the peoples behind the Iron Curtain.

And no one in the West considers the possibility—and rightly so—that in the event of a victory on the part of the German Socialist Party (SPD) or the British Labor Party, the collectivization of agriculture will be enforced in their countries. But for the countries behind the Iron Curtain and, above all, for Ukraine, with its thousand-year-old affinity with the soil as private property, the West propagates a "corrected" system of collectives. The SPD is in favor of a shareholding (i.e., participation as regards private property) on the part of the workers in industrial enterprises, which fundamentally means the end of socialism. A concrete example of this is the private right of participation, introduced at the initiative of the CDU (the Christian Democratic Party), in the state "Volkswagen Works," as well as new projects of the same type on the part of the SPD. In spite of this, however, the West advocates the idea of preserving a socialist system in a corrected form in the countries behind the Iron Curtain, even though it is precisely this Marxism which is hated most by the peoples subjugated by Moscow.

In the West liberal capitalism has been transformed into the so-called "people's capitalism," and in the course of this process Marxism has suffered a downfall. But in spite of this obvious fact, the West is determined that socialism should be preserved in the countries behind the Iron Curtain after their liberation from Bolshevism—that is to say, a socialism with collectives possibly reorganized somewhat on Rosenberg lines, as was practiced during the brief German occupation period.

Lord "Haw-haw," Quisling, and Laval were hanged or shot as German collaborators, whereas General De Gaulle and men like him were acclaimed as freedom fighters. And the West likewise regards the Russian collaborators who, together with Stalin, Molotov, Vyshinsky and the Russian occupation army, in harmonious agreement with all the Gottwalds, Bieruts, Dimitroffs, and other agents of the Kremlin, forced their peoples to put their necks in the noose, as acknowledged champions of the freedom of the peoples in question and as partners of the Western world.

The former Vice-President of Gottwald's Government and until recently President of the "Assembly of Captive Nations" (ACEN) was one of the originators of the agreement between Czechoslovakia, Poland, and the Soviet Union which was concluded in 1947 and was directed against the Ukrainian Insurgent Army (UPA). As Gottwald's representative he declared in the Czech parliament: "...Never against the USSR, but always shoulder to shoulder with it.... Great Russia is our friend and brother. The friendship of the Czechoslovak Republic with the Soviet Union is unswerving and of vital importance both to the Czechs and to the Slovaks...."

This politician maintained friendly relations with the Bolsheviks and helped them to exterminate the fighters for the freedom of Ukraine and of all freedom-loving mankind. He is now regarded as a champion of the freedom aims of the subjugated peoples and is encouraged and aided by the Western "anti-Communists." This also applies to a certain NKVD captain, who is made much of in the West even though he recently murdered hundreds of freedom fighters. It may be right to afford asylum to such criminals (if there is no other alternative), but it is indeed scandalous that former tyrants and their henchmen who go abroad are regarded by the West as champions of the freedom of the enslaved peoples.

General De Gaulle, whose attitude towards Nazism was uncompromising, was rightly regarded by the Allies as the champion of the freedom aims of the French people. Why do the leading political circles in the West not apply the same standards to the Ukrainian nationalists, who, after all, are uncompromising fighters for the freedom of Ukraine against Russian Bolshevism?

For negotiations with France, the FLN and Ferhat Abbas are regarded as fitting partners, but not pro-French or treacherous Algerian elements.

No one regards a colonial official appointed by the occupant as a genuine representative of the enslaved peoples in question. Why then should a certain Hulay, or some other person won over by money, or some Russian of the Russian Solidarists' Organization (NTS)—that is to say, a Russian colonial official—be the spokesman of the Ukrainian people? The whole world would scoff if General De Gaulle were to negotiate on the final solution of the Algerian problem with the French colonists and ignore the Algerians themselves. But no one scoffs when Kennan refers to Ukraine as the Texas of Russia, or when "leading" Western circles designate such gentlemen as Stolypin, Kerensky, or Poremsky as "co-advocates" of the freedom aims of the Ukrainian people.

What a "confusion of tongues"! In fact, a Tower of Babel of ideas, conceptions, trends, and movements! Dark forces are creating chaos and evil in the West!

While the Western empires are disintegrating, the West is determined to save the Eastern Russian empire from destruction at any price. Marxism has proved to be a complete failure in the Free World; but it is precisely this Free World which is determined to force it on other peoples at any price, after the latter have been liberated from Bolshevism. In the West socialist parties are renouncing the these modern mass media of influence, are open to those who propagate the putrefaction of society. These same public media, however, almost always deny access to those who speak up on behalf of patriotism, self-sacrifice, heroism, high Christian ideals, or even for the national and moral education of youth. How many ridiculous films are produced? How many similar books and articles are written? Yet—where can one find a film or an article which glorifies patriotism and high human ideals?

The death of Stepan Bandera and the trial of his murderer in Karlsruhe, for example, were of interest to television producers: not from a lofty point of view, however, but solely from the sensational. The West German press proves clearly how a society is fed on demoralizing propaganda, and how difficult it is to publish an article that advocates great ideals, national and human values. This is not a mere accident—it is a consequence. The former occupational administrators required a license to transmit radio broadcasts to Marxist inmates in Nazi concentration camps, or to leftist "democratic" elements. At present, however, one is simply not allowed to speak up against the Soviet Russian domination over nations which were once free and independent. One is not allowed to advocate greater sacrifice for one's own homeland and the fight for religious ideals. Hence, the freedom of the press is only for those who share the views held by the owners and their supporters—not for the intellectual elite who think otherwise.

He who endeavors to defend long-cherished ideals, morals in politics, literature, and art, the ideals of a militant church idealism, is soon labelled a "fascist," a "Nazi," an "enemy of democracy" and "peace." The prevailing mood is cynicism and nihilism; he who speaks up against them is denied access to press, radio, and television. He who advocates a moral and spiritual rebirth of the world and an ideological march against Russian Communism is called a "warmonger," a medieval "crusader." (Today, crusades are equated with Nazism and Fascism).

In the Western world of today, hardly anyone is interested in the necessity of a new crusade, a new Peter of Amiens, without which a rebirth is impossible. It is prohibited even to mention such things in the public media: such ideas are silenced—their authors are stigmatized.

The young live in a spiritual vacuum. They are offered material wealth and luxury—but they are given no notion of the higher and nobler purposes of life, of genuine patriotism. The love of one's homeland and the love of God are ridiculed.

All ideology is without appeal; religion is without significance. Science alone is still fashionable. No doubt, however, it too will soon be thrown into the rubbish heap by the cynics. Even at that, science is not faith, not ideology. It cannot offer a solution to the cause of being. It cannot develop moral laws; it can only help to demonstrate their eternal value. Religion alone can decide moral values.

Today the prevailing view is that it is better to die of surfeit than in the struggle for higher human values, for the love of one's homeland, for God. Hence we have the popular phrase: "Better Red than dead." People have lost their character; they no longer have a dynamic moral sense. Without these, there cannot be a creative power. While running after the "new," the "modern," the "progressive," people lose sight of the "old," the eternal, and the unchangeable. There are no new ideas—only new perspectives. The aim, therefore, should be to

program they have followed so far, and in the system of "people's capita
there is a mass application of the principle of private property to meai
production. On the other hand, the West would like to see a "corrected" s(
ism, a "democratized" Marxist totalitarianism, Titoism, or some other nat
Communist bogy preserved in the future in the countries of the peoples ens
by Moscow.

No one in the West would dream of collectivizing agriculture, but the
nevertheless propagates the idea of preserving the collective system i:
countries behind the Iron Curtain, and all that is to be done is to corre(
"harmful excesses" of this system. As "leading" Western circles rightly as:
this is the "Eastern" form of democratic socialism.

The ideas of Marxism are outmoded on this side of the Iron Curtain anc
are likewise falling to dust in the countries enslaved by Moscow. But, unf
nately, the West refuses to acknowledge this fact. What's more—all the c(
empires in the world are falling into decay, but the West still advocat(
preservation of the most ruthless of all these empires, namely the Russian
though it is precisely this empire which is digging the grave of the West. O1
indeed say, *quo vadis occident?*

ABN Corresponden(
July-August 1961, pr

Lack of Ideology

The Occident without Sails and Helmsmen

From time to time the question arises whether it is possible to defenc
beliefs in the Free World openly, whether the democratic right to freec
expression is a right for everyone, or only for those whose thinking is in c
with that of the press, radio, television, and other modern media of propa

We do not deny that freedom of the press exists in the West; but we d
that their freedom is vouchsafed to those who defend beliefs that are not :
by the owners of the press and the radio. It is permissible, for example, tc
up for the preservation of the Russian empire in almost every press
whereas it is very difficult to find a newspaper that will give one paragr
present the thesis that the Russian empire should be dissolved into n
independent states. One can defend the coexistence policy—indeed, ever
price of surrender, as is done by the hopeless British pacifists led by Lord F
One cannot, however, define the liberation aspiration of the enslaved nat
the Soviet Union. Press space is given to those who propagate demor
trends: homosexuality, the primacy of material values over spiritual valu(
appeal," gangsterism, the "heroism" of Red Spanish brigades, frivolo1
adventures, sensational crimes, etc.—all this can be read in the daily press
one takes exception to it. The press, the radio, television, and the cine

realize and perfect the ideas which have always been with us. The ideas of God, homeland, human dignity, freedom, glory, faith, honor are not accidental and temporal ideas. They represent the eternal foundation of human existence. We must not discard them, as we would an old pair of gloves. We must continue to derive courage and faith from them; to realize our human dignity with them.

Lack of character is becoming ever more prevalent in the West. Everything is mixed together—a hodgepodge prevails: revolutionaries together with opportunists, honest men together with those who have no character; the courageous together with cowards; altruists together with egoists; ascetics with sybarites; abstinents with alcoholics; socialists with capitalists.

The capitalists in the West, for example, consider themselves progressive because they have Marxists in their enterprises who serve for money. Marxists infiltrate the capitalist press; everything is intermixed. Road signs on which people could orient themselves are simply not clear. Ideology as such is denied on the grounds that it contributed to the growth of Nazism and Fascism and produced a blood bath of hatred. Prayer is now forbidden in American schools on the grounds that it is contrary to some religious convictions. The fact that prayer is a direct communication with God and not the expression of any one Church belief is completely overlooked. That Christianity elevated men is forgotten: that without religion, the world becomes a human jungle.

Indispensability of Ideology

Without an ideology there cannot be any great social movement for the same reason that a boat without sails will not move. Without something to catch the wind and direct it, there can be no great and consistent movement. An ideology is the world's sails, without which it would find itself in a state of nirvana. World politics cannot be based solely on actions suited to the requirements of the moment, nor can it be based on a policy of reacting to another's moves. He who simply tries to extricate himself from unpleasant situations by the use of clever pseudo-ideas will lose in the long run. Since the aim of Soviet Russian imperialism is to conquer the world, the West must have its own mission: to spread and defend Christian ideals, truth, freedom, and justice the world over, to counteract evil everywhere. The creative and noble ideas of Christianity, heroic humanism, and nationalism must oppose Communist Russia's messianic imperialism.

It is true enough that Nazism and Communism were the outgrowth of ideologies—but this is no reason to deny the value of an ideology altogether. The problem lies not in ideology as such, but in the aim and intent of an ideology. The Christian ideology, for example, preaches self-renunciation, self-sacrifice, negation of egoism, and promotes the realization and fulfillment of higher and just values—all of which tends to the betterment of mankind as a whole. The Nazi and Communist ideologies, on the other hand, embody precepts and tendencies that are vividly opposed to human values. At present, the West is ashamed of its past; of its crusades, its noble ideals, its concept of chivalry. Dark forces are at work which scorn and ridicule everything that was once lofty in the life of the Occident. Ideology itself is flatly renounced as the crime of some peoples. But what is offered in place of ideology? Cynicism, nihilism, sensualism. In short, faith in God and in Man is rejected, and the "golden calf" is once again placed at the basis of life. Perhaps we will have full stomachs, but our hearts will be empty.

What we need is a return to a national Christian ideology, which is a return to eternal spiritual values, to morality, altruism, self-sacrifice, to a stern tradition: a return to God and homeland.

He who propagates "freedom for all," and understands by this freedom for cynics and nihilists to poison the soul of man and to demoralize society, is a hypocrite. The cynics and nihilists set up on their pedestal not God and godlike men, but the animal-like, the sexual, the demoralizing concept of man; they are doing everything in their power to divide and suppress those who defend healthy, creative ideas based on God's Commandments and love of one's homeland. Only when such animal-like beings are curtailed in their demoralizing activity can real freedom for true men, the godlike beings, exist.

And just because mediocrity reigns in the arts nowadays, just because people no longer dedicate themselves to great ideas and have lost profound faith, our epoch has not yielded such great artists as Michelangelo, Raphael, El Greco, Leonardo da Vinci, Shakespeare, Shevchenko, Beethoven, Bach, etc. The great artists' sources of inspiration were always *great* ideas: belief in Divine laws and in the homeland.

The present social-political order in the world, including the West, is not the last word in the construction of a healthy society. We are witness to the fact that the distorted democratic system is unable to preserve the many-sided freedom of man. A proof of this is the fact that the press of the Free World does not allow the freedom of all nations and of all men to be defended. For example, the spokesmen for the liberation aspirations of the nations enslaved within the Soviet Union are not given a voice in the press, radio, television.

In the past, international conflicts occurred when a gentleman's character was insulted. Today, the most serious insults to one's person are allowed to pass without a consequential retaliation. When, for example, Khrushchev did not give his hand to General Eisenhower, at the time President of the United States, the incident was simply allowed to pass.

During his World War II crusade in Europe, Roosevelt saw one tyrant only—Hitler. He did not see the other one—Stalin. He did not see the necessity, therefore, of destroying two empires, the German and the Russian, to restore real freedom and security in the world. It is to be regarded as the gravest tragedy of recent times that the most ruthless of tyrants of all times was allowed to dictate *his* terms at Teheran, Yalta, and Potsdam, notwithstanding the fact that without US aid Russia would not have been able to hold its fronts. At Potsdam, President Truman held two aces in his hands: the atomic bomb and the subjugated peoples. Both Truman and Eisenhower, however, were walking in the footsteps of a degenerating Occident. F.D. Roosevelt surrendered to Stalin; President Truman ignored even Mr. Churchill and later Mr. Bevan, and walked in one front with Stalin, who dictated his terms, which President Truman accepted notwithstanding British protests. In spite of his various mistakes, Prime Minister Churchill foresaw the threat of Russian Communism. He still had a sense of ideology; he had not become a cynical pragmatist and empiricist. However, the "spirit of Yalta" triumphed. It was the triumph of the demon Stalin, empiricism, pragmatism: the view that "somehow it would be possible to coexist with the devil."

Churchill did not heed the warning of General Franco, and replied that after the war Great Britain would be the most powerful nation in Europe. And today? Probably Churchill himself would laugh at his wartime prognosis. General Eisenhower did not grasp what was happening at that time. To him, the fight against Communism was an "abstract" fight. To Roosevelt, it did not matter where Moscow trod wth its boots.

A "democratic" system in which the decisions are no longer made by the responsible representatives of the people, but by anonymous power groups is a completely irresponsible democracy. Such power groups deck themselves behind the "will of the people"; they cannot be as easily exposed as totalitarian tyrants. Their actions are based on parliamentary resolutions. Members of Parliament themselves seldom have the slightest idea what these power groups are deciding.

Moral Foundations in Politics

In criticizing various governmental aspects of American policy, we do not want to lay any blame upon the American people themselves, who are concerned with upholding moral principles in politics. On this ground the USA did not recognize the USSR before Roosevelt's presidency. The enslavement of peoples by tyrants was contrary to American moral convictions.

A typical contradiction of American politics is the disrespect demonstrated by the State Department towards resolutions adopted by the Congress of the United States, although the latter represents the desires of the people. The American people, as we have already pointed out, preserves traditions of morality in politics. The Captive Nations Week resolution which was adopted by the US Congress is a good case in point. In this resolution, the liberation of the nations enslaved in the Soviet Union is supported. The Secretary of State, Mr. Dean Rusk, on the other hand, regards Ukraine, Georgia, Armenia, and Byelorussia as "integral parts of traditional Russia."

In 1918-19, a US committee which investigated the question of Ukraine distinctly supported Ukraine's right to independence, including within its ethnographic limits Galicia and the Crimea. The Committee's motives were of a strictly moral nature. It was the belief of President Wilson's Government that even if the Ukrainian state should fail to retain its independence, Eastern Galicia should not remain a part of Poland. When Ukraine's independence is again restored, the status of Eastern Galicia will once again be a question. This fact indicates that at that time there was more harmony between the will of the American people and its Government.

Americans returned home after the Second World War from the European battlefield as fighters for ideas, for the rights of the individual and of nations, although these ideas had not been realized. They would have been real crusaders, if President Roosevelt had inspired the Americans with crusading ideas. Instead of concerning himself with a crusade against both tyrants, he turned his attention to coexistence with the Russian Antichrist. It did not help him to sing the fighting Christian hymn "Onward, Christian soldiers," for the battlefield had already been shared with the collaborators of Antichrist. The Atlantic Charter and the fighting hymn were only symbols of that lack of faith which sold half the world to Russian tyrants, instead of destroying all tyrannies and giving the world lasting peace.

Today we are witnessing the results of a policy without "ideological foundations." Where is the world being led by people who do not uphold faith in truth and justice? Not peace but triumph of truth on earth is the highest value. Christ did not teach us to surrender to the forces of evil, nor did he teach us to associate with them. He taught us to propagate and to defend God's truth and Commandments. God is eternal and his Commandments are unchangeable. God is not dead notwithstanding the fact that thousands of nihilists have proclaimed His "death." Our planet cannot be preserved against destruction by the negation of divine Commandments. The world will not be saved from ruin by "coexisting" with the Antichrist—as is presently practiced by some short-sighted Western politicians. The fear of the use of nuclear weapons is pushing humanity into an abyss from which there will be no escape. He who, out of fear, renounces the dignity of godlike creatures and God's Commandments as just ideas is doomed to an infamous death. The preconditions for victory over the nuclear blackmail consist, first of all, in the understanding that without God's will humanity cannot be destroyed at random. The White House "brain trust" will not save the world, for it lacks the most important ingredients: faith, ideology, and a political mission—without which a strategic plan is in vain. With tricks and experimentation with the Antichrist the "brain trust" will not overcome the forces of evil. *A moral rebirth alone can save the world: a return to great ideals.*

The question of defending the Free World against the Communist Russian tyrants depends, first and foremost, upon individuals who are capable of organizing and directing this defense. When this defense, however, is left in the hands of people who have no faith in what they are defending, who do not acknowledge unchangeable ideas and laws, who do not have a sense of responsibility for the traditions of their own nation, who have no moral principles—then a grave threat to humanity arises.

Just a few years back, Senator J.F. Kennedy supported the Congressional resolution with regard to the right of all subjugated peoples in the USSR to national independence. But after he had become President, he accepted the fact that his Administration would go so far as to refuse to acknowledge the existence of these nations. The same Administration once promised to destroy the Communist regime of Fidel Castro in Cuba. Cuban freedom fighters were encouraged to invade the island. When the situation became more complicated, however, this Administration betrayed them, and left the Cuban people to tyranny under Russian overseers. Somewhat later, it proposed to exchange Cuban free-dom fighters for tractors. What humanism! It is not to be wondered that men of character like Admiral Burke, the commanding officer of the US Navy, resigned his post. In his letter of resignation to President Kennedy, Admiral Burke wrote that the USA floats on waves of dreams. He pointed out that the military power of the US was being undermined by "disarmament committees" and that atomic missiles were subject to regulations that ruled out the very thought of war. We are a threat to the world, he stated. No one knows our policy, because we ourselves do not know it. For similar reasons, General Norstad resigned his post. He found himself in total disagreement with the policy of his Government.

In defending moral foundations in politics and in defending the liberation struggles of the subjugated peoples we are often reproached on the grounds that we "break the rules of hospitality" in the countries of our residence. Of all such reproaches, the most surprising are those heard in Western Germany. Let us take a closer look at this "rule of hospitality."

At the end of 1962, the Bavarian radio reviewed the most important events of the previous year. The court trial in Munich of the sexual murderers Ferbach and Vera Bruene was mentioned twice, but not a single word was said regarding the historically important trial of the Soviet Russian agent Stashynsky, at Karlsruhe, at which the criminal activities of Shelepin, Voroshilov, and Khrushchev were brought out. Such is the nature of "objective information"!

Protests against this kind of "objectivity" are often regarded as "breaking the rule of hospitality." The German press seems to forget that political emigrants are living in Germany as a result of the Germans' own faults: some of these political emigrants were taken by force for the purpose of slave labor during the war, others were transported to German concentration camps. If the Germans had heeded these same political emigrants during the war, there would be no Russian prison of nations to be liquidated today. Hence, there would be no political emigrants from Eastern Europe living in Germany.

Backward mentality is presented in the book *Summing Up the Second World War* in the chapter on "guerrilla warfare" in France, Poland, Greece, Yugoslavia, and Ukraine—not, however, the "guerrilla warfare" of the UPA but that of the Red Army. For General Rendulic, the author, the national insurgent war "did not exist." He exculpates all the methods used to combat the guerrillas. As far as he is concerned, guerrillas are not soldiers and therefore, in his opinion, the rules established by the Hague Convention regarding military usage do not apply to them. In General Rendulic's eyes, any opposition after a country has been occupied by a hostile army is illegal. It would follow, according to his opinion, that the uprisings in East Berlin, Poznan, and Budapest were all illegal. In other words, for him might is right. He believes that occupation becomes lawful after the conqueror's military victory, and that guerrilla warfare is "illegal," "per-fidious," and "criminal." Hence, according to his arguments, the occupation of Eastern Germany by Russia is legal, and the fight against it illegal. From his point of view, no people has any right to liberate itself because forceful action is illegal. Nazi units which plundered and murdered during World War II were acting in accordance with his criteria of lawfulness, whereas the insurgents who fought against these units were outlaws! "Experts" such as General Rendulic advocate slavery for their own people. The East Germans have no right to fight for their own liberation. Hitlerite reasoning still lingers in authors such as General Rendulic and in publishers of books such as *Summing Up the Second World War*.

Quo Vadis, Occident?

Many journalists became hysterical over President Kennedy's handling of the Cuban conflict in autumn of 1962. There is a saying that when there are no fish, even crabs are fish. In other words, better such a "victory" than complete surrender.

Let us examine the facts. The greatest world power, the USA, allowed a provocateur, assisted by Moscow's gangsters, to set up a nest at its own back door. Instead of destroying this pygmy in its own hemisphere, the USA left the organizers of a Cuban invasion in the lurch. Afterwards, an unbelievable trade transaction was proposed: human beings for tractors. Hence, human beings became a commodity: Cuban freedom fighters became the object of trade between the USA and the Cuban dictator, Fidel Castro. A typical commercial approach to politics!

In the meantime Moscow turned the Cuban island into one of its forts and set up one of its missile bases there. American public opinion, however, was not going to put up with the President's policy of allowing an avowed enemy to set up a military base in its own backyard. The President ordered a blockade of Cuba and sent an ultimatum to Khrushchev, who, avowedly, "took away" his missiles from Cuba. The world press immediately proclaimed a triumphant victory.

But how real is this "victory"? Moscow "took away" its missiles from Cuba, in return for which the US Government signed a statement guaranteeing "peace" and non-intervention in Cuba. Until that time, Communist regimes in the Western hemisphere had guarantees from Moscow only—now they had a guarantee from the US Government also. The success of the US Government consists in the fact that Moscow "removed" its missiles from Cuban soil, Moscow's success in the USA's pledge not to intervene in Cuba. Before the Cuban blockade was initiated, the USA did not recognize Castro's regime, and did not have any obligation to Moscow with respect to its Cuban policy. President Kennedy's negotiations with Khrushchev over Cuba, however, were a kind of *de facto* recognition of Castro's regime. It is of not great importance that the USA does not have diplomatic relations with the Castro Government. For Moscow's purposes it is sufficient that the US has pledged not to intervene in Cuba's affairs, for in the meantime it can turn Cuba into a Russian expansionist base. The pseudo-removal of Russian missiles from Cuba is being treated as a Western "victory" in the Caribbean area. As long as a Communist Government remains in control of Cuba, however, there can be no thought of a real US victory. In April 1965 Castro made a statement to the press that the rockets were still in Cuba for its defense.

What is Moscow looking for on the American continent? What right does it have to speak up on behalf of and to decide matters on Cuba? No one could accuse the USA of an imperialist adventure if she should undertake to liquidate this Russian foothold. The Cuban people must be given the opportunity to choose their own government and their own national policy. The anti-Bolshevik forces the world over are highly in favor of such a move and would regard the USA as a real defender of human rights and people's rights, if it should show determination to remove Communism from Cuban soil.

The exact opposite has been the case, however. Moscow took two steps forward and one step backwards, inasmuch as the US Government acknowledged Moscow's right to intervene in the affairs of the American continent instead of demanding its *complete* withdrawal from Cuban soil. If the US Government's promise not to intervene in Cuba is to be regarded as binding, then it is easier to speak of the USA's defeat and Moscow's victory. How can we speak of a meaningful victory on the part of the West merely on the basis of Moscow's temporary restraint in setting up a military base on Cuban soil, when almost half of the earth is still groaning under the yoke of Russian Communism. Moscow has the acknowledged right to participate in decisions concerning Africa, Asia, Europe—and now in America. And yet the Western press speaks of a "victory" over Russia. By such recklessness, the defensive attention of the Free World is being lulled to sleep, and the fact that many peoples are still languishing under Russian slavery is simply forgotten. In the meantime, the Communists seek new objectives: Berlin, Laos, Vietnam, the Congo.

History proves that Russia always retreats under the pressure of force. She fears an out-and-out war, for she knows that the nations she holds in suppression would immediately come to the defense of the West. In its expansion policy, Moscow always stops when it senses that the Western powers will defend their position, even at the cost of a nuclear war. Under the guise of retreating in the name of peace, it begins negotiations, grabbing whatever it can in the bargain. As soon as the West show signs of loosening up, however, Moscow immediately proceeds to advance again. Such was the case in Korea, for example. When it became clear that the United States was determined to defend South Korea, Moscow took the first opportunity to stop its miscalculated adventure.

Indeed, the menace of a new world war exists only because the West is opportunistic. It does not have its own convictions. Inasmuch as the USA does not show any inclination to support the national liberation revolutions on the part of the peoples subjugated within the Soviet Russian bloc—a revolution, which threatens to destroy its empire—Moscow can provoke conflicts and gain wider possessions in other parts of the world.

Moscow cannot risk a war, for it needs its military to control the unrest which exists in every part of its empire. If the West would once realize this, it would adopt a far firmer policy in Eastern Europe. Its fear of Russia is without basis, for the Soviet Russian empire is a giant on clay feet. Moscow is a bluff in international politics.

Cuba was one of Moscow's most recent examples of a great bluff. Moscow would never have dared to go to war over Cuba. But neither Mr. Rostow nor Mr.

Rusk understood this. They did not grasp the essence of the Cold War, for they do not have their own system of ideas and their own positive plan of action. They rely upon a policy of reacting to Soviet Russian moves. They have momentary designs, but no long-range objectives.

The United Nations' action in Katanga did not offer a brighter future. The impression exists, not without foundation, that the US Government began a policy of agreeing to spheres of influence between the USA and Russia. Katanga was indeed a chance for the Free World. By the use of force, the USA liquidated the regime of Katanga's President, Tshombe, who is the one African politician who does not regard all white men as devils. Tshombe was not taken in by the promise of "neutrality." In opposition to the advice of his African colleagues, he did not embrace Russia as his ally. Together with white men, he wanted to build a well-organized and independent Katanga. He tore down the wall of hatred between white and black, and preferred to ally himself with white men against Communism, rather than with black Communists against white men. By way of thanks, however, the white men of the UN, led by the USA, destroyed his achievements and his loyal forces—solely because Katanga aspired to independence. Katanga had a full right to independence, for the Congo is not a homogeneous nation. She was a colony under administrative rule formed by the Belgian King Leopold II. It is sheer nonsense to speak of the Congo as a nation. And Katanga did not threaten anybody. Her only desire was independence. But the USA refused to recognize Katanga's independence, thinking to save the Congo from chaos thereby. The truth of the matter is that chaos has been introduced into an ordered Katanga.

It is even more regrettable that the independence of Katanga was maintained by a cooperative act between the USA and Moscow—a fact which suggests that the USA has more interests in common with Soviet Russia than it does with its allies in NATO or SEATO, whose objective is to defend the Free World against Soviet Russian aggression.

The Katanga affair compels us to draw unpleasant conclusions with respect to the future. By the same token, for example, the USA Government could oppose the independence of Ukraine or Azerbaidzhan. Russia, as is well known, needs the oil, coal, and iron which are to be found in these countries. Along the same lines it is argued that the Congo cannot exist without the natural resources of Katanga. This argument sufficed to destroy Katanga. In whose interest? we must ask. Perhaps only in Moscow's, which is supporting U Thant, who was punishing Tshombe on Lumumba's behalf. Whereas the UN does not show any inclination to come to the defense of the nations enslaved within the Soviet Union, it was very active in liquidating Katanga's independence, completely disregarding its statutory and organizational obligation to defend justice and peace the world over.

In a similar way, the West assisted various Wrangels and Hallers to drown Ukraine's independence in blood. The year 1918 is being repeated on the African continent. Hence, the UN comes through as a purely militaristic organization of cowards who attack a weaker foe but run from the stronger foe.

Only a few months had elapsed before the USA invited the emigré Tshombe to save the Congo—the whole Congo this time, after they themselves had liquidated the bastion of anti-Communism in Africa—Katanga. Really, a ship without sails and helmsmen.

Only Moscow and Washington were satisfied by the action in Katanga, while London and Paris were indignant. Behind the back of NATO, the leaders of the USA were conducting negotiations with Moscow. More than anything else this was consequence of agreements over Cuba: the US Government's tribute to Moscow for the latter's consent to "remove" its missiles from Cuban soil. The problem of Hungary has vanished from the agenda of the United Nations. The Hungarian uprising was drowned not only in blood, but in the unprincipled action of the UN. The tyrants in Budapest have made it quite clear that U Thant will always be an honored guest in Hungary. The US Government's policy leads one to the belief that the USA is giving up its role of defender of freedom, and its policy is causing the loss of moral stability.

A detente between Moscow and Washington has come into existence, while a state of tension is growing up between Washington and her West European allies. Before Senator Kennedy became President, he wrote that it was nonsense to withhold nuclear secrets from France, while Moscow—the enemy of man and mankind—knew all of them. Today, on the contrary, France cannot obtain information on the production of advanced nuclear hydrogen bombs and has to spend millions of her own research in this field. So it comes about that the monopoly on nuclear weapons, upon which the future of the world depends to a large extent, remains solely in the hands of the USA and the Russians. It is a tragic partnership. Are the tyrants in the Kremlin closer to Washington than the latter's allies in free Europe? How will the American policy develop next? We will have to wait and see. But at present it is hopelessly strange. *Quo vadis, Occident?*

ABN Correspondence,
June-July 1965, pp. 6-9

Western Alliance with the Subjugated Peoples Needed

Our Prognosis Has Proved Correct

We regard it as our duty to subject the foreign policy of the United States to a critique, for our prognoses have proved to be true—as a matter of fact, more than once. Let us but recall our explanation of fifteen years and more ago to the effect that in the atomic era revolts constitute an alternative—at that time, the press, the politicians, and many others laughed at us. But we witnessed one revolt after another: in the East Zone of Germany, in Hungary, in the concentration camps, and later in Vietnam and in Cuba—in short, it turned out that our military, political, and strategic prognoses were right. Our conception of the modern conduct of war has been widely acknowledged, even by such highly qualified men as Liddell Hart, Professor Teller, and General Fuller.

With respect to this, Liddell Hart wrote: "The atomic bomb is neither a good policeman, nor a good fireman, nor a usable border station. It is also a questionable means of suppressing a revolt; it can prove deadly for both sides...."

Professor Teller, who made valuable contributions to the creation of the atomic bomb, wrote as follows: "The United States will have to train guerrilla units if it wants to win in bush-fighting.... These units would have to be armed with small, clean atomic weapons, which are necessary for a limited atomic war. But the final victory will depend upon the people for which we are fighting.... *It must be on our side....* It must take up arms and attack the enemy, which our partisans will have dispersed.... The battlefield of a limited atomic war [with limited, tactical atomic weapons] will not become a wasteland.... But we can only win such a war if the people of the country in question are on our side...."

Moscow and Marshal Sokolovsky are aware of this danger. Sokolovsky knows where the Achilles' heel of the empire and Communism lies. Since he is at a loss to defend the Soviet Union in the event of internal revolt, he plans—as a means of intimidating the West—the following: "To achieve the most effective results in the shortest time in a future war, the Soviet war machine and that of the Socialist camp will have to apply its full military force from the first moment on, literally in the first hours and minutes. As far as weapons are concerned, a third world war will be fought with rockets and nuclear warheads. Accordingly, the strategic rocket troops will be of supreme importance in the war machine, whereas the other parts of the armed forces will be fundamentally changed. The final victory, however, will be won as a result of the joint efforts of all parts of the armed forces...."

From these reflections of Marshal Sokolovsky, it is clearly to be seen that Moscow is afraid of a drawn-out war, for it is aware that the fall of the empire and the destruction of the regime will come from the inside.

But the French sociologist R. Aron is right when he writes in his book *War and Peace*: "If the Soviet bloc should convince itself that it possesses an incontestable superiority, either in terms of the passive or active means of deterrence, then the danger would be deadly."

At present, the situation appears to be as follows: the USA has become entangled in peripheral, hopeless wars whereas it was not even capable of coping with Cuba. Now, it is going through the same thing in Vietnam, whereby the possibility of a direct confrontation with Red China becomes more and more real. And to top it off, on the advice of men like Kennan and Rostow, the United States is making efforts to secure a non-aggression pact wth Moscow—just as Hitler did.... In short, not only the West's "active" but its "passive" means of deterrence is becoming more and more lame; in short, the perspective danger of Moscow looms larger and larger, though the internal situation in the Russian empire, owing to the enormous intensification of the offensive resistance, has become hopeless. But this the West does not at all take into account. *Ceterum censeo—* Moscow's power lies in the weakness of the West's political ideas, in its lack of a clear perspective, as well as in its failure to grasp the contradictions and irrationalities of the Russian empire and of the regime; furthermore, it is a grave mistake on the part of the West to refuse to exploit the revolts within the empire.

"Russia's weakness is our strength," said General Fuller, "but her strength is our ignorance." He further writes that "the psychological center of gravity of the Soviet Empire is to be sought in the hearts of the subjugated peoples within the USSR and behind the Iron Curtain. Further, it should be borne in mind, and it seldom is, that this psychological 'bomb' is as great a deterrent to the Soviets' resorting to actual war as the hydrogen bomb itself." (*The Conduct of War*, p. 352).

What solution does the State Department have to offer for the world crisis and the threat to mankind? When it becomes apparent during a talk with a high official of the US State Department that my line of argument was having no effect on the prejudices of his attitude, I posed a question bordering on desperation—namely, how did the United States intend to subdue and defeat Communism? With a disarming naïveté, this high-ranking man answered: "*The liquidation of Communism is not at all a part of the plans of the USA.*" This explanation brought our talk to an abrupt end.

The Political Conception of the State Department

Notwithstanding the above, I pose this question: How does the State Department conceive of victory? How does it conceive of the fight against Communism, when it does not even want to hear anything against Russian imperialism, which indeed it takes under its protection? Moscow knows what it wants. Moscow has a plan and it acts according to this plan.

The political conception of the West does not go beyond peaceful coexistence, which was foisted upon it by Moscow, on Lenin's inspiration. It does not go beyond "evolutionary liberalization of the regime," democratization—or, to state it in general terms, not beyond the conception of converting the devil to a belief in God. In fact, it sometimes appears that the conception of the West reads as follows: "Let Moscow swallow as much as possible, then maybe it'll choke." Indeed, it appears to me that this is the real political conception of the State Department. Whether this conception is to be regarded as a responsible one is another matter; but reduced to a simple formula, it is very likely as I have stated it!

Otherwise, how is it to be explained that it is constantly repeated in the West that the Russian empire—or, as it is called, the Soviets—has ceased to constitute a danger? It appears to be completely forgotten that Russia's borders have extended far beyond those of 1939, that Moscow's "way of life"—Communism—dominates the Chinese mainland, half of Europe, numerous countries of Asia, Cuba, and other areas. In addition, we have to take into account Moscow's political influence and military maneuverings on various continents, then, for the first time in history, "the visit" of Moscow's naval force in Alexandria (Egypt)—and, consequently, its presence in the Mediterranean. Even Catherine II's wishes to build up Russian influence in Latin America appear to be in the process of realization—cf. Venezuela. Through the Communist Parties which are subservient to it, through fifth columnists, and through its political weight, Moscow is in a position to make itself felt in every continent and in every matter that is of importance in the world—as a matter of fact, more forcefully than the largest empire of yesterday, Great Britain, could. Moscow influences the revolts of the Negroes in the United States. Moscow is present everywhere but, according to Rostow and Kennan—indeed, according to Senator Fulbright—Moscow's influence is on the wane. Hence, according to this view, it would appear that the best advice is to capitulate to Russia altogether in all parts of the world, let it grab the whole world, then it will choke, for it would not be capable of digesting all that it will have seized. It sometimes appears to me that the so-called "Brain Trust" in the United States must have reached such conclusions in the process of formulating its policies. As a matter of fact, we have even heard the view expressed that it would not be so bad if West Germany also were to be occupied by Moscow, for in that case Red Berlin would get involved in a conflict with Moscow similar to the Moscow-Peking conflict. If one pursues this view a bit further, one would have to conclude that some Americans must be of the opinion that a Red America would be more likely to fight against Moscow.

Such a perverse line of argument on the part of America's and the West's gravediggers would find its logical conclusion in the following statement: "In defiance of the Russians, we agree that, after they have succeeded in occupying the whole world and have arrested and imprisoned all the freedom fighters of the West, they will have difficulty in guarding all these imprisoned people and will, moreover, begin to suffer pangs of remorse owing to the murder of fresh millions of the 'bourgeois,' the 'fascists,' and 'agents of the Vatican and Wall Street.' And a time will come when it will be too boring for them to hold us confined in prison, or to murder us, and their pangs of remorse will become intolerable—then, owing to our endurance in suffering, we will conquer the Russians." Do not think that these are fantasies on my part.

S. King Hall, an important politician and publicist, who began his career as a high-ranking Marine officer, wrote such absurdities and such nonsense in his book *To Win the War in Peace* (1958). I am quoting from the German edition; but perhaps there is a purpose in repeating this stupid nonsense. "Do you believe, my critics ask me, that Khrushchev or anyone of his successors would be afraid of occupying England—for fear of the consequences? Yes, I reply, I believe they would be afraid if we could succeed in carrying out the necessary preparations. I mean that it would be possible to make the occupation of Western countries by Russian troops very dangerous for the Communists—in the psychological sectors. I am of the opinion that it would have to be thought out very carefully. In any case I am convinced that psychological deterrence is more important than the deterrent effect of hydrogen bombs.... The first condition of my resistance without the use of force is that it must be psychologically thought out.... The basis of psychological resistance, and also the attack on the whole moral position of the occupiers depending upon it, lies in the conduct of every single individual, who, as long as he lives, must not renounce his right to be a free man, but must stand up for his principles with his conduct and his character in every way possible.... Civil resistance is not based on armed power, but it is nonetheless offensive from a psychological point of view...."

"We should defend the idea and spirit of democracy," the author writes, "indeed by passive resistance, for resistance by sabotage or terror, etc., would only mean the continuation of organized military resistance...." The author is of the opinion that every form of physical resistance in the atomic era is nonsense. Therefore, his direct advice is to capitulate to Moscow, and "by passive resistance to show Moscow what we can do...." *O sancta simplicitas!* There are still old, naïve numbskulls to be found in the Free World! If they were merely numbskulls! But I am not of the opinion that Rostow and Kennan, Lattimore and Lippmann belong to this category of naïve simpletons....

Such prospective capitulations to Moscow are recommended by those men who no longer believe in the world of ideas of the West, who have lost the belief in their own truth and are merely impressed by what comes from the East—*ex Oriente*—but not by the creative conceptions which stem from the underground of the East, but by that which comes from the Kremlin or from Mao's palace....

What Do We Have to Suggest to the West?

Nothing more than what we declared during World War II and during the two decades since then. A common front consisting of the free nations of the world, led by the United States, together with the peoples subjugated by Soviet Russia and Red China, *against both tyrannies*—Moscow and Peking—with the intent of bringing the empire to ruin and disaster and of destroying Communism from within. We are for the realization of the idea of national, independent states of all the peoples subjugated by Russian and Chinese Communists, for the freedom of individuals, respect for all of their rights, for human dignity and social justice.

In his book *The Conduct of War* (London, 1964, p. 352), the highly gifted military theoretician General Fuller writes precisely to the point in the sense of the principles which we have been representing for decades. "Therefore, in the Cold War, the psychological center of gravity of the Soviet Empire is to be sought in the hearts of the subjugated peoples within the USSR and behind the Iron Curtain. Further, it should be borne in mind, and it seldom is, that this psychological 'bomb' is as great a deterrent to the Soviets resorting to actual war as the hydrogen bomb itself. Russia's weakness is our strength, and her strength is our ignorance; no man realizes this more fully than Nikita Khrushchev...."

The eager efforts of the West to put an end to the Cold War at all costs by no means constitute the precondition of the West's success in the Cold War. On the contrary, fuel should be added to the Cold War in all possible ways. The Russian empire and the Communist complex must be attacked politically, economically, and psychologically, and it must be borne in mind that within the Russian empire there are countless millions who are on the side of the West, despite the fact that the West has forgotten them and casts them to the tyrants as victims. In short, it

has not the least interest in their fate. The road to victory is through a reorienta-
tion in terms of the subjugated peoples. Where are the dozens of radio and
television stations, the dozens of infiltration points which were set up and
directed by us to have our ideas transmitted through them? For decades we have
been repeating the same thing: many are pro-West—the peoples subjugated in
the USSR, the peoples in the satellite countries, in Asia and in Europe, the
Chinese are on the side of the West, the Vietnamese, the Koreans, the Tibetans,
Mongolians, Turkestanis, and countless others. But the West has no use for
them, whereas Moscow, which has only fifth columnists in the West, executes
fantastic wonders with their help. Isn't it time to examine this situation very
carefully?

   We want to give a direct answer to one other question. Let us assume for a
moment that there really is a dreadful "Red-yellow" danger, or really a "yellow
danger," which has to be averted to save the world from being swamped. We ask
whether a prison can be defended with the prisoners contained in that prison
under threat that otherwise another prison would be set up in its place in their
country. Prisoners have never defended their prisons. On the contrary, they
break out of prison without regard to the risk that perhaps death or an even
worse prison awaits them. The Ukrainians, Turkestanis, Georgians, Azerbaidzhanis, Armenians, Lithuanians, Byelorussians will never defend the Russian
empire aganst a Chinese attack; on the contrary, they will rise up against the
Russian prison of nations and against the Red Chinese avalanche. They will carry
on a fight against both sides. In no case will they take up arms against the
anti-Russian front to save "the unity and indivisibility of Russia." We by no
means have in mind to exchange our fetters. We do not want to defend the
Russian fetters to keep ourselves from being placed in Red Chinese fetters!

   Do the allies not want to learn a lesson from World War II? Millions of soldiers
of the Red army escaped to the German side, though they could not expect any
good from the Germans. And the revolutionary elements of Ukraine and other
nations began a *war on two fronts* against *both* tyrannies, the Russian and the
German. The same will be the case in the future. The Russians were trying to
win over the Ukrainians to their side by fictive palliations; for instance, they set
up a "Ukrainian front" and established a "Foreign Ministry of the Ukrainian
Soviet Socialist Republic," introduced the "Khmelnytsky Order" in the army and
promised to form a "Ukrainian Soviet army." The Russians prompted the Ukrainians to write Ukrainian patriotic poems and songs (i.e., "Love Ukraine" by
Sosiura), and the Ukrainian SSR has been accepted as a member by the United
Nations.

   Can anyone deceive himself into believing that the Ukrainians or Turkestanis,
Georgians or Lithuanians, Byelorussians or Hungarians will defend the Russian
prison of nations and peoples against the Red Chinese avalanche? Is it at all
possible that the Hungarians or Ukrainians, the Poles or Georgians will ever be
able to forget the terrible mass murders in Budapest or in Vinnitsa, the mass
starvations of 1932-33 and the genocides of 1937-38 and 1945-1950, Katyn or
other places where murders and tortures were carried out? No subjugated
people trusts the Russians; no subjugated nation will ever defend the prison in

which it is confined against foreign invasion, no matter who the invader might be. On the contrary, it will fight a war on two fronts against both foes, just as it did in World War II.

The only possibility and the only solution to this situation is the destruction of the Russian empire and the establishment of independent, national states of all the subjugated peoples which, worthy of this great and holy cause, tenaciously and determinedly, in friendly alliance with one another and in military and all other forms of alliances with the West, will defend their freedom and independence against any new occupier. But we must stress this point again and again: a prisoner will never defend his prison, but will make use of every opportunity, whether rational or not, to free himself from his confinement.

Incidentally, if the United States has indeed suddenly and unexpectedly become afraid of Red China, why doesn't it help Chiang Kai-shek to initiate a preventive war in the form of a civil liberation war? Just as before, Chiang Kai-shek greatly desires to land his troops on the Chinese mainland. Even a sixth-grade schoolboy would have been able to foresee that sooner or later Red China would have an atomic bomb! Today, Mr. Rusk declares that troops cannot be landed on the Chinese mainland because Mao possesses atomic weapons—but yesterday, Mao did not have any atomic weapons! To be sure, one always has an excuse handy. The main cause of all this is the division of the world into two blocs, and no desire to crush Communism and the Russian empire; on the contrary, a desire to help the Russian empire and Communism to spread. Were not President Truman and General Marshall able to foresee the meaning of Communist domination on the Chinese mainland? Chiang Kai-shek had the situation in China well in hand. Why did the United States help to overthrow him? Why did it promote Mao's seizure of power? And after this first, crude, criminal mistake, why didn't the United States make use of any other opportunity to overthrow Communism in China? Why did it choose instead to do away with General MacArthur and to liquidate the far-sighted attitude and plan of McCarthy, who purged America of its Lattimores, Hisses, Whites, and Rosenbergs? But these mistakes are repeated again and again: witness Cuba, where Fidel Castro was held to be a democrat and a modest social reformer. I refuse to believe that those people whose duty it was to know what Castro was really up to were not aware of the real situation. If we, who live thousands of miles from Cuba, who have access neither to research institutes nor to special foreign agents in China, were nonetheless capable of seeing Castro, as well as Mao, as Communist guerrilla leaders, then how is it to be explained that the United States, with its unrivalled possibilities of obtaining information, did not see it? We are to believe that President Truman did not know who Mao was. And we are to believe that President Eisenhower did not know who Fidel Castro was. If this was really the case, then we ask how such leaders in the ranks of the American political elite can lay claim to the political leadership of the world. If the President's advisors give him such information, then we should like to ask: "Who are these advisors? Whom do they serve, Moscow or Washington?!"

Now, a new speculation already offers itself: Moscow has to withdraw at least a part of its troops from Germany and Poland, for Soviet border troops in Siberia and Turkestan have to be strengthened against Red China. The US is also strengthening its troops in Asia against Red China. Hence it appears that interests agree. The danger of an attack from Red China brings the USSR closer to the West. However, these calculators don't seem to realize this simple truth— namely, that neither Mao nor Kosygin is so naïve as to have the USA stand by as a laughing third party which will liquidate both the USSR and Red China after they have exhausted themselves in a war against one another.... The "cleverest of the clever" resolutely declare that Red China could never come closer to the United States because it belongs to the yellow race, whereas Russia can more easily relate itself to the US because it belongs to the white race.

But who is it that incites the Negroes against the whites? Is it Russia or not? The mentality of the peoples of the white race is foreign to Russia. And Japan and China, with Confucius and Sun Yat-sen, with their ideals of freedom stand closer to the peoples of the white race than Russia, with its ideal of crushed individuality, a *kolkhoz* man, in contrast to the private ownership mentality of a Chinese or Japanese farmer and the Japanese and the Chinese respect for tradition, ancestry, the heroism of the kamikazes and samurais.... Furthermore, it must be remembered that the world is divided into nations, not into races. Most of the wars have been fought between peoples of the white race, and not the white race against the yellow. Japan fought a ten-year war against yellow China, but the matter of race was of no importance. It is the nation that matters.

Spiritually, culturally, philosophically, and socially, Russia is another world which is fundamentally foreign to the peoples of the white race, as well as to the peoples of the yellow, the black, or the red races. Aggressive godlessness has nothing in common with the yellow race; the yellow race never proclaimed godlessness. On the contrary, there is no other people which would be more tolerant in terms of religion than the Chinese. Aggressive godlessness was instilled into the Chinese Communists by Russia, by Communism. In this matter, not even Marx went so far as Moscow, which murdered millions of people because of their belief in God. I as a Ukrainian feel culturally more related to the world of the high, social ethics of Confucius, as well as to the world of heroic Shintoism, of the cult of ancestry, than to the harmful principle of Tolstoy— "Don't resist evil"—or to the apotheosis of a criminal, or to the Idiot of Dostoevsky. "All people must become Russian, above everything else, they must become Russian. Since all-inclusive humanity is a Russian national idea, every single individual must become, above all, a Russian...." So said Dostoevsky in *The Journal of a Writer*.

In 1881, Dostoevsky wrote: "Why is the future conquest of Asia necessary for us? What have we to do with Asia? We need Asia because Russia lies not only in Europe but also in Asia, because the Russian is not only a European but also an Asian. And more than this. Perhaps we entertain greater hopes for Asia than for Europe. I will even go a step further: Asia is perhaps the most important road for our future destiny." Dostoevsky was not a Communist, but he was a Russian messianist.

He declared the poison, not only of Bolsheviks, but of every individual Russian. He is fundamentally in error who thinks of signing a pact with one tyranny against another—he will never be victorious, as the history of all time teaches us. Empress Catherine II supported the left elements in Western Europe against the "God-embalmed" European monarchs, who regarded this as a desecration at that time. With respect to means and measures, Russia is not very particular whether a Lenin, a Peter I, a Kerensky, a Khrushchev, or a Kosygin is at her head. Only a front against *both* tyrannies, simultaneously active, can save the Free World. If the West does not want to suffer a defeat, as it did in World War II, it must form an alliance with the subjugated peoples. World War II is not yet over; it is still being fought, albeit in a nonconventional form....

ABN Correspondence,
March-April 1967, pp. 1-7

On the Threshold of a New Yalta

Ukraine has never counted on liberation with the help of intervention of foreign bayonets. It always oriented itself to its own strength. Numerous immigrants to the USA from the subjugated nations cast their votes for the Republican Party, in particular for Nixon, because they expected a change in the American foreign policy to the advantage of Ukraine and other subjugated countries. But things took a different turn. Nixon is conducting "his policy" and is not concerned with nations subjugated in the USSR. When he visited Ukraine, he did not even dare to do what de Gaulle did in Kyiv, mentioning the separate history of Ukraine in the Princely Era and the marriage ties between the Ukrainian and French monarchs. Nixon, as an ordinary tourist, holding hands with his wife, had a picture of himself taken in front of St. Sophia in Kyiv, which for him is "the mother of Russian cities." He was taught nothing by the "Ukrainian Republicans."

Against the background of such experience by Ukrainains and members of other subjugated nations—now citizens of the USA, it is mandatory to advocate a different concept of domestic American politics. The division of Ukrainians in the USA into supporters of Democrats or Republicans is unjustified. It is the same as sitting on two chairs. The Ukrainian Congress Committee of America, the American Friends of the ABN, the Organization for the Defense of the Four Freedoms of Ukraine, the Ukrainian Youth Association of America, and other organizations should examine their policies concerning the Government of the USA and initiate a joint action of national groups from behind the Iron Curtain in order to establish their own third force in the USA, not a pro-Democratic or a pro-Republican force, but one which embarks from its own position and advances its own concept, as a new political orientation.

Under certain conditions, the present US parties will be forced to reckon with this third force, which will have an influence on the formulation of American policies benefitting nations enslaved or threatened by Russian imperialism. Nixon does not respect the resolutions of the US Congress dealing with the subjugated nations, although these resolutions are binding on each American government. Basing itself on such a Congressional resolution, the third force has good starting chances. It is just as necessary for Germans, Lithuanians, Byelorussians, Cubans, and other nationalities, together with Ukrainians, to create the action center of this third party which will proclaim its political program: a practical realization of the Captive Nations Law and a rejection of the US appeasement policy toward the Russian empire and Communism. During Congressional elections it will put up its own candidates. It can also nominate its candidate for President. Even Negroes and Puerto Ricans, who by their resoluteness have achieved considerably more in the US than have the Ukrainians or the Germans, the Poles or the Lithuanians, the Cubans or the Bulgarians, can serve us as an example.

Nixon has ignored the ideals of the Occident, although the US sprang from its sources and traditions. As a travelling salesman to Brezhnev and Mao Tse-tung, he only embarrassed the United States. If Nixon expects that Brezhnev will save him from the Watergate affair, he is gravely mistaken, for provocateurs and lackeys of Moscow are the hidden arrangers of this affair. Through his agreement with Brezhnev, Nixon is helping to save the Russian empire. It is well known that Roosevelt saved Stalin and Eisenhower saved Khrushchev during the Hungarian Revolution, and now Nixon is saving Brezhnev. Nixon shares the responsibility for the intensification of terror to Russian-subjugated countries, just as he shares the blame for the Russian armed occupation of CSSR. Moscow does not take any risks without the tacit consent of Washington. Simultaneously, in line with its plan of psychological warfare, it now synchronizes scandalous affairs, arranged and inspired by it, which are intended to expose the "decadence" of the West and its "decaying" elite.

Upon the heels of the Watergate affair, there "suddenly" came to light an affair involving two British ministers with call girls, as well as the Steiner scandal in West Germany. Steiner was a representative the *Bundestag* (parliament) and a KGB agent who sold his vote to Brandt for an additional 50,000 DM. Thus Brandt won the balloting by one vote, remained Chancellor, won the elections, and gave half of Germany to Moscow.

At the same time, the Italian police revealed that three Communist electrotechnicians bugged Pope Paul VI's private telephone network and registered texts of all his secret conversations with the heads of the curias and other Church and state dignitaries. All these "incidents" occurred simultaneously.

Decisions affecting the fate of nations are hidden behind such "incidents." Brezhnev and Andropov want to show the moral worth of the leading elite of some Western states. Brezhnev travelled to the White House because he knew that the ground for the realization of his plans had already been prepared psychologically. And Nixon is saving the USSR, with grain, technology, and loans.

Today, Brandt and Wehner—leftist Sovietophile socialists who neglect their own nations—are symbols of the West. And Nixon, allegedly from anti-Communist positions, helps to consolidate Russian tyranny.

Great statesmen of the West are a thing of the past. They do not exist today.

The West is waiting for another anti-Bolshevik Clemenceau, an anti-Russian Churchill, a nationalist de Gaulle, an Occidental-in-spirit Adenauer.

The peoples of the West do not need parties, but renaissance movements, primarily ethical and ideological as well as political. If nationalism and the heroic concept of life are not reborn inside Western nations, then Moscow will triumph over them, not because of its might, but due to the weakness of the West. Nixon and Brandt are dictating dark pages of Occidental history.

President Nixon followed in Roosevelt's footsteps and, in spite of the sad experience of cooperation with the Russian empire, he negotiated with Brezhnev a new version of the old agreement made at Teheran and Yalta.

It is an agreement about "peaceful coexistence" about the renunciation of atomic weapons, about mutual cooperation and support, about joint intervention and division of the world into spheres of interest of the two superpowers. Two policemen of the world, striving to establish a global condominium, are conspiring. From this it follows that the two policemen are ready to intervene against China or France, for example, if those nations, defending their own interests, threaten to resort to nuclear arms.

The two technological superpowers will supposedly preserve a lasting peace, with a basic difference. Moscow is aggressive, aiming to conquer the entire world, while Washington desires "peace and quiet." Of course, Nixon's obligations provide Moscow with an opportunity to increase its pressure against Peking, all the more so since Brandt has become a friend and a collaborator of Moscow. Thus the Western flank of the Russian empire is secured by Brandt and Nixon.

Nixon is totally disregarding the present moral superpower—the nations subjugated inside the Russian empire—just as Metternich had done in the past. For him, a man without vision, a technocrat and an admirer of technology, the national and the human soul do not exist. *Newsweek* reports that political advisors and experts from the secret service have warned Nixon that Russia can use this situation for a "surgical operation" so as to get rid of the nuclear power of China. Other "experts" believe that through such an agreement Nixon wants to "encourage" Brezhnev to attack China just as Stalin had done with the Molotov-Ribbentrop Pact, and to be the survivor, benefitting from the clashes of others.

This view is false, however, for there are no grounds to trust in the farsightedness of Nixon's policies or in his long-range planning. Furthermore, the agreement contains clauses which exclude such a possibility. Instead, they compel the USA to help Moscow or to hinder any counteraction by China that might threaten the USSR. Nixon has also recognized Brezhnev's intervention in the CSSR and Moscow's domination over the subjugated nations, and he has betrayed the ideas of the Free World in favor of a tyranny.

Essentially this infamous treaty has the character of police control over the whole world, supposedly a joint police supervision, and over Western Europe as well. But all the geopolitical, ideological, political, and strategic chances of modern guerrilla warfare remain on the side of Russian Bolshevism. The free countries of Europe and the world increasingly become an open terrain for Russian aggression, while the USA even pledges to expand the economic potential of the aggressors and to defend them from "adversaries."

But no peace is possible between a static and a dynamic, aggressive, and destructive force, particularly when the USA recognizes and confirms the aggressive starting positions of the USSR, thus weakening even more its ideological, political, and military positions.

The concessions of the USA and of other Western governments in favor of the Russian empire were initiated by Brandt, while the treaty between Nixon and Brezhnev weakened the positions of Red China, which can be forced to be more conciliatory toward Moscow. Nevertheless, Nixon's agreement with Brezhnev weakens the anti-Russian potential of Western Europe and certain Chinese forces and reduces the significance of those arms and technological elements which Moscow fears most. The Americans and their allies together have an advantage over Russia with respect to nuclear weapons. On the other hand, Russia has an absolute advantage over the West in conventional arms. The agreement with the USA consolidates its power even more and gives it an opportunity to extend its subversion to the whole world.

That same agreement also weakens all other Western states and their partners, with the exception of the two policeman. In the end, however, it considerably weakens the potential of the second policemen, America, because it undermines the potentially anti-Russian forces in the world, including the USA. Nixon failed to take this fact into consideration, just as Roosevelt had failed to do so in the past.

The suggestion that Nixon will allegedly maneuver Brezhnev into a war with China is unrealistic, for Brezhnev is no Hitler. For Brezhnev, an agreement with the "capitalists" is mandatory because he must have a gendarme for crushing the national liberation uprisings of the nations subjugated in the USSR. He plays the role of a new Metternich, who needed Russian troops to combat Kossuth. Khrushchev won US consent for crushing the Hungarian Revolution, while Brezhnev won it for a possible uprising of Czechs and Slovaks....

The agreement between Nixon and Brezhnev is a conspiracy against the nations subjugated in the Russian empire, a guarantee that Nixon will not meddle in the "domestic affairs" of the USSR and, if need be, will even help to crush those who strive for freedom and independence. All present "agreements" with Brezhnev as well as the so-called disarmament conferences are water for the mill of the Russian empire.

The expansion of NATO forces and the nuclear might of Western Europe will be torpedoed, for both policemen have pledged "to eliminate the threat posed by atomic weapons." Without the development of these arms, Western Europe will be forced to seek protection from the USA—that is, become its satellite and make its interests dependent on those of the USA.

What is the benefit of NATO's concept of nuclear strategy when its very essence is being denied by the agreement? What is the point of NATO planning in general?

Agreements with Moscow and disarmament will not save the world from Russian tyranny, but the building up of nuclear and conventional weapons by

West European nations and a stake on nations subjugated in the USSR will do so. In other words, the policy of liberation of the subjugated nations and dependence on their own forces. Otherwise West Europe will find itself in the role of a satellite of one or the other superpower. The downfall of Brandt's government—an outpost of the Russian empire in Western Europe—thermonuclear armament, in particular the expansion of conventional armed forces, orientation the insurgent armies of the subjugated nations, a systematic and planned consolidation of their liberation revolutions—all this is the sole road to liberation of the still-free nations of Europe from the satellite status which is inevitably waiting for them. Here a special role falls to Ukraine and the ABN, to England and France—but a national France, a patriotic and anti-Russian France which understands the fundamental threat and the spirit of the historic epoch.

Our thesis that Ukraine is the revolutionary problem of the world is justifying itself more and more. And it is surprising that Nixon does not disregard this revolutionary force, that he does not rise in defense of its cultural leaders and freedom fighters who are also defending the liberty of the United States.

It is difficult to grasp what is happening around those having power in the West. Why do they let themselves be slaughtered like calves? Churchill once said that only the most stupid slaves choose their own butchers. This is taking place right now. The Russians shout about the necessity of a conference of so-called European security, and the USA and other Western states follow that call as calves to a trough. Why is Moscow so interested in the "disarmament conference"? Does it fear an attack? After all, everyone knows that nobody in the West even dreams of attacking the Russian empire. Here people are happy chewing gum, drinking Coke and Bavarian beer, dancing sexy dances; these are the dreams of a decadent society. Dancing boogie-woogie they are rolling down to the abyss. Who is preparing an attack against the Russian tyrants? Brandt, Mitterand, Fanfani, Nixon? Nixon has even capitulated in Vietnam.

"The conference of security" is needed by the Russian chieftains in order to protect themselves from the uprisings of nations they oppress, to gain a lasting guarantee of territorial status quo, a guarantee in international law, a permanency of the status quo of subjugation of nearly a quarter of a billion people—members of nations subjugated in the USSR and its satellites—in order to be able to extend further its aggression and conquests.

For these reasons, it is not the Western states which need a "security conference" but the Russian empire, which is threatened by insurrections in Ukraine, Turkestan, Hungary, in the Caucasus, and in other countries it suppresses. It is not the US or Europe which have a common border with China, but the Russian empire. Why is the West rescuing the empire's tyrants? This can be answered only by the Russian espionage network which infiltrates Western states.

In this situation there are no grounds to have confidence in Western states and to orient ourselves on their "liberation policy." Therefore, we must orient ourselves only on the forces of nations subjugated in the USSR, upon our own forces, as the sole guarantee of national and social liberation from the Russian yoke.

A conflict between the Russian empire and Red China is not the object of our orientation, since it might have an unpredictable end, resulting even in an integral *coup d'etat* in China by the pro-Russian elements (a new Lin Piao and Liu Sao-chi) and their reconciliation with Russia.

Moscow is incapable of conducting a conventional or a thermonuclear war with Red China. Therefore, it is counting on a civil war in China, provoked by the pro-Russian elements. Such pro-Russian Chinese elements can be found on the territory of the USSR as well. Their main concentration is in Tashkent and in other centers of Turkestan, as well as in Siberia. In the event of internal disturbances in China, they are ready to take power into their own hands, with the help of the Russians, and to reorient Chinese politics on Moscow. The Kremlin is awaiting this very opportunity.

The Russian chiefs are not afraid of any US intervention to the disadvantage of the Russian empire, for they know that the so-called treaties with Western states, especially the USA, are like a new Yalta or Teheran. Moreover, Moscow can rely on the precedents and experience of Budapest, Prague, Bratislava, the Berlin wall, and the uprising in East Germany.

Although Moscow's gamble on Lin Piao has failed, it is nevertheless counting on a similar situation after Mao's death. Therefore, the expectations of some Western opportunists that the Chinese will take their chestnuts out of the fire for them are completely unrealistic. There is no guarantee that Peking will go to war with Moscow. The subjugated nations alone are the true, irreconcilable enemies of the Russian empire. And they are the hope of the world.

The struggle of nations subjugated in the USSR for liberation is at the same time a bulwark which saves the Free World from a Russian deluge. The Russian empire is a colossus on clay feet which finds itself on top of a volcano: the liberation revolutions of the subjugated nations.

The Ukrainian Review,
No. IV, 1973, pp. 30-36

The Road to Ideological Victory Over Marxism and Bolshevism

How can we find a way out of the contemporary ideological, moral, religious, and spiritual crisis that has enveloped a great part of mankind? The nations subjugated by Communism and Russian imperialism are not undergoing such a crisis, for in the cruel struggle for self-preservation they have found their identity, their eternal values and beliefs, which have given them strength in their fight for national independence and freedom. Their faith is sustained by their suffering and martyrdom, by their heroic lives, which are filled with the belief in the victory of truth and God's justice, with the concept of God and Country as "the thought of God."

Today mankind awaits leaders of vision, not necessarily pragmatists or vote-getters, but men with a sense of mission, men who commune with God about saving mankind from the Communist and Russian-Bolshevik flood. Such people exist in the subjugated nations. They are warriors of the spirit; they are in concentration camps, prisons, and psychiatric wards, but they are indomitable, like Dantons of national and religious ideas, like inspired soldiers of faith. One of them is Lev Lukianenko, who, after fifteen years of prisons and prison camps, has been arrested once again for defending the idea of Ukrainian independence. Lev Lukianenko writes: "Even if I were the last man on earth, I would fight for Ukraine." Lukianenko is now in prison for his participation in the Kyiv Group for the realization of the Helsinki accords. In his Christmas address to militant atheists, Lukianenko writes:

A human being is always a part of God and that which unites him with God is a great sphere of spiritual life. The soul of man, which lives and feels godlike, attains its deepest unity through communion with God and draws from this that idea of the sublime and beautiful which cleanses a person and lifts him above material and bodily needs. It makes of him a real human being that senses beauty and wants to become something better by striving eternally towards God and by an eternal recognition of God through his works.

God, Ukraine, and the nation—these are the fundamental ideas of faith and rebirth, the revitalization of individuals and whole societies.

Valentyn Moroz, the Ukrainian philosopher and historian sentenced to fourteen years of prison, writes:

Wake up! Open your eyes! Throw into the trash your "progressive" rose-colored schemes. Then you will see the living reality. Then you will see the greatest event in the world, beautiful and formidable in its grandeur—the march of a nation through history. Its mighty rhythms dominate everything. Mountains tremble from its heavy steps and Jericho's walls, built on lies, tumble down.... There is no full worthwhile life without death. There are no true values without the possibility of their loss. A nation is a rock which Atlas must eternally support on his shoulders. This is its goal—to carry on its shoulders something great, special, unique, holy. To feel responsible for not letting it fall. This can only be a nation, a sacred vessel in which the most valuable treasures have been kept for ages. One can get rid of this burden and ease one's biography, but then life will become empty and senseless.

Ideas for the Spiritual Renewal of Mankind

Two fundamental ideas, the national and the religious, are emphasized by Ukrainian cultural leaders and political prisoners. Joseph Slipy, the Patriarch of the Ukrainian Catholic Church, a martyr and a defender of the faith, speaks of the rebirth of nations and people, of heroic Christianity, religion, belief in God, patriotism, and the struggle for one's country. The age of national liberation, of new values, new concepts of life and struggle, the age of new people, great in their faith and noble of heart, an age of heroic humanism that is brought before the world by a liberating nationalism—such an age is still before us. Mankind is waiting for a new world order which will combine in itself the best achievements of the human spirit in all areas of life. Nationalism as a new national and socio-political system of life has not yet been realized anywhere in the world. It has already begun to revive nations with its ideological, ethical, and cultural value. Yet nationalism was neither Nazism, which was national *socialism*, nor was it fascism, which, although in principle distinguishing itself from racism, is not related to nationalism because of its single-party totalitarianism, negation of social development, and imperialism. Nationalism is anti-imperialism, anti-chauvinism, anti-racism, anti-colonialism. It respects the right of every nation to its statehood within its ethnographic boundaries. Nationalism, because it is the rule of the people, will save the world from slavery. Is it not strange that out of 145 sovereign nations in the world only about 30 have democratic governments? Communist totalitarianism and colonialism continue to rule an ever-growing number of the nations of the world. The independence of nations and the realization of human rights can, in our era, be acheived only by a nationalism of liberation which draws its strength from a heroic humanism and a solidarity of all levels of society. Valentyn Moroz writes, and history confirms, that all great cultures have a religious and national foundation. There are no national geniuses without national cultures. There are no world geniuses unless they are national geniuses first and unless they grow and mature in the spiritual environment of their nation. There is no world culture without separate national cultures that comprise a universal world culture. Imperialists and colonialists, especially those of the Bolshevik kind, perpetrate a crime against world cultures when they attempt to denationalize and assimilate the peoples of the world.

Denationalization is a deheroiazation of life; denationalization is the destruction of the cultural life of man; dechristianization is barbarism, as can be seen by the Bolshevik system of the Russian empire, a prison of nations and people.

There should not be and there cannot be a Soviet nation: there can only be Ukraine, Georgia, Byelorussia, Lithuania, Latvia, Estonia, Azerbaidzhan, Turkestan, Armenia, North Caucasus, Russia, and other nations. The attempt to create a Soviet nation means the destruction of national cultures and their thousand-year-old traditions and religious and national identities. To deprive nations of their spiritual roots means the destruction of morals and civilized life and the regression to a barbaric age.

Communism—The Most Retrogressive System in the Development of Mankind

Bolshevism, as a synthesis of Russian imperialism and Communism—that is, Leninism, of which Marxism and Communism are integral components—is not progress in the history of nations and people but a reactionary movement, a regression to the morals and culture of the jungle. Lenin and Marx are the greatest criminals in the history of humanity. Their pupil was Stalin, the mass-murderer.

Although Bolshevism, Communism, and Marxism have been responsible for the killing of over 60 million people in the Bolshevik empire in the course of sixty years, their ideas are supported by many in the Free World, especially by young people. The reason for this is not only Moscow's propaganda about the "achievements" of Communism but mainly the facts that:

1) Western democratic liberalism places in the center of its value system the hedonistic and material well-being of the individual; and 2) official Christianity, as formulated by the Vatican and the World Council of Churches, has abandoned the ethics and beliefs that made Christianity an unmatched revolutionary force in the history of mankind. The greatest revolutionary event in the world was the birth of Jesus Christ. Out of the first thirty-two Popes, twenty-nine died the death of martyrs. Neither Peter nor Paul bargained with the tormentors of Christ, the Neros and Diocletians, as do their modern successors under the directives of today's Pope. Only martyrdom provides a religion with strength and victory. The Patriarch of the Ukrainian Catholic Church Joseph Slipy, Cardinal Mindszenty, the Reverend Vasyl Romaniuk, Pastor Vins, the clergy of the Lithuanian Church and the other underground churches—these are the true Christian alternatives to the official imitations of the West. The more hedonism spreads in individuals' lives, the more the modern Church eases its demands upon the faithful. This is a great mistake. The essence of the religious life is self-abnegation and self-sacrifice, simplicity, strictness of tradition. Monasteries and monks—these are the proof of the strength of religion and the church!

The Church of the Catacombs is the true Christian Church and not the World Council of Churches or the Vatican, which collaborate with the ungodly Communist regime and its "religious" hierarchy. Let us support the Christianity of heroes and martyrs and not capitulate before militant atheists.

The Occident Has Abandoned Its Values and Ideals

The official ideology of the West has rejected the idea of nationalism and patriotism. The nation is no longer considered to be an organic community or the highest social ideal in the world, but rather an isolated unit of egoism. The idea of national heroism is no longer a subject for enthusiasm and emulation of youth but rather a cult of the Golden Calf. The downgrading of the heroic concept of life in conjunction with one's native land is the most important reason for the spiritual and moral decline of the West. "Better Red than dead"—this is the motto of the decadent hedonism of the official West. Because the leaders of the West have rejected the idea of the heroic life in defense of one's country, a great part of youth has lost its ideals, for the path to God leads through the nation, through one's native land. And one's homeland is not wherever one feels well; one feels well where one's homeland is. The West lost its power of attraction when it lost its ideals, its sense of mission, and its faith in itself and its culture. It lost its power of attraction when its leaders began to believe in ideas of ruin and destruction: dialectical and historical materialism, Marxism, Communism, Leninism, and the new prophet of the West—Mao! The Middle Ages, a magnificent page in the history of heroism and creative energy of the West based on national and religious beliefs, are still regarded as the "Dark" Ages, although those were times of heroism and the concept of *noblesse oblige*. The officialdom of the West, with its democratic liberalism, its cult of egoism, and anti-Christian and anti-national tendencies, has resulted in the intellectual and spiritual demoralization of the younger generation. No research institute can find the reason for this demoralization and communization of youth because those organizing inevitably look in the wrong place. The real reasons are the disbelief in the nation, in heroism, in heroic humanism and heroic Christianity. One has to believe in something, one has to know what to live and what to die for. As one Ukrainian hero stated as he was about to perish at the hands of the invading enemy: "I know what awaits me and I am not afraid of death. I am only sorry that I will no longer be able to serve my country—Ukraine." Until the West once again acquires ethical, spiritual, and religious values, it is doubtful whether it will be able to achieve victory over dialectical and historical materialism.

Communism never achieved a single victory in the subjugated nations by means of its slogans and ideas, but rather by means of its use of national and social ideas drawn from the arsenal of liberating nationalism. Today Russian imperialism, whose instrument is Communism, used ideas of national liberation in its ideological propaganda and the private use of land and property in its socio-political propaganda. Only after gaining power does Communism forcibly take away the land from the people and institute collectivization—as happened in Ukraine, for example, forty-five years ago. And those countries with strong national leanings Communism turns into colonies of Moscow—as, for example, Poland, Hungary, Latvia, Byelorussia, Georgia, or Ukraine.

The Question of the Concept of Eternal Values

The ideological and military struggle against Bolshevism and Russian imperialism can only succeed under the following conditions:

With the help of Marxism, Communism, Leninism, and dialectical and historical materialism, Moscow presents humanity with a pattern of social and national existence that leads to collectivization of the economy and a dictatorial form of government. The goal is a worldwide Communist Russian empire of totalitarian despots with the aim of destroying the nation, the family, and the individual.

Is this a new Babylon? Valentyn Moroz, the Ukrainian historiographer sentenced to fourteen years of prison, foresaw this possibility when he made a symbol of the little town of Kosmach with its thousand-year-old Christian and national culture as opposed to the merging of nations for which Moscow, as the center of the world empire of non-nations, is striving. Our answer to the question is that it is not enough to do what the officialdom of the West does when it attempts to oppose the idea of the freedom of the individual to the ideas propagated by Marxism-Bolshevism. Freedom is merely a frame, a necessary condition; it is the possibility of choosing from among different values and ideals and of being able to put these values into action. It is not only a question of freedom, but a question of the nature of the values and ideals that the West represents.

One must oppose the ideas of Communism, Marxism, and all of their offshoots with ideas for which the West is ready to struggle, which it defends, and which it can present to the subjugated nations and peoples. Without this kind of opposition it is not possible to be victorious. To be more concrete, against the denial of God one must affirm the conception of God as the creator of the world; against the idea of an international and anti-national class rule one should affirm the national principle as a means of world order and sense of community; against social realism in culture one should support the idea of freedom of cultural creativity based on religious and national concepts; against the destruction of individuality, the affirmation of man as an image of God; against the dissolution of the family as an organic national unit, the realization of the family as necessary to the moral and physical health of the nation; against agricultural collectivization, the idea of private ownership of land and the means of production; against "étatisme," a triple organization of economic activities: the private sector, the cooperative sector, and the government. But the most important idea is to uphold the nation against the empire. The central concept necessary to the realization of the potential of each nation is the breaking up of the Russian Communist empire into independent states. Only nationalism with its ideal of liberation and the ideal of heroic Christianity can accomplish this.

I realize that I am proposing unpopular ideas, but behind these ideas stand the nations enslaved by Communism and Russian imperialism. Not every authoritarian regime is opposed to democracy. When a democracy needs to be saved through the suppression of Communist activity that may threaten fundamental freedoms, then such an authoritarian regime cannot be regarded as an evil but must be helped to make the transition to a normal guarantee of basic human rights. Today, many condemn General Franco, but if it were not for his help, it is possible that Russian Communist divisions might be stationed on the shores of the Atlantic. Let us be fair in our judgment of historical events. The freedom fighters in the subjugated nations are dying for the cause of national and democratic ideas, for the rights of nations and the fundamental rights of individuals, and for the ideals of nationalism.

U.S. Human Rights Policy and the Imperative Needs of Freedom Fighters

The United States, in the continuation of its anti-colonial struggle of liberation and in its traditional role as representative of aspirations for freedom and national independence, has been uneven in its defense of the universal ideals of freedom of nations and individuals. President Wilson initiated the idea of the self-determination of nations, but did not put it into effect. President Eisenhower took up the idea of the liberation of the subjugated nations, and the US Congress, with its 1959 Public Law concerning the Captive Nations, set the tone for US policy in regard to the liberation of the nations enslaved in the Russian empire and the restoration of their national rights. However, this law has remained an empty declaration that has a moral rather than a political effect at the present time. President Carter has taken a step backwards. He has not combined President Wilson's position with the stand of President Eisenhower, but has substituted instead the idea of human rights as the main drift of US foreign politics. Yet is this declaration a religious and ethical one only or a political one? Will it have practical results concerning the Russian Communist empire? The capitulation of the West in Belgrade makes this rather doubtful. The unwillingness of the US to support the Helsinki groups in Ukraine, Lithuania, Georgia, and Armenia in their demands for human and national rights shows that at present President Carter's declarations have only a moral aspect and not a concretely political one. The harsh sentencing of the leaders of the Ukrainian Helsinki group—Tykhy, Rudenko, Marynovych, Matusevych, and Lukianenko, who was re-arrested after fifteen years of imprisonment and is being threatened with incarceration in a psychiatric prison—without any reaction from the US Government, emphasizes the lack of conviction concerning the problems of human and national rights. Many Ukrainian political and religious prisoners treated President Carter's defense of human rights very seriously, and openly supported the President, with the result that they have suffered a great deal at the hands of Brezhnev. If the US Government has no serious intention of beginning an ideological offensive against Bolshevism, then it should not create illusions among those who are struggling against it. The fighters for freedom could do more for the liberation of their nations than the mere assertion of solidarity with the President of the US—who has left them to the mercy of the KGB. President Carter has received many appeals from Ukrainian political and religious prisoners asking for US citizenship. As the Prime Minister of the last independent Ukrainian Government on Ukrainian soil, I have received an appeal from Ukrainian political prisoners which reads, in part:

> During the last several years a significant number of people, among them particularly Jews and Russians, have been able to leave the USSR. Since the majority of them come chiefly from the ranks of the open opposition, which, regardless of the increasing repression by the regime, has grown intensely in the last two decades, world public opinion received eyewitness reports about the existence of totalitarianism in general, its practices, the situation of the individual, and the enslavement of whole nations.
>
> The world is especially well informed about the state of affairs and the oppression of Jews in the USSR, and this helped to mobilize the world community, mass media, and the Governments of many countries against such violence. At the same time there are almost no Ukrainians among those leaving.
>
> There is, in this, also a positive factor, since this numerically small (percentage-wise) but nationally highly conscious part of the population remains in Ukraine. Nevertheless, in my opinion, an active involvement of this segment of Ukrainians in the national liberation process, culture, and science would bring Ukraine incomparably greater benefit were they in the Western countries and in our diaspora. It is a matter of saving the people who are already unable to work in Ukraine. There are many who desire to leave, but there are no possibilities of doing so.
>
> Realizing the complexity of the situation (and in order to establish a precedent), we, the Ukrainian political prisoners, have requested the President of the United Statest to grant us American citizenship. Being political prisoners, this may complicate the decision. But there are thousands of people who are "free" and who have

been ruthlessly repressed by the KGB for many years. Consequently, they find themselves in a hopeless situation. This is the second and personal aspect of the problem.

Talented literati, artists, and scientists suffer personal tragedies, or are unable to work creatively. To condemn to inactivity, to kill talent is a more subtle but no less cruel method of destruction of the treasures of Ukrainian culture. Examples: Opanas Zalyvakha, an artist of European stature, has not been allowed even one personal exhibit; talented poets like Lina Kostenko and Ihor Kalynets have not published a single collection of poetry in the past ten years, Ivan Svitlychny, a renowned literary critic, prior to his arrest was unemployed for approximately ten years and could not publish a single article; Mykhailo Horyn, a talented psychologist, is employed as a stoker, and in twelve years has not even had one publication; Yevhen Sverstiuk, a known Ukrainian (literary) critic and psychologist, had been persecuted even before his arrest by being dismissed from his job, and could not publish a single work; Vasyl Stus, one of our better poets—not even one book. The following scholars were dismissed from learned educational institutions: R. Krypiakevych, M. Braichevsky, and Y. Leshkevych, as well as other writers whose works have never been published, such as V. Ivanysenko, B. Horyn, M. Kosiov, V. Badzio, and R. Kohadsky. The talented writer R. Kudlyk has been silenced, as well as scores of others who have refused to compose party odes and panegyrics. Because of this, their works do not appear on the pages of newspapers and periodicals. The list of such people can be complemented with hundreds of names.

Each of us in his own way joins in the process of creation of Ukrainian culture and the rebirth of the nation—a new wave of upheaval for our freedom.

From all the facts cited here, it can be concluded that under conditions of absolute tyranny and the arbitrariness of the KGB, a Ukrainian cannot be useful to Ukraine in Ukraine. This is exactly why we are turning to you, Mr. Premier, with the request to strengthen with your authoritative recommendation, as well as the influence of the organized Ukrainian diaspora, our request to the President of the United States of America to grant us the citizenship of that country.

Once again we would like to bring to your attention that it is not a matter of individual cases. The previously cited facts about the life of each of us is only a small illustration of the exposure which threatens us with the loss of freedom.

But in Ukraine there live thousands of people with similar biographies whose creative potential is doomed.

Repression for beliefs and for the creation of spiritual values is varied: concentration camps, prohibition of writing and painting, confiscation of works already created, etc. The methods are varied, but the objective is the same—to destroy Ukrainian spirituality.

Our conclusion is that the West, in order to attain victory, must wage a planned ideological battle in which it opposes Russian Communism by its own view of life, its own concept of world order and world values. We have already suggested the contents of such a view.

ABN Correspondence,
March-April, 1967, pp. 1-7

For the Global, Ideological Warfare of the Occident

Moscow treats the inherent problems of its ideological war and especially the problem of the movements of national liberation very seriously. Moscow's concern shows itself in the fact that the main part of the Soviet Constitution is the following postulate of Soviet Russian politics, as stated in the preamble: "This victory [in the Great Patriotic War] made possible new, favorable circumstances for the growth of socialist strength, for *national* liberation...in the whole world." And in Section 28, under the title of "Foreign Policy," we read: "The foreign policy of the USSR is directed toward the *strengthening* of world socialism, the support of the struggle of peoples for national liberation and for social progress...." Hence, wars of expansion, imperialist aggression, interference in the social and national process of all nations and continents—all this was foreseen and recorded in the Soviet Constitution, a document which provided for imperialist wars and the conquest of the whole world. Hitler presented his whole program and plan of aggression in *Mein Kampf*, just as Lenin did. The only difference lies in the fact that Rosenberg's speech in London was boycotted by Englishmen and thus rendered ineffectual, in the same way that during the French Revolution the Jacobins could not propagate their views in the United Kingdom. But the ideas of the enemy, the entry of Moscow's Trojan horses in the form of Leninism, Communism, and Bolshevism, are received in the West with enthusiasm. The ideas of the enemy are propagated in churches and universities, and the leaders of the Communist parties in the West travel to Moscow to make plans to enslave their own nations! The betrayal of one's country has today become a self-evident phenomenon.

The ideas that ought to be launched against Bolshevism have already been referred to. These ideals, especially those of national and human rights should be a politically functioning aspect of US foreign policy and not just a humanitarian gesture. The concept of national and human rights, must be an integral element of US foreign policy just as Marxism-Leninism is an integral element of Russian policy and planning, including the exploitation of the ideas of national liberation movements. One and a half billion people live in Communist totalitarian countries. National and human rights, in a specific context, and of the sort that we have already mentioned, are also major weapons in the defense of the West. For a long time now the US has ignored the national and human rights of the captive nations within the USSR. In this respect the US must play a more aggressive role after the total defeat of the West in Belgrade. Moscow has received assurances concerning the boundaries of its empire. The West, however, has received no assurance from Moscow concerning the human rights question, let alone the national rights one. The newly developing nations must realize that the attitude of the free nations toward them will depend on whether they support and defend the agents of totalitarian Communism or whether they are the champions of national and human rights, of democracy and national liberation. International treaties and international law are on the side of the free nations.

However, the constitutions of the US and of the other free nations are not suitable for an ideological global war against Bolshevism. In order to succeed they

A Policy of Detente Leads to War,
A Liberation Policy Leads to Peace

The ABN's Conception of Liberation

The synchronized national liberation revolutions of the subjugated nations, directed against Russian occupation and Communist totalitarianism, will destroy, from inside, the Russian empire and the Communist regime.

The isolated uprisings of separate nations cannot be successful, as they could easily be suppressed by Russia—*e.g.*, the uprisings in East Germany, Hungary, and Poland in the past. On the other hand, a synchronized chain of uprisings of the subjugated nations, supported by a liberation policy of the Western countries in favor of the subjugated nations, would be successful and would bring the revolution against the Russian occupants to a victorious conclusion.

We feel that the Western countries, in helping the nations oppressed by Russian Communism, would also be serving their own interests.

The subjugated nations form a first line of defense for the Free World. Had it not been for the resistance and liberation struggle of these nations in the past, the Russian aggressors would by now have dominated all of Europe.

The Achilles' heel of the Russian empire and the Communist system is the liberation struggle of the subjugated nations and oppressed peoples. As the ratio of Russians to non-Russians in the Russian spheres of influence is one to two in favor of the subjugated peoples, the only way in which the Russians can keep the empire together is by a policy of terror.

The Russian Empire Is Not Invincible

The ideals of freedom, which motivate the subjugated nations, are stronger than terror and mightier than any nuclear weapons. The essential point is that he would be aware of the weaknesses of the Russian empire and awkwardness of its system. The West should recognize these weak points of the Russian empire and thus remove the myth of the "invincibility" of Communism and the Russian empire.

To attack the weak points of the USSR, and especially its nationality policy, is a procedure which we recommend to the governments of the Free World.

Nuclear weapons cannot be used against revolutionaries for obvious reasons. On the other hand, simultaneous revolutionary struggles in many subjugated countries give the insurgents a chance to destroy this prison of nations and peoples without a world war and nuclear holocaust. There is no other more appropriate way (with the fewest sacrifices and dangers involved) than the path of liberating revolutions to get rid of the last major aggressor and the last, most serious colonial empire of all times. For this reason, the liberation movements should have the moral and material support of the Free World.

The other alternative, the policy of cooperation and detente which the West

must be changed to meet the exigencies of a global war with a global
which has shaped the constitution of his empire to wage aggressive, expan
wars. The Western nations are unable to even grant citizenship to fi
fighters and cultural workers who defend the very essence of natic
individuals. Only Winston Churchill received US citizenship! Yet citi
should be available to everyone in the ideological war who represents th
of humanity. The foreign policy of the US must be based on ethical co
tions if it is to unite and appeal to the multinational roots of its citizei
constitutions of the free nations must allow the use of all legal means t
the fighters for national and human rights and to support the national l
struggle of the enslaved nations in the Russian empire and in the Co
sphere of influence and control. It is necessary to make use of political, e
and military means, similar to those of Moscow and Cuba in Angola, i
make the transition from ethical and religious sentiments to politic
There is an opportunity here to make use of a whole arsenal of
maneuvers in accordance with internationally legal decisions and law
the Russian empire has become entangled in its attempt to undermin
nations. This has boomeranged against Moscow from the viewpoint
tional law and from the viewpoint of the insurmountable contradict
the empire itself. This boomerang is not being exploited at present.

The charter of the UN and its statement concerning the indepen
nations of the world, the Universal Declaration of Human Righ
declaration about the dissolution of all the empires in the worl
resolution about the need and duty of providing captive nations with
against the colonial yoke, the 1977 Geneva ratification of internatic
times of war and the Geneva Convention of 1949 concerning the ju
of prisoners of war from insurgent armies identically as well as
armies—all those "boomerangs," to which Moscow has been a sig
attempt to weaken the West, must be used against it and its empii
ideological war. This is of the utmost importance.

Until the West realizes that it is not only a question of the enslave
of its very own existence, it will remain in a state of continual r
remember that in our subjugated nations Communism has becom
is powerful only because of the ideological weakness of the W
strength of the Communist, pro-Communist, anti-national and
elements of the West. The way out lies in the ideal of heroism
patriotism and the nation, in the belief in God and in the idea of
the image of God, in the struggle against hedonism and egoism, a
ism, against the desire to exploit and dominate. The surviva
without the victory of nationalism and an ethic based on religic

Address Delivered at th
Anti-Communist League
Washington, D.C., April

now practices, will never stop the Soviet-Russian aggression, as it did not stop Hitler's aggression, and will consequently lead to war. Right now a policy of détente makes it possible for Moscow to infiltrate the free nations and conquer them later at an appropriate moment.

George Meany, the President of the American Federation of Labor and Congress of Industrial Organizations, in an interview on May 30, 1973 with the German Television Network, gave an accurate analysis of Russia's world expansionist policy:

> Brezhnev himself explained what détente means to the Kremlin and what the Soviet rulers are trying to get out of it. Addressing a conference of select Communist representatives at Karlovy Vary, the Soviet dictator said on April 24, 1967:
>
> Experience teaches, in particular, that the Cold War and the confrontation of military blocs, the atmosphere of military threats, seriously hampers the activity of revolutionary, democratic forces. In conditions of international tension, in bourgeois countries, the reactionary elements become active, the military raise their heads, anti-democratic tendencies and anti-Communism are strengthened.
>
> And conversely, the past few years have shown quite clearly that in conditions of slackened international tension, the pointer of the political barometer moves left. Certain changes between Communists and Social Democrats in certain countries, a noticeable falling off in anti-Communist hysteria, and the increase in the influence of West European Communist parties is most directly correlated with the reduction in tension which has taken place in Europe!

There can be no lasting coexistence, not to speak of cooperation, between tyranny and freedom. Sooner or later, it will come to a conflict, because they are two totally contradictory worlds. To prepare a victory for one's own plans is sensible, but to wait for a chance outcome when the enemy is already actively engaged in a course of action is suicide.

We consider that the West, in its policies towards the present-day Russian empire, should take note of some existing facts. The age of empires has passed; there are no more Western empires. The UN Charter and the Universal Declaration of Human Rights condemn in principle any imperialism or colonialism. Why then defend the Russian colonial empire in Europe and Asia?

The constant and persistent efforts of Western governments should be directed toward the restoration of national independent states of the subjugated nations in the USSR and the realization of human rights in Ukraine, Estonia, Lithuania, Latvia, Turkestan, Byelorussia, Georgia, Armenia, Azerbaidzhan, Northern Caucasus, and elsewhere.

The West should aim for the restoration of full independence and the realization of human rights in Bulgaria, Poland, Hungary, Slovakia, Czechia, Romania, and other satellite countries.

The West should stand for the reunification in freedom and independence of the German people and the removal of Russian occupation forces from all the subjugated countries, so that the liberated nations can have free elections and recover all the attributes of sovereignty that every independent country in the world enjoys.

Without the fulfillment of these conditions, no agreements or talks with the Russian imperialists should be indulged in. Such an attitude, if adopted by the Free World, would create an unbearable atmosphere of pressure on Russian and other Communist tyrants and would drive them into a dead end. Simultaneously, the nations subjugated by them, having regained their strength and confidence, would disintegrate the empire from within. Then the free nations would gain lasting allies in the subjugated nations and, last but not least, a true and just peace.

Unfortunately, the present-day policy of the Western world towards the Russian empire is inconsistent, often contradictory, and does not serve its own best interest. As a consequence, the Western policy is leading toward war as surely as our liberation policy leads toward peace. Why? Because the strong national revolutionary liberation movements inside the Empire paralyze the aggression of Russian imperialism and Communism.

On the other hand, the weakening of the revolutionary movements within the Russian empire, via a policy of detente, creates for that empire a possibility of consolidation without any danger from the outside, and this inevitably lead to the extension of aggression to ever new territories. The time will come when, as in the case of Nazism, the West will not be able to retreat any further and war will be the only solution.

Hence, supporting the revolution within the USSR by the ways and means stated above means supporting peace; supporting a policy of détente means encouraging war or capitulation.

Ours is the age of ideologies; it is also the age of thermonuclear weapons, of national liberating and anti-imperial revolutions, and the age of guerrilla warfare. Along with the development of military technology, the meaning and importance of guerrilla warfare is also growing.

In conclusion it should be emphasized that the Helsinki Conference surpasses all other previous international conferences or agreements with Moscow, for it acknowledges all the Soviet Russian conquests in Europe and Asia and gives Moscow a free hand to carry out acts of terror, Russification, and extermination against the subjugated nations, acts needed by the empire for furthering its existence.

The hope that such a confirmation of the status quo at the Helsinki Conference will provide "the possibility of an exchange of ideas information and people" between East and West and thus lead to a lasting peace is merely an illusion.

No country in the world is intending to attack the USSR! Should the Soviet Russian aggressors be standing on the very shores of the Atlantic, they would still not feel "safe" and would then perpetually desire new guarantees of their current conquests, until they had captured the whole world.

A compromise will always be to the detriment of the Free World and the subjugated nations.

As the crude facts of the present day have demonstrated, the treaties with Moscow have caused greater intensification of the terror against the subjugated nations.

Since the official circles of the Free World render neither practical assistance nor human compassion and moral support to those who suffer and fight, we appeal to the Western man in the street, to the young people, to the mass media, and to the intellectuals to support the subjugated nations in their fight for national independence and human rights.

We especially appeal to the press, radio, and TV to come to the defense of all those who have been incarcerated, banished from their homelands, or locked up in psychiatric clinics because of their uncompromising stand against all violators of national and human rights.

We give our full support to an appeal recently received from Ukraine by Mr. David Floyd of *The Daily Telegraph*. The full text of that appeal is available for your kind attention and consideration.

The Ukrainian Review,
No. I, 1974, pp. 19-23

The "Afghan Crisis" or the Global Crisis of the West?

What Has Come of the Political Will to Fight?

In view of the recent Russian imperialist aggression in Afghanistan and in conjunction with the weakness of the West, including the USA, the crisis of the Free World was exposed with all its far-reaching consequences. First and foremost, this is a crisis of incapacity, a lack of the will to pose any sort of opposition, a crisis of being lulled to sleep in one's prosperity, a crisis of frightening disinterest in the future. The Western powers have concentrated all of their attention on the endless agglomeration of luxuries, of ever-burgeoning wages, without giving a second thought to the future, without any vexation over the possibility that in one night the wave of Bolshevism might drown their material riches and a great concentration camp of destitution, suffering, terror, and despair might be erected.

Intoxicated by its hedonism, the West is sleeping. A candidate for political office does not have any chance of victory in any type of election if he or she does not make promises to aggrandize every citizen's prosperity. The will to fight has become nonexistent. The idea of the nation, patriotism, a burning faith in some higher ideal, the idea of heroic Christianity—are all weakening, and instead we have a Christianity of comfort which disdains any self-sacrifice or self-negation in the name of a higher ideal. Hence, the West is faced with a grave crisis of spirit, morality, and world-view (Weltanschauung.). Elections are won by those who conceal from the people the severe problems of this era of turmoil, danger, and the Bolshevik threat of world annihilation. He who has the courage to point out the threat of the Bolshevik deluge is labelled a "fascist," a "warmonger."

The noble attempt of President Carter did not receive the necessary understanding and "support." Mr. Carter was unprepared for the highest office of the greatest superpower in the world, since he was unacquainted with the history of the Russian imperialist nation. This lack of knowledge was exposed when President Carter made the statement that he had only recently realized that he had been fooled by Brezhnev. This statement is without parallel in the historical annals of world statesmen and leaders. The entire history of Russia is a factual attestation to the inevitability and historical determinism of the further development of Russian expansionism. President Carter should have at least read one basic historical primer on the Russian empire, which was and continues to be a deadly threat to the world. It would seem that he never even read the smaller but essential studies identifying the Russian spirit, such as the writings of N. Berdyaev, who was born in Kyiv, considered himself to be Russian, and was an analyst par excellence of the integral Russian spirit, as well as one of the few Russians who denounced the Russian nation for its intrinsic imperialism.

Afghanistan—A Historical Goal of Russian Aggression

Afghanistan has always been in the historical plan of Russian imperialism, regardless of whether this plan was formulated by the Russian tsarist or Bolshevik regimes. This has been historically proven. Presdient Carter has declared that he had warned Brezhnev with regard to Afghanistan, but in truth, this is a very naïve position. What is essentially needed is not some secret warning, but the capacity to create some sort of military resistance. Why did President Carter not issue a public warning? We are very skeptical as to whether any warning whatsover was issued by President Carter, who has gravely compromised himself in this crisis.

Because of a total lack of the will to fight, the West, therefore, also lacks a global strategy, especially in regard to the Russian empire. All these so-called doctrines of Truman, Nixon, or Carter, Dulles' containment policy, the policy of coexistence, or détente—all this amounts to nothing in the face of the systematic realization of Moscow's global strategy. Afghanistan is only the next step in the logical development of the political-strategic concept of Moscow. This is not simply the outcome of some spontaneous decision, nor is it due to some fear of a "threat" from the West, but, quite simply, this is the consequence of the plan of Russian imperialism, which has been systematically realized beginning several centuries in the past. The national liberation movements continuously threaten to destroy the Russian empire from within. So, to keep this empire intact, it is necessary to mobilize the chauvinistic, messianistic instincts of the Russian masses for ever-greater conquests.

Russia's current plan is clear and simple: to seize the oil fields of the Near and Middle East by overpowering them and occupying the countries of Africa, thereby gaining control over the natural resources of these countries, on which the industrialized West, especially Western Europe, is highly dependent. Moscow intends to sever Western industry from these resources and, consequently, bring the West to its knees. Hence, the capitulation of Western Europe will be achieved without a thermonuclear war, or, for that matter, without any war whatsoever. Their aims are obvious and simple. It is inconsequential whether Moscow will occupy a country or, instead, place it within its sphere of influence, whether this be Cuba, Ethiopia, Angola, Mozambique, South Yemen, or some other country in South America, or in Southeast Asia, Vietnam, Kampuchea, Laos. This is all academic from the point of view of *Moscow's general political strategy*—the conquest of the entire world.

Moscow seeks out the most vulnerable spot on every continent, or geopolitical complex, and when a vacuum appears it is quick to fill this vacuum with its military subversion and disintegration. In the end, "a friendly invitation" is issued from the "Government" of this new "satellite," or rather from Moscow's gendarme regime in this colony, calling for "aid," which is then rendered in the form of military occupational troops—and in a short period a new victim has fallen within the Russian jaws while the rest of the world looks on. And then we find people like Mr. Brandt, Mr. Bahr, Mr. Wehner, General Bastian, who are ready to justify Moscow's aggressions in any way possible. Several German and French politicians are political illiterates with regard to their knowledge of the *national* complex of the USSR. For them, Ukrainians, Byelorussians, Russians— this is one and the same people! Furthermore, Chancellor Helmut Schmidt and even F.J. Strauss always use the queer label—"Soviet," or "Soviet people," etc., which only further confuses and deceives the general populace. There is no greater nonsense in the world. "Soviet" is the Russian equivalent of the English word "council." Hence, how is it possible for a nation to be a nation of councils, or, for instance, a nation of committees? How can a nation be erected out of local, regional, or national councils, or out of a "Supreme Soviet" (Council)? This is the kind of naïveté that the politically ignorant West allows itself to be caught in. How can a "Soviet"—that is, a council—attack another nation; how can a nation, a people of councils, exist? Nowhere in the world has there been an instance in which some administrative or legislative forum created a nation! Mr. Schmidt declared that he is waiting for the "Soviets" to retreat from Afghanistan, and other such nonsense. There are no "Soviets" occupying Afghanistan, or any other country for that matter. What we have are *Russian* occupational forces threatening every freedom-loving people in the world. Here we are attempting to point out an essential and elemental detail. This detail, however, or rather the total lack of comprehension of its basic significance in the West, points out the West's complete ignorance of the most important complex in any future victory over the USSR—*the subjugated nations!*

For a Global and Political Strategy of the West

Once we accept the fact that the Russian plan is to conquer the entire world, then we must formulate a global counter-strategy. An "Afghan crisis" as such does not exist, instead there is a crisis of the West—a crisis of a lack of leadership. Afghanistan is an historically determined step in the process of Russian expansion. The next step will be Iran, Saudi Arabia, Thailand, Latin America, Africa. It is unimportant who is to be the next victim. Any global strategy depends to a large extent on the element of surprise. Should the not-so-distant events in Angola and Ethiopia have not been enough to point out to the Pentagon the proper direction to be taken? What about Vietnam, Kampuchea? Should it not suffice to mention the fact that the Russian empire has the largest modern land-based army in the world, the most powerful nuclear potential, the greatest military naval fleet and air force strategically positioned in all the oceans and seas of the world, which allows it to forcibly appropriate, on every possible occasion, new seaports for itself—as was most recently shown in the Indian Oceans? Only a Bolshevik agent, or a political illiterate, or an electoral candidate for political office who desperately wants to be elected even at the cost of deceiving the public will persist in maintaining that the USSR has constructed an all-powerful military machine which it only intends to use for defensive purposes.

From whom must the Russian empire defend itself? The USA is neither attacking anyone nor is it a threat to anyone. It is a crime to equate Afghanistan with Vietnam. The Americans were *defending* South Vietnam and lost this war because of their politically naïve position. By no means can the Americans be considered oppressors in Vietnam. Their elemental mistake was that they continued to adhere to their agreements with the Bolsheviks, against the will of the Vietnamese people, when the Russians, on the other hand, never manifested any intention to adhere to their part of these agreements. Instead of permitting President Diem to march on the North with the idea of liberating it—the Americans were hopelessly bickering among themselves as to their aims in Vietnam, only to capitulate totally in the end, never taking the crucial and decisive decision to initiate a serious offensive, and, more importantly, never giving Diem the change to launch an offensive on his own. All those who at one time condemned the United States are now silent, when hundreds of thousands of Vietnamese workers are drowning on the high seas after having to escape from their hell, or when millions of Cambodians are dying from an artificial plague organized by the Communists!

It is unimportant whether the Russians will next attack in the Persian Gulf or Central Asia or the Near East (they are already preparing an attack on Iran and/or Turkey) or in some other country of South America or in the Pacific Ocean. For all these various aims, they have their naval fleets, their fifth columns, and all the necessary weaponry. The West will not be able to salvage anything without its own global concept! Any attempt to put out the flames which periodically flare up here and there is worthless. That power will actively pursue the actualization of its global strategy concept! The West must formulate a more sophisticated and wide-ranging strategy which must also include other elements besides those strictly military in scope—that is, the West must identify and utilize the Achilles' heel of the Russian empire—*the subjugated nations!*

Strictly military strategies, which, in any case, the West does not have, will be rendered useless unless the West seriously considers and analyzes the idea of the political liberation of the subjugated nations of the Russian empire. This was best proven by the events in Afghanistan, Angola, Ethiopia, Mozambique, South Yemen, and Cuba. Even the best military strategy or doctrine of war is not viable if it is not a *function of political aspirations* to fundamentally change the existing, tyrannical, imperio-colonial order, which enslaves whole nations. Without the inclusion into this global military strategy of the political factor, without the construction of this strategy on the concept of the liberation of the subjugated nations—the defeat of the West is assured.

NATO, as a regional military alliance, will never reach its goal, since it must become integrally imbedded in the global military and political strategy and system. Moscow is actualizing its global strategy, when NATO, in comparison, is antedated and antiquated. The viewpoint of the German Government—namely that it is only interested strictly in the geopolitical complex of NATO—is evidence of its total lack of comprehension of Moscow's global aims. It is not possible to resolve regionally the problems of Europe, since the Russian empire stretches far beyond Europe. Who, if not NATO, is supposed to counterpose Russian aggression in Africa, Asia, and Latin America? Yet the Germans feel that this is beyond the competencies of NATO. The Russians are presently occupying, not a part of the USA, but a part of Germany, and their empire is global and not limited to Europe! Hence, NATO has become antiquated without its inclusion in the global center of strategic planning and action.

Furthermore, due to the Europeans' lack of political will to fight, NATO is completely dependent on the decisions and risk of the USA. The European member states of NATO (including Germany) must begin financing their own, more sophisticated atomic weapons arsenal, and not only depend on the sacrifices of the American people. Not being included within the global context, NATO leaves all the continents outside of Europe to be defended by the USA. The relations between the USA and China, the defense of the Near and Middle East and Africa—crucial geopolitical areas for Western Europe—are potential components of a global strategic doctrine of the USA, which as yet does not exist! It is not surprising that De Gaulle developed a separate atomic weapons system for France, despite US opposition. And it turns out that this move was justified when we look at the increased aggression of Russia. This is not to be understood as saying that we support the opportunistic pro-Russian politics of the French Government, which is egoistically hoping that the US will pull the chestnuts out of the fire in the interest of France. Western Europe must understand that it must become a partner of the US, it must develop its own weapons system, so that together with the US it can pose some viable opposition to the Russian global strategy. There cannot be any third power, which will be the beginning of the finlandization of Western Europe; instead, Western Europe must become a partner of the US with the same aims: *the dissolution of the Russian empire with the aid of the subjugated nations*, as the key factor in a new global strategy, as a partner, as a new political superpower.

For the Development of Conventional Forces,
a Naval Fleet and Especially Guerrilla Forces

A new military strategy of a global nature must primarily develop conventional military forces, a naval fleet, an air force, and a strategic "alarm force" of several parachutist divisions, which would be always on alert to liqudate future Russian aggression on defenseless countries, such as Afghanistan, Angola, or Rhodesia. In the general plan of this global strategy, various roles can be instituted, if we were to regard the necessity of including the so-called "Third World" into a military and economic alliance of friendship and mutual benefit with the West, respecting the sovereignty of the white countries of Africa and other continents outside of Europe. Western Europe, for example, should pay great attention to Africa, the Near East, and Latin America, whereas the USA ought to interest itself more with both continents of North and South America, as well as with the Far East and the Pacific Ocean. The Americans and the Western Europeans should apportion between themselves the responsibilities of defending the Indian Ocean and the Persian Gulf. This is not to be regarded as a mechanical apportionment of responsibilities, but ought to be understood as a means of accenting the necessity of acting in *unison*, whereas, within the various specific complexes, some will have relatively greater or lesser responsibilities. Only within such a construction can there be a victory over Russian imperialist aggression! However, even the most far-reaching and thought-out strategy will be rendered useless in the long run if it does not take into account the most significant factor—the superpower of the nations subjugated by Russia in the USSR and satellite countries. Any military plan that does not include this superpower as the crucial variable will end in defeat, as did Hitler's or Napoleon's military strategies. "Ceterum censeo": *without the national liberation revolutions— armed insurrections—of the subjugated nations, the West can never be victorious over the Russian empire!*

Without a Concept of the Dissolution of the Empire
There Can Be No Common Front

In its global military and political strategy the West must include the guerrilla-revolutionary concept of a liberation war—armed insurrections—of the subjugated nations. There is no chance of victory over any empire, and all the more against the Russian empire, without the consideration of this decisive factor. It is indeed possible that a situation may arise which will force the subjugated nations to take up arms against Russia and the West, as was the case with imperialist Nazi Germany, if the West chooses to ignore this political and spiritual superpower. It may happen that the soldiers of the so-called Soviet Army will fight against the Western forces instead of deserting to the side of the West if the West does not proclaim as its military and political goal the idea of the dissolution of the Russian empire. In the Red Army forces which were invading Berlin, there was a considerable number of non-Russians, who were simply taking revenge for the genocidal policy of the Germans throughout the war; by no means were these troops attacking for reasons of allegiances to the Russian empire and the Communist system.

On the other hand, the Ukrainian Insurgent Army and the Organization of Ukrainian Nationalists—the UPA and OUN—actualized their own concept of liberation in a common front with the subjugated nations, in a two-front liberation war—and this concept remains unalterable for the OUN. This means that if an analogous international situation should arise, the OUN-UPA will continue to actualize its self-inherent and self-authorized Ukrainian political liberation concept with its own military-insurrectionary, guerrilla, and political strategy, regardless of whether China or the US or some other bloc of powers should enter into a war against Russia. Without the prior recognition of the concept of the dissolution of the empire and the reestablishment of a sovereign and independent Ukrainian Nation-State and independence of other subjugated nations—there can be no common front! The West must finally realize this fact. The revolutionary forces of the subjugated nations will never enter into a common alliance with anyone who will fight to keep the empire intact.

Therefore, the key variable in the global strategy of the West must be a strike at the very heart of the empire and system and not only at the peripheries; the policy of containment or balance of power is "peripheral," since every defensive concept of the West is doomed to be defeated. During Truman's term in office, the West was in sole possession of the atom bomb and, hence, was capable of forcing the USSR to retreat; the West was powerful enough to destroy the Russian imperialist system. This was not to be, and through various phases of "containment," "coexistence," "détente," the West finally regressed to the point of having to accept and formulate a policy of balance of power between the two superpowers, which has already been transformed into the military ascendancy of the Russian empire! The only possible solution (from the point of view of the West) to this disadvantageous state of affairs lies in the dissolution of the Russian imperialist system from within, and not in some "arms race" with the USSR. The key to the final resolution of this global crisis is the liberation nationalism of the subjugated nations! It is absolutely absurd to claim that some "one-world" utopianism (a world government) can be this key. Neither can this key be the military-technical superiority of the West, but, as a primary factor, the subjugated nations armed with the idea of national liberation. A crucial and significant function will also be carried out by the religious sphere in conjunction with the national Holy Wars for the nation, for the Fatherland, for God.

The Russian empire is surrounded by inimical forces from without and from within: Japan, China, the Western nations, the peoples of the Near, Middle, and Far East, Central Asia, Southeast Asia.... Those who presently do not understand the Russian threat, or are blinded and deceived by fanatics inspired by Moscow, such as a Khomeini, will sooner or later come to their senses. *The decisive factor is the enemy within—the subjugated nations!* The tragedy of the West is that it does not want to understand the key position of this force. It is indeed surprising that, despite the liberation of the African nations from the imperialist fetters and the establishment of their role in the world, the West remains incapable of formulating a parallel deduction with regard to the liberation of the nations currently subjugated by Moscow, in spite of their ancient, traditional heritage. What sort of strange blindness is this?

For the Immediate Implementation of Anti-Russian Measures

Currently, the matter of discontinuing all technological, financial, and economic aid for the empire, including all grain sales, is becoming an actual necessity; the West must utilize the internal weaknesses of the empire just as Russians utilize the weakness of the Western nations on the military, socio-political, and other levels, exploiting every open flaw in the West. Hence, the West ought to utilize every economic weakness of the empire, *but its primary focus ought to be geared toward supporting the revolutionary national liberation struggles of the subjugated nations!* Let us look at Moscow's actions in Africa, for instance.

In regard to the Russian occupation of Afghanistan, the boycott of the Moscow Olympics is a bare minimum, of which the West is not even capable! This is frightening and is proof of the total moral degradation, the loss of all honor and dignity—not only national honor, but human honor as well! The vital factor in strengthening the liberation revolution is the psychological, ideological and political war in the spirit of the subjugated nations!

The Western states must organize an all-out campaign among their citizenry, especially the youth, in the area of their militarization and patriotic upbringing, informing them of the fact that the USSR is a multinational empire and not a monolithic state. The fact that even some Western journalists and parliamentarians are completely unaware that *the USSR is the Russian empire* is beyond comprehension! The various means of mass communication must finally begin informing the people of the horror of Bolshevism, about the concentration camps, genocide, and Russification, rather than simply continuing to condemn the crimes of Nazism, which is long since dead, when, at present, humanity is threatened by the Father of Nazism—Bolshevism! It is horrifying that not one demonstration of Western youth against the genocide in Vietnam, in Kampuchea, in the USSR has yet taken place.

The Western European nations must cease in their role of an intermediary between the USA and the USSR. All this amounts to the demobilization of a common front and the repudiation of a common global strategy!

The most shameful role in this regard was played by France and Germany. The statement by Mr. Brandt or Giscard d'Estang to the effect that the Near East complex in conjunction with Afghanistan is simply a point of conflict between two superpowers is a manifestation of either an unbelievable political naïveté, megalomania, or malice, which can only be to the benefit of Moscow.

The US declaration, in which it was stated that it will treat the Persian Gulf as a matter of its national security, ought to be accepted with great gratitude by the entire Free World. Here the US is not defending *its national interests*, since it has enough oil for itself in the USA and Latin America, but, instead, the US is defending the interests of the Near East, of Germany and France and their further existence.

The statement of leading German Social Democratic politicians, claiming that Germany must defend strictly its interests separate from those of the US, is bordering on capitulation to Moscow. The oil of the Near East is in the national interests of Germany, and not the USA. This is not an "imperialist" target of the USA, but a matter of life and death for German industry, a matter of whether Germany will or will not capitulate to Moscow. The interests of free Europe are, first and foremost, being defended in Afghanistan, and not strictly the interests of the USA! The USA is not so much defending itself in the Persian Gulf, as all the Western European nations! If the Persian Gulf should fall under the direct control of Russia, then Germany, France and Italy will also become dependent on Russia's whims and wishes. Therefore, the refusal of Chancellor Schmidt to boycott the Olympic Games is not simply a blow for the US, but is against the interests of Germany! It turns out that the interests of Germany are being defended by Moscow and are being harmed by...Washington! This is nonsense. If Bonn were to eventually decide, sometime in May, to boycott the Moscow Olympics in solidarity with the US, what significance will such a belated action have when their current refusal to boycott has created a situation which demobilized other Western nations such as Norway, whose Olympic Committee has already decided to participate in the Moscow Games? This position of Bonn is in support of the politics of Paris in this and other matters. However, in the final outcome, Germany and Berlin will not be defended either by Paris or Rome, but primarily by Washington. How is one to comprehend the current politics of Bonn? In whose favor is it? And the statement of the head of the socialist parliamentary faction, Wehner, demobilizes every patriot; he justified Moscow's move in Afghanistan, claiming that Russia was forced to occupy this country so as to undercut the revolutionary aspirations of the Turkestanis and other Islamic peoples in the USSR. Since when do socialists stand up in defense of subjugators, even justifying their actions, in the manner of Wehner and Brandt, forgetting their traditions, established by Bebel, a great defender of the nations subjugated by Russia? This is similar to the actions of various Communist leaders of the Russian fifth columns throughout the world. There is no correlative precedent in the history of movements for national and social justice to justify the subjugation of ever more *new* peoples by the necessity to keep those *already* subjugated within the imperialist yoke. We must assume that tomorrow a new statement will come from some socialists in the SPD, claiming that the Russians must occupy Pakistan or Iran because they are being threatened by the Islamic peoples of these countries. Furthermore, we will see the justification of *tomorrow's* occupation of West Germany for reasons of a threat of revolution in *East* Germany. It will then become necessary to occupy France because France will constitute a threat to the Russian empire with its border on the Rhine, and, hence, it will become necessary to expand the empire to the Atlantic and, thus, the conquest of the entire world will have been achieved! Then, perhaps, the threat to the prison of nations and people will be liquidated. And so, we have reached our end.... Where are you heading, Occident? What has become of the great, noble tradition of the Europe of yesteryear? Where is your love of freedom and independence, respect of human dignity, respect for the nation and the individual? Where is your Christian spirit?

The subjugated nations must carry the burden of a great, revolutionary responsibility: the spiritual, moral, idealistic, patriotic, and religious rebirth of free nations. Perhaps this was the mission given to us by God—through the sufferings and thorns, to the laurel wreath?

ABN Correspondence,
May-June 1980, pp. 1-8

U.S. Ambassador to the U.N. Jeane Kirkpatrick with Yaroslav Stetsko. (1983).

Yaroslav Stetsko with Vice President George Bush. (1983).

XI
The National Liberation Struggle

How to Localize and Win the War against Russia

Introduction

The following brochure by the last Prime Minister of free Ukraine is so lucid and all-embracing that little introduction is needed.

Mr. Yaroslav Stetsko, the writer, must surely be recognized as an unquestionable authority on the subject on which he has written so admirably.

I have not gained what knowledge I possess of Central and East European affairs from reading books written by other people. My professional work happens to have entailed my traversing much of Soviet Russia, far from the visitor or tourist track, and living in countless homes of peasants as one of themselves. In the years between the two wars, that same business caused me to be, for a considerable part of each year, in the independent states on Russia's western frontiers. I had, therefore, unique opportunities for acquiring personal knowledge and experience of Russian policy and actions in the past, as well as imbibing the feeling of peoples whose ancestors had been in the closest contact with their eastern neighbor for centuries.

I think Mr. Stetsko's work, short as it is, is one of the most important yet published on the subject of Russia. If anyone thinks the present world situation can continue indefinitely, I can only say that I differ; the explosion will come, and we, as usual with Britain, will not be prepared for it unless we follow Mr. Stetsko's advice; and there will be no time to recover this time. Whom are we fighting in Korea? Russia!

I endorse every word of this brochure, but I would like to draw special attention to the section "Unauthorized Dabblers in Politics." The resistance movements in the non-Russian states of the USSR and their struggles for freedom have one obvious enemy in Moscow. But, to my mind, a less obvious but no less dangerous enemy exists in the many societies professing to aim at the freedom of the Russian peoples. Incidentally, there are no Russian *peoples*; there are Russians and peoples who are not Russians. These societies, although professing to be prepared to consider some kind of freedom for the non-Russian peoples some time, all have one thing in common—the indivisibility of "Holy Mother Russia," that is, the maintenance of the Russian prison of nations with the non-Russians, as at present, prisoners within it. Many of these societies have almost unlimited funds at their disposal, funds which are applied to the suborning of nationals of these non-Russian states, for there are traitors in every land. It is satisfactory that they will be dealt with as traitors should be when they fall into the hands of those fighting for the cause they have betrayed.

To my mind, there is a most sinister power behind these societies, whether the latter know it or not, and, as no good can come of avoiding plain speaking, that power is New York finance, which is seeking world conquest just as much as Moscow. That power will never give freedom and independence to the non-Russian countries; its object is to obtain control of the enormous potential wealth of these states, to exploit it, not for the benefit of their own peoples, but for a cruel money-power. It is obviously much easier to control one central concern than a number of smaller ones seeking to exploit the wealth with which God has so bountifully provided for their own folks.

In this connection I cannot do better than quote a very great and surely unbiased authority, Clarence Manning, the distinguished Professor of Slavic Studies at Columbia University. He says:

> The West has not yet faced the rolling back of the Iron Curtain. Meanwhile there is the story of execution, deportation, and annihilation of the non-Communist elements, there is the same appeal from leaders abroad, from the population at home, and the same feeling of helplessness which allows the Kremlin-selected envoys to roam at will through the United States, Great Britain, and France in the name of an international law in which the Russians do not believe.
>
> The West still listens to the siren song of the anti-Bolshevik Russians. Those of the conservative-military class and of the Social Revolutionists and their allies both agree that Russia is one and indivisible; that all the various peoples that exist within the territory of the once-Russian empire must be treated as a unit. It makes no difference that Stalin proclaims the dangers of the various nationalisms within the Soviet Union. It makes no difference that he appeals for membership of the various Soviet republics in the United Nations as a new sop to this national agitation. The West hears only the voice of some Kerensky or tsarist who proclaims the opposite, and they forthwith believe that a free Russia, one and indivisible, is the only solution. It makes no difference that Stalin proclaims the annihilation of whole groups for their opposition to Russia; that he announces that it is only the Great Russians who are loyal to the Soviet state and are responsible for Soviet victories. That means nothing as compared with the word of a tsarist general or a Kerensky who proclaims the opposite.

It is a dangerous error on the part of the West to try to put aside the resistance movements in the various non-Russian states. It is only through collaboration with them and not through any atrocious scientific weapon that Russia can be conquered, and I do commend Mr. Stetsko's arguments to the most serious consideration.

For the rest, I would only wish to add that I have long had the honor of close friendship with Yaroslav Stetsko, and no one could meet him on the intimate terms I am proud to enjoy without recognizing in him a great and unselfish patriot and a statesman of the highest ability.

May God reward him in his work, and his people for their unanimous, unswerving support of their leader.

John F. Stewart, Chairman, Scottish League for European Freedom

Worse than Bolshevism

The fear of Bolshevism in the West is worse than the evil itself. Indeed, the fear of Bolshevik Russia is the West's most dangerous enemy, paralyzing its will, driving it to compromise and preventing it from doing anything positive to put an end to Russian aggression.

"Fear has big eyes" is a Ukrainian proverb. The Bolsheviks are only too familiar with the West's paralyzing fear of Russia. It is systematically fed by fifth columns which spread rumors of the incomparable strength of the Soviet Union, its masses of fanatic soldiers, deadly Russian weapons, the omnipotence of the MGB-MVD, etc. By means of such legends the Bolsheviks hope to suggest invincible strength and thus paralyze the West's will to fight.

It is, of course, good if the West is mobilized by the danger threatening it. But if fear of this danger calls forth defeatism in the West, then it no longer benefits the West but the enemy. Though the West recognizes the danger of Bolshevism, it does not take the necessary steps to meet it. Many Western politicians repudiate the policy of the strong hand because they are afraid of irritating or provoking Moscow. That is hiding one's head in the sand like an ostrich, or something worse; it is the policy of a man hypnotized by a boa constrictor's venomous eye and unable to avert death.

It is high time that the West realized its chances of victory if it unites with the nations subjugated by Moscow. Such an alliance would make it not only superior to Bolshevism, but invincible. Cooperation with the subjugated nations would also give the West the confidence in its strength that the Free World needs, and must develop if it is to be victorious.

The Real Enemy

Just as in World War II the real enemy of the Allies was Germany, but not the many countries occupied by Germany—France, Belgium, Holland, Denmark,

Norway, Serbia, Greece, Poland, Czechia, etc.—the present enemy of the West is Russia alone and not the non-Russian countries occupied by Russia, such as Ukraine, Byelorussia, Turkestan, Georgia, Armenia, Azerbaidzhan, North Caucasia, the Cossack Republic, Idel-Ural, and Siberia, countries that declared their independence in 1918-21 and had their own governments.

In the Soviet Union today, the Russians play the part of a *master people*, and it would be a great mistake to put them on the same level as the non-Russian peoples of the USSR and regard them as equally subjugated. It would be just as much a paradox to maintain that, for instance, the Germans under Hitler were just as much "subjugated" as the Poles during the last war.

No plans for world conquest are cherished either by the Ukrainians, the Bulgarians, or any other non-Russian people under the dictatorship of Moscow. But the Russian people, which has always proclaimed a messianic mission, is still striving for world hegemony. If the West, therefore, seeks to put up a defense against this aggression from Moscow, it must first be quite sure who its real enemy is, where he is, what his plans are, what his strength is, and on whose power he depends.

It would be tragic if the West were to swallow Russian bait and consider all the nations in the East as equally to blame for Bolshevism. In reality, Bolshevism was introduced into the world by the Russians alone and is merely a continuation of 500-year-old Russian imperialism, as Dean Acheson, Secretary of State in the USA, very rightly confirmed. It is not an "international clique" but solely Russians that are responsible for Bolshevism, a specifically Russian phenomenon, a system of world policy that is not even identical with Marxism or Communism.

Up till now, the Russian people have made no great attempt to destroy Bolshevism. Why is there no resistance movement in Russia proper, no insurgents like the Ukrainian Insurgent Army (UPA) created by the Ukrainian people from its own resources? Why is there not a single sign of anti-Bolshevik resistance in Russia, such as the UPA in Ukraine, the Basmachi in Turkestan, the White Partisans in Slovakia, and other fighting organizations in the non-Russian countries under Moscow's occupation?

Natural Allies

In organizing its fight, the West must be sure with whom and against whom it intends to fight. It must and can fight only in cooperation with the peoples subjugated by Russia, and *against* Russia. Another question to consider is what propaganda is called for if, in addition, diversion is to be created in the enemy's ranks; and still another is to decide if the real enemy may be regarded as a potential friend and if the non-Russian peoples in the Soviet Union should be lumped together with the Russian people on the false assumption that they have a common fate.

A clear distinction must be made between oppressors and oppressed. This alone will permit a clear strategy of battle and reveal where the real enemy is. The decisive blow against the heart of the enemy's power is always the most important part of wise strategy. The proper knowledge and use of allies widens the front of attack and opens new possibilities. Unwise strategy may lose the support of potential natural allies and drive them into the arms of the enemy, as Hitler did in his Eastern campaign.

The enemy in the East is, and will always be, Russia alone, in its ethnic frontiers, a fact Western strategy must always remember. In World War II, for instance, it never occurred to any of the Western Allies to fight against France, Belgium, or Poland merely because these countries were occupied by Germany and might possibly be transformed into friends of that country. On the contrary, every normal person was certain that opposition to Germany in those countries had grown as a result of occupation. And the Allies quite properly did not fight against peoples under the power of Germany; they supported the resistance of De Gaulle in France, or Bor Komorowski in Poland, of General Mykhailovich in Serbia, etc. Similarly, the West today ought to support the organizations of resistance among peoples oppressed by Russia, if it wants to ensure victory over Russian imperialism.

An Absurd Attitude

The attitude of present-day Western politicians towards the peoples subjugated by Moscow is absurd. The Western allies considered it quite natural for France or Holland in the years 1940-44 to desire liberation from the yoke of Germany and independence, and all their plans were based on this natural assumption. Why, then, do they not consider it equally natural that, for instance, Georgia or Ukraine or Turkestan should desire liberation from the Russian yoke?

Western politicians are putting up gigantic plans for Western defense and strategy. Anyone with the slightest idea of the national liberation movements among the non-Russian peoples in the Soviet Union and their potential is horrified at the thought of the methods employed by Western politicians against Russia.

And the solution is as simple as child's play. Treat our peoples as you did those of the countries occupied by Germany in the last war and you will not go wrong. That is all we ask of the West.

Untenable Arguments

The answer will perhaps be: you want us to fight, not only against Russian imperialism, not only against Bolshevism, but also against the Russian people as the instruments of Bolshevism. And we maintain that you must have courage to look at the truth. The aim of the conflict must be victory.

Against whom did the Allies fight in World War II? Only against national socialism, or against Germany? And against whom in the First World War? Against the Kaiser, or against Germany? If the fight was against national socialism only, why the dismantling of industrial plants, why the demand for

ethnographic German territory in the East, and why the complete demilitariza-
tion of Germany? Why has a central state been replaced by a federation? In
putting those questions we do not wish to pronounce any judgment on the policy
of the Allies towards Germany. We wish only to state facts and draw conclusions
at a time when the world is threatened by a far greater enemy than Germany—
namely, Moscow. If such preventive measures seem called for against Germany,
are they not far more justified against imperialist Russia?

The very existence of Bolshevism, which always was a more dangerous enemy
than national socialism, ought to have been sufficient reason for the Allies to
treat Germany differently during and after the war. At any rate, no one can deny
that in the Second World War the Western Allies fought not only against
national socialism but against Germany as a whole, just as Germany fought
against France, and not merely against the Second or the Third Republic, and
against Great Britain, and not against the British monarchy.

An Inexorable Historical Fact

In expressing these indisputable facts, we do not want to advocate the extirpa-
tion of the Russian people or even their annihilation by atomic bombs in a future
war. We merely wanted to show *who is on the side of the West and who is not* in this
historical conflict and to draw therefrom conclusion as to strategy. We wish to
state unequivocally that a Third World War must attack not only Bolshevism but
Russia, whereby we do not mean the entire territory of the Soviet Union, still
less its sphere of influence and its satellites, but only the territory occupied by the
Russian people.

But we should like to point out to Western politicians that the situation in
Russia is quite different from that in all non-Russian countries in the USSR,
which fact should greatly influence the strategy of the West.

As in World War II, the propaganda meant for the German people was different from that for the French, Belgian, Dutch, or other peoples under Germany,
the propaganda of the West today must vary according as it is directed to the
peoples of non-Russian countries or only to the Russian people itself.

As long as the Bolsheviks parade the power of their countless divisions before
the eyes of the Western world, and as long as the press in the West continues to
alarm the peoples on this side of the Iron Curtain by reports about the divisions,
the West will be too overwhelmed by the Russian "superiority" to produce any
satisfactory program to meet it. Nor can Western Europe's efforts to put thirty
divisions against the advancing massed armies of the Soviet Union be of much
value in strengthening the West's self-confidence and hope of victory.

A comparison of the two sides from the numerical standpoint reminds us of
the meeting between David and Goliath. Russia has always depended on the use
of masses. The problem, therefore, is to find the proper method of destroying the
numerical superiority of the USSR and to apply it with due skill at the right time
and place. The only weapon capable of blowing the Russian prison of nations up
from within is not the atomic bomb but the idea of the national liberation of the
peoples oppressed by Russia. And the support of the liberation movements of

these peoples and the satellite states is the weapon the West must seize, if it would be victorious against Moscow at minimum cost. Cooperation with the Anti-Bolshevik Bloc of Nations (ABN), the common front of these peoples, is in the interest of the West.

The Peoples behind the ABN

There may at present be gaps in the organization and structure of the ABN but that is unimportant. The decisive point is that it represents fighting organizations and liberation movements of various peoples that are already operating. It is of little account which nations are represented by a definite organization in the ABN and which are not. The main thing is that all the non-Russian peoples in the Bolshevik empire are behind the ABN as a factor of great potential power, since no nation has ever abandoned, can never abandon, its rights of sovereignty and claim to freedom. Even if recreant representatives of these nations in exile have deserted the banner of independence for their nation, this banner will be held aloft by the ABN and the nation in question will throng to support it in the decisive hour. That is why the ABN holds fast the slogan of independence for every people within its ethnic borders, no matter whether emigrés of one or the other people may support federation with Russia, thus betraying their people's cause. The ABN, for instance, is firmly convinced that neither the Azerbaidzhani, the Byelorussians, or any other of the subjugated nations will consent to federation with Russia, but will continue the fight for complete separation from Moscow and thus realize the sacred right every independent state has of deciding its own affairs.

Unauthorized Dabblers in Politics

We know very well that these peoples would never approve a resurrection either of the "Vlasov Movement" (KONR) or of the "Kerensky Movement." Dabblers in politics in exile who accept as representatives of the non-Russian peoples in the Soviet Union the ideas of the "Council for the Liberation of the Peoples of Russia" automatically forfeit all authority to represent their peoples. Should the West attempt to introduce by bayonets the idea of an indivisible Russian empire into the Soviet Union, and should the KONR with some non-Russian dabblers in politics appear in their native countries, they will be received as traitors in the service of the enemy and treated accordingly.

These traitors among non-Russian emigrés are being paid with American dollars today. But we warn the Western world against cultivating treason in these circles. That Russian imperialists are ready to play the part of Judas is not reason why Americans should do so. Sooner or later these traitors will appear before the court of their own peoples and they cannot escape punishment. Their doings in exile are not fundamentally different from the practices of the NKVD and the MVD at home. Should they appear one day in their native countries in the ranks of the Russian "liberator" they will be confronted by the national divisions of their own people, who will sweep them and their protectors out of existence.

The Oath Will Be Kept

At the foundation of the ABN in 1943 in Ukraine in a meeting at a place that was occupied by the Ukrainian Insurgent Army (UPA), the latter and the insurgent troops of other non-Russian peoples in the Soviet Union swore an oath of mutual loyalty and help, an oath sealed by blood. This oath will be kept, till the hour of freedom strikes, not only in Kyiv, but also in Minsk, the capital of Byelorussia, and in Baku, the capital of Azerbaidzhan, and their national flags fly as a symbol of liberty in all the capitals of the non-Russian peoples. That is why the ABN holds fast to the slogan that alone represents the inflexible will of all peoples subjugated by Moscow: "Our own life in our own country, free of federal interference from Russia! Our own life in our own state, with an army, a parliament, a government of our own, independent of Moscow or any other alien power!" And that is what will come!

Just as the giant Goliath was brought low by the boy David, "Great Russia," a colossus on feet of clay, will one day be conquered by the united strength of our peoples—of 3 million Azerbaidzhani, 8 million Byelorussians, 45 million Ukrainians, and all the other non-Russian peoples in the USSR. Our idea of national liberation is so powerfully explosive that it will inevitably bring about the fall of the Russian empire. It is the guarantee of victory over the giant Goliath. The intrigues of certain Western circles, which try to purchase the services of collaborators among non-Russian exiles for a new Russian imperialism and tyranny, put obstacles in our way, thus undermining the West's chances of victory from the outset. Such attempts will not help to localize the conflict between the East and the West. On the contrary. They will expand it all over the world.

A Tragic Paradox

It is a tragic paradox that the Western world should make every effort to avoid war while the attitude of its politicians towards the decisive problem of the non-Russian peoples must inevitably lead to a worldwide expansion of the war.

All who are serious about avoiding war keep their eyes on the Achilles' heel of the Russian dungeon of nations—i.e., on the possibility of utilizing the explosive power of the idea of national liberation among subjugated non-Russian peoples. For this would, if not avoid war, at least localize it. It is therefore in the interest of the West itself to support these peoples in their fight against Russian imperialism, to attract them from the Russian front into their own. It is here that a blockade of the enemy can be successful by a concentrated attack.

The West should not leave the entire burden to us while it stands aside and watches us bleed to death. Russia today is not only our enemy, but the enemy of the whole world. We don't want to be made a cat's paw, and the West itself must takepart in the fight and make sacrifices which can be reduced to a minimum only if the struggle is coordinated with the strength behind our liberation movements. The foundations of the Russian empire are by no means firm and it would not be difficult to shake them if this were gone about in the right way.

The West must do something to give the non-Russian peoples in the Soviet Union some concrete hope and destroy their feeling of isolation from the Western world.

A Voice in Support of Our Ideas

General Fuller, the English military writer, launched the following proposal in his article "What the Kremlin Fears Most":

> Lastly, I will end with a concrete proposal. Because from past history there is no reason to suppose that a change of regime in Moscow will call a halt to the age-old urge of Russian expansion, the aim of the Western powers should coincide with the aim of the ABN. This means that the Soviet Empire must be dealt with as was the Turkish—that is, split up into its component parts, each part becoming an independent country.
>
> The first step towards achieving this end is the formation of all freedom-loving peoples on both sides of the Iron Curtain into a common anti-Bolshevik front. The duties of this front should be to plan and organize partisan activities within all subjugated countries and train refugees and form them into the nuclei of national armies, around which the enslaved peoples can build up their fighting forces on or after the outbreak of war.

If these things are done, the Western nations need have no fears. But if they are not done, though the West may win the next war, in its winning it will reap its own destruction and may well end in Bolshevizing the world.

The ideas for which we have been fighting for years are evidently gaining ground in competent Western circles. The sooner the West takes practical steps, the surer the localization of the war. If the biggest radio stations in the world begin to broadcast not only in the language but also in the spirit of the ABN, if our fighters behind the Iron Curtain feel that they are being supported everywhere, and if all these programs are coordinated with our center of planning and we are recognized as an ally of the West with equal rights, then cracks in the structure of the Soviet Union will begin to appear. Even if the USSR should reply to such measures by a declaration of war, it would not be able to conduct a war of aggression because the Soviet army would begin to disintegrate in the first weeks of the war, just as it did when Germany invaded the country.

Instead, therefore, of puzzling about how to avoid the war that the Soviet Union is systematically preparing for, the West ought to be planning how to win it with the minimum of casualties. But if the West, for instance, approves a new edition of the "Council for the Liberation of Russia" (KONR) and supports a policy of Russian imperialism, it will play into Moscow's hand just as surely as

Hitler did when he refused to recognize the independence of the non-Russian peoples in the Soviet Union, thus paving the way for Stalin's "Patriotic War."

The Duty of the West

General Fuller showed great wisdom and farsightedness when he wrote:

> If the West is to gain the sympathies of the enslaved peoples, it must inspire them. To think in terms of the atomic bomb is autocratic, to think in terms of liberation is democratic.

The limitation of the war in time and place lies, therefore, in the hands of Western politicians if they will appropriate the ideas of the ABN.

In conclusion let us repeat: the realization of democracy in the East is unthinkable without the disintegration of the Russian dungeon of nations into the national independent states within their ethnic frontiers of the subjugated peoples, the first condition for the complete development of the character of the individual. For us, the democratic idea cannot be separated from the idea of national liberty, a principle that is expressed by the slogans:

Away from Russia!
Freedom for peoples!
Freedom for the individual!

The West can gain a permanent victory over the USSR only if a second front of the subjugated peoples can be erected behind the Iron Curtain throughout the entire country. If it does not coordinate and synchronize its actions with those of such a second front, the West will scarcely win any war against the Bolsheviks

Conditions for Formation of a Second Front

The first condition for this coordination is that the West should recognize without reserve the conception and the ideas of the subjugated peoples—the disintegration of the USSR and the reconstruction of its various independent states—and that it should help the satellite states to recover their sovereignty; further, that the West should refrain from interfering directly in our internal affairs, but help us to build up our sovereign democratic national states.

To realize these aims, it is essential:

(a) to contact representatives of the resistance movements behind the Iron Curtain who have formed the ABN, to recognize them as entitled to speak for our subjugated peoples and to launch a great political and publicity campaign behind the Iron Curtain. In other words, the center of coordination in the free nations would have to cooperate closely with the centers of coordination for the subjugated peoples, in order to organize campaigns and draw up plans of strategy, etc;

(b) for the West to contact the coordination center of military operations for the subjugated peoples, in order to draw up plans for common military and political campaigns.

Military and Political Strategy

The following points are important for military and political strategy:

(a) In order to meet the Bolshevik tactics of war on two fronts—aggression abroad and civil war at home—and Bolshevik methods of involving the West in peripheral wars (Korea, China, etc.), the following strategy is indicated: first, the second front of all subjugated peoples should be consolidated by a proclamation by the West in support of their aims; secondly, an attack must be launched on Moscow, the bastion of Bolshevism, and on the Russian ethnographic territory, in order to liquidate the hinterland of Bolshevism.

Whenever the West attacks Bolshevism in its stronghold, the subjugated peoples will be able to cope with the Russian occupation troops, provided they receive support from the West. If the strategy of the Allies is coordinated and synchronized with that of the subjugated peoples, it will be able to cut off Russian troops in central and western Europe from their bases by the formation of a front in their rear—i.e., in the Baltic states, Byelorussia, Ukraine, Turkestan, Caucasia, Idel-Ural, Cossackia, Bulgaria, Romania, Hungary, Slovakia, Czechia, Poland, etc.,—the Allied fleets giving support from the Black Sea;

(b) Logical conclusions must be drawn from the fact that the Soviet army is composed of soldiers of different nationalities. Bolshevik armies in the Far East, for instance, are largely composed of members of subjugated nations. We should even now launch an ideological attack by broadcasting, and it should be possible for us to spread messages throughout the Soviet Union and its satellite states by means of pamphlets, thus closing the grip of psychological warfare round the USSR. In Bolshevik divisions, not far from the Korean theater of war, there are freedom-loving Turkestanis, Byelorussians, Tatars, Georgians, Ukrainians, Azerbaidzhanis, Cossacks, North Caucasians, men from Idel-Ural, Armenians, Lithuanians, Latvians, Estonians, and other anti-Bolsheviks. Secret stations in Japan, Australia, Western Germany, Turkey, and elsewhere ought to speak to the subjugated nations in our name. But the speakers must not be exiled politicians of the past, who are regarded by our peoples with irony and contempt, but uncompromising anti-Bolshevik champions of freedom, who appeal to our peoples in the name of their organizations and movements and from the stronghold of the ABN.

Coordination Essential

To sum up, victory over Bolshevik world aggression and imperialist Moscow will be assured only if the plans of the Free World of the West can be coordinated with the will and political aims of our peoples.

Yaroslav Stetsko
Foreign Affairs Information
Series, No. 12, Edinburgh:
Scottish League for European
Freedom, August 1952

Subjugated and Free Nations in a Coordinated Freedom Campaign

In order to be able to fight Russian imperialism and Communism successfully, *it is necessary to unite the efforts of the subjugated and of the free nations in a single, coordinated, and systematic freedom campaign;* for Russian imperialism, which world Communism nowadays serves, directs a subversive campaign against the entire free and enslaved world through its center, the Kremlin.

On the other hand, there is no world center for the coordination of the anti-Communist campaign of the Free World and of the nations subjugated by Russian imperialism and by Communism, neither with respect to support for the revolutionary liberation movement in the countries behind the Iron Curtian, nor as regards the coordination of the anti-Moscow campaign with the national political organizations in exile, which are the representatives of the fight for freedom of the subjugated nations.

There are two trends in the anti-Communist fight in the world on the one hand, the uncompromising line which definitely rejects any possibility of a "peaceful coexistence" with Russian imperialism and international Communism and, accordingly, fights for the complete annihilation of Bolshevism and for the disintegration of the Russian-Bolshevik peoples' prison into independent national states within their ethnic frontiers; and, on the other hand, the efforts of most official circles in the Free World to find some common modus vivendi with Moscow and its satellites. The numerous uncompromising anti-Communist organizations of the Free World are endeavoring to change this wrong attitude on the part of the official circles of their peoples, for it is an attitude which is undermining the force of the anti-Bolshevik fight of the subjugated nations. It remains a decisive fact that the subjugated nations are concerned almost exclusively with the practical policy of the Western governments and with the consequences of this policy—as, for instance, the failure to support the Hungarian revolution.

And the so-called psychological war in the concrete sense is also determined by the governments of the free nations and is adjusted to the status of the relations existing between the independent states or the major powers and Moscow. Thus, the psychological war by no means corresponds to the prospects of a large-scale campaign, which would destroy Bolshevism by disintegrating its

Soviet Russian bulwark into independent national states, but solely aims to check Bolshevik and other Communist aggression and to arrive at a compromise with Moscow.

In view of this situation, it is impossible for the major Western powers to find a basis for cooperation with the national revolutionary liberation forces of the peoples subjugated by Russia and by Communism. The aim of the subjugated peoples is not merely to check or curb Bolshevik aggression, still less to establish "Titoism" in Poland or Hungary or to liberate the so-called satellite states alone, but, above all to liquidate Communism-Bolshevism in the USSR itself and to break the USSR into independent national states with democratic forms of government.

A precondition for the coordination of the anti-Communist fight of the free states and of the subjugated nations must be *agreement on the aims of the fight*, as well as the coordination of the practical plans of the liberation movement and of the war, the mutual dependence of these two factors on each other, and the mutual assistance of the free and the subjugated nations against their common enemy. The representatives of the national revolutionary liberation organizations should therefore be treated by the Western powers as *contracting parties* and not as agents.

In order to win over the subjugated peoples to the side of the West and in order to gain their confidence, the free states of the West must definitely adopt a positive attitude towards the aims of the fight of these peoples and must actively support their fight for freedom. The decisive active force of the revolution rests with the individual, who carries on his fight against Russian imperialism and Communism in the name of the highest national and human ideals. The revolutionary process must liberate both the people and the individual from the power of the Communist regime and must make them both conscious and active fighters for freedom and justice. This process must deprive the entire mechanism of Soviet Russian power—including military strength—of its force. Soviet military science will be paralyzed if the men who are responsible for and engaged in it cease to carry out the orders of the Bolshevik regime and, united in their revolutionary campaign, direct this same military science to the destruction of the headquarters of the Soviet Russian occupants and aggressors and those of the executive and fighting units under its command.

The most important thing, therefore, is to win over the *soul* of the individual. This can only be achieved by *ideas* for which *men*, as members of their *nations*, live, suffer, and fight. Without a definite and clearly crystallized system of ideas there can be no victory for the anti-Communist fight behind the Iron Curtain.

Practical Support of the Anti-Communist Revolutionary Fight

It is necessary in particular to take into account the possible practical and effective support of the anti-Communist revolutionary fight by the Free World; for this is the precondition for a genuine victory over Bolshevism. Apart from manifestations of sympathy towards the ideas of the revolutionary fight for freedom, it must also receive practical assistance and must gain genuine allies for the common fight.

Whereas the forces of the subjugated peoples which are striving for national independence regard the problems of the war and of the national revolution as the two factors which, in the event of their mutual coordination, are most likely to bring about the overthrow of Bolshevism, these problems are considered in an entirely different light by political circles in the West. There, interest in a possible anti-Bolshevik revolution in connection with the problem of war is concentrated on the question of whether such a revolution would safeguard the West against a Soviet offensive. Inasmuch as certain circles in the West allow themselves to be swayed by their wish to avoid a war, they regard the fight for freedom of the peoples subjugated by Russia merely as a factor which hampers the Bolsheviks and prevents them from starting a large-scale war; these circles affirm that the situation which is acting as a brake on Bolshevism has been caused by the fact that the fight for freedom is already absorbing the attention and power of the regime, and, further, that the danger of a revolution flaring up in the Soviet world once a war is started is in itself a brake.

But it is precisely this dread of a war with the USSR and the wish to avoid it at any price that is the factor which constantly paralyzes the policy of the West towards Soviet Russian imperialism and robs it of initiative and determination in all the vital problems of the present international situation. And it is precisely for this reason that various possibilities of cooperation of the anti-Bolshevik fight for freedom of the enslaved peoples and the Western states in their efforts to stop the further expansion of Russian imperialism are not utilized.

If the Western powers support the fight for freedom of the peoples enslaved by Moscow with all the means at their disposal, they will be able to free themselves from the Bolshevik danger at a considerably lower price than they would be forced to pay if the USSR itself were in a position to force them to choose between war or capitulation. But any support on the part of the West can only be completely successful if it is given on the strength of a firm decision—namely, to let the cause of freedom be victorious and to annihilate Bolshevism-Communism by every possible means. The risk of a war and Bolshevik threats must not prevent the West from giving the revolutionary fight of the subjugated peoples its active support, for if Soviet Russian imperialism should confront the Western powers with the unavoidable prospect of a military clash, then it would be better for the West to take up the fight in a situation which is more favorable for it; that is, while the Bolsheviks are still engaged in dealing with another front, the internal front, rather than to wait passively until Moscow itself chooses the most favorable time and opportunity to settle up with the West. In any case, an armed conflict on the grounds of active—or even armed—Western support of the revolutionary fight behind the Iron Curtain would be less dangerous and easier to bear for the West than a conflict forced on it by Bolshevik aggression; and in particular, as regards the use of the so-called super-modern weapons, Bolshevik efficiency and strength in this respect would, in the event of an external conflict connected with the anti-Bolshevik internal liberation movement, at least be considerably impaired, since the military-scientific mechanism can be paralyzed soonest by revolutionary campaigns within its own camp. From this point of view the anti-Bolshevik national revolution may actually afford the West considerable chances to evade a Bolshevik atomic offensive or to suffer to a far less extent in this case—but, of course, only provided that the Western powers wholeheartedly support the national revolution in every way and, if needs be, take upon themselves the risk of a military clash with the USSR.

The aims of the Anti-Communist World Congress shall be as follows:

a) to formulate the ideological and political principles of the anti-Communist fight of the free nations and of the nations subjugated by Russian imperialism and by Communism, and to start a universal movement of resistance against Communist infiltration and against the depreciation of those values of the Free World which are based on the organic and spiritual elements of religion, tradition, social reform, and the universal freedom of the individual;

b) to bring about a rebirth of the faith of a free society in the higher values, as, for instance, in the ideas of the nation, in a spiritual and social culture born of the national mentality of the peoples;

c) to mobilize the free communities for the protection of the eternal values of mankind which are endangered, and to call into being a leading intellectual class which in each nation by its united efforts should take the initiative in preserving the eternal values of mankind and of its own nation and should promote the idea of the liberation of the subjugated peoples in the common fight against Russian colonialism;

d) to make all the free peoples of the world realize the unavoidable danger of Russian imperialism and colonialism, which uses Communism as its means of power and which, as long as it continues to exist, will not desist from its predatory policy of conquest until it has conquered the whole world;

e) to expose the cunning tactics of the Kremlin as regards the so-called "peaceful coexistence," the aim of which is to lull the vigilance of the free nations in order to crush them unexpectedly at the opportune moment;

f) to stress the inseparability of the interests of the free and of the subjugated world in their common fight against Communism and to emphasize the terrible danger which threatens the Free World as a result of the "without-me-tactics" which the latter employs, above all inasmuch as the subjugated nations are merely left to fight their unequal struggle against Bolshevism alone;

g) to draw up the basic principles for a joint political strategy and liberation idea, which must be pursued in coordination by the Free World and the subjugated nations;

h) to set up a coordination center on the basis of the cooperation of the representatives of the national revolutionary organizations of the nations subjugated by Russian imperialism and by Communism with the anti-Communist organizations of the Free World;

i) to influence the governments of the free nations so that they abandon the policy of coexistence, which is being pursued at the expense of the subjugated nations (both in the satellite states as well as in the USSR);

j) in the event the official circles of the Free World continue to pursue their policy of coexistence—with the help of the masses of the nations of the Free

World, to organize a campaign of universal support for the revolutionary fight for freedom of the subjugated nations, without taking into account the tactical measures of the official policy of the governments concerned;

k) to make the Free World realize the vital significance of the fight for freedom of the subjugated peoples as regards the protection of free mankind, inasmuch as this fight is preventing Russia and her Communist bloc from carrying out an offensive against the nations that are still free;

l) to analyze the present situation behind the Iron Curtain on the strength of the fight for freedom of the subjugated nations and to draw conclusions accordingly as regards the development of a joint action on the part of the free and the subjugated nations, in connection with the success achieved so far in this fight for freedom, which the subjugated nations are conducting entirely alone without any support from the Free World;

m) to draw up a historical survey of this forty-year struggle against Russian colonialism (in its recent Bolshevik form), taking into account in particular the activity of the Ukrainian Insurgent Army (UPA), and giving a prognostication as to the future form which this fight will take, both in the event of cooperation and joint action on the part of the Free World and without such cooperation;

n) together with the emigrants of the nations subjugated by Russian imperialism and by Communism, to put up a resistance against Communist infiltration and the subversive activity of the "fifth columns"—of the Communist parties in the Free World—and thus expose the latter as an instrument of Russian imperialism and colonialism;

o) and in this connection to expose the other internal contradiction in the Bolshevik system, taking into account in particular the difference between reality and phraseology which this system has inherited from traditional Russian imperialism and from the tactics of its predatory policy of conquests;

p) to fight for the exclusion of the USSR and its satellites' governments from the UN and for the severance of all diplomatic relations with these countries, in connection with which action the UN, by admitting the national representatives of all the nations subjugated by Russian imperialism and by Communism, must be transformed into an organ of struggle against Russian colonialism and world Communism;

q) to proclaim, in the form of a freedom manifesto, the *Magna Carta of the Independence of Nations*, in which not only the destruction of Communism as a social and political system is to be declared as the aim of the policy of liberation but also the disintegration of the Russian colonial empire in order to restore the independence of the nations subjugated by the USSR—Ukraine, Byelorussia, Turkestan, the Caucasus and the Baltic states, etc.

This freedom manifesto shall define the positive aims, which will be pursued by the Free World in supporting the national revolutionary fight for freedom of the subjugated nations and by the realization of which, after the liquidation of Bolshevism, the Free World intends to give assistance to these nations. The fight is nowadays not being fought between empires for the expansion of the territories, but is being fought for their *freedom*. In view of this fact, the aims of the common anti-Communist fight of the Free World and of the subjugated peoples must be based on purely absolute values—complete freedom and independence for all nations, social justice in the name of higher ideals, and universal freedom for the individual, which can only be realized in an independent, democratic, constitutional state based on the recognition of religious principles, which come into conflict with Communist atheism.

In connection with this freedom manifesto, the following proclamations must be drawn up and issued:

1) *Proclamation to the Free Nations of the World*, in which the obligations of these nations towards the subjugated nations must be defined, since the latter by their fight for freedom are preventing the Bolsheviks from carrying out a general offensive—though the fact must be borne in mind that the Communist danger does not cease to exist but, on the contrary, continues to grow as long as the Free World fails to launch a counterattack. In addition, this proclamation must also contain an analysis of the present tactics of the Kremlin on the strength of the Russian imperialist and colonial tradition, an analysis of the internal crisis in the USSR which has been caused by the partial successes of the fight for freedom of the subjugated peoples, and a criticism of the policy of concession pursued by the Free World and of the vague character of the latter's political aims.

2) *Proclamations to the Subjugated Peoples*—an assessment of the significance of their fight for freedom and of its prospects in a possible common anti-Bolshevik front, an analysis of the present Soviet Russian policy from the point of view of the revolutionary fight for freedom of the subjugated nations, an account of the national struggle in all spheres of life, etc.

3) *Political Resolutions*—directives for the joint anti-Communist campaign, demands, addressed to the governments of the free nations, plans for the anti-Bolshevik strategy, decisions regarding the combative means of the common front of the Free World and the subjugated nations, plans for the psychological war, prognostications on the possibility of avoiding an atomic war by a universal and military counterattack (in connection with the development of the revolutionary campaign of the subjugated peoples), criticism of the policy pursued so far by the Free World towards Russia and Communism (from the ideological, political, economic, and military point of view).

On the strength of all these facts, a practical campaign shall be undertaken by the politically and socially interested circles of the Free World, in the following directions:

1. the setting up of radio stations for national liberation movements (out of private means if the governments concerned cannot be persuaded to do so), in particular in regions which border on the USSR, its satellites, and Red China;

2. financial support for the revolutionary movements behind the Iron Curtain, out of funds departed voluntarily;

3. the founding of a political planning institute for the permanent cooperation of the Free World and the subjugated nations;

4. the founding of a propaganda center for joint action on this side of and behind the Iron Curtain as well as universal support for the expansion of the propaganda bridgeheads of the national revolutionary organizations of the peo-

ples subjugated by Russia and by Communism in the region bordering on the Russian sphere of influence;

5. the expansion of the centers of action of the national revolutionary organizations in the countries which tend to so-called "neutralism";

6. the expansion of the representative missions of the national revolutionary organizations in the Far East (namely, in South Korea and Vietnam, similar to the mission which already exists in Taiwan), for the purpose of effecting a more intensive penetration than hitherto beyond the so-called Bamboo Curtain (all the more so as the principles of the revolutionary liberation campaign in South Korea, Vietnam, and Free China tally with those of the subjugated nations in the USSR and in the European satellite countries);

7. the founding of a center for the intensification and expansion of humanistic sciences on the basis of the organic elements of the mentality of the subjugated nations, for the purpose of training an intellectual elite which could exert its moral and philosophical influence on the younger generation behind the Iron Curtain that has been infected by dialectical and historical materialism;

8. the expansion of publishing activity for the purpose of informing the Free World about events and conditions behind the Iron Curtain, as well as the reprinting, in the languages of the free peoples, of illegal anti-Bolshevik publications in existence behind the Iron Curtain;

9. a systematic attack on Communist propaganda in the Free World, with the help of trustworthy eyewitnesses and qualified experts from the ranks of the political emigrants of the nations subjugated by Russia and by Communism;

10. the expansion of the existing centers of the trade unions of the emigrant workers of the subjugated nations and universal support for their propagandist activity among the trade unions and the entire working class of the Free World (taking into special account radio programs in this connection behind the Iron Curtain);

11. a particularly intensive campaign among the students and the younger generation as a whole (who, as is known, are frequently more susceptible to Communist propaganda than the older generation) and universal support for the youth center in exile of the subjugated nations.

Our fight against Russian colonialism and international Communism can only be successful if it is based on the ideas just expounded, for the present epoch is an epoch of the victory of the national idea over the imperialist idea.

As regards the *organizing* work of the congress, the following points must be taken into consideration;

The essence of the matter of the organization of the World Congress lies not in the greatest possible number of participants, but in the justice of the ideas which are to arouse the enthusiasm of the subjugated nations and stir the free nations to action. We exclude no one from our world bloc, provided that he does not exclude himself by refusing to acknowledge the fundamental ideas of the present anti-Bolshevik fight.

In the first place, the enemy that is to be fought must be defined precisely. It is Russian imperialism, whose instrument is world Communism. Russia is the bulwark and the source of world Communism, which she has nurtured. Once the Soviet Russian empire is disintegrated into independent national states, Communism will be deprived of its main base; for once it no longer has the political, military, and economic power of the Russian peoples' prison behind it, every people will be able to deal with it in their own country. The disintegration of the Soviet Russian empire, the last and most terrible empire in the world, and the restoration of independent states, not only in the satellite countries but, in particular, of the subjugated nations in the USSR—this is the fundamental idea on which the political program of our world center must be based. Without this fundamental idea, there can be no victory over world Communism, for the subjugated nations cannot take part in a common front with the free peoples if the latter do not support their efforts to attain complete national state independence.

Those who refuse to acknowledge this idea exclude themselves from the common front. Peoples cannot fight for new fetters, still less so if they regard Bolshevism as a form of Russian imperialism, which in the past, under the guise of Pan-Slavism or of the "defense of the Orthodox faith," etc., subjugated them.

It is a question of a selection among *ideas*, and in this respect there can be no compromise.

ABN Correspondence,
July-August 1958, pp. 7-8, 10

European Thought and the Ukrainian Idea of Freedom

In September 1870, Ernest Renan wrote:

> The spiritual and moral strength of Europe lies in the cooperation between France, Germany, and England; united, these powers will in an effective way concentrate their attention on another power, on Russia. Russia would not be a big danger if it were repulsed from Europe and if it were to allow the peoples of Central Asia to exist within the structure which is in keeping with their common interests. But Russia is influenced by the old desires and aims which she continues to cherish. Moscow is like the dragon in the Apocalypse and will one day assimilate the former subjects of Genghis Khan and Tamerlane. By the union of the European powers the old continent will keep its equilibrium and will possibly master new situations....

Renan exhorts the descendants of his contemporaries to think about the near future as regards to Slav peoples who have been conquered by Russia and who, as he says, "are all heroic and courageous and have no desire to be ordered about and to be incorporated in the big Russian conglomerate."

These words express a profound European thought. The remarkable foresight of this outstanding French thinker regarding the European idea, which now more than ever is occupying the minds of the Europeans, is extremely interesting and informative. Perhaps the European movement will succeed in bringing about a big reconciliation between the Western and Central European peoples and forming a radiant center of regenerated European values for the enslaved peoples of East Europe. The idea of the ancient heroic Christian culture and way of thought, and not the policy of living in the present without thought of the morrow, can become the basis of the rebirth of militant Europe. Europe will be lost if its elite is not regenerated in the spirit of the ancient Crusaders, of Aetius, of Karl Martel, and of Peter of Amiens, and in the spirit of Palmerston, Clemenceau, Foch, Charles XII, and of the Ukrainian Hetman Mazepa—the staunchest opponent of Peter I. Up to now, whenever Christian Europe was threatened by deadly danger, men with a profound faith and a victorious idea always appeared to guide its destiny. The Russian Genghis Khan of today dreads a revolution on the part of the enslaved peoples. Does the West, does free Europe, intend to help these nations and thus help itself to overcome the Apocalyptic dragon? The fate of our continent depends on the answer to this question.

European thought and the European movement must not allow themselves to be swayed by any tactical and political considerations as regards the peoples subjugated by Russia. The frontiers of Europe must not be shifted arbitrarily. At one stage in history the frontiers of Europe extend as far as the Oder-Neisse, at another stage as far as the Vistula or, at most, as far as the Soviet frontiers of 1939. But the profound thought that Europe is where the peoples profess their adherence to European values and suffer, fight, and die for these eternal European values is constantly ignored in diplomatic considerations. Europe is not confined either to religious or Romano-Germanic limits. Preponderantly Anglican England, Catholic Austria, preponderantly Orthodox and partly Catholic Ukraine, and Orthodox Greece—all are equally part of Europe. Whether Russia, as a spiritual phenomenon, belongs to Europe is a question which is not for us to decide, but which must be decided by the Russians themselves. Europe is not exclusively a geographical but, to an even greater extent, a cultural and ethnical conception, built up on the basis of the Greco-Roman cultural circle and the Christian mentality. And it was precisely the nations of East Europe, such as Ukraine, for example, who, by warding off the onslaught of the Mongols and Tatars, preserved the ideas and principles of Christianity with its essential traits of human dignity, freedom of the individual, and voluntary social solidarity, and with its clearly marked sense of honor and heroic attitude to life under the common and binding law of the Divine Will.

It would be wrong to exclude someone from the family of European peoples who actively supports the European community at risk to himself. If we really try to understand the mentality of the Ukrainian, Georgian, or Lithuanian people, for instance, and take into consideration the outstanding characteristics of the European spiritual values and social institutions, we shall have irrefutable proof that these peoples form an integral part of Europe as a spiritual unit. And, incidentally, they are surprised when this right is denied to them. We are not hostile towards the Russian people and likewise wish that they obtain their independence within the limits of their own ethnic territory If we consider

Europe objectively, however, we cannot disregard the attitude of the intellectual elite of the Russians in historical retrospect, an attitude which, as is well known, differs entirely from European views. It is certainly no disgrace for someone to refuse to profess his adherence to our European values, but in order to have an objective basis for an analysis and a knowledge of how far Europe extends, we must take facts into account. If a Japanese affirms that he does not belong to Europe spiritually, this does not in any way makes us discriminate against him.

If we consider historical processes objectively, we shall realize that it was precisely the Russian lust of conquest which suppressed various European nations whose standard of culture and civilization was far higher than that of Russia. This was and still is a conquest of the type carried out by Genghis Khan and Attila. This was the case in the days of the tsars and still is the case today, and in this respect no one will deny the cultural superiority of the Ukrainian or Georgian people as compared to the Russians. In this connection mention must also be made of the occupied East Zone of Germany and of the high standard of civilization of the Czech people.

Whether Russia belongs to Europe in the spiritual sense must be decided by the Russians themselves. Let us now consider what Russian and other thinkers, historians, and politicians have at various time said about Russia's affinity to Europe.

Professor Smolka, who most certainly cannot be regarded as a friend of Ukraine, is convinced that the architecture of the Ukrainian churches reveals Florentine motifs, while the Ukrainian roadside shrines resemble the motifs found in the Vorarlberg, in the Italian Campagna, and in France. These Ukrainian works of art which were found at crossroads were unfortunately prohibited by the tsar in 1843. In his work, comprising three volumes, Leroi-Beaulieu also mentions the European character of Ukraine; and the candid Russian Pan-Slavist Leontiev, in the fifth volume of his collected works (*Sochinieniya*, p. 138) writes about the Ukrainians in the same manner as he does about the Dutch and the Germans and shows that *they are exactly the opposite of the Russians.*

All traditions and historical developments were quite different in Ukraine than in Russia proper, not only now but also, for instance, when the Ukrainian Catholic Church was liquidated in Central Ukraine in 1839 in that part of Ukraine which was under Russian rule. Writing about Ukrainian Orthodoxy, the famous Pan-Slavist said that Ukrainian Orthodoxy, its ideas, its culture, and organization had been latinized. He affirmed that "the introduction of theology as a subject of instruction at the Kyiv Academy was carried out under the influence of the West. The works of the Ukrainian theologian Prokopovych could safely take the Jesuits under their protection or the Holy Congregation 'Propaganda Fidei' " (Vol. V, p. 32).

There are two kinds of Orthodoxy: the Caesaro-papist Russian Orthodoxy and the autocephalous Ukrainian Orthodoxy, which today still continues to exist underground as a Church of the catacombs, just as does the Ukrainian Catholic Church in Western Ukraine. Ukraine is likewise the *Far East of the Occident,* but *never the Far West of the Orient.*

Herzen said: "It is most fortunate for the Russian people that they were not changed adversely by Catholicism...."

In *A Writer's Diary*, Dostoevsky wrote: "Why do practically nine-tenths of the Russians when travelling abroad always seek to establish contact with European radical leftist circles, which, as it were, disdain their own culture? *Is this not an indication of the Russian soul, to whom European culture has always been something foreign?* I personally am of this opinion."

And the Russian emigrant Alexander Herzen cursed the Western world with these words: "Long live chaos, vive la mort!"

The tsarist Konstantin Leontiev wrote in the last century in his book *The Orient, Russia, and the Slav Elements*, "I believed and I still believe that Russia, which must take the lead in a new formation of the Eastern states, is to give the world a new culture too, and is to replace the decadent civilization of Romanic-Germanic Europe by this new Slavic-Eastern civilization." In giving reasons for his political theory, he wrote as follows about the European-minded Slav peoples: "For all these peoples [he is referring to the Southern and Western Slavs] as far as their intellectual classes are concerned represent nothing more than the *most ordinary and most commonplace European bourgeoisie in the history of the world."*

And since it was precisely France which in the nineteenth century played the part of the chief representative of this European "bourgeois culture," he expressed the following opinion on this subject: "If it is necessary for the further independence of Eastern-Russian thought from Romano-Germanic thought and for the adoption of new cultural forms and state forms that the dignity of Romano-Germanic civilization should be lowered in the eyes of the people of the East, if it is necessary that the judgment of values regarding that civilization should become violently prejudiced against it as rapidly as possible, then it is to be desired that precisely that country which has taken the initiative in the present progress should compromise its genius as speedily and as finally as possible!"

And he revealed his opinion and that of his Russian contemporaries even more emphatically when he wrote at the time of the Paris Commune: "Would it be possible to imagine the victory and the rule of the Commune without vandalism, without the material destruction of buildings, cultural monuments, libraries, etc.? Surely not; and in view of the present means of destruction, it is much easier to reduce the greater part of Paris to dust and ashes than it was in ancient times to destroy other great centers of culture—as, for instance, Babylon, Nineveh, or ancient Rome. And this should be the wish of everyone who aims to introduce new forms of civilization."

Such is the profound opinion of a Russian patriot and loyal tsarist, who is fully aware of the irreconcilable hostility of his country towards Europe. What interests him most is the kindling of a world conflagration which should destroy European culture.

It would be a big mistake to regard Bolshevism in its origin and developments as an extra-Russian phenomenon. The Russian philosopher N. Berdyaev characterized Bolshevism as follows: "...Bolshevism is a *purely national* phenomenon; he who wishes to penetrate its depths must uncover the national roots of Bolshevism and must explain its origin on the strength of Russian history.... Bolshevism is a distorted and perverse realization of the Russian idea, and that is why it has been victorious. The fact that *the hierarchic feeling among the Russian people is only very weak, but the urge to an autocratic government, on the other hand, is very strong*, has contributed to this victory. The Russian people would not hear of a constitutional legal state.... Bolshevism is in keeping with the mentality of the Russian people" (*The New Middle Ages*). Berdyaev admits that there is a distinct difference between Europe and Russia: "The Russian people cannot create a humanistic empire of a moderate kind and they do not want a legal state *in the European sense* of the word.... The feeling of affinity with property, family, rights, furniture, and old customs has never stirred the hearts of the Russian people.... The European, on the other hand, regards his possessions as sacred; he will not allow himself to be deprived of them without a hard struggle...."

The West European powers expanded their empires pyramidwise. The upper part of the pyramid has remained standing, but the foundations of the economic development, which for the most part were to be found overseas, are gradually beginning to crumble. It is therefore imperative that some other kind of support should be found for the organic foundations of European unity. The "remnant of Europe" which still remains to us is economically dependent on America and under America's military protection. For this reason it can only establish its own independent economic policy if the East European countries—and by these I mean not only the satellite states, but also Ukraine, Caucasia, Byelorussia, and other countries—detach themselves from the Russian empire and set up their independent states once more and in this way creates the precondition for the formation of a sound Europe as a complex whole. As long as the Russian empire is not disintegrated into independent states, our peoples have no possibility of reaching a free decision, as Italy, Germany, or France can do, regarding Europe and integration.

We must likewise bear in mind the fact that every federation or union in East Europe was imposed on the peoples by cunning and coercion. I refer to the treaty of Pereyaslav in the 17th century between Ukraine and Russia, according to which two states enjoying equal rights formed an alliance out of which a compulsory federation was later forged. Or another example: in 1783 a protectorate treaty was concluded by Georgia and Russia, according to which Georgia was to remain an entirely sovereign state with its own king and only a joint foreign policy was to be observed.

In 1801, however, Georgia was occupied and transformed into a Russian administrative province.

At the peace conference at The Hague in 1907, which was convened on the initiative of the Russian tsar, the petition of the Georgian people demanding that the independence of the Georgian state be restored was submitted to all the delegates.

In 1916, a conference of the representatives of all the peoples subjugated by Russia was held in Lausanne. These peoples again repeated their demand that their independence should be restored. It is thus obvious that there can be no question of forming a federation with Russia in East Europe as a preliminary stage for a European community. For Russian coercion would always be behind such a federation and Russian imperialism would once more use it as a powerful means of ruling Europe and the world. *The fact must be emphasized that the integration of Europe can only be achieved by the disintegration of the Russian empire into independent states, for only in this way would the nations of East Europe become independent and regain their freedom of decision.*

It would be wrong to condemn the idea of liberation nationalism amongst the East European peoples. Liberation nationalism is by no means identical with chauvinism, exclusivism or imperialism. It consists exclusively in the will to self-assertion of a people and in their will to freedom and independence which goes hand in hand with patriotism. This liberation nationalism also characterized all the underground movements of the West European countries which rose up in opposition to Nazi occupation. It was also the fundamental principle on which the large-scale resistance movements of the Dutch and the Norwegians were based. The peoples of East Europe who are still enslaved are perhaps even more sensitive to the idea of national freedom, and for this reason one must not, when propagating the European idea, allow the latter to become a contradiction of the idea of national freedom in the East European countries, especially not as it has always been a characteristic trait of the European element since time immemorial to advocate national freedom and independence. *The key to the victory of the European idea in the East lies in bringing this idea into harmony with the idea of national freedom of the East European peoples, by acknowledging the latter idea and integrating it in the entire European ideological campaign.*

It would be wrong of the European movement to rely only on those elements of East Europe which, from the start, accept the ideas formulated so far by the European movement without any objection. It is more advisable to rely on and include those forces which remain faithful to the historical and permanent European values in the struggle against barbarity, and do so under the banner of the idea of national freedom, which they do not regard as a contradiction of the European idea, but, rather, as an integral characteristic of the latter. It is understandable that certain "white" Russian circles are likely to adopt a positive attitude towards the European movement for opportunist reasons. These circles want to preserve the regional East European coercive federation, under Russian domination, and already regard it as a future part of the European federation. But there can be no question of this, as far as the East European peoples are concerned. The Russian paper *Posev* said in its edition of November 10, 1957:

"The protest against Communism in Russia is more definite in character. It contains nothing of the national factor. But the protest against Communism in Hungary, for instance, contains also the elements of a fight for national independence."

In order to be successful, one must take into account as the primary factor the European idea, which is decisive for the fate of every individual European, the fact that our peoples in the USSR and in the satellite countries are fighting for national independence, and must incorporate this fundamental demand on the part of all peoples who desire to regain their freedom in the overall European movement as a prerequisite for the realization of the European integration.

It certainly seems somewhat strange that even the ideological European movements should show consideration for the opportunist political factors of the Cold War. It is a known fact that an "Assembly of Captive Nations" is held from time to time in Strasbourg, to which only the exiled representatives of the satellite countries are invited. At a congress of the European Movement in Augsburg, the president of the German European Movement answered the question as to whether the Ukrainians are to be regarded as a European people in the negative. And one has sufficient reason to be pessimistic if one also considers the motives behind the Yalta policy, in which it was decided to do everything possible to appease Moscow and to allow only such servile Governments to be set up in the present satellite countries as would not be too frightening for Moscow. The European movement can only fulfill its historical task if it abandons all tactical and opportunist considerations, if it concentrates its attention on the noble aim of a European spiritual and economic regeneration, if it is based on the Christian philosophy of the world and supports the national-state disintegration in East Europe as a precondition for a future European integration.

The Communist materialistic system of evil and crime must be opposed by a uniform system of good and nobility. The achievement of a spiritual regeneration is the precondition for the annihilation of Bolshevism. It does not suffice to preach the slogan of a freedom which is neither determined as regards quality nor precisely defined as regards content. A formal freedom is no longer adequate, and the value and the ideas which one is trying to realize within its framework must be explicitly stated and defined. Freedom is an essential basis for the realization of noble ideas. Freedom is a precondition for the realization of the idea of justice, which represents man's highest possession on earth. And justice demands that one should accord the East European peoples the same preconditions for a free decision as are afforded to the West European peoples who are now free.

The idea that, if only Western Europe unites, it will be able to form a third force is in our opinion not based on genuine preconditions. The Marshall Plan has definitely contributed to the economic prosperity of Western Europe, not to mention American military strength, which for the time being is protecting the present "remnant of Europe" against a Russian attack. In view of this absolutely necessary dependence on America, how can one talk about Western Europe's independence? Without the disintegration of Soviet Russian-ruled East Europe and without the organic incorporation of the East European countries—on the basis of equality of rights—in Europe as a whole, and without the East European sales and import markets, Europe can never become a permanently sound organism relying on its own strength. Europe can only assert itself as a whole and not if it is divided into East and West Europe.

Nor must we overlook spiritual culture. If we consider the ideas which today are a living force in America or Australia, we shall see that they are still our European ideas. If we compare the spiritual world of these continents with the spiritual world of Russia and if we do not place too much emphasis on geographical position as the criterion of Europe, it becomes obvious that the Americans or

Australians are in every respect more European than the Russians, irrespective of whether the latter are Communist or anti-Communist.

Europe's mission failed because European ideals were not faithfully observed. Just as Europe hundreds of years ago started a world revolution, so too European ideas still live on today in all continents. In order to seize the opportunity of this new division of nations unhesitatingly and courageously, and in order to establish contact with this world historical process, the European movement must assume its fitting role, above all as regards the East European peoples, and it is in this respect that an offensive spiritual advance is imperative. Never before in the course of history has the European mentality felt that it was being forced into the defensive and was being defeated to such an extent as is at present the case! The spiritual world of Europe always steered a progressive course. Why then should one now timidly want to limit the European movement to the remnant of Europe? Europe is becoming more and more limited, but *not in the sense of the spiritual experience* of the peoples incarcerated in the USSR who obviously continue to fight for European values, but in the sense of the narrow-mindedness and biased attitude of some West Europeans, who have already lost faith in the European mission and would like to limit Europe to the remnant of Europe for opportunist reasons.

Another factor which reveals the conflict of interests in Europe is the second industrial revolution. Strange to say, in this atomic age a division of the nations throughout the world and, in particular, behind the Iron Curtain is now in progress. It is precisely the idea of national freedom which, if rightly conceived, can counteract the agglomeration of thermonuclear weapons as a means of destruction in the hands of the Moscow tyrants, can disintegrate this colossus, and, in this way, will be able to wrest its material and human potential from it.

These are some of the ideas for which the peoples behind the Iron Curtain are suffering and fighting.

From the point of view of the subjugated peoples, we thus consider that the future of the European movement lies in the fact that it should detach itself from every kind of opportunist policy and should definitely and wholeheartedly support the aims which the nations incarcerated in the Russian peoples' prison are pursuing. These are as follows:

1) The precondition for the all-European integration is the disintegration of the Russian empire into independent national states.

2) By means of freely elected parliaments the independent national states are to be allowed to reach a free decision (just as the German, Dutch, French, and Italian people were allowed to reach a free decision, for instance, with regard to the European Coal and Steel Community or the EURATOM) with regard to the European Community.

3) Every state, irrespective of its size, wealth, and population, shall be represented equally in the European bodies. The nations are to be regarded as communities and no nation may predominate since otherwise integrated Europe will become a new European empire with the strongest nation ruling over the others.

4) More emphasis must be placed on the positive possibilities to be developed

out of the European community and less on the limitation of sovereignty, a question which is a sore point with the peoples incarcerated in the Russian empire. The peoples of East Europe enjoy no real sovereignty. It would, therefore, be inappropriate to talk about the limitation of sovereignty.

On the basis of these principles, it would be imperative that:

a) Without taking the various policies of the Western governments towards Moscow into consideration, one should admit the representatives of the nations incarcerated in the USSR—as, for instance, Ukraine, Byelorussia, Georgia, etc.—into the European movement—that is, into the advisory European bodies—on the basis of equal rights for all;

b) The representatives of these peoples should be invited to all the congresses of the European movement and the right should be conceded to them to discuss European integration in detail from their point of view, which advocates the disintegration of the Russian empire;

c) One should abandon the policy which is based on tactical considerations and still cherishes the hope that there can be a tenable basis—in reality, however, long since outmoded as a result of events—for an understanding with Soviet Russia;

d) The aims of the national fight for freedom of the peoples incarcerated in the USSR should be included in the program of the European movement. In this way the Free World will win back the shaken confidence of the enslaved nations, and the European movement will assume a role that is missing in the West, that of the champion of the freedom of the East European peoples, and will thus fulfill its historic and international political function in the anti-Bolshevik fight;

e) The leading bodies of the European movement should be extended by including the representatives of the peoples enslaved in the USSR who support the above-mentioned ideas, and this should be done on the basis of equal rights for all;

f) The publications of the European movement should report in detail on the fight for freedom in the satellite countries and the nations incarcerated in the USSR and should adopt a positive attitude to this problem. One must not dispose of this matter by classifying it under the general heading of "Russia." Neither Ukraine, Georgia, nor Byelorussia nor any other of these countries has anything in common with Russia, just as Holland, France, and Poland during the Nazi occupation were not identical with the German Reich;

g) It would be extremely important for the European movement to have its own radio station and, linking up with the national fight for freedom of the peoples subjugated by Russia and in conforming with their aims, to expound its ideas through this medium. For this purpose the spokesmen of the fight for freedom of the subjugated peoples who are now living in the Free World and who have always opposed Communism uncompromisingly should also be rallied.

If the European movement, which seeks to overcome national egoism and aims to arouse understanding for the other nations and for Europe as a whole, is not willing to take on this task, who else is there at present who would do so?

Europe's misfortune lies in its retreat. But the question at issue is the regeneration of the eternally valid European values. The profounder motives which have prompted the West European Monroe Doctrine in the political, ideological, and spiritual sense, a doctrine which is gradually being applied in practice and which also accepted a coexistence and containment policy not only in the political sense, lie in the fact that Western Europe has lost faith in itself. In order to survive, one must not isolate oneself from the great and decisive world processes. The great American democracy is Europe's daughter, and, in any case, it would be too early for the motherland of world progress to start becoming resigned.

The Ukrainian Review,
No. III, 1958, pp. 3-16

Possibility of National Revolutions Behind the Iron Curtain

The principal unchanging aim of Russian policy is world conquest. This is the essence of Russian imperialism. Especially in its modern form Bolshevism is the synthesis of Russian imperialism and Communism. The union of these two phenomena has greatly advanced the cause of Russian aggression. Therefore, one must consider both of these phenomena in order to realize the practical program of the liberation policy towards them, and to counterattack Russian aggression.

In order to conquer Bolshevism a universal solution to all vital problems must be found. Bolshevism is a menace to the entire world; the resistance which is offered must, therefore, be universal. The countries which are still free must not continue to live in false complacency while our national struggle goes on and our freedom-fighters protect them, or they will themselves be drowned in the near future by the Bolshevik flood, after the champions of our cause have laid down their lives.

In order to justify the millions of victims of the two world wars before God, mankind, and history, in order to perceive a deeper significance in the deaths of countless innocent women and children, old and young alike, and in order to escape the depths of despair when pondering on the senselessness of all these sacrifices and self-sacrifices, it is imperative that the fight which is in progress should represent the settling of the last big account with the forces of evil, crime, imperialism, barbarity, and cruel and satanic tyranny, and that this fight should result in a genuinely better, more just and noble life, and should be followed by a permanent peace. This peace must not, however, involve tyranny and misery, but must be a just peace with freedom and equality of rights for all, so that all nations and men may feel that they have been liberated from fear, need, cruelty, national subjugation, and social injustice for all time, and all peoples and nations may lead a free, happy, and independent life.

This is the higher and deeper meaning of our fight, and it is not concerned with political hatred!

Mankind today must be more interested in the ethics of this fight, in its moral aspect, and in its spirituality, than in its political significance, for only then will man's political attitude change and will he cast aside all that is bestial, cruel, and inhuman, since he has been created in God's image.

A nation which has been subjugated has a deeper and more sensitive awareness of right and wrong than one which is free. A prisoner longs for freedom more than he does for bread. Once the Western world understands this spiritual attitude and adjusts its way of thinking and its ideals to that attitude, it can rely on the unity of the unwavering front of the free and the subjugated nations.

Communism has become a "religion" of evil and a faith for fanatics who have lost their sense of values, which, however, they believe they are preserving, though in reality they are devoting themselves to false ideals with a zeal worthy of a better cause. For this reason the idea that atomic bombs and military supremacy will suffice to exterminate Bolshevism must be rejected. Bolshevism can still be conquered by the faith and conviction of those who take up the fight against it—a fight which will not remain an empty threat but will be victorious!

Bolshevism destroys all sublime, divine, and human values, denies God, kills religion, destroys churches and undermines Christian morals; that is why the anti-Bolshevik revolution for liberation must put God first and, before anything else, take a stand for the protection of religion, and place human actions on a heroic moral basis. A deepening of religious experience and a revival of religion in practical life will then be a positive result of the new revolution, so that man, even in an age of brutal sadism and barbarism, will be revitalized by an atmosphere of the good and the noble. Persecutions have never been able to wipe out religion, but have only strengthened it, for it is better for religion and the church to be persecuted than to be mere protégés of a state. Every religion contains elements of martyrdom for the sake of truth.

The most vital problem in the present-day world is that of the enslaved nations and their struggle for independence and democracy. In Asia, in Africa, and in Eastern Europe, many people are fighting for freedom and independence. Great empires are disintegrating because of this desire for individual and national freedom. Russia is trying skillfully to use the power of nationalism outside the Iron Curtain against the West. She knows that the nationalism of the peoples inside her empire is her Achilles' heel and her greatest potential enemy. The West will win only after the destruction of the Russian empire and the establishment of independent states of all the people at present enslaved by Russia and by Communism. The enslaved nations are the real third force; whichever bloc wins their potential to its side, this bloc will triumph in the end.

Khrushchev the New Tsar

The period of "de-Stalinization" or of the so-called collective leadership is definitely over in Moscow. Authoritarianism or one-man rule, which is the characteristic traditional trait of the Russian Government, is securely in power. In Russian history an unstable period of slightly liberal policies has always followed the death of a dictator-tsar, enabling the next emperor to consolidate all available powers. After this happens the old tyrannical centralized regime returns to its traditional tactics.

After Stalin's death, Khrushchev, the new tsar, had to give illusory concessions to the enslaved nations until he had eradicated all personal rivals for the throne. Having secured absolute control after expelling from Moscow's power center the Malenkov-Molotov group and after liquidating Zhukov's ambitions to leadership, Khrushchev is now proceeding with the removal of all fictitious "liberties"; he even liquidates Bulganin. The trend toward so-called national communism in the satellite countries is being eradicated and Tito-like concepts of a Communist "bloc" of equals are rejected. Other roads toward socialism are rejected and all Communists are reminded that Moscow is the only "Mecca" of Communism, and there is no other equal to Moscow. Khrushchev's new and fanatical ambition is to neutralize the United States in order to gain freedom of movement for the subjugation of Indonesia, the Arab States, India, Free China, and others, as well as for further efforts in the fight with the liberation movement in countries already subjugated.

The National Liberation Struggle
against Russian Imperialism and Communism Today

When it became obvious to the leading active forces of the national revolutionary movements after World War II that the policy of the USA and of the other major Western powers was directed towards a peaceful settlement and was not in the least disposed to consider seriously the question of supporting the national fight for freedom of the nations subjugated by Russia, a change took place in the fighting methods of these liberation movements. In place of the strategy and tactics of armed insurrection, underground tactics and an underground resistance on a broad front, in the political, economic, cultural and religious fields, were adopted and these were supplemented by armed action within certain limits and of a purely defensive nature as in Ukraine. The OUN, the UPA, and the UHVR concentrated their activity in Ukraine—and similar liberation organizations of other peoples did the same in their lands—on the intensification and extension of the fight in all spheres of life and among all social groups in order to combat the enemy in all fields of national life with all the forces available. Underground propaganda, underground publications—political, educational, and even literary (including the collected works of the underground poets), journals for youth and for children—all this is preparing the people for a long-range fight for a long-range goal. Propaganda was disseminated in the ranks of the Soviet Army in order to undermine its strength and morale from within, to aggravate its internal conflicts, and, finally, to cause it to disintegrate into its national elements. Further features of this underground activity were: resistance to collectivization, economic sabotage, and a constant fight for private property for the farmers; support in Ukraine for the two catacomb churches— the Ukrainian Catholic Church and the Ukrainian Autocephalous Orthodox Church, for influence on the legal forms of cultural activity, resistance against forcible Russification, moral, psychological, and political training, and preparation of the masses for an insurrection. In addition, deportations to Siberian concentration camps and to Kazakhstan were used in order to form new resistance centers there, for the purpose of destroying the Soviet Russian peoples' prison and the Communist system from within. The riots of the Ukrainian and other non-Russian prisoners in Norylsk (June 1953), in Vorkuta (July 1953), in Kingiri (Kazakhstan, June 1954), in Mordovia (September 1955), and in Tachet (1956) are known to the whole world.

Thus, on principle, the internal contradictions in the Soviet system are utilized to bring about its disintegration, as can be seen from the fact that deportations to Siberia, which was formerly the safest center of Soviet industry, are now taking an unfavorable turn for Moscow's tyrants inasmuch as they are in this way now helping to undermine Siberia's industry and are making Moscow's strategic position more complicated; but Moscow can see no way out of its difficulties.

Armed political action is now entirely subordinated to expediency, and not, as was formerly the case, strategic rather than defensive. The long-range task of this action consists in expanding and protecting the political revolutionary underground organization and the smaller, armed auxiliary units, which, if necessary, could develop into an important political, revolutionary, and military force.

Because the revolutionary organizations for national liberation feel that they have been sadly disappointed by the West, they are working systematically on the fulfilment of a plan for a simultaneous and coordinated anti-imperialistic and anti-Communist revolution for national liberation in all countries and in the concentration camps. Moscow's policy of dispersing the best elements of every non-Russian nation is taking a dangerous turn for Moscow itself; for in the new regions to which they are sent, these rebellious elements are rousing the indifferent and are strengthening the faith of the hesitant; they are the yeast which is helping the national and social resistance to grow and which is systematically guiding it in the right direction.

The idea of a common anti-imperialistic and anti-Communist front of all the subjugated nations is thus assuming a real form—that of a planned, systematic, consistent, and continuous preparation for the disintegration of the Bolshevik empire from within and for its partition into independent national states, each with a democratic constitution. The ideological, political, psychological, and ethical revolution is taking place in all social groups of the peoples subjugated by Russia, and people are becoming more and more aware of the fact that there can be no social revolution without a national political revolution, no freedom for a subjugated nation without self-government, no overthrow of Communism without the collapse of the empire, which at present exists in Communist form for subjugation of the individual, for a universal collectivization of life, for an absolute state omnipotence, for totalitarianism, and through the concomitant, complete enslavement of the individual for the enslavement of the entire nation. The national liberation revolution is the national liberation war of the subjugated peoples against the foreign conquerer—against Russia!

The confidence of the subjugated nations in the West has been sadly shaken since Hungary was abandoned to Russian tanks. Synchronized and coordinated anti-imperialist and anti-Communist revolutions for national liberation—such is the conception of liberation held by the subjugated nations today. To what extent such revolutions can be successful without help from the West is a question the leaders of the West must answer before God and history—and, in this connection, it must be borne in mind that Bolshevism is as great a danger for the West as it is for our nations.

To quote a typical example: the revolutionary detachments for national liberation which in Ukraine waged a two-front war against both Nazi Germany and Soviet Russia—the OUN, the UPA, the UHVR, the underground governments of Ukraine which opposed the Kyiv government, and the ABN, which was founded on the initiative of the UPA in the forests of Ukraine in 1943, during the two-front war, and which united the uncompromising and sovereign organizations of the subjugated nations—are ignored by certain circles in the USA, in spite of the fact that they play a very significant part in the anti-Bolshevik campaign. The Communist gangs and the sham government of Ho Chi Minh, for instance, were, it is true, not recognized by the West, but they were acknowledged as "lawful" by the USSR, while at the time of the greatest military action of the UPA not a single Western state made the least effort to recognize either the UPA (on the strength of The Hague Convention of 1899 and 1907, par. 1 and 2) as a belligerent army, or the UHVR as an independent Ukrainian government which opposed the same government of Kyiv—even though this government relied on its own fighting strength and operated on its own native soil.

A similar situation in the fight for freedom also exists in other subjugated countries, in Turkestan, Caucasia, Byelorussia (White Ruthenia), Lithuania, Estonia, Bulgaria, Czechia, Cossackia, Latvia, Albania, and many others—not to mention the magnificent example of Hungary.

It is by no means a coincidence that the propaganda of the Kremlin constantly stresses the "friendship of the peoples in the USSR," which, according to Lenin, should be cherished like the apple of one's eye. It is obvious that there is something wrong with this "friendship of the peoples" and that it is precisely the *national problem* which is the vulnerable spot of the Russian empire and of Bolshevism; and it is precisely on this problem that the liberation policy of the USA should concentrate.

The nationalism of the subjugated nations which aims at the liberation of peoples is the key to the destruction of the Russian empire and of Communism. And this nationalism has remained invincible.

Although deeply and bitterly disappointed in the West's inaction and indifference to their plight, the enslaved peoples inside the Iron Curtain are keeping their spirit of resistance high and are not wavering from their anti-Communist position. The brutal policies of Moscow which rely on mass deportations to Siberia have proved ineffective, because these recalcitrant peoples spread seeds of discontent and rebellion wherever they go.

The ideal of a common cause of all the nations enslaved by Russia has taken root behind the Iron Curtain and no form of Russian tyranny can ever destroy it.

The Soviet Russian system has failed and continues to exist only because it is supported by Russian bayonets. The case of Hungary in the fall of 1956 bears this out most eloquently.

ABN Correspondence,
May-June 1959, pp. 7-8

What and How?

For the goal of liberation of the nations enslaved by Russia to have any chance of success, the Western action directed against Bolshevism will have to develop along different lines from those followed up to now. It will have to be based on different political principles, different military and political strategy, and will have to take into account the decisive factor—the enslaved nations in the USSR.

As regards the West's policy towards the Soviet Russian empire, there are two possibilities: one, the entire system of Western policy will be basically altered in the sense of a total negation of Bolshevism and the Russian empire—the latter's complete isolation, rupture of every connection with it, its expulsion from the United Nations, with the intensification of a consistent diplomatic pressure and blockade of the Russian Communist bloc and the simultaneous universal support of the national liberation struggle of the subjugated nations. This pre-supposes taking a decision to help, if necessary, national liberation revolutions militarily in order to disrupt the present Soviet Russian empire from within. The other possibility is the present policy of hesitation and half-measures.

The primary objective of Western policy, in my opinion, should be to bring about a total coordination of political and military action of the Free World with the national-liberation, revolutionary formations behind the Iron Curtain. In this respect cooperation between the relevant circles of the West, particularly the United States, with the national liberation movement's representatives in exile, who have never been tainted with collaboration with Bolshevism and who are fighting for the cause of splitting up the Russian empire, is a necessity. The principal aim should be a synchronized and concerted action of the two sides, not only in the political, but also in the strategic and military spheres.

In case a war should break out, the Free World ought to concentrate its military action against Russian ethnographic territory. In such a situation the subjugated nations, such as Ukraine, Poland, Hungary, Turkestan, or the Caucasus, will be able to deal on their own with the Russian occupation troops stationed in their territories. With the help of the national uprisings, supported by the West, it would be possible to cut off the Russian troops in Central and part of Eastern Europe from their bases.

Without systematic support of the revolutionary movements behind the Iron Curtain on the part of the West, it would be unwise to expect a sudden explosion there In order to bring about a collapse of the Russian threat the West ought to render every possible political support to the revolutionary liberation organizations of the non-Russian nations. Nor should technical and material support be lacking. A close contact should be established between the revolutionary underground and the Free World through the national liberation movement's representatives in exile. Moscow has at its service fifth columns and Communist parties all over the world and renders them support and acknowledges them quite openly. The United States and the Free World have true friends and partners in all peoples behind the Iron Curtain, but, unfortunately, do not recognize them! Russia predicts a victory of Communism in the entire world and openly propagates it, while the West is afraid to hint, for example, that the independence of Ukraine and of the other peoples enslaved by Moscow lies in its own interests. Khrushchev interferes quite blatantly in the internal affairs of free and sovereign nations. Where is the Western statesmen who would ask frankly why there is no independent Ukraine, Byelorussia, Turkestan, Georgia, Armenia, Azerbaidzhan, etc.? This is not a question of interference in the internal affairs of a foreign power, because the problem concerns the restoration of independence to nations whose sovereignty has been internationally recognized, some of whom even today are members of the United Nations! The West lacks courage enough to urge, even on the basis of the UN Charter, the independence of Ukraine and Byelorussia. Can there be any offensive policy of liberation when even the UN, which Russia belongs to, is interpreted to the latter's full advantage?

The West has to draw practical conclusions for the liberation action from the fact that the Soviet Army is composed of soldiers of various nationalities, and it has to find ways and means to attract them, by a corresponding propaganda action from outside and from within, to participate in the revolutionary activity aimed at liberation.

In our view the Russian Bolshevik empire should be encircled by offensive centers of action in all the countries adjacent to its sphere of domination in Europe as well as in the Near, Middle, and Far East. In this work political formations of the national liberation movements of the subjugated nations, which are active in exile and which so far have not been taken into consideration for these purposes, should be included. However, it must be brought out that not the people of the past, not those who have linked their names with the Bolsheviks and have been discredited among their nations, not the opportunists who are willing to sell their services for money, not those who lack the courage to defend their convictions, not the political agents, but the free political partners of the West should be listened to. Such people ought to be given the use of radio stations in order to broadcast in their nation's interests, without being obliged to submit to a political line dictated from above. They ought to be given the opportunity to maintain contacts with the underground movements within their nations in the home countries. Through them the underground movements should receive every support and their opinions should be heard even if they are sometimes bitter. The situation and the needs of the nations among which they have grown up as revolutionaries are known better by such people than by any outside agencies.

By the political content of their programs and by the composition of their personnel, neither Radio Liberty nor Radio Free Europe, as the alleged spokesmen of the subjugated nations, correspond to the desires and aspirations of the enslaved peoples. The American Committee for Liberation from Bolshevism is conducting a policy which runs counter to the interest of the nations enslaved in the USSR. Likewise the political line of The Institute for the Study of Culture and History of the USSR, with headquarters in Munich, is alien to the enslaved nations.

The anti-Communist action in the Near and Middle East should have been carried out directly by the political representatives of the nations subjugated behind the Iron Curtain, for the simple reason that they know the situation and would have more easily gained the confidence of the local population—as, for instance, if it had been conducted among Moslems by a nationalist Moslem from behind the Iron Curtain who is now in exile. The ABN is prepared to undertake such an action, because it has within its ranks some prominent representatives of Islam. This can be done on the condition that the ABN be free to carry out its propaganda activities, including radio broadcasts, in accordance with its political program with regard to the captive nations behind the Iron Curtain. It would be worthwhile for the West to try this approach, and we are convinced that, after some time, they would realize how much greater repercussions the actions of the ABN would cause in the Russian empire, compared with the activities of the so-called American Committee for Liberation from Bolshevism, Radio Liberty, Radio Free Europe, etc. Moscow incessantly attacks the nationalism of the subjugated peoples; it is the force which is most dangerous to its dominance. Why is the West reluctant to use this powerful weapon against Russia?

Siberia is inhabited by millions of non-Russians who have come there as deportees, settlers, concentration camp prisoners, soldiers of the Soviet Army. In the Maritime Provinces (the so-called "Green Wedge") in the vicinity of Vladivostok, bordering on Korea, Ukrainians predominate. A similar situation prevails in the so-called "Gray Wedge" in the south of West Siberia. In the Far Eastern countries, particularly in Korea, it would be extremely advisable to establish special centers for the penetration of this area with the help of radio propaganda, literature, etc., and in general to work out a military parachute drop in Siberia in case of an armed clash. In planning these measures the emigrants from Ukraine as well as from other enslaved countries now settled in Australia should be taken into account, for Australia occupies a prominent position as regards anti-Communist action in the Far East. To support the idea of Siberian independence would be in the interest of the United States, with the aim of eliminating Russia from the Far East. Siberia borders—across the Bering Strait—on Alaska, the United States. From Taiwan, where an ABN mission is located and supported exclusively by the modest means of the Ukrainian emigrants, propaganda action can be carried out behind the Iron Curtain, not only by means of radio but also by printed propaganda. Pakistan lies near the border of Turkestan (USSR) and from there too penetration of ideas, as well as technical penetration, is possible. In Kazakhstan there are hundreds of thousands of deportees, mostly Ukrainians, some of whom belong to the most reliable anti-Russian underground.

In Turkey, too, a reservoir of people who would be able to penetrate the regions of the USSR, especially Ukraine and the Caucasus, can be built up. This reservoir, in case of war, can play a particularly important role.

In Berlin an ABN center can also be established. It would have the task of disrupting the Soviet Army as well as manning a radio station of the ABN.

The Russian policy of deportation and dispersion of the best elements from among the enslaved nations should be answered by an idea, an idea which would unite all these fighters in a common front, so that, wherever they come in contact with other non-Russians who fight for their national independence, they fight united against their common enemy, Russia and Communism. The political concept of the ABN provides a suitable solution to this problem. This is a concept of envisaging a common revolution which should bring about the collapse of the Russian empire and the establishment of national democratic independent states.

The universal attack by Russia ought to be answered by a correspondingly universal counterattack. Within the broad plan of the encirclement of the Russian empire and its Communist allies, such as Red China, North Korea, North Vietnam, the task of building up a revolutionary force on the territories of the enslaved peoples, such as Ukraine, the Caucasus, Turkestan, Bulgaria, Hungary, etc., should be placed in the foreground, and to these countries the activities should be directed. On this score, so far, nothing serious has been done on the part of the United States. The activities of the American Committee for Liberation from Bolshevism, Radio Liberty, or Radio Free Europe cannot be considered seriously, for they, as a rule, lavishly adjust their policy to every tactical need of official circles. The policy of liberation cannot be directed by factors of monetary expediency, but should be conducted systematically in a planned fashion, taking into account the situation and the demands in the subjugated countries. It has to be determined by the national liberation centers and organizations of the subjugated nations and coordinated with the competent circles of the Free World, provided that the latter recognize their aims and principles

The United States and the Free World are, unfortunately, doing exceedingly little for the mobilization of the internal forces of resistance of the enslaved peoples. At the same time the work of the fifth columns, the Communist parties, and the entire subversive machinery of Moscow in the Free World is carried out systematically and is directed from a single center. Moreover, the attitude of the United States to the objectives of the struggle of the subjugated nations is far from certain. A "non-predetermination" policy propagated by the American Committee for Liberation from Bolshevism, or the evidence of cooperation with and support of some Bolshevik collaborators as well as the policy of fighting Marxism with Marxism and the Red Russian empire with the concept of another Russian empire of a "White" type, cannot satisfy the aspirations of the enslaved nations.

In the Middle East, in Asia and Africa, Communism is wary of using its usual slogans. Instead it makes use of national revolutionary and anti-feudal slogans which have nothing in common with Communism as a doctrine. In their strategy, however, the Communists keep to one principle: "bourgeois" reforms must be introduced and carried out by them, for they hope thus to get themselves into power. Once there, they begin to introduce the Communist system, total collectivization and centralization, and, remaining true servants of Moscow, they subordinate their country to the Kremlin. Communism in Asia ought to be unmasked as an instrument of Russian colonialism and imperialism. This, unfortunately, is neglected. The distribution of the feudal estates for private ownership among the working peasants, propagated by the Communists, is not a Communist slogan. Similarly, the idea of national independence, and the liberation of the colonial or dependent countries are not Communist, but national slogans. To oppose these slogans would be unwise. What is necessary, however, is to unveil what goes on behind the stage, to show that this is an intrigue of Russian colonialism and imperialism, which is a relatively easy matter, because, to give an example, the democratic slogans being as noble as they are, the colonial peoples reject colonialism and imperialism on the part of the democratic great powers.

The connection between Russian colonialism and Communism is evident. It is incomprehensible why the West takes every care to avoid unmasking this connection. Instead it fights a fiction, so-called "international Communism," which, deprived of the support of Russian bayonets, would have survived as just another doctrine, like anarchism.

This function of unmasking Communism in these areas could very well be fulfilled by the representatives of the nations enslaved in the USSR and, in general, by the representatives of the peoples subjugated by Russia and Communism, if the United States on its part would show a more favorable attitude to the cause of national liberation and would support actively the liberation struggle of the subjugated nations.

The World Anti-Communist Congress for Freedom and Liberation is particularly timely. A preparatory conference was held in Mexico City in March 1958. Representatives of anti-Communist organizations from various parts of the world were present, representing sixty-five nations in all. Among them were: the APACL, the Inter-American Confederation for the Defense of the Continent (Latin America), the ABN, and other well-known anti-Communist organizations. This effort should be given full and enthusiastic support by the United States and other free countries of the world.

The Ukrainian Review,
No. III, 1959, pp. 6-11

I Accuse Khrushchev of Mass Murder of the Ukrainian People

> "Three-quarters of mankind may
> perish so that the rest may
> experience Communism!"
>
> —Lenin

The Ukrainian Attempt to Use the German Campaign in the East to Advantage for the Restoration of an Independent Ukrainian State

For centuries Russia was the deadly enemy of Ukraine. After the unfortunate battle of Poltava in 1709, in which the head of the Ukrainian state, Hetman Ivan Mazepa, together with his ally King Charles XII of Sweden, was defeated by the huge armies of the Russian Tsar Peter I, Russia restricted the rights of the Ukrainian people to an ever-increasing extent until eventually Ukrainian was even prohibited as a written language. Again and again the Ukrainians revolted, until in 1917-18 they succeeded in regaining their independence for a short time. As a people oriented to the West with a thousand-year-old national culture, history, and state tradition, the Ukrainians constantly hoped for the support of the Occident in their fight against the Russian-Eurasian "urge towards the West," all the more so since they were convinced that with the restoration of the Ukrainian state, with its population of over 50 million, Russia's pressure on Western Europe would be broken for good. As Germany at that time was the only anti-Russian power, the Ukrainians took this objective fact into account in their liberation plans.

After the Ukrainians realized that the Western allies had no intention of relying on the fight for freedom of all the peoples subjugated by totalitarianism (both Nazi and Soviet Russian), in the future campaign against Hitler, they sought to use the German-Soviet war to advantage for their own interests—that is to say, for their national state independence. On June 23, 1941, the leaders of the OUN handed the German Government a memorandum which not only clearly formulated the principles for possible cooperation but also contained certain warnings if the German war aims in the East should not be in keeping with the Ukrainian ideal of freedom.

This memorandum contained the following statement:

> Even if the Germans on entering Ukraine are naturally welcomed there as liberators, this attitude may soon change if Germany does not enter Ukraine with the aim of restoring the Ukrainian state and with the appropriate concepts in mind. A new order in Europe is unthinkable without an independent national Ukrainian state. For centuries the Ukrainians have revealed their infinite love for freedom. It is this urge for independence, this fighting spirit, and an attitude of constant defense against foreign influence that have created the typical Ukrainian as he is today— namely an individual who adopts an attitude of distrust and opposition to all foreigners....

It was further stressed in the OUN memorandum that a military occupation in East Europe would eventually prove untenable, and the Hitler Government was warned against pursuing occupation policy based on violence and disregard of the national rights of the East European peoples. The memorandum then added:

> The Ukrainian military powers will have to defend the East European continental front when Ukraine, released from its two-front war, is able to use its entire military potential against Russia. An independent Ukrainian military power, which would be in keeping with the mental attitude of the Ukrainians, will put a stop to Russian pressure on Europe.

It was clearly emphasized in the memorandum that Ukraine would not conduct a war against the Western allies but solely against Soviet Russia.

The Organization of Ukrainian Nationalists systematically organized its cadres for the independent revolutionary fight for freedom (training in Ukraine and abroad), in order to use these cadres independently of the Eastern policy of the German Reich. The main factor of the liberation campaign of the OUN was thus not reliance on foreign support but on one's own forces, on a Ukrainian insurgent army, and on the national revolution of all the peoples subjugated by Russia. And it was this same idea which prompted the intention of not letting soldiers of Ukrainian nationality in the Red Army fall into the hands of the German troops but instead making them members of a Ukrainian insurgent army before they were taken prisoner.

The Ukrainian Legion

Quite apart from all this, however, the decision was also reached to form a Ukrainian legion within the German army, for the following reasons: on the one hand, relations with pro-Ukrainian German Supreme Command circles would in this way be strengthened and activated politically and, on the other hand, the legion would under favorable circumstances fulfill the role of a collecting point for prisoners-of-war and deserters of Ukrainian nationality. Should it transpire that the German policy in the East did not intend to effect a disintegration of the Russian empire into independent national states and thus oppose the vital interests of the Ukrainian people, the Ukrainian legion might then play an extremely important part in turning the active Ukrainian national revolutionary groups into a regular army (a measure which was to a certain extent carried out later in 1943).

Neither Churchill nor Eden became quislings when they made a military alliance with Soviet Russia in order to defend their own country against Hitler's advance; why then should the Ukrainian partner have acted differently when there was still a prospect of helping Ukraine to regain its national state independence with Germany's support? Surely the Ukrainians were not in any way to blame for the fact that Hitler's policy with regard to the East later turned out to be completely mad!

Prof. Theodor Oberländer, Prof. Hans Koch, and Prof. Georg Gerullis, who at that time belonged to the German Supreme Command as reserve officers, conducted the negotiations and completely agreed with the Ukrainian political aims. In an arrangement agreed upon, the following points were stipulated:

1) The Ukrainian Legion is a unit which was formed to fight for the Ukrainian state;

2) The legion swore allegiance to the Ukrainian State but not to Germany and not to Hitler as the latter's representative; accordingly, the political training of the soldiers in absolute loyalty to Ukrainian political aims would be guaranteed;

3) The legion would be commanded by Ukrainian officers; the German officers would only be in charge of the general supervision. Every day military training would begin with the hoisting of the Ukrainian flag and would end with the singing of the Ukrainian patriotic prayer. German political or ideological subjects of instruction would not be included at all in the curriculum of training.

A few days after the outbreak of the war the Ukrainian Legion was used in active service, and on June 30th it entered the capital of Western Ukraine, Lemberg (Lviv). Joyously and hopefully, the people of the town welcomed the Ukrainian soldiers of the "Nightingale" Legion and the German troops. The fact that the Ukrainian Legion had been incorporated into the German army was regarded by the population as a sign of Germany's friendship in the Ukrainian fight for freedom.

When Hitler's government revealed its true intentions as regards Ukraine by its policy, Captain Roman Shukhevych, the Ukrainian commander of the "Nightingale" Legion, which at that time was stationed in Vinnytsa, decided to send a memorandum to the German Supreme Command in which he stressed that under the given circumstances the legion did not feel that it could continue to fight on the German side.

On August 28, 1941, the German Supreme Command replied that the "Nightingale" Legion was to be withdrawn from the fighting front. It was then transferred to Neuhammer (in Germany). The same thing happened to the "Roland" Legion, which was operating in South Ukraine. On September 15, 1941, the two legions addressed a memorandum to the German Supreme Command in Berlin. It was signed by every soldier and contained the following demands:

1) Independence for the Ukrainian State, which was to be subsequently recognized by Germany;

2) All Ukrainian political prisoners, headed by Stepan Bandera, and all the members of the Government in Lemberg, headed by Yaroslav Stetsko, were to be released from custody;

3) The legion was only to be used for active service on the Eastern Front and on Ukrainian territory;

4) The legion was to be led exclusively by Ukrainian officers; the duties and rights of the Ukrainian officers were to be equal to those of the German officers;

5) The relatives of soldiers who had been arrested were to be released from custody and were to have the same rights as the Germans;

6) The soldiers of the legion must not be expected to swear allegiance to Germany;

7) The legion would be prepared under these circumstances and preconditions to sign a contract of service for one year, which contract would be signed by each soldier in his own name;

By way of answer the legion was moved to Frankfurt on the Oder. On November 1st a reply to the memorandum was received from the German Supreme Command. It declared that it was not competent to deal with political demands. As regards the other points in the memorandum it was stated: "The legion is only to be used for active service on the Eastern Front: an additional oath of allegiance to Germany need not be sworn"; other demands were also agreed to.

Although the political points of the memorandum were not dealt with, the members of the legion nevertheless decided to sign the contract of service, since they foresaw the necessity of an armed fight against Hitlerite Germany and at the same time against Russia; a thorough training of a military character in practical service in the Germany army would be of decisive importance in the future fight for freedom.

After a year of fighting against Red partisans in Byelorussia, in the course of which the legion won the friendship of the Byelorussian population and full recognition on the part of the German army command, all the legionnaires on October 31, 1942, rejected the German suggestion to renew the contract of service; the legion was disbanded, the officers of the legion were arrested by the Gestapo, and all the non-commissioned officers and soldiers were placed under police surveillance. Captain Shukhevych, who had already been arrested prior to this date, escaped during transport and a few months later became the commander-in-chief of the UPA under the name of Taras Chuprynka.

Practically all the legionnaires went over to the UPA, where they immediately assumed important posts. In the course of time the UPA developed into a large army, 200,000 strong (a fact which was even corroborated by German sources at that time).

The Ukrainian Two-Front War against Soviet Russia and Hitlerite Germany Developed on a Large Scale

In the fight against the UPA under the command of General Taras Chuprynka, the Chief of the Nazi Sturm Abteilung (S.A.), Viktor Lutze, was killed in May 1943, near Kovel; on March 20, 1944, the Soviet Marshal Vatutin was killed in North Volhynia; on May 3, 1946, Colonel General Moskalenko of the NKVD was killed in the neighborhood of Stanislav; on March 28, 1947, the Polish Vice-Minister of Defense, General Walter Swierczewski, was killed; on May 12, 1947, the USSR, Poland and Czechoslovakia signed a tripartite agreement to combat the UPA—so great and dangerous did the power of the Ukrainian Insurgent Army seem to Soviet Russia.

(From the report of the U.S. Congress Committee of December 31, 1954, Rep. No. 2684, part 7, Congressman Kersten's Report, p. 31.)

The Discoveries Made by the "Nightingale" Legion in Lviv on June 30, 1941

In a special edition we published accurate reports of the mass murders of Ukrainian political prisoners by the NKVD committed in Lviv prior to the entry of the German troops. Numerous witnesses who have survived and who were in Lviv prisons at that time, as well as other trustworthy persons, reported at length on these atrocities committed by the Bolshevik criminals. We also included the testimony of the Ukrainian Greek Catholic Metropolitan, Archbishop Count Andreas Sheptytsky, who mentioned as many as 6,000 murdered persons in one prison alone and definitely accused the Russians of having committed these atrocities. The great Patriarch of the Ukrainian Church and the greatest moral authority for 45 million Ukrainians accused the Soviet Russian NKVD units of the mass murders in Lviv and other towns in Ukraine. There is no one in the Free World who would doubt the accusations made by the aged Patriarch of the Ukrainian people, who is soon to be canonized by the Apostolic See, or who would question the truth of his words. For he is the man who, during the Soviet Russian occupation of Ukraine, had the courage to ask the Pope to give him his apostolic blessing and send him to a martyr's death for the faith and unity of the Church. "The Church has nothing to lose by this: it can only gain by such a step; as the spiritual father of the poor people who are obliged to endure so much suffering, have I not the right to die for their sake?" And he also had the courage to intercede with Hitler himself for the persecuted Jews, a fact on which Rabbi Dr. Herzog in Palestine commented as follows:

> When the Germans carred out a pogram against the Jews in Rohatyn, Metropolitan Sheptytsky addressed a petition to Himmler in which he emphatically objected to the murder of innocent and defenseless persons. This action on his part caused a considerable sensation for it was definite proof of his great courage. There was no one in Europe at that time who ventured to openly support the Jews against the ruthless Gestapo. *And the entire Ukrainian people took his action as an example and helped the persecuted Jews in every way possible, and, at risk to their own lives, frequently hid them in their own houses, a measure which was prohibited under penalty of death. It must also be pointed out in this connection that the Ukrainians themselves had to endure great suffering and hardships under the terrorism of the Gestapo.*

When the Ukrainian Insurgent Army (UPA) defended the rights of the Ukrainians, Himmler requested the Metropolitan on the strength of his authority to inform the Ukrainian Insurgent Army that their activity was a violation of the Fifth Commandment. To which the Metropolitan replied: "The National Socialists do not believe in God and hence have no right to refer to God's Commandments!" When Himmler thereupon answered that for every German or every person of German descent who was shot, twenty Ukrainians were to be shot, the Metropolitan addressed a sharp pastoral letter to the occupation army in which, among other things, he declared: "God will punish those who disregard His Divine laws!" If the Metropolitan showed such courage in censuring the crimes of the Gestapo, he would most certainly not conceal any of the mass murders which, so it is alleged, German units committed when they entered Lviv. *On the other hand, however, the Metropolitan, in keeping with the true facts, accused the Soviet Russian NKVD units and held them responsible for the mass murders in Lviv—murders which the Russians, in a mendacious and defamatory manner, are trying to blame on the "Nightingale" unit and Prof. Oberländer.*

The Soviet Russians, incidentally, contradict themselves in their accusations against the "Nightingale" unit and accusations against Prof. Oberländer.

The *Krasnaya Zvezda* (the official organ of the Ministry of Defense in Moscow) of October 20, 1959, *Radianska Ukrayina* of October 21, 1959, and *Komsomolskaya Pravda* of October 22 and 25, 1959, accuse the "Nightingale" battalion and Prof. Oberländer of murdering over 310,000 persons in the district of Lviv; they insinuate that Bandera was in command of the "Nightingale" and was in Lviv together with Prof. Oberländer. Bandera is supposed to have known certain secret details about Oberländer's alleged crimes and for this reason was murdered at Oberländer's instructions. Actually, Bandera was not in Lviv at the time, but in Cracow, where he was under the surveillance of the Gestapo. He had already been arrested on July 5th and taken to Berlin. He was never a soldier, nor did he ever command the "Nightingale." The Ukrainian commander of the "Nightingale" was Roman Shukhevych, who found the body of his brother in a Lviv prison among the corpses of the persons murdered by the NKVD, a fact which became generally known.

The shameless manner in which the Soviet Russians lie can also be seen with regard to another point mentioned in *Krasnaya Zvzda*, which, among other things, accuses Bandera of having "joined the service of Nazi espionage as early as 1936 under the name 'the grey man' [Siry]." The actual truth is that from June 1934 onwards Bandera was in the worst Polish prison, the Swiety Krzyz, to which he had been sentenced to life imprisonment on account of his revolutionary activity.

Only fools believe the Kremlin liars!

The fact must also be mentioned that the "Nightingale" legion was organized by opposition circles of the German Supreme Command, including Canaris, who naturally did not set up this legion in conjunction with the German army for Himmler's purposes, but with the intention of supporting the Ukrainian independence aims.

The Case of the Polish Professors

The Soviet Russians are now blaming the "Nightingale" legion and Professor Theodor Oberländer for the murder of the Polish professors in Lviv, in spite of the fact that the Soviet Russians themselves recently accused not the German army but, quite definitly, the Gestapo of having committed these murders. The Russians trip up on their own lies and defamations.

We should like to quote from the previous accusations made by the Soviet

Russians as quoted (in the Polish periodical *Kultura*, Paris, No. 1/147-2/148, p. 176, 1960):

> ...The case of the professors who were shot in Lviv also caused a sensation in the Nuremberg trials. In the collection of documents on the Nuremberg trials, published in several volumes in the Soviet Union, we find a precise report on pages 243-245 of volume 3: "At the orders of the Reich Government, the Gestapo authorities, prior to the capture of Lemberg, made a list of all the leading members of the intelligentsia who were to be liquidated.... [A list containing the names of thirty-eight professors in Lemberg is then given.] Immediately after the capture of the town of Lviv, mass arrests and executions were carried out. The Gestapo arrested...."
>
> "On February 15, 1946, during the afternoon session of the Nuremberg tribunal, the Soviet prosecutor Smirnov read out testimony by Prof. Groer of the Faculty of Medicine at Lviv University, who escaped death only by a stroke of luck, in which testimony Prof. Groer definitely states that the Gestapo arrested and ill-treated Polish professors on July 3, 1941, and in this connection mentions his own case and that of Prof. Bartel.
>
> There is no mention of any army unit or of the "Nightingale." Thus, during the Nuremberg trials no one accused Prof. Oberländer or the "Nightingale" battalion of these crimes.... Prof. Sosnicki told me in the winter of 1941/42 that some of the families of the professors had received an official confirmation to the effect that their husbands or fathers had been shot on the strength of a special order by the security headquarters.

In a pamphlet published by the Bolsheviks under the title *Pidchuzhmy propa roa my* ("Under Foreign Flags"), the security service units are likewise held responsible for these murders and no mention whatever is made of the "Nightingale" in this connection.

Incidentally, Himmler organized special security police units and security service units which were designed as "action groups" and divided into "action commandos, special commandos, and part commandos." They were intended to be used for the so-called pacification of the occupied East territories. In sections 2b, 4, and 5 of the directives for special regions in connection with Regulation 21 (the "Barbarossa Case"), the army was informed of Himmler's independent action as regards the security service (of March 13, 1941) as follows:

> 2b) In the theater of operations of the army the Reich Leader of the SS, in order to prepare the political administration, has, on the orders of the Führer, been entrusted with special tasks, which arise out of the fight that must ultimately be fought between two opposite political systems. As far as these tasks are concerned, the Reich Leader of the SS is acting independently and on his own responsibility.
>
> In the rear theaters of operations of the army the action groups and commandos had only subordinated to the field army in so far as service with the troops was concerned, but as regards commands and their scope they were under the RSHA [Reichssicherheitshauptamt].

This was the declaration under oath by Lieutenant-General Heusinger, Chief of the Operations Section of the German Supreme Command, on February 1, 1945.

The entire police force depended exclusively on Himmler. The action groups which operated in West Ukraine were under the command of the higher-ranking SS and police leader Korsemann. Otto Ohlendorf, commander of the Action Group D, declared under oath: "As Chief of the Security Service, Section 3, of the head department of the security police and of the security service (RSHA), I declare that the action groups and action commandos were led by the personnel of the Gestapo, of the Security Service, and of the criminal investigation police."

It is thus obvious to everyone who is unbiased that the liquidations were carried out not by army formations, but by security police and security service units; and in the case of the Polish professors in Lviv, too, there can be no question of the murders having been carried out by army units.

Furthermore, there appeared in the Polish daily published in London, *Dziennik Polski*, of August 18, 1958, a letter by a Mrs. W. L. Chomsowa of London, who was in contact with the family of Prof. Bartel from the outbreak of the war until January 1944. She writes that Prof. Bartel was shot on July 22, 1941, by personal order of the Reich Leader of the SS, Himmler. At that time, the "Nightingale" and Prof. Oberländer had for the past sixteen days been hundreds of kilometers away from Lviv in the east. At that time there was a special SS commando unit under Eberhard Schöngard and Heinz Heim, which had come to Lviv via Rudky. These two Gestapo officers were responsible for the physical liquidation of the Polish professors and for the political liquidation of the Ukrainian National Government.

It is likewise obvious beyond all doubt to anyone who is unbiased that—as the Swedish, Swiss, Portuguese, and American press reported in this connection—the mass murders of the political prisoners in the Lviv prisons were carried out by the NKVD at the personal orders of Khrushchev, the First Secretary of the Communist Party of Ukraine at that time and Stalin's governor there, before the Germans entered the town.

We hardly venture to put a rhetorical question: why should the Ukrainian nationalists of the "Nightingale" have committed mass murders against the other Ukrainian nationalists in the Lviv prisons; and why should Roman Shukhevych have murdered his own brother, whose decomposed body he found among the corpses of those who had been murdered?!

Such shameless defamations and lies can only be invented by the criminal minds of the Kremlin murderers.

Why should the Ukrainians shoot the Polish professors and thus open an additional and third front at a time when they already had Soviet Russia and Hitlerite Germany as their enemies?! It was, on the other hand, precisely in the interests of Ukraine to form a joint front with all the subjugated peoples against the oppressors, a fact which is explicitly stated in the political resolutions of the OUN conferences and congresses.

In an article entitled "Oberländer from Berlin's Perspective," which was published in the Polish periodical *Kultura* (No. 3, 1960, p. 138), a statement by the Polish professor Sokolnicki, who still lectures at the Technical College in Soviet-occupied Lviv, is quoted. In this statement he quite plainly and definitely holds the Gestapo responsible for the murder of Prof. Bartel and the other Polish professors, and blames neither the Ukrainian nationalists of the "Nightingale" battalion nor the German army for these murders.

It is obvious to any objective-minded person from the gross contradictions in the Soviet sources that have been published at various times that the Soviet Russian accusations are based on lies.

The Neutral Press on the Russian Mass Murders in Lviv in 1941

The Ukrainian socialist periodical *Vilna Ukrayina* ("Free Ukraine", No. 25/1960, Detroit) definitely accuses the Soviet Russians of having committed the mass murders in Lviv in June 1941. It also quotes the Swiss paper *Die Tat* of July 6, 1941, which contained the following comments:

> When the Soviet Russians were no longer in a position to assert themselves in Lviv, the NKVD, prior to its flight, carried out a terrible massacre of innocent prisoners. According to the reports of neutral press correspondents, this massacre is one of the most dreadful and ruthless massacres ever heard of in the history of the world. In the police prison twenty prisoners were crowded together in each of the smallest cells; they were then shot through the spy holes. Two thousand to twenty-five hundred persons were murdered in this way.

On July 7, 1941, the *Stockholms Tidnigne* wrote as follows:

> Prior to their retreat the Russians, giving vent to their hatred a last time, carried out mass murders with inhuman brutality in many of the prisons. Shortly before they retreated, they set fire to Brygidky prison. In the cellars the Communists stacked up the corpses of the murdered like blocks of wood. On each layer of corpses they strewed sand so thickly that one could walk on it. On this layer of sand they then spread another layer of corpses. I found no one alive among the prisoners.

In the book *Genocide in the USSR*, published by the American Institute for the Study of the USSR in Munich (in July 1958), the following facts are stated regarding the NKVD crimes in West Ukraine:

> In 1941, when the German army began its Eastern campaign, the Bolsheviks murdered prisoners on the spot or during transportation. In Lviv, Stanislav, Chortkiv, Berezhany, Stry, Ternopil, Berestya, Rivne, Kremyanets, and Lutsk, mass executions of thousands of prisoners were carried out at that time....

Wherein Lies the Primary Motive of the Kremlin's
Defamatory Campaign against the Ukrainian "Nightingale" Unit
Incorporated in the German Army?

The primary motive of Moscow's defamatory campaign against the "Nightingale" unit is to defame the symbol of the armed Ukrainian fight for freedom and the heroic commander-in-chief of the Ukrainian Insurgent Army (UPA), General Taras Chuprynka.

Roman Shukhevych, later known as General Chuprynka, was the Ukrainian commander of the "Nightingale." After the Reich's government had refused to recognize Ukraine's independence, Shukhevych and his unit broke with the Germans, and practically all the members of the "Nightingale" went over to the UPA; the latter was strengthened with these new cadres, and soon afterwards, Roman Shukhevych assumed command of the UPA!

The attempt to brand the "Nightingale" soldiers as mass murderers was intended as a deadly blow to the UPA, which has become the immortal standard-bearer of the Ukrainian fight for freedom, and to the memory of the former Ukrainian commander of the "Nightingale," General Chuprynka.

To this end a systematic defamation campaign has been carried on in the Soviet press for over a year. This press accuses the members of the OUN of having committed unthinkable crimes against the innocent population during the time of the German occupation of Ukraine. In this way the Ukrainian freedom fighters are to be held to blame for the Bolshevik mass murders!

A further aim of this campaign is to create a false picture of the Ukrainian liberation movement in the minds of the young Ukrainians to whom the traditional ideas of freedom and liberation of the Organization of Ukrainian Nationalists and of the Ukrainian Insurgent Army have gradually become an ideal.

When the staff of the KGB (Committee for State Security) in Moscow planned the murder of Stepan Bandera, its intention was to divert public attention from itself to the Germans. For this reason the murder of Stepan Bandera was planned in such a manner as to be able to lay the blame, later, on Prof. Oberländer and thus kill two birds with one stone. The intention was, of course, to defame Adenauer's government!

Federal Minister Oberländer was to be the scapegoat for the perfidious game of the Russians, which aims to defame and discredit the Ukrainian revolutionary fight for freedom in the eyes of the youth of Ukraine and of the public in the Free World.

The German side, led by former Federal Minister Oberländer, however, defended itself very unskillfully; for it would have done better to start a large-scale counterattack and, in doing so, make use of the very accusations which the Russians are bringing in against it; namely, that the Germans actually did not commit any mass murders in Ukraine at that time, but that the Russians did; and the German side should also support the Ukrainian fight for freedom, which later was also directed against the Nazi occupation. But, unfortunately, nothing whatsoever is being done in this respet in Germany. In fact, some Germans even joined in the Moscow defamation campaign against their own Federal Minister and, like the Communists, demanded his resignation, instead of exposing the mass murderer Khrushchev, who at that time was Moscow's governor in Ukraine and gave orders that these mass murders were to be committed there. Side by side with this new defamatory campaign against the Ukrainian unit "Nightingale" the Soviet Government naturally has continued its constant campaign against the Ukrainian National Government of 1941, which was and is accused of having consisted entirely of quislings.

What Were the Real Facts of the Situation?

In the early morning hours of June 30th, 1941, a group of leading OUN men headed by Yaroslav Stetsko, who were disguised as a propaganda unit and had false identity papers, after an adventurous journey from Cracow, drove into Lviv in cars. On the way to Lviv they held rallies in all the villages and places that they passed through and proclaimed the restoration of the Ukrainian State to the inhabitants; the administrative power was taken over by the Ukrainians and in this way a *fait accompli* was established. In Lviv the OUN, with the help of its local organization, took over the broadcasting station, and at a rally of the leading Ukrainians there, held that same afternoon, the mayor and the town council were appointed and the administration of the town taken over by the Ukrainians.

Although the OUN in Lviv had suffered considerably as a result of the revolt crushed by NKVD units on June 27th, it was nevertheless still powerful enough to effectively and actively aid and support the OUN elements that arrived there on June 30th. After Yaroslav Stetsko had discussed the plan for the proclamation of the restoration of the Ukrainian State and the formation of the national government in all its details with the Metropolitan Count Andreas Sheptytsky, he convened the National Assembly in the venerable building of the oldest Ukrainian national society of recent times, the Prostiva, on the evening of June 30th. This Assembly consisted of the leading politicians who had remained in Lviv: economists, scholars, clergymen of both confessions, and other prominent personalities in Ukrainian public life who had managed to survive Russian terrorism; these persons were headed by the former President of the Government of West Ukraine in 1918, Kost Levytsky, and the envoy of the Metropolitan, Bishop Joseph Slipy. On the following day, the Metropolitan announced the joyful news to his people, in a pastoral message, that the independent Ukrainian State had been restored once more, and he exhorted the citizens of Ukraine to prove themselves worthy of their freedom. He recognized the new government and expressed the hope that all citizens, irrespective of their origin, nationality, race, and religious faith would enjoy equal treatment and prosperity. The same attitude was also expressed by the head of the Ukrainian Orthodox Autocephalous Church, Metropolitan Polikarp, who gave the Lviv Government his blessing.

The National Assembly unanimously approved the proclamation proposed by the OUN of the restoration of Ukrainian national independence and appointed

Yaroslav Stetsko head of the government. Towards the end of the meeting, the authorized representative of the German Supreme Command and of the German Ministry for Eastern Affairs, Prof. Dr. Hans Koch, suddenly appeared, and the opposition which he expressed in his address clearly revealed the true intention of the Nazi Government.

The original plan of the OUN leaders to hold the proclamation of the Ukrainian Independent Government and of the restoration of the Ukrainian state in Kyiv, was, however, changed by Yaroslav Stetsko at the last minute when he realized that the deferment of the proclamation until July 2nd in the opera house, a suggestion made by his comrades, would undoubtedly be prevented by the Gestapo, which would be sure to hurry to the scene.

The proclamation of the independence of Ukraine was intentionally held in Lviv, to compel Germany, even at this early stage in the war, to adopt a clear and definite attitude with regard to the question of Ukraine's state independence. It would have been impossible to have waited until Kyiv had been taken by the Germans and then hold the proclamation in the capital of all Ukraine, because by that time the Nazi Government would have taken steps to prevent this. The formation of the government in Lviv was intended to make Ukraine the main center of events from the very outset. And this was, in fact, accomplished. The government in Lviv always acted as the government of the whole of Ukraine and it was likewise regarded as such at that time and later by the outside world.

It became the symbol of the will of the Ukrainian State. By means of a plebiscite, which was carried out spontaneously in every village and town and which expressed approval of and enthusiasm for the proclamation the state action of June 30, 1941, gained the approval of the entire people.

The broadcasting station and all the public buildings in the town were in the hands of the Ukrainian nationalists, the insurgents of the armed Ukrainian militia; Ukrainian insurgent units, which on June 27th had engaged in street fighting with Soviet Russian tanks in Lviv, were stationed in the forest near the town. There was also a Ukrainian unit in German uniform ("Nightingale") in Lviv. Under these circumstances it was impossible for Himmler to resort to any measures of violence before stronger units of the Gestapo and the Security Service were brought up. It was only ten days later, when the Security Service had completed its preparations, that violence was resorted to.

On July 10th, in the evening, there was an attempt to assassinate the head of the government in which his chauffeur was seriously wounded. It was assumed that this attempt was carried out either by NKVD agents who had remained behind, or by some Gestapo center.

On July 11th, the head of the government was arrested and taken to Berlin, where, together with Mr. Bandera, he was placed under police surveillance. Various means were now resorted to in order to persuade them to revoke the action of June 3, 1941. When all these efforts failed, however, Bandera, Stetsko and thousands of other Ukrainian nationalists were arrested on September 15, 1941, and taken to Sachsenhausen and other concentration camps. On September 30, 1944, Bandera and Stetsko were taken to a villa near Berlin. That the Germans had made certain mistakes was admitted, and an attempt was now made to find a basis for cooperation by recognizing Ukrainian independence, but in view of Hitler's ruthless terrorist regime in Ukraine, this suggestion was once more turned down by the two spokesmen of the Ukrainian liberation movement. After Bandera and Stetsko had once more been put under the surveillance of the Berlin police they managed to flee, with the help of members of the Ukrainian underground movement, who were employed as civilian workers from the East in Germany (see also *Germany and Ukraine* by R. Ilnytsky, Munich: East Europe Institute, 1958).

The Democratic Basis of the Ukrainian Government of 1941

The defamatory character of Soviet Russian propaganda in its discriminatory campaign against the Organization of Ukrainian Nationalists can be seen from its lies about the alleged one-party composition of the National Government of June 30, 1941. This government was not a one-party government, but was composed of the representatives of various political trends in Ukraine, socialists, national democrats, Catholics, non-party representatives and nationalists. Although the overwhelming majority of the population supported the OUN, the latter decided to take over only a certain number of Ministries. In addition to the office of Prime Minister, the police administration, the post of the second deputy of the head of government and the department of political coordination which the territorial leader of the OUN Evhen Lehenda, who was later murdered by the Gestapo, took over, OUN member V. Stakhiv took over the Ministry of Foreign Affairs. There were two Deputy Ministers of War one was General Taras Chuprynka, and the other (later Chief of the UPA General Staff) Colonel Hasyn; the Minister of War was a social revolutionary, the famous Ukrainian general of the war of liberation 1918-20, General Petriv; and the Minister of the Interior was a socialist and the Minister of the Economy a national democrat. In number the nationalists were in the minority in the Cabinet.

In addition, a provisional parliament, the Ukrainian National Council, under the honorary presidency of the Metropolitan Count Andreas Sheptytsky, was formed, and here too the representatives of the OUN were likewise in the minority. Dr. Kost Levytsky (a national democrat), who had spent two years in Lubianka prison in Moscow, was elected President of the National Council.

After the head of government had been arrested, the other nationalist members of the government, who had not gone into hiding, were arrested and put in concentration camps. It was only the nationalists who at that time actively combatted the Nazi occupation. Neither the socialists nor the national democrats nor the non-party representatives were arrested.

Of the nationalist members of the government, the following were murdered by the Gestapo: as already mentioned, the Minister of Political Coordination and territorial leader of the OUN, Evhen Lehenda Klymiv; the Deputy Minister of Economy, Yatsiv; and the Minister of Forestry, Piasetsky (from the Front of National Unity, a small nationalist-minded group).

The following persons were arrested: the deputy head of the government and member of the OUN, Dr. Lev Rebet; the Minister of Foreign Affairs, V. Stakhiv, as well as other OUN members of the government and, of course, the president of the Organization of Ukrainian Nationalists, Stepan Bandera, who at that time was in Cracow and was arrested there on July 5th.

We have intentionally reported on the events in Lviv on June 30th and at the beginning of July, 1941, in detail, in order to prove, on the strength of these irrefutable facts, how defamatory and treacherous Soviet Russian propaganda is. In defaming the Ukrainian Government of 1941 and also the "Nightingale" detachment and Prof. Oberländer, it ruthlessly resorts to its usual methods of attack—namely, that if one repeats the same lies a thousand times, then some of them will eventually make an impression.

Khrushchev gave orders that the mass murders in Lviv and in other places in Ukraine were to be committed at the time in question. And he alone bears the whole blame!

The Ukrainian Review,
No. 1, 1960, p. 3-19

The Danger of World War

In discussing the danger of a new world war, one must in the first place refute certain mythical ideas about the alleged incompatibility of a just defensive war with the Christian doctrine. War as such is by no means to be condemned as immoral, insofar as one does not completely reject the idea of defending one's justified rights against a wanton aggressor. Nor is the use of atomic weapons to be condemned as absolutely immoral: it all depends on the motives and the aim. Otherwise the Free World would be obliged to let its aggressors use these atomic weapons—namely, for the purpose of overthrowing in a most criminal way all the foundations of ethics and law and of destroying every kind of legal order. The defenders of law and order and of truth must not substitute for their risk the idealization of defenselessness or passive waiting for criminal acts of murder. The defense of law and order and of truth must take precedence over the personal instinct of self-preservation.

The Italian Minister of Foreign Affairs recently said in Washington: "Italy would be better able to bear destruction by atomic war than by Communism." Mr. Dulles, too, when he resigned from office, wrote: "The American nation does not merely constitute a self-satisfied community, but it has been created with the mission of building up a world in which freedom and justice are to rule." And elsewhere he said: "It is difficult for us to stand up for our national idealism and our national mission unswervingly and, at the same time, prevent a terrible world catastrophe," for "nowadays this our ideal confronts the alarming and relentless provocation of Communism." Thus, no capitulation to the forces of evil at any price, but a fight against them, even in the face of catastrophe!

A number of Western statesmen are well aware of the danger which threatens from Moscow and also of the fact that one must sometimes sacrifice temporal things for the defense of eternal truth and for the defense of the good. Gustav Gundlach, S.J., interprets the address of Pope Pius XII to the 6th International Congress for Penal Law as meaning that even the downfall of an entire people in manifesting their loyalty to God against an unjust aggressor can constitute such an important fact that it would justify a terrible defensive war.

In defending truth and our rights, we must not be guided by a utilitarian point of view, but, above all, by ethical principles. Right and truth are worth more than life. In any case, the world will probably not last for ever, and the "responsibility for the need of mankind" by no means rests with us, as all the pacifists and defeatists would have us believe. Should Providence decree that the just are forced to prove their loyalty to the principles of the divine order in the world with the aid of atomic weapons — namely, by defending their freedom and their rights against the aggressor—then God will take the responsibility, and not we.

The West should thus put a stop to its pacifist propaganda, anti-atom hysteria, and its demand for a one-sided disarmament; for all this is only likely to prompt the Moscow aggressor to launch an attack. Fear of atomic war as a form of universal destruction is not justified, inasmuch as we—provided that we fulfill our ethical duties towards God and our native country—cannot possibly become the object of destruction. One should not ascribe to the criminal Khrushchev an all-destructive power, as if the key to the existence or non-existence of the human race rests solely in the hands of godless Moscow.

There is, however, a way to achieve a clear victory without having to resort to the use of atomic weapons—namely, by means of the national liberation movements of the peoples subjugated by Moscow, coordinated as a simultaneous revolution and supported by a joint anti-Bolshevik world front. The essential point is not so much to seek to surpass the war potential of the so-called Communist bloc solely by technical means or by the number of soldiers, but, rather, to undermine to a decisive extent the *human* potential of the armies that Moscow has at its disposal; and not merely because the West cannot hope to exceed the human reserves of the Moscow-Peking bloc, which amount to astronomical figures, but, above all, because this bloc constitutes the last and most ruthless empire in the history of the world, and, moreover, like every empire inevitably suffers from the same vulnerable weakness—the most important task is to win over the souls of these other nations and individuals. They possess weapons—the weapons that have been placed in their hands by their subjugators; the important point is that these weapons should be used against the subjugators at the right moment. Moscow is forging weapons against itself and this is the vicious circle from which Moscow will never be able to escape, provided that the West sets its hopes on these decisive forces by adopting the ideas of the liberation revolutions of these nations and actively supporting the national revolutionary processes behind the Iron Curtain. The competition between the rivals must, in the first place, be carried on for human souls, and then, secondly, for human bodies. The superiority of the West as regards atomic weapons by no means guarantees its security for any length of time, since it would disarm itself ethically if it were forced to use its atomic weapons without taking into consideration other factors—*ideological* and really decisive factors—namely to win anew the sympathy of the subjugated nations by actively supporting their anti-Bolshevik fight and its aim, the disintegration of the Russian empire into national, independent, and sovereign states within their ethnic territories and the final liquidation of every type of Communism; and in this respect it is to be left to the peoples themselves to choose their own political and social regime, in keeping with the fundamental principles of their religion and their internal national solidarity and the principle of respecting the *individual* as a being created in the likeness of the Divine.

This would be the essential ideological and ethical action to be adopted by the West: the practical and technical action, however, would consist in allowing the so-called conventional or classical fighting forces of the West (all the services) to remain at least proportionately equal in strength to those of the Moscow bloc.

And in this respect the West can set its hopes on the national revolutionary action of the peoples subjugated by Moscow; but, of course, this does not mean that only these peoples would wage war while the Free World looked on passively. No, the Free World will have to support the liberation action behind the Iron Curtain actively and, if necessary, with armed force, for its cause, too, and not only the cause of the subjugated peoples is at stake. The latter are not dependent on anyone's favor and do not beg for favors. They appeal to the Free World in its own interests to support their revolutionary fight for freedom since, in doing so, it will be rendering itself a service. If the leading statesmen of the West do not want an atomic war—and quite rightly so—and, in fact, no world war at all, and if, at the same time, they fail to support the national revolutions behind the Iron Curtain, what other way to bring about the destruction of Bolshevism and of the Russian peoples' prison do they visualize? Neither war, nor revolution—as the passive attitude of the West during the Hungarian revolution clearly showed—so what other way is there? A miracle, although none of these leading statesmen believe in miracles! Indeed, no miracle is likely to happen.

Conscious of these principles and facts, the ABN has always considered not utilitarian motives, but ideological and ethical values, which must be defended, as the most important principle in determining its foreign policy—that is to say, absolute values, which the common effort of freedom-loving mankind should set up against the materialist attitude to life on this side of and beyond the Iron Curtain.

An anti-materialist spiritual revolution is also the precondition for victory against Moscow.

Thus, the foreign policy of the ABN has always been determined by the following principles:

Consistent defense of the national idea as a motive power of our historical epoch, against every form of totalitarianism and imperialism; it has taken decades for the world to realize that nationalist liberation movements cannot be evaded and that even the major powers are powerless in the face of such movements. It is, however, imperative that this attitude should become a guiding principle for the practical policy of the State Department.

The resolution recently adopted by the U.S. Congress—both by the Senate and by the House of Representatives—regarding the introduction of a "Captive Nations' Week" is, in any case, highly commendable, especially as this "week" is to be proclaimed every year by the President of the USA as a declaration of solidarity with the peoples subjugated by Russian imperialism and Communism and in honor of their national fight for freedom; in a special statement President Eisenhower has already proclaimed that this "week" shall begin July 20th. American solidarity with the fight for independence of Ukraine and other subjugated nations within the Soviet Union is expressed without any discrimination, without any mention of so-called "non-predetermination." This resolution on the part of the US Congress, together with the decree issued by the President of the US, is of far-reaching ideological and ethical significance; it will remain a highlight in the history of the USA, insofar as its government gradually adopts the right course of a genuine liberation policy—that is to say, one that is directed against the "indivisibility" of the Russian empire. Unfortunately, this is at present only being done on the ethical level, but not on the practical and political one; for the so-called American Committee for Liberation from Bolshevism is still conducting a policy which is opposed to our demands. And yet, the steps recently taken by the US Congress and the President give us certain grounds to hope that the USA in the course of time will change its policy towards Russia—a policy which has so far not been formally determined and is vague in content.

For the US Government is gradually beginning to realize that in practice the foreign policy of the Soviet Government is, above all, determined by the indomitable pressure of the national anti-Russian liberation movements in the Russian imperium and by the increasing military strength of the Free World. The aim of the Soviet game of speculation with the Western sector of Berlin is to obtain from the major powers of the West a joint guarantee for the status quo of subjugation, in order to shatter the hopes of support from the West which are entertained by the subjugated peoples. The least concession regarding West Berlin would automatically compromise the possibility of any Western liberation policy—namely, as regards all the subjugated nations. On the other hand, resolute measures on the part of the Allies to effect the inclusion on the basis of international law of West Berlin in the German Federal Republic as a whole, together with the necessary retention of the same numbers of allied troops in Berlin, as well as the annulment of the Potsdam Agreement, would destroy all of Khrushchev's lying arguments based on the pseudo-sovereignty of the so-called German Democratic Republic, without the danger of war; for Moscow, for the time being at least, is not likely to want to risk a war, since it knows that it would be threatened by internal paralysis in that case. The Berlin conflict is actually diverting the attention of the West from other sore spots and Communist Russian aggressions, as, for instance, Iraq or Laos. The Berlin Blockade in 1947 and its failure, incidentally, were also intended to make the West indifferent to the loss of the Chinese mainland, which at that time was finally "liberated" by Moscow. Perhaps the present Berlin maneuver is a similar one and the actual attack will be carried out somewhere else.

Moscow's offensives are always global, both as regards the "external" and, particularly at present, the "internal" fronts; for "internal" fronts occasionally enable Moscow—as the recent example of Vietnam proved—to extend the external boundaries of its domination without any very great risk. Moscow's global offensive must be repulsed with an equally global counteroffensive. There is a front against Moscow, against Communism, and against the present form of Russian imperialism everywhere; and the counteroffensive must be carried out in various territories in order to encircle Moscow's spheres of dominion on all sides by our counteraction.

In occupying the Eurasian continent, Russia left numerous positions open, which can easily be attacked. And in this connection Khrushchev introduced his well-known policy of economic decentralization which aims to transfer the important centers of the war industry to various regions in order to lessen the danger of their being destroyed by American atomic weapons from the widely distributed American air bases—or, possibly, by American submarines, which recently crossed the Arctic Ocean at record speed and thus now represent a deadly danger to Russia's war industry in the north.

Not only the Ukrainians—though predominantly the Ukrainians—have been scattered throughout Siberia, Central Asia, and the Far East by the Soviet regime; and this fact dictates that we should plan anti-Russian action accordingly. Hence, too, our cooperation with the APACL—that is to say, with Free China (Taiwan); with Free Korea, which practically borders on the regions of the Far East which are populated by Ukrainians; with Pakistan, which is so close to Turkestan (where, incidentally, there are at present millions of Ukrainians living in the so-called "virgin regions"); with Vietnam; and, of course, with Turkey. The distribution of the concentration camps in Siberia and Kazakhstan is an established fact. For this reason, one must not underestimate the importance of the ABN broadcast programs transmitted from Taiwan and of programs transmitted from any of these other countries of Asia. An insurrection in the territory of Siberia, Kazakhstan, or the Far East (it would, of course, have to be initiated at a suitable opportunity) is by no means entirely out of the question. Hence, our cooperation with Free China, South Korea, or Pakistan has an added significance.

The problem of Ukrainian independence is not a local problem, and, accordingly, the Ukrainian liberation action must neither be planned nor assessed from a local point of view. If there were no Russians across the Black Sea, there would be no Russian pressure in the Near and Middle East, for Russia would then also be evicted from the Caucasus and from Turkestan. Russia's absence from the Carpathians would liberate the whole of Central Europe from pressure.

The Ukrainian problem in the complex of the nations subjugated by Russia constitutes a world problem; for with the liberation of Ukraine— which would inevitably lead to the liberation of all the other nations subjugated by Russia— the political map both of the European as well as of the Asian continent would have to be completely changed. The assumption that the Russian empire will bring the future offensive on the part of China against Europe, the offensive of the yellow race against the white, to a standstill is not justified, for its is precisely Russia and none other that has provided China with an ideology of destruction and a false faith. In any case, history shows us that no colossus with feet of clay has ever been able to hold up an invasion by new conquerors, but has always fallen apart; for the peoples subjugated by it have always used the first opportunity possible to shake off their fetters. Neither the Ukrainians, the Georgians, nor the Turkestanis would ever think of defending the Russian empire against a Chinese invasion; but, once they have become independent, the Ukrainians, the Georgians, and the Turkestanis will defend their own independence on a common front against anyone who attempts to attack them—even China. Incidentally, the Chinese have for centuries—apart from the lust of conquest of foreign occupants—been a peaceful people, and their famous Great Wall was erected as a defense; and it is highly improbable that—once they have recovered from the Communist pestilence—they will seek to conquer or annex foreign countries. At present, Peking is, in any case, actually dependent on Moscow, and it is Moscow that dictates its conduct in the Communist bloc.

A great conflict is at present being enacted in Asia between Russia and its direct and indirect satellites, on the one hand, and the freedom-loving nations of Asia, on the other hand, and neither the Ukrainians nor other peoples subjugated by Moscow can afford to stand aloof.

In keeping with our principle of a global fight against our common enemy, we have also established our cooperation with the Inter-American Confederation for Defense of the Continent, which is comprised of the representatives of the anti-Communist organizations of twenty-two nations of America. In the USA— which is at present the most powerful country of the Free World—we also have sincere friends, who recently made it possible for the first time for a Ukrainian to testify officially before two committees of the House of Representatives of the US Congress—before the Foreign Affairs Committee and the Un-American Activities Committee. Our view of the future, inevitable disintegration of the Russian empire, is gradually gaining more and more supporters. The fact that at the Preparatory Conference for the Anti-Communist World Congress (in Mexico City in March 1959), at which the delegates of the anti-Communist organizations of sixty-five nations were present, the political platform of the ABN was adopted by an overwhelming majority as the basis for convening the Congress is still yet another proof of the strength and compelling force of our ideas.

The 6th Inter-American Conference in Guatemala in October 1958 likewise adopted our conception of the national and social liberation policy in its programs for the anti-Communist fight. And our participation in the Anti-Communist Conference of the Asian Continent in Saigon, in 1957, also brought us success, for it was not the ideas of the so-called "White Russian" solidarists—the NTS— but our ideas which gained the approval of those present. In view of the success with which we have disseminated our ideas, the advocates of the NTS persuaded certain financially powerful Western circles to debar us from the recent Anti-Communist Conference in Korea (in June 1959). But precisely these efforts to prevent us, against the wishes of the Asian natives from attending this year's conference are proof of the power of our ideas; certain "private" American Russophile circles are afraid to have their views confronted by ours, since they know that the unprejudiced delegates of the countries of Asia and Latin America who are present at such conferences, though they may sometimes not be particularly well-informed, would not be able to resist the strength of our arguments and the justness of our principles. The fact that the Russophile circles in the Free World seek to avoid a free exchange of ideas in the presence of delegates of other nations is clear proof of the ideological weakness of these circles. But no one is any longer in a position to exclude us from the freedom-loving communities of the Free World; we have already entered the world arena and no one can hurl us out of it into non-existence or oblivion!

In view of all these facts, our tasks abroad are constantly increasing. Our great emigration from our native countries will be justified when we, those who took part in this emigration, are inspired by the thought that we did not leave our native countries merely to save ourselves from being physically destroyed, but, above all, to help our people to attain freedom and independence and to further the disintegration of the Russian empire by also winning over active friends for our just cause in the Free World.

ABN Correspondence
January-February 1960, pp. 3-8

The Role of the Subjugated Peoples in the Anti-Bolshevik World Struggle

Khrushchev Is Digging His Own Grave

In order to be able to combat the enemy successfully in psychological warfare, it is imperative that we should be able to define him exactly so as to recognize the historical processes which are taking place before our very eyes.

What is happening in the world around us? We are witnessing two opposing processes; on the one hand, a drive to form a world colonial empire—that is to say, a world Union of Soviet Socialist Republics; on the other hand, a universal fight to form national independent states. In this polarization there is no room for a middle course. The national liberation idea must be victorious throughout the world—that is, not only in the disintegrating Western empire but also in the Russian prison of peoples.

In this connection I wish to quote some excerpts from the new program of the Communist Party of the Soviet Union, Paragraph 6.

> The world is experiencing an epoch of stormy national liberation revolution. The mighty wave of the national liberation revolutions is sweeping the colonial system away and is undermining the pillars of imperialism. In place of former colonies and semi-colonies, young sovereign states have been and are being created. Their

peoples have entered upon a new period in their development. They are asserting themselves as creators of a new life and active participants in world politics as a revolutionary force which is destroying imperialism.... The peoples of the countries that are formally independent but actually politically and economically dependent on foreign monopolies are rising up to fight imperialism and the reactionary pro-imperialistic regimes. Those peoples who have not yet cast off the fetters of colonial slavery are fighting heroically against their foreign subjugators.... Political independence can only be consolidated by a people that has attained democratic rights and freedom and takes an active part in the administration of the state. The fundamental precondition for the solution of the all-national tasks is a consistent fight against imperialism....

The imperialists are resorting to every means (colonial wars, military blocs, conspiracies, terrorism, subversion, economic pressure, bribery) in order to keep the countries which have liberated themselves under their dominion, to make their independence merely a matter of form or to deprive them of their independence...to put tractable puppets in the leading governmental posts.... Imperialism continues to be the main enemy and the main hindrance on the path to the solution of the general national tasks which confront the young sovereign states and all independent countries....

So much for the program of the Communist Party of the Soviet Union!

If we now add the little word "Russian" in the right place and, instead of "dependent on foreign monopolies" say "dependent on Russia," we have the precise diagnosis of the world situation on the part of the 22nd Congress of the Communist Party of the Soviet Union.

It is entirely correct that Russian imperialism is the main enemy and the main hindrance on the path to the solution of the national tasks.

It is entirely correct that the Russian imperialists resort to every means in order to subjugate peoples.

It is entirely correct that the fundamental precondition for the solution of world problems is a consistent fight against Russian imperialism and that the peoples who have not yet cast off the fetters of colonial slavery are fighting against the Russian subjugators.

The "Conference on the Political Warfare of the Soviets" in Rome, however, rejects a political offensive against the Russian colonial empire on the basis of acknowledgment of the national liberation idea.

There is a glaring contradiction between the excerpts quoted above and the words of Paragraph 4 of the program of the Communist Party of the Soviet Union, which reads as follows: "to combat all phenomena and remnants of every kind of nationalism and also to endeavor to bring about the liquidation of nationalist phenomena" and "to overcome the trends to local patriotism and national egoism, as well as to relentless combat, the trends to national narrow-mindedness and exclusiveness, to idealization of the past, and outmoded customs and usage."

This is additional proof of how powerful and how dangerous liberation nationalism is in the interior of the Soviet Union.

Russian arrogance is clearly expressed in the following paragraph of the program of the Communist Party of the Soviet Union:

The process at present in progress of voluntarily learning Russian in addition to the mother tongue has a positive significance since it contributes to the exchange of ideas as well as to the fact that in this way every nation and every people become participants in the cultural achievements of all the other peoples of the USSR and in world culture. The Russian language has in practice become the joint language of communication and the language of cooperation of all the peoples of the USSR.

Russian chauvinism could not have been expressed more plainly than in this program. And it clearly transpires from the latter that the works of world culture are only made available in Russian in the USSR and in no other language.

"The National Union for Peace and Freedom" of Bonn Advocates the Disintegration of the Russian Empire

The National Union for Peace and Freedom, a member of the CIAS, under the chairmanship of Mr. Fritz Cramer, Germany, stated as follows in its official organ, *Der aktuelle Osten*, of October 10, 1960, in an excellent article by H.R. Alscher entitled "The Vulnerable Spot of the Soviet Union" (a "Comment on the Soviet Declaration on the Concession of Independence to the Colonial Countries and Peoples"):

Wherein lies the danger for the Soviet Union? It lies in the fact that the Soviet Union itself is a colonial empire. Its non-Russian constituent parts are striving for independence in the same way as the former colonial territories of the West have done. The consequence for the Soviet Union would be disastrous if it were to be drawn into the eddy of the liberation movement.... Prime Minister Diefenbaker of Canada has undoubtedly defined the colonial character of the Soviet empire most aptly and has thus dealt Moscow a blow in its most vulnerable spot. And this weak spot in the imperialist system of Moscow must be attacked again and again.

By doing so, a threefold aim can be achieved:

1) Moscow can be forced to abandon its offensive and assume a defensive position;

2) The developing countries can be enlightened as to the colonial and imperialist aims of Moscow's policy and can to a large extent be made immune against Communist propaganda;

3) The colonial and semi-colonial peoples of the Soviet empire can be won over to resistance against Moscow's colonial rule.... Colonialism is the vulnerable spot of the Soviet Union.

Addressing the United Nations Prime Minister Diefenbaker said:

Since the last war seventeen nations have been brought to freedom by France. In the same period, fourteen colonies and territories, comprising half a billion people, have achieved complete freedom in the Commonwealth.

Together, these thirty-one countries, most of them now members of the UN, have gained freedom through the encouragement, approval and guidance of the United Kingdom and France.

These facts of history invite comparison with the record of Soviet domination of peoples and territories, sometimes gained in the name of liberation, but always accompanied by loss of personal and political freedom.... The Assembly is still concerned with the aftermath of the Hungarian uprising of 1956.... How are we to reconcile that tragedy with Mr. Khrushchev's assertion a few days ago in this Assembly when he said: 'It will always be the Soviet stand that countries should establish systems of their own free will and choosing....' What of Lithuania, Latvia, Estonia? What of freedom-loving Ukrainians and other Eastern European peoples? Khrushchev has said, at the same time, that the course of history indicated that the end of colonialism must come unconditionally and immediately.... Then there must be no double standard in international affairs. I ask him here and now to give those nations under his domination the right of free election to give them an opportunity to determine the kind of government they want under genuinely free conditions. Then, indeed, will his words result in action carrying out the obligation of the United Nations Charter.

The official organ of the German sector of the CIAS states: "In his speech before the United Nations Khrushchev has completely corroborated our theory that the Muscovite empire [of tsarist days] was a continental colonial empire...." Khrushchev said: "In accordance with the Constitution, each of our fifteen Constituent Republics has the right to remain in the Union or to secede, if it wishes to do so. The fact that there are nineteen Autonomous Republics, nine Autonomous Regions, and ten National Areas makes it possible to preserve the national characteristics, the cultural peculiarities, and the independent existence of every nationality and every ethnic group. Khrushchev must indeed have regarded his audience on this occasion as being extremely naïve, since he had the audacity to tell them a fairy tale about the right of states to secede from the Soviet Union. He talks as though the story of Moscow's wars of colonial conquest from 1918 to 1924 were not known to the world. He talks as though no one knew that after the collapse of tsarism in 1917 all the former colonial territories proclaimed their independence and detached themselves from Moscow—as, for instance, Finland, Poland, Estonia, Latvia, Lithuania, Ukraine, Georgia, Azerbadzhan, Armenia, Turkestan, and even Siberia...."

The official organ, Der Aktuelle Osten, then continues: "Colonialist from the outset, Moscow is today as imperialist as it was in the days of Ivan, Peter, Catherine, Nicholas, Lenin, and Stalin. Colonialism is the leitmotif of Moscow's policy, and anti-colonialism is nothing but a diversive manuever on the lines of the 'Stop, thief!' method. Today, the colonial thieves are to be found not in London or Washington, but in Moscow."

In conclusion Der Aktuelle Osten suggests that the "Declaration on the Concession of Independence to the Colonial Countries and Peoples" submitted to the General Assembly of the United Nations by Khrushchev on September 23, 1960, should be worded as follows:

   1) To all colonial peoples, dependent and non-self-governing territories (as, for example, Ukraine, Turkestan, Poland, and the Soviet Occupied Zone of Germany), must be conceded without delay complete independence and freedom for the setting

up of their own national states in keeping with the freely expressed will and wish of their peoples (the Ukrainians, Turkestanis, Poles, Germans, etc.).

The colonial regime, colonial administration in every form (whether as a Soviet Socialist Republic, an Autonomous Soviet Socialist Republic, a People's Republic, or a Democratic Republic, etc.) must be abolished completely in order to enable the peoples of these territories (the Latvians, Tatars, Romanians, Mongols, Germans, etc.) to decide their fate and the form of their government themselves.

2) At the same time all the bases of colonialism on foreign territory (and also the bases of the Soviet Union in Outer Mongolia, in North Korea, in Central Germany, and elsewhere) must be abolished.

3) The Governments of all countries (in particular the Government of the Soviet Union) are requested in all inter-state relations to strictly and faithfully observe the UN Charter and the Declaration on the Equality and Respect of the Sovereign Rights and the Territorial Integrity of all states without exception (in particular of the states in East Europe and Southeast Europe, in the Caucasus, and in Central Asia). No aspects of colonialism (nor of Soviet colonialism) shall be permitted. Nor shall any special rights and privileges whatever of any states at the expense of other states (e.g., special rights and privileges of Soviet Russia at the expense of Poland, Germany, Hungary, Bulgaria, etc.) be permitted.

The time has come to demand the complete and final liquidation of the colonial regime in every form and variation.... This disgrace, this barbarity, and lack of culture must definitely cease for good.

I am of the opinion that the fundamental ideas of this publication of the German sector of the CIAS and the demand that the Russian colonial empire be disintegrated into independent national states of all the subjugated peoples (regardless of the date when they were subjugated) should be included in the resolution adopted at the 2nd International Congress in Rome in order to be used as a transition to an offensive against Russian colonialism. This has, however, not been done, since the organizers of the Congress in Rome, Mme. Suzanne Labin and Minister G.M. Lombardo, are in some way or other under an obligation to the White Russian aspirants to colonial rule.

Marx versus Russia

Not only has Khrushchev, however, so daringly corroborated and criticized the Russian imperialism of tsarist days and the existence of the Russian colonial empire at that time, but Karl Marx has also done so in the brilliant reports which he wrote during the years 1853 to 1856, when he was an exile in London, for the *New York Daily Tribune*. (They have been published in the book *Marx versus Russia* by the Seewald Verlag, 1960).

In an inimitable way Karl Marx in these reports exposes the ideologically tinged expansion urge as a constant that has always existed in Russia's policy: "What has changed? Nothing at all! Russia's policy is unchangeable. Russia's methods, tactics, and maneuvers may change; but the lodestar of Russian policy—world domination—is a fixed star."

Marx also exposed Pan-Slavism as a form of Russian imperialism when he wrote:

> Pan-Slavism is a form of Russian imperialism—it is not a movement that strives for national independence, but a movement which, directed against Europe, would destroy all that history has created throughout thousands of years. This could not be achieved without eradicating Hungary, Turkey, and a major part of Germany from the map....
>
> Alexander II will set himself at the head of the Pan-Slavist movement and will change his title of Emperor of all Russians to that of Emperor of all Slavs....
>
> The Russian bear will certainly be capable of anything as long as he knows that the other animals with which he is dealing are not capable of anything.

I should also like to quote some other brilliant thoughts by Karl Marx, since they have so far been omitted from all Soviet Russian editions of Marx's works. For it is essential that public opinion in the West should also become acquainted with the other aspects of his ideas.

> There is only one way of dealing with a power like Russia and that is by fearlessness.
>
> The system of intimidation is far less expensive than actual warfare.
>
> Russia only hands the Western diplomats so many notes—like throwing bones to a dog—in order to give them some harmless pleasure whilst she herself used this opportunity to gain more time.
>
> Inasmuch as Russia counts on the cowardice and fear of the Western powers, she intimidates Europe and asserts her demands as far as possible in order to pretend later that she is generous since she contents herself with more immediate aims.

It is obvious from these reflections alone that the main enemy is Russian imperialism and colonialism. Communism is merely an idea employed in the service of Russia—an idea which is in keeping with the Russian mentality.

These lucid thoughts by Karl Marx are rejected by Marx's supporters, Mme. Labin and Minister Lombárdo, as far as combatting Russian colonialism is concerned!

Berdyaev and Bunin Identify Russian Imperialism with Bolshevism

In his work *The New Middle Ages* the Russian philosopher N. Berdyaev writes as follows:

> Bolshevism is in keeping with the mentality of the Russian people; it is merely an expression of the spiritual disunity of this people, of its apostasy of faith, its religious crisis, and its extreme demoralization. Bolshevik ideas are completely in keeping with Russian nihilism.
>
> Dostoevsky was the prophet of the Russian revolution and he realized that socialism in Russia is a religious problem, a question of atheism, and that the

Russian revolutionary intelligentsia, is not concerned with politics but solely with the question of saving mankind without God.

The Russian emigrants [the NTS] are not sufficiently aware of the fact that in the case of the Russian problem it is by no means a question of a small group of Bolsheviks who happen to be in power and who can be overthrown, but of a new and infinitely large class of persons who have now become the rulers of the country and cannot be easily overthrown. The Communist revolution has, above all, materialized out of Russian life.

Berdyaev also deals at length and in detail with the organic connection between Russian imperialism and Bolshevism. He identifies the latter with Russian imperialism and describes Bolshevism as the most exaggerated form of aggressive Russian expansion.

In his work *The Meaning and Destiny of Russian Communism*, Berdyaev characterizes Bolshevism as follows:

Bolshevism is the third form of Russian imperialism, of the Russian empire.... Bolshevism is a purely national phenomenon; he who wishes to penetrate its depths must uncover the national roots of Bolshevism and must explain its origin on the strength of Russia's history.

This idea is also taken up by the famous Russian author and holder of the Nobel Prize I. A. Bunin. In his book *Vospominaniya* (Memoirs) he completely corroborates Berdyaev's theories, adds to them, and elaborates them. In this work Bunin presents the reader with a whole gallery of intellectual instigators of Bolshevism in the Russian literary "brotherhood" at the end of the 19th and beginning of the 20th century. Whereas Lenin and the Russian social democratic revolutionary party endowed Bolshevism with its theories, political aims, ideology, and strategy, it was Tolstoy, Chekhov, Andreyev, Mayakovsky, Blok, Yesenin, Byedny, Gorky, Kuprin, Petrashevsky, Voloshin, and their like who imbued this treacherous and perverse Bolshevik idea with an evil soul, which made it dynamic and caused it to infect a huge proportion of the Russian intellectuals.

If we sum up the sharp-sighted observations made by Bunin in his memoirs, we arrive at the following picture of the spiritual fathers of the Russian October revolution:

They constituted a society of destroyers, blasphemers, rogues, clowns, braggarts, insolent creatures, barbarians, and tramps, who were possessed of diabolical mendacity and paranoia. To this coterie—as he says—also belonged mendacious decadents, persons who were hysterical, mental defectives from birth, persons who were insane, psychopaths, and cynics. And this entire coterie, according to its own admission, constituted the intellectual vanguard of the "new Russia"!

They were the same "demons" that Pushkin visualized, that Dostoevsky saw in flesh and blood, and that Muscovy (ethical Russia) in our era has turned loose on Europe in the person of Lenin, Stalin, and Khrushchev, in order to crush Europe under the heel of the modern hordes.

But what do the Frenchwoman Mme. Labin and the Italian Mr. Lombardo say to these views expressed by the Russian thinkers? Are they determined to hold Karl Marx responsible for the atrocities of Lenin, Stalin, Yezhov, Yagoda, and Khrushchev, or the Russian criminal tyrants as defined by Berdyaev or Bunin?

Hugh Seton-Watson on the New Imperialism

The famous Frenchman the Marquis de Custine and the Englishman Fletcher (in the old days of Theodore, son of Ivan the Terrible, in the 16th century) give an account of intellectual conditions, or rather, of Bolshevism in the intellectual sense, in that era of Russian history. It is only on the strength of an historical analysis that one can rightly assess and combat the phenomenon of the present form of Russian imperialism—i.e., Bolshevism. It is erroneous to regard Communism as something that has been imported to Russia. It is, however, correct to treat it as a phenomenon of modern Russian colonialism. For this reason one must, above all, consider the national liberation idea as the permanent, explosive force in the Russian colonial empire.

In his recent book *The New Imperialism* the famous British historian Hugh Seton-Watson expresses views on Russian colonialism which we also hold and affirms that as always the basic idea in the new Russian colonial empire is nationalism. He writes as follows:

> In view of the past experience of all colonial empires, and the role played by the intelligentsia in so many countries of Asia and Africa in the last decades, it would be astounding if the intelligentsia of the non-Russian nations of the Soviet Union were not affected by nationalism, did not cherish the hope that one day they may achieve independence.

It is indeed regrettable that the Frenchwoman Mme. Labin does not identify herself with the ideas of the famous Frenchman de Custine, or of the clear-sighted Englishman Seton-Watson, with regard to the fight for freedom of the subjugated peoples, but with those of the Russian colonialists—namely, the NTS—who in Hitler's day included an anti-Semitic paragraph in their programs and now want to continue subjugating other peoples.

Major-General J.F.C. Fuller: "The Most Explosive Force Is in the Hearts of the Subjugated Peoples"

How could the Free World, in view of its inferior strength as regards classical weapons, withstand a war of aggression on the part of Russia with conventional weapons, without being the first to resort to nuclear weapons, if it misses the only opportunity of destroying the Bolshevik empire from within—namely, by supporting the national liberation revolutions?

Major-General Fuller answers this question thus:

Because both America and Great Britain realize that they cannot hope to rival Russian fighting manpower, they have decided to make good their deficiency in it by relying on what they call tactical nuclear weapons; in other words, less powerful nuclear weapons than atomic and hydrogen bombs, which they call strategic nuclear weapons. This is to tackle the problem the wrong way round. The correct solution is not to increase weapon power, but to reduce Russia's superiority in manpower, and so indirectly increase Western manpower. This can be done by subverting the Russian fighting forces, which are largely recruited from the subjugated peoples within the U.S.S.R. and the satellite countries. Be it remembered that during the first few months of Hitler's invasion of Russia in 1941 well over 2,000,000 prisoners were claimed by the Germans. This is an unbelievable figure until it is realized that the vast majority of these men were deserters—Ukrainians, Byelorussians, Cossacks, Tartars, Turkestanis, and other subjugated peoples. There can be no doubt that, had Hitler welcomed these droves of deserters as allies, and proclaimed that his policy was to liberate their countries, the Soviet Empire would have collapsed through lack of fighting manpower. Instead he treated them as subhumans, and thereby lost the war. Though nuclear weapons have their use, more especially as a threat, the surest way of overcoming the manpower of Russia is to support the national liberation revolutions, and attack the Soviets on their inner front—in Marshal Pilsudski's words: "that most dangerous of all fronts."

And a further question: is it not true that the only guarantee for a lasting peace and for the security of the whole world lies in the disintegration of the Russian empire into independent national states for all the subjugated peoples, all the more so since Russia is the last and most terrible colonial empire in the world? For what reason is the disintegration of the British and French empires approved whereas the idea that the Russian Empire should continue—at least within the frontiers of 1939—is supported?

To which Major-General Fuller's answer is:

My answer to the first part of this question is—yes! To the second, that the ignorance of the Western peoples, particularly the Americans and British, is so profound that they are blind to what Russia is and always has been. This ignorance is largely due to the fact that Russia has never belonged to Europe; her civilization owes nothing to Latin culture; she never took part in the Crusades, the Renaissance, the Reformation, and the Thirty Year's War, and was unaffected by the discovery of the New World and the French Revolution. Also it is due to the secrecy in which the Muscovites have always wrapped themselves. In 1823 the Abbé de Pradt, at one time Napoleon I's ambassador at Warsaw, wrote: "On the other side of the Vistula falls a curtain behind which it is most difficult to see clearly what is happening within the Russian Empire. In the manner of the Orient, from which it has derived its character, the Russian Government is concentrated in the court of the prince; he alone speaks, writes little, and publishes nothing. In a country constituted to hide everything from public knowledge, one is more or less limited to guess-work, and this limitation also applies to the Russian army.... Since the days of Peter the Great, the policy of Russia has never ceased to be one of conquest; one might say that for a whole century her Government has consisted in one and the same man, with one and the same idea—methodical aggrandizement." Unfortunately, Western statesmen do not read Russian history.

Since the days of Ivan III (1462-1505) Russia has been the most persistent colonizing power in the world, and unlike the British imperial system, the urge of which was mainly commercial, the Russian has always been based on subjugation and terror. These means are so antipathetic to Western imperialism that Western peoples fail to see them. They look upon Russia as the land of 200,000,000 Russians, whereas actually over half her population consists of non-Russians, the majority of whom are violently opposed to Russian rule. Thus, though in this age in which the self-determination of nations has become a leading political ideal, the disintegration of the British and French empires is welcomed by the liberal-minded peoples of the West, their ignorance of Russia and her history like an iron curtain obscures from them the truth that Russia is not only the most extensive colonial empire in the world, but the most brutal.

Whether the dissolution of this slave empire will guarantee lasting peace is a hypothetical question which the future alone can answer; but that it will set free in all some 200,000,000 European and Asiatic people, and allow them to govern themselves is an uncontrovertible fact. If the West really believes in freedom, then the Russian Empire must go.

Major-General Fuller has not only diagnosed the political situation correctly, but has also elaborated a military and political plan of promising results for the counteroffensive, which is above all determined by the idea of the disintegration of the Russian empire. At the same time, he had also suggested concrete measures of the psychological and political fight, of which we should like to quote the following. In his article entitled "For What Type of War Should the West Prepare?", Major-General Fuller summarizes his views on political warfare as follows:

(1) In an ideological age wars take on an ideological character.

(2) They are conflicts between ideas in which bullets play a secondary part.

(3) The Cold War is the real war, and its aim is internal attack on the enemy.

(4) Ideas are largely impotent unless backed by force—the threat of actual war.

(5) The greater the threat, the more audaciously can the Cold War be waged, hence the importance of scientific superiority.

(6) As this may lead to the outbreak of actual war, the West must be prepared, not only to fight it, but to convert its cold war into civil and guerrilla war within the enemy's country.

(7) These things the Western nations will never adequately do unless: (a) Western Germany is fully re-armed, and (b) they cooperate with the resistance movements behind the Iron Curtain.

Finally, let us remember this: in the mobile and scientific warfare of today, he who prepares for the defensive digs his own grave.

I have omitted military considerations and suggestions, since this is a matter for the military general staff to decide.

In an interview in *US News and World Report* Major-General J.F.C. Fuller gave the following answer to the question as to what concrete action he would recommend the Allies to take in the Cold War. He said that there were vast areas in the interior of the USSR where discontent prevailed, and added that there were strong insurgent movements in all the satellite countries and in Ukraine. What was needed in the first place was an extensive and better information service. At the same time he stressed that an effective Western Charter with a similar psychological appeal to that of the old Communist Manifesto should be proclaimed. Subsequently our work could then begin. He went on to emphasize that it would be unwise to start a revolution too soon, but said that the Allies could really give the discontented peoples hope of freedom. It was possible to ascertain what line the respective regional conditions called for and which persons were most susceptible to our ideas of freedom. In the meantime, he pointed out, use could be made of wireless transmitters and propaganda literature.

Ukrainian Concentration Camp Prisoners' Demands to the Free World

The demands put to the Western world by the Ukrainian political prisoners during the insurrection in Vorkuta in 1953, and also the demands expressed in the appeal by the Ukrainian political prisoners in Mordovia to the United Nations are in line with the suggestions made by Major-General Fuller.

In his book entitled *Vorkuta* (p. 194), which he wrote on his return from the slave camp there, Dr. J. Scholmer, a noted German doctor, enumerates the demands of the insurgent prisoners to the Western world during their riot in the camp:

1. The dropping of leaflets over all camps giving the signal to the prisoners to call a general attack.

2. The dropping of arms, radio transmitters, explosives, medical supplies, and food. This is to be done not only at Vorkuta, but in all the forest camps along the railway leading southward.

3. Immediate formation by the prisoners of partisan groups which would be in a position to cut the 1,500-km.-long railway line at given points.

4. Creation of a separate republic, independent of Moscow, which would embrace the whole vast forest network of European and Asiatic Russia. If the prisoners had arms, this would be quite unassailable. No tanks, aircraft, or artillery can operate in this gigantic partisan terrain.

5. Intensive radio propaganda to the peoples in the Soviet Union from this independent republic with the aim of bringing about:

    a) A peasant rising under the traditional slogan "Land for the Peasants."

    b) A workers' rising under the slogan "Factories for the Workers."

6. Proclamation of the national independence of Ukraine, the Baltic States, Byelorussia, the peoples of Caucasus, Turkestan, and the Far East.

7. Ultimate creation of conditions similar to civil war by an aggravation of the tension between the hard core of the army and the peoples of the Soviet Union.

This plan of action has been corroborated by the military theoreticians of the West through the fighting insurgents.

U.S. Congress in Favor of the Disintegration of the Russian Empire

The Congress of the United States of America has rightly comprehended and assessed the political character of the global anti-Bolshevik offensive, even though the practical policy of the State Department and of various American semi-private organizations is not in keeping with the wishes and principles of the US House of Representatives.

I was pleased to see the names of Senator Dodd, Paul Douglas, and Kenneth B. Keating, who in the US Senate on June 22, 1959 recommended the famous resolution on "Captive Nations Week" and got it unanimously adopted, on the list of persons invited by the International Invitation Committee to the Congress in Rome.

I am of the opinion that it would be appropriate for the international Congress in Rome to support this Resolution and to adopt it as a guiding principle in political warfare—that is to say, in the sense of advocating the disintegration of the Russian colonial empire. At the same time, it should be stressed that no miniature colonial empires should be allowed to exist in the future in Europe. Thus, Czechoslovakia for instance should be dissolved and an independent Slovakia and Bohemia restored again. The same also holds good in the case of Yugoslavia, where an independent Croatia, Serbia, etc., should be set up again. Such territories as the Congo, Mali, Nigeria, Liberia, and Katanga should be given their independence!

The text of the US Congress Resolution is worded as follows:

Joint Resolution providing for the designation of the week following the Fourth of July as "Captive Nations Week."

WHEREAS the greatness of the United States is in a large part attributed to its having been able, through democratic process, to achieve a harmonious national unity of its peoples, even though they stem from the most diverse of racial, religious, and ethnic backgrounds; and

WHEREAS this harmonious unification of the diverse elements of our free society has led the people of the United States to possess a warm understanding and sympathy for the aspirations of peoples everywhere and to recognize the natural interdependence of the peoples and nations of the world; and

WHEREAS the enslavement of a substantial part of the world's population by Communist imperialism makes a mockery of the idea of peaceful coexistence between nations and constitutes a detriment to the natural bonds of understanding between the people of the United States and other peoples; and

WHEREAS the enslavement of a substantial part of the world has resulted in the creation of a vast empire which poses a dire threat to the security of the United States and of all the free peoples of the world; and

WHEREAS the imperialistic policies of Communist Russia have led, through direct and indirect aggression, to the subjugation of Poland, Hungary, Lithuania, Ukraine, Czecho-Slovakia, Latvia, Estonia, White Ruthenia, Rumania, Bulgaria, East Germany, mainland China, Armenia, Azerbaidzhan, Georgia, North Korea, Albania, Idel-Ural, Tibet, Cossackia, Turkestan, North Vietnam, and others; and

WHEREAS these submerged nations look to the United States, as the citadel of human freedom, for leadership in bringing about their liberation and independence and in restoring to them the enjoyment of their Christian, Jewish, Moslem, Buddhist, and other religious freedoms, and of their individual liberties; and

WHEREAS it is vital to the national security of the United States that the desire for liberty and independence on the part of the peoples of these conquered nations should be steadfastly kept alive; and

WHEREAS the desire for liberty and independence by the overwhelming majority of the people of these submerged nations constitutes a powerful deterrent to war and one of the best hopes for a just and lasting peace; and

WHEREAS it is fitting that we clearly manifest to such peoples through an appropriate and official means the historic fact that the people of the United States share with them their aspirations for the recovery of their freedom and independence: Now, therefore be it

RESOLVED by the Senate and House of Representatives of the United States in Congress assembled, that the President is authorized and requested to issue a proclamation on the Fourth of July, 1959, declaring the week following such day as "Captive Nations Week" and inviting the people of the United States to observe such week with appropriate ceremonies and activities. The President is further authorized and requested to issue a similar proclamation on each succeeding Fourth of July until such time as freedom and independence shall have been achieved for all the captive nations of the world.

In spite of the fact that Senator Dodd, the initiator of the US Congress "Captive Nations Week" Resolution, was a guest speaker in Rome, and in spite of the fact that my suggestion in this respect was accepted by acclamation at the plenary session of the Congress, under the chairmanship of the delegate of the German Federal Parliament Neumann (of the CDU Party), Mme. Labin and Minister Lombardo completely ignored the resolution, since Mme. Labin had declared herself the "dictator" of the Congress and had appointed herself head of the resolution commission, which was nonexistent and had not been elected by anybody!

Liberation Nationalism as the Most Effective Weapon in the Fight against the Last Colonial Empire in the World

As already mentioned, Prof. Hugh Seton-Watson has rightly assessed the situation behind the Iron Curtain in his book *The New Imperialism*, and Major-General J.F.C. Fuller has in an exemplary manner drawn the logical conclusions, from the practical point of view, from this situation and has set them up as guiding principles for the military and political strategy that should be followed.

So as not to miss the opportunity of establishing contact with the universal national liberation movement in order to use it for its own advantage, Soviet Russia is trying to pose as the champion of the national liberation of the peoples of the Western colonial empires, which are disintegrating with the aid and consent of the mother-countries, for in the majority of cases the former ruling nation concedes independence to the formerly ruled and dependent peoples without war.

At the same time, however, the Russian despotic empire is conquering and subjugating more and more peoples and countries. And the 22nd Congress of the Communist Party of the Soviet Union has meanwhile issued the following proclamation:

> In many countries the liberation movement of the developing peoples is being effected under the banner of nationalism. The Marxist-Leninists distinguish between the nationalism of subjugated nations and the nationalism of subjugating nations. The nationalism of subjugated nations is democratic in its general purport and is directed against subjugation, and the Communists support this form of nationalism since it is, in their opinion, justified in a certain historical stage. Its purport is expressed in the striving of the subjugated peoples for liberation from the imperialistic yoke, for national independence and national regeneration....
>
> The national states are asserting themselves more and more actively as an independent force in the world arena, and seen objectively they are essentially a progressive, revolutionary, and anti-imperialistic force....
>
> The days are past when imperialism was still able to make unhindered use of the masses and the material resources of these countries in the predatory wars that it had started....
>
> The countries of socialism are the sincere and loyal friends of the peoples who are fighting for liberation from the imperialistic yoke or who have liberated themselves from it, and give these peoples their universal support. They support the abolition of every form of colonial subjugation and in every way do their share towards consolidating the sovereignty of the states which are being created out of the ruins of the colonial empires.

It is extremely regrettable that the "Conference on the Political Warfare of the Soviets" in Rome did not support the liberation nationalism of the countries in the last, most ruthless, and largest colonial empire in the world. Instead of which, Mme. Labin and Minister Lombardo tried to propagate the idea of non-predetermination as regards the independence of the people in the USSR, as well as the idea of the preservation of the Russian empire according to the frontiers of 1939. It looks as though the West is willing to accept the present frontiers of the Russian sphere of influence, as long as Moscow leaves it in peace.

Here and there in the West there are indications now and then that some realize the importance of nationalism in the fight against Russian imperialistic subjugation. At a press conference on August 5, 1958, President Eisenhower himself declared: "I believe in nationalism and I support it for the good of all the peoples." And Ex-President Harry S Truman wrote in an article on August 25, 1959: "In this era of the abolition of the old colonialism and of transition to the independence and nationalism of peoples, we must not overlook the menacing growth of a new type of colonialism—Red, exploiting colonialism."

It would have been of decisive importance for the idea expressed in this treatise to have been included in the resolution of the Congress in Rome, so as to influence the public in this direction and also to launch appropriate campaigns to support the fight for freedom behind the Iron Curtain. This was not, however, done, since the organizers of the Congress, Mme. Labin and Minister Lombardo, have aims in mind which are not connected with the liberation of the peoples from the Russian yoke.

In conclusion I wish to stress that we must always bear in mind the words of the British Air Vice-Marshal E.J. Kingston-McClough in his book *Global Strategy*:

> The enemy here considered is not simply embodied in an ideological threat but rather it is the state called Russia—that is, Russia as a power: a Russia expanding and desiring to extend her sphere of influence, a state posing as the symbol of all manner of ideals. It is Russia as a fighting force, an organized community, and a power or state in the most autocratic and absolute sense with which we are concerned.

Mme. Labin and Minister Lombardo have rendered the world fight against Bolshevism a disservice in refusing to attack Russian colonialism.

Another disappointment and another unsuccessful, negligible, nondemocratic initiative on the part of the anti-Communist world league!

Moscow has no reason to be afraid of the undemocratic anti-Communists who reject the national independence of the peoples—as, for instance, Mme. Labin, Minister Lombardo, and others. They will never succeed in rousing the enthusiasm of peoples and individuals for the fight, even though they have the necessary funds. For it is not money but ideas which are decisive in this case! And the ideas of Mme. Labin and Minister Lombardo are false, and their methods are the totalitarian methods of a secretive coterie and clique which conspire with undemocratic anti-Communism behind the backs of the peoples.

The Ukrainian Review,
No. IV, 1961 pp. 6-22

The Steps to Victory

Aims and objectives of a world center against Russian imperialism can be classed in two groups. The first group consists of all efforts and activities that should have as their aims the following:

1. To organize and assemble under one banner the main centers of intransigence in the Free World against the policies of conquest and national oppression combined with social subjugation that are furthered by Moscow. The action should be taken in accordance with the principles outlined in the section on the ideological and political platform, with the purpose of influencing in an organized way various governments so that they change their policies in regard to the Russian subjugation of nations and to Communism. Also, to educate a new generation of Western leaders to replace those who are only too willing to compromise with the tyranny and conspiracy of Moscow.

2. To stimulate the organization of a new order on a worldwide scale of firm believers in God and country, whose ideals and ways of life would illuminate society and who would be the standard-bearers of the rebirth of the Free World.

Only with this rebirth can the victory of these ideals be achieved behind the Iron Curtain. This is what is urgently needed. We should not forget that the strength of ideas of the Western world, indeed the strength of the West itself, always lays in its expansive spirit.

3. The aim of the Rebirth Movement of the Free World—i.e., the movement rooted in faith in God and nation—would be to bring about the victory of our ideas behind the Iron Curtain—i.e., the liberation of the nations subjugated by Russia, the restoration of their independence and realization of social justice in those sovereign states.

The second group of aims and objectives pertains to political propaganda, financial, and military aid that should be granted to national liberation revolutionary movements inside and outside the USSR.

The sovereignty of each nation must be guaranteed—i.e., the donor of this help cannot interfere in the internal affairs of the recipient nation—aid should be given to the central organ of each movement, and the center in turn shall distribute that help through its own channels and according to its own independent plans.

Two-fold actions are indispensable: a) in the West—i.e., in the Free World—and b) for the subjugated nations directly. Yet both these actions are indissolubly united. An action which is not based on centers of the Free World that have a strong faith in basic values, such as independence for nations and freedom for the individual, but instead has its source in material interests, is of an ephemeral nature—i.e., it can always be beaten by higher bids or can be sold at auction for a higher price. We need in the West champions of definite ideas and a strong faith in them. Only then can the action have a lasting foundation, and will not depend, for instance, on change in tax allowances.

An ideological and political struggle, a spiritual crusade based on high principles must begin immediately—an ideological and political assault on the centers of evil, of defeatism, marasmus, decay, falsehoods, and misinformation. Such an aggressive attitude ought to be based on a thorough knowledge of the real conditions and aspirations of the subjugated nations gained from studies and knowledge of primary sources.

From the above statements it follows that a CENTER OF IDEOLOGICAL AND POLITICAL COORDINATION OF ACTIONS, composed of sovereign spokesmen of the subjugated nations and new forces of the Free World, is urgently needed. And these spokesmen should be treated as parties to an aggreement and not as agents of intelligence services.

A CENTER OF POLITICAL-MILITARY ACTION should be created with the purpose of developing the new strategy of struggle in the sense of the insurgent-revolutionary concepts of General Taras Chuprynka and General J.F.C. Fuller, and for training the cadres accordingly. The cadres of the subjugated peoples should be at the disposal of the sovereign spokesmen of respective peoples alone, and must not be treated as saboteurs of various intelligence services.

There should be a RESEARCH INSTITUTE OF THE IDEOLOGICAL, POLITICAL, ECONOMIC, CULTURAL, AND RELIGIOUS STRUGGLE behind the Iron Curtain, in opposition to the Institute for the Study of the History and

Culture of the USSR, which is an illusion devoid of objective scientific endeavor. The concept of an Institute of Soviet Studies deludes us into believing in the existence of a new area of learning, worthy of research. "Soviet Studies" is nothing but a study of the Russian mentality, methods of deception used by Russian imperialism and Communism. It is more important that everyone should understand the spirit of resistance of the subjugated nations and in connection with this the Russian methods of deception and extermination.

Instead of an Institute of Soviet Studies there should be an Institute of Research into Russian imperialism that would examine and expose colonialism, genocide, ideas of the Third Rome, and Pan-Slavism, and show the duplicity of the so-called liberation of the proletariat or colonial nations and other similar ideas of Russian imperialism.

Moscow maintains that the nations of the world have accepted two different ideologies and two social-political systems—capitalist and Communist—thus trying to place them on the same level as merely competitive ideas. In doing this Moscow attempts to hide the fact that the nations where Communist ideology is dominant have been subjugated by Russia by force of arms. Moscow tries to create the impression that these nations voluntarily chose the so-called socialist system of life. The fact, however, remains that not a single nation subjugated by Russo-Communist imperialism after World War I and World War II, except the governing Russian nation, voluntarily accepted the Communist system, and none of them accepts Moscow as its metropolis in any respect.

Publications by this new Institute in various languages of the world should expose the true character of the Russian evil. Such an institute ought to employ a new type of personnel—i.e., people who until now had to remain silent in the West but who are at the disposal of the ABN.

At the same time the struggle of the subjugated nations against enslavement and Russian tyranny and the analysis of official announcements made by Russian imperialists and their stooges in combination with information gathered through other channels must be presented in their true meaning.

The national fight and the manifold manifestations of national life, including the ideological struggle, should be clearly defined, because up to now they were concealed or distorted and interpreted as opposition to the regime. The great revolution of nations that is at present unfolding must now be revealed to the Free World to its full extent. Similarly, the negation of the liberating nationalism of subjugated nations should cease, for no one disclaims the nationalism of the Afro-Asian peoples. At the same time these publications should reveal to the Afro-Asian nations the true character of Moscow and of Communism in general.

The Press Agency should spread information and communications with new contents and tendencies which differ from those that have been disseminated so far in the Free World. This ought to be the agency of truth, which hitherto has been distorted in the Free World.

Radio stations and television programs should have the purpose of propagating ideas, explained on an ideological level, to reveal the truth about the struggle of the enslaved peoples and to enlighten the societies of the Free World, particularly its youth. Therefore, new radio stations and new television programs are indispensable. They should be combative, propagating idealism, loftiness, great-ness, showing the life and heroism of the enslaved peoples, the great personali-ties of General T. Chuprynka—Commander-in-Chief of the Ukrainian Insur-gent Army—and Stepan Bandera, and the underground Church; they should reveal the genocide inspired by Moscow, the Muscovite man-made famine in Ukraine and in other countries of the USSR, Khrushchev's warfare against the Ukrainian insurgents, conditions in the concentration camps of the USSR, the Hungarian uprising, the heroism and martyrdom of all nationalities and their great leaders, as well as the sacrifices of great men of the West—in general, to disseminate another type of content by means of these communications, to influence the masses.

The official political journal of the center should shape different political attitudes of the Free World toward the Moscow-Peking tyrants from those prevailing up till now. This journal should be published in many languages. It would have to be a militant journal, campaigning for the ideas and concepts defined in the platform of the Mexico conference of 1958 by the ABN and in the addendum to this plan.

The ideological journal of the Center would have to further the moral and ideological renaissance of the Occident and the whole Free World in the spirit of faith in God, heroic humanism, and nationalism, to bring about a moral revolu-tion in the ideological realm.

The journal would have to give a new interpretation to current events. The problem of a moral rebirth of the Free World is inseparably tied up with the liberation of the enslaved peoples from Russian imperialism and tyranny. This issue of mutual interdependence should remain paramount and be proclaimed as dominant. A rebirth is not possible by accepting the thesis of a passive tolerance of evil—namely, that the enslaved can be exterminated as long as we can enjoy a life of comfort.

The whole action cannot be limited to simple education; its end is a campaign against Moscow and its fifth column by all possible means in the Free World.

Mass demonstrations, manifestations, marches in solidarity with the libera-tion struggle of the enslaved nations, as well as protest rallies against tyranny and the false policies of the governments of the free countries, mobilization of the masses for such a campaign, rallies of youth in front of consulates and embassies against Khrushchev's or Gromyko's visits, against friendly gestures toward the tyrants, for a complete rejection of coexistence and compromise, which always result in the capitulation of the West.

Furthermore, the journal should campaign against the subversive and terror-istic actions of the KGB which are directed against a possible unified action of the enslaved and the Free World.

It would be necessary to organize international conferences on various conti-nents to strengthen the front against the common enemy of the enslaved and the free.

An international congress should be organized to develop world-wide action on the basis of the Mexico conference of 1958.

The fighters for freedom and political independence should visit various countries with lectures and public appeals for cooperation in the struggle for independence of the enslaved nations. Participants in the struggle should be invited to speak about this struggle and about the Golgotha of the subjugated peoples in concentration camps and prisons.

It would be a mistake to hope that Moscow will not succeed in its propaganda, which aims to undermine the prestige of the USA and other Western powers in the eyes of the subjugated nations, especially now during the realization of the contemporary policies of Messrs. Rusk and Rostow.

It should be realized that failure is bound to attend a propaganda which concentrates on exaggerated praise of something which is against human nature—for instance, of the view that religion is superfluous, that the national idea is something old-fashioned, that collective farms are justifiable; on the other hand, a thousand-fold repetition of the possible consequences of the coexistence policy—i.e., the loss of Hungary, Cuba, Laos, the extradition by the American authorities of thousands of refugees in 1945 to the Russians, etc.—will be crowned by success.

The highest achievement in Russia's plans for world domination was the recognition and tacit acceptance by the West of the status quo—that is, the status of enslavement of the non-Russian nations, the establishing of diplomatic relations with the Western world, and the legal recognition granted to Moscow's agents in the capitals of the captive and subjugated nations.

A further important concession on the part of the official West to Moscow is the actual isolation of the national political spokesmen of the subjugated nations and discrimination against them by branding them, in the spirit of Bolshevik intentions, as fascists or anti-Semites, despite the fact that many of them, as for instance the chairman of the ABN himself, for years suffered in Nazi concentration camps. The voice of these people is not only unheeded, but in practice it is being suppressed and negated.

The national political emigrants, the champions of the ideas of national liberation and of the uncompromising fight against Bolshevism and Russian imperialism, will continue to be the means through which a proper liberation policy on the part of the West could start a chain reaction and release immense explosive powers behind the Iron Curtain against the oppressive domination of Russia.

America lost a great opportunity for the whole global, moral, and cultural development, for it neglected the immigrants from behind the Iron Curtain by letting them live in New York slums and by letting former college and university professors, well-known intellectuals, and cultural workers become cleaners and floor-sweepers in factories and similar establishments.

Toynbee was right when he designated the emigrants as the yeast of the rebirth of the West, but...

Bitterness, nihilism, acute disappointment seized most of them. Nothing would have been easier than to have created opportunities at well-established institutions and schools for these thousands of intellectuals and cultural workers of East European extraction to study and teach; in this way they would have been able to use their cultural potentialities for the purpose of spreading the new ideals which are old truths; and they would have contributed towards deepening

the idealistic sentiments within American society whilst at the same time revealing the truth about Russian tyranny. All these forces should have been included
in the psychological battle carried on by the Free World against tyrants, but such
actions should have been determined not on an ideological and philosophical
basis dictated by experts of the Harvard type or by Russophiles of the Rostow,
Kennan, Bohlen type, but by an independent authority, without any binding
instructions from above.

All is not yet lost, however....

One of the important objectives of the World Center must be to include in an
appropriate way the potentialities of our political emigrants in the total fight of
the Free World.

It was a lost opportunity on the part of the West that the extraordinary fact of
the bravura raid (1948-1949) across the frontiers of three countries performed
by a detachment of 500 members of the Ukrainian Insurgent Army—who under
dangerous and very difficult conditions carried out the order given by General
Taras Chuprynka to spread the truth about the reality of the struggle and
slavery under Russian domination—was neither exploited nor even publicized.
These 500 insurgents, now organized in the Association of Former UPA Fighters, in our opinion constitute an ideo-political potential similar to the Hungarian
insurgents of the so-called satellite complex.

In addition to the matters mentioned just now, the following additional problems must be mentioned:

1) The encirclement of the USSR and the so-called satellite countries by ABN
missions with the aim of ideological, political, and propagandistic penetration by
means of people and literature. Furthermore, the setting up of radio stations of
the ABN in countries adjoining the Russian Communist empire   for instance, in
Germany (West Berlin), Turkey, Pakistan, Taipei (where an ABN mission is
already active and is at present broadcasting), in Korea, Vietnam, Japan, the
Philippines, Greece, etc.

Strategic radio stations should be so powerful that the possibility of being
jammed would be minimized and, accordingly, the means of penetration behind
the Iron Curtain maximized.

Transportation by planes of leaflets and various kinds of revolutionary propaganda material, which should be dropped in the territories of the countries
within the USSR, including Siberia. Here the experience and technique of
Nationalist China in its raids over Mainland China could be used and perfected.

2) Provided political conditions were fulfilled, training and supply of technical
equipment and technical knowledge needed for those destined to be dropped
behind the Iron Curtain should for various reasons be placed in the hands of the
respective national organizations. From outside authorities only technical assistance and the training of instructors (or advisors) would be expected but not
direct contact or supervision of those individuals who would be dropped over the
territory.

A separate objective should be the training of the organizers of guerrilla
warfare in the event of a third war, but this requires that our political platform be
recognized and accepted. Without political guarantees it will not be possible to

obtain people for sabotage actions. In other words, without a clear statement of specific political commitments on the part of the West, no manpower could be enlisted for subversive and sabotage actions.

In this context a selection of young men capable of military service from the nationalities behind the Iron Curtain and formation of separate combat groups are inavoidable, since otherwise, if dropped as individual saboteurs on the territories of their origin, they will be seized by the insurgent units, for the simple reason that the insurgents would like to free themselves from Bolshevik provocations and counter-saboteurs such as the Soviet bands led by Kovpak before and after 1945, who tried to deceive the UPA commanding officers by disguising themselves as nationalist guerrillas.

3) A research institute in the national languages of the peoples behind the Iron Curtain to edit publications which are to be sent to these peoples.

4) Infiltration and enlightenment during Youth Festivals, Olympic Games, among Soviet seamen and tourists who visit the West or who ask for political asylum, special training for those who intend to tour the countries behind the Iron Curtain—all this should be done confidentially but according to a definite worked-out plan or system.

5) Writing, editing, and publishing of strategic and political material to be ready in the event of a war and thus to be able to influence by this material members of the Soviet armed forces, party members, members of Communist youth organizations, collective farmers, cultural workers, but above all and especially addressed to the nations as a whole. This is an important task.

6) Strengthening the already existing ABN missions and establishing new ABN missions in various countries of the world including Africa, in order to expose Russian imperialism through these nations. In addition, a mission working with the United Nations and intended to denounce Russian aggressive policies must be set up in order to attack Russian imperialists from all sides. Books about the national problems in the USSR, their colonial character, and the struggle of these nations against the USSR should be published in various languages. Similarly, the *ABN Correspondence* should appear in large editions in various languages, since the unique approach of the ABN to different cardinal issues is not expressed by any other journal or publication.

7) A staff preparing plans for combating the KGB (Soviet secret police) is indispensable.

8) Instead of the puppet governments of Moscow the free nations should recognize the revolutionary centers as legitimate spokesmen of the independent strivings of the subjugated peoples until such time as sovereign governments shall be formed on liberated territories.

9) The free Governments should proclaim a great Charter of national-state independence and individual freedom for all the enslaved within the USSR and the Communist sphere. This charter should serve as a manifesto of the struggle of all freedom-loving mankind, and the policies of the Free World in respect to Russia should be formulated accordingly. The dismemberment of the Russian empire as well as the destruction of Communism, by means of which Moscow conceals its imperialism, should become the dominant slogans of all the freedom-

loving peoples. The liquidation of this empire will bring the end of Communism. It should be unmasked everywhere and at all times.

10) In opposition to the present United Nations Organization there should be formed another UN with equal rights for its members and UN fighters for the liberation of all colonially enslaved nations and the establishment of independent states within their ethnographic boundaries. Such a UN organization should not, however, become a kind of world government, since otherwise the principles of national sovereignty and national entity will be negated. But the sovereignty of nations should be the central idea of the new United Nations Organization, as a fighting movement for the national idea, the freedom of the individual, faith in God, and social justice. There must be no room in the new United Nations for tyrants, neutralists, and coexistentialists.

The vital need of our day is the formation of a worldwide front of free and subjugated nations, with a closely coordinated strategy of struggle against Russian imperialism and Communism, a front which would originate from a global coordinating center on the basis of the political concept of the national liberation movements of the subjugated peoples, which form the first front of combat.

The entire activity, particularly in respect to the areas of the subjugated peoples, cannot be directed by any foreign body; its content and scope must be determined by the national revolutionary centers or liberation organizations which are sovereign in their decisions. The West can only supply technical opportunities for its unfolding but not the political directives or policies, as is the case with the Free Europe Committee, or the ACLB, which realize the political line of the State Department but not of the subjugated nations fighting for national independence.

The Ukrainian Review,
No. IV, 1963, pp. 16-24

Principles
of the Anti-Communist World Movement

The Importance of Europe

Before there can be any discussion about the political and organizational principles of an anti-Communist world movement, it must be clearly established that Europe is neither a subsidiary of America nor of Asia, but a separate force. The prerequisite in the process of Europe's separate role in a political, economic, and military respect must be the assurance of its own spiritual, moral, and ideological strength. It is the latter which we have set as our task in our present-day activities. Under no condition can we relinquish the ideological-political power positions of Europe and consider her as an appendage to America or Asia. Already now the new Russian imperialists define Eurasia, the so-called "All Russia," as a center of the two continents, relegating Europe to a small peninsula and Asia to the periphery of All Russia-Eurasia. That Europe has a future as a leading ideological-political power of the world, as a constant source of new ideas and concepts, and as a source of immortal spiritual values cannot be disregarded in the formation an anti-Communist world movement. In view of its economic, geopolitical, and human potential and especially in view of its genius, Europe has unlimited possibilities to play a decisive role in world politics. On one condition, however, that which we call Europe today is not Europe at all, but only its rump. The peoples subjugated within the USSR from Ukraine to Estonia, from Slovakia to Georgia, form an internal part of Europe. The subjugated people regard themselves as propagators of the cultural European heritage and defend European values. The Russians have distanced themselves from Europe, especially so by their concept of Eurasia. Europe is not exclusively a geographic concept. Even the remaining free part of Europe is a power, if it relies upon its own forces.

The consciousness of Europe's power must influence and decisively determine our thoughts in regard to a world anti-Communist movement.

The Importance of the Subjugated Peoples and of Their Liberation Struggle

a) *The opinion of General Fuller and of other scientific and military experts.*
The peoples and individuals subjugated and enslaved by Russian imperialism and Communism are the second power factor to be taken into account with reference to the anti-Communist world movement. It is they who are the Achilles' heel of the Communist system—not the hydrogen bomb. Their resistance to the Russian empire, and to the regime from within, is a guarantee of success and the alternative to a nuclear war. In his book *The Conduct of War, 1789-1961* (p. 320), General Fuller, the most famous and profound military theoretician of the world, wrote:

> It is this inner front—rather than first line—which is the Achilles' heel of the Soviet empire. Not only are half of the inhabitants of the USSR non-Russian, and many of them are nationally minded and antagonistic to Muscovite rule; but it has also been estimated that less than five percent of the peoples behind the Iron Curtain are in sympathy with their draconic Communist regimes. As we have seen, whenever a crisis has occurred within the Russian Empire, whether in tsarist or Communist times, the 'minority' nations have revolted, and whenever oppression has appeared to weaken in the countries behind the Iron Curtain, disturbances or revolts have followed. In the Hungarian uprising of 1956 it should not be forgotten that the only non-Hungarian people who fought on the side of the rebels were deserters from the Soviet army.
>
> Therefore, in the Cold War, the psychological center of gravity of the Russian Empire is to be sought in the hearts of the subjugated peoples within the USSR and behind the Iron Curtain. Further, it should be borne in mind, and it seldom is, that this psychological "bomb" is as great a deterrent to the Soviets resorting to actual war as the hydrogen bomb itself. Russia's weakness is our strength, and her

strength is our ignorance; no man realizes this more fully than Nikita Khrushchev—what, then, is his Cold War policy?

General Fuller's ideas are confirmed by the most famous atomic scientists and military experts.

Max Planck, one of the pioneers of modern physics, said in 1962 in *Chance*, (published in Munich):

> With traditional political concepts, we will not be able to cope with this situation. The bankruptcy of the traditional idea of war, attack and defense, is obvious. Without a reappraisal, there is no possibility of averting the danger.... Today, the greatest danger is represented by the people who refuse to recognize that the era which is now beginning is fundamentally different from that of the past.

B.H. Liddell Hart wrote that the atomic bomb is an uncertain means of suppressing a revolution; it can be deadly for both sides.... "It is neither a good policeman, nor a good fireman, nor a usable border station." (Quoted from *Deterrence or Defense*).

In *A Forward Strategy for America* (1961) Robert Strauss-Hupe stated: "The Communists have been able to carry out the fight against the West through numerous auxiliaries and representatives.... In this way they put the West under constant pressure, without employing the last provocation—the causus belli— which, from historical experience, is absolutely necessary to cause Western nations to go to war against the main enemy."

The Frenchman, Raymond Aron, stated: "If the Soviet bloc convinces itself that it possesses an incontestable superiority, either in terms of passive or active deterrent instruments, or in terms of the totality of all military means, the danger would be deadly."

Therefore, the subjugated peoples must be a decisive element in the formation of the World League and in the analysis of the power elements of the anti-Communist world struggle. Hoelderlin rightly stated· "But where danger exists, there are also saviors."

b) *The ABN and the Anti-Communist World Movement.*

Starting from this position, the ABN formulates its views on the anti-Communist world movement as follows:

The ABN has always been in favor of the idea of creating a world anti-Communist movement, and itself had raised this matter as early as 1949 at the International Conference in Edinburgh. The ABN considers such a body very necessary, but maintains that the success of its action is dependent on a clearly defined political content. This world center must contain in its program of action not only the destruction of Communism, but also the breakup of the Russian Empire, regardless of its ideological base, into independent national states, each of which would encompass its presently subjugated people within its ethnographical boundaries—in other words, Ukraine, Byelorussia, Lithuania, Latvia, Estonia, Georgia, Armenia, Azerbaidzhan, North Caucasia, Turkestan, Bohemia,

Slovakia, Hungary, Poland, Bulgaria, Romania, Albania, Croatia, Serbia, and other nations subjugated by Russian imperialism and Communism. The ABN opposes not only the Communist system but also Russian imperialism in any form.

Neither the ABN nor any national liberation revolutionary organization—any member of the ABN—will ever cooperate with any Russian anti-Communist but imperialistic organization which will not actively support the breakup of the Russian Empire (the USSR and its satellites) into independent states. Therefore, it is in the very nature of things that no Russian imperialistic non-Communist organization which aims at destroying the Communist regime while preserving the Russian Empire under a so-called democratic system can ever be a member of the world anti-Communist movement. No action which does not clearly support the concept of independent nation-states and the breakup of the Russian Empire will ever be successful in countries subjugated by Russian imperialism.

The ABN rejects in principle the idea of a common front with the USSR against Red China which is advocated by certain official Western circles, but supports simultaneous action against *both—Moscow and Peking*. The ABN opposes the neglect of a front against the Russian empire, while concentrating only on the threat from Red China.

In principle, we are against a common front with one tyranny against another. We also are opposed to a common front of America with the Russian empire— such a front appears to be developing against China as the so-called main enemy. From a world political view, however, Red China is by no means to be considered the main enemy. We conceive of a common front of the Free World with the subjugated world against both tyrannies simultaneously. We must not forget August 23, 1939, when Stalin and Hitler signed a non-aggression and friendship pact.

The ABN rejects in principle all uncertainties concerning the future fate of nations subjugated by Russian Communist imperialism. These uncertanties are cause by the avoidance of the question of the breakup of the Russian Empire and by promising instead the Russian formula for plebiscites, "self-determination" or so-called "non-predetermination"—because never yet has any nation had to question the right to its own freedom and national sovereignty. Moreover, in conformity with the concept of disintegration of all Western empires, the Russian Communist Empire must be destroyed and a *new* empire must not rise on its ruins!

The ABN considers that the organizational statutes and the political platform which were chosen at the 1958 conference in Mexico should be the basis for the world center especially as they represent the positions agreed upon by sixty-five national delegations from several continents. The ABN does not consider that the geographical principle of representation by continent should be included— because, for example, half of Europe is subjugated.

Hence, a continental representation cannot be a fair representation.

In the opinion of the ABN there is a main front consisting of captive nations, and a secondary front made up of free nations. Each of these fronts has a very different understanding of the danger involved and the degree of effort needed to oppose Russian or Chinese Communist aggression. The ABN stands in the main front, having as members national liberation revolutionary organizations from Asian nations also subjugated by Russian imperialism, such as Turkestan, for example. The principle of continental representation by itself will not take into consideration the interests of those who are in the main front. For example, in Ukraine, a nation having a population of 45 million, a great battle is being waged against Russian Communism. The organizers of this battle, the Organization of Ukrainian Nationalists, and the Ukrainian Insurgent Army, known throughout the world, are dynamic members of the ABN. However, in accordance with the continental representation such a force would not be separately represented in the executive committee. Even the ABN, as the strongest coordinating center of nations subjugated by Russian imperialism, would not be represented, because probably there would already be a representation from Free Europe in the executive committee.

Therefore, in our opinion, we should adopt the position accepted by the 1958 Mexico Conference, where both the organizational structure and the political platform were approved. Moreover, the resolutions concerning Russian colonialism which have already been accepted by the Asian Peoples' Anti-Communist League are a basis for cooperation for the ABN, because there is no doubt that these decisions will be included in the political platform of the world league as the point of departure in any stand towards the Russian Empire. The US Congress's Captive Nations Resolution (Public Law 86-90, 1959) should be regarded as a political platform of the world anti-Communist movement. If the highest legislative authority of the American nation—the US Congress—in spite of possible diplomatic difficulties passed a resolution on the disintegration of the Russian Empire unanimously eight years ago and three consecutive presidents of the USA proclaimed this public law again and again, then how can a world anti-Communist movement composed of unofficial organizations be afraid to accept this resolution as a political basis for its activities?

It is necessary to accept this conception of ABN—that is to say, its general, basic ideas on the world struggle against Russian imperialism and Communism. Otherwise, the subjugated peoples cannot be won over to the West, and these peoples constitute the main front against the Bolshevik world-enemy.

Ideological Principles of the European and World Anti-Communist Movement

In the fight against Communism and Russian colonialism and imperialism, it is absolutely necessary to stress the problem of nation-state independence, the national idea, the freedom principles of a new world order, and to counterpose it to the imperialistic ideas. In view of the fact that today the Communists and the Soviet Russian imperialists hypocritically fight against colonialism and imperialism and speak up on behalf of national independence, *it is impossible that our efforts will be successful if we fail to lay the main stress on the most just and most progressive idea of our century, the national idea, the idea of national independence of all the peoples subjugated by Russian imperialism and Communism. This idea must become the motivating power.* It is absolutely necessary that we incorporate this principle in the charter of the world anti-Communist movement so that we shall succeed in overthrowing the Russian empire and the Communist system in all its forms.

A moral revolution is an indispensable prerequisite of a successful struggle against the world evil of Communism, whose main center is Moscow. A spiritual rebirth of humanity and renewed faith in the unchangeable and eternal truths, faith in God and country, and, finally, the de-barbarization of humanity—these are the values which humanity needs today. The time has now come for a great spiritual and ideological revolution recalling the greatest epochs of human upsurge. It is high time that the process of erosion of idealism and humanism in the Free World be halted, for society cannot exist without faith and eternal truths. Without an ideology based on faith in God, humanism, and patriotism, there can be no victory over the ideology of evil propagated by Moscow today. In our century, a century full of fear, it seems paradoxical to die for a cause, for an idea, for the eternal values, for a definite and determined way of life, for freedom, for God and country—it seems paradoxical because cynicism and nihilism have engulfed the entire Free World.

Our world is very old. The important thing is not to invent a new ideology; almost every worthwhile idea has already been expressed. What is needed is to defend the very old ideas. What is needed is character, courage, loyalty, and determination in the realization and application of the old ideas. History has always reacted favorably to courage, moral qualities, character, faith in God and country. Ephemeral ideas, on the other hand, have disappeared without making any significant inroads in mankind's history. If the West continues to underrate moral values and ideology and shies away from an ideological contest, it will cease to be what it has been, since the West collectively has represented a synthesis of the old Greek, Roman, and Christian values, just as the Oriental civilization represents the harmonious synthesis of ancient values of the Chinese, Japanese, Confucian, Buddhist, and Shintoist cultures.

It is because it has been based on these eternal values that the West has become the freest and the richest society. But this society is doomed to perish within a short time, if Western man ceases to aspire towards high ideals, ceases to struggle for true values, and ceases to believe in and aspire to a higher moral and spiritual order. It is up to the free man. Moscow is certain to emerge victorious if the free man does not return to moral values as the dominant factors in life, to faith in the eternal truths, and to an appreciation of a life of moral ideologies. Whoever depreciates these idealistic qualities will also lose his material possessions. To value the heroic over the preservation of one's own egotistical life, which is not so precious that it cannot be risked—to rate effort and struggle on behalf of one's friends above one's utilitarian profit, to struggle for the great and the supreme in life as opposed to the cult of the little man, to place sacrifice and devotion above amour-propre, and to find the meaning of life in service to an ideal—these are the elements of a new anti-hedonistic revolution of spirit which are sorely needed in today's world. Faith in God, patriotism, love of one's country, morality based on religion, the ideal of the nation as a cornerstone of the world order, the national principle of the organization of the world, respect for man created in the image of God, the freedom of man's creative work, and the ideals of social justice as opposed to dialectical and historic materialism, to internationalistic Communism, and to the ideology of the herd, which is a creation of the Russian Communist spirit—these are the ingredients of the anti-materialistic and anti-Communist revolution of the spirit, an idealistic and moral revolution of freedom-loving mankind.

The principles just outlined do not contradict the fact that free societies are pluralistic and this accounts fundamentally for their freedom. In pluralistic societies there cannot exist one single ideology. There might be many ideologies, as well as many creeds, as well as many ways of approaching spiritual problems. We must uphold moral values—so underrated today—but we ought not to seek a single ideology. The very fact that those of us who are worth their salt turn out to be believers and defenders of the perennial and supreme values contradicts the concept of a single ideology.

The existence of common eternal values of all humanity cannot be denied. They have to be defended from Communism.

Freedom is the necessary prerequisite for competition of various ideologies. If we want to win, we should have our own vision of values and qualities which are worth fighting for, and the freedom achieved will be the precondition of this competition. The pluralistic society approves of the contest for the higher values! Above freedom stands justice. Freedom permits us to fight for the higher ideal— justice. We know why we want to be free and what we are striving for. The pluralistic society means the common struggle of all religions against militant atheism.

Besides, from a merely religious point of view, Communism ought to be attacked at the same time by Christians and Moslems and Jews and true Buddhists, etc. Whoever believes in the supremacy of the Almighty, of the Creative Spirit, must single out the Communists as enemies. But there is no oneness of religious faith but plurality and consequently there cannot be a single ideology.

Political Concept on Liberation from Fear and Slavery

The enslaved nations in the Russian prison of nations are a component and integral part of freedom-loving mankind, and so are those captive peoples that are under the domination of other Communist regimes. The ideological revolution, the moral, anti-hedonistic, anti-materialistic, and anti-imperialistic revolution takes place in the spirituality and in the struggle of the captive nations and peoples in the Russian prison of nations. The ultimate objective of this revolution is a total negation of Communism as a system imposed on the captive nations by the Russian totalitarians. Communism is a modern form of Russian imperialism, a national imperialistic Russian idea under the guise of which Russia endeavors to conquer the whole world. The national liberation idea, and freedom struggle of the captive nations in the Russian Empire—i.e., in the USSR and the so-called satellite countries—constitute the Achilles' heel of this despotic and tyrannical edifice. Moscow uses the policy of genocide for the purpose of destroying nationalities, independence, and freedom.

The atomic age is accompanied by a process of disintegration of empires and by the victory of the national principle and the ideology of national statehood as the most just and the most ideal. The captive nations enslaved in the Russian Communist sphere of domination are a third sovereign force dependent on no one on the world's chessboard. They constitute the key force around which all international problems and politics of necessity must revolve. Humanity's road to liberation from fear lies in the national revolution of all the captive nations directed against Russian imperialism and Communism.

National uprisings—that is, national liberation wars of the captive nations enslaved by Russian imperialism and Communism—are a possible alternative to an atomic war, which can be averted through the active support by the Free World of the national liberation movements in the captive countries. In any future armed clash the decisive role will be played by the people who are adequately prepared militarily. With the development of military technology, the significance of the armed forces of peoples, especially of revolutionary guerrillas, assumes a great and important meaning. In parallel with the development of its thermonuclear and conventional arms in order to counterbalance the Russian Communist and satellite-bloc armaments, the Free World should endeavor to diminish the human war potential of the Russian Communist bloc by winning over to its side the souls and minds of the soldiers of the captive nations.

The assurance of success lies in synchronized and coordinated national revolts and in a chain of revolutionary uprisings. In order to disrupt and destroy the Russian prison of nations from within, an entirely new idealistic, moral, and political atmosphere with respect to the captive nations has to be created in the Free World; moreover, a new attitude toward the captors and oppressors of the former has to be adopted by the Free World.

Above all, the present policy of the West should undergo certain important changes which would attune it to the service of new ideas and a new way of life. To bring about a national and political revolution which would embrace all phases of life—culture, religion, the social and economic complex, and the whole gamut of a nation's life—the policy of "coexistence" has to be rejected in principle because it enables Moscow to gain recognition of the status quo of the captive nations as a startng point for other conquests. A new hope and confidence has to be aroused in the captive nations. They should become convinced that the West will not betray them, but will support their struggle for freedom and national independence. The international institutions should be reorganized and reconstructed for the purpose of conducting an effective struggle against Russian imperialism and colonialism, with the participation therein of the liberation spokesmen of the captive nations. The Free World must have more faith in the ideals of sacrifice and heroism, and ideological growth of the Free World must be sympathetic to and consonant with the moral values and political objectives of the captive nations.

Thus, the alternative to a thermonuclear war is not a policy of "coexistence," which leads necessarily to the outbreak of an atomic war, but a policy of liberation. Liberation of the captive nations and not disarmament of the Free World, bold and decisive resistance to Russian Communist aggression and not appeasing it—this is the urgent requirement for the West today. Any local liberation, isolated and limited to a certain area or country, is a pernicious illusion. The problem of liberation is at present an integral and inseparable problem encompassing all the captive nations. Such is the spirit of the "Captive Nations Resolution" enacted by the US Congress in 1959. In essence, this resolution supports the breakup of the Russian empire, the restoration of state sovereignty to all the captive nations in the USSR and in its extended territorial empire. It is precisely this concept that should mold the basic offensive of the free world against the forces of Russian Communist imperialism and colonialism.

Moscow cannot risk a war, for it needs its military forces to keep in check the unrest which exists in every part of its empire. Indeed, the menace of a new world war exists only because the West is opportunistic. It does not have its own convictions, its own positive plan of action, relying instead on a policy of reacting to Soviet Russian moves. History, however, suggests the opposite approach. There are many examples which show that Russia always retreats under the pressure of force. This was the case in 1918 at Brest; in 1920 after the victory of Pilsudski and Petlura at the Vistula; in 1925 upon the determined stand of Kemal Pasha; in 1948 in Berlin; 1950 in Iran, when Anglo-American divisions appeared; in 1958 in Lebanon, when American Marines landed there. In short: in every instance where it was clear that the West was determined to fight, Moscow fell back. In 1956, had President Eisenhower come to the defense of the Hungarian revolutionaries instead of telegraphing Tito that the US was not interested in Hungarian affairs, Hungary would be an independent nation today. The same holds true for Berlin. If timely and proper assistance had been offered, there would not be a wall of shame to attest to Western indecisiveness. And there would not have been the Russian invasion of Czechoslovakia.

The Ukrainian Review,
No. III, 1968, pp. 9-19

The Present Stage of the National Liberation Struggle of the Subjugated Nations

The Nations Rise

Stalin died on March 5, 1953. In the summer of 1953 the Russian empire was shaken by uprisings in the concentration camps of Vorkuta, Norylsk, and Karaganda. They were followed by uprisings and disturbances in Kingir, Balkhash, and other places, which were crushed by the MVD-MGB troops in 1954. A leading role in the organization of these uprisings was played by the Ukrainian nationalists (Bandera followers), as well as prisoners of other nationalities.

On June 17, 1953, the Germans revolted, while in Magdeburg the Chekists shot eighteen soldiers of the Soviet Army who helped the insurgent workers.

In 1956, there was a revolution in Hungary and disturbances in Poland. Ukrainian, Turkestani, Byelorussian, and other soldiers sided with the Hungarian freedom fighters, turning their tanks against Russian aggressors. On the foundation of the nationwide uprising in Ukraine

(1942-1953) and Lithuania—for both of these nations waged guerrilla-type warfare on two fronts, against Soviet Russia and Nazi Germany—in line with the traditions of armed struggle of the UPA (Ukrainian Insurgent Army) and OUN (Organization of Ukrainian Nationalists, Bandera followers), on the foundation of the struggle in concentration camps and the uprisings in 1953-1959 of prisoners, the revolutionary liberation movements increased in strength in the subjugated countries.

At the 20th Congress of the Communist Party of the Soviet Union (February 1956), Khrushchev was forced to "dethrone" Stalin, while on June 30th, the Central Committee of the CPSU adopted a resolution "on the combatting of the personality cult and its consequences." To save the empire he began to reorganize the concentration camps, fearing a chain reaction of uprisings of 17 million prisoners. The young generation of the subjugated nations, hand in hand with the unyielding older generation, launched the struggle on a broad front.

Fear Has Been Overcome

The possibility of uprisings even inside a totalitarian empire has been documented by facts. Only a lack of synchronization, coordination, and their extension to other subjugated countries prevented the downfall of the empire and the system. A realistic guidepost, however, has remained; simultaneous and not separate, isolated revolutionary uprisings of the subjugated peoples are the surest road to liberation. The occupation regime will be powerless when confronted with such uprisings for it will not be able to use nuclear arms, which would be self-destructive due to radioactive fallout. Moreover, the administrative machinery itself is infiltrated by anti-imperial and anti-Communist elements. The Soviet army is composed not only of Russians but also of soldiers from the subjugated countries, while the satellite armies—as shown by the Hungarian revolution, the disturbances in Poland, and the events in Czechia and Slovakia—will not take a stand against their own rebelling compatriots, but on the contrary will themselves rise against the occupant. What is more, the soldiers of the Soviet army, which is based on universal, compulsory military service, are tightly bound with their nations, living by the same ideals as their fathers and mothers. It is not an isolated incident that three years ago, on August 31, 1970, in a military court of the Baltic Military District, there ended a trial of an underground organization inside the army which had its branches in Poland, Azerbaidzhan, and other places. The resonance of the national liberation struggle of the subjugated nations will be heard in the armed forces. Neither the KGB nor the party will be able to protect it against this, since the soldiers of the Soviet army are an inseparable part of the nations from which they come. It was not a chance occurrence that in the first half of 1973 over 15,000 young Ukrainians of military age were thrown into punitive detachments along the Sino-Soviet border.

It is worth recalling that the March 1917 revolution which toppled tsarism was effected in Petersburg by three regiments composed of Ukrainians (the Volhynia, the Izmailiv, and the Preobrazhensk). The present-day army with its technology and modern weaponry, with the concentration of material and firepower in individual, strategically important locations, but primarily because of its multinational, heterogeneous human component, the majority of which is from the subjugated nations, has its special role and significance. In addition, the army is particularly important because it provides a meeting ground for the young people of various strata, including the professional intelligentsia, the workers, the collective farmers, and so on.

The fact that the highest-ranking spokesman of the Armed Forces Command (Marshal Grechko), the KGB chief (Andropov), and the administrative chief (Kosygin) are in the new Politburo of the Central Committee of the CPSU speaks for itself. All elements of violence have been united in the center of the empire.

A characteristic of the national liberation struggle of the subjugated nations is its nationwide scope. The struggle is not limited to a narrow circle of intellectuals. A massive counteroffensive is being waged against the occupant's drive to destroy the way of life of the subjugated nations. This means that there is in progress a struggle for a farmer's right to the private ownership of land, at least for an increase in the size of so called private plots of land, versus the collective system imposed by force and terror. There is a return to national traditions, to the individual sources of spirituality of each nation; in opposition to militant atheism there comes the cult of the ancestral religion, the millenial or centuries-old traditions; against the Orthodox Church, subservient to the Kremlin regime, which serves the atheist government and whose mission is to become the Third Rome, each nation's own religious traditions combined with the national idea are fearlessly defended. Side by side with the ideological, cultural, intellectual, literary and artistic struggle in the sphere of the humanities which encompass the entire complex of spiritual creativity, side by side with philosophical idealism, with so called historian—i.e., and the cult of great national figures during the period of state independence and the historic grandeur of past centuries—there come the student rebellions (Tahanrih, August 9, 1956), in which the students openly took an anti-government stand at seminars. There are also disturbances among the peasant youth, as confirmed by the Soviet press, while revolutionary attitudes become rampant among former prisoners (*Izvestia*, April 19). In the Chernihov region, collective farmers refused to give up their private plots of land, winning an increase in their size (*Izvestia*, May 19). In some state farms of the Kazakh SSR, the workers systematically reduced their time of work (*Selskoe Khozyaystvo*, July 17). In the Stalin region the miners forced the management to increase their wages (*Pravda Ukrainy*, March 6). In Dniprodzerzhynsk the workers of a metallurgical plant protested against the increase of work norms. Beginning with 1956 and up to 1973 there were countless such examples. What is the heart of the matter?

The decisive factor, it must be emphasized, is that various strata within the subjugated nations have joined in the struggle. They are fighting to realize fully their idea of the substance of each sector of life. Such a fulfillment can be achieved only in their own independent states. A precondition of essential changes in every sphere of life is each nation's own government in its own land. Without the sovereign rule of a given nation there is no land and no freedom. Therefore the new slogan is not "land and freedom" but "sovereign rule, land,

and freedom." This is self-evident to all strata of the subjugated nations. Without a political revolution—that is, without the assumption of power by those staging it, the subjugated nations—there is no fulfillment of the aspirations of any stratum of a people. The essence of the present stage of the liberation struggle is a spontaneous and systematic mobilization of the broad circles within the subjugated nations in order to reach the zenith—the renewal of national statehood, which only then will make an all-round development of a modern nation possible. The slogan "freedom" is insufficient. Freedom is a framework which must be filled with content. Freedom is a prerequisite, an opportunity to make a choice among diverse values, with a guarantee of the possibility of realizing the chosen values. It is mandatory to define clearly for what values and for what qualities one stands. The peoples have been deceived for many decades. A struggle for justice, for lawfulness—this is a revolutionary slogan which mobilizes the moral sentiments in a system of "legalized" lawlessness and disenfranchisement. Political self-determination is not a mobilizing slogan, for Lenin even added "including secession" to it, yet he was able to deceive the people. Therefore, the only rallying cry is national independence—complete separation from Russia. There is no other alternative. The disintegration of the empire and the reestablishment of independent national democratic states is the goal. A struggle is being waged for sovereign rule, for freedom and justice, for the realization of the nations' own ways of life in their own states. In this aim there is simultaneously concentrated the definition of the contents of every phase of national life, the principles of its organization. In history (e.g., the history of Western empires) a subjugated nation had to fight not only against military occupation and economic exploitation, but also against a hostile spirituality, sociality, a contradictory way of life, an entirely different system of life and beliefs. Bolshevism, Communism, Sovietism, the Russian way of life, spiritual, cultural, and religious Russification are neither a Lithuanian, nor a Georgian, nor an Estonian, nor a Byelorussian, nor a Turkestani, nor an Azerbaidzhani, nor a Ukrainian way of life. A characteristic phenomenon of the contemporary era of the liberation struggle of the subjugated nations inside the Russian empire and in the Communist-dominated countries is that hand-in-hand with the direct forms and methods of struggle, such as demonstrations, strikes, revolts, mass actions, and armed clashes, goes the ideological, political, cultural, and religious struggle, a struggle of two opposite concepts of life; the Russian, Bolshevik, Communist concept and that of the subjugated nations. It is a clash of total national organisms, of the captor and his captives, who are not only physically oppressed and economically exploited— attempts are also being made to deprive them of their national soul. And this is essential in that struggle. The struggle for the souls of nations!

The greatest achievement of our liberation struggle, a guarantee of our victory, is the fact that the struggle for the soul of the subjugated nations was taken up by the YOUNG generation, many of whom were born of parents who had grown up under the Bolshevik occupation, a generation which has never seen the Free World, but on the contrary was reared in an atmosphere hostile to its own nation, in the spirit of the occupant.

The banner of a 1000-year-old traditionalism, the primacy of the spirit, the immortality of the soul, the banner of the nation, of the eternity of a nation was raised by the generation of the sixties and the seventies and carried by sons and daughters not only of inmates of prisons and concentration camps, but also of average workers, collective farmers, and even technocrats.

This is the greatest blow suffered by the Communist ideology and system of life, the Russian system of occupation, in recent decades. This is all the more so since the realization of one's own national quality, of one's own inherent substance, of one's own values of traditional spirituality, culture, lawfulness, society, and the statehood of the past, the reawakening of national self-respect, the discovery of one's own millenial tradition of statehood, the treasures of one's own land not only of the present but also the richness of all-round state— political, cultural, and socio-political creativity of the past make for the final ideological victory over the enemy's system of ideas.

For this reason, it will be impossible to crush national aspirations. As a rule the revolution of soldiers has been preceded by the revolution of poets and creators of spiritual values.

The ideological, spiritual, moral, and political revolution is a precondition of armed revolution. The creativity of the young generation has a clear national political aim: the national state.

The so-called *samvydav* (self-publication) from the subjugated countries, widely known in the world, is proof of this. The *Ukrainian Herald*, an uncensored publication of the Ukrainian patriots, besides political statements and documentation also carries literary works, while the *Chronicle of Current Events* limits itself only to an informative content. The *Exodus*, dealing with Jewish affairs, and other periodical and non-periodical publications published in Estonia, Lithuania, Armenia, Georgia, Turkestan, and Latvia, reveal a similar purpose as that of the *Ukrainian Herald*.

Metaphysical and Ethical Concept of the Liberation Struggle

The facts of struggle are deeply rooted in its ideological and political motivation. It also determines the quality and the substance of freedom towards which the young fighters of the subjugated nations aspire. The struggle is neither being waged from the positions of dialectical and historical materialism, nor from positions of philosophical materialism, but just the opposite. Two concepts of the world, two systems of value, are clashing. This is no longer the question of "pure" and "betrayed" Communism, of "pure" and "betrayed" Marxism, but of Christian—or more broadly—of religious metaphysics and philosophy, of religious faith, of theism vs. atheistic materialism. This is the ideological and philosophical backbone of the struggle. It did not help any that in the textbooks of world history the Russians did not dedicate a single line to the greatest revolutionary event in the history of the world: the birth of Christ, whose religion encompassed more than half a billion people. They also disregard other religions— Islam, Buddhism, Judaism—persecuting them as the "opium of the people." It is not an accident that the intellectual elite of Ukraine, for instance, cultivate the Christian philosophy of H. Skovoroda (1722-1794).

The young generation asks:

"What have you created for your people in exchange for persistent agitation against religious beliefs and rites, ancient customs, traditions, and holy days— i.e., all that which in the past a foreigner had to respect if he wanted to show his respect for the people?"

Religion has been placed at the foundation of cultural creativity: "It is impossible to imagine traditional cultural treasures outside the Church.... A struggle against the Church means a struggle against culture.... How many times was the nation saved by the Church alone.... Under the conditions [prevalent] in Eastern Europe, the Church was the only force independent of the government...."

In the face of these and similar documentary revelations of the point of view of the young generation inside the subjugated nations, the Sovietology of most Western research institutes with their thesis about the "new" Communist and later even the "Soviet" man can declare their bankruptcy. For us, Sovietology is the study of lies and deception, the exposure of falsehood. Regrettably, this is not so for Western statesmen.

Fifty years must have done their work, maintain the Sovietologists—i.e., they must have re-educated man. But they forget that Christianity has been re-educating man for two thousand years and has not transformed him into an angel. Why should a diabolical system be more successful, provided such comparison can be drawn?

The National Idea and the Heroic Concept of Life

To our regret, we cannot cite the author's names, for some of them are languishing in prisons while others are still free. Nevertheless, the authenticity of all the quotations is guaranteed by our conscience.

A young underground author says the following about the national idea:

"The national idea exists and will continue to exist. It is real for us today and means the fullness of the sovereign state and cultural existence of the Ukrainian nation.... The national idea...encompasses countless other ideas common to mankind.... And the very absorption by the national idea, a dedication to it, leads at the same time into the most secret depths of other social and spiritual needs...." "The national question is knitted together by thousands of the finest threads with the most essential questions of human conscience.... Nationalism is an inseparable part of the nation itself. Without nationalism there is no progress; without nationalism there is no nation....

The liberation movement in the whole world—the most outstanding phenomenon of the present—is occurring under the banner of nationalism. More than half of mankind considers it as its banner.

A young Estonian prisoner in Mordovia proudly declared: "Do you know Estonia is one thousand years old? Once, there were sixty Estonians and Estonia survived. Estonia has survived in camps as well." And on one occasion, presenting a bouquet to a representative of the government, which when unwrapped turned out to be a mesh of barbed wire, a prisoner shouted: "Long live free Estonia!" This incident from camp life is related by Prof. Osadchy, sentenced to ten years after already having served two years of imprisonment, for the essay "Cataract.""The Ukrainian Kalynets, a poet sentenced to twelve years, creates a new model of the world," says the brave Latvian poet Knut Skuenis, a prisoner himself in a Mordovian concentration camp.

Or Ali Khashakulhov, a North Caucasian (Ingushet) sentenced as a young boy for anti-Russian nationalist (Ingushet) activity, says mournfully:

> If our nation does disappear, a skeleton of a wolf will harden high up in the mountains. Of a giant wolf. This will be the last wolf of the world. Wolf means the native land, its symbol, its flag. When the Ingushets were deported to Kazakhstan during the war, the wolves also disappeared from the Waynakh hills. The wolves could not live without the Ingushets, who were deprived of their fatherland. The wolves did not wish to become a flag for foreigners.... "If I knew," says Ali, "that my language would die tomorrow, I would die today....

The wolf and the native land.... The Russians—foreigners. Where can one find Bolshevik "successes" here? These are testimonials to the total bankruptcy of Communist Sovietism and the Russian "big brother" theory.

"If Yurko, the son of Gen. R. Shukhevych, commander-in-chief of the UPA, had denounced his father he would have been in the Crimea long ago...." "Go away, scoundrel," says Yurko to an overseer from the KGB who tries to talk him into signing a statement renouncing his father, "go away or I'll send you to a mausoleum...." And his father told him: "You grow up, it is not yet certain what will happen in your lifetime...." And since the age of fourteen, Yurko has languished for his father nineteen years in camps under severe regime [as of 1968]...." After serving his twenty-year sentence, Yurko Shukhevych was sentenced anew on Sept 9, 1972, to fifteen years

The young people have revised, have renewed themselves, have gained new life. They have grasped the great idea and revived faith in it.

"A nation is a temple, the desecration of which constitutes the greatest crime.... Let the tenth part of a nation remain, but with full-valued spirituality this is not yet fatal. A whole willow grove grows from a piece of a full-valued willow twig. We live in the spontaneously irrational, in the depths, by roots alone, which continuously sprout but rarely reach normal blossom," said one of the greatest heroes in the field of cultural creativity, Valentyn Moroz, sentenced to fourteen years. "Denationalization," teaches one underground author, "is tantamount to deculturalization.... Denationalization is deheroization.... Dechristianization, collectivization, colonial industrialization, mass resettlements from village to city—all this constitutes a destruction unprecedented in Ukraine's history of traditional Ukrainian structures, catastrophic results of which have not yet been fully revealed...."

This formula summarizes the position of the young generation so far as its program and outlook on the world are concerned. It is deeply rooted in the traditional national spirituality.

An individual who respects, knows, and loves the history of this nation lives not only his own lifetime but as long as his people and his land.... The nation is immortal, it will live.... Know yourself in your people....

The young generation is captivated by the heroism of its ancestors. It gave rise to legends which were revived by the young people. "Legends which cultivate and raise our spirit above this abyss," writes a young author, "legends about the transmigration of souls, contemplation of the soul's immortality, legends about the continuity of the kin, about the immortality of a people... We are speaking about the legend of the nation's eternity...."

The entire class theory, Marxism, Sovietism with its theory of the tradition-less "Soviet" people, the world proletariat, the withering away of nations, the class struggle—all are useless!

The Contrasting Worlds

In 1825 Herzen wrote, "Centuries of self-dependence were not able to eradicate everything independent and poetical in the celebrated Ukrainian nation. It has more individual development, more local coloring than we [the Russians]; in our country the ill-fated uniform carelessly covers national life. Our people have no knowledge of its history, while every village in Ukraine has its own legend. The Russian people know only Pugachev and the year 1812."

And in 1971, the *Ray of Freedom*, an uncensored Russian periodical criticizing "The Program of the Democratic Movement" of the USSR of Sakharov and Co., said that

The Russian people is the only one in history which destroyed its genuine intelligentsia or permitted it to be destroyed, in 1918-1921, 1928-1931, 1937-1939. The people as a whole are philistine slaves who often idealize their slavery and are at the same time capable of being cruel tyrants. If we were to establish a democratic order, then, filled with vengeful hatred toward their 'nachalniks' of yesterday and contempt for today's 'soft' Government, they would start a vicious blood orgy, as was the case in 1917-1921. And then the newly emerged political adventurers, playing upon the evil passions of the mob, will thrust aside the 'slaverer' democrats in order to institute a new tyranny, with a new evolution of terror and cruelties in the course of decades.

The traits of the Russian Church: cringing before the state, inactivity, and non-resistance to evil, religious egoism, and anti-sociality. At this time, can voices of protest of the clergy be heard against the harassment of the dissidents? Do we hear anything about self-immolations, hunger strikes, demonstrations, attacks on illegality, arbitrariness, imperialism, the invasion of Czechoslovakia, the persecution of religion, and so forth?

In the country half the population is non-Russian, having its own interests and expectations. The question must be raised concerning the realization of the right to separation of developed peoples into independent states. In our everyday life there is alcoholism, sexuality, epicureanism. In the event of the first hard test there is repentance, testimony against friends. Dobrovolsky against Ginsburg and Galanskov, Zinovyeva against Pimenov, and so forth. A moral and political renaissance is needed...cultivation of moral purity in oneself...spiritual depths ...unyielding courage...indestructable energy.

Fearing unity of the national and the Christian ideas, *Robitnycha Gazeta* of March 13, 1973, wrote: "Priests and former Ukrainian Uniate monks attempt to conduct illegal religious activities, disseminate religious leaflets, small calendars, and prayerbooks with anti-Soviet and anti-Communist contents, urge [people] not to work in Soviet institutions, refuse to accept passports, military cards, and other Soviet documents."

The Road to Liberation

The spiritual and moral revolution is a real fact. It is a precondition of a political revolution. The national political revolution is unconquerable provided it grows out of the traditional original elements of the spirituality and sociality of a given nation. Synchronization of the national and social revolution is a guarantee of its success. Cultural revolutions do not occur; culture is created in the course of centuries. What occur are the culturally political revolutions—i.e., a forceful removal of the enemy occupant, who makes impossible the development of national culture from the nation's own traditional historic roots.

Now a particular struggle is being waged in the cultural sphere, for it is a battle for the national and human soul. Before the soldiers take up arms, a revolution is staged by poets and artists. There was Shevchenko before the year 1918 in Ukraine. Without Petofi and his brilliant revolutionary songs and deeds, there would not have been a Kossuth. Without Mickiewicz and Slowacki, there would not have been a Pilsudski. Nevertheless, parallel to this struggle of ideas, there is an active struggle in various spheres of life, including armed clashes and mass demonstrations, strikes, and resistance to a hostile occupation and system in life generally.

A consequence of this is the inclusion of the spokesman of the extensive police and terror apparatus, Andropov, and the Bonapartist, Marshal Grechko, in the highest party organ. The presence of Gromyko in that body testifies to the success of the policy of weakening the West. This policy also furthers the intensification of terror inside the country. Brezhnev (Party) and Kosygin (Administration), Andropov (KGB), Grechko (the military), Shelepin (trade unions), and so forth—all organized forms of violence are united in the highest body of the party. Their chief aim is to save the empire from revolts of the subjugated nations. Re-Stalinization, intensified Russification, mass imprisonment of fighters for national and human rights, national and cultural genocide, linguicide, modernized methods of terror; psychiatric clinics, chemical and medical means of breaking an individual's will power; the use of arms in crushing national and social resistance, as well as open revolt of the masses (e.g., Lithuania)—all this characterizes the era of Brezhnev.

Hoping for national and religious rights through reformism, evolution, constitutionalism, and democratization from above has proved disappointing. Those who fought for the fulfillment of rights guaranteed by the Constitution are behind bars.

There is one noticeable, basic difference between dissidents and fighters for national rights, between reformists and nationalists. The former strive to repair the existing empire and system; the latter wish to topple it, by reestablishing independent national states. For this reason many of the former belong to the so-called third Russian emigration, while the latter are either executed or languish in concentration camps for fifteen to twenty, and even thirty-five, years, as the Ukrainian nationalists Oleksa Bilsky, imprisoned since the age of nineteen and now in Potma, who went blind while in prison. Oleksa Bilsky, fifty-five, is suffering imprisonment solely for his nationalistic views, for which he refuses to repent.

The appearance of DARING individuals who stand up for their convictions, defend human and national rights, and risk their own lives and freedom—all this is of crucial importance. Of course, if the struggle were limited only to the forms and methods employed by them, it would have no prospects. It must always be borne in mind that these figures could have appeared only on the foundation of the two-front struggle of the UPA-OUN, the Lithuanian insurgents, the nationwide resistance of the Georgian, Turkestani, Armenian, North Caucasian, Azerbaidzhani, and other nations.

The underground organizations continued to exist and still exist. Some were short-lived, others not. The OUN in Ukraine and anywhere else where Ukrainians live is consistently active in the underground.

If the essence of an underground revolutionary organization is primarily ideological unity and political guidelines for action, to be followed later with technical contacts for the sake of following these guidelines, which to a large extent can be done openly, then it is impossible to destroy it. If our concept of liberation is not a palace revolt but a general revolt of nations, then the guidelines for their mobilization must be transmitted openly. A description of mass armed action in Novocherkassk, Nalchyk, or Tiflis broadcast over the radio constitutes a guideline for analogous actions in Dnipropetrovsk, Tashkent, or Kaunas, and vice versa. In such actions, new leaders emerge. Underground organizations provide an ALTERNATIVE AUTHORITY to that of the occupant. It is created by LEADERS of spirit and action who have come to the fore openly. This results in the occupant's attempts to force statements of repentance and to discredit the underground as a foreign agency in order to do away with SYMBOLS, with ALTERNATIVE leadership, with the ALTERNATIVE OF THE SUBJUGATED NATIONS' SOVEREIGN RULE.

In order to prevent the enemy from resorting to his wicked techniques of deception, the Lithuanian heroes took out medical certificates prior to their self-immolation attesting that they were MENTALLY healthy. Such instances of courage as that of the young student-worker Kalanta, or student Palach, or the UPA-OUN fighter Makukh are rare in history.

In the main, the liberation movements of the subjugated nations are nationwide movements. This is confirmed by those who appeared in the West, particularly the Jews.

The 1972 disturbances in Dnipropetrovske and Dniprodzerzhynsk (Ukraine), Nalchyk (North Caucasus), Kaunas (Lithuania), Moldavia, Tashkent, and Bukharra (Turkestan), in 1973 in Tiflis (Georgia) and Erivan (Armenia) and earlier along the Don (Cossackia); or the toppling of Gomulka in 1917 following a workers' revolt; the student disturbances in Budapest in 1973; the posture of the Czechs and Slovaks who have not given up their struggle for independence in 1968, and later the Bulgarians and Romanians who resolutely combat imposed Communism just as the Poles or the Germans who perish at the Berlin Wall—all prove that the liberation movements of the subjugated nations are not only movements of the intelligentsia but of the people in general. The fact that the young intellectual elite is united in a common front with workers and collective farmers is a guarantee of the invincibility of the popular revolution. In his book *Will the USSR Survive until the Year 1984?* Andrey Amalrik mentions that, out of 134 signatures protesting imprisonments in Kyiv, 25 percent were those of workers.

" 'Glory! Glory! Glory'! shouted the crowd which filled the entire Pekarska street in Lviv (this occurred throughout the five days). Flowers were tossed to us. They fell on the metal roof of the car, through the crack in the door upon us. When we proceeded to the court building, we walked on a carpet of fresh spring flowers," writes M. Osadchy about the trial of the cultural leaders (*Cataract*, p. 42).

Without discrediting anybody's struggle for freedom we would like to recall that in Moscow only a few persons demonstrated against the sentence passed on Bukovsky, the majority of them being Jews.

The world-renowned Estonian declaration of the spokesmen of national freedom about the fact that all three Baltic states are resolutely in favor of independence, that Marxism is bankrupt, while Christianity is invincible, that the time will come when tanks will not be marching on Prague or Bratislava but on Moscow or Leningrad, proposes the only realistic road to liberation: the armed struggle.

To Expect or to ACT?

The maneuvers of MVD troops held in the fall of 1970 near Moscow under the motto "Crushing Revolts in Concentration Camps" point to the preparations of the occupant for a confrontation with its greatest threat. Vasyl Symonenko points to armed struggle as the only road to liberation. "Oh Kurd, save your cartridges, but do not spare the life of killers!... CONVERSE WITH THEM WITH BULLETS... Oh, Kurd, save your cartridges. Without them you will not be able to protect your kin!"

There is no path to liberation other than the simultaneous national liberation of nations subjugated in the USSR, and the guerrilla strategy is the only realistic one. Nuclear bombs cannot be dropped on revolutions and revolutionaries, for this is tantamount to the occupant's committing suicide. The greater the growth of classical military technology, the greater becomes the significance of armed people, the "primitive" method of warfare. On the heels of the general call for further development of conventional arms, there will come a time when voices will be raised in support of uprisings inside the empire of tyrants, as a way of avoiding a nuclear war.

In the nuclear age, ideological, psychological, and political warfare is becoming more intensive. In military technology and strategy, this is reflected by guerrilla warfare. Both Moscow and Peking are aware of this. This awareness, however, is still lacking among the official circles of the West.

The process of development inside the subjugated countries normally proceeds along the lines of popular uprisings and a joint front of the captives against their captors. It was not by chance that, while in a concentration camp, a young Ukrainian poet dedicated to Jan Palach his poem "about a virgin killed by the occupants in Golden Prague."

Another dedicated his poems to Georgia, Latvia, Moldavia, and Byelorussia, and still another wrote: "If you want your nation to be free, express solidarity with those who are liberating themselves and you will find support among them."

The invincibility of the spirit and a joint front of struggle of the subjugated is a guarantee of victory.

"Long live free Ukraine," said Vasyl Makukh;

"Long live independent Lithuania!" said Romas Kalanta;

"It is better to die in flames, than to live under the Russian yoke," shouted Czech Jan Palach.

How deeply were they inspired by an idea when they were capable of this kind of sacrifice.

The Ukrainian Review,
No. I, 1974, pp. 3-18

The National Liberation Struggle within the Russian Empire

In my deliberations I would like to proceed from the assumption of our common fears and expectations and to attempt to find a way out of the critical situation in which not only the nations subjugated within the Russian empire find themselves. I am not speaking about the cause of one part of the world—the subjugated world alone. I am speaking about our common cause—of the free and enslaved people, and more—of the free and enslaved nations.

It is said that mankind is on the brink of possible destruction by a thermo-nuclear war. Does such a threat really exist? Is there really no other solution than capitulation before tyrannies or appeasement and detente at the expense of hundreds of millions of subjugated people and dozens of enslaved nations, acknowledging their slavery, the domination of Russian tyrants over them? Is there not one more "overlooked," neglected superpower, not so much material and technological as spiritual, moral, and political, which plays a decisive role in events which are implacably approaching? Detente with tyrannies and the balance of power on a global scale—i.e., capitulation before despotic governments— or a wager on spiritual, moral, eternal values of man and nations as a way out of the critical situation in which the world finds itself? Besides the technological, in particular the thermonuclear, element of a superpower, more important is the moral, spiritual element, or more precisely: the spiritual superpower is of greater importance. It is composed of individuals and nations subjugated in the Russian empire and under the Communist yoke which are thirsting for freedom and justice, ready to sacrifice everything material. After all, why should the lawful process of the dissolution of empires on a world scale stop at the orders of the Russian prison of nations? Why is the absurd, unnatural concept of the Russian Empire, which, in a way unprecedented in history, imposed upon the nations and individuals it subjugates to its own way of life from metaphysics to the system of collective farming, not to become finally bankrupt instead of preserving itself as some "new world, a new system of ideas and values?"

The spiritual, moral, and political superpower of our epoch is the billions of subjugated people and dozens of enslaved nations within the Russian empire and other Communist states. This is the true reality, the real factor of world politics which will decide the future of mankind.

It is not enough to possess the most modern weapons and military technology. One must have the souls of nations and individuals on one's side. Are the souls of the Ukrainians, Turkestanis, Georgians, Poles, Azerbaidzhian, Lithuanians, Estonians on the side of Russia, on the side of Communism?

Even the Russian Sakharov must acknowledge the powerful, dynamic force of the concept of national liberation, although he champions human rights, not the rights of nations.

But we place national rights, liberation nationalism, as a central issue, for at no time were human rights achieved in a subjugated nation without the fulfillment of a prerequisite: an independent, democratic, but above all a sovereign state of each nation.... We sympathize with the human rights movement, but the ideas of this movement will never be realized in nationally oppressed countries, in an empire. Sakharov and Solzhenitsyn—in spite of all our sympathy for their limited aspirations—are not on our side for their goals are the rights of the Russian individual, while ours are the rights of people of the subjugated nations in their own independent states. Human rights of a subjugated nation can never be realized without the achievement of its national state independence. Both of them are striving for the impossible—to preserve the empire and to achieve human rights, unless only the Russian people are meant. In order to gain human rights Washington had to win national independence for America. Today, there are no individuals in the world defined in a way other than by their nationality. Hence, no human rights can be achieved without the rights of a nation to which an individual belongs.

Had the so-called democratic empires guaranteed human rights in the nations which they oppressed? We do not think so. Recapitulating: only a nation's own national state with a democratic system of government guarantees human rights in a given nation, having first fulfilled a precondition: national sovereignty.

The slogan of our epoch is independence vs. empire. Nation vs. the prison of nations! Human rights as a consequence of the national right and a democratic system! Self-determination is not a revolutionary slogan of our time. Lenin put forth a more far-reaching slogan, self-determination including separation, and deceived the peoples. Not a plebiscite of paper ballots, but a plebiscite of blood dating back a thousand years, repeated time and again in liberation and defensive wars against aggressors and conquerors of Ukraine, Georgia, Lithuania, Latvia, Turkestan, Bulgaria, Estonia, Hungary, etc., has self-determined these nations with millenial or centuries-old traditions as nation-states. Border villages can self-determine themselves, but not entire nations.

The ratio of forces in the Russian Empire, including the satellites, is one to two to the advantage of the subjugated nations. Not only the oppressors but also the oppressed carry arms in the course of their general military duties. A democratic system and modern technology have in fact made classical warfare in line with the Clausewitz doctrine impossible, to be supplanted by a modern type of warfare: guerrilla warfare. The "absolutist-aristocratic" doctrine of warfare propagated by Clausewitz is outdated now.

In a given case it is not a question of compromise between two governments on one territory, a compromise between the oppressor and the oppressed, but of the expulsion of the occupying power and the establishment of the occupied nation's own government. The problem is not one of imposing one's own will upon the vanquished, in the sense of the Clausewitz doctrine, in a limited framework, but of a total driving out of the aggressor from one's own land by an all-out guerrilla war of nations subjugated by Russia in synchronized, coordinated national liberation revolutions which would pass into or be accompanied by a conventional war.

Since the concept of war has changed in the thermonuclear and ideological age, in the age of the downfall of empires, as a lawful development of history, in the age of the armed people, when atomic armament ceases to be a privilege of the superpowers, when its quality is changed into quantity—for even tiny Israel already has its own atomic bomb—then the horrible problem of atomic war will of itself cease to exist, creating a global stalemate. Both individuals and nations will again place their bets not on a homunculus—a narrow-minded intellectual-technician who allegedly has the fate of the world in his hands, but on man. Man will again become a human being with his own free will, his own morality. Mankind will find itself in a blind alley if ethical and cultural progress do not go hand in hand with technological progress. The former lagging behind. The dehumanization, deheroization and dechristianization with a lack of religion and morality and a barbarization of humanity have reached an unprecedented peak....

Yet, in the face of all this our cardinal question is: does the fate of mankind lie in the hands of the Kremlin criminals and mass murderers of nations and individuals who possess thermonuclear arms? Our reply: no! The thermonuclear age is a blind ideological age. Hence we are not only faced with a political, strategic question, but with a metaphysical one: to be or not to be for mankind? Individuals and nations must realize the ideals of freedom, truth, justice, human and national rights with God's teaching on earth by fearlessly striving for their fulfillment, for this is their duty as higher beings.

A great shortcoming in the West today is the absence of great statesmen—ideologists, visionaries, charismatic men of words, faith, and heroic concepts of life. Technocrats and pragmatists—often with the best of intentions—hold sway now. In the age of thermonuclear arms and ideological wars this is a tragedy. James Reston aptly comments in *The International Herald Tribune* of March 4, 1974, under the heading "The World Crisis of Democracy": "It is true that the men of eloquent idealism are gone—the Churchills and De Gaulles. They have been replaced on the whole with political technicians.... There is a problem...." And he ends his article as follows: "The political 'decline of the West' is no longer a subject for theoretical debate, but an ominous reality, particularly when the leader of the West, the United States, has so much trouble of his own...."

The Present Forms and Methods of Struggle

Observing the present stage of struggle in Ukraine, it must be stated that moral and political struggle, conceptual and cultural strife, and attempts to assert Ukrainian qualities and values are continuing and intensifying. This period will not end since the stress on spiritual formation and assertion of the nation cannot be extinguished in spite of the various phases of liberation struggle and an accent on its different aspects— as, for instance, the socio-political, economic, and military. After the period of mass popular uprisings of 1942-1953, the emphasis was placed on a multifaceted underground struggle, including the armed defensive, and particularly on a conceptual-political and cultural-religious and socio-political struggle of a limited scope. With the change of forms and methods of transition to a longer period of struggle, armed struggle was relegated to a secondary position, while the political concept of a revolutionary guerrilla struggle extended not only to the Ukrainian people at large but to other nations enslaved in the Russian Empire, including the satellite states.

The essence of the present state of struggle is a conflict between two contradictory national organisms—the Russian and the Ukrainian—in all phases of struggle; it does not mean the exclusiveness of only those elements defined in a given stage. As we have already mentioned, the emphasis on mass armed struggle of the 1942-1953 period in no way signified a neglect of the elements, the culminating mobilization of which was the concentration of all forces and energy upon a decisive armed struggle. A changeover to other forms, which had been made by General Roman Shukhevych, did not mean a failure of that stage, but rather was caused by the turn of events in the world, in the USSR, and Ukraine.

Depending on the phase of struggle in Ukraine, there exists a corresponding assistance campaign from abroad; in the phase of stress upon the moral and political fight major efforts are turned to strengthening this form as much as possible, although this does not mean that in a different phase this work would be less intensive. And so, at present it is absolutely necessary to disseminate our own and other literature which corresponds to our ideas, concepts, viewpoint, faith, and our road to liberation. Mandatory are radio broadcasts, the erection of our own radio station, verbal and written information, mass and militant actions and acts in foreign countries as forms of support for the struggle in Ukraine and within the empire, the formation of a global anti-Russian front, international conferences directed toward our ends, a joint anti-Russian action with those in the Free World sympathetic to our cause, in particular with emigrations of the ABN peoples, and so forth.

In Ukraine and the empire, there continues a campaign in defense of Moroz, Shukhevych, and other imprisoned cultural and political leaders and the ideas and principles of the ABN are being propagated as a realistic method of liberation through our own efforts. Some of these methods are demonstrations of workers, strikes of workers and collective farmers lasting one hour, one day, or even several days. An appropriate gradation of actions is also actualized here and there by attacking the enemy in various spheres of life, including the economic one.... All of us remember the events in Novocherkassk in 1962 and Dnipropetrovsk and Dniprodzherzhynsk in 1972.

Reports are reaching us that during court proceedings against political, cultural, or religious leaders, short-term strikes of students, workers, and collective farmers were held. We have read the "The Cataract" that those being tried in Lviv were showered with flowers by the crowd on Pekarska Street as they were led from the automobiles to the courtroom...that Lina Kostenko strewed flowers in their path and that the defendants walked on a carpet of flowers to their trial....

We know about the organization of protest letters to the press from plants or collective farms, which also exerted pressure on opportunistic cultural leaders who were forced to "protest" on their part because the fear for their own skin in the situation of mutual responsibility created by the KGB did not diminish, but increased when they were silent. When people like Svitlychny were active, Vinhranovsky felt freer; when Moroz was active, Lina Kostenko felt freer; when Vinhranovsky was active, Drach created more freely; when Drach is free, there is a lesser threat to Honchar, and so forth. Honchar defended Kosmach. He defended the stolen iconostasis, thus defending himself, the author of "Sobor" (Cathedral). Sverstyuk defended Honchar's "Cathedral" in his "Cathedral in Scaffolding." Paradzhanov belonged to those petty thieves who concealed the theft of the Kosmach iconostasis. What happened? With the imprisonment and torturing of Moroz, Paradzhanov also fell from power because the circle of responsibility is narrowing.... It is mutual responsibility which is the characteristic of the present era of Russian terror. Concealment of the theft of the iconostasis did not help Paradzhanov. For this he and Lyubchyk were aptly and severely criticized by Moroz....

Slogans Pertaining to Dynamic Life

The liberation struggle in Ukraine is not an abstraction which is suspended in the air of theoretical slogans. There the people are mobilized by vivid slogans growing out of real life. The traditions of the nationwide struggle of the Ukrainian Insurgent Army (UPA) have not been forgotten. They are being perpetuated.... The UPA is ingrained in the memory of the people because it united into one whole struggle all spheres of life—national coupled with social, cultural with religious—but everything is brought down to the national denominator—that is, without a sovereign national state, without the Ukrainian sovereign and united state it is not possible to attain a picture of Ukrainian content in any sphere of the life of the nation.

We can see how resistance is developing under the slogan "Down with deportation of our youth to Kazakhstan, Siberia, Mongolia." Let us recall the resistance put up by new draftees who were forced to serve on the Chinese border. The slogan resounded: "Let's perform our military duty in Ukraine!"

Now the Russians are transporting 25,000 skilled construction workers from Ukraine and other subjugated nations, including professional engineers, to build the infrastructure of Mongolia. We can hear the cry: "Let's remain in Ukraine, let's not go to Mongolia!" In Ukraine and Kazakhstan, in Siberia and on the Russian territory there resound the following slogans among the members of the subjugated nations: "Let's return home from Kazakhstan, Siberia, and Russia! We demand Ukrainian newspapers, books, libraries. Let's return from Poland and the so-called retrieved lands to the Lemky or to the Kholm region. These are not our lands. We have our own native territory of the Lemkos or the people of Kholm. We request a bishop for our Greek Catholic Church in Poland." All these slogans are spread spontaneously, for the nation lives and thinks. The OUN (Organization of Ukrainian Nationalists) and the UPA leave their traces everywhere. Decades of sacrificial acts, self-sacrifice, thousands of the fallen and tortured-to-death members of the OUN-UPA have not remained in vain on the road of struggle.... Acts of sacrifice are never futile; they always serve as guideposts....

We hear from tourists how the young people demonstratively sing Ukrainian patriotic songs on Dnipro boats and buses. We can hear the slogans: "Down with discrimination against Ukrainians in Ukraine! Ukrainians for Ukraine—Ukraine for Ukrainians! Let's demonstratively sing Ukrainian songs in streetcars, buses, and trains! Let's recall the observances at the grave of Taras Shevchenko in Kaniv. Let's recall Alla Horska and her call to courageously defend Ukrainian Ukraine." On walls and facades of buildings we can read the inscriptions: "Communism equals Nazism! The Bolsheviks are Nazis! Brezhnev is a new Stalin! Brezhnev is a racist Hitler!" In factories of heavy industry, in particular in the armament industry, we can hear whispers: "Let's work slowly." This slogan was promoted by the British in the war against Hitler for the countries which he enslaved. They are recalling it in Ukraine and Lithuania, in Georgia and Turkestan, and are applying it against the Russian occupants. "Let's slow down in the factories, on the collective farms"—this slogan resounds spontaneously.

Let's remember that even tiny Estonia raises her head. Only recently forty Estonians were arrested on the streets of Tallinn because they demonstrated under these slogans: "Russians get out of Estonia! Long live free Estonia! Estonia for Estonians!" Thousands of demonstrators in Kaunas protested religious persecution in Lithuania. "Let's not marry Russians" is a slogan in Turkestan. It is true in Ukraine as well. At an ABN Conference in London in 1973, a Turkestani author emphasized the Turkestanis' feeling of superiority over the Russians. Hence the slogans prevalent in Turkestan: "Moscow is savage! Turkestan—the culture of centuries!" Such a slogan is even more frequent in Ukraine. When Kyiv was already a cultural center the wolves were still howling on the site where Moscow now stands. The idea of cultural superiority penetrates and is reflected even in literary creativity. ˇSklyarenko is dead. Therefore he will not be hurt anymore by a mention of his work "Svyatoslav." There are many more such works, but their authors are still alive so we shall not mention them. Or, is not Skovoroda the pride of Ukraine? Or the novels about him?

But the battle is unfurling not only in the cultural sector, it encompasses the economic and socio-political sectors as well. Russia has imposed its socio-political and economic system and its institutions, which contradict the Ukrainian nature and spirituality. For this reason about 8 million Ukrainians perished in the struggle against the system of collectivization in Ukraine. For this reason, unchanged to this day, there resounds a slogan in Ukraine, spontaneously, naturally, lawfully: "Down with kolkhozes. Let's have decollectivization, land for private tilling ownership by the peasant"—these are timely slogans even today.... Kolkhozes are a Russian invention. Kolkhozes are a means of national and social enslavement. "Let's have bigger private plots! Let's have private ownership of land of the farmers! Down with kolkhozes, as it had been down with landlords! Russian and Communist sharks get out!"

It is not by chance that such slogans are becoming more and more widespread since collectivization is an unnatural phenomenon in Ukraine. One of the prominent Ukrainian cultural leaders wrote that dechristianization, collectivization, colonial industrialization, and resettlement from the village to the city have ruined the traditional Ukrainian structures of centuries and this will have far-reaching negative effects on the Ukrainian people. This is not a rhetorical or a literary phrase. Some statistics: Soviet agriculture employs about 30 percent of the entire work force of the USSR, five times greater than West Germany. The farmers of Western Europe are capable of producing enough foodstuffs to guarantee the feeding of the European Community. The USSR manages not to import grain only in exceptional years. Industrial progress is manifested by the fact that a smaller number of farmers suffices to feed the other fellow-citizens. Recently Brezhnev boastfully declared that they had managed to supply the population with agricultural products from the 42 million hectares of cultivated land in Kazakhstan and Siberia. Upon the orders of Khrushchev, Brezhnev, then Secretary of the Communist Party of Kazakhstan, had been developing the "virgin lands" until the wind scattered the top soil, and this became one of the reasons for the fall of Khrushchev. In any event, the allegedly good present harvest of Brezhnev makes it possible to barely feed the population without imports. But why is it so? In the past, Ukraine alone was the granary of Europe, but Brezhnev kept silent about another proof of complete bankruptcy of the collective system. The West European farmer, for instance, in particular the West German, harvests 43 double centers of grain from one hectare while in the USSR one hectare yields a bit less than 15 double centers of grain, two and a half times less. The farmers in the USSR on the average get 2000 liters of milk from one cow, while the West German farmers get 3,600 liters.... Compare the private and the kolkhoz economy. The Soviet farmer can cultivate on his own a maximum of 5000 sq. meters of land. These small parcels of land and tiny gardens amount to no more than 1 percent of all cultivable land in the USSR, yet they take care of 12 percent (12 percent!) of all food needs. Is this not a catastrophic figure for all admirers of the kolkhoz system, which more than all theories points to the absolute bankruptcy of the kolkhoz economy?

Concretely speaking, for Brezhnev the problem of the subjugated nations, including the Baltic states, has been solved. In the next fifteen years, he is planning to make 50 million hectares of land between the Baltic and West Siberia suitable for either grain production or pasture land—i.e., cultivable land four times that of West Germany. These are the new virgin lands. A gigantic sum of 35 billion rubles is being set aside for this purpose. Brezhnev talked about this in Alma Ata in connection with the twentieth anniversary of Khrushchev's "opening of the virgin lands" in Kazakhstan.... The sum of 35 billion rubles is 25 percent of all agricultural expenditures for the years 1971-1974. Brezhnev stated that this was a decision of the Central Committee of the Communist Party of the Soviet Union and that the present "virgin lands"—42 million hectares which were made suitable for agriculture in the last twenty years—today supply 27 percent of all USSR grain. The question arises, how is it possible that 50 billion hectares of land suitable for agriculture just lay about without "being seen" by the brilliant Central Committee of the CPSU and its chiefs? It must be assumed that for the drying out of swamps, cutting down of forests, and so forth Moscow will "recruit" new prisoners, as had been the case with the infamous construction of the "unique" canals in the Stalin-Beria period.... Brezhnev also remembered the need for the reorganization of Soviet agriculture on a "modern, industrial" basis. Therefore, recalling the "agrocities" of Khrushchev, he announced the merging of collective and state farms, their fusion into "large production companies" which should apply "industrial methods to agriculture," adapting the achievements of science and technology.... The same process of centralization is taking place in industry.... Hence, the new Bolshevik cartels, trusts, and monopolies.... The ownership "for life" of the kolkhoz is disappearing and in practice everything will become state farms....

A new deception of the peoples... A new method of putting the blame on someone else... A new imperial policy in the economic sector as well... A new centralization of the occupying power's government in the agricultural field.... Hence, completely natural and spontaneous are the slogans "Down with kolkhozes, down with sovkhozes, 'agrocities,' or other 'large production companies,' or 'economic regions,' The process of national and social liberation revolution unfolds normally and naturally. The kolkhoz system is failing, although the occupation regime keeps it through terror, not only as an economic system of occupation, but also as a system dictated by military considerations.... The struggle in this segment of life is of primary importance, for this is the struggle against the anti-Ukrainian, Russian way of life imposed on Ukraine by force.

Bolsheviks Were Unable to Change the Soul of the Subjugated Nations

The struggle is deeply rooted in its ideological and political motivation. It also determines the quality and the substance of the freedom toward which the young fighters of the subjugated nations aspire. The struggle is being waged neither from the positions of dialectical and historical materialism, nor from positions of philosophical materialism in general, but just the opposite.

I shall not use my own words, but those of representatives of the young generation in relating what they write and say regarding ideological, political, and strategic positions. I regret that I am not able to give their names; some of them have still managed to escape arrest.

This is what the young generation proclaims: "God has created man.... When there is no God, there are no people.... While building the kingdom of God Christians have resurrected the dead spirituality.... Happy are those who have God.... The basis of morality is the idea of God and the immortality of the soul.... Spiritual life is the only genuine life.... The Church, the bearer of the spirit, must be preserved.... The main thing is to defend the Church...."

The young generation has reached the level of ontology. In the face of imposed Marxist materialism it would be a mistake to remain without an answer to the problem of man's origin and being.

Ethics motivated by religion has a lasting foundation. It is not by chance that one underground author in Ukraine wrote: "We shall build the holy cathedral, send our spirit to heaven, and it will stand for centuries.... How much did our ancestors have to sacrifice while inculcating in their children human ideas, beliefs, selfless love of truth, and respect for the God of their ancestors...."

Religion has been placed at the foundation of cultural creativity: "It is impossible to imagine traditional cultural treasures outside the Church.... A struggle against the Church means a struggle against culture.... How many times was the nation saved by the Church alone.... Under the conditions [prevalent] in our countries, the Church was the only force independent of the government...."

"The apothosis of man as a creature like unto God and not a cog. How can stone-age despotism be ingrained in the soul of a Ukrainian, who as early as the Middle Ages elected and deposed the Cossack chief 'Koshovy' and could himself become a 'Koshovy,' who gave birth to the philosophy of Skovoroda—a hymn to human individuality, with the maxim 'know thyself'...philosophy for which the Ego is the basis of everything, even of the kingdom of God, and even God himself, is nothing other than the fully developed Ego. He who knows himself has found the desired treasure of God... The true man and God are one and the same!"

Traditions of the Subjugated Nations and Their Own Way of Life

In their literary, historical, philosophical, and sociological works, the young, persecuted authors express the following views: the past is our greatest treasure, a spiritual shield, a highly tested experience. An individual with just the present is like a tree without roots.... We deposit into the immortal national treasury our very best and take from it as much as one can.... We pour ourselves as a drop into its [national] sea and think about the eternity of the sea...." And an underground author makes a typical assertion: "Our nation did not follow the big brother [the Russian people]...but chose a difficult, thorn-covered spiritual path—but its own...."

The young generation discovers the road of reawakening in the struggle for the assertion of its own values. It declares, "The present events in Ukraine are also a turning point: the ice of fear which firmly bound the spiritual life of the nation for many years is breaking...."

"Spiritual slavery," says another author, "is the greatest national calamity; prosperity makes a man neither great nor happy. What is it all worth in comparison with freedom, with the life for which you strive, and with the right to think! Wealth is to be found within ourselves, and not in money, property or deeds.... Conscience is the worst torture...."

No matter where you go, writes still another author, "there are foreign bayonets.... The Russians stand in regiments. The stronger think, strive to counteract evil.... The weaker only pray.... We have no right to die as long as our people live in slavery.... The earth will not receive us, will throw us out...."

In the face of Brezhnev's neo-Stalinist terror, another wrote: "But, why do they now fear the Word more than hundreds of swords?.... The bonfires...were turning into ashes, concealing every spark of the conflagrations to come, which will yet raise the flames as crimson banners and herald the great day.... All of us are precursors.... The messiahs will follow in our footsteps.... They cannot help coming.... Nothing is permanent in the world, including falsehood.... The Messiah will come soon and through his sufferings save the people and their freedom...."

Persecution, suffering, and death are the road which leads toward resurrection. "Jesus was seized...and crucified...and he rose forever in the hearts of the unfortunate.... We are but precursors," say the unsubdued of our days about themselves. We live in the pre-revolutionary era in the Russian prison of nations and individuals, a colossus on clay feet, a colossus on a volcano.

And today our purpose is to point out its weak spots in order to help liberate the Free World from the fear of a rabbit hypnotized by a boa constrictor.

"Tyrants love tears and repentance, while somebody's uncrushed dignity is the same for them as a knife in the heart!"

Just as in the early stages of Christianity, the enemy tyrant is afraid of the word—that is, of ideas and of the faith backing them. The thermonuclear age is an ideological age and requires an ideological struggle.

The young generation of the subjugated nations has been reborn. It has stood up in ideological and active defense of national traditionalism, of the national heroism of life, of heroic religiosity, and heroic humanity, of the individual.

"It is impossible to break people, to turn them into slaves, until you steal their holy days, until you destroy their traditions, until you trample on their cathedrals...." states a contemporary Ukrainian intellectual.

And in contradiction to the thesis about the so-called Soviet fatherland, the young generation firmly declares in the words of V. Symonenko: "One can choose one's friends and one's wife, but not one's fatherland; a human being has but one mother, or none at all!"

After 40 years the nations still hate the collective system which suppresses man's ego, individualism, and creative initiative and transforms people into a herd, the individual into a "small cog," as a well known writer from Ukraine puts it. One of the young poets—presently in prison—wrote: "...and the soil became a torment for Ukraine, just as the kolkhozes, [became] a modern compulsory service for a landlord...compulsory service—three days, kolkhoz—seven days...."

V. Moroz, the defender of the national principle of world organization, of traditionalism, of Christian—or rather religious—foundations of culture, and the defender of one of the oldest centers of Ukrainian pre-Christian and Christian culture, Kosmach, contrasts Kosmach to Babylon—the organic, natural, and national concept of world organization to the fusing-of-nations concept. The megalopolis effaces the individual and kills freedom. As Ihor Kalynets, poet and philosopher, proposes a new model for world order, Moroz, an historian, advances a universal conception for saving the word, in another complementary aspect. However, neither of them has been offered the Nobel Prize as yet.

Truth Is Dead without Its Carriers

Truth does not triumph of itself. It triumphs when its carriers are ready to sacrifice their lives for it. "What is important is to believe, the arguments will find themselves.... No apostle has ever converted anyone by arguments. Not a single spiritual revolution has occurred without apostles. Contemporary renaissance is also impossible without them..." writes the unbroken Valentyn Moroz.

And Ivan Dzyuba said: "There are epochs when decisive battles are fought in the sphere of social morality, public conduct, when ever the elementary human dignity resisting brutal terror can become a revolutionary force. Our age also belongs to such epochs...."

Valentyn Moroz continues: "It is possible to have great spiritual treasures, but they simply will not be noticed if they are not taken by an inspired person and melted down in the furnace of his inspiration.... Contemporary Ukraine needs apostles, not accommodators, not realists with their arguments. Not one spiritual revolution has taken place without apostles.... If we want to be Ukrainians, let us fear a 'realist' like fire.... Ukraine is a flower which has grown in the midst of the snow.... An idea is not enough. An idea is bare and dry—what is needed is its living embodiment...."

"The truth is known—what is needed is faith.... Faith needs absolute truth, dogmas. Dogmas," says V. Moroz, "are gladly criticized by all, and this is understandable in our reality, but while pursuing this petty occupation they somehow failed to notice that an individual without any dogmas, an individual who does not believe in anything, has become the main danger. Nihilism has set in—a product of mass culture.... In a human being the technical function is being developed hypertrophically at the expense of the spiritual, and this for some reason is called progress."

"Let us look at national history," writes a young philosopher of history currently in prison. "Have not those become its heroes who with a child's smile have passed over abysses and have raised highest the spirit of national immortality? Have not the practical, the down-to-earth, and the ill-adjusted been forgotten... who ridiculed the Don Quixotes? For legends are created by a Don Quixote, who glance with a fiery look beyond the summits of life. And the rash Don Quixotes become heroes of folk tales [sagas] and national history...but the people collect the traces of the great, often futile, efforts of a Don Quixote, into a legend singing praises to the madness of the courageous...."

When I. Dzyuba issued a statement of repentance, V. Moroz declared to the court: "Well, we shall fight. Just now, when one has signed a statement of repentance, another one reclassified himself as a translator—just now it is necessary for someone to give an example of firmness.... The lot has fallen on me.... It is a difficult mission. To sit behind bars is not easy for anyone. But not to respect oneself—this is even more difficult. And therefore we shall fight!"

As can be seen from the facts of the direct struggle, the subjugated nations possess those who believe in the idea of national liberation, its apostles and carriers. Therefore, neither the idea nor its carriers can be killed anymore.

Nationalism—an Unconquerable Force

How inflammatory is the national idea is evidenced by protest self-immolations:

On November 5, 1968, Vasyl Makukh, fifty, the father of two children, a fighter of the UPA and the Organization of Ukrainian Nationalists (OUN), long-term prisoner of Russian prisons and concentration camps, burned himself in Kyiv with this exclamation: "Long live free Ukraine!"

—On January 20, 1969, the Czech student Jan Palach immolated himself in Prague while shouting: "It is better to die in flames than to live under the Russian colonial yoke!"

—On February 10, 1969, the Ukrainian patriot and former prisoner of concentration camps Mykola Beryslavsky, fifty-five, the father of three children, attempted self-immolation as a protest against Russification, for which he was sentenced to two and a half years' imprisonment.

—On May 14, 1972, the Lithuanian nationalist student Romas Kalanta burned himself in Kaunas with the exclamation: "Long live independent Lithuania!"

—On May 29, 1972, the Lithuanian worker Stonis, twenty-nine.

—On June 3, 1972, the Lithuanian worker Andrus Kukavicious, sixty-one.

—On June 9, 1972, the attempted self-immolation of the Lithuanian Zalizh Kauskas.

The heroic conduct before the court of the Lithuanian sailor, Simas Kurdirka, sentenced to ten years of harsh imprisonment, who greeted his verdict with this exclamation: "I demand freedom for my fatherland, Lithuania!"

—The heroic conduct of the young Ukrainian historian Valentyn Moroz in a

Russian court, with his by now famous expression: "If, having placed me behind bars, you were counting on creating something of a vacuum in the Ukrainian renaissance, then you will be disappointed. Try to understand that there will not be any vacuum any more!"

The national idea is embodied in concrete action, in the direct struggle of the subjugated nations in their native lands and in the concentration camps—as, for example, the much publicized hunger strike in Potma in March 1972, in which Ukrainian, Lithuanian, Jewish, and other political prisoners participated; street revolts and disturbances in Dnipropetrovsk and Dniprodzerzhynsk in 1972; the armed clashes of Georgian nationalists with the Russian occupation detachments in Tiflis; armed clashes in Erivan, Armenia, of recent years....

In June 1971, a revolt broke out among the Kabardinians (of the North Caucasus) in the city of Nalchyk. It was crushed by military units of the Russian KGB, and a woman was even executed by a firing squad after a closed trial. In December 1972, in Derbenti, in Dagestan (in the North Caucasus), armed kolkhoz workers forced the KGB to release the head of the kolkhoz, who had given meat to starving peasants. In June 1971, in Tyraspol, Moldavian students demonstrated for two days in favor of the secession of Moldavia from the USSR and its annexation to Romania.... During the 1972 Jewish Passover, the KGB organs provoked racial disturbances between the Kabardinians and the Jews in the course of which the KGB killed eight Kabardinians and two Jews in Nalchyk.

In Estonia, there appeared the renowned letter of the representatives of the Estonian intelligentsia defending the right of the Estonian people to independence, and threatening that the time would come when the tanks would not be marching on Prague and Bratislava but on Moscow and Leningrad.

In Turkestan, in May 1969, the Uzbeks—shouting, "Russians, get out of Uzbekistan"—revolted in the concentration camps. These disturbances spread across Taskent and Bukhara. The famous struggle of the Crimean Tatars, defended by General Hryhorenko (a Ukrainian), is by now widely known throughout the world. The Armenian groups "Shand" ("in the name of the fatherland") and "Paros" ("torch") fought from 1919 to 1970 for the independence and unity of Armenia, publishing a periodical and leaflets. Their members included students and workers.

The heroic national and religious efforts and the decisive resistance to Russification are renowned throughout the subjugated world. Lithuania has not and never will lay down its arms in its struggle for independence and the Christian religion.

In Byelorussia, the writer Bykov strongly protested against the Russification of his country. Byelorussian youth raised its voice in protest....

An underground organization was founded by Latvians in 1952 called the "Baltic Federation." Its aim was to fight for independence of the Baltic nations—Lithuania, Latvia, and Estonia—and to jointly counteract the Russian occupants....

In Bulgaria and Romania, national resistance is constantly growing. In Hungary, there were new student disturbances in 1973! In Poland, a revolt by workers in 1971 was responsible for the toppling of Gomulka.

Is it possible to stop the process of disintegration of world empires for any conceivable reason whatsoever at the frontier of the totalitarian, anti-religious Russian Empire?! The fundamental contradictions of the empire and the system are realized and felt by the subjugated nations every day; they are no longer illiterate but, on the contrary, every average person is literate, all the more so as these captive nations (such as Georgia, Ukraine, Lithuania, Turkestan, Armenia, and others) are in possession of ancient cultures over a thousand years old. Does the permanent Soviet and Communist propaganda with respect to the attributes of sovereignty for the newly created states—e.g., on the African continent, with armed forces of their own, separation from the "metropolis" and from the empire, a sovereign foreign policy, withdrawal of imperialist armies from the former colonies, etc.—not remind even a pupil of a primary school in Byelorussia or Azerbaidzhan, Estonia or Latvia of the complete contradiction between windy rhetoric and reality—i.e., the colonialist situation of those nations which are constantly exposed to the Russian KGB, Russification, the Russian occupational army, the lack of any sovereignty as to decisions concerning their own affairs, etc.?! In the mentality of even the subjugated nations' children the question of national independence is always on the order of the day, even being supported by official propaganda. When attacking the Western states' nonexistent colonialism and imperialism the Russian occupants are employing a two-edged sword.

Consequently, the liberation nationalism of the subjugated nations in the Russian Empire is not only stimulated by the inborn striving towards the creation of their own way of life but is also conditioned by international development. The national principle as opposed to the imperialist one is the slogan of the present era.

V.A. Kapshytsei, a recent Jewish emigrant from the USSR to Israel, writes: "One of the major questions facing us is the national question.... The national forces are breaking the Communist empire apart...."

Brezhnev denotes "local patriotism" as related to "nationalism" in the economic sphere After the mass arrests in Ukraine the First Secretary of the Central Committee of the Communist Party of Ukraine, Shcherbytsky, the successor of Shelest, stated during the April assembly of the Central Committee of Ukraine in 1973 that many authors revealed national conceit and limitation, idealized the patriarchal system, interpreted the history of Ukraine in the light of depraved ideological views on "originality." The party secretaries of Georgia, Lithuania, Latvia, Uzbekistan, Armenia, and other pseudo-republics were removed from their posts because they had not been successful in fighting their nations' liberation nationalism. The *Ukrainian Historical Journal* (No. 3, 1973) states, in the essay entitled "Anti-Sovietism—The Chief Trend of Ukrainian Bourgeois Nationalist Subversive Activity," that nationalism cannot be repressed. The author, V.P. Cherednychenko, quotes Lenin: "Bourgeois nationalism and proletarian internationalism are two slogans which irreconcilably oppose each other, expressing two policies [rather: two world outlooks] with respect to the national question." In order "to overcome any manifestations of nationalism in the economy" the Russian imperialist leadership is also forcefully unifying the economic regions according to the Tsarist model. The theoretically existing sovereignty of the "republics" is being violated. Seven economic regions are to be created: the Far East, Siberia, Kazakhstan, the Northern Center, Volga-Ural, Central Asia, and the South. The so-called "Ug" (South) of the USSR corresponds exactly to the "Ug" (South) of tsarist Russia. It includes, among others, Ukraine, Georgia, Azerbaidzhan and North Caucasus. The food shortage in Ukraine in 1973 proves the bankruptcy of the system. So does the purchase of grain in the USA, Canada, and Germany.

The empire is also undergoing a period of economic recession.

W. Kolarz says: "Nationalism is a kind of explosive against Communism" and "finally Communism may capitulate before nationalism on the international scale" (see *Communism and Colonialism*," London, New York: 1964, p. 13).

Popular Nationwide Movements

It must be stated that the national liberation movements of the subjugated nations are popular movements, in which an active part is taken not only by students and intellectuals, but also by workers and collective farmers.

According to Andrei Amalrik, out of the 134 signatures appearing under one Kyiv protest letter in defense of prisoners, 25 percent were those of workers of the Kyiv factories.

The strength of our movement was always to be found in the people, who continuously produce ever new heroes.

It is significant that the city is also becoming a part of the liberation struggle. This is an important phenomenon. The countryside was the mainstay of the OUN-UPA. It is a good turn of events that the city is taking over its due role. To demoralize the village is the enemy strategy. Ukraine's reply: while defending the village, a successful advance upon the city. The intellectual elite, the students, the workers are standing on the frontlines. Not only an ideological but also an active struggle has developed—e.g., the actions of students and workers. The same is occurring in Lithuania, Estonia, Georgia, Turkestan, Croatia, North Caucasus, Byelorussia, Poland, Slovakia, Czechia, Hungary, Romania, and Bulgaria.

What is the heart of the matter? Yuriy Yofe, an emigrant from the USSR to Israel, stated: "The Democratic Movement in Russia is a purely intellectual phenomenon, which has been never so popular as, for instance, the Ukrainian Nationalist Movement...."

Revolution Possible

In the thermonuclear and the ideological age, the most timely and real is the liberating, revolutionary, insurgent concept, which will destroy the empire and the system from within. In the fall of 1970, maneuvers of MVD forces took place near Moscow under the slogan "Suppression of Uprisings in Concentration Camps."

The uprisings of Ukrainian, Lithuanian, Turkestani, Georgian, Armenian,

Byelorussian, and other prisoners in concentration camps in 1953-1959, the disturbances and revolutionary upheavals in East Germany, Hungary, Poland, Czechia, and Slovakia, the nationwide insurrection in Ukraine in 1942-1953, and the partisan warfare in Lithuania have established that revolutionary struggle is possible even in the totalitarian, Russian, imperialistic system. The courageous acts of Croatian nationalists have proven the weakness of Yugoslavia as an artificial, forced, colonial structure in Europe.

Simultaneous, not separate and isolated, revolutionary uprisings of the subjugated peoples are the surest road to liberation. The occupational regime will be powerless when confronted with them for it will not be able to use nuclear arms, this being self-destructive. Moreover, the administrative machinery itself is infiltrated by anti-imperial and anti-Communist elements. The Soviet Army is composed not only of Russians but also of soldiers from the subjugated countries, while the satellite armies—as shown by the Hungarian Revolution, the disturbances in Poland, and the events in Czechia and Slovakia—will not take a stand against their own rebelling compatriots, but to the contrary will themselves rise against the occupant. What is more, the soldiers of the Soviet army, which is based on universal, compulsory military service, are tightly bound with their nations, living by the same ideals as their fathers and mothers.

It is not an isolated incident that four years ago, on August 31, 1970, in a military court of the Baltic Military District, there ended a trial of an underground organization inside the army which had its branches in Poland, Azerbaidzhan, and other places. The resonance of the national liberation struggle of the subjugated nations will be heard in the armed forces. Neither the KGB nor the party are able to protect it against this, since the soldiers of the Soviet army are an inseparable part of the nations from which they come. It was not a chance occurrence that in the first half of 1973 over 15,000 young Ukrainians of military age were thrown into punitive detachments along the Sino-Soviet border.

Not only the captive nations' aspiration for freedom and independence makes them strong, but also the fact that their fighters dispose of technological weapons as well, including the most modern type thereof, as it is impossible to exclude over 200 million captive nationals from technological production. It is the unsolvable contradictions of the imperialist Russian and the Communist system that constitute a decisive weakness on the part of the subjugator. Openly turning to Russian chauvinism and attempting to completely Russify the captive nations proves the weakness and bankruptcy of Communism in the USSR.

Can one expect any self-respecting nation, even the most insignificant one, to idolize its subjugator and exploiter as "big brother" as the Russifiers are constantly demanding? The young Ukrainian intellectual Ivan Dzyuba dared to describe and condemn this situation in his work "Internationalism or Russification?".

The Russian occupants are frightened by the fact that American and British intellectual elites are beginning to understand and appreciate liberation nationalism. Nationalism is not Nazism, Fascism, imperialism, colonialism, anti-Semitism, and the like, but their opposite, an ideological and political philosophy. It implies the independence of each nation, patriotism, true democracy residing in the nation and including the entire people—not just a stratum, class, or group; it also means respect for the right of even the smallest nation, to independence and freedom from exploitation; it is an anti-Communist and anti-totalitarian ideology stressing heroic humanity and social justice, idealism, anti-Marxism, the primacy of the national and social elements over egoism, and of national heroism of life. Therefore, nationalism, frightens Moscow. An American sociologist quite often referred to by Bolshevik theoreticians, Hans Kohn, says that nationalism is a social phenomenon "wherein all problems of recent and contemporary history are condensed." The well-known English economist, investigating the problems of international politics, Barbara Ward, maintains that "nationalism is undoubtedly the most powerful political force today" (in *Five Ideas That Change the World*, New York, 1959, p. 19). The former executive director of the CIA, L. Kirkpatrick, Jr., shares this view; in 1959 he wrote: "We no longer doubt that nationalism is the most powerful explosive force in world society...."

An Appeal from the Underground

An Appeal from Ukraine, smuggled to the West, appeared in *The Diary Telegraph* on the 16th of August, 1973:

Our front is compelled to act illegally, and that is why we mail this appeal without signatures. We appeal to the public opinion of the world to raise its voice in defense of the Ukrainian people, and against Russian despotism.

The UN Charter and Declaration of Human Rights, which were also signed by the Governments of the USSR and Ukrainian Soviet Socialist Republic, guarantee to each and every nation the right to national independence and individual freedom. However, the Party and Government of both the USSR and Ukrainian SSR completely disregard their own laws. The latter is, actually, the colonial administration of Ukraine receiving direct orders from Moscow.

The Government of the Ukrainian SSR did not even obtain the privilege for Ukrainian convicts to serve their sentences on Ukrainian territory, for here they are citizens and here they could obtain better assistance from their families. For attempting the realization of just rights, Ukrainian community leaders were sentenced, some to death (L. Lukyanenko, I. Kandyba, whose sentences were commuted to fifteen years' imprisonment in concentration camps with a severe regime); for attempts to free cultural creativity and for opposing Russification, several hundred cultural workers, poets, artists, scientists, and scholars (such as V. Moroz, Y. Sverstyuk, V. Chornovil, I. Svitlychny, Ihor and Iryna Kalynets, W. Stus, Iryna Senyk, Mykhaylo Osadchyi, I. Hel, and others) were punished by heavy sentences of up to fifteen years of imprisonment in concentration camps and exile; for protesting against unlawful court proceedings and for the defense of the rights of individuals, punishments in the form of unspecified terms within special psychiatric asylums under KGB supervision were imposed (L. Plyushch, professor of cybernetics; A. Lupynis; Gen. P. Hryhorenko, and others); for religious convictions I. Moyseyev, Mykola Khmara, and others were beaten to death; Rev. V. Romaniuck has been sentenced to a long prison term; for refusing to denounce his father, Yuriy Shukhevych was sentented to fifteen years of imprisonment, after he had previously served twenty years; for defending her husband, the microbiologist Nina Strokata-Karavanska was sentenced to four years of imprisonment; for defending the rights and freedom of their nations A. Oliynyk, P. Kovalchuk, I. Chayka, and others were executed; M. Soroka, V. Malchuk, and others were tortured to death.

For defending the rights of the Ukrainian, Tatar, Jewish, and other nations, S. Karavansky, Gen. P. Hryhorenko, and Ivan Dzyuba were punished with extreme severity.

For defending the Jewish people who have been discriminated against, Petro Yakir and others were again put behind bars.

In order to break the will of resistance, the KGB is using modern chemicals and medical drugs manufactured by its professional staff, or is systematically poisoning foodstuffs (P. Starchyk, I. Dzyuba, V. Moroz, L. Lukyanenko, I. Kandyba, and others).

Through the application of modern methods of breaking the will power of a human being, the terror of Brezhnev-Andropov surpasses that of Stalin-Beria.

"We warn you that if national rights and freedom of individuals, freedom of creativity and religion are not defended not only by us, who are at present suffering persecution and cruel treatment, but also by the entire cultural world—then a massive and intensive terror will gain the upper hand in the whole world, for Russian chauvinists and Communists will not stop and will not be satisfied with what they have conquered.

We call upon workers, writers, artists, scholars, students, and young people, women and churches and all people of good will to demand the immediate abolition of the use of chemical and medical means and the application of malpractice, including psychiatric methods, and furthermore the release of all political and religious prisoners, the liquidation of concentration camps, the end of Russification, and the realization of national independence for the nations subjugated in the Soviet Union in accordance with the UN Charter and the Universal Declaration of Human Rights.

The letter was signed by the Front of National Defense of Ukraine and dated July 1973.

In conclusion, I would·like to express our bitter disappointment. Only a few people in the West raise their voice in defense of nations and human rights, for the freedom of religion and cultural creativity of members of subjugated nations; Ukraine or Latvia or Lithuania or others. Neither the press, nor politicians, nor governments, nor the Vatican, nor the churches , nor humanitarian or judiciary institutions do this—they all remain silent and do not condemn the draconic sentences of Moscow against one of the most famous cultural leaders of Ukraine, Valentyn Moroz, who is sentenced to fourteen years' severe regime, or the Lithuanian Simas Kudirka. No Western publisher published the works of Valentyn Moroz or Yevhen Sverstyuk or Ihor Kalynets or Vasyl Stus, whose works are of great artistic value. The reason for this is that the authors from Ukraine or Latvia stand not only for human rights, but also for the rights of nations.

It is a kind of "decline of the West" when it defends the representatives of the ruling Russian nation and not the subjugated nations. The West is indifferent to the lot of hundreds of millions of oppressed peoples and dozens of subjugated nations.

Urgent Action Needed in Defense of the Persecuted

In news just received from Ukraine we have learned about a new Russian-Bolshevik crime:

At present Svyatoslav Karavansky (writer and literary critic, sentenced to twenty-five years in concentration camps, released 1960, but again arrested in 1965 to serve the rest of his sentence, in 1970 his term prolonged for another five years of imprisonment) is serving his unlawful imprisonment in a political concentration camp with an especially severe regime. Such a concentration camp, where people are buried alive, could only have been thought up by the devil himself. In this concentration camp the prisoners constantly live and work under lock, without any fresh air, because they are never taken out for exercise.

In this concentration camp the prisoners are forced to work long hours in glass-grinding workshops, from which dangerous dust unceasingly penetrates the lungs of the undernourished prisoner and seriously threatens his life. This threat is increased also by the fact that the glass-grinding workshops are situated in buildings adjacent to the prisoner's living quarters. The cells, polluted by this poisonous dust, are also a hazard to human life. This dust is everywhere: in the air, on the beds, in the clothes, and in the food. In comparison Vladimir prison was a real blessing.

Another report from behind the Iron Curtain reveals that three prominent Ukrainian women, Stephania Shabatura, Nina Strokata, and Iryna Kalynets, imprisoned in Soviet Mordovian prisons, have appealed to the Secretary-General of the United Nations, Mr. Waldheim, by letter dated 10th May, 1973, in which they protest against the enslavement of the Ukrainian nation and demand for themselves an open trial in the presence of a UN representative. The text of their appeal is as follows:

To the Secretary General of the United Nations.

An Appeal

Stephania Shabatura, born 1938, sentenced to five years' imprisonment in camps and three years' forced exile, an artist from Lviv.

Nina Karavanska-Strokata, born 1925, sentenced to four years' imprisonment in camps, a scientific worker from Odessa.

Iryna Kalynets—Stasiv, born 1940, sentenced to six years' imprisonment in camps and three years' forced exile, a poetess from Lviv.

The day 12th January, 1972 was the beginning of a new wave of repressions against the Ukrainian intelligentsia. We are being persecuted and imprisoned simply because we, as Ukrainians, stand for the preservation and advancement of the Ukrainian national culture and language in Ukraine. All arrests conducted during that year in Ukraine are violations of the Declaration of Human Rights by the Soviet authorities.

We are defenseless before the unlawful Soviet court. We were tried illegally and at present are serving our sentences in the Soviet political camp No. 3 in Dubrovlag, Mordovia. We refute all the charges that were brought against us. We are not asking for a favor, only for a normal, fair, and open trial in the presence of a representative of the United Nations. 10th May, 1973.

During the last months in prison Anatoliy Radygin (his memoirs, *Episodes from Mordovian Concentration Camps*, were published in Naharia, Israel, in October 1973) repeatedly asked Valentyn Moroz what message he could deliver to the Free World. Pain-stricken as he was Valentyn Moroz frowned and repeated insistently:

"Let people know only one thing: I am being kept together with insane people and my life is like hell! They are trying to make me mad just like those who are thrown into my ward. They are assassins and cannibals! I do not have any air to breathe!"

Radygin, the author of the memoirs, adds the following.

Thus I repeat, too: one of the most honest and talented Ukrainian publicists is reduced to a state of complete exhaustion approaching insanity. His present existence comprises a frightful mixture of hungry life in jail and miserable existence in a room of a mental asylum, where he is constantly attacked by semi-animals that have completely lost their human look and have no distinguishing national or social features whatever. Valentyn Moroz is being physically and morally tortured day by day.

Remember this!

Appeal to the Conference

In view of these alarming reports, we ask the Conference to:

Severely condemn and together with us urge the liquidation of all concentration camps!

Demand the release of all prisoners condemned and imprisoned for their national, political, and religious convictions!

Demand the termination of the application of chemical and medical means of breaking the will power of political and religious prisoners in order to extort statements of repentance from them!

Vigorously denounce the practice of confining fighters for national and human rights in insane asylums!

Demand an end to persecution of believers in God and cultural leaders who defend the essence and spirituality of their own nation, without which a nation perishes!

Demand the withdrawal of Russian occupation forces and the Communist terror apparatus from the Russian-subjugated nations within the USSR and its satellites!

Demand a return of national sovereignty to all the nations subjugated by Russian imperialism and Communism in the USSR and the satellites, as well as for those nations enslaved in the artificial state of Yugoslavia!

Without national culture there is no world culture!

If you don't want to see a KGB gun and the law of the jungle prevail in the world, fight for humanism and for morality based on religion!

We ask you to join in the protest against Russian and Communist crimes for the defense of the imprisoned and persecuted fighters for human and national rights!

> Address Given to the Seventh WACL
> Conference, Washington, D.C.,
> April 8-11, 1974

Revolutionary and Reactionary Forces in the World

We would like to express our deep gratitude for this great honor, which you—our dear compatriots from various nations—bestow upon us. We hardly deserve these accolades of honor, since we are simply fulfilling our sacred duty towards our Fatherland, towards our common front against our common enemy, towards the ABN, and towards yourselves, who for many decades have shared in our achievements and even in our unfulfilled hopes in our national liberation struggle against the Russian oppressor. We would rather not dedicate today's festivities to separate individuals, who have not yet given the greatest sacrifice on the altar of freedom and independence for their Fatherland; instead, let us dedicate this occasion to the national liberation, revolutionary movements of our nations, by again demonstrating our solidarity and determination in the anti-Russian and anti-Communist liberation struggle. But if we are to mention individuals, let us today again commemorate our leaders and brethren in arms of our revolutionary liberation struggle who have fallen in battle—individuals such as Osman Batur, the leader of the Turkestani insurgents—Basmachi, the leader of the North Caucasus freedom fighters—Shamil, the Commander of the Lithuanian warriors—the Byelorussian insurgents' leader Vitushka—General Maleter, the hero of Hungary—the presidents and martyrs for freedom of Estonia and Latvia—the heroes of Bulgaria, Croatia, Romania, Cuba, Poland, and the courageous Afghan revolutionaries—and last but not least the heroic Commander-in-Chief of the Ukrainian Insurgent Army General Roman Shukhevych-Chuprynka, and the symbol of the national liberation struggle, Stepan Bandera. We also bow our heads before the countless national heroes known only to God—the unknown soldiers of the liberation revolution of nations. They are all known to God and therefore they will always live amongst us in spirit.

The essence of the matter is not in the tragic element of dying for an idea, but rather in the element of human greatness manifested by their death, by this manifested apogee of heroism!

We do not believe in the illusion that the epoch of wars for one's Fatherland has long since passed, erased by the dawn of a new thermonulcear era. With the specter of the thermonuclear Armageddon notwithstanding, we must remember that the world is ruled by the irresistible will of the Providence of God. Nations not only learn from this will, but God always comes to the behest of those nations which resolutely affirm God's will of justice by defending their Fatherland. *Liberation wars are holy wars for freedom and justice*, for the sovereignty of one's country. They attest to the desire of all free men to glorify their Creator against Russian atheistic Bolshevism and genocide. Such wars of liberation have God's blessing, because they are just.

There can be no end to wars of liberation as long as there continue to exist imperialism, colonial occupation, and exploitation and the desire of imperialistic nations to rule over the rest of the world, or over other nations. Pacifism can only be tantamount to capitulation in the face of this evil. This Bolshevik evil has become very aggressive in its desire to eradicate all nations, their culture, and everything that is sacrosanct and holy in them. Everything noble and majestic in life is now being grossly challenged by a hedonistic lifestyle. For the Free World to be victorious in this struggle against the Bolshevik evil it needs, above all, to nurture a rebirth of patriotism, of a heroic spirituality, and a heroic humanism, of a heroic Christianity, of religion in general, of the severe traditions, morals, and ethics of the first Christians. There can be no political and military victory without an ideologico-moral rebirth. An individual will only sacrifice his life for something eternal! A national principle of world organization against imperialism and the destruction of the Russian empire from within by way of national-liberation revolutions is the only alternative to a thermonuclear war. The re-establishment of democratic nation-states within their own ethnographic territories—this is our goal! Our liberation cannot come as a consequence of international agreements, "evolution," or "liberation," of the Russian empire and its Communist regime, which is a typical product of Russian imperialism in its modern form. The democratic system of an imperialist nation was never a factor in the realization of democracy in the nations subjugated by the imperialist power, since democratization is only possible after the dissolution of empires into sovereign and independent nation-states. The world has yet to know of a democratic empire. Every subjugated nation was always oppressed by national enslavement and the total repression of all human rights and fundamental liberties. The realization of these rights and freedoms is predicated on the establishment of national independence, of a sovereign nation-state with a democratic order, formed by the will of the nation in accordance with its own system of values.

The so-called Helsinki Accords, of which the Russian empire is a signatory, are a contradiction in themselves. They are simply a reaffirmation of the inviolability of the borders of the empire and its totalitarian, anti-democratic Communist system. The Russian empire is the most barbaric system in history. For this reason alone *the Helsinki Accords should be annulled*. While debates are being held in Madrid, the Russians are arresting and sentencing the members of the Helsinki Monitoring Groups, most recently the Ukrainian jurist Ivan Kandyba. All discussions with such a partner should be immediately terminated, especially when one side brutally tramples upon the fundamental tenets which serve as the foundation for these discussions.

There are two fundamental issues which the West must resolve: to identify the enemy and to find a consistent solution to the world crisis.

It would be completely reactionary to formulate a global political strategy by imitating the imperialistic concepts of balance of power, emasculated at one time or another by the British, by Metternich, and later by Bismarck, and to place these imperialistic regional concepts of the past within a global context, particularly in the relations between the Russian empire, its Communist system, and the Free World.

The present era is particularly characterized by the collapse of empires and the primary prevalence of the national principle in all spheres of international politics throughout the world.

Furthermore, a concept of arms limitation at the lowest possible level, in reality, does not resolve anything. This process cannot be controlled, especially if one takes into account the fact that Moscow has never respected any agreements. The most important factor to be considered, however, is the extremely perilous situation within the Russian empire, which is being threatened by the centrifugal revolutionary forces of the national liberation movements of the subjugated nations. This unstable situation within the empire cannot continue for much longer, and the 1980s may witness a revolutionary explosion of the national potential of the subjugated nations. All the efforts undertaken by the West to maintain the existing status quo, ranging from the policy of containment to that of detente, have only served to buttress and promote Russian aggression in Asia, Africa, and Latin America.

Was the West able to foresee that Ukraine would be capable of leading a war on two fronts against Germany and Russia? And yet, not only did Ukraine lead such a war under the leadership of the UPA and the OUN, but this revolutionary-guerrilla war continued well into the 1950s. Lithuania also led a guerrilla war on two fronts. Byelorussia also had its insurgents! Similarities can be drawn from other nations. At that time the Allied forces refused to believe in this miracle, but once it became a reality—they neglected even to consider it. *This war on two fronts against Nazi Germany and Russia of the subjugated nations, and in a common front with the Western Allies, would have been the decisive factor in the Second World War, which would have saved the world from both Nazism and its original prototype—Bolshevism.*

Will the present leaders of the West learn from their past mistakes? Will history be our teacher, particularly this year, when Ukraine is commemorating the fortieth anniversary of the reestablishment of an independent Ukrainian State, proclaimed on June 30th, 1941? This historical Act was born of the will of the Ukrainian nation and laid the foundation for the ensuing war of liberation on two fronts. Lithuania also proclaimed its independence in 1941.

Presently, the heroic Afghan nation has taken up arms against the onslaught of Russian imperialism. And at this crucial juncture in history, the West's reaction is limited to a disconcerted boycott of the Moscow Olympics, or to the institution of a number of economic sanctions which are paralyzed by several loopholes. Instead, the West ought to have immediately liberated Cuba, buttressed by the Russian agent Fidel Castro, from under the Communist yoke.

The United States can either become the vanguard force of the Free World in supporting the national liberation, anti-colonial, anti-imperialist revolutions of the subjugated nations against the most tyrannical and brutal empire the world has yet known—the USSR, the Russian prison of nations, which would be in accordance with its own American Revolution of 1776. Or, in contradiction to these noble traditions, the United States can become a global, anti-revolutionary, reactionary power, continuing to defend the existence and stability of the Russian empire.

If the United States continues to ignore the Congressional Resolution on Captive Nations of 1959, if it continues to ignore the resolution of the United Nations on decolonization by refusing to apply it to the Russian colonial empire, demanding its immediate dissolution, if it continues to refuse to apply to the USSR the UN resolution of 1976, which required, from the standpoint of international law, that all UN member states render military aid to the subjugated nations fighting against colonial enslavement—then Moscow will be able to maneuver the US into a reactionary position, on the nominal assertion that the US is against independence and freedom for nations, while Russia itself will continue to render military aid to the Kurds, the Baluchis, the southern Azerbaidzhanis, the Arabs, and to other nations from one or another geopolitical complex. The United States can avoid this dilemma by including as an integral component of its international policy the necessity of the dissolution of the Russian colonial empire and by actively supporting the national liberation struggle of the subjugated nations in that empire, leading to the reestablishment of national independent and sovereign states within the ethnographic boundaries of these nations.

Such a position of principle will automatically resolve any derivative questions dealing with the artificial constructs of multinational states. Thus, *the United States will become the revolutionary liberating force in the world, and the USSR its reactionary adversary.*

We fear that if the United States agrees to continue its discussion with the USSR, without establishing any preconditions to these talks, then for all intents and purposes this will be tantamount to its acquiescing to the military occupation of Afghanistan in exchange for a temporary concession on the part of Moscow not to militarily intercede in Poland.

Weakness of the Prison of Nations

Afghanistan was a well-regulated step on the road to oil and the mineral wealth of Asia and Africa.

At the end of the eighties the Russians will have exhausted their oil reserves. They will have the oil of the Middle East and thereby the key to the satellitization of the rest of Europe. Demographic changes are occurring at a quicker rate: Russians are already a minority in the USSR, and in a decade every third inhabitant of the USSR will be Islamic.

Moscow knows that it can buy anything for oil—electronics, technology, bread—and it is therefore ridiculous to think of it giving up Afghanistan, which is the key to oil. Oil is the key to the highly industrialized West. If Russia were to establish control over the oil fields of the Persian Gulf area, then it could hold the West hostage, despite its own underdeveloped and primitive economic system.

It is meaningless to conclude all these SALT II or III treaties. In reality this is simply a disarmament farce in which the *west* arms the USSR. This comedy takes place in the following way: the West supplies the Russians with electronics, technology, grain, various economic aid, and even conventional arms in modified form. The West thus creates a base for rocket, atomic, and conventional arms and, through its senseless yet assiduous economic and trade policies, aids the Russians by allowing them to concentrate on the development of their own heavy arms industry, indeed even strengthening it.

The empire sits on top of a volcano. Any attempt on its part to somehow resolve the crisis in Poland threatens the further existence of this empire. An occupation of Poland by additional military forces will bring about a Russo-Polish war, which will subsequently have its repercussions in the international sphere and in the USSR itself, further complicating the already tenuous internal situation in the empire, regardless of the probable brevity of military hostilities in Poland. If the revolutionary processes in Poland are further tolerated and allowed to develop, without being countered by force or subversion, then the power and authority of the Communist Party—i.e., the Russian imperialists—will be irrefutably broken, with all the evident repercussions in other subjugated nations. *We must remember that the liberation processes are a power, and power means authority.* Can the imperialist colonial regime share authority? Can the imperialist-colonial regime share authority with those that it has enslaved and colonized? We think not! The empire is losing itself in its own contradictions, which it cannot resolve in any of the subjugated nations.

The world is excited and surprised by the events in Poland, but does not understand that all this has happened before. The forties and fifties were teeming with strikes and uprisings of Ukrainians and other political prisoners in the forced labor camps. The fifties, sixties, and seventies saw numerous workers' strikes in Ukraine—in Donbas, Odessa, Novocherkassk, and other cities and provinces of Ukraine, Lithuania, Latvia, Estonia, Byelorussia, Georgia, and many more areas.

In 1962 workers in Novocherkassk were killed by the MVD, which crushed the strikes and uprisings of the workers after the commanding officer of the Red Army refused to give the order to fire on the workers and shot himself instead. A number of strikes, clashes with the militia, and deaths occurred in Kyiv, Sevastopol, Krasnodar, and Kryvyi Rih.

In the seventies there were sporadic strikes in Dnipropetrivsk, Dniprodzerzhynsk, Kyiv, and many other cities in Ukraine, accompanied by bloody clashes with the Russian occupation troops. There were student demonstrations in many Ukrainian cities, protests against Russification, and various forms of struggle and resistance. The groundwork for the creation of free trade unions was also laid by Ukrainians, in particular by the Donbas worker Klebanov. The workers and urban guerrilla forces are a new factor of great importance.

The geopolitical situation of Poland is without any doubt better than that of Ukraine. Nevertheless, it is not to be expected that without synchronized actions in other enslaved nations and without the help of other nations in the empire Poland will be able to attain independence.

The 1980's will be a decade of volcanic explosions. A threat based on strength by the West, along with the concurrent determination to use this strength, will undoubtedly have a decisive effect on the gerontocrats of the Kremlin.

In this dilemma, the United States has only one available solution: *to clearly and openly proclaim a Great Charter of Independence for all the nations subjugated by Russian imperialism, thereby promoting the complete dissolution of the Russian empire into nationally independent and sovereign states.* The United States must discard the antiquated and reactionary policy of detente and balance of power, substituting for it a consistent, progressive, and dynamic *concept and policy of national liberation.* Only then will Moscow be forced into a position of being the most reactionary force in the world.

In refraining from exposing the USSR as the most tyrannical colonial empire in the world, the USA is creating the illusion of a homogeneous and nationally uniform "Soviet nation" as a new "historical formation." The United States is thereby justifying Moscow's deceitful and deceptive political strategy of being the supporter of the rights of the nationally and socially subjugated and oppressed peoples of the world, whereas in reality Russia is itself the most brutal subjugator of nations and peoples. In short, the United States, by its fundamentally unsound and inconsistent policies with regard to the ideals of national and social liberation, has incredibly given Moscow its "carte blanche" in these crucial and historically key political areas.

As long as the United States continues to pretend that the national liberation struggles of Ukraine, Georgia, Turkestan, Byelorussia, Bulgaria, Azerbaidzhan, Lithuania, Latvia, Estonia, Croatia, Czechia, Slovakia, Armenia, Cuba, Poland, Hungary, Romania, Albania, North Caucasus, Vietnam, Idel-Ural, and the other subjugated nations in the Russian empire do not exist as the central problem in the struggle for a new and just restructuring of the world political international order, the future cannot be theirs!

What Is Necessary at the Present?

1. *A center of psychological warfare must be created,* founded on the political and ideological concepts of the ABN, and at the disposal of the ABN, directed at the subjugated nations in the USSR and the satellite countries, with branches established in:

a) One of the countries of the Near East, perhaps Egypt, directed particularly to Afghanistan and the African nations presently controlled by Moscow and its puppet states, such as Cuba, the "DDR," and other satellite countries;

b) Latin America, particularly Cuba;

c) Southeast Asia, with Vietnam as the focal point;

d) The Far East, with Siberia as the focal point.

The major objective of this center would be the promotion of the idea of national liberation on all levels of society in the subjugated nations, particularly the Soviet army, on the basis of political cooperation with the national liberation centers or organizations of the subjugated nations.

2. *Military training in guerrilla warfare* must be offered to the Afghan revolution-aries, as well as to the émigré members of the nations subjugated in the USSR and the satellite countries. *We demand that the West immediately give military aid to the Afghan freedom fighters—the Mujahaddin,* in the form of arms, anti-helicopter and anti-tank weapons, surface-to-air missiles, mine detectors, radio broadcasting sets, etc.

3. In the forum of the United Nations and elsewhere in the international sphere, *the West must recognize the true representatives of the subjugated nations—i.e., the representatives of the national liberation movements*—as the only real representatives of the will and aspirations of these nations, rather than continue to recognize the imperialist lackeys of Moscow.

4. The representatives of the national liberation struggle of the subjugated nations *must have* at their disposal *the various modern, technical means of promoting their struggle* in a number of forms in their respective countries, on the basis of their concept of liberation, without them having to meet any preconditions effected by changes in policy by the Western countries.

By utilizing the existing media of mass communication to the fullest, *the West must propagate our forms and methods of waging a national liberation struggle, formulated by ourselves*, not restricting the ideas of this struggle by accommodating or adjusting them to the momentary tactical and situational exigencies in the relations between the Western countries and the USSR.

The West must actively support the Cuban freedom fighters, so that they may overthrow Castro's regime in Cuba, which will immediately resolve the numer-ous problems of diversion in Latin America, and all the more in Africa.

In the forum of the United Nations, the West must resolutely pursue the issue *of condeming Russian emperio-colonialism, questioning the right of lackey governments to speak in the name of the subjugated nations*. Also, as a concurrent measure, the West must give the national liberation organizations of these nations similar status to that of the PLO, demanding the expulsion of the USSR and the satellite countries from the United Nations.

These are our initial demands, predicated by our belief that a reversal of policy is necessary in the West.

5. We are also convinced that the great Chinese nation, with its culture of many millennia, will return to its intrinsic Confucian traditions and the national-political concepts of Sun Yat-sen, and will overcome the Marxist-Leninist way of life forced upon it with its own integral forces.

6. We support and recognize the legitimate Japanese claim to the Kuril Islands and Sakhalin, occupied by Moscow. We fully support the idea of unification in freedom of Korea and Germany. We call on all of the world to actively support the Vietnamese insurgents, and all the patriotic anti-Communist fighters for freedom and independence of the nations of Africa, who are defending their Fatherlands from Russian imperialist aggression.

Our demands are not simply the demands of our respective émigré communities, but rather they emulate the demands of those who are on the first front of the struggle. During the uprisings in the concentration camps of Siberia in the 1950s during the Stalin era, the political prisoners demanded that the West support their revolutionary aims, as was outlined by Joseph Sholmer in his book *Vorkuta*.

The political prisoners demanded arms, medical supplies, radio broadcasting sets, food, and the like, which were to be delivered by the West through parachutists. But, more importantly, *the prisoners demanded that the West proclaim its support for national independence of the subjugated nations in the USSR!* The fact that Khrushchev deemed it necessary to reorganize the concentration camps and even freed many prisoners was no coincidence. *The conflagration of the empire could have easily begun in the concentration camps!* The initial phase in this action was to be a general strike! The organizers were Ukrainian nationalists, Lithuanians, Turkestanis, and freedom fighters of the other nations.

We must nevertheless remember that these demands were born from the reality of the struggle.

Let me conclude my address with the well-known ABN slogan: *"He who liberates himself will be free; he who poses as a liberator of others will lead them into slavery!"*

ABN Correspondence,
May-August 1981, pp. 6-7

An Analysis of Russian Expansionism

Allow me to begin with a few comments concerning the ideological aspect of Russian expansionism:

In 1878, Dostoevsky wrote that "all people should become Russian, particularly Russian, because the Russian national idea is universal."

Russian literature to date invariably continues in this colonial genre. During the past years many books have appeared about the undercutting of Turkestan by "progressive" tsarist generals; about the battles with the Basmachi (Turkestani freedom fighters) in the nineteen-twenties; about the colonial war against the Organization of Ukrainian Nationalists and the Ukrainian Insurgent Army in the nineteen-forties. Alexander Prochanov's novel *A Tree in the Center of Kabul* is one of the latest additions to Russian colonial literature. It is a story about the Russian nation's "brotherly" assistance provided to the "oppressed Afghan nation" in which Prochanov ideologically justifies war with the whole world and armed intervention wherever a Russian can set foot. Volkov, a journalist and hero of the story, rides through the streets of Kabul in a tank crushing the residents; rides in a helicopter shooting at caravans of women and children convinced that he is "bringing happiness, goodness, and unprecedented life, love, beauty...." Prochanov is in dispute with those fascinated only with the Russian tsarist past.... In his opinion, the current mission of the Russian empire in the form of the USSR is much broader and much more important, because the spread of the "idea of Bolshevism, of Soviet ideals, will bring the world as a whole inevitable happiness...."

The narrative, published in the journal *Oktiabr* in 1982, supports the predictions of the Russian writer Evgeniy Zamiatin made in his 1920 narrative *We* about the "Sole State of the Future" in which the residents "found happiness beneath the iron fist of their benefactors" (the Good Samaritan).

In Zamiatin's daily *State Newspaper* there is an announcement, with which the story begins, informing all that the construction of the cosmic ship has been concluded. Its mission: to subject unknown beings living on other planets, possibly still in the wild state of being free, to the divine restraint of reason. The announcement emphasizes: "If they do not understand that we are bringing them unmistakable happiness, then it is our responsibility to force them to be happy...." In 1920, the *State Newspaper* proclaimed: "Prior to weapons we try words." It was at that time that the Red Army was engaged in battles with the Army of the Ukrainian National Republic, and then with the Polish Army, in order to "bring happiness" to those "unknown beings from other planets" living in the "wild state of freedom" or, in other words, in their own independent states. Prochanov continues to describe the next attempt at "forcing a nation to happiness." In Afghanistan, the Russian "word" is not effective, is without power, and the Russian army establishes "happiness through force...."

Without an understanding of the spirit of the bearer of Russian imperialism, it is impossible to understand Russian politics or the strategy of Russian aggression. Lenin incorporated Marxism into his complex of imperialistic ideas because it was a justification for using Russian force to bring about "happiness for creatures on other planets."

Russia aspires to conquer the entire world. Each one of its conquests must be secured by another conquest in an infinite progression. Such a progression can only lead to the conquest of the whole world. Moscow will only feel secure when Zamiatin's "Sole State of the Future" of the 1920s becomes a reality.

The 1980s will be a decade of volcanic explosions in the Soviet-Russian prison of nations.

On numerous occasion, the Russians have declared their aims. In 1921 Lenin said:

> Western Europe and America have closed their eyes before the facts and reality and will support the Soviet war industry with the materials and technology that we need to defeat them.

In 1973 a member of the Politburo of the Communist Party of the Soviet Union stated in Prague:

> With detente we have achieved more in a short time than in all the years of political confrontation with NATO. Comrades, through detente we will be able by 1985 to attain a position we consider indispensable.

A few years ago Brezhnev said to the President of Somalia. General Mohammed Siad:

We must acquire the two things that mean life or death to the West: the oil of the Persian Gulf and the minerals of Africa.

There are two fundamental issues which the West must resolve: to identify the enemy and to find a consistent solution to the world political crisis.

British Air Force Vice-Marshal, E.J. Kingston McClough, appropriately identified the enemy in his book *Global Strategy*:

> The enemy here considered is not simply embodied in an ideological threat but rather it is the State called Russia: that is, Russia as a power, a Russia expanding and desiring to extend her sphere of influence, a state posing as the symbol of all manner of ideals. It is Russia as a fighting force, an organized community, and a power or state in the most autocratic and absolute sense with which we are concerned.

General J.F.C. Fuller expressed his views as follows:

> No power the world has ever seen has been more vulnerable to internal attack than the Bolshevik empire. It is not a national state, but a state of nationalities. As Theodore Mommsen wrote nearly a century ago: "The Russian empire is a dustbin that is held together by the rusty hoop of Tsardom. Rip that hoop and its empire is at an end." In 1956, when the Hungarians rose against their tormentors, the shock to the Kremlin was so great, I am convinced, that had America and Great Britain flown a provisional Government into Hungary, which upon arrival would forthwith have called upon them for military support, then rather than risk a nuclear war, the Russians would have evacuated Hungary. The reason should be obvious. It is that the Kremlin is living on a volcano, and it knows that the most explosive force in the world is not to be found in the hydrogen bomb, but in the hearts of the subjugated peoples crushed under its iron heel....
>
> Because both America and Great Britain realize that they cannot hope to rival Russian manpower, they have decided to make good their deficiency by relying on what they call "tactical nuclear weapons"; in other words, nuclear weapons less powerful than atomic and hydrogen bombs, which are called "strategic nuclear weapons." This is tackling the problem the wrong way round. The correct solution is...to reduce Russian superiority in manpower, and so indirectly increase Western manpower. This can be done by subverting the Russian armed forces, which are largely recruited from the subjugated peoples within the USSR and the satellite countries. Be it remembered that during the first few months of Hitler's invasion of the Soviet Union in 1941, well over 2,000,000 prisoners were taken by the Germans. This seems an incredible figure until one realizes that the vast majority of these men were deserters—Ukrainians, Byelorussians, Georgians, Turkestanis, Cossacks, and other subjugated peoples.

I would like to underline that the excellent military theoretician General Hackett, in his book *The Third World War*, written in conjunction with other renowned military theoreticians of NATO, predicts that the subjugated nations in the Russian "prison of nations" will play a crucial role in the future clash between the world of freedom and the Russian world of tyranny. He pays particular attention to the anti-Russian revolutionary potential of Ukraine, which he posits as the decisive factor in the victory of the Free World.

It would seem that the political and military strategy of the West is founded upon the expectation that a miracle will happen of and by itself. *This real miracle will be the revolutionary uprisings of the subjugated nations.* This miracle will come with the appearance on the international global area of this neglected power.

I would like to bring to your attention the role of the Ukrainian Insurgent Army in World War II and the related fault in Allied strategy.

Ukraine is a wealthy country in many respects. Her wealth is attributable to an abundance of grain, raw materials, natural resources, and in general, her geo-political position. She also possesses a dynamic, revolutionary potential in her huge and creative population. Her system of values and ideals of renewal are diametrically opposed to the Russian system of ideals; the Russian way of life. Other subjugated nations are no less important, for instance, Turkestan, Azerbaidzhan, Byelorussia or Georgia. The two-front liberation war of Ukraine, Lithuania, and the other subjugated nations, in a common front with the Western Allies, against Nazi Germany and Russia, would have been the decisive factor in World War II. It could have saved the world from both Nazism and its original prototype—Bolshevism. Later, when it was clearly too late, Winston Churchill reached a similar conclusion, stating that the Allies ought to have "slaughtered" both "pigs" when they had the chance.

Another theatre of Russian aggression is present-day Afghanistan. In 1912, the far-sighted American General Homer Lea stated the following:

> There are two lesser known cities in the world, which are of enormous significance for all of humanity—Herat and Kabul.

The General then underscored the significant words of the Russian tsar, Peter I. taken from the tsar's final testament to his successor. In this testament the tsar stated that India would be the key to Europe. Then he continued:

> Do not waste any possible opportunity of provoking war with Persia, so as to quicken its destruction and to make possible our conquering of the Persian Gulf.

It is important to note that the Islamic nations in the USSR have a combined population of approximately 50 million people and they are rapidly outnumbering the Russians. Afghanistan is also an Islamic nation and the ideological-political consequences of its anti-Russian liberation struggle are already evident in the USSR.

What, in fact, is the Communist system?

We must remember that the liberation processes are a power, and power means authority. But it is impossible for two powers to reach a compromise when the powers concerned are those of the occupied and the occupier. A good example is Poland.

The essential fact to be remembered is that the Communist system is an integral component of the imposed system of Russian occupation. It is impossible, for example, to maintain the stability of an occupational system, imposed upon an occupied nation by Russian armies and the KGB, and to simultaneously maintain free and independent trade unions. The Communist Party is the inevitable and concomitant agent of foreign occupation. This occupation is made possible not only by Russian troops, but also by the Communist terror apparatus, the party and its administrative organs and various branches.

The Church also has a leading role in the liberation process, because religion is in opposition to the militant atheistic Russian system of occupation. The national and social liberation processes are in continuous opposition to the national and socio-political Russian totalitarian system. These revolutionary tendencies, when aroused in all spheres of life, will exert increasing pressure resulting in a radical change of the whole system, including the expulsion of the occupational forces.

We understand the policy of detente very well in all its variants, including the politics of balance of power. We all wish to avoid a Third World War, especially a thermonuclear war. We are all opposed to it but we, the subjugated nations, comprise the most determined opposition because it is on our land that the war will be played out.

Now there is only the question of whether the policy of detente and balance of power are preventative measures, are an alternative to atomic war. If the parties in question are not aspiring to identical goals, there can be no balance of power. In comparison to the so-called period of Western power politics, the policy of detente brought with it an unparalleled expansion of the Russian empire across all continents.

The USSR cannot win an arms race with the West. But it is not necessary to create tragicomic situations— with one hand to arm the USSR and with the other to beg the Russians for "arms parity at the lowest level," while at the same time creating the groundwork for a maximum arms build-up. Western world markets indirectly arm the USSR while their governments concurrently conduct disarmament talks. At the end of the 1980s the empire will be at this end of its technological armament potential and will be in the midst of an oil crisis.

The Ukrainian Review,
No. IV, 1982, pp. 6-10

The Liberation Struggle of Nations—The Path to a Just Peace

Ours are the aspirations of all freedom-loving and peace-loving humankind. We seek to avoid World War III and a thermonuclear holocaust. The primary issue that we must all address is how we are to attain these objectives.

The policies of detente and "balance of power" have not justified themselves as satisfactory means to reaching this end. Paradoxically enough, it was during the era of detente, and not the Cold War, that the Russian empire extended its boundaries beyond its previous acquisitions of World War II and established its hegemony over many countries in Asia, Africa, and Latin America. It was during the period of detente that various struggles for freedom of the nations subjugated in the USSR and the "satellite" countries were forcibly repressed. It was only recently that Moscow invaded Afghanistan and undertook a military intervention by proxy in Poland.

A "balance of power" concept is viable only when the partners are striving for common aims. The West does not have territorial encroachment as one of its policy objectives whereas Moscow aims to conquer the world. These are two opposite vantage points.

In Helsinki, the substitute for a post-WWII peace treaty was Western recognition of the inviolability of the borders and the indivisibility of the Russian prison of nations. It is contradictory to demand human rights and self-determination, while simultaneously recognizing the inviolability of the borders of the Russian colonial empire. An essential precondition for the fulfillment of fundamental human liberties in the subjugated nations is a national, independent, and democratic state. There can be neither a just nor lasting peace without national independence of the subjugated nations in the USSR and the "satellite" countries. Permit me to elaborate on how this aim can be achieved:

1. The West should discontinue all forms of economic aid to the USSR, such as transfers of electronics and technology and grain sales. In other words, all mutual economic relations with the USSR should be terminated. Western aid strengthens the military-industrial sector of the Bolshevik prison of nations, whereas without it Moscow would be incapable of militarily surprising NATO or even maintaining the present pace in the arms race.

We are voicing our protest particularly with regard to the construction of the natural gas pipeline from the Gulag Archipelago by Western European nations. Our reasons are as follows:

a) The pipeline is being built by at least 100,000 political prisoners from the subjugated nations, who are being persecuted for their political and religious beliefs. This is especially true of Ukrainians, who constitute approximately 60 percent of the political prisoners of Russian concentration camps. Does the West want to become an accomplice to these crimes of genocide against humanity?

During the last two years several new centers of slave labor camps have appeared along the pipeline route. In Ust-Ischim alone there is a center with eight such camps. More centers may be found in Urengoi, Surgut, Tawda, Tiumen, Irbit, and Lyswa. These centers consist of destitute barracks or wagons which serve as living quarters—hardly sufficient protection in freezing temperatures of minus 30-40 degrees Centigrade. This work is done without sufficient machinery. Heavy burdens are moved by hand. Women are often found working with crippled hands. They suffer from various skin diseases resulting from exposure to asbestos. Lung diseases are a fact of life. Their food is atrocious. Due to a lack of vitamins the loss of teeth is a common ailment among the prisoners. These camps are a type of hell on earth.

Public opinion must also bear some of the responsibility for this situation because it is the public which demands that governments trade with the Bolshevik nation-killers for the sake of a more comfortable lifestyle.

b) With the completion of this pipeline, the West European countries will become more dependent on the USSR, thereby allowing themselves to become the future objects of blackmail.

c) The pipeline will supply Moscow with billions of dollars of hard currency, which will be used for the further armament of the USSR against the West.

d) The West European countries will create the impression that they are stabilizing the Russian empire by financing and building the pipeline through the occupied territories of the subjugated nations at the cost of the genocide and torture of the best sons and daughters of these nations. To this day, huge constructions across the Siberian wasteland are built almost exclusively by our prisoners, just as Petrograd was erected by Peter I on the corpses of Ukrainian kozaks, who rose up against Russian occupation.

2. The West ought to discontinue technological and other aid to the USSR and "satellite" countries, without which Moscow would no longer be able to maintain its present pace in the arms race. Within several years the internal weaknesses and contradictions of the Bolshevik system will surface. To conduct disarmament negotiations with your adversary, while simultaneously arming him, is ludicrous. Our appeal to the West is that it a) stop arming the tyrannical Bolshevik system indirectly with Western aid, and b) invalidate the gas pipeline agreement on humanitarian and military grounds, leaving West Europe considerably less vulnerable to Russian blackmail.

3. The West should morally and politically support the liberation struggle of the subjugated nations and individuals so as to hasten the dissolution of the Russian empire and the Communist system from within. This would lead to the reestablishment of independent nation-states of the peoples presently enslaved in the USSR and the "satellite" countries.

Moscow cannot use its thermonuclear arsenal on the insurgents of the subjugated nations, since this would also lead to the destruction of its occupational forces and terror apparatus. This fact was underlined by General Hackett in his book *The Third World War*, and elaborated upon by J.F.C. Fuller in his works, most notably *Russia Is Not Invincible* and *How to Defeat Russia*. Moscow's inability to conquer Afghanistan, the recent events in Poland, and the mass strikes and uprisings of Ukrainian, Lithuanian, Latvian, Estonian, Turkestani, Byelorussian, and their political prisoners (17 million in Stalinist concentration camps) are all evidence of the weakness of the Russian empire and its Communist system.

The decade-long war of liberation fought on two fronts by the Ukrainian Insurgent Army (1942-1953), whose fortieth anniversary we are commemorating this year, serves as testimony to the indomitable perseverance of nations that have risen against Russian tyranny. Ukraine's Proclamation of Independence of June 30, 1941 was the beginning of her two-front war of liberation against Nazi Germany and Bolshevik Russia. After the defeat of Nazi Germany in World War II, Ukraine continued this armed struggle against Bolshevik Russia, which was victorious only because of Western aid. The USSR was forced to enter into a tripartite pact with Communist Poland and Czechoslovakia (CSSR) in 1947 in order to militarily defeat Ukraine's armed forces, led by the OUN and the UPA.

The salvation of the world from an atomic war and World War III lies in the liberation struggle of the subjugated nations. The significance of an insurgent concept of liberation as a modern type of warfare was also confirmed by General Fuller. The present Afghan insurgent war of liberation further underlines this point. The heroic Afghan people should be helped by the West in every possible way. As the American General Homer Lea stated in 1912, he who controls Kabul and Herat has the key to Asia.

5. NATO needs to continue its armament program, especially with regard to conventional weapons, because otherwise the West will be vulnerable to Russian expansionism. It is better to lower the Western standard of living now as opposed to living under severe Russian domination and repression later.

6. Western moral and political support of the subjugated nations' liberation struggle will decrease the human potential of the military personnel of the Soviet army, since the West will then be able to gain the allegiance of the soldiers from the subjugated nations.

7. The West should proclaim a Great Charter of Independence for the nations subjugated in the USSR and the "satellite" countries. The Western democracies should raise the issue of Russian imperialism at all international forums, demanding that the United Nations Resolution of Decolonization from 1960-72 be applied to the Russian prison of nations, and not to nonexistent British or French empires. Moreover, the UN resolution on Namibia from 1976, which calls upon all UN member states to actively support an anti-colonial liberation struggle, should also be applied by the West to the nations subjugated in the USSR and the "satellite" countries. West European parliaments should pass a law stating the necessity of political and moral support for the national liberation struggles of all nations subjugated by Bolshevism, thereby confirming their solidarity with the United States Congress, which unanimously approved a resolution in July 1959 with respect to the captive nations, known as Public Law 86-90. The President of the United States, in accordance with the resolution, annually appeals to the American people to manifest their solidarity with the liberation struggles of Ukraine, Poland, Lithuania, Hungary, Latvia, Estonia, Byelorussia, Slovakia, Czechia, Turkestan, Georgia, Armenia, Azerbaidzhan, Bulgaria, Croatia, Romania, Albania, North Caucasus, and all other nations subjugated by Bolshevism and Communism.

Slava Stetsko, ed.,
The West's Strongest Allies,
Munich: Press Bureau of the Anti-Bolshevik Bloc of Nations, 1985, pp. 14-17

On the Liberation Front

It is noteworthy that in 1983 the Free World in general had strengthened its resolve to counter Russian imperialist aggression throughout the world. This, in turn, has spurred greater interest in the liberation struggle of the subjugated nations in the USSR and the "satellite" countries. The numerous commemorative observances of the ABN's fortieth anniversary that were held last year in Washington, London, Bradford, Detroit, Chicago, Toronto, Montreal, Munich, and elsewhere underscore the growing interest in our concept of liberation, as an alternative to nuclear war.

1983 also marked the tragic fiftieth anniversary of the Ukrainian Holocaust of 1932-33, in which 10 million Ukrainians starved to death as a result of a deliberately instituted famine. Western interest in this heretofore little-known Holocaust is an indication of rising indignation over Russian genocidal practices that Moscow employs to suppress the liberation struggle of the enslaved peoples. In an article that appeared in the *Washington Post* on January 5, 1984, columnist George Will described Moscow's genocidal practices in Afghanistan by drawing a parallel to the Ukrainian Holocaust of 1932-33. The primary lesson that the legacy of Stalin and his pupil, Hitler, has indelibly imprinted on the minds of the present-day rulers in the Kremlin is that an occupational system requires the application of indiscriminate terror and even a deliberate genocide of mass proportions; any lessening in the degree of terror will result in its inevitable failure.

The Russians cannot achieve their ultimate aim in Afghanistan by conventional military means. Hence, they lead a war of attrition against children, women, and the elderly. Small toy-bombs have left countless Afghan children maimed and crippled for life. Since they cannot defeat the Afghan insurgents, the mujahedeen, in open battle, the Russians choose to destroy or terrorize the entire nation.

The war in Afghanistan is brutal. But the Afghan people remain unvanquished chiefly because of their strong faith in God and their nation. The Russians cannot triumph on this front. Just as in 1940 in Finland, similarly now in Afghanistan, an insurgent strategy has proved to be superior to Moscow's modern military strategy. Afghanistan will continue to be the Achilles' heel of Russian aggression and our strategy must be incorporated within the complex of psychological warfare in Afghanistan.

The situation in Poland in somewhat different. The concept, promoted by *Solidarność's* leader Lech Walesa and Cardinal Glemp, to share authority with the colonial regime, has not justified itself. Bolshevism precludes any possibility of applying Montesquieu's classic three-tiered division of power (*L'Esprit des Lois*, 1748), or even a dual division of power between the enslaved people and their oppressor. The Communist military regime in Poland is an extension of Moscow's colonial power and, therefore, any negotiations with this regime cannot be valid: a system of dual authority with an occupied people, represented by *Solidarność*, and the occupying power, represented by the Communist Party and Jaruzelski's military regime, is *a priori* impossible. Polish national structures cannot exist parallel to Russian, Bolshevik structures. This was also recently asserted by *Solidarność's* underground leader, Zbigniew Bujak ("Polish Fugitive Urges 'Long March,' " *New York Times*, December 19, 1983, p. 8).

Several Variations in the Occupant's Strategy

We must always bear in mind that the Russian General Staff of the Armed Forces, the KGB, and the Politburo have provided for a number of contingency plans in their general strategy to suppress the liberation struggle of the enslaved peoples. Past experience has shown that Moscow can always implement these contingencies with the tacit consent of the West. The Hungarian uprising of 1956 was crushed by direct military intervention. Moscow employed different methods in Czechoslovakia in 1968, in 1961 in the Berlin wall crisis, and in 1953 in the Berlin uprising. In 1968 in the CSSR Moscow deceived the architects of the "Prague spring" (Dubcek and Smrkovsky) and suppressed the people's aspirations for freedom from above. For their subservience, the reform-minded Communist leaders in the USSR were granted their lives, but were rendered completely powerless. In Poland, the overt threat of direct Russian military intervention diverted the attention of *Solidarność's* leaders from the covert betrayal that Jaruzelski and Moscow's other agents were preparing. The euphoria that was created in the false hope that the negotiations with Vice-President Yagelsky would bear fruit blinded Walesa, Bujak, and others as to the possibility of a betrayal, which had already been prepared by Jaruzelski and his benefactors in Moscow. It was also in Moscow that the entire propaganda campaign in justification of the subsequent proclamation of martial law was prepared. During the half year prior to the institution of martial law in Poland, special military "ZOMO" and militia units were being secretly trained in isolation, so that in a few days these same well-trained units were able to drive millions of *Solidarność's* adherents into the underground, thereby striking the death knell for open, "legal" dual authority in Poland.

A different variation of the Politburo's general strategy was applied in the CSSR and in Hungary. In Afghanistan we find yet another variation: the prelude to the Russian military invasion was the outright execution of the "disloyal," pro-Communist government. In Grenada, President Reagan's rescue mission forced Moscow to abort its plans for a military invasion by proxy. Moscow's unexpected response to the three-day-long strike in Kyiv, fulfilling most of the worker's demands, was yet another variation of this general strategy.

Bujak's recent appeal to begin building Polish national structures not parallel to, but in opposition to the Bolshevik structures of the occupational regime further confirms our concept of liberation. Although the Church in Poland is also a decisive factor in the liberation struggle, it has nonetheless become an inhibiting factor as well, since it has placed itself in the position of a partner of the occupation regime. The Pope's recent visit to Poland was interpreted by Jaruzelski as a bestowal of "legitimacy" to the PPR—i.e., an independent state of the Polish people endowed with a rightful place in international forums. However, we feel that only the Polish people, and not a satellite state of Moscow, can be accorded a legitimate place in an international forum. The Pope's visit has resulted in an undercutting of *Solidarność's* authority, and buttressed the colonial pseudo-authority of the occupation regime. The moral strength of the Church is great, but it has become politically incongruent with the revolutionary liberation movement. Moreover, the Church's orientation is not directed towards forging a common front of liberation among the subjugated nations, but it seems to think that the Polish nation can liberate itself on its own.

On the Situation in Poland

The situation in Poland is, in general, also a result of the deliberate policy of the Vatican's Secretary of State, Cardinal Casaroli, who seemingly has accepted the existence of the Communist system and, in particular, of the Russian empire with its ever-increasing expansionist capabilities as a stable, immutable *fait accompli*. This view is apparently also shared by Cardinal Glemp and the Vatican, which is planning to establish diplomatic relations not only with Warsaw but with Moscow and Zagorsk. It is interesting that the Pope has expressed little concern over the genocide in Afghanistan and even less concern over the genocide in Ukraine. Furthermore, placing President Reagan and Andropov on an equal footing in the Vatican's appeals that both Washington and Moscow make mutual concessions is in itself tantamount to identifying a genocidal regime with the humane and democratic US Government. The Church's position in this regard has led to a considerable degree of disorientation, particularly among the Third World, and most of all in the overwhelmingly Catholic Latin American countries.

In his clandestine interview, Z. Bujak, the leader of the Polish underground, confirms our concept of liberation by opposing any dialogue with the occupation regime. He calls for a "long march" for resistance to the colonial regime, building clandestine organizations in schools, factories, and scientific, academic, and cultural institutions. Bujak believes that any legal forms of struggle are not now feasible. He stated in the interview that "there exists a very strong resistance movement...a very strong movement of rejection, a movement to boycott all institutions of the regime, and I regard this element as very significantly changing the classic system of Communist rule." *The New York Times* writes that "despite the setbacks in the streets, Mr. Bujak said in the interview, the opposition was building clandestine structures that would enable it to survive.... The strategy of the 'long march,' Mr. Bujak said, consisted of 'ignoring all the actions of the authorities, with the exception, of course, of those directly affecting us, such as the police, which have to be counteracted, and organizing various forms of social life—independent union activities, independent activities in science, education, and culture—outside the influence of the authorities.

"The idea, he said, was to put 'permanent pressure on the authorities in all areas of social and political life.'" Bujak further states: "The strength of the regime and of Moscow comes from using oppression against society, an oppressive system built into all possible areas of social life."

Bujak does not agree with Walesa, who recently suggested that US sanctions be dropped since they are too harmful to the Polish economy. "As long as the decisive policy of Western governments is maintained," according to Bujak, "the policy based on respect for human rights, we can cherish hopes our efforts will not go to waste.... If this support and this decisive policy of the Western governments is replaced by a policy of concessions and the closing of eyes to what is happening in our country, this will threaten us with the danger of the breakdown of resistance."

In quoting at length from this *New York Times* interview with "Poland's most wanted fugitive," our aim was to demonstrate that the present events in Poland substantiate our paradigmatic revolutionary concept that perceives the revolutionary processes primarily as a struggle between two diametrically opposed conceptions of life, two ways of life, two cultures, two polar world-views, two antithetical moralities, two inimical national organisms: a Russian, Bolshevik system of values against the national value system of each subjugated nation. This revolutionary concept is presently being applied in part by the Polish underground. In an interesting poll recently conducted among Polish students, we find that ninety percent of them openly stated that they were religious and anti-Communist. This is a reflection of the complete state of bankruptcy of Communism in Poland, despite the fact that it has been in existence there for almost forty years.

Several Characteristic Elements of the Ukrainian Liberation Struggle

With regard to the situation in Ukraine, we have in the past drawn attention to two intersecting phases in the revolutionary processes: a) the continuity of the ideological-political struggle, and b) the formation of Ukrainian national, social, cultural, religious, and other structures in polar opposition to the Russian, Bolshevik structures forcibly implanted in Ukraine. Given a system of totalitarian terror, it is completely unfeasible to establish an organizationally centralized, revolutionary network with a central headquarters that would regularly send out special instructions to its clandestine units. The revolutionary processes themselves mobilize the wider strata of society, which on their own initiative create groups of like-minded people that are not organically or technically connected, but whose activity is directed towards the same ideological-political aims. The very form and substance of the occupational system, which is forcibly imposed, in itself evokes a resistance movement. This struggle does not need clandestine instructions, but first and foremost it needs vital mobilizing ideas and slogans that would be in consonance with the spontaneous vital life-forces of the nation. Moreover, these revolutionary ideas must continuously stress that only by achieving national independence, sovereignty, and statehood can the nation as a whole truly prosper on every level of its own inherent creativity. National independence and statehood are the primary preconditions for the fulfillment of all of the people's desires and aspirations.

In our struggle, the ideals for which we are fighting are specified in our program of action. Our strategy must be applied to an occupational totalitarian system that is in its essence a Russian, Bolshevik system of occupation. The

Russian artificial famine in Ukraine in 1932-33 was not only an economic policy, a result of Moscow's collectivization drive; in fact, its primary aim was to physically liquidate the Ukrainian nation and to break the Ukrainian will to fight for its national independence. Collectivization, as an anti-Ukrainian social ideal and system, was the means by which this aim was to be achieved.

We must demonstrate that in our liberation struggle we seek to bring about a revolutionary change on all levels of life in accordance with our national values and ideals. The revolutionary processes will continue to grow, as our nations continue to grasp the true national essence of all aspects of life, and as groups of like-minded individuals continue to be created, popularizing our liberation ideals by means of modern technology and electronics. The various smear campaigns that Moscow has led against us, in which it even resorts to falsifying our publications (e.g., the most recent provocation by Moscow's lackey Kukhtiak, who is known in Ivano-Frankivsk as an agent provocateur), all have one aim: to compromise our liberation struggle in the eyes of the Western world. On the one hand, Moscow desperately wants to cut all possible political contacts that we may have with Western democratic governments, and on the other hand, to create an illusion behind the Iron Curtain that the ABN and the OUN have been in contact with KGB centers and are in the service of Western intelligence agencies, all of which is nothing more than a pack of lies and provocations.

The Need for a Psychological Offensive

Afghanistan, Finland, the PLO, or the insurgencies in Latin America and Africa are a clear indication of the modern significance of an insurgent guerrilla strategy. For over four years the Russians have been desperately trying to salvage their colonial position in Afghanistan, with no end to the war in sight.

From the perspective of our strategy, it is vital to mount a political-psychological offensive, particularly by means of radio broadcasts behind the cIron Curtain. Unfortunately, in the context of the West's political strategy, the significance of this factor is not yet fully appreciated. Until now Radio Liberty has not been broadcasting into Afghanistan. If Radio Liberty is truly founded upon principles of democratic pluralism, then its personnel composition should be reflective of the proportionate strength of a given political movement or orientation, and not of a strictly leftist-liberal coloring.

Solidarność would never have grown into an all-national movement of mass social proportions had it not been for the broadcasts of Radio Free Europe. The Polish radio broadcasts provided a crucial organizational link of communication. For example, a detailed description of a strike in Gdansk over the radio waves of Radio Free Europe was, in fact, an instruction for the Solidarność groups in Warsaw, Cracow, Lublin, Poznan, and elsewhere that the same methods should be applied there. Modern technology and electronics are also a means of revolutionary struggle and not only a means of repression of the occupational regime.

The Mujahedeen in Afghanistan need anti-helicopter rockets. They do not need foreign armies, but they lack the crucial types of weapons necessary for leading a modern insurgent guerrilla war of liberation. Furthermore, a most decisive form of Western assistance would be to equip the Mujahedeen with the modern technical means for leading a political-psychological war among the soldiers of the Soviet army. This would have to be coupled with a means of transporting Soviet POW's somewhere to the Free World.

The Afghan front of liberation remains unvanquished, in spite of the fact that there are over 3 million refugees that have escaped from the invading Soviet army. It is unlikely that there were 3 million bourgeois capitalists in Afghanistan. Are the millions of Afghanis who are actively supporting the Mujahedeen also bourgeois capitalists? Is it true that the Mujahedeen have an "extreme constriction of the social base of the objective process"? These are the words that one of Moscow's agents uses to describe Ukrainian nationalism (*Ukrainian Historical Journal*, No. 10/83). In a recently published book. O.V. Kartunov expresses concern that "the nationalist leadership has begun very heated activity, with the aim of enlarging their nationalist groups with young people that have become poisoned with the ideology of bourgeois nationalism." This ideology, the author continues, "has long since and forever lost its social base in Ukraine and has become an émigré phenomenon." These statements contradict the assertions of Andropov and Chernenko, who in their keynote addresses have called upon all party cadres to maintain a strict vigilance against the threat of nationalism and religion.

Paying the required tribute to the "indomitability of proletarian internationalism," Kartunov states that, nonetheless, "nationalism has attained a social base among the Ukrainian émigré community...which lives in the spirit of the ideology of bourgeois nationalism and cultivates ethnic separatism." In these words we find the real goal of the Russians: to bring about the assimilation of the Ukrainian *emigre* community, so that there will remain nothing of the nationally conscious *diaspora* that has been the vanguard of the nation's struggle for independence and statehood in the Free World.

The author is acutely perturbed that "the Ukrainian nationalists have borrowed and utilized the experience of international Zionism with regard to creating a spiritual ghetto...." He is concerned with "common subversive actions that have been co-organized by the nationalists and the Zionists, their participation in anti-Soviet rallies, the publication and distribution in our country of provocative literature, the preparation of threatening radio broadcasts, etc." And another factor that really hurts is the fact that "the ringleaders...have utilized clericalism for the dissemination of their anti-Communist, nationalist ideas among the youth." This is a reference to the documents of our churches that we have been smuggling into Ukraine by the thousands. Repeating for the tenth time the phrase about "the construction of the social base and the deepening of the ideological-organizational crisis of bourgeois nationalism," the author recapitulates that "one should not underestimate it [nationalism] in the present ideological struggle," because (in conclusion) "the nationalists are becoming more active and aggressive."

These same ideas and formulae can be found in all of the Russian-Communist, Ukrainian-Communist, and Polish-Communist press and journals. Evidently,

Moscow issued directives to all of its colonies in the USSR and the "satellites" to raise the level of vigilance regarding the threat of Ukrainian nationalism. In an article in the *Trybuna Luda* (People's Tribune), the author, Jerzy Wisnowski, expresses concern with President Reagan's words: "Your struggle is our struggle. Your dreams are our dreams." He agitated over the growing understanding in the West of the significance of Ukraine and the subjugated nations, and particularly of Ukrainian nationalism. He writes: "So much has been written about the fascist [sic] Stetsko and his comrades from the OUN, UPA, and ABN...." And further, "There is absolutely no social, or political, or any other basis for the realization of their insane aspirations either in Ukraine or in Poland.... However, any underestimation of this small, albeit determined and fanatical, enemy would be a grave mistake...." Here again, the true fears of Moscow are fully revealed. On the Kremlin's orders, the various Bolshevik periodicals have literally copied verbatim in a number of languages Moscow's anti-OUN-UPA-ABN smear campaign and have revealed their fear of the threat that awaits the empire from the liberation struggle of Ukraine and the subjugated nations.

The subjugated nations are the Achilles' heel of the Russian empire!

The Ukrainian Review,
No. 1, 1984, pp. 10-16.

Glossary

Persons

Badzio, Iuriy (1936-   ), Ukrainian philologist, literary critic, translator, writer, and political prisoner.

Bandera, Stepan (1909-1959), member of the OUN and the UVO; became head of the Homeland Executive; sentenced for his revolutionary activities by the Polish authorities; participated with Yaroslav Stetsko in proclaiming the re-establishment of the independent Ukrainian state on June 30, 1941; for refusing to rescind the proclamation he was arrested and interned in Sachsenhausen concentration camp, assassinated on October 15, 1959 in Munich by KGB agent Bohdan Stashynsky.

Bereslavsky, M., attempted self-immolation at the University of Kiev; prior to attempt distributed leaflets protesting national oppression in Ukraine, arrested and imprisoned.

Bilsky, Oleska, Ukrainian patriot imprisoned at the age of nineteen, fate unknown.

Boieslav, Marko, poet and playwright, member of the OUN and the UPA; his writings reflected the liberation struggle of the Ukrainian people during World War II; fate unknown.

Boretsky, Mykola (1879-   ), Metropolitan of the Ukrainian Autocephalous Orthodox Church; arrested in 1930 and perished in the labor camps.

Braichevsky, Mykhailo (1924-   ), noted Ukrainian historian, archeologist and senior scientific research associate of the Institute of History of the Academy of Sciences of the Ukr. SSR; suffered reprisals for scholarly objectivity and defense of persecuted Ukrainian intellectuals.

Chornovil, Viacheslav (1938-   ), Ukrainian journalist and activist in the human rights movement, member of the Ukrainian Helsinki Group, political prisoner.

Chuprynka, Hryhoriy (1879-1921), Ukrainian modernist peot; executed by the Bolsheviks.

Dontsov, Dmytro (1883-1973), noted Ukrainian political theorist, publicist, editor, and literary critic; his ideology based on principles of voluntarism and idealism had great impact on the generation of the 30s and on the members of the OUN; advocated Ukrianian state independence.

Drach, Ivan (1936-   ), Ukrainian poet, screenwriter, and literary critic, one of the leaders of the Ukrainian cultural renaissance in the 1960s initiated by the *shestydesiatnyki*.

Diak, Mykhailo (1935-   ), a Soviet police lieutenant who became a member of the underground Ukrainian National Front in the 1960s; sentenced to a labor camp.

Dzyuba, Ivan (1931-   ), Ukrainian literary critic and publicist, member of the *shestydeisatnyki*; wrote *Internationalsm or Russification?* a criticism of Russian nationality policy; sentenced to a labor camp; later recanted.

Franko, Ivan (1856-1916), poet, writer, publicist and civic leader, Western Ukraine's greatest writer and poet.

Fuller, John (1887-1966), British officer, military theoretician and historian; understood threat of USSR and role of subjugated nations as allies of the Free World.

Hasyn, Oleska (1910-1949), colonel, Deputy Minister of Defense in the Ukrainian National Government (1941), Chief of Staff of the UPA (1945-1949); died in action against Russian security forces.

Horobovy, Volodymyr (1899-1985), jurist, senior member of the OUN; served long term in Soviet labor camps.

Horska, Alla (1929-1970), artist; designed in 1964 for Kyiv University with three other artists a stained-glass panel which was destroyed for being "ideologically subversive"; murdered by the KGB.

Horyn, Bohdan (1939-   ), Ukrainian literary critic, political prisoner.

Horyn, Mykhailo (1930-   ), industrial psychologist, political prisoner.

Hryhorenko, Petro (1907-1987), Soviet major-general, founding member of the Ukrainian Helsinki Group; confined to psychiatric hospital in the USSR; emigrated and died in the USA.

Hrytsay, Dmytro (1907-194?), leading member of the OUN, general and Chief of Staff of the UPA (1943-1945), executive member of the UHVR; died in prison in Prague.

Iefremov, Serhiy (1876-1939?), scholar, publicist, political leader; arrested in 1929 as leader of the Union for the Liberation of Ukraine; perished in the labor camps.

Kalynets, Ihor (1939-   ), one of the most gifted contemporary Ukrainian poets, a political prisoner.

Kalynets, Iryna (1940-   ), Ukrainian poet and writer, wife of Ihor, a political prisoner.

Kandyba, Ivan (1930-   ), lawyer, advocated secession of Ukraine from the USSR, founding member of the Ukrainian Helsinki Group, a political prisoner.

Karavansky, Sviatoslav (1920-   ), poet, writer, linguist, translator, member of the OUN in the 1940s; sentenced to twenty five years in the labor camps; emigrated to the USA.

Khvyliovy, Mykola (1893-1933), Ukrainian writer; originally supported the Bolsheviks, later openly advocated independence for Ukraine; commited suicide as a protest against Russian policies in Ukraine.

Klymiv-Lehenda, Ievhen (1915-1942), head of the Homeland Executive of the OUN (1939-1941), Minister of Political Coordination in the Ukrainian National Government established by Yaroslav Stetsko.

Kolodzinsky, Mykhailo (1902-1939), colonel, member of the UVO and the OUN, chief of staff of the armed forces of the Carpatho-Ukrainian Republic in 1939; died in combat against the invading Hungarian army.

Konovalets, Ievhen (1891-1938), colonel, commander of the *Sich* corps of the Riflemen in the Ukrainian Army, leader of the OUN; assassinated on 23 May, 1938 by a Soviet agent in Rotterdam.

Kosiv, Mykhailo, lecturer in literature and head of the Institute for the Study of Ivan Franko in Lviv University, a political prisoner.

Kossak, Zenon (1907-1939), Lieutenant, member of the OUN, staff officer in the headquarters of the armed forces of the Carpatho-Ukrainian Republic in 1939; died in combat against the invading Hungarian forces.

Kostenko, Lena (1930-   ), noted Ukrainian poet, one of the *shestydesiatnyki*; participated in protests against arrests of intellectuals in Ukraine.

Kotliarevsky, Ivan (1769-1838), the "father" of modern Ukrainian literature, author of *Eneida*, a burlesque travesty of Virgil's *Aeneid* and the first work to be written in the vernacular Ukrainian.

Krasivsky, Zynoviy (1930-   ), poet and writer, a political prisoner.

Lukianenko, Lev (1928-   ), jurist, author of a draft constitution of the Ukrainian Workers' and Peasants' Union which included secession of Ukraine from the USSR, member of the Helsinki Group, a political prisoner.

Lupynis, Anatoliy (1937-   ), Ukrainian poet and political prisoner.

Lypa, Iuriy (1901-1945), physician, sociologist, publicist, member of UPA; died in action against Soviet security forces.

Lypkivsky, Vasyl (1864-1938), Metropolitan of the Ukrainian Autocephalous Orthodox Church, arrested in 1930 and perished in the labor camps.

Makukha, Vasyl (1918-1968), former Ukrainian political prisoner; committed self-immolation in Kyiv on the fiftieth anniversary of the Bolshevik revolution.

Maletar, Pal (-1956), commanding general of the insurgent forces during the Hungarian Revolution in 1956; lured to a conference by the Russians, arrested, and executed.

Marynovych, Myroslav (1949-   ), engineer, member of the Ukrainian Helsinki Group, a political prisoner.

Matusevych, Mykola (1946-   ), historian, member of the Ukrainian Helsinki Group, a political prisoner.

Mazepa, Ivan (1644-1709), Hetmen of Ukraine; joined King Charles XII of Sweden in a war against Russia; defeated at the battle of Poltava in 1709.

Moroz, Valentyn (1936-   ), Ukrainian historian and publicist; served many years in Soviet prisons and labor camps; now resides in Canada.

Oliynyk, Volodymyr (1920-   ), member of the OUN and the UPA, a political prisoner.

Omelianovych-Pavlenko, Mykhailo (1878-1952), general and commander of the armed forces of the Ukrainian National Republic in 1918-1920, author of many books on modern military history.

Petlura, Symon (1879-1926), leader of the Ukrainian Social Democratic Party, head of the government of the Ukrainian National Republic (1918-1920) and commander in chief of its armed forces; assassinated in Paris by a Bolshevik agent, Samuel Schwartzbard.

Petriv, Vsevolod (1883-1948), general, commander of the Ukrainian army of the National Republic and minister of defense in the National Government of 1941.

Piasetsky, Andriy (1909-1942), engineer, lecturer at Lviv Polytechnic, minister of agriculture in the Ukrainian National Government; executed by the Nazis.

Rebet, Lev (1912-1957), publicist and leader of the OUN; assassinated by KGB agent Stashynsky in Munich.

Romaniuk, Vasyl (1925-   ), Ukrainian Orthodox priest, member of the Helsinki Group, a political prisoner.

Rudenko, Mykola (1920-   ), poet and writer, founding member of the Ukrainian Helsinki Group, a political prisoner; now residing in the West.

Senyk, Iryna (1925-   ), nurse, member of the OUN, worked with the medical services of the UPA and later the Ukrainian Helsinki Group, a political prisoner.

Shabatura, Stefania (1938-   ), artist, member of the Ukrainian Helsinki Group, a political prisoner.

Sheptytsky, Andrey (1865-1944), Metropolitan and primate of the Ukrainian Catholic Church (1900-1944) in Western Ukraine.

Shevchenko, Taras (1814-1861), born a serf; became a painter, Ukraine's greatest poet, and the key figure in the Ukrainian national revival; was punished for his writings with exile and compulsory military service by the Tsarist regime.

Shukhevych, Roman (1907-1950), commander in chief of the UPA, deputy minister of the Ukrainian National Government, leader of the OUN and secretary-general of the UHVR, brilliant military tactician and strategist in insurgent warfare; killed in action against Soviet Russian security forces.

Shukhevych, Iuriy (1934-   ), son of Roman; imprisoned in 1948 at the age of fourteen for refusing to denounce his father; member of the Ukrainian Helsinki Group.

Skovoroda, Hryhoriy (1722-1794), greatest Ukrainian philosopher, referred to as the "Ukrainian Socrates."

Slipy, Joseph Cardinal (1892-1984), Patriarch of the Ukrainian Catholic Church; spent eighteen years as religious and political prisoner in Russian labor camps; released on intercession of Pope John XXIII to live in Rome.

Sokulsky, Ivan (1940-   ), poet and journalist, member of the Ukrainian Helsinki Group, a political prisoner.

Soroka, Mykhailo (1911-1971), architect, member of the OUN and the UPA; spent thirty years in Russian labor camps where he died.

Sosiura, Volodymyr (1898-1965), Ukrainian romantic poet of great lyrical power.

Stakhiv, Volodymyr (1910-1971), leading member of the OUN, minister of external affairs in the Ukrainian National Government; imprisoned in Sachsenhausen concentration camp during the war.

Strokata-Karavanska, Nina (1925-   ), microbiologist and physician, dissident activist in Ukraine, a political prisoner; currently resides in the USA.

Stus, Vasyl (1938-1985), one of the greatest contemporary Ukrainian poets, member of the *Shestydesiatnyki* and the Helsinki Group; perished in a Russian labor camp.

Sverstiuk, Ievhen (1928-), psychologist, literary critic, and writer, prominent Ukrainian dissident activist, political prisoner.

Svitlychna, Nadia (1936-), philologist, member of the Ukrainian Helsinki Group, a political prisoner; now resides in the USA.

Svitlychny, Ivan (1929-), Ukrainian critic, publicist, translator, political prisoner.

Symonenko, Vasyl (1935-1963), outstanding Ukrainian poet and a member of the *shestydesiatnyki*; died from cancer.

Terelia, Iosef (1942-), leading Ukrainian Catholic lay activist; imprisoned in psychiatric prisons and labor camps. Now living in Canada.

Tkachuk, Iarema (1933-), member of the United Party for the Liberation of Ukraine the aim of which was independence for Ukraine, a political prisoner.

Tykhy, Oleska (1927-1984), teacher, member of the Ukrainian Helsinki Group; perished in the Russian labor camps.

Tymkiv, Bohdan (1935-), member of the United Party for the Liberation of Ukraine, a political prisoner.

Velychkovsky, Vasyl (1903-1973), bishop of the Ukrainian Catholic Church secretly ordained in Ukraine in 1963; spent fourteen years in Russian labor camps; emigrated to Canada and died in Winnipeg.

Virun, Stepan (1932-), member of the Ukrainian Workers' and Peasants' Union which advocated secession of Ukraine, a political prisoner.

Voloshyn, Rostyslav (1911-1946), leading member of the OUN, one of the founders of the UPA and the UHVR.

Yatsiv, Dmytro, member of the OUN, secretary of the Ministry of the National Economy in the Ukrainian National Government; perished in Auschwitz.

Zalyvakha, Opanas (1925-), Ukrainian artist participated with Alla Horska in producing stained-glass panel; a political prisoner.

Zarytska, Kateryna (1913-1986), leading member of the OUN and the UPA, founder and head of the Red Cross service of the UPA, a political prisoner.

Organizations, Places, Terms

Act of June 30, 1941. Proclamation of the reestablishment of Urkainian statehood on the initiative of the OUN under the leadership of Stepan Bandera; Yaroslav Stetsko elected head of the Ukrainian National Government by the National Assembly.

Anti-Bolshevik Bloc of Nations (ABN). An umbrella organization of liberation movements of the nations subjugated by Soviet Russia, had its inception at the First Conference of the Subjugated Nations of Eastern Europe and Asia in Ukraine on November 21-22, 1943.

European Freedom Council (EFC). An organization founded in 1967 and dedicated to the promotion of national independence of nations under Russian and communist domination in Europe.

Golden Gate. Ukrainian historic monument in the form of a defensive tower with a triumphal entrance and a church above it built in the Kyiv ramparts in 1037.

Kaniv. Ancient Ukrainian town founded in the eleventh century in the southern part of the Kyiv region on the right bank of the Dnipro River, the burial place of the greatest Ukrainian poet, Taras Shevchenko.

Konotop. Town in Eastern Ukraine near which Ukrainian forces under Hetman Vyhovsky defeated an invading Russian army of 10,000 on 8 July, 1659.

Lviv Council. Assembly of the Ukrainian Catholic Church convened in 1946 by the Soviet Russian authorities in which it "joined" the Russian Orthodox Church.

Organization of Ukrainian Nationalists (OUN). Movement founded in 1929, dedicated to the reestablishment of an independent Ukrainian state within its ethnographic boundaries, successor of the Ukrainian Military Organization (UVO); on June 30, 1941 proclaimed restoration of independent Ukrainian state and established Ukrainian National Government headed by Yaroslav Stetko; most of its members arrested and some executed.

Samvydav, literally "self-publishing." Various materials, typed or handwritten, critical of the regime and circulated illegally in Ukraine.

Shestydesiatnyki, literally the "Generation of the Sixties." A group of younger Ukrainian writers who emerged after Khrushchev's speech at the Twentieth Congress of the CPSU in 1956 denigrating Stalin; ushered in a Ukrainian literary renaissance.

Sich. Ukrainian Cossack fortress on the Dnipro River (1552-1775), destroyed during the reign of Catherine II.

Supreme Ukrainian Liberation Council (UHVR). Organized by the OUN on July 11-15, 1944 to lead the struggle for independence against Germany and the USSR; functioned as Ukrainian government.

Trident. The Ukrainian national emblem.

Ukrainian Insurgent Army (UPA). Formed in 1942 from insurgent self-defense groups and military and paramilitary units of the OUN, by 1944 had a fighting force of 200,000; fought on two fronts against Nazi and Soviet forces; opposition to the latter lasted into the 1950s; commanded by General Roman Shukhevych.

Ukrainian National Government. With the Nazi invasion of the USSR on June 22, 1941, the NKVD forces began massacring or deporting Ukrainian political prisoners from Western Ukraine; OUN units seized power in Lviv on June 30, convened a National Assembly, and proclaimed the restoration of the independent Ukrainian state; the Nazis responded with mass arrests; Yaroslav Stetsko, Stepan Bandera, and about 1,000 others arrested; many were executed or perished in concentration camps; these events marked beginning of resistance to the Nazis and the creation of the Ukrainian underground state which lasted a decade (1941-1951).

Ukrainsky Visnyk (The Ukrainian Herald). Underground publication which reported on Soviet violation of human rights and the struggle to maintain Ukrainian identity and national rights.

Index